Education in Democracy:

SOCIAL FOUNDATIONS OF EDUCATION

FOUNDATIONS IN EDUCATION

HAROLD BENJAMIN, *Consulting Editor*

EDUCATION IN DEMOCRACY:
Social Foundations of Education

Philip W. L. Cox
PROFESSOR EMERITUS OF EDUCATION
NEW YORK UNIVERSITY

Blaine E. Mercer
ASSOCIATE PROFESSOR OF SOCIOLOGY
UNIVERSITY OF COLORADO

McGRAW-HILL BOOK COMPANY, INC.
New York Toronto London 1961

EDUCATION IN DEMOCRACY: SOCIAL
FOUNDATIONS OF EDUCATION

Preface

The dynamics of American life derive from continuing experiences, experimentation, and energetic endeavors to do something about whatever seems less than satisfactory. The criteria by which these experiences, experiments, and endeavors are judged are seldom verbally formulated except as catch phrases. They are, nonetheless, among the most potent aspects of the nation's social life. They require that individual yearnings for freedom, security, and self-respect be accorded a high place in the national scheme of values.

All experiences, including teaching and learning, have social foundations. Even though experience may be biologically derived, its effects on persons determine its acceptability and, hence, its repetition and modification.

By *education* is meant those experiences that a society intentionally fosters among its members in the expectation that thereby, under the control and guidance of its selected social agencies, its values, purposes, and organization will be molded and stabilized.

Obviously, the character of a society determines, in the long run at least, what educational experiences and institutions will be approved or even tolerated. Thus a relatively static society will give priority to training and indoctrination in order to inculcate the customs, beliefs, skills, and behavioral practices that characterize each class or status in that society.

This is not the case in so industrialized, polyglot, transitional, but democratically oriented a society as twentieth-century America. To be sure, over-all values and purposes, such as the pursuit of universal happiness, are given verbal assent by the people who may publicly approve or reject any specific educational measure. Nevertheless, there is no *certain* sanction for any specific American societal characteristic educators may favor as means for achieving the verbalized values and purposes. On the contrary, the range of approved customs, beliefs, skills, and behavioral accommodations in our fragmented and mobile society is great, and the approvals themselves are often inconsistent, transitory, and of varying potency from day to day.

The facts about these characteristics of community life are readily available to men and women of college age. Moreover, the standards by which college students are inclined to evaluate them are, in large measure, already conditioned by community aspirations to stability and mutual welfare. Even though they frequently avoid facts, most Americans do find themselves living under rules which call for self-restraint, at least temporary acceptance of majority and of official decisions, and the proscription of domestic violence. These rules for social living, whatever the extent of their violation, do foster the appeal to reason as a method of making decisions.

For the most part, the behavior, attitudes, and beliefs of Americans have been derived from trial-and-error experiences among what may be called a somewhat "self-selected" people. They have evolved, and continue to evolve, in response to the necessities and opportunities inherent in everyday life. If these behaviors and attitudes seem to the majority (or even a sufficiently powerful segment) of citizens to be useful (or even minimally harmful), they are socially tolerated or approved. At any time, the dominant standards and aspirations of American citizens can be said to be the products of a truly American experience in an American cultural milieu. This is not to deny the influence of other factors. The Christian ethic, Puritan morality, aristocratic tradition, the teachings of John Locke, and the exaltation of free enterprise, for example, do provide ideological frameworks for the justification, explanation, and systematization of standards and aspirations; they also provide some of the shibboleths used in rallying support for programs of action. Nonetheless, even these influences are interpreted in the context of the American experience. They take on an "American look" as they are applied in judgment of behavior and beliefs in the community.

Education in a democracy must, therefore, find its social foundations, not in a firmly entrenched body of customs, beliefs, skills, and accommodations, but in their tentative adaptations to a constantly changing civilization. There are, of course, some universals without which there could be no society, the basic affection and accommodation practiced in most families, neighborhoods, audiences, work groups, and political units, for example. Even the continuing existence of schools as instruments for meliorating the individual and social lives in the always transitional American civilization may be assumed.

If the school is to fulfill such a complex function, however, the faculties, boards of education, and other representatives of the public who guide and execute the meliorative measures must act in the light of the multifarious, transitional, and often conflicting prestiges implicit in the contemporary patterns of culture. But the schools have a far more positive mandate than that of meliorative accommodation; they are, above all else, agencies for the construction of a humane world order, with America as potential forerunner and exemplar.

During the final years of the decade of the 1950's, much adverse criticism of American education developed in the United States. In large measure, as a result of the shock of learning about Russian technological advances, many critics engaged in agitation for extremely narrow intellectual and "scholastic" emphases. They insisted on a narrow standard for evaluating social efficiency which subordinates learnings derived from associational life to the relatively rare self-realization derived strictly from "book learning," laboratory techniques, mathematical reasoning, and abstract philosophical and aesthetic judgment. The "intellect" was to be trained somewhat esoterically by taking courses in liberal arts, mathematics, and exact sciences (the latter somehow including history, but not the social sciences).

For many of these critics, excellence meant cloistered knowledge and facility in the manipulation of symbols; the application of this excellence was merely to seek for more and more such knowledge and facility. Humane values were to be obtained second hand by reading the judgments set forth by esteemed writers of history, poetry, fiction, philosophy, and the rest, and—to be sure—through reflection stimulated by lecturers and discussion sessions.

Needless to say, we do not number ourselves among these critics—though critics of another sort we sometimes are. We cannot accept, as we emphasize on the many pages of this book, such a narrow conception of education. The American society is heterogeneous. The men and women who contribute to the national welfare are of many and varied talents. From our view, therefore, the mission of the public school at all levels is relatively easy to describe: It seeks to foster the self-discovery of talents and the selective self-creation of abilities of every individual. The job of the school is to influence such self-development in the direction of the social welfare. One needs no special insight, in the light of this assumption, to know that the proper subject matter for the American schools is as broad as life itself, as Alfred North Whitehead wrote so eloquently three decades ago.[1]

> There is only one subject matter for education and that is Life in all its manifestations. Instead of this single unity we offer children
>
> [1] *The Aims of Education*, The Macmillan Company, New York, 1929, pp. 10–11. By permission of the publisher.

—Algebra, from which nothing follows; Geometry, from which nothing follows; Science, from which nothing follows; History, from which nothing follows; a Couple of Languages, never mastered; and lastly, most dreary of all, Literature, represented by plays of Shakespeare, with philosophical notes and short analyses of plot and character to be in substance committed to memory. Can such a list be said to represent Life, as it is known in the midst of the living of it? The best that can be said of it is that it is a rapid table of contents which a deity might run over in his mind while he was thinking of creating a world, and had not yet determined how to put it together.

The problem of the American educational system, of course, is not to find new substitutes for mathematics, science, history, philosophy, and literature but, rather, how to make knowledge come alive for young people. In this volume, we explore the successes and failures of many attempts to incorporate the knowledge and wisdom of the ages into the processes of associational living of students and teachers. And, as to the charge that the schools must somehow produce "great leaders" to save the nation in an age of crisis, we—like Whitehead—are more concerned with the production of a great society.[2]

If mankind can rise to the occasion, there lies in front a golden age of beneficent creativeness. . . . The problem is not how to produce great men, but how to produce great societies. The great society will put up the great men for the occasions.

A book dealing with the social foundations of American education should aim at helping readers comprehend the major social dynamics to which schools necessarily respond and at helping them make judgments regarding the probabilities of the continuing force of these dynamics. It cannot, however, limit its treatment to exposition because it has the further responsibility for fostering perspective and evaluations regarding these dynamics and for stimulating in the readers readiness to participate as teacher and as citizen in shaping the culture so that the ideals to which the society is dedicated may increasingly be realized.

To do this effectively requires more than the transmission of ideas. For ideas cannot be communicated from one person to another except by means of common symbols. In a real sense, ideas cannot be communicated from a person who has them to a person who does not have them. Each person, in other words, must create his own.

[2] Alfred North Whitehead, *Science and the Modern World,* The Macmillan Company, New York, 1926, p. 295. By permission of the publisher,

This is not at all to say that an individual's ideas are not influenced by the exposition and argument presented by other persons. However, idea making is an active process of the mind; hence, if tenable, the conception must correspond to the facts of the individual's experience. Significant ideas, indeed, generally issue from efforts to understand causes, effects, or other concomitants of a fact or an event; they rearrange or reconstruct some aspect of the world in which we live.[3]

In this book, therefore, we have endeavored to foster a spirit of inquiry on the part of each student. We have sought to encourage in the student a readiness to create, however tentatively, his own ideas. The experience and many of the data he needs for such creation are at hand. Not only is his own adolescence recent (perhaps contemporary) and his awareness of community influence keen, but also his family relations and his contacts with the life of his college are daily experiences. He knows the school as it has helped or hindered him in self-fulfillment.

In a spirit of active inquiry and hypothesizing, stimulated and at least partially modified and validated by reflective reading and group dialectics, the student is encouraged to evaluate educational institutions as he understands their functions in American society. How are American schools at sequential age and grade levels endeavoring to carry out their meliorative mission? And with what success is the coordination of positively oriented institutions of our democratic society being achieved? How best can those institutions which are functioning effectively be drawn upon as examples to stimulate and guide the efforts of civic and professional leaders in other communities?

The foregoing explanation will, we hope, make understandable the organization of this book. The sequence of parts and chapters follows a spiral plan: that is, in Parts 1 to 3, the student is encouraged to apply his thinking to aspects of the community, the individual, and the school with which he is, presumably, already somewhat familiar. Parts 4 and 5 carry him beyond the areas of knowledge that the instructor may safely assume are commonly possessed and agreed to; they present those aspects of contemporary American culture which peculiarly illuminate the social and individual challenges that demand responses and adaptations by social institutions. Parts 6 and 7 carry the student into the examination and evaluation of significant trends and practices of schools and cooperating community groups seeking to deal melioratively with those challenges described in Parts 4 and 5. Thus, community life itself tends to become a "school"—a "concrete dynamic whole" in which the "group atmosphere" is characterized by benevolence, by

[3] Cf. John Dewey, *How We Think,* D. C. Heath and Company, Boston, 1910, p. 273.

alterations in the power structure, and by the emergence of dynamic democratic leaders.[4]

The many and varied sources of published material from which we have consciously drawn information and inspiration are acknowledged in footnote citations. Suggestions and criticisms have been made by several professional colleagues. Harl R. Douglass, University of Colorado, urged that the preparation of the book be undertaken, and he read critically several versions of Parts 2, 3, and 4. Frank L. Parks, Oregon State College, contributed criticisms, suggestions, and material used in Parts 2 and 3. James H. Buchanan, Kansas State Teachers College, contributed to the preparation of Chapter 14. Mrs. D'Arcy McNickle, Boulder, Colorado, gave much editorial assistance, and Edwin R. Carr, University of Colorado, read portions of the manuscript. Harold S. Sloan, New York University, scrutinized one version of Chapters 10 and 11. We are also grateful for the help given us by the many students and by the members of committees and audiences with whom we have worked over the years. All of these persons, and more, have influenced the organization and content of this book. We, of course, accept full responsibility for the text as it stands.

Philip W. L. Cox
Blaine E. Mercer

[4] Cf. Kurt Lewin, *Resolving Social Conflicts,* Harper & Brothers, New York, 1948, p. 49.

Contents

xv

PART ONE

Introduction: The American Setting

1

The Dynamic Character of American Society

THE AMERICAN SETTING

With rare exceptions, Americans, whether native-born or coming from lands across the sea, have striven for what they individually conceived to be the "better life." To most of her citizens, the United States has always remained a new and unfinished country; she has, in unusual degree, offered men and women chances to possess material things, to seek and to win independence, and to maintain dignity and self-respect.

Survival in this new nation required, and therefore developed in common people, the ability to participate in the institutional activities of the communities in which they lived—there were wages to be earned, crafts to be mastered, commodities to be made and marketed, and children to be reared and educated. Through mischance, bad judgment, or lack of physical stamina, many, of course, have failed to achieve even their smallest goals. But, throughout the history of their country, large numbers of Americans have been characterized by great energy, persistency, courage, ingenuity, and, often, by audacity. Small successes have fired the imaginations of ordinary men and women and have kindled hopes of far greater achievements both for themselves and for their progeny.

3

Whether as farmer, homemaker, unskilled laborer, factory worker, clerk, frontiersman, or professional, the American has typically been an aspirant, an inventor, a purposer, and a planner.

American ambitions and ingenuities have been stimulated by the remarkable increase in production during the last two centuries, by the vastness of the continent with its resources to be exploited, and by the minimizing of authoritarian restraints by which, in other lands, the common man has traditionally been kept in his "proper place." Into this dynamic milieu of opportunity and challenge, there have entered wave after wave of immigrants and generation after generation of youth.

Two interrelated quandaries have faced Americans: on the one hand, how can they survive and prosper individually, as families, and as ethnic groups; and on the other hand, how can they persuade or compel other men and groups to approve, or at least to tolerate, their efforts to better their economic status and prestige. The uneasy outcome of this dilemma in the United States has been a morality that subordinates socially inherited patterns of attitudes and behavior to estimates of individual worth. Somewhat reluctantly, it accords both approval of, and condescending toleration for, economic self-seeking and status-striving by ambitious men and women.

The Necessity of Ground Rules

In general, the great majority of Americans has come to realize that there can be little security for anyone unless there is a reasonable degree of security for everyone. Hence, if conflicting purposes and activities are inevitable among so dynamic and heterogeneous a people, some ground rules acceptable to the majority are necessary. And since, in the United States, no secular ruler or ecclesiastical authority has the power to superimpose such regulations, the legal and moral codes derive from the consensus of those having enough prestige and power to make their voices heard among their fellow citizens.

In important respects, these codes have had to apply to the entire society in order that great segments of the population be not arrayed against each other. Social mobility has been general throughout the nation. The development of the frontier, urbanization and industrialization, and the building of complex financial resources and instruments have become inextricably interrelated. Ingenious men, for their own purposes, have sometimes directed their talents and incredible energies to circumventing and manipulating the codes of their society. For these and other reasons, a strong national government became a necessity in the United States: to serve as a clearinghouse for public information and as a forum for debating the various, and frequently conflicting, beliefs and desires of different interests. It legislates, administers, and adjudicates, however faultily, on behalf of the society as a whole.

However, the American economy, although regulated by the national government, has been neither homogeneous nor static. Customs and traditions, as well as hopes and grievances, have differed widely among people. So, too, have their economic interests, and these differences are vigorously expressed in the wide variety of pressures brought to bear by individuals and groups seeking to influence the decisions of legislators, administrators, and justices.

Decisions and the Future

Every significant decision by any branch of the government is almost certain to be influenced by the resultant of three general factors: the responsibilities, powers, and limitations of the national state set forth, explicitly or implicitly, in the Constitution; the appeasement of sectional and segmental sentiments; and the dynamic immediate pressures and plausible arguments favorable and unfavorable to the decision.

However, once the decision is made, it is more important for its effect on the course of future events than for the immediate satisfaction or dissatisfaction produced among groups of the people (although such responses are obviously important also). It is in the next year, the next decade, sometimes even further in the future, that an economic boom or bust, an international crisis, a threat of social upheaval, or an era of diffused well-being, hope, and harmony permit evaluation of the decision made by government. In a mobile, dynamic, and only dimly predictable world, every policy decision is made with reference to the future; it is an adventure and an experiment. Indeed, it is the tentativeness and the experimental character of social policies and programs which encourage people to accept them even before their effects have been determined. Such application of the pragmatic criterion parallels the common practices of individuals and groups in a dynamic society—practices that are roughly analogous to the procedures of science.[1] Decisions, whether of individuals or of legislatures, may be thought of as hypotheses to be tested by future applications and to be reconsidered and modified if found inadequate.

What is true of policy and program determination by agencies of the national government applies equally, if somewhat less compre-

[1] We use the term "pragmatic" here, and elsewhere in this book, to refer to the principle that the truth or value of an idea is to be tested in terms of its consequences in action. And by "truth," we mean, with Charles S. Peirce, "a state of belief unassailable by doubt." *Collected Papers*, vol. 5, *Pragmatism and Pragmaticism*, Harvard University Press, Cambridge, Mass., 1934, paragraph 415.

hensively, to state and local governments and to all nongovernmental social establishments. Executives, boards of directors, councils, and membership assemblies, however named, though accommodating their decisions to their characters and bylaws and to the immediate pressures and tolerances of their publics, take action on policies and programs whose adequacy can be judged only in the future. And, since the relative strength of the various factors in a future situation can never certainly be foreknown, flexibility in application and frequent reconsideration of decisions are required.

Much of the same kind of process characterizes every individual who adapts his behavior and modifies his conclusions in the light of what he considers his present needs and of what he estimates his potentials and limitations to be. Though his day-by-day adaptations are not rigorously controlled, they are of the nature of hypotheses to be tested through application.

Individual Adaptations

What we have been saying comes down to this: in our open society, man must venture, must find what security he can in his capacity and readiness constantly to reassess the factors that importantly affect the milieu in which he and all his establishments function and to use these reassessments to formulate new hypotheses. Even though man's adaptations be made at the level of trial and error, with a minimum of reflective thought regarding their probable effectiveness, they are in some degree experimental and adventurous. The diversity and unexpectedness of situations that must be faced strengthen, weaken, or otherwise modify behavior, attitudes, and beliefs.

Only the emotionally mature individual can face the uncertainties of a changing world which calls for daily, even hourly, revisions of responses that have, theretofore, been adjudged the "right" ones. Fortunately, the individual's adaptations are usually made in company with other persons; they are institutionalized changes.

The American society is always in process of change, always becoming something different from what it has been, and always future-minded. Individuals, faced with the necessity of conforming to the usages and outlooks of those with whom they are in communication, must constantly engage in modifying their own personalities. In the United States, therefore, the very socialization processes through which more static societies maintain their fixed customs and values encourage individuals to develop a capacity for adaptation.

An understanding of the processes by which Americans adapt to their changing environment is important to the development of principles and techniques for democratic education. Hence, these principles deserve a systematic summary.

THE COMMUNITY AND THE INDIVIDUAL

Each individual lives in a world of people, with their ideals, customs, and institutional practices. The food he eats, the clothing he wears, the house he lives in, the family in which he grows up, and the language and symbols he uses—all condition him from birth. He cannot escape from these, or from the form of government under which he lives, the technologies of production, consumption, and finance, and the hundreds of associations, traditions, customs, prestige values, and standards of his time.

All these circumstances require some degree of conformity, the price that the individual must pay for the freedom of will or of action he may hope to achieve. Compromises and accommodations between his own drives and the conditioning factors of his society are essential to the development of every individual.

His response to conditioning varies, however, and in that variety he discovers individuality. It is quite as individualistic for one person to seek to lose himself in the crowd, making himself as indistinguishable as possible from his fellows, as it is for another to strive for uniqueness of dress, behavior, or expression. Biological inheritance, childhood experiences and relationships, adolescent stresses and resulting frustrations, victories, and later adjustments, all interact day by day and hour by hour with the "oughts" and "musts" of decisions growing out of one's immediate surroundings in time and space.[2]

The Community as a Social Dynamic

These surroundings, which have so profound an effect upon every individual, are usually thought of as his "community." But community is more than a place. It is also a process.

The community is a social dynamic, a process of producing change in its members. It consists of the language, the symbols, the institutions and loyalty to them, the techniques of social intercourse, the *mores* (obligatory behavior), the *taboos* (forbidden behavior), the standards of living in houses, clothing, food, and mechanical gadgets. It also includes the prestige attached to the stereotype of "success" in the roles of its various members—the manager, the artist, the states-

[2] Cf. David Riesman and others, *The Lonely Crowd*, abridged ed., Doubleday & Company, Inc., New York, 1955, pp. 70–77.

man, the good parent, the good neighbor, and even the gangster, where he is important to the group.

In a word, the community is a complex of information, habits, techniques, institutions, and standards that in their intercommunication make individual minds tick. Interacting with the original biological equipment, this community complex to a great degree determines what a man is and what he shall become. It controls the pattern of morals and aspirations to be encouraged, accepted, or tolerated by the immediate social order.

Immediate surroundings and events, while of great direct importance in affecting communication of information and mood, seldom determine what aspects of community life are *most* important. The family, the school, the church, the political party, or another institution or agency often becomes the most influential force in the establishment of attitudes and behaviors, thereby setting particular patterns acceptable in a given locality. But it is obvious that these patterns of beliefs, attitudes, and behaviors have backgrounds as well as applications that are, in most cases, far removed in time and space.

Examples of temporary or permanent supremacies of the remote over the immediate are almost unlimited in number. Jesus of Nazareth, Shakespeare, Karl Marx, and Galileo are not our contemporaries, but they are very important members of our community; the influence of these individuals in our lives today is far more real and significant than that of millions of our contemporaries. Events in the U.S.S.R., China, and Africa influence attitudes and actions of Americans as effectively as do events in neighborhoods and in state capitals. Ethnic and religious prejudices and practices, established far away and long ago, are maintained in the present. Modern society has indeed become so intricate in structure, so cosmopolitan in character, and so interdependent in its activities that it is difficult, if not impossible, to draw a distinction between national and international problems, much more difficult to do so between problems of the local and of the national community.

Community Processes and the Child

No one, at any age, altogether escapes the community processes. Asleep or awake, in rest or in activity, in work or at leisure, at home or outside it, the practices and feelings of the individual are in large measure his ways of responding to the patterns of his community. What is permissible? What promotes prestige? How can frustration be avoided? How can affection and approval be gained? These and many other questions confront the individual as he attempts to adjust his behavior to community standards.

It must never be overlooked, moreover, that, even during school years, when growing physically and socially is the main business of living, the child is controlled by the community process far more than by the so-called "disciplines" of the scholastic institution that he attends physically for twenty-five or thirty hours a week for forty or fewer weeks a year. The child is seldom under school discipline as much as one-sixth of his waking hours.

More important than the limited time under the influence of school disciplines is the relative emotional intensity of out-of-school and in-school experiences. Greater emotional intensity is likely to be attached to success and failure in the neighborhood or community than in the more restricted environment of the classroom. Both inside and outside the school environment, young people are largely preoccupied with such activities as playing, working, idling, self-decoration, day-dreaming, athletics, organizing collections, running with the gang, reading, flirting, and practicing numerous skills. Every community provides, for these activities, some expressions of approval (or, at least, toleration) which are quite as welcome to children as school rewards could possibly be. The thousand and one uses to which children, youths, and adults put their time and energy determine to a great extent the influences brought to bear upon personality development.

Development, Education, and Training

The educator who seeks to understand and utilize the conclusions of scientists is much concerned with the relative values of these developmental influences. He accepts the fact that the *development* of human beings is significantly conditioned by the multifarious aspects of community life. The educator welcomes some forms of this conditioning and exploits it for ends that seem good to him. He may deplore other elements in community life; he devises means whereby they can be minimized and, if possible, eliminated. He sometimes finds developmental influences which he considers neutral or ambivalent; he seeks to modify these selectively.

The social process, for example, is likely to transmit three sets of conditionings: (1) the mother tongue, love of one's fellows, technical ingenuity, dependability, courtesy, and sympathy; (2) selfish indifference, cruelty, and lying to gain immediate ends; and (3) newspaper reading, political and ecclesiastical loyalties, patterns of aggression and dominance, and pride in physical appearance and competence. The first set is obviously welcomed by the educator. The second he would seek to redirect or undermine. The third he would exploit selectively, seeking to increase those expressions that seem likely to enrich, and to minimize those that seem likely to impoverish, the lives of the individual and of the groups of which he is a member.

Under the complex of encouragement and restraint of cultural influences, such as family, neighborhood, church, television, and advertising, the child grows and matures. He more or less unconsciously absorbs the values and practices of his culture.

Much of what the child learns, therefore, is in no sense through conscious *education* by adults. He picks up information, techniques of doing things, ideals, prejudices, and hopes through a complex process of trial and error, accident, and purposiveness which, taken all together, comprises his experience of living in his community.

From his birth, he also submits to *training*. This training is imposed upon him by those who believe that he and his immediate groups are benefited by the practice of such virtues as personal habits of hygiene and manners, religious observances, promptness, and truth telling (perhaps only selective). Conscious teaching of this nature, begun generally in the home, is continued by the school, the gang, athletic teams, church, police, and employers. Through indoctrination, regimentation, and a system of rewards and punishments, the code of each group to which the individual belongs is enforced. The elements of this code derive from traditions and prejudices, from "the rules of the game," from regulations to promote safety, to protect property, and to maintain orderliness, and from the technical skills required for particular patterns of living.

Throughout the history of formal education, a considerable proportion of school time and effort has been devoted to training young people in the "right" information and skills, "right" beliefs and values, and "right" behavior. Within limits, this emphasis on training is not only inevitable but also justifiable. In general, adults may be assumed to know better what is "good" for the child, both in the present and in the foreseeable future, than he himself does.

Nevertheless, the pervasiveness of the training concept has at least three seriously unfortunate concomitants. First, many of the adult trainers may erroneously interpret social values and, thus, hold to standards which are seriously out of harmony with the contemporary and future social needs of young people. Indeed, their standards may be (and often are) self-contradictory[3] and confusing. Second, trainers all too readily confuse ends and means. They are likely to value docility, obedience, and faith somewhat more highly than honesty, judgment, and independence. All social leaders, especially teachers, who consider edu-

---

[3] Cf. Margaret Mead, *And Keep Your Powder Dry,* William Morrow & Company, Inc., New York, 1942, esp. chap. VI, "Parents, Children, and Achievement."

cation as training, are prone to assume that acquiescence is synonymous with assent. Third, and most serious, is the danger that an early fixing of stereotyped mores and prejudices may unfit the individual for the toleration and freedom essential to modern liberal democracy or to future social change.[4]

Social Ends and Education

Education is a term properly applied to a far broader process than training and to one much more selective than development.[5] Life may stultify and distort individuals and groups as truly as it may ennoble them. The individual develops largely by process of trial and error in relation to the culture pattern that surrounds him. If this culture pattern preponderantly exalts humane values and relationships, the evolution of the individual will be of great educational significance for the realization of democratic ideals. If the culture pattern is unjust or cruel, the results are likely to be undesirable and, in some situations, tragic.

Education is more telic[6] in its orientation than is development. It assumes that goals believed to be socially desirable can be well established. It utilizes both training through exercise of authority and development by encouraging or frustrating experiences in such a way as to promote those values and responses that support educational ends agreed to be desirable.

To be more specific, let us assume that the goals for education in a liberal democracy are self-realization, civic competence, economic efficiency, and friendly human relations. For the attainment of each of these goals, experience fosters both positive and negative adaptations.

[4] Riesman and others, op. cit., pp. 57–64.

[5] Development is akin to, and yet more inclusive than, the anthropological and sociological concept of socialization. This latter term refers to all the social processes through which an individual at the same time "learns" a personality and is inducted into the membership of his society. The concept of development, as the authors use it, emphasizes, more heavily than does socialization, the biological and psychological bases of personality formation without, however, slighting the social aspects. Cf. Blaine E. Mercer, An Introduction to the Study of Society, Harcourt, Brace and Company, Inc., New York, 1958, pp. 70–73, and Blaine E. Mercer and Edwin R. Carr (eds.), Education and the Social Order, Rinehart and Company, Inc., New York, 1957, pp. 30–32.

[6] The terms "telic" and "teleological" refer to distant or long-term purposes as differentiated from immediate goals; for example, a spirit of fair play versus the catching of a flyball or other desired skills in baseball.

And for each goal there are techniques, and perhaps faiths, that may wisely be superimposed through instruction, example, and ritual.

Education, whether it takes place in the school, the home, the church, or any other associations, incorporates the kinds of development and training which foster growth toward one or more of the above-named goals.

However, education goes further. It sets up restricted and planned social environments wherein youths and professionally prepared adults share in the setting up and completing of projects. These adults seek to help each young person to contribute to the success of the class, the club, or the troop, to realize positive social benefits thereby, to act cooperatively and generously within the group, to develop both technical skills and personality traits characteristic of economically efficient persons, and to behave (and, in some degree, to feel) both humanely and objectively toward persons unlike themselves. Some of the projects, lessons, or other group-learning experiences furnish greater opportunities to advance toward one of the goals than toward another; hence the variety of classes, clubs, teams, and other activities. Nevertheless, every unit provides many chances for training, for development, and for education which are designed to promote telic purposes.

Folkways, Mores, and Social Stereotypes

The degree to which training, development, and education can be utilized in terms of such goals as self-realization, civic competence, economic efficiency, and friendly human relationships is conditioned by the potency of those patterns of standards, values, and customs variously called "folkways," "mores," and "social stereotypes," which so significantly guide thought and behavior in a society. The folkways are basic to social organization. They probe deeply into the emotional, as well as into the intellectual, life of man. They furnish him ready criteria for feeling that an institution,[7] course of action, expression of sentiment, or aesthetic arrangement is to be approved or disapproved.

[7] In sociological parlance, the term "social institution" refers to the habits and customs which have been sanctioned, regulated, and established by group authority and which have developed into formal social structures. The term "institution" is, however, properly applied also to an establishment of public character which fosters and authorizes such habits and customs. A useful distinction is made between the *patterns* of behavior standards (institutions) and the social *groups*, such as the family and school which they organize (institutional associations). Cf. R. M. MacIver and Charles H. Page, *Society*, Rinehart and Company, Inc., New York, 1949.

They help him maintain standards, faiths, and group pride by the exaltation of common beliefs, acts, relationships, and precepts that are felt, rather than reasoned, to be "right."

Social establishments provide both stabilizers and lags in an otherwise dynamic society. Their loyal adherents frequently assume that the glorified "truths" and standards of morality transmitted to them are not open to question. Hence, objective inquiry regarding the meanings and justification of stereotyped beliefs makes them emotionally uncomfortable. It is perhaps trite to observe that, today, vast numbers of the young people react with deep emotion rather than with critical thought when such subjects as sex relations, freedom of religious belief, racial equality, and biological evolution are mentioned.

Despite these factors making for social inertia, educational institutions have no alternative but to foster independent judgment and critical attitudes among young people. Such traits are likely to conflict both with the traditional institutional regimen and with the stereotypes that many adults use as criteria for judging whether scholastic institutions are to be supported morally and financially. The responsibility of education in a dynamic democratic society is quite different from that which exists in authoritarian states, where emphasis is placed upon the acceptance of established values; hence, educational institutions must encourage pupils (at appropriate ages) to examine and judge institutions and beliefs. At the same time, their work must also receive the general approval of many people who may not appreciate the importance of the teacher's role as social critic.[8]

Institutional Resistance to Change

Science (by which is meant objective and rigorous inquiry) and *technology* (by which is meant all planning and experimental improvement that tests scientists' hypotheses and applies them to human affairs)

[8] In practice, the dangers potential in the conflicting values of educators who are devoted to science and democracy, on the one hand, and of some religious sects, nationalistic organizations, and other ideological groups, on the other hand, are generally resolved by compromises. The spirit of denial of religious sectarian instruction in the public schools is likely to be extended either to the avoidance of reference to specific ideas, "facts," and data regarding which patrons disagree emotionally, or to making voluntary the attendance in class, the answering of examination questions, and (in high school and college) the choice of elective subjects and club memberships whenever and wherever topics that seem likely to arouse public controversy may be presented. In some public schools, of course, the issue is met by the simple expedient of avoiding controversial matters in so far as it is possible.

have advanced the physical and ideological potentialities of social life far beyond the immediate capacity of any inflexible social institutions to deal with them.

Our political institutions, for instance, with their national loyalties and stereotyped slogans, reflect the attitudes of the eighteenth and earlier centuries when, in Britain, France, the United States, and other countries, nationalism was a particularly potent and revolutionary form of popular reform. In the mid-twentieth century, however, jingoistic nationalism seems obviously inadequate. The present conflict between institutional support for an outmoded nationalistic stereotype and the changes implicitly required by the modern world is itself a social fact which educational thinkers must face and with which enlightened educators, statesmen, publicists, and other social leaders must deal.

What is true for the stereotype of nationalism today has analogies and implications for other social institutions and establishments. Family life, for example, with its patterns of authority, divisions of labor, and multifarious rituals, developed in domestic economies. Such activities as food procurement and preparation, the bearing and rearing of children, recreation, culture transmission, and protection against enemies and adverse forces of nature, impressed the individual with the importance of the relationship which existed between group effort and the satisfaction of individual physical and social needs. Under our modern economy, however, these services are bought and paid for; they are rendered, in greater or lesser degree, by outsiders, and paid for by the earnings of family members, whose jobs, in factory, shop, office, farm, or other places, are only of remote interest to the family as a whole. Moreover, the family, especially in the Old World and in our own Eastern states, was formerly characterized by continuity of habitat and social status. In the United States especially, there is geographic and social mobility which has greatly attenuated the traditional family "virtues," such as obedience, loyalty, and fellowship.

Similarly, ecclesiastical institutions are rooted in antiquity. Rituals and responses that have had intellectual justification in pre-scientific cultures have less significance for many enlightened individuals today. It is recognized, of course, that many religious groups have made significant gains in the direction of tolerance and have partially succeeded in giving modern interpretations to ancient principles of faith. However, the advantages derived from these steps toward rationality have scarcely compensated for the losses in emotional fervor and certainty of belief—two pronounced characteristics of the faithful during earlier ages in religious history.

Courts of law, also, developed principles and precedents under economic and political conditions far less impersonal and abstract than are human and institutional relationships today. In many situations, modern tribunals base their decisions on reasoning quite removed from the implicit facts of the existing relationships. Precedent and custom are thus respected while the realities which have come as a result of change are adapted to fit them. Hence, in legal procedure, the advantage which we derive from respect for earlier interpretations of justice is modified by the difficulty in making modern practices realistic and useful.

Nevertheless, institutional slogans and the beliefs they reflect retain great emotional strength even though they may no longer correspond to realities. Children are told to honor and obey parents even though parental failure may have to be offset by the school. Obedience to law is praised in a society in which clever legal manipulations are often admired and rewarded.

School children and their elders, regimented in posture and gesture, repeat in concert the Salute to the Flag. Although they may not understand the literal meanings of the phrases they repeat, they are likely to feel a patriotic glow from participating in the ceremony. Too often this pleasant feeling also is invoked by men and organizations that, "wrapping themselves in the flag," advocate the antithesis of the noble sentiments expressed in the Salute.

Language itself is so shot through with obsolescent implications that it is difficult to find words to express the nature of ordered relationships among adults and young people of today. The school teacher, serving *in loco parentis,* may get little understanding and support from parents in imposing a type of discipline that few of them feel secure enough to use. Parents remain guardians of their children until they are twenty-one, though these minors may work, fight, and bring up children, independent of family restraints, in environments strange to their parent-guardians.

Church, law, government, family, and nation do adapt laggardly to a changing world, because people find that continued resistance produces futility and chaos. But these changes—necessary, even inevitable, as they are—cause great moral shock in minds attuned to slogans and "principles" of diminishing application. Infallibility of authority, *caveat emptor,* states' rights, filial respect, "America first," are examples of appeals used to justify nostalgic demands for a return to an obsolescent world.

SUMMARY

The immediate and compulsory orientation for educational institutions in the United States is based on two fundamental and interrelated qualities of our culture. On the one hand, there are the complex outcomes of development and training of young and older people of heterogeneous backgrounds and diverse environments; these outcomes are made somewhat consistent, nevertheless, by such common factors as the potential of material plenty, freedom from Old World social stratification, and a high level of mobility. On the other hand, there are the dynamic aspirations to achieve personal security and recognition for oneself, one's progeny, and other in-groups; there is an awareness, often dimmed by rivalries and fears, that the welfare of the individual is fostered by the fellowship of all. This awareness fosters a readiness to compromise opinions in order to get on with a job, to judge policies and acts by their results, and to abide by social decisions lawfully made.

On the whole, American experience and potentialities justify an optimistic philosophy of education. For three hundred years, the remarkable energy and dynamism of an adventurous people have been restrained and coordinated in and by a society which looks to the future. Abuses of freedom have been regrettably frequent and serious, to be sure; dangerous crises have occurred, and may occur again; and social understanding and moral responsibility remain inadequately developed. Nevertheless, the pragmatic criterion constantly applies: the abuses, threats, and obduracies conflict with the purposes of the great majority of men in our society; whereas reasonableness, fellowship, legal restraints, open-mindedness toward change, and accommodation to circumstances, whether advantageous or disadvantageous, all are favorable to the common welfare.

American education is emphatically experimental and instrumental and, in degree, reconstructive, not because the values and truths sought or ascertained through scientific inquiry are more or less certain or ultimate than those of metaphysical systems, but because the genius of American civilization is experimental. Education has a function to perform in order to meet promises and threats here and now.

Consonant with American experience and the Constitutional prohibition, education, as differentiated from training and development, leaves all unexaminable faiths (except that of national patriotism) to ecclesiastic and ethnic organizations. Education does indoctrinate the socially useful arts and information, the fundamental tools of our culture; but beyond them, it seeks to foster the readiness and ability to inquire, to cooperate, to create, and thus to live abundantly in the favorable climate of a civilized society.

Such a society exists only partially and spasmodically. But our philosophy postulates that because it does characterize our humane aspirations and because there are enough exemplifications of it, however fragmental and of brief duration, to justify a belief in its achievability, the social mission of popular education is clear. Education seeks to help persons of all ages to create ego ideals that exalt reason, self-responsibility, fellowship, civic competence, and economic adequacy.

Because much of the training and developmental experiences of young people reflects unexamined and unevaluated adult prejudices and customs, the school's educational program is peculiarly focused on the traits and values that they will carry forward into adult life. These traits and values, which can come to characterize them as young adults, will, in turn, enrich social life as a whole and hence the social inheritance as reflected in the training and development of oncoming generations.

SELECTED REFERENCES

Cooley, Charles Horton: *Human Nature and the Social Order,* Charles Scribner's Sons, New York, 1902. A classic work in sociology which explores the relationship of personality and society.

Gabriel, Ralph Henry: *The Course of American Democratic Thought,* The Ronald Press Company, New York, 1940. An authoritative intellectual history of the United States.

Mercer, Blaine E.: *The American Community,* Random House, Inc., New York, 1956. A general, brief work on American communities.

————: *An Introduction to the Study of Society,* Harcourt, Brace and Company, Inc., New York, 1958. An introductory sociological analysis of the American society.

Myrdal, Gunnar: *An American Dilemma,* Harper & Brothers, New York, 1944. An excellent work on many facets of American life with especial attention to the complexity of choices of beliefs and values. Perhaps the most detailed analysis of Negro-white relations published to date.

Riesman, David and others: *The Lonely Crowd,* abridged. Doubleday & Company, Inc., New York, 1955. An insightful analysis of American personality as it reflects and is reflected in the social order.

Williams, Jr., Robin M.: *American Society,* rev. ed., Alfred A. Knopf, Inc., New York, 1960. A widely respected sociological study of American institutions.

DISCUSSION QUESTIONS

1. The technologies of civilized people are the media they use to achieve their purposes. Show that this statement is true of the alphabet, Arabic notation, parliamentary procedure, due process of law, and the recognition of the individual's right to self-expression. Is the school unconsciously passing on to young people techniques that our society has renounced?

2. "Uniformity has always been the reliance of the autocratic temper. . . . The democratic principle in action is never a formation of any kind, but rather a mode of associated life." (Harry L. Miller and R. T. Hargreaves, *Self-directed School,* Charles Scribner's Sons, New York, 1925, p. 9.) How true of contemporary American public schools is the second sentence quoted? Explain one change that the school might undertake to promote the democratic principle.

3. John Dewey proposed two criteria by which a democratic society might be judged: How numerous and varied are the interests which are consciously shared? How full and free is the interplay with other forms of association? (*Democracy and Education,* The Macmillan Company, New York, 1916, p. 96.) Do you know of a school organization which approaches this implied standard? Set up about five desiderata by which a democratically oriented school might guide its evolution.

4. Is there necessarily opposition between individual self-expression and effective social control? Between social integration and individual differentiation? Between conformity to moral restraints and institutional rules, on the one hand, and self-reliance and scientific attitudes, on the other? If so, what compromises are required for effective institutional organization?

5. If activities alone educate, and if every impression should be accompanied or followed by expression, what does a pupil learn from reading about the institution of slavery and reciting back to the teacher what he has read?

6. William H. Kilpatrick has called attention to the many incidental learnings that go on during a class period. (*Foundations of Method,* The Macmillan Company, New York, 1925, chaps. 8 and 9.) For example, it is the aim of the school to teach, not only how to derive the formula for finding the area of a trapezoid, but courtesy, interest in mathematics, and pleasure in school membership. Further, the ability to sustain effort may be strengthened, weakened, or otherwise modified. Of what importance is this fact to a teacher? How may a class period be controlled if more good than harm is to result?

7. Is there a cause-and-effect relation between the rigid regimen typical of authoritarian school administration, pupils' ennui, daydreaming, breaches of discipline, and truancy? Do schools which provide opportunity for varied approaches to the search for prestige find themselves also characterized by pupils' ennui, daydreaming, and breaches of discipline? If so, is there any solution to the quandary?

8. The legal definition of the teacher's function and authority is that they are those of a substitute parent. But, obviously, the parents of the children for whom the teacher is held responsible differ widely

among themselves regarding norms for personal behavior and views concerning child training. How can a teacher discover or create a feasible role as the representative of such heterogeneous personalities?

9. Some conservative educators, noting that constructive critical thinking is impossible unless the necessary facts are known, advocate major effort by elementary school teachers to inculcate factual knowledge and fundamental skills rather than to encourage immature and inadequately informed children to engage in critical thinking. Do you agree with them in part or in whole?

10. Does the right to life, liberty, and the pursuit of happiness imply an experimental approach to seeking solutions for personal and social problems? If so, may we expect to find many adults and children responding to challenges and opportunities by trying out one mode of behavior after another to see how each one works? In that case, what becomes of "fixed" patterns of child discipline, especially those that have characterized patriarchal or matriarchal authoritative families? Is permissiveness by the family in child training inevitably accompanied by permissiveness in school regimen?

11. To what extent is it feasible or desirable for teachers and parents to reverse the roles assigned them by law, that is, for teachers, in the light of their special training and experience, to guide the parents of their pupils toward the understanding and encouragement of children's efforts to use their liberties wisely in their pursuit of happiness? How else can the teacher hope to find sympathetic reinforcement from parents for his efforts to give educational direction to children's developmental tasks?

2

The Education of Americans

THE COMMON SCHOOL AND ITS STUDENTS

Planned education in the United States, though it includes important programs directed toward the enlightenment of adults, focuses its main efforts on the preparation of children and adolescents for effective membership in a humane society. It is generally recognized that the continuity of our society depends largely on the favorable development, training, and education of young people. Our society is heterogeneous and fluid, shot through and through with nostalgic images of the dimly remembered past and with aspirations for future personal liberties and pleasures. The preparation of successive generations of youth for participation in it requires more than a transmission of knowledge and skills. It is also very important that young people be encouraged to value America's humane ideals and to adopt attitudes and behavior which conform to them.

The Decisive Importance of Young People

American children vary not only in their biological inheritance but also in their memberships in the diverse and overlapping geographic, ethnic, and class segments composing the American population. It is sufficient here merely to recite some of the obvious social groups whose environments in great measure shape their personal traits and their values. One example is some of the people of the Deep South who are

20

dominated by the residuals of white supremacy and of xenophobia. Another example is that of migrant workers, both those engaged in agriculture and those in industry, whose children can have little familiarity with stable community life. A third example is that of the people of metropolitan areas characterized by rapid technological change, expansive public health and sanitary regulations and services, conflicts among different ethnic and occupational groups, and an alienation of work from its final products. A fourth example is that of village and rural populations, less and less self-subsistent as crops, machinery, and commercial services become specialized and as transportation and communication facilities improve and result in the rapid urbanization of their tastes.

Children growing up in these and other definable subcultures, however greatly affected by their environments, still have much in common. Social and geographical mobility, favorable for the freeing of youthful minds from arbitrary authority and from encrusted customs, is all about them. Technological change invades the farm, the home, the factory, the office, the service shop, police and fire departments, and welfare agencies; hence, new and different forms of efficiency are highly valued and so are in demand. The authority attached to parental and other adult statuses weakens as admiration for the power and effectiveness of the technician increases. Prestige is attached to the machine operator, the exemplar of technology.

The sense of power potential and freedom which characterizes the American society has many and ambivalent effects on the youth's self-image. Whether he envisions himself as armed gangster, daring automobile driver, sophisticated lady-killer or predatory beauty queen, or as inventor, junior executive, aspirant for scientific, artistic, or other honors, he exercises his freedom to choose and, with the aid of technological products, to achieve.

The Common School

One experience that most young people have is attendance in public school. Schools differ from each other in various localities and in the population segments they serve. It may be presumed, however, that there is something in the learning of scholastic skills and knowledge, in the rhythm of the school day, week, and year, in the association of age and grade groups with selected adults, and in the regimen of the institutionalized environment that acts as a stabilizing and directive influence on social attitudes and behavior. Consequently, all normal children are required by the several states to attend school from the age of six or seven until they are sixteen or older. And, in keeping with the presumption, schools are mandated to promote in their pupils those traits which are believed desirable for members of the American society.

THE FLUIDITY OF THE SCHOOL

Conservatism and Progressivism in Educational Institutions

In a fluid society, the progressive modification of educational institutions is essential, if social values and civic virtues are to be conserved. The school would be impotent if it should cut itself off from the dynamic community processes which are shaping youthful characters hour after hour, week in and week out, year after year. Hence the seeming paradox: progressivism is the only effective conservatism.

Progressivism is, however, not a stereotyped form of education. Rather, it is characterized by a persistent experimentalism. Its adaptations are planned and undertaken to deal with problems, many of which are not of the school's making. In most cases, the solution of these problems challenges the community as a whole rather than the school alone.

No two progressive communities, hence, no two progressive schools and no two progressive teachers, are faced with the same problems and opportunities as they endeavor to transmit the American heritage to children and to their adult associates who have not adjusted to it. Where, for example, the poor and underprivileged are herded together, as they are in many metropolitan areas, juvenile gangs and delinquency may be rampant, cultural conflicts acrimonious, ill health widespread, and family life and ecclesiastical leadership fragmentary. In such a situation, the problem is one that faces the community as a whole; the school is merely one of the community's several social establishments engaged in meeting the challenges. It therefore transmits to pupils and, so far as it can, to their adult associates a selected culture, one that is in harmony with what enlightened civic establishments are endeavoring to foster. Thereby, the school aids in the conservation of order, tranquillity, and common welfare.

The freedom from traditional authority and the sense of power which is part of a machine age provide a social momentum that the school cannot disregard. How to elicit creativity and how to funnel interests and energies toward the attainment of educational objectives are immediate and almost overwhelming challenges to the community and, hence, to its school. Appropriate responses to these challenges require far more than the transmission of the obsolescent cultural patterns of docile obedience, acceptance of established authority, and pretechnological attitudes and skills.

Education Versus Fixed Institutions and Values

Liberal democracy does not depend on a monolithic belief in a just God, a just state, just officials, or a "true" doctrine—even the "doctrine" of liberal democracy is the subject of polemics. Rather, liberal democracy finds its stability in a tolerance of diversity of opinion and behavior to the limits of overt acts of violence, in the canceling out of extreme opinions and social programs, and in the ideals of gentle conduct, friendly cooperation, and mutual interdependence.

Under democracy, youth does ask itself the very question that Plato feared. He has Adeimantus state the question:[1]

> And now when the young hear all this said about virtue and vice, and the way in which gods and men regard them how are their minds likely to be affected, my dear Socrates—those of them, I mean, who are quick witted, and, like bees on the wing, light on every flower, and from all that they hear are prone to draw conclusions as to what manner of persons they should be and in what way they should walk if they would make the best of life? Probably the youth will say to himself in the words of Pindar:
> "Can I by justice or by crooked ways of deceit ascend a loftier tower which may be a fortress to me all my days?"
> For what men say is that, if I am really just and am not also thought just, profit there is none, but the gain and loss on the other hand are unmistakable. But if, though unjust, I acquire the reputation of justice, a heavenly life is promised to me.

Self-determination: Asset and Liability

In democratic societies, all ambitious, energetic youths must ask themselves that question and face that quandary: How ascend "a loftier tower which may be a fortress to me all my days?" In what way should I walk if I would make the best of life—"by justice or by crooked ways"? If they are to find answers and solutions that are not harmful to themselves and to society, people from childhood must practice making decisions with freedom to make mistakes. The crucial problem of education of young people in a democracy is how best to aid them to find satisfying solutions to this quandary.

Many adults, even in the teaching profession, fear to permit children to make significant choices; to them the possibility of "wrong" decisions seems fraught with danger. They do not grasp the meaning of self-education as the reconstruction of experience. Without con-

[1] Plato, *The Republic*, trans. by Benjamin Jowett, Heritage Press, New York, 1944, p. 54.

sciously recognizing the similarity, they would prepare children for a predetermined adulthood just as they would train a dog for a pre-determined maturity as a hunter or as a house pet. Teachers and parents who would be truly democratic in method and objective cannot afford to sacrifice the opportunity for growth which freedom of choice provides, either in order to save time or in order to shield the learner from embarrassing mistakes.

Predetermination is, however, as impossible as it is undesirable in a world of accelerating change. Civic training and character training may unfit children and youths for the business of living which calls for constant choosing and active adaptation.[2] The practices and re-sultant habits and attitudes which ought to be promoted in childhood and youth should, as maturity advances, increasingly approach those that typify effective adult life in a democracy. But democracy exalts the individual; it requires tolerance toward divergencies of belief and behavior; it recognizes that many persons who have seemed "wrong" to their generations have, through their "errors," made most valuable contributions to human progress.[3]

The preceding paragraph may seem to overstate the case against predetermination. Perhaps, in one sense, it does. Every individual certainly carries throughout life some tendencies to behave in accordance with instructions and even with the unspoken preferences and values transmitted by his parents, his siblings, and others. The nature of our success-oriented society is such, however, that these "inheritances" are radically modified through selection, repression, and adaptation according to their survival values. Indeed, they are often so self-contradictory that they may cancel each other or it may be necessary to choose among them.[4] They inevitably influence, but seldom if ever control, the resultant attitudes and practices of older youths and adults.

Democracy requires more than the people's consent to comply with established rules and manners. It assures the right and encourages the practice of each individual's participation in the processes of government. And since the government of behavior resides in the family, school, church, coterie, and economic organization as truly as it does in municipal, state, national, and international administrations, the right to consultation and to consent apply to all of them. The greatest feasible freedom from outward compulsion for every individual

[2] Or, to borrow a phrase from Burke, to make them "unfitted by being fit in an unfit fitness." Quoted in Robert K. Merton, *Social Theory and Social Structure,* Free Press, Glencoe, Ill., 1949, p. 154.
[3] For example, Socrates, Jesus, Columbus, Copernicus, and Luther.
[4] Cf. Margaret Mead, *And Keep Your Powder Dry,* William Morrow & Company, Inc., New York, 1942, esp. chaps. 3–7.

is central to the democratic purpose and process. But, obviously, every free individual is assumed to be intelligent and enlightened enough to recognize the reciprocal character of his rights and of those of all other persons of his society, and to behave in such ways that the common welfare shall not be seriously abridged by his acts. This recognition and such behavior are basic to democratic morality.

Specific and Evanescent Moralities

If the laws, rules, and codes of the American society were entirely consistent and uniform for all of the population, they might be transmitted from generation to generation as a morality, thereby ensuring the establishment of justice, tranquillity, and a perfect union. Such is obviously not the case. The wide variation among approved attitudes, beliefs, and behavior among different families, sects, and occupational and regional groups makes moral sanctions rather specific for situations wherein one or another code is dominant. Moreover, the ephemeral potency of events which accentuate fear, hostility, hope, and confidence complicate the "musts" and "oughts" of life almost from day to day.

The lack of symmetry and the transitory character of moral patterns in the American culture are, however, somewhat redressed by three factors, all of them aspects of attitudes whose effects will influence the future:

First, as young people and their families move from place to place and from one occupational and social setting to another, their acceptance by their new associates depends largely on their conformity to a basic morality, including financial honesty, respect for privacy, and good will toward their associates. Such morality, although at first fragmentary, tends to establish approved patterns for a wide range of behavior.

Second, hope and the ambition to better their lots in life foster a readiness among people to cooperate with others whose help, or at least whose toleration, is necessary to the fulfillment of aspirations. Cooperation itself dictates mutual adherence to trustworthiness and considerable toleration toward minor differences, whether of race, creed, or other background.

Third, the ramifying effects of the continuing economic revolution are as significant as is adjustment to social imperatives and as is mutual aid in fostering a common acceptance of basic morality. Parochial loyalties, prejudices, and belligerencies are weakened as factory, office, and service employment come to dominate population areas that formerly have been primarily devoted to agriculture, mining, or fishing. Public service and regulations, provisions for patrons, and safety of persons and property foster urbanity, nonviolence, and at least an outward show of good will.

THE CHILD, DEMOCRACY, AND THE SCHOOL

Youth's Responses to the Ambivalent Cultural Environment

Adherence to cooperative and humane norms is, of course, shot through with failure. Violent outbursts and other expressions of fear and hatred occur all too frequently. In-group loyalties and group rivalries foster morally sanctioned intolerance, suspiciousness, deception, and lawlessness; their intensity often overrides the mandates of a humane civilization, and, unfortunately, they are peculiarly powerful in their effect on adventurous youths and young adults to whom they offer immediate group recognition and approval.

Nevertheless, these loyalties and rivalries, however deep-rooted, are in time restrained by an awareness among more intelligent and sophisticated individuals that they are harmful to the social order and, hence, to the welfare of all. It becomes imperative for alert, informed citizens to endeavor to direct and coordinate human energies and dynamisms away from futile and obsolescent antipathy and overt hostility, and toward attitudes and behavior consonant with a democratically organized industrial society. In carrying out this imperative, they find moral support in the harmony between their efforts and the ethical mandates of religion and of the canons of American democracy —the Declaration of Independence, the Preamble to the Constitution of the United States, and the pronouncements of our national heroes. The purpose and direction of these ethical edicts are in common with the dynamics of the American society; hence, they provide a criterion by which events and trends are to be evaluated.

Education in its broader meaning applies to all efforts of these concerned and enlightened citizens, individually and in groups, to promote morally sanctioned attitudes and behavior that are consonant with the purpose and direction of American ideals. Indeed it is only within a society which encourages the advocacy and practice of such a morality that young people can evolve personal codes in accord with American aspirations.

Schools for children, youths, and young adults in this society, whatever other special functions they may seek to fulfill, are under moral obligation to foster attitudes and behavior that comply with the democratic ethic. It is, therefore, a selective culture that the school seeks to reproduce within its own environment; one wherein the participants, whether kindergartners or university graduates and their teachers, find incentives for action and satisfying rewards in accom plishments which are consonant with the general welfare and with liberty for all to pursue happiness.

THE MEANING OF DEMOCRATIC EDUCATION

In the United States, educators are therefore committed to one supreme purpose—to help our society make its great experiment in democracy work successfully. Every adventure involves uncertainties and insecurities, outcomes cannot be surely predicted, and measures for attaining society's goals require frequent adaptation as new insights evolve and new factors become potent. We do not *know* for certain, but we seek to find out, if a government of, by, and for the people can provide the things that justify its endurance—tranquillity, justice, and common welfare.

The Supreme Commitment of American Educators

It may be that human associations are best controlled by some other form of organization than popular consent and participation, perhaps an overlordship by an industrial oligarchy, a tyranny by a benevolent autocrat, a persuasive leadership by a scientific, intellectual, or aristocratic elite, or a garrison state dominated by a military cult. It is even possible that a return to a classical or feudal structure controlled by an aristocratic leisure class, which softens its parasitism with *noblesse oblige* sentimentality, might prove more manageable for planning and achieving these social goals. But the American experience thus far gives fair reason to doubt that any of these would be better.

Whatever the predilections of individual educators, however, their major obligation is to the society that installs them, provides them with prestige and authority, and directly and indirectly grants them economic support. They are morally bound to make intelligent and earnest effort toward assuring the success of the democratic experiment. If our adventure fails, failure must not be justly attributable, even in small part, to negligence on the part of professional educators.

Means and Ends

The goals toward which a democratic society moves in large part determine the means by which progress toward those goals is made. Education, as a major means, must, therefore, exemplify democratic processes and, so far as feasible, democratic objectives.

Democracy is neither utopian nor a far-off civilization to be sought through generations of authoritarian discipline. It is a way of living here and now, a means to attaining present civic competence, humane attitudes and behavior, individual creativity, and economic efficiency for all persons who undergo educational experiences. The constant reconstruction of these experiences with their attendant partial failures and partial successes provides a wholesome self-discipline; it fosters the emergence of a self-image attuned to the individual's own capacities, the approval of associates, and opportunities for further attempts to realize the selfhood.

The democratic virtues, such as tolerance of others' ideas, behavior, and origins, readiness to participate and cooperate, and ability to think objectively and reflectively, cannot be learned in a social vacuum. These attitudes, habits, and skills are embedded in undertakings that arouse personal and social enthusiasm. It is because these character modifications, which are part of the community processes, are valuable at all ages that their development in educational environments takes on a special, dynamic quality.

Education as Transmission of Values

The thesis of the education of children and youths in any society, relatively static or dynamic, must postulate that the emotional, intellectual, and physical habits and attitudes which youths practice will make a significant contribution to the character they will exemplify as young adults. The traits of young adults give color and direction to the standards and aspirations of the society in which they are always the most potent, and often the decisive, element. If young men and women preponderantly support the *status quo,* then ordered change is unlikely, if not impossible. If they preponderantly criticize and challenge the mores, then fashions and customs crash. If they preponderantly demand political and economic changes, then political parties and economic leaders compete to woo and persuade them and, to some degree at least, seek to meet their demands. If they are preponderantly for national imperialism and war, then peaceful solutions to international problems are next to impossible. If, on the other hand, they are for peace, national aggression will not be tolerated.[5]

How may a society influence, even if it cannot control, its own stability and progress? It may do so if it can entrust the education of its youth to men and women of understanding and competence, the majority of whom are in sympathy with its aspirations. Society may thus hope to predispose youth and young adults toward achievement of its goals.

But the number and variety of such educators are great, and their relative influence varies with time and circumstance. They include not only those connected with formal systems of schools, colleges, and

[5] Cf. A. M. Schlesinger, *New Viewpoints in American History,* The Macmillan Company, New York, 1948, pp. 103–125.

adult centers, but also the clergy, officers of youth organizations, directors of recreational programs, editors of newspapers and magazines, and many others. Obviously, the school, by itself, is almost helpless if it runs counter to the more potent extra-school programs and influences.

Confusion of Means and Ends in the Liberal Democracy

Democracy's great dilemma may be expressed as follows: How can these in-school and extra-school influences be controlled for the invigoration of values and processes favorable to the achievement of democratic goals? Would not any effective control require the denial of the democratic right of those enterprising individuals who seek to influence the public mind toward standards that suit their deleterious purposes—the fostering of preoccupation with gambling, sexual allure, wasteful consumption of goods, and frenzied distrust of certain disparaged individuals and groups? Who indeed can be trusted to decide what influence is deleterious and to enforce censorship of the agency that exerts it? And in what instances would public opinion tolerate such censorship? [6]

The dilemma is further complicated in a society which exalts science and technology as ours does. The stream of discoveries and inventions and their influence upon social life become powerful factors in the modification of the conduct and attitudes of young and old alike. One has only to consider the effects on the public mind and conduct of motion pictures, television, the automobile, and contraceptive devices to appreciate how greatly knowledge, habits, and attitudes may be modified by technological changes.

One may reasonably sympathize with those of conservative temper and training who fear that science and technology may so mechanize and dehumanize man that, like Frankenstein's monster, he will crush everything civilized and decent in his life. So it may prove. Certainly applied science has the potentiality for destruction of all that Christianity and democratic ideology hold dear. [7]

It is, however, impossible to avoid this danger. For good or for ill, science and technology are real. They have at least as great a

[6] In limited fields, including sex morals, safety and health hazards, national loyalty in times of tension, protection of property, and threats of mob violence, responsibility for decision is, of course, assigned to appropriate civic agencies.

[7] George A. Lundberg, Can Science Save Us?, Longmans, Green & Co., Inc., New York, 1947, pp. 16–34. For a frightening expression of the fear of the destruction of all life, see the novel by Nevil Shute, On the Beach, William Morrow & Co., Inc., New York, 1957.

potential for making radical changes in the future as they have had in the recent past—changes that affect minds and hearts as truly as they do architecture and the material possessions.[8]

A democratic people, therefore, can only look to the future hopefully in full knowledge of the difficulties that await them. Perforce, a democratic society has to face frankly *all* the facts and trends of social life, as far as they can be ascertained. However reluctantly, it is eventually compelled to take bold measures to deal correctively and constructively with social forces. Intelligence and reason must emerge superior to mysticism or mere institutional loyalty if democracy is to continue to be a dynamic, constructive form of social organization.

It is obvious that purposive agencies and associations cannot possibly deal with the specific problems involved in a technological society before they occur. It is basic to democratic ideology, however, that the stimulus to inquire, experiment, reason, and act within the limits of mutual freedom will tend to solve this quandary. In most cases, young people, if not already malconditioned biologically or socially, will develop active, adaptable personalities as they engage propulsively in the business of living.

Lasting Influence of Education

Because the impact of the attitudes and behavior of adolescents and young adults on our complex society is overt and obvious, there may be a tendency to overestimate the significance of the individual and social development of young people in their teens and twenties. If so, an appreciation of the great, perhaps the equally great, importance that should be attached to the plasticity of free adults is needed.

Competent child psychologists have argued, and adduced somewhat convincing evidence, that personality is largely determined at a very early age. Psychological maturity is achieved by the individual

[8] A rather academic question may occur to the reader at this point. If social psychology, applied sociology, or another social science should ever perfect the instruments by which popular attitudes and efforts might be controlled by whoever might manage the state, would not the precious spontaneity and inventiveness of youths and adults be vetoed in our society—except in the nooks and crannies of hobbies and aesthetics? In other words, will not the advance of the social sciences, even in democracies, lead inevitably to fascism or some other form of absolutism? Affirmative answers to these questions are plausible. They certainly are possible, however unlikely even in a distant future. Indeed, as will be explained in later chapters, the conclusions of the sociologist, Pareto, like those of the earlier political philosopher, Machiavelli, have been used to rationalize authoritarian government.

only if his satisfactions are earned by "mature" behavior even in baby-hood. Averill has stated the case for early determination thus:

> If a child is indulged and catered to by his parents, if his every whim is noted and satisfied; if he is babied and sheltered and spoiled; if he is allowed to have his own way, is given no duties or responsibilities, meets no crossings and rebuffs—then the adult product is inevitable: a physically mature person, with the emotions and feelings and social niceties of an infant. If, on the other hand, he is given early responsibilities; if he is trained to meet his problems and face them; if he learns to control his emotions, respect the wishes and interests of others, cooperate with parents, teachers, friends and mates—then the adult product is equally inevitable: a person not only physically mature, but mature in his social and emotional nature as well.[9]

On the other hand, the world has had in adult education a brilliantly successful example built upon a very different hypothesis—that no matter how inadequate may have been his childhood education in home and school, the destiny of no human being is fixed so long as he has questions that require answers and has the opportunity and the need to make decisions. This Grundtvigian hypothesis[10] has been the basis of the content and method of the Danish Folk High School and of its counterparts in Sweden, Norway, Finland, and elsewhere, which enlighten young adults with little regard to earlier schooling and training. Directly or indirectly, this hypothesis underlies the content and procedures of all effective adult education; its application varies according to social philosophies, but socialism, fascism, and democracy all build upon it.

Adolescent Developmental Patterns and Education

However important may be the place of childhood and adult education in supporting social stability and orderly progress, the crucial significance of the adolescent period cannot be questioned. Adolescence is the growing-up age; it is peculiarly the period of initiation into the "great society" with its standards, customs, atavism, aspirations, doubts and fears, conflicts and cooperations, and blind changes and wavering experimentations. From primitive societies to the most modern and sophisticated ones, the importance of the adolescent period for institutional and individual stability has been recognized.

[9] Lawrence A. Averill, *Adolescence,* Houghton Mifflin Company, Boston, 1936, pp. 106–107. Used by permission.
[10] Attributed to Bishop Nicolaj F. S. Grundtvig, of Copenhagen, 1783–1872.

In a mobile society, such as that created by the American frontier, by the assimilation of large numbers of migrants, and by rapid scientific and technological change, effective adult control over adolescent activities is difficult to manage. Neither unconcern nor regimentation is likely to promote constructive self-realization of the individual and reasoned social behavior. Adolescent delinquents defy law-enforcement officers. Young sex offenders flaunt the rules of parents. Adolescent skeptics disregard the scholastics and undermine orthodox creeds. Fraternity members ignore adult efforts to control their organizations. Zealous bigoted youth groups—religious, political, and economic—act overtly in defiance of custom and regulation. Excessive withdrawal and daydreaming characterize some individual response; groveling sycophancy characterize others. Lust to domineer over associates by means of audacity, cleverness, or conspicuous behavior is another form of overadjustment.

Emotional Maturity Characteristic of Most Individual Adjustments

Conversely, wherever *intelligent, consistent,* and *moderate* adaptations to normal adolescent desires and needs are made by adults, there is likely to be found respect for law as an expression of public opinion. The church will probably be regarded as an instrument for good, and the canons of good taste, supplemented by challenging opportunities for athletic, civic, and aesthetic accomplishments might be expected to reduce the storm and stress of sexual maturation common to Western youth. Faiths and creeds inculcated by families and religious bodies, for example, frequently prove embarrassing when social sanctions reward tolerance of difference, critical analysis, and sympathy for variant opinions.

One may indeed wonder at the general freedom from emotional strain which characterizes most American youths and adults in spite of the hodgepodge of nonrationalistic faiths and loyalties with which they must contend. The conflicts among our sectarian, nationalistic, political, and ethnic stereotypes and standards are many and serious. Occasionally, to be sure, these conflicts are evidenced in bitterness and violence, but such expression is sporadic and unusual.

Whence comes the readiness of most Americans to substitute a quip, a grin, a toss of the head for an insult? One wonders how it is possible for the children of polyglot, multisectarian, nationality-conscious immigrants to grow up into young adults who are so much alike, whether from Georgia or from Oregon, whether met in Saipan or in Rome.

Something little less than miraculous happens in our society; something gives young people a new start in human relationships and in personal values. Quite obviously, the miracle is not complete; vestiges of Old World antagonisms and hangovers of prescientific mysticism are ghosts that scare up present emotional conflicts over obsolete stereotypes and slogans. Indeed, the flippancies and the superficially common interest in sports, television performances, comic strips, fashion, mechanized gadgets, and social acceptability that so effectively blanket open expressions of bias and suspicion are not altogether ennobling.

It might be wished that the explanation for the miracle could be found in our ideals and in the practices of liberty and brotherhood. And in some degree, one is justified in so explaining it. But feelings and behavior are only in part responses to ideas. On the whole, we may welcome the common interest of youth in activities, jobs, recreation, and adornment in so far as they conform in a measure to our liberal ideas, hoping that they will serve as a background of common experience from which rational acceptance of the rights of all men to life, liberty, and the pursuit of happiness will emerge.

Education Not Limited to Schools

Our common life of association in such places as trains, restaurants, stadia, stores, theaters, and factories, and in radio and television audiences, is almost all-embracing. There are, however, a number of rather specialized agencies, segments of our common life, that deserve special mention and treatment. Among them are family and neighborhood, youth-serving organizations, leisure-time activities, labor union activities, governmental programs, economic and business processes, and publicized reform movements. Youth organizations, frequently fostered by adults, wherein young people themselves launch and manage projects varying from selfish enjoyment to "world-saving" services and propaganda are also important. These organizations are often ephemeral, but frequently they are very potent in shaping the character of the active members.

In later chapters, many of these agencies and activities are examined in more detail. Together with the school, they exemplify most of the processes through which young Americans undergo their initiation into adult membership in our society. Out of them come our heritages of work, of thrift and conspicuous consumption, of individualism and voluntary cooperation, of attitudes toward invention and change and toward nationalism, internationalism, and world government. From them, also, we derive attitudes that are obsolescent, if not altogether obsolete, especially stereotypes of bygone economies, for example, individual entrepreneurships, exploitable immigrant labor, rapacious mortgage holders, shiftless carefree Negroes, radical agitators, effete Europeans, and docile, fatalistic Asiatic peoples.

These varied, conflicting, and confusing heritages constitute the fabric of our culture. The designs and orientations change as wars are succeeded by uneasy peace, booms by busts, trust in central government by distrust, parochial pride by the desire to aid the sick and hungry wherever they may be, and the fervors of world-championship contests by worry over race riots. The student of education is concerned with the fabric rather than its more obvious manifestations. He seeks to understand and to evaluate the elements which compose the social heritage of beliefs, attitudes, and behavior in order to discover methods for utilizing them beneficently.

The Democratic Frame of Reference

In the United States, a democratic frame of reference for the educator's philosophy is taken for granted. Hence, his understanding and evaluation of people's beliefs, attitudes, and behavior are affected by his ideas about how they ought to be in order to preserve and promote a democratic society. In a word, his own attachment to the democratic ethic underlies his criteria for determining what is just, right, desirable, good, or the opposite. The democratic ethic also underlies the degree of intensity with which he approves or condemns. His judgments and opinions are therefore frankly and openly biased by his responsibility as an *American* educator.

Within this important limitation, he strives to be rational and objective as he examines the reasoning by which he and other educators justify their judgments. He asks that others be consistent, logical, and honest, and that the facts with which they deal be representative ones, that is, not selected simply to bolster their hypotheses. If these conditions are met, he respects the judgments of other educators even though his own opinions be very different.[11]

SELECTED REFERENCES

Brogan, Denis W.: *The American Character*, Alfred A. Knopf, Inc., New York, 1944. A favorable appraisal of the contribution of the American public schools to the democratic way of life.

Brookover, Wilbur B.: *A Sociology of Education*, American Book Company, New York, 1955. A competent textbook on the sociology of American education. Contains a good discussion on "Education in American Culture," pp. 37–57.

[11] For a clear and succinct exposition of the complexity of beliefs and value choices, see Gunnar Myrdal, *An American Dilemma*, Harper & Brothers, New York, 1944, pp. 1024–1028.

Butts, R. Freeman: *A Cultural History of Education,* 2d ed., McGraw-Hill Book Company, Inc., New York, 1955. A useful book on the cultural history of education in the Western world. Chaps. 9, 11, and 14–17 deal specifically with the American experience.

Commission for the Defense of Democracy through Education: *True Faith and Allegiance,* National Education Association, Washington, 1952. Argues that realizing the American Dream is the paramount mission of education.

Cox, Philip W. L., and F. E. Long: *Principles of Secondary Education,* D. C. Heath and Company, Boston, 1932. Parts 1, 3, and 4, present materials pertinent to the present chapter.

Dahlke, H. Otto: *Values in Culture and Classroom,* Harper & Brothers, New York, 1958. Part 2 of this fine book contains informative chapters on the social and cultural contexts of the American school.

Dewey, John: *Democracy and Education,* The Macmillan Company, New York, 1916. A searching discussion of the relation of education and democracy.

Edwards, Newton (ed.): *Education in a Democracy,* University of Chicago Press, Chicago, 1941. A stimulating series of lectures.

Hansen, Allen Oscar: *Liberalism and American Education in the Eighteenth Century,* The Macmillan Company, New York, 1926. Historical study of the Colonial and Revolutionary philosophical backgrounds of the American educational system.

MacLean, Malcolm S., and Edwin A. Lee: *Change and Process in Education,* The Dryden Press, Inc., New York, 1936. Emphasizes the role of social change in the educational process.

Mead, Margaret: *The School in American Culture,* Harvard University Press, Cambridge, Mass., 1951. Provocative lectures on cultural aspects of American education by a leading anthropologist.

Riesman, David: *Constraint and Variety in American Education,* Doubleday & Company, Inc., New York, 1958. A series of essays on American education in the 1950s.

DISCUSSION QUESTIONS

1. Make a list of social establishments in your local community which strongly influence the behavior of the inhabitants. Compare your list with similar lists made by your classmates.

2. What is your interpretation of the concept *social change*? Can you give some concrete examples of changes which have taken place in your community which might be said to have affected *all* of its members?

3. Name ten or more established moral imperatives characteristic of your neighborhood or social set, for example, those affecting dress, etiquette, religious practices, property rights, privacy, and patriotism. What special penalties are enforced against breaking these standards?

4. Which of the prescribed or approved behaviors and attitudes that you have named were taught and enforced by the schools you attended? Did school membership at any level decrease or otherwise modify your responses to the mores prevalent in your neighborhood or social set?

5. What seem to you to have been the underlying assumptions regarding the nature of the school and the purposes of school education (whether consciously or unconsciously held) that dominated the persons who controlled the program of the secondary school you attended?

6. Statements are frequently made that anxiety is common among contemporary youths and adults. Various causes are assigned and many undesirable results are alleged. From your experience as a member of social groups, do you believe that anxiety is a norm for individuals? If so, does your conclusion conflict with the authors' statement on page 32 that "a general freedom from emotional strain . . . characterizes most American youths and adults . . ."?

7. Is the public school mandated to teach morality? Is there a community consensus as to what constitutes morality which the school is expected to foster? If moral means ethical, does the contemporary exalting of tolerance make moral training unrealistic? If moral means customary, what becomes of ethical discrimination; that is, is it a hidden assumption that it is ethical to conform to custom? If moral is equated with spiritual, does that tend to glorify emotionalized attitudes rather than reflective thinking? Is the quandary resolvable?

PART TWO

Socialization: Processes and Establishments

3

Culture Worlds of Childhood
and Youth

BASIC CONCEPTS

The topography, climate, and fertility of the habitats of human beings are obviously important conditioners of both individual lives and social organizations; so, too, are the biological inheritances of mankind. In combination, these factors both foster and restrict man's individual and social development. They stimulate his courage, ingenuity, and industry. They also compel him to accept and to adjust to his geographic and biological limitations.

The primary concern of the professional educator, however, is with people themselves—in their individual and collective behavior and valuations as they respond to the customs, traditions, and aspirations, and to the material accomplishments and technical processes of the society of which they are a part. The social inheritance to which the people of a society must respond constitutes their *culture*.

What this culture may be at any time or place is obviously affected by the physical environment and the inborn characteristics of the inhabitants. What children learn and enjoy will differ according to whether they grow up in urban or in rural areas, in Southern states or Northern, in city slums or in middle-class suburbs, and according to

39

their pigmentation and their physical and mental capacities. In great degree, however, the interaction of these factors and the development of young people and adults are influenced in fundamental ways by the man-made heritage of customs, inventions, and aspirations. Indeed, the buildings, roads, and even the scenery of a community are, in varying degrees, expressions of human culture. The educator, therefore, deals with physical and biological factors within a culture complex.

From the fetal stage on, every human life is influenced by the cultural environment as well as by its strictly biological inheritance.[1] Adaptive responses begun *in utero* become vastly complicated and multiplied after birth. The individual's natural drives to alleviate his accumulating tensions involve responses to human beings and to his cultural and social environment. As he grows up, feeding processes, voices and gestures, language, customs, and a host of complex relationships and stimuli pour in on the individual from his family and playmates. He lives in the context of institutions, organizations, and accepted social practices. While he must live and grow according to the potentials and limitations of his biological heredity, the human individual may still be viewed as chiefly the product of his learned responses to the attitudes and behavior of the groups to which he belongs. They dominate his social environment.

Cooperation and Social Life

It is a complex and often contradictory social world to which the individual responds. Its primary, though not always overt, characteristic is cooperation, both personal and organizational; else there would be no society. Even compulsion and competition are forms of interdependence, for obedience implies the acceptance of a superiority-inferiority relationship, and competition implies that rules be followed.

As a society increases in complexity, cooperative behavior and attitudes among its members come to include both those which are characterized by alternating leadership[2] and by extrafamilial brother-

[1] The fetus responds to external stimuli, such as noise, and to those mediated through the mother's mental and emotional states.
[2] S. A. Courtis and others, *Cooperation, Its Principles and Practices,* Eleventh Yearbook, National Education Association, Department of Supervisors and Directors of Instruction, Washington, 1939, esp. chap. 2. Varying with the kind of problem to be dealt with, groups express their confidence in one or several individuals who are judged most capable of meeting the challenge competently. Such leadership acceptance is likely to be tentative and specific; it varies with continuing confidence and with peculiar needs as circumstances change. For a more recent statement which empha-

hood. The social maturity of individuals may be evaluated in large part on the basis of these two sets of behavior and attitudes.

As the individual develops, therefore, it is probable that he will increasingly not only recognize the mutual benefits to be derived from compromising, bargaining, consenting to leadership, and exemplifying brotherly attitudes, but that he will also more frequently feel and act in accord with this awareness. The individual learns the processes of democratic cooperation almost unconsciously for the most part. He may learn them as parts of such values as being a good sport or a square shooter. These learnings are demanded by code or vogue within many social situations. Thus they meet the pragmatic test; life is pleasantest and most satisfying if one plays the game according to the rules. Cheating, stinginess, self-seeking, and bullying, the antitheses of democratic cooperation, are generally disapproved by the individual's peers.[3]

To be sure, such moral conditioning is not universal among all groups within a society or in all the social settings of any one group. Deception and clever evasion may be highly regarded in some organized sports and card games and in "horse-trading" forms of business practices. Small-group loyalty to family, gang, or work associates is often accepted as justification for lying and sharp practice. Nevertheless, the culture as a whole tends to set limits on the situations wherein such noncooperative behavior is approved or tolerated.

Living together requires that constructive social behavior and attitudes outweigh negative and harmful ones. Not only is violent revenge forbidden and sullen withdrawal censured by civilized people, but in many situations, friendliness and readiness to forego unequal advantage are expected. It follows that honor is extended unreservedly for individual courage, effort, and resourcefulness only if their expression does not seriously harm other persons or the community as a whole. Even in the case of differences of opinion or of religious faith, there is much moral sanction not only for tolerance for all to hold and practice according to their beliefs but also for encouraging individual expression and persuasion.

---

sizes the roles of expert "change agents" in the leadership of planned change, see Ronald Lippitt, Jeanne Watson, and Bruce Westley, *The Dynamics of Planned Change,* Harcourt, Brace and Company, Inc., New York, 1958.

[3] That is, those persons whom he recognizes as his equals and, therefore, whose opinions he respects. It hardly need be emphasized here that "the game" is *democratic* cooperation. Thus, blind conformism, which negates the dignity and the function of the individual personality, violates the most fundamental of the rules.

TRANSMISSION OF CULTURE THROUGH GROUP LIFE

Obviously, there are strong and disconcerting exceptions to the characteristic patterns of moral sanction in the United States. There are groups composed of individuals not yet reconciled to the ways of democratic living. Zealous adherents of "one true religious faith" sometimes resent the assertions by those who hold to other "truths." Some immigrants from the Old World retain their grievances and loyalties for several generations after coming to the United States, occasionally transferring old resentments to new objects in their adopted land. People of one region frequently hold hostile and suspicious attitudes toward people of another. Members of one ethnocentric group often feel certain that their race, former nation, national ancestry, or other "we-group" is superior to all others. And among all groups are "me-firsters" who seek self-advantage without regard for the welfare of others.

Close association within groups dominated by prejudices and self-seeking does predispose members to inimical attitudes toward out-groups. In the United States, nevertheless, it is difficult for anyone consistently to maintain hostile patterns of feeling and behavior. In the first place, most persons belong to several groups, so that exclusive loyalty to any one becomes impractical. Furthermore, parochialism is out of keeping with the general American spirit of accommodation, good-natured tolerance, and avowal of human rights to life, liberty, and the pursuit of happiness.

The groups to which an individual belongs are seldom homogeneous. His religious associates, for example, are usually heterogeneous as to wealth, national background, occupation, political affiliation, recreation, and aesthetic taste. Similarly, his neighbors, his fellow workmen, the members of his clubs, and all his other associations include persons who differ among themselves in appearance, preferences, and viewpoints. Among young people, similar differences exist among schoolmates, playmates, and among the families they come to know. Moreover, the vicarious experiences people have through reading, attending movies, and watching television extend and vary their social relationships. The social heritage of most Americans is thus conditioned by the necessity for forbearance and accommodation if any individual is to find peace and prosperity.

The Social Heritage in Relatively Static
and in Dynamic Societies

The newcomer to the United States enters a society marked by fluidity and mindful of the future. Almost everything he sees, hears, feels, and tries to comprehend is in some degree in the process of change, is passing and giving place to something new. There is no one absolutely stable "right way" of doing most things. Individual preference and accommodation to circumstance are everywhere in evidence—in personal appearance, in mode of transportation, in language use, in domestic life, in religious practice, in the manipulation of tools and techniques, in employment, in building design and construction, and in practically everything else that is directly or indirectly man-made.

The term *social heritage* refers to all aspects of the environment other than those of nature. It includes all material items such as buildings, roads, and mechanical instruments, customs and modes, morals (which form a society's concepts of proper behavior), and nonmaterial ideas and aesthetic spiritual valuations. To this man-made environment, social scientists apply the term culture; its connotations are vastly broader than those of the popular usage of the word, referring to refinements of taste and manners.[4]

In a relatively static society (one that is most likely to be primitive and isolated), culture consists largely of accustomed things, behavior evaluations, and ideas. Alternatives, if not unknown, are strange and seemingly uncertain. Safety and personal security are found in conformity to established things, modes, and beliefs. Venturesomeness is approved by one's associates only within specific situations—courage in the warrior, ingenuity in the artisan, and self-reliance in the hunter—and only as the initiative applies to his specialty. Within the static society, a close-knit morality controls adults and, hence, children who inherit the culture through imitation of, and discipline by, the family and other institutional associations. Within the narrow framework of family, clan, tribe, or village brotherhood, these in-group virtues include loyalty, honesty, consideration for one's fellows, and the unquestioning acceptance of all other moral behavior and ideas as *right* ones. Heresy endangers the stability of a static society; it is, therefore, generally severely punished by ostracism, imprisonment, or death.

In the static society, the "right" attitudes and behavior directed toward outsiders are very different from those expected to be directed to those within the society. Loyalty to the in-group carries with it the implication of nonacceptance of the ways of life of out-groups. Since "our" beliefs are considered the *true* ones, "our" language, "our" architecture, and "our" foods the *standard* ones—indeed all "our" ways of life the *right* and *proper* ones—different beliefs, costumes, and tastes

[4] Similar distinctions must be made between the social scientists' use of the terms *social* and *society* and the applications of these words to esoteric, pseudoaristocratic coteries, such as the Social Register group in New York City.

are at best strange, probably wrong, and quite likely evil.[5] Altruism toward "foreign devils" implies disloyalty toward one's own associates. To harm the out-group members, except when they come as guests or traders by the in-group's consent, may be morally approved by family and tribal standards.

The Enlargement of In-group Memberships

Social evolution has been largely comprised of progress in enlarging the individual's in-group membership so that the virtues of mutual helpfulness, loyalty, fair dealing, brotherliness, and empathy may apply to members of wider and larger communities.

It is, of course, quite obvious that mankind—even the American people so favorably situated geographically and economically—has not progressed consistently in this respect. Intolerance of the different, the strange, the heretical, the "disloyal" still characterizes most men. We are still, in varying degrees, chained to our cave-man morality. Whether man, especially American man, can free himself before he uses his scientific, technological, and economic power to destroy himself (and perhaps all life on the planet) depends in large measure on his emancipation from his deep-seated tribal morality.

The outcome may be decided by the success or failure of the policy makers of technologically and educationally advanced nations in creating a world in which bargaining, leadership, and brotherhood are possible. It is a complex, almost paradoxical, task they face. They must maintain popular support and consent if the policies they espouse are to be instrumented. Such popular consent, however, requires the communication of ideas to, and through, men whose minds are conditioned by in-group morality, whose emotions demand the approval of the crowd, and for whom expressions of hate and fear are more typically the outcome of the tension they experience than are expressions of love and empathy.

THE NATURE OF THE AMERICAN CULTURE

Contemporary social scientists are rather likely to tread cautiously when they treat of social values. Textbooks in sociology, for example, frequently emphasize the subjective, philosophic character of the valuing process, how specific any value is to time and place, its

[5] Margaret Mead points out that it is indeed common for primitives to regard "themselves" (that is, their tribe or their clan) as "human," while considering all the rest of mankind as "nonhuman." "Our Educational Emphases in Primitive Perspective," *American Journal of Sociology*, vol. 48, no. 6, pp. 633–639, 1943.

frequent impracticality, and the compulsion of democratic governments to improvise means of meeting occasional needs and opportunities.[6]

However justified such caution may be for the pure scientist, it fails to explain the great dynamic of the American society. Pecuniary values, for example, are so highly regarded that whoever does not seek, as a minimum, the American standard of living is regarded either as queer or shiftless; bettering one's lot accounts for much of our characteristic, restless energy. Freedom and self-respect are interrelated aspirations which economic sufficiency aids in fulfilling; they are socially valued goals, even if paradoxically we have to compromise with public opinion in order to gain them. Freedom and self-respect also foster ingenuity, initiative, and competence in some form of activity—in mechanics, artistry, science, sports, or aesthetics. Most Americans believe that they have a high regard for beauty, artistry, and altruism. Appropriate behavior, though rooted in conformity, is itself both a goal and an instrument for attaining other ends. Finally, approachability and friendliness are elements of the self-portrait of most Americans.

All these values are the practical manifestations of those transcendental values given verbal expression in our canons—the Declaration of Independence, the Mayflower Compact, Lincoln's Second Inaugural Address, and the rest. They constitute an important background for the stage on which we play our parts. As Americans, our "looking-glass selves" [7] must conform—or must at least be so rationalized as to satisfy us that they do conform—to these agreed-upon values.

Community Values in an Expanding Society

There is much truth in Margaret Mead's assertion that oft-repeated, emotionally charged slogans are what little Americans are made of.[8] But these rallying cries are potent just because they correspond to the deep desires of the American people. It is the common man,

[6] Cf. William F. Ogburn and Meyer F. Nimkoff, *Sociology*, 3d ed., Houghton Mifflin Company, Boston, 1958, p. 721, and George A. Lundberg, Clarence C. Schrag, and Otto N. Larsen, *Sociology*, Harper & Brothers, New York, 1958, pp. 15–16. The junior author of the present book hastens to point out that his own position in a recent textbook is similar. Cf. Blaine E. Mercer, *An Introduction to the Study of Society*, Harcourt, Brace and Company, Inc., New York, 1958, pp. 14–15.

[7] Charles Horton Cooley, *Human Nature and the Social Order*, Charles Scribner's Sons, New York, 1922, pp. 183–185. William James presented a related concept, the "I" as judge of the "me."

[8] Margaret Mead, *And Keep Your Powder Dry*, William Morrow and Company, New York, 1942.

engaged in acceding to a social power, to whom freedom, equality, and fraternity are meaningful concepts.[9] He is often confused (as are statesmen and scientists) as to what measures are propitious for realizing his desires. Again and again, he has been sidetracked and his crusading zests exploited for irrelevant purposes. In the long run, however, "fact, the dictator" has compelled him to support his own aspirations for happiness through security, opportunity, and recognition of others. Hence, these related conditions have become basic community values.[10]

The American community may, indeed, be best treated as a group-valuing entity. Common interests, the hallmark of community, are not localized in our society. Communication is so vigorous, our economic and intellectual interests so nationwide, and our organizational loyalties so complex that local control over social values, though still important, tends to be limited to folkways, for example, manners, costumes, and ritualistic and moral conformities.[11] Industrialists, investors, machine operators, teachers, farmers, merchants, government agents, and social reformers—although individually they may have many local concerns and associations—belong to nationwide, even to worldwide, communities whose valuations affect their ideas, aspirations, and behavior in important ways, regardless of local residence.

Folkways and Technicways

As long as local and regional populations retained important economic, political, linguistic, and other social relationships that were *peculiar to them,* they kept readily distinguishable behavior and values. But the numerous migrants into and out of these localities and regions throughout our history have tended to destroy the local barriers of custom and belief. During the past half-century, moreover, certain aspects of the complex American technological, industrial, and scientific changes have in large degree revolutionized the outlooks of people of all but the most isolated localities.

[9] Howard W. Odum and H. E. Moore, *American Regionalism,* Henry Holt and Company, New York, 1938, pp. 627–628.

[10] E. L. Thorndike, seeking standards for evaluating the "general goodness" of larger American cities, selected thirty-seven criteria: five dealing with health; eight with educational opportunities; two with recreation; eight with social-economic conditions; five with physical comforts; three with reading habits; and six with other living conditions. *Your City,* Harcourt, Brace and Company, Inc., New York, 1939.

[11] In some cases, these nationwide concerns evoke moral compulsions more aggressively potent than those of local folkways, for example, economic and political expressions.

Odum[12] has applied the term *technicways* to the individual and group adaptations men make to machine technology and its accompaniments. He asserts that they transcend and supplant the mores and tend so to modify human behavior and institutions as to outmode the earlier, natural rate of societal evolution. Technicways are not to be clearly distinguished from folkways. The advertising agencies, for example, though an obvious example of an agency popularizing the technicways, make much use of folk art, both graphic and musical.[13] The near universality of the automobile, while it undermines many folk standards of behavior and of class distinction based on conspicuous consumption, does nevertheless build upon such age-old folkways as courtship, family common ownership, neighborliness, and travel. Similarly, in the cases of clothing, food preparation, shelter, and health protection, innovations change established procedures, but they do not actually *replace* the fundamental needs and processes.

Groups, Crowds, Publics, and Individual Adjustments

Technicways and folkways are communicated to individuals in much the same manner, even though the former are served by a technology which, historically, has not been attached to folkways. In combination, they largely determine group vogues.

The merchandising of commodities is addressed to group standards and vogues which it selectively manipulates and exploits. It encourages the individual to identify himself with group-honored figures and with common or specific success symbols which seem to assure him emotional security and probable recognition by his actual or hoped-for peers.

Technicways thus build up and give direction to the desires and feelings of the people of the communities that they are so constantly and vigorously expanding and complicating. These desires and feelings, to the degree that they are aroused and satisfied, provide the energy and create the means for their own gratification. Thereby, the intrusion of technicways into the folk processes of control becomes so universal that the two merge.

Man's fundamental desires for adventure, security, recognition, and response limit and condition each other in obvious ways. Adventure enhances recognition, but it threatens security. Affectionate response,

[12] Howard W. Odum, *Understanding Society: The Principles of Dynamic Sociology,* The Macmillan Company, New York, 1947, pp. 364–368.

[13] F. P. Keppel and R. L. Duffus, "The Arts in American Life," in *Recent Social Trends in the United States,* McGraw-Hill Book Company, Inc., New York, 1933, pp. 958–1008.

while it fosters security, may inhibit adventuresomeness and striving for recognition. The fulfillment of desires is always conditioned by the reactions of one's associates, one's audience; it is they who provide recognition and response; it is they who control one's emotional security.

Whether the audience is a single person—wife, friend, or hero—or the whole of mankind, the evocation of response and recognition, the granting of emotional security, and the patterns of adventure are socially conditioned. The audiences themselves reflect standards learned from social usages. And these usages represent both face-to-face groups and those which are more attenuated and vicarious, perhaps nationwide or even world-wide. Indeed, the actor himself seeks adventure, security, recognition, and response that conform to the standards by which his multiple audiences are likely to judge him.[14] Each such audience thus takes on "group" character.

It is the group that inspires, tolerates, and approves both the goals sought by the individual and the means employed to attain them. If he would avoid isolation, each person must adjust to the standards of the groups whose good opinions he cherishes.

Every individual belongs to many groups. Often these groups vary significantly in what they value and approve. The family and the gang, the church and the night-club set, the art coterie and the football team, are unlikely to reward the same traits and accomplishments. The individual meets such dilemmas by differentiated behaviors, each adapted in some degree to the specific group's pattern of approval. The challenge to adaptability is further complicated by the fact that each group may have different valuations under different circumstances —the family entertaining guests, the football team at a victory dinner, the art coterie holding a dance.

Collectivities other than those made up of one's immediate associates also call for personality adjustments. They sometimes foster the abnegation of individual judgment and action, as in the case of the mass behavior of a crowd or mob. In other mass situations, one may conform outwardly without seriously modifying his customary personality attributes; for example, as a subway passenger, an observer of an accident, or a member of a waiting line.

Then there are those rather amorphous phenomena called publics. Even when one is a member of a public, his relations with his fellow members are usually impersonal. All have a common interest, of course; else, there would not be a public. But the chief concern is

[14] Erving Goffman has written an original and provocative study of human behavior using the metaphor of theatrical performance as his major analytical tool, *The Presentation of Self in Everyday Life,* Doubleday & Company, Inc., New York, 1959.

in the object of interest—the actor-idol, the political victory, or the sports contest; self-identification with other members is usually half-hearted. One member may not even agree with others regarding a specific, desired outcome or the issues connected with the object of common interest. Often he does not even know who many of his fellow members are. Nevertheless publics are important; they elect Presidents, create policies, and build popular reputations.

On occasion, a public, or a segment of one, may become a crowd; indeed this transformation is precisely what the public-relations employee frequently strives for on behalf of his employer. Publics usually are poorly informed regarding the issue or person they support or oppose; they communicate among themselves in clichés justified by accepted but unexamined assumptions. Despite these shaky foundations, however, the most vocal members of publics usually speak and act rationally. Publics become crowds when they are emotionally aroused to the point that they are unified in support of, or in opposition to, a man or an issue that "isn't there"—a symbol to hate or to adore, to fight for or against.[15]

Religious revivals, political mass meetings, prize fights, and military marching exemplify the exploitation of human suggestibility by means of rhythm, color, noise, and participation (both personal and vicarious) and by partial breakdowns of the cultural regulations that prescribe self-restraint, good taste, and rational judgment. But crowds need not be gathered in one place. Mass media can foster crowd-like behavior for brand-named soap, for fashions, and for or against symbolic ideas, slogans, and persons. Cults can exhibit crowd behavior in their ceremonies and rituals.

The pressure to transform publics into crowds is somewhat offset by the ordinary social intercourse of Americans at work, at play, and in most other daily experiences. As noted above, multifarious associations tend to undermine militant loyalty, pugnacious intolerance, and the security implicit in doing and believing what "everybody" is doing and believing. The formation of crowds is further weakened by conflicts between beliefs and symbolic behavior in different mass situations to which an individual is subjected; for example, his religion emphasizes universality while his ethnocentrisms are segmental. Moreover, the self-pride in individualism, backed by the desire for adventure and recognition which is characteristic of the American dream, fosters

[15] Walter Lippmann, *The Phantom Public*, Harcourt, Brace and Company, Inc., New York, 1925, pp. 65–74. For a stimulating discussion of the role of mass opinion in recent American history, see also his *Essays in the Public Philosophy*, Little, Brown & Company, Boston, 1955, esp. chap. 2.

resistance to crowd pressures. The right of every man to decide for himself what to believe and to do, and the assumption that he has the capacity and willingness to do so (however limited the right and the assumption may in fact be) are supported in the American society by such instruments as public debates, forums, and secret ballots.

Class, Status, and Role in the American Society

Other fragmentations than groups, crowds, cults, and political parties have significant places in the United States. It has come as somewhat of a shock to discover that our "classless" people are actually classifiable in terms of anthropological analogies. The studies of local populations in cities, suburbs, and villages by W. Lloyd Warner and his associates and by numerous later investigators have shown convincingly that consciousness of social status is present throughout our society. The phenomenon of the American class structure will be discussed in detail in later chapters. Here it is sufficient to note that, except for people of different color, immigrant and migrant segments, and the defeated men of the "skid rows" of the large city, the American class structure reflects only dimly its Old World counterpart. In this country, the delineations of the class system are vague; the system interposes relatively few obstacles to social mobility. Class identifications have little in common with the dynamic forces that shape our national destiny.

The *status* structure in the American society is far more significant than the *class* structure. Statuses are multifarious and alternating.

In the hierarchies of business, government, military forces, most churches, and numerous other organizations, superior-inferior status relations are a constant. Such status is, however, specific and functional, rather than personal; the superior official in a lodge may be an inferior in employer-employee relationship; the captain in the national guard may be the janitor in an apartment house. Within a single family, the mother and the wife may hold separate statuses without distorting her personal relationships.[16]

In a word, class status is only one of many statuses in our society. Indeed, one of the most striking phenomena in the contemporary United States is the frequent change of role and status among people. Expertness and self-confidence in almost any role assure high status

[16] One leading sociological theorist uses the family as a test of whether or not a given status position figures prominently in the stratification system. He writes, "if different statuses may be combined in the same family and must be so combined to operate properly, they cannot be the basis of social stratification." Kingsley Davis, *Human Society,* The Macmillan Company, New York, 1949, p. 365.

and respect. The surgeon readily accords superior status to the auto mechanic when his car needs "doctoring." The upper-upper-class socialite, disturbed about the condition of the road near his residence, acknowledges the superior status of the politician or municipal superintendent of streets with respect to having it repaired. Almost every individual is accorded superior status in some role. He may be the toughest rowdy, the coolest gambler, the cleverest pickpocket, the best-dressed woman, or "always good for a laugh." Or he may be an able lawyer, an erudite professor, or a civic leader. Indeed, he may attain high status in several varied roles independent of each other and with little relation to his social-class status.[17]

Role-, status-, and class-mobility patterns change with the times. The acceleration of change and the unevenness in the rates of change are so great in the contemporary United States that new dilemmas, new experimental solutions, and new triumphs and disappointments constantly intrude into the configurations of daily life. Whoever has, or seems likely to develop, a skill, a method, or special knowledge that in any way contributes toward meeting the challenges of the day may, at least temporarily, play an eagerly acknowledged role and may find respected status within some group.

Status Seeking and Personality Adjustment

One other aspect of the interplay of role, status, and social class should be mentioned. No matter how specifically the high status accorded to an individual is related to his role, its effect on his personality usually increases his general self-esteem and self-confidence. Because of this, he seeks and frequently attains recognition in related roles and functions. Success makes personality dynamic and propulsive. Moreover, popular recognition of his elevated status, however specific to a single role, fosters a readiness of his publics to look to him respectfully for competence and leadership in other roles and, hence, to accord him special status. Furthermore, because social class is rather artificially superimposed on our technologically conditioned society, there develop many significant situations wherein members of the upper social class have much lower social status in certain circles than middle-class people who have special competencies to meet emergencies.

Failure to win status may also stimulate effort. The major observable effect to compensate for disappointment may be discouragement

---

[17] Continuing recognition accorded to superior status of any role player generally requires that he frequently give evidence of his special competence in the role. The professional boxer must fight; the statesman must take action; the mother must love and protect. Every privilege and prestige carries corresponding responsibility.

and withdrawal or a wounded aggressiveness. Whether in fantasy or in active membership in other fields of endeavor, however, the ego seeks to find status. The roles sought and played under the "secret control" [18] of the wound inflicted by failure often are disruptive to the social order. Such roles are exemplified by behavior associated with courtship and marriage without regard to social-class lines, extreme concern for recognition of beauty or athletic prowess, and even clever and risky delinquency—in so far as they grow out of failure in business, academic tasks, and the like.

Adaptations which grow out of success and failure in status-seeking roles take place from birth to old age. The individual is seldom conscious of the causes of his tensions, of why he drives himself to find and fulfill roles that will bring recognition and status. The causes are deeply and complexly embedded in the interaction of self and group during infancy, childhood, youth, and adult life; each successive event engages a differently conditioned self and a differently perceived audience.

It is indeed by these interactions that the individual reconstructs experiences and so becomes a status-seeking person. The responses of others to his behavior so stimulate and modify his personality that they are embodied in his later feelings and actions. Herein is found the justification for the cliché that the personality is socially conditioned.[19]

The Local Environment

Competition for self-expression by individuals is a constant in any social organization. Where the social environment is relatively homogeneous—as it may be in a family, a neighborhood predominantly of one religious sect or of one national origin, or a small country village—the patterns of approval and rejection are likely to be more

[18] H. G. Duncan, "Secret Control," *The Journal of Educational Sociology,* vol. 2, no. 1, pp. 300–309, 1929.

[19] The following deal with various aspects of role, status, and social stratification: W. Lloyd Warner, *American Life: Dream and Reality,* University of Chicago Press, Chicago, 1953; Richard Centers, *The Psychology of Social Classes,* Princeton University Press, Princeton, N.J., 1949; Bernard Barber, *Social Stratification: A Comparative Analysis of Structure and Process,* Harcourt, Brace and Company, Inc., New York, 1957; and Joseph A. Kahl, *The American Class Structure,* Rinehart & Company, Inc., New York, 1957. For a brief summary of important researches on social mobility, see Blaine E. Mercer, *An Introduction to the Study of Society,* Harcourt, Brace and Company, Inc., New York, 1958, pp. 499–505.

nearly consistent than in the heterogeneous groups characteristic of much of modern American urban and surburban life. In the former, the folkways and mores are more compulsive; individuals are likely to conform more strictly to patterns of belief, loyalty, speech, and manners; security, recognition, and kindly response are withheld from the nonconformist. In the latter, traits which adhere only to a segment of the population may be assessed as peculiarities, parochialisms, and gaucheries, to be sure, but occupational and political associations are likely, with little regard to peculiarities of culture, to award status for individual contribution to some common end. Hence, social adaptability, rather than moral assuredness, is rewarded.

The social and spiritual values characteristic of the differing American communities can be assessed only within the frame of reference of the American dream in a technological society. If our destiny is to be roughhewn by conserving the "virtues" that are sometimes assumed to have made our country great, then parochial moralities may in fact keep us on course since frequent adaptations for immediate ends, besides being superficial, may be devoid of a sense of direction. Conversely, adaptability seems imperative if life, liberty, happiness, justice, tranquillity, the common defense, and the general welfare are to be worked for anew in situations of kaleidoscopic change. The flexibility that subordinates "fixed ideas" and "old-fashioned" moral sanctions to current exigencies, however shallow-rooted it may be, seems inevitable.

The transition is occurring, in any case. The techniques of communication and transportation, occupational requirements, the cycles of war and uneasy peace, inflation and depression, and geographic and social mobility all accentuate the emphasis on adaptability. The only constant is change!

The "eternal verities" may still hold, but their attainment must be sought always in new environments. Educational agencies, in fact, are but intentionally controlled environments, where individuals under guidance can reconstruct their experiences and so re-create themselves. In so far as families, neighborhood groups, governmental agencies, political and economic associations, social service organizations, churches, and other social establishments perform such functions, they are as truly and significantly educational as the school.

Some of these establishments deal directly with young people; all of them bring indirect influences to bear on children and youth. In certain respects, each of them may well provide a more auspicious developmental environment than the school is allowed to offer; this is because the school is severely limited both by legal restrictions and by the traditions and stereotypes of its staff and its publics.

CULTURAL TRANSMISSION IN THE UNITED STATES

Culture Modified in Transmission

The transmission of culture in societies that are dynamic and constantly growing takes on a peculiar characteristic. It is inevitable in such a society that youth learn to use knowledge, instruments, and beliefs that are themselves changing from year to year. The youth often inherits, therefore, not an attitude of respect for the erudition and mastery of his elders, but admiration for their adaptability, their readiness to examine new hypotheses and proposals and to adopt and utilize those that seem most likely, by their superiority, to replace the ones previously believed to be true. Hence, most youth become concerned with the use of accurate information experimentally employed for the establishment of new values and concepts, which in turn must be subjected to the most rigid and constant reexamination in the light of experience.

Conservative Exploitation of the Spirit of Inquiry

There is, moreover, an acceleration of change in the society which is due to questioning attitudes on the part of its more vigorous and more admired adults and which is, therefore, inevitably transmitted to the young. Questioning attitudes and experimental hypotheses lead out in many directions. New forms of crime, new experiments in finance, new missions for the church, new apparatus for fighting wars, new instruments and methods for propagandizing and indoctrinating the people for selfish or for unselfish ends, new ways of spending increased leisure time, new forms of exploiting the ignorant and the socially aspiring, new discoveries by scientists, new techniques for engineers and physicians—these and hundreds of other innovations and experiments are going on all of the time.

In some significant cases, however, the very processes of inquiry and experiment may be exploited to foster conformity among the youth and adults whom the innovator seeks to influence. The inquiring and innovating mind of the tory, for example, may evolve methods and instruments which tend to make passive the minds of the common people—at least regarding political and economic questions, for example, party labels, pageantry, trivial gossip, slogans, and repeated assertions. The active orthodox religionist may popularize his orthodoxy through appeals to fear, rivalry, revivalist excitement, social aspirations, and even economic survival, or he may so structure his organization that great numbers of people feel that they have a share in creating and maintaining it. Leaders who find expression for their talents in politics, business, or labor, often are similarly ingenious. They are equally resourceful in impressing the membership of their organizations —and through them the public at large—with the positive relationship which, they assert, exists between their privilege and power and the general welfare of the community.

Such soporifics for the popular mind—myths, patriotic fervor, loyalty, excitement, diversion, conformity, economic success—have been known and used since social organization began. Plato, who looked forward to a static society, would have had philosophers create a social inheritance that would keep the "silver" (inferior) men content and docile. The transmission of an idealized culture, he believed, could only be had through censorship; only by purifying the social inheritance and teaching it as a code could a state develop in which injustice would give way to justice.[20] The medieval church and the modern totalitarian state are both examples of this same thought pattern, that is, that people are benefited through a government which induces conformity of belief and behavior in civic and economic matters while encouraging vocational and recreational diversity.[21]

Science as a Way of Life in the United States

In most realms of behavior and ideas, Americans make choices regarding what they shall do and what they shall believe. Such choices are hedged about by moral considerations; they are subject to crowd pressures and stereotypical values; they reflect the individual's innate qualities as shaped by previous experience. Often, however, these influences are ambiguous and conflicting. His choices are, therefore, seldom altogether predetermined. Generally he selects his responses from among a number of alternatives.

Willingness to conform to an institutional pattern, whether of clothing, etiquette, religious belief, national myth, or pursuit of "success," is a choice, even though the decision be negative. So, too, is defiance of a conventional belief, especially if it is a protest against anonymity.

In an open society, every person is free in some degree to create his own self. He adjusts day by day to the exigencies of life, partly to minimize obstacles and partly to grasp opportunities for self-assertion. Thereby he develops his distinguishing character, his uniqueness as an individual.

[20] Plato, *The Republic*, trans. by Benjamin Jowett, Heritage Press, New York, 1944, pp. 86–119.
[21] R. M. MacIver, *The Web of Government*, The Macmillan Company, New York, 1948, pp. 46–47.

Obviously, there is no single pattern of American character; indeed, even the categories into which Americans are sometimes classified are ambiguous. Nevertheless, there are central tendencies toward plasticity caused by the accessibility of new forms of experience. Each exposure to changing opportunity fosters, if it does not quite require, some modification of thought and behavior.

The process of determining what modification is likely to suit the occasion is experimental. Though influenced by imitation of others' adjustments, conformity to instructions, and the acceptance of advice, the actual adaptation of an individual to meet a new challenge involves at least a modicum of reflective thinking.

Reflective thinking is scientific, no matter how it enters into the process of adaptation to our rapidly changing culture. It is an attempt to predict the effect of whatever adjustment is to be chosen or discarded. The prediction utilizes those factors which can be readily identified and whose potency may be measured or estimated; these factors are supplemented by what is recalled from similar past experience. The choice arrived at, to the extent that it is affected by reflective thinking, is the individual's hypothesis. He tries out this hypothesis, modifying it as he makes further adaptations of his behavior and beliefs to meet contingencies.

Science and the Nonspecialist

Many opportunities as well as many difficulties face young people as they develop socially from infancy to adulthood. It is well worth the student's time and effort to explore and seek to understand these opportunities and difficulties. The data and techniques of the sociologist, anthropologist, psychologist, physician, and others are useful in the refinement and correction of whatever tentative conclusion may already have been reached. Many scientific data, generalizations, and techniques will be presented in later chapters of this book.

Science is not esoteric and mysterious, reserved for specialists and experts. Doubtlessly, experts use it more skillfully than nonspecialists and achieve ends that are denied the latter. Nevertheless, science as a way of life—an attitude favorable to objectivity and logic, a practice of seeking causes for phenomena and of estimating present and future outcomes of the interplay of forces and events—is a social heritage in which all men share in greater or lesser degree and in some or many activities.[22] In the realms of competitive sports, love-making, finessing at bridge, designing costumes, cooking a meal, telling a story, solving

[22] Cf. James B. Conant, *Science and Common Sense,* Yale University Press, New Haven, Conn., 1951, esp. pp. 258–353.

a puzzle, or making investments, men seek in some degree to estimate outcomes that will result from those antecedents which they recognize and to which they assign importance—whether these antecedents be astrologers' prophecies, analogies drawn from previous successful experiences, or the construction of trend graphs.

Moreover, each has a private domain for data-gathering, analysis, comparison, application, and formulation of hypotheses—the memories of his useful experiences and those of his companions. However inaccurate these memories may be, and however suffused by auras of pleasure and anguish, they are his own. And yet, those who seek to recall the past in an effort to attain objectivity are frequently surprised to discover how generally adults have shared in experiences similar in kind and in intensity to those that characterize the young people of the present. Consider the following:

1. Suppose that you first turn to your own school days. What can you recall about the school buildings, school organization, teachers, custodians, fellow pupils, and out-of-school companions, and the patterns of their homes in those days?

2. Did you learn as much from living with others and from the total school activity (associational living and school regimen) as from learning school subjects?

3. Did you admire, perhaps develop deep affection for, older young people, such as upperclassmen, teachers, older members of your own or of your friends' families? For those of your own age? Of one or of both sexes? Simultaneously or at different stages of your development?

4. Did you skip classes, play truant, daydream, escape to imaginary adventures? How often? With whom? For what reasons?

5. Have you, or have any of your friends so far as you know, been deeply affected by the literary and intellectual masterpieces, for example, great books, the intellectual disciplines (such as mathematics, linguistics, and science) that you have studied in school and college?

6. To what autonomous groups did you belong as you grew up, such as family, neighborhoods, churches, play groups, clubs, athletic teams, stamp collectors, orchestras, and campers?

7. What of the loyalties and antagonisms that were associated with membership in each of these groups? Were they personal-psychological ones? Were they caused by the mores of the groups? Or were they responses to outside influences, such as hostility, fear, or jealousy on the part of nonmembers toward the group?

8. Can you recall the emotional coloring of attitudes and behavior toward members of these in-groups as compared with those

exemplified in relation to nonmembers of the same and of different age levels?

9. Whom did you recognize as peers among your associates at different stages? What places did age, race, ethnic background, religious affiliation, sex, economic status, special competencies, and sophistication of dress and conduct play in your acceptance of associates as peers rather than as inferiors or superiors? Were peers more likely to be siblings, athletes, members of the gang, school classmates, members of the same sex, or sophisticates rather than their opposites?

10. What of the sex mores? How early and in what sequence did they affect you? Can you recall other early conditionings by parents or other adults regarding what you, as a little girl or a little boy, were supposed to do, to like to respond to, or to wear? What is your earliest memory of awareness of the subtleties of the pursuit-and-being-pursued game prescribed by the sex mores of the American society?

11. Can you recall childhood examples of instruction and imitation that made you conscious of the roles of etiquette, posture, dress, conversational "lines," and other sophistications as they accentuated masculinity and femininity?

12. At what age did you first recognize the peculiarly moralistic fervor of judgments regarding sex and "sin"? What were the origins of this impact? Were they from family? Religion? Literature?

13. Aside from striving to conform to the appearance and other standards of admired peers and elders of one or both sexes, what other adult stereotypical models influenced you temporarily or lastingly? What of athletic heroes? Political fixers and big shots? Military figures? Civic leaders? Club women? Labor organizers? Homemakers? Musicians, actors, and other artists? Can you identify any aspects of the pattern of prestige that led you to emulate them?

The above questions suggest only a few of the many experiences shared by the vast majority of people of college-age or over. Though they grew up in a different time, young people ought not to underestimate the extent of common experience they and their elders have had—and their own children most probably will have.

We grow into our society by entering many aspects of it rather simultaneously. We cannot escape any of them altogether. But we have come a long way toward understanding what our personalities are and how they are formed. We can estimate the relative potency of the elements of nurture and nature that interact to make us and our contemporaries what we are and what we are likely to become.

SUMMARY

In this chapter we have attempted to demonstrate that young people live in a cultural world of their own which relates closely to the accumulated and changing heritage of their whole society, and, indeed, of all mankind. This culture is not of their making, but at the same time, it is the one in which they grow up, mature, and take their places as citizens, living more or less adequately in the present, and predisposing themselves willy-nilly toward the adaptations they will be required to make in the future.

The various ways in which the individual interacts with his social surroundings and the part played by these surroundings may well be manifested in the organizations and institutions with which he identifies. Of one thing we may be sure: whatever the individual may eventually become in the maturing process will result from interaction with his immediate environs and his resulting interpretation of these interactions as they relate to the social standards he knows.

The chapters immediately following deal, therefore, with some selected, rather primary groups that condition young people and with some secondary institutions that less directly and immediately control their moods and their minds.

SELECTED REFERENCES

Albig, William: *Modern Public Opinion,* McGraw-Hill Book Company, Inc., New York, 1956. An able treatment of public opinion and its formation.

Benedict, Ruth: *Patterns of Culture,* Penguin Books, Inc., Baltimore, 1956. This anthropological study in comparative cultures has been widely influential in the social sciences. A good place to start for an understanding of the influence of culture in personality development.

Dewey, John: *The Public and Its Problems,* Henry Holt and Company, Inc., New York, 1927. An insightful essay on the thesis that democracy is not simply a political system, but a way of life.

Handlin, Oscar: *The American People in the Twentieth Century,* Harvard University Press, Cambridge, Mass., 1954. A fascinating study of the American character.

Martindale, Don: *American Social Structure,* Appleton-Century-Crofts, Inc., New York, 1960. A competent textbook on the American society, with emphasis on community analysis.

Mercer, Blaine E.: *The American Community,* Random House,

Inc., New York, 1956. A brief survey of research and theory on the American community.

Queen, Stuart A., William N. Chambers, and Charles M. Winston: *The American Social System,* Houghton Mifflin Company, Boston, 1956. An interesting and informative textbook on American social and cultural patterns.

DISCUSSION QUESTIONS

1. Assuming that it is true that two infants of seemingly equivalent capacities will most likely grow up to be very different persons during their mature lives, is the differentiating factor more likely to be one of immediate cultural environment (family and neighborhood during childhood) than it is the complex and frequently contradictory prestige patterns and rules of the game to which one must adjust as he grows up? Or is it because of some innate, latent ability which eventually springs forth from heredity?

2. Is it feasible (and if so, desirable), that children of school age attempt directly to judge and to influence the provisions of home and neighborhood for health, recreation, and beauty, for example, campaigns for playgrounds and parks and agitation for new public buildings? Do such activities demoralize the relationships between children and adults? If the effects vary, what are some of the determining variables? Are the adult world and its standards ever challenged by youth? With much success?

3. Is social ignorance (as reflected by admiration for big-shot cleverness and ruthlessness, by superstition and fatalistic attitudes toward matters of health and safety, and by emulation of superficial qualities of much-publicized individuals) more or less frequent among the more highly educated than among the less educated parents of a neighborhood known to you? Is school education an antidote for social ignorance? Might it be?

4. Marxians generally argue that the individual is so largely the product of his environment that punishing him for illegalities and immoralities is pointless except as it restrains him temporarily from further depredations and, perhaps, warns others that such acts are not tolerated by society. In effect, according to this position, the justice or injustice of a punishment for an offense is less important than its influence in modifying community tolerance and moral standards and in developing moral integrity. How does this outlook compare with your own? With that generally reflected by American judicial opinions? With that usually found in newspaper editorials dealing with crime? Is the individual

will equally as important as social conditions in determining morality and obedience to law?

5. Despite multifarious upbringings in families and neighborhoods, people of Western culture are assumed to be much the same everywhere in their desire for security and dignity and affection. Are they? Despite great differences in current behavior, attitudes, and aspirations among individuals and social segments the world over, has the faith of liberal democracy in the right of the individual to *his* life, *his* liberty, and *his* pursuit of happiness a chance of success if used as the primary guidepost in determining social policies and programs? Consider this in connection with the treatment of lawbreakers, both wealthy and poor. In the conscious and unconscious neurological character of an individual whom you know well, what part do the adjustments of babyhood seem to you to play? How does it come about that there is so great a degree of uniformity among adults, in view of the unique combinations of social conditioning and biological potentialities that might be expected to make everyone very different from everyone else?

6. Life adjustment is a matter of continuing reconstruction of experience. Basically it is developmental and experimental rather than consciously educational in character. Is it possible under the conditions of contemporary institutional life for any specialized meliorative social agency to influence in significant degree the processes of family and neighborhood life adjustment? What of playgrounds and athletic contests? What of censorship? What of religious training?

4

Family and Neighborhood

THE FAMILY AS A UNIVERSAL INSTITUTION

One of the institutions common to all mankind is the family. It varies greatly in specific form and function from one society to another and even from one group to another within the same society, but it exists in some variation everywhere and among all people. The dependence of the infant on the protection and nurture of older persons assures very intimate associations of the child with parents and, usually, with siblings during his early, most formative years.

Both biological adaptation and social learning take place in the young child from hour to hour. His learning is chiefly by trial and success or error, but his biological equipment is such that these successes and errors are largely functions of his intimate relationship with older associates.

Babies differ by nature in spontaneous bodily movement (mobility) and in emotional expression (temperament). Their patterns of interaction with other human beings and with material objects, as well as with their physiographic environments, are learned through practice. Habits of adjustment (which appear about the fourth month) are, therefore, products of learning, but biologically inherited predispositions determine in considerable degree which habits will be learned and which rejected.

62

In a relatively homogeneous society, the sum total of inter-actions results in behavior patterns that are more alike than unlike because the social environment to which individual children must adjust is similar. The student of the social foundations of education deals with personality traits which are common to all normal persons just as he does with any other facts of human development.

Nevertheless, the specialist in this field is usually peculiarly cautious where such generalizations are concerned. Two reservations are in order. First, he is keenly aware that some patterns which are almost universal in one society may be unusual or nonexistent in another; consequently, they must be treated with reference to social conditioning in the family and the community rather than to biological equipment. Second, in common with modern psychologists, he is skeptical of any specific cause-and-effect relationship that might be inferred from the relating of feelings to behavior.[1]

Innate capacities are widely agreed to be less potent drives to human conduct for the great preponderance of men than are the social customs that condition the individual. "Men spring from culture." [2] These reservations do not mean the denial of the universality of certain equipment or the reality of the driving effect of emotion. They do mean that biological inheritances are frequently less important than culture in determining individual and group attitudes and conduct. The student of personality formation finds a major concern, therefore, in drives which have to do with the way men relate to one another, whether these drives spring primarily from the inherent nature of the person or the customs and taboos of the social group.

Approached in this way, the questions of what comes first in time and in importance, nature or nurture, and of the actuality of three, a hundred, or no inherited patterns of behavior become academic. Fear, anger, sex feelings, and other emotions are realities, and to understand personality is to understand the characteristics, the causes, and the effects of their varied manifestations in the social environments where they occur. *Effects are further causes*—there is a chain reaction. Each type of manifestation is to be evaluated in terms of its probable influence on individual and, for the educator, on social welfare.[3]

[1] Cf. Clyde B. Moore and William E. Cole, *Sociology in Educational Practice,* Houghton Mifflin Company, Boston, 1952, pp. 57–78.

[2] Leonard W. Doob, *Social Psychology,* Henry Holt and Company, Inc., New York, 1952, p. 46.

[3] For more detailed and comprehensive treatment of original nature and social conditionings, see Gordon W. Allport, *Personality: A Psychological Interpretation,* Henry Holt and Company, Inc.,

THE AMERICAN HOME

The family, functionally and structurally, is the most important conditioner of the child's personality. The infant comes into the world with relatively few inherited behavior patterns and with a great capacity for variety in adaptation to his environment. The acculturation process in the family depends upon the plasticity of the child.

It is almost inevitable that there should be considerable conformation of the baby's habits and attitudes to the family's functional requirements. Feeding, sleeping, dressing, comforting, and all other aspects of infant care involve human beings and their natural and acquired traits. Some of these traits relate to voice, skills, gestures, moods, and standards of hygiene, noise, orderliness, and other behavior characteristics.

There is, of course, great diversity in these matters, not only among different homes, but also within any home from one time and occasion to another. In most American families, home regimen and domestic values are not inherited en bloc from ancestral customs and standards. Home life is itself plastic, reflecting not only the frequently unlike mores of parents and other adults, but also the many other factors that arise in the modern society. Among these factors are various technological gadgets in the home (such as nursing-bottle warmers, thermostatic controls, portable telephones, cooking timers, and plastic toys and containers) and also the influence of individuals and agencies concerned with child welfare. At one time, child specialists and agencies recommend early habit formation and impersonality in child care. A few years later, they advocate flexibility of schedule, postponement of some aspects of training, and much mothering (fondling, singing, talking) by adults.[4]

Nevertheless, these variations are but deflections of the stream of acculturation by which most children learn the conventional practices

New York, 1937, Charles Horton Cooley, *Human Nature and the Social Order,* Charles Scribner's Sons, New York, 1902, John Dewey, *Human Nature and Conduct,* Henry Holt and Company, Inc., New York, 1922, Clyde Kluckhohn and Henry A. Murray (eds.), *Personality in Nature, Society, and Culture,* 2d ed., Alfred A. Knopf, Inc., New York, 1954, and L. P. Thorpe, *Psychological Foundations of Personality,* McGraw-Hill Book Company, Inc., New York, 1938.

[4] Cf. Martha Wolfenstein, "Trends in Infant Care," *American Journal of Orthopsychiatry,* vol. 33, pp. 120–130, 1953.

and standards of American life (for example, eating at table, sleeping in a bed, control of elimination, cleanliness, dress, and forms of address). And the child's nervous and organic system responds to this inculcation of culture in such ways that his personality emerges as a pattern of habits, adjustments, standards, and beliefs. This pattern is, for good or for ill, not fixed in childhood or even in adulthood; but it does underlie the feeling of "fitness" or "unfitness" by which many later experiences and standards are judged.

Growing up is an age-old and very complex business for the human being, endlessly varied as the individual experience is. The regimen of child-care institutions, however intentionally and intelligently organized and administered, has not been so successful as home rearing has been. Despite the frustration, disharmony, punishment and reward according to whim, and the frequently unhygienic conditions of home life, somehow the child who grows up in his home is more likely to survive as a reasonably normal individual than one brought up in a child-care institution.[5] There are subtleties in the relationships and mutual adjustments of the child-parent-sibling complex that seem almost to defy analysis.[6] These subtleties are parts of the social inheritance, through which responsiveness, security, adventure, and recognition are sought and found, hour by hour and day by day. Ego shapes itself in a world it never made but which it in part accepts and in part rejects progressively, experimentally, selectively, and continually.

INTERRELATIONS OF FAMILY AND NEIGHBORHOOD

Neighborhood Influences

What has been said regarding family life is, in greater or less degree, true of the neighborhood. Of course, the relatively homogeneous neighborhood, where most families have similar customs, values, antagonisms, and fears, reinforces the individual family's patterns more strongly than does the more heterogeneous neighborhood. But whether a neighborhood is fragmented or unified in any and all respects, other than nearness of residences, it affects people's attitudes and behavior. Propinquity to play areas, gang hangouts, churches, and police stations, for example, deserves serious attention in the study of forces which stabilize or disorganize family life.

[5] James H. S. Bossard, *The Sociology of Child Development,* Harper & Brothers, New York, 1954, pp. 51–72. See, also, René Spitz, "Hospitalism," in *The Psychoanalytic Study of the Child,* vol. I, International Universities Press, New York, 1945.

[6] Bossard, *op. cit.,* pp. 91–118.

No neighborhood exists in a social vacuum. Generally, indeed, the standards and behavior of the cohesive neighborhood are more varied and responsive to the patterns of the general community culture than those of any one family are likely to be. Even if all residents are Negroes rather than whites, Orthodox Jews rather than Protestants, or middle-class rather than lower-class, they share many interests and experiences with residents of other neighborhoods. Many of them see the same movies and television programs, follow the same comic characters in the same newspapers, root for the same athletes, are confronted with the same advertising displays, are allured by the same factions, and are appealed to by the same political devices.[7]

Moreover, the same individualistic impulses and urges that make growing children respond by a mixture of acceptance and rejection to the standards and practices of home life, characterize their maturation as members of local groups. The neighborhood usually provides the early out-of-home environment wherein the adaptation mechanisms are developed in contrast to those patterns learned in the family circle. Here, the family patterns are modified, avoided, or vigorously asserted. Experience is often a tough school, with frustration, deprivation, and physical pain exacted as the price for gaining status in one's age group. In extreme cases, indeed, the experience compels the child to lead a double life or, more accurately, multiple lives.

He may be timid, but compensate for it by "acting tough" or "covering up." He may be a gentle, cooperative brother and yet belong to a destructive, callous gang. He may be a devout "Christian" and yet hate all who are not recognized as members of his own groups. He may be a bitter rebel in his own home, and yet a docile member of his team, class, or "set." He may be meticulously honest under one set of conditions but a liar and thief under another set.

Family and Neighborhood Influences Not Clearly Distinguished

The dilemmas related to conflicting and evanescent selves are exceedingly complex and often lead to frustration. Both the family and the neighborhood are human environments into which practically all children are introduced for development. They provide the face-to-face relationships that serve as a nexus between infancy and maturation.

The means by which acculturation is fostered provide one way of distinguishing family processes from those of neighborhoods. Means characteristic of the family are sibling- and parent-child relationships,

[7] Although the neighborhood exemplifies the local community, it is the intensified *process of communication* due to propinquity that must be emphasized. Neighborhood and family mediate between the community's values and behavior and those of individuals.

sleeping, eating, and dressing customs, expressions of affection, scolding, and rewarding. Processes of the neighborhood are those connected with church, school, gang, team, corner gossip groups, play field, movie theater, parties, and excursions. Obviously, there is much interpenetration between family life and neighborhood life. Older brothers and sisters, and sometimes parents, may participate in the same neighborhood institutions and practices as does the individual child who is striving for his own adjustment.

As has already been pointed out, moreover, both family and neighborhood absorb many of the values and stereotypes that are "American." The climate of opinion, in so far as it fosters attention to personal appearance, social and economic rivalry, self-assertion, and voluntary conformity to language, dress, and other behavior patterns, controls in large degree the standards that are exalted in the home and the neighborhood.

Even within families and relatively homogeneous neighborhoods, the inevitable conflicts between the values and the practices approved by adults (many of which are likely to be accepted by children as standard patterns) often have serious repercussions on group unity, loyalty, and authority. In the American melting pot, the potent instruments of communication penetrate almost irresistibly the ego ideals of young and old.

Variety of Family and Neighborhood Acculturation Processes

If the individual child were standardized in native equipment and early experience, it might be possible to classify the processes and effects of family and neighborhood upon his development. Of course, this is not the case. The securities and insecurities of childhood, the fears and frustrations, the affectional experiences and the successes, the early or late development of abilities to walk, speak, and read, and the successive states of health of any individual are too numerous and varied for it to be possible to make other than very crude categories of environmental settings or of types of personality development.

Nevertheless, such classifications aid in understanding the ways in which primary group processes condition the mental, emotional, and physical growth of the individual. It should be kept in mind that there are some important constants in these interpersonal processes: the helplessness and consequent dependence of the young child; the plasticity of the human infant and his potential for conditioning and learning; the mores that exalt obedience, affection, kindliness, parental authority, individualism, and conformity; and the moral drive of habits and standards built into the individual mind of childhood, chiefly by parents and their substitutes.

The varied, and often elusive, effects of family and neighborhood influences on the development of the individual personality are further complicated by the patterns of mobility in the United States. Transiency of residence in a neighborhood is one form of mobility. Identification of self with a coterie not confined to the home community is another form of mobility. School attendance and membership in youth-serving organizations selectively enlarge the neighborhood experiences of boys and girls and constitute still another form.

The efforts of the larger community's constructive social agencies (such as governments, churches, and welfare agencies) are necessarily adapted to the conditions and trends of family and neighborhood life. There are two major reasons for this. In the first place, the effects of their homes and neighborhoods on young people determine in large part the occasions and opportunities for these agencies to function. In the second place, the success of the methods available to meliorative agencies depends on the primary groups' understanding of, and support for, their ends and efforts.

SIGNIFICANT MOTIVATIONS CONDITIONING FAMILY AND NEIGHBORHOOD

In the modern world, no family lives to itself. Its internal relationships and practices merge with the social organization and the general style of life which characterize the community. The family in a depressed neighborhood adapts itself to slum facilities, standards, and emotionalized attitudes; its members may accept or reject, but they cannot ignore, their neighbors' ways of life. The same holds true for families in other types of residential areas. Children who grow up in one type of social and economic environment are in varying degrees products of their neighborhoods as well as of their families.

Most of the social-class characteristics identified by recent sociological investigators are products of such adaptations. They are the result of the interactions of individuals and groups in the context of the customs and value systems of their neighborhoods. The personality outcomes, though individually unique, are similar enough to justify classification. And the advantages are not all with middle- and upper-class neighborhoods.[8] The lower-class environment, in general, favors "more gratification and easier outlet for children's organically based drives"—rage expressions, aggressive behavior, and sex expressions. The middle-class neighborhood mores restrict physical aggressions to patterned forms, either rule-controlled contests or subtleties of posture

[8] Allison Davis and Robert J. Havighurst, *Father of the Man*, Houghton Mifflin Company, Boston, 1947, pp. 17–29.

or gesture. Overt sex expression and fist fighting are discountenanced and so overcontrolled that children's personality problems focus about aggression and sex. Compensations and sublimations for these repressions take many forms, among them initiative and skill in social and economic competition, ambition for class prestige, and fear, anxiety, and guilt about sexual and crass physical behavior.[9]

Among the small [10] and rather esoteric upper class, "good form" in manners, taste, and accomplishments outweighs overtly expressed competitive ambitions. Family pride and class awareness, subtly transmitted, make for dependency on parental approval. Upper-class neighborhoods tend to be coteries or cliques, self-sufficient and mildly individualistic, influential in artistic and intellectual affairs, but somewhat outside the stream of the dynamic social life of the community. Boys and girls are frequently trained and educated separately, especially during adolescence. Engaging in competitive behavior which is obviously for self-advantage is "not done"; etiquette, "honor," and discretion are mandatory.

Numerous sociological researches have shown that, while social-class membership has especially important ramifications in the lives of children and youth of the lower and middle classes, as compared to the upper class, it is, nonetheless, important in the lives of all three. Although the findings of research on child training, as it is influenced by social class, are somewhat conflicting,[11] there can hardly be doubt of

[9] *Ibid.*, pp. 24–25.

[10] W. L. Warner and P. S. Lunt report that, in Yankee City, the upper-upper class contained 1.4 per cent, and the lower-upper class 1.6 per cent, of the population. *The Social Life of a Modern Community,* Yale University Press, New Haven, Conn., 1941. "Five per cent of the respondents in a Gallup poll said they were upper-class. George Gallup and Saul F. Rae, *The Pulse of Democracy,* Simon and Schuster, Inc., New York, 1940, p. 169. Similarly, Richard Centers found that 5 per cent of a cross section of American males categorized themselves as "upper-class." *The Psychology of Social Classes,* Princeton University Press, Princeton, N.J., 1949, p. 77.

[11] Studies of Chicago and Boston families, while revealing some disagreements, showed a much clearer relationship between social-class and child-rearing practices (for example, greater severity with respect to toilet training among lower- than among middle-class families and more freedom of movement for children among the middle-class families) than indicated by other studies in New Haven, San Francisco, and Eugene, Ore. See Allison Davis and Robert J. Havighurst, "Social Class and Color Differences in Child-rearing," *American Sociological Review,* vol. 11, no. 6, pp. 697–710, 1946.

the general significance of class to the life ways of American young people. Irregular employment in a slum area makes hunger, cold, and sickness experiences to be dreaded and compensated for. Hence, the neighborhood tolerates acts and attitudes that shock the prudent and responsible bourgeoisie. Children running loose, violence and disorder in the crowded homes, recourse to orgies, predatory gangs, cleavages and segmental prejudices, narrow loyalties to leaders and institutions, all these complicated and inconsistent phenomena have survival values within some neighborhood frames of reference. Where and under what conditions one develops and adapts determines what his personality will be far more truly than the reverse.

Many questions that are matters for individual decision in the middle-class neighborhood are economically resolved among the poor. Woman's place is more likely to be where she can help stave off hunger and cold. Children more frequently must care for themselves and for their younger brothers and sisters if there is to be any care at all. The sacredness of private property is little esteemed among the propertyless. Law-enforcement officers are often resented as representative of middle-class standards that seem to have little application to slum neighborhoods. This attitude is accentuated among immigrant groups who retain a fear of governmental supervision.

Status and Role as Determinants of Choice

An urge for self-expression is an attribute of every human being. Indeed, several selves generally characterize an individual, one being dominant in one situation, another in a different circumstance. An aggressive star on the athletic field may become a gracious host in the evening. One selects the role that he will assay in the light of his estimate of his capacities, his "audience's" supposed receptivity, and some ego ideal that he hopes to achieve. Success in fulfilling his chosen role, he expects, will in degree bring recognition by whatever "audience" he courts.

Robert R. Sears and others, *Patterns of Child Rearing,* Row, Peterson and Company, Evanston, Ill., 1957, Martha Sturm White, "Social Class, Child Rearing Practices, and Child Behavior," *American Sociological Review,* vol. 22, no. 12, pp. 704–71, 1957. George Psathas, "Ethnicity, Social Class, and Adolescent Independence for Parental Control," *American Sociological Review,* vol. 22, no. 8, pp. 415–423, 1957, and Richard A. Littman, Robert C. A. Moore, and John Pierce-Jones, "Social Class Differences in Child Rearing: A Third Community for Comparison with Chicago and Newton," *American Sociological Review,* vol. 22, no. 12, pp. 694–704, 1957.

The "audiences" which are valued vary for different individuals and for the same individuals at different times and in different settings. The often-heard generalization that the individual tends to be group-satisfied must be cautiously applied. The specific group settings to which he responds are ephemeral and varied. On occasion, the dominant group influence may be that of a coterie (a gang, clique, an ethnic or religious segment). At another time or in another mood, group satisfaction may be sought somewhat imaginatively and vicariously in a group ideal, myth, or stereotype (behavior believed becoming for a Baptist, a musician, or a spaceship pilot).

To be sure, all the varied forms of approval which the individual seeks are conditioned by his culture and so, in a broad sense, group satisfactions are implicit. Roles and statuses that arouse individual enthusiasm in a slum quarter are likely to be different from those that stimulate members of an upper-class neighborhood. In neither case, however, is there uniformity for all persons in the neighborhood.

The concept of the special potency of the peer group in influencing an individual's attitudes, beliefs, and behavior is fruitful in that it properly emphasizes a somewhat specific in-group acceptance and toleration. But here, too, caution is needed, for the individual usually belongs to several peer groups, the members of each of which may be superiors or inferiors in other settings. Football peers are not necessarily social-class peers or musical peers.

Irrational Authority of Group and Institutional Figures

Habitual behavior and its accompanying attitudes are generally unreasoned, though they may be reasonable or, at least, amenable to rationalization. They are adopted and practiced because conformity to the ways of the family, neighborhood, and other groups with which the individual identifies himself maximizes security. "Right" and "wrong," "fitting" and "unfitting," "loyal" and "disloyal" are terms of great moral significance. But they reflect the essentially irrational authority of the mores. Affection, approval, and hence security within family and other primary associations require at least some compliance with the standards accepted by the groups. Failure to conform is met with disapproval, perhaps by punishment; certainly it results in social isolation, at least temporarily.

The moral structures of the family, the gang, the athletic team, and ethnic, religious, and occupational groups are not altogether compatible. So each person learns to differentiate among the "right" and "fitting" behaviors and the "wrong" and "unfitting" ones for each occasion. To tell the truth, for example, is moral in general. In specific situations, however, withholding the truth or even lying to protect one's fellows is morally approved; in such cases, loyalty supersedes honesty, becomes "more moral." Moral development, then, comes out of the subtle process of compromising and resolving the conflicting, irrational elements of the moral structure the individual necessarily obtains from his social experience.

Irrational and incompatible as these complex adjustments are, they are of prime importance. Throughout history, the family and its immediately associated groups have been universal conditioners of individual personality patterns. The subtleties of human adjustment to the ways of life of parents, siblings, and neighbors are neither clearly nor completely understood. It is known only that stable home and neighborhood conditions are necessary for the preservation of the texture of stable societies.

The conflicting currents of rapid social and cultural change often disorganize long-established family and neighborhood patterns and so sacrifice something of their stabilizing influence. The effects of these disorganizing forces are, however, ambivalent. Outmoded in-group prejudices and narrow loyalties may help the individual in identifying with his childhood and parochial peer groups, but they are likely to unfit him for membership in the broader community which is characterized by diversity of association and outlook. Nevertheless, family and neighborhood conditionings are so potent that social changes are likely to be insignificant unless they affect, or find support in, these primary groups. Hence, the efforts of reformers, merchandisers, social workers, and educators are likely to fail if they do not gain the cooperation of families and neighbors.

The interpenetration of broader social movements and organizations and of local communities has gone so far in the modern world that some authorities believe it is almost necessary to initiate reforms in family and community patterns before attempting to interpret them as general social norms.

Ideas crystallized in national and world organizations are in many cases hatched and nourished in numerous small communities. Some totalitarian states have quite successfully used the concept of planting germinal ideas in small communities so that they may "catch fire" and appear later in national concepts. The Russian rulers may still be pondering why the Ukrainian farmers have not wholeheartedly taken over the notions of collectivized agriculture injected into their centuries-old way of life, which is characterized by a closely knit family-neighborhood-community structure. Some effort has been made, of course, to identify the collective farm with the historic *mir* (village) in the minds of peasants. In Nazi Germany, slogans and rituals were effectively related to warmly remembered village ceremonials and traditions. The father concept and the authoritarian patterns of German family life are reflected in the words patriotism and fatherland; the priest and the monarch are "father figures." The term "fireside talks," popularized by President Roosevelt in the 1930s, was analogous to the family council.

Most successful state reforms have come through the local channels first. Historic examples of this sequence are those of the Gracchi brothers of Rome, the Napoleonic Code in France, the socialization of Mexico, and the breakdown of the sharecropping system in the Deep South. The degree of success of the reforms has depended largely upon the amount of interpenetration existing among the local communities involved.

National policies, if they are to become permanent and basic to the life of the people, must have their roots in local community organization. Open forums and town halls are still necessary and basic to the "jelling" of concepts due to become national issues.[12]

SUMMARY

To understand youth and its world, it is almost an absolute necessity that the chief concern be with processes since young people's interests most surely lie in the future. An understanding of the dynamics of social and cultural change is indispensable to the educator who seeks to know how the family experiences of young people link them to peers and adults outside their own families. The family, the school, and the community exemplify constantly changing and intricately interwoven life processes. The interaction of the individual with these processes will be treated in detail in a later chapter.

It is obviously impossible, in a short treatise such as this, to treat in full the family influence upon an individual's development. The intent has been to orient the reader in the areas of family and neighborhood organization as the essence of human society in general and to show some of their important influences upon the individual in particular.

[12] Recent communications research indicates the importance of group memberships and communication in the acceptance or rejection of messages which come to an individual via the mass media. Group norms and the patterns of person-to-person communication (especially through "opinion leaders") suggest the importance and potentials of public forums in a democracy. Cf. Elihu Katz and Paul F. Lazarsfeld, *Personal Influence: The Roles Played by People in the Flow of Mass Communications,* Free Press, Glencoe, Ill., 1955, pp. 130ff., 331–332.

SELECTED REFERENCES

Anshen, Ruth Nanda (ed.): *The Family: Its Function and Destiny,* rev. ed., Harper & Brothers, New York, 1959. A scholarly and informative collection of papers on the family.

Baber, Ray E.: *Marriage and the Family,* 2d ed., McGraw-Hill Book Company, Inc., New York, 1953. A good, easy-to-read book covering courtship, marriage, and a multiplicity of family interrelationships. Chaps. 8 and 9 on parent-child interaction are especially helpful.

Barnes, Harry Elmer, and O. M. Ruedi: *The American Way of Life: An Introduction to the Study of Contemporary Society,* 2d ed., Prentice-Hall, Inc., Englewood Cliffs, N.J., 1950. Chap. 4 has a clear presentation of the concept of neighborhood.

Becker, Howard, and Reuben Hill (eds.): *Family, Marriage, and Parenthood,* 2d ed., D. C. Heath and Company, Boston, 1955. A large, informative collection of papers by twenty-three experts on the family.

Butler, George D.: *Introduction to Community Recreation,* 2d ed., McGraw-Hill Book Company, Inc., New York, 1949. A general discussion of neighborhood and community recreational organization and activities.

Goode, William J.: *After Divorce,* Free Press, Glencoe, Ill., 1956. One of the most important empirical studies of divorce and its effects yet undertaken.

Kirkpatrick, Clifford: *The Family as Process and Institution,* The Ronald Press Company, New York, 1955. Perhaps the most encyclopedic of textbooks on the American family.

LeMasters, E. E.: *Modern Courtship and Marriage,* The Macmillan Company, New York, 1957. A good text on the American system of courtship and marriage.

Martinson, Floyd M.: *Marriage and the American Ideal,* Dodd, Mead, & Company, Inc., New York, 1960. A well-organized and researched textbook on marriage and the family.

Sanders, Irwin T.: *The Community: An Introduction to a Social System,* The Ronald Press Company, New York, 1958. Contains an informative chapter on "Family, Religion, and Morality."

Sirjamaki, John: *The American Family in the Twentieth Century,* Harvard University Press, Cambridge, Mass., 1953. A sprightly, brief description of the American family in the mid-twentieth century.

DISCUSSION QUESTIONS

1. Have you known, rather intimately, young people who as children spent considerable periods in institutional homes? Do these young people now believe that something desirable was missing in their childhood that most of their contemporaries who were brought up in families experienced? Or the reverse? Do any of these young people give evidence of characteristics that may have been intensified because of institutional life in childhood? Are cause-and-effect relationships identifiable?

2. "In the family a home atmosphere holds the same place as executive ability in business"; that is, it keeps the home going as a creative, attitude-developing environment. Thoughts and attitudes are shaped in the momentum of family activities and relationships. Can you exemplify this process by reference to your own experience? Or find an exception to the generalization which, in degree, invalidates it? It may be suggested that you explore your enthusiasm for, and avoidances of, food, furnishings, types of play, social relations, and aspects of beauty. Can you refer any of them to the attitudes, words, or other behavior of members of your childhood home? How were the authority patterns set?

3. How much of your individual uniqueness is due to biological inheritance, to social learning during childhood, and to experiences since adolescence? Do your tentative conclusions lead you to question the emphasis sometimes placed on early childhood conditioning as a prime factor in character formation? Is there conclusive evidence for assigning greater importance to early experience rather than to later influences? Consider the following aspects of uniqueness in selection of examples for examination: attitudes toward property; docility or resistance under conditions of authority and regimen, as in military service or in the classroom; extreme introversion or extroversion as compensation for insecurity in family and neighborhood life.

4. Reflect on the neighborhood conditions, standards, and prestige of the members of a class, club, team, or other small group known to you. What can you learn about tolerance of uncleanliness, disorder, strident voices, and interruptions of conversation? What of open or unacknowledged admiration for cleverness (within or outside the law), ruthlessness, publicity seeking, and defiance of law-enforcement officers?

5. Within a neighborhood known to you, list the centers where children of various ages congregate; for example, sidewalks and streets near homes, backyards and alleys, open lots, candy and soft drink

shops, street corners, club rooms, settlement houses, church parish houses and grounds, playgrounds, swimming places, and movie theaters. Try assigning values ranging from +3 for the most beneficent environment, with 0 standing for ambivalent balance (as much good as bad), to −3 for the most undesirable environment. Make a sketch map of the neighborhood area showing the location of these evaluated centers, indicating the more remote gathering places by arrows at the edge of the sketch. Comment on the planned efforts of public and private schools, social service organizations, businessmen, trade unions, and law-enforcement agencies to suppress or minimize the importance of some gathering centers and to foster and heighten others. What are the criteria by which you judge what is and what is not desirable and effective?

6. In the light of your experience, can you formulate any more definite statement about the human mind than the cliché that "nature and nurture" both condition its development and its qualities? Does the presence of one or more defective members of a family increase the likelihood of low mentality among others of the group because of imitation and limitations of the social milieu or because the biological heredity of all members of the family are similar? Perhaps you might conclude that biological inheritance determines an upper or a lower limit for individual intelligent behavior. Or that biological inheritance furnishes the drive to solve problems and to overcome obstacles that characterizes intelligent persons. Do you have difficulty in differentiating between "intelligence," "personality," "aptitude," and "native ability"?

7. Parents are occasionally convicted in courts and sentenced to jail or to pay fines because of negligence in fulfilling their responsibilities to delinquent minors. Under modern urban conditions, can all, most, or some parents justly be held responsible for the attitudes and behaviors of their children? Consider such cases as the following: (a) both parents employed outside the home either by necessity or by choice; (b) broken families in overcrowded quarters where conditions are not conducive to "normal" family living; (c) one or both parents accept ruthlessness or cleverness as normal and approvable standards for successful and satisfying life.

8. From your own observations and from such information as you can obtain regarding families known to you, what is your conclusion concerning a possible causal relationship between delinquency of young people and economic irresponsibility of their parents as reflected by their neglect of property, unwise spending of money, and readiness to go on relief? Between delinquency of young people and mental or emotional inadequacies of their parents?

9. Is moral and legal delinquency more frequently a cause of poverty in families than a result of it? Cite one or more examples to support your judgment.

10. What is eugenics? What measures, if any, are taken in your state to deter persons with syphilis or with genetically transmissible feeble-mindedness from becoming parents of children? On what grounds do some religious groups oppose proposals for the sterilization of adults who are judged by physicians to be physically unfit for parenthood, or the practice of contraception by potential mothers and fathers who believe themselves unfit for the production of healthy offspring? Do eugenists and biologists know enough to formulate rules for barring individuals from parenthood? In general, or just in extreme cases?

11. Are divorce laws and public attitudes toward separations of married couples, with and without children, too rigid or too lax in the state and community best known to you? Are law and tolerance out of harmony with each other? [13] If so, what are some of the effects of laws lacking moral support in the community?

12. What special problems and opportunities for family life have the recent increases in marriage and birth rates introduced or intensified? How does economic inflation affect this new turn in family life? How have depressions affected family formation and stability?

[13] See Howard Becker and Reuben Hill, *Family, Marriage, and Parenthood,* 2d ed., D. C. Heath and Company, Boston, 1955, pp. 694–707.

5

Other Social Establishments

Many facets of cultural and social organization, in addition to the family and neighborhood, are of interest to the student of the social foundations of education. With the increase of wealth and its social influence on the family and neighborhood, new problems of stabilization have arisen. The accompanying occupational and residential changes and vertical mobility, often associated with economic rivalry and assertiveness, have caused social unrest which has been felt in group structures, in the functions of the family, and in neighborhood processes. Every major change in one social establishment modifies the interplay of behavior and attitudes within and among related institutions.

What now constitutes worthy home membership is, therefore, somewhat changed from patterns of the past. One obvious example of such change is to be found in the increase in frequency of age-level grouping for leisure-time activities; that is, cooperation among children of approximately the same ages belonging to several families. This change accentuates horizontal age groupings and diminishes the effects of vertical ones.

Changes in the structure of the family in Western societies are significant, though less dramatic than changes in function. The extended family (parents, children, and close relatives living in one home), frequently exemplified in village and rural areas in the nineteenth and

78

earlier centuries, has largely given way to independent, geographically separate family units.[1]

The functions and processes of family life have changed in important respects in response to contemporary social and economic needs and opportunities, as has already been noted. Conflicts resulting from these changes[2] have too often emerged as jealousies, rivalries, and extreme forms of competition among the various members, leading to suspicion and undermining group solidarity.[3]

Religious and civil governments, combined in many societies, have in the past been effective stabilizing social instruments; they have usually supported the conservative functions and structural patterns of the family. For reasons having to do mainly with urbanization, however, these social establishments are today quite as influential in accelerating the changes in familial and neighborhood behavior patterns as they are in supporting those already established.

Social change makes fundamental modifications in religious and governmental establishments mandatory if these establishments are to maintain public confidence. Hence, while church and state tend to preserve the stability of family and neighborhood through creeds, laws, and the like, they also respond to the temper of the times by making provisions to meet newly arisen needs for individual self-expression and social welfare. Thereby, they accelerate changes in outlook and custom.

Many American religious groups have supported social legislation requiring child-protection and welfare programs, shorter working hours, minimum wages, minimum housing standards, pure food, and old-age pensions. Such social legislation has, in considerable degree, limited parental authority regarding health measures, economic exploitation, and the discipline of children. It has also superimposed and somewhat replaced standards of conduct which in an earlier day depended on the moral sanctions of like-minded neighbors. Moreover, there are many extrafamilial groups today, such as Boy Scouts and approved and unapproved cliques, coteries, and gangs, which serve the juvenile mores and satisfy the desires of young people. Simultaneously with the increase of state intervention and extrafamilial moral controls,

[1] Talcott Parsons asserts that the typical American family is an isolated, "open, multilineal, conjugal unit." *Essays in Sociological Theory Pure and Applied,* Free Press, Glencoe, Ill., 1949, p. 234.
[2] Anna M. Kross, "Conference on Divorce No. 9," University of Chicago, The Law School, February, 1952, pp. 77–91.
[3] Judson T. Landis and Mary G. Landis, *Readings in Marriage and the Family,* Prentice-Hall, Inc., Englewood Cliffs, N.J., 1952, pp. 160–165.

truly authoritarian families and highly cohesive neighborhoods have become increasingly rare.

SOME CHALLENGES AND PROBLEMS RAISED BY RAPID SOCIAL CHANGE

Americans have created a society which is less closely kin-centered than are those of many other parts of the world. Numerous ideas are transmitted by the family, such as the expectation that children will leave their parents, socially, geographically, and occupationally, that would never be tolerated in a more traditional society.[4] These children will inevitably live in a different world, and their progeny, in turn, will spring from a different culture than did their parents. This is an extraordinary fact which educators too often overlook.

The break in continuity is peculiarly dramatic in the case of first- and second-generation families. In recent years, for example, many Puerto Ricans, Mexicans, Negroes, and white "hillbillies" have moved from rural communities into large cities, such as New York and Chicago. Many of their children have seriously taxed the ability of social welfare workers and police in keeping order. In schools and other establishments, many of these young people are learning behavior and attitudes characteristic of the new urban communities in which they dwell. Simultaneously, however, they retain membership in families and, frequently, in ethnically cohesive neighborhoods which are characterized by mores transplanted from their former homes. Unlike their counterparts in many other societies wherein children seldom oppose parental wishes, young people in the United States seek and attain acceptance and prestige among a wide variety of heterogeneous associations. Increasingly, young adults court and marry with little regard for religious affiliation or national origin, live where and how they please, and visit parental homes as often or as seldom as they choose.[5] These changing patterns are very significant for those youths who find themselves in a school situation related to the modern American culture but live at home in a culture transplanted by immigrant parents and grand-

[4] Robert F. Winch, *The Modern Family*, Henry Holt and Company, Inc., New York, 1952, esp. chap. 11.

[5] A study of the patterns of interaction between middle-class married children and their parents found, however, that there remained in the 1950s a high rate of mutual aid. "Apparently the middle-class family as represented in our sample is not as independent or isolated a unit as it is generally thought to be." Marvin B. Sussman, "The Help Pattern in the Middle-class Family," *American Sociological Review*, vol. 18, no. 1, p. 28, 1953.

parents.[6] Nor must the great variations in familial and neighborhood patterns between different localities of the United States be overlooked. Equally significant variations can be found among sections of any large city.

All such cultural and social fragmentations bring new patterns of behavior and attitudes in a highly mobile society. They bring new and difficult problems to public and private social agencies—law-enforcement agencies, schools, and churches. Every new occasion brings unique problems. Veterans of the Korean conflict, for example, presented patterns that differed from those of World War II veterans. When the Korean veterans went back to school, fewer of them were married and they were much closer to their high school academic experience. Hence, it is probably true that adjustment to college life required much less effort for most of them.

It becomes obvious that the comfortable stereotype of family and neighborhood developmental experience in the United States of a generation or more ago is no longer valid. It is sometimes asserted that American parents attempt to exemplify the virtues which they commend to their children, such as seating females at the table first, eating promptly what is set before them, upholding religious concepts, and approving successful work in school. Doubtless, there are American families of which this is true, and there are neighborhoods and subgroups typified by such familial patterns. But social establishments must deal with many Americans who do not conform to this stereotype. Their unconventional moral sanctions and predispositions require patient understanding as well as restraint and correction in those instances in which the welfare of their fellow citizens is endangered.

ESTABLISHMENTS AND PERSONALITIES

Social Establishments

A social establishment, as the term is used in this book, is any organization whose effects on social behavior, attitudes, and knowledge are such that it significantly conditions the development of children and adults. Social establishments include organizations as varied as official state agencies, religious sects, radio-broadcasting stations, political machines, department stores, youth-serving organizations, houses of prostitution, banks, and public parks. They may be good, bad, or indifferent, as judged by educators who must deal with them all, selectively; ignoring or evading them is, of course, one form of dealing with them.

[6] Oscar Handlin, *The Uprooted*, Atlantic Monthly Press, Boston, 1951, pp. 259–285.

Such social establishments as those listed above relate to the family and neighborhood, as well as to the schools. They provide selective, if often contradictory, impacts on children and adults. Governmental, religious, and civic organizations generally teach obedience to established authority and advocate honesty and reason. By precept or example, however, they sometimes also encourage people to "succeed at all costs," to be clever, and to be loyal, even when such success, cleverness, or loyalty involves a degree of disobedience, dishonesty, or even avoidance of reason.

These indirect impacts of social establishments on individual minds are reinforced, or otherwise affected, by the direct transmission of ideas between institutions and personalities. Through numerous instruments, the state contacts the individual; policemen, postmen, inspectors, election agents, and other officials are met in person, and also vicariously, through billboards, radio, newspapers, and mass meetings. Through church attendance, union membership, magazine reading, the consumption of goods and services of many kinds, and association in varied groups, the individual absorbs a hodgepodge of prejudices, faiths, opinions, and knowledge.

Whether for good or ill, the resulting patterns of attitudes, creeds, and actions are endlessly fragmentary and usually evanescent. Not only do the standards, prestige values, and slogans of any one social establishment conflict with those of other institutions and organizations, but they are, in effect, often self-contradictory. Moreover, their interpretations vary widely both because the mediating instruments differ and because the individual varies in readiness and background experience.

The American State as a Social Establishment

Let us get down to some concrete examples. Because the state seems so obvious, and relatively so precise, a social establishment, we will start with it. It is probably unnecessary to warn the reader that the term "state" refers to any body politic, that is, "any body of people occupying a definite territory and politically organized under one government." [7] The territory may be as restricted as a ward or a village, or it may be much larger. While political organization is of major importance in defining the state, sociological, economic, historical, and geographic factors provide its *raison d'être*.

It is obvious that the individual belongs simultaneously to several states—the city, the county, the state or province, the nation,

[7] Robert H. Lowie, *Social Organization,* Rinehart & Company, Inc., New York, 1948, p. 317.

and international organizations—each with its locale, and all with overlapping, sometimes conflicting, purposes. Furthermore, as with all social establishments, the sanctions and assumptions that characterize any one state are complex and variable in space, time, and special circumstances.

Suppose we examine first of all our nation-state, the United States of America. What are the impacts that its legal structure and agencies and its ideology and shibboleths make on individual Americans?

Allegiance to and protection by the nation's government are reciprocals which are explicitly stated in both public opinion and national law. Allegiance implies obedience to legally constituted authority—the nation's lawmaking, law-interpreting, and law-administering officers. It also includes military service, the payment of taxes, and the willingness to participate in expressions of respect for national symbols. Protection implies that citizens' persons and property will be safeguarded by federal courts and agents in so far as the Constitution of the United States has not delegated these functions to its subdivisions.[8]

The concept of this mutual relationship between the citizen and the nation is almost universally held throughout the civilized world and has been so held through recent centuries. The tenet itself is a major social inheritance, reiterated and repledged year after year.

Nevertheless, a considerable part of our social inventions consists of evasions of this obedience and of the efforts of individuals to get their full share of protection. Unquestioning submission to authority sometimes conflicts with self-interest and independence. Such counterpoise to the threat of an all-powerful state is itself, historically, a social heritage. It is nearly universally asserted and defended in democratically oriented societies.

Liberalism, the hallmark of democracy, exalts individual skepticism, enlightened self-interest, and resistance to regimentation of thought and action by the state or by any social establishment within the state —whether it be economic elite, political party, ecclesiastical hierarchy, or ethnic group. This freedom of thought and action, so honored in democracies, provides more than a safeguard against governmental authoritarianism and coercion. It fosters frequent, though sometimes uneasy, regroupings among people who, in spite of varying purposes and orientations, find themselves in agreement on an immediate objective. On almost any matter of state policy or practice—tariff, internationalism, social security, internal improvements, child welfare, labor

---

[8] See Learned Hand, *The Spirit of Liberty*, Alfred A. Knopf, Inc., New York, 1953, esp. no. 10, "Democracy: Its Presumptions and Realities," and no. 27, "A Pledge of Allegiance."

relations, or control of commerce—such partnerships are likely to include those whose self-interest would be served by the action they espouse, those who favor or fear the effect on human dignity and freedom of the line of action in question, and, of course, those moved by combinations of these attitudes.

The assertion that the American national state is characterized by checks and balances is true of the structure of our constitutional government; legislative, executive, and judicial organs can and frequently do interfere with the programs or specific acts of one another. What is not so often asserted, however, is just as true and in the long run more fundamental: The American citizenry is characterized by diverse individual and group advocacies and resistances that are ever checking each other and ever creating new balances in the body politic, and in American life in general.[9]

It may be hyperbolic and picturesque to claim that every American citizen is "an uncrowned king." It surely is true, however, that great numbers are so conditioned by poverty, fear, stereotypes, narrow loyalties, and "social" ambitions that they do not perform their sovereign functions very vigorously. So long as they get along, the majority of human beings are inclined to go along, as H. G. Wells has asserted.

Nevertheless, the potentialities of sovereignty are always there. The American nation-state is a social establishment that depends on almost daily plebiscites. Radio, movies, newspapers, billboards, letters, and conversations dealing with issues impinge on the background of information, prejudices, vested interests, and reasoning habits of considerable proportions of the population. And state action is modified in terms of what "the public" will support, or at least tolerate. Even the Supreme Court, however it patterns its decisions in terms of legal principles and precedents, takes account of public opinion; else it would surely lose its prestige and strength—as at times it has partially lost them.

THE INFLUENCE OF GOVERNMENT AND PRESSURE GROUPS ON PERSONALITY

The student of the social foundations of education is primarily interested in those aspects of the nation-state which significantly affect

[9] "Roman Catholics, for example, have tended to vote Democratic in the United States; businessmen have traditionally voted Republican. But there are many Roman Catholic businessmen who are pulled in two directions at the same time." Blaine E. Mercer, *An Introduction to the Study of Society,* Harcourt, Brace and Company, Inc., New York, 1958, p. 540.

personality development. How do the typical American boy and girl and their adult relatives differ from their counterparts in the Soviet Union, in prewar Germany, and in other nations? Are the differences matters of degree or of kind or both? Are they due chiefly to traditions that determine the form of the nation-state and other social establishments amid which the people live, are they chiefly the result of the character of those establishments, or both? Answers to these questions would undoubtedly aid in formulating opinions regarding the often-asked question: Can some determined and resourceful groups "take over" and recondition American social establishments? Can it happen here?

Types of Nongovernmental Social Establishments

No satisfactory answers to this most important speculation can be given without an examination of important nongovernmental establishments in the United States. These establishments may be roughly classified in three types: (1) those that influence by their efforts to affect the nation-state and to persuade people to support the changes they seek in legislative, administrative, and judicial behavior; (2) those that exert their influence with little reference to state action (except by permission or avoidance), appealing for direct action to support their primary purposes; and (3) those which carry on some activities of both types, either at different times or simultaneously.

Examples of the first type are economic pressure groups and most social reform organizations. To the second belong nonprofit social service and recreational organizations. Religious sects, groups advocating intercultural cooperation, and educational organizations belong to the third type.

As the impact of each of these types on the American mind is examined, it should be remembered that educators are not only concerned with the facts and their interpretation but, also, with judging the *educational* effects of these establishments. Values based on social purposes are concerns of all educators.

Conflicting Interests as Factors in Political Development

The clashes between individuals and groups with different interests in tribal, regional, state, church, and other institutional policies and programs are so universal that Karl Marx, a century ago, could assert that class struggle was the key to understanding human society. No student of history doubts that there is a measure of truth in the thesis that class struggle is a great mover of men, even though many believe it to be too sweeping in the claim that it is the *only* mover.

In the United States, both because of the extraordinary natural resources and the geographic and social mobility that have always characterized the population, enduring class conflict has not been maintained, although some elements of it persist in connection with farm tenantry, migrant labor, and city slums. Nevertheless, throughout the history of the American nation, groups who thought themselves at a disadvantage have been remarkably able to challenge existing social arrangements. Through impact on public opinion, through new forms of association, and by means of the ballot, they have frequently succeeded in insuring for themselves a fuller participation in the national life.

Changing Concepts of Government and the Governed

With relatively little regard for social-class origin, military, administrative, artistic, and technological abilities have been used, encouraged, and recognized not only in the United States but in many other countries of the Western world. A collection of related qualities has also been held in high regard. "Cleverness" in the governing of men has often supplemented administrative, artistic, and technological abilities. Shrewdness, showmanship, and verbal facility have provided in many instances the means for acquiring positions of leadership and power over the masses of men.

Sometimes such cleverness has been combined with more than average ability in military, administrative, artistic, or technological fields. Too often, in addition, such cleverness has been peculiarly highly developed in psychoneurotics—a kind of compensation for seclusiveness, childhood antipathies, and inferiority feelings. Fortunately, such cleverness has been most potent when used by wholesome men who have been demagogues in the historical sense of the term—leaders truly identified with the people.

With the development of city-states and nation-states in Western Europe in the fifteenth and sixteenth centuries, there developed a new area for the application and refinement of the art of cleverness.[10] Loyalty and obedience, later euphemized as "citizenship," became institutionalized and stereotyped as "morals," and even as "ethics." They were obligatory on the part of the "people." Overt violation was frequently punishable by death—a punishment which the thoroughly conditioned populace enthusiastically acclaimed.

In great degree, therefore, the intellectual aspects of statesman-

[10] The arts of political-power attainment and maintenance, set forth by Machiavelli in *The Prince*, chap. 3, have been practiced by political leaders from antiquity until the present day, despite frequent disavowals and ethical condemnation by the practitioners.

ship, diplomacy, and intrigue were focused on the sovereigns and their bureaucracies of administrators, military officers, economic advisers, and courtiers. For the mass of the people, drama and ritual were superimposed on economic and personal insecurity. They were not expected to understand, or to pass judgment on, the decisions of their masters; in fact, they were psychologically conditioned so that they could not.

Elites and the Common Man

Even in the sixteenth century, a new eddy was forming in the social current that further complicated the class relationship and also brought new hope to the common man. This vortex of activity was due to the rise of the *bourgeoisie,* the middle classes in the towns—technicians, bankers, traders, managers, entrepreneurs—and a "fourth estate" composed of publicists of press, platform, pulpit, and stage, who provided information, ideas, propaganda, and battle cries for the ordinary man.

Into the resulting vortex of social revolution were drawn many men not of the bourgeoisie, who were dazzled by the slogans and ideals of the bourgeoisie leaders. The English revolutions of the seventeenth century and the American and French Revolutions of the eighteenth century were fomented and led by men of the middle classes, with the support of laborers and peasants who, although they eventually gained political recognition, failed to find the social and economic security for which they had hoped.[11]

The nation-state remained a major locus for the activities of clever men, and the so-called "popular revolutions" provided them opportunities. The leaders of the middle classes of Europe and America found it difficult to appease the disappointed artisans, small landholders, and tenants who had taken their promises literally. Popular demand for immediate changes in social arrangements (for example, restriction of claims against future income, economic freedom to produce, buy, and sell to the best advantage of the individual immediately concerned, and limitations on legal penalties that bore especially heavily on the humble) could be neglected only at the risk of militant challenge to middle-class establishments.

Men who live by their wits have continued to outguess and outwit their less clever fellow citizens. Through all the years of American history, however, many of their maneuvers and angles have been brought under state control, thereby driving such men to invent more chicaneries.

[11] Erich Fromm, *Escape from Freedom,* Rinehart and Company, Inc., New York, 1941, esp. chaps. 2 and 3.

The result is a continuing demand for the services of ingenious lawyers, witty entertainers, mass-diverting sports promoters, persuasive publicists, political manipulators, sometimes even for fear-inspiring vigilantes and gangsters, and, indeed, for vociferous patrioteers to divert popular attention from the purposes and projects of the clever schemers. This constitutes a major malady of the postrevolutionary world.

Varying Impact of Elites on American Society

The degree to which the various segments of American society are infected by these agents of clever elites varies greatly in both time and place. Although the same fashions and sports, detective stories and funnies, radio, television, and movie programs tend to stultify rural people just as they infantilize urban dwellers, the impacts of these agents are more likely to be offset by contacts with realities in rural settings than they are in cities. Weather and crops, construction, trade, and neighborly amenities are matters of first-hand experience in small communities to a greater degree than under the tenuous social relationships of urban life. Though conservative stereotypes (for example, race prejudice) may retain potency longer among rural than among urban people, the former, historically, have been less likely to be swept off their feet by military propaganda, fashionable crazes, and political claims. As mass communication becomes even more pervasive, of course, these differentials will become smaller.

As the pendulum of economic plenty and poverty swings, residents of urban centers may feel the impact before those of rural areas. Mass unemployment, loss of property, restriction of credit, and exhaustion of savings undermine security and tend to foster critical inquiry. Frequently, popular protests arise more insistently where the intermediate steps between production of wealth and its consumption are difficult to distinguish than they do where the credit nexus is less vague. Nevertheless, rural populations, once aroused by the foreclosure of mortgages (caused in large part by the loss of effective urban demand for rural goods and services) and the consequent fear of want, have, historically, reacted quite as vigorously and, perhaps, with even less restraint than their city cousins.

The interest of students of social phenomena and their educational implications in those establishments that directly affect the state is obvious. Children and adults are partial products of diverse and ever varying climates of opinion. Where and when the climate is dominated by charlatans and schemers in the employ of political parties or economic pressure groups, few if any individuals can or will risk ostracism by frequent overt (or even concealed) acts of disbelief and challenge.[12]

[12] *Ibid.*, chap. 4.

The Shifting Alliances of Economic and Reform Pressure Groups

There are always groups of people who seek, directly through use or alteration of government, what they believe to be desirable changes in the social order. Some of these groups are made up of people who have special interests and who seek their own advantage; others are genuinely concerned with reforms for altruistic purposes. Of course, still other groups combine the qualities of both special interest and altruistic reformers and, therefore, the lines which divide them are not always clearly distinguishable.

It often happens that a specific end sought by a reform group is identical to an advantage desired by a special-interest organization. Occasionally, indeed, there occurs in a single establishment an ambivalence of motive and advocacy; desires for social betterment and for special advantage may mingle. Economic organizations and political parties that favor intervention by the national government in the affairs of people of other countries may honestly and simultaneously be concerned both with the promotion of human welfare and with the effects that such intervention would have on the future of the individuals and groups who advocate it. Similarly, we find "public relations officers" attached to social service, military, governmental, university, and reform organizations; it is their function to develop not only strong public sympathy for the goals and methods of their organizations, but, in addition, it is their aim to earn a high popular regard for their leaders, symbols, and services.

Resulting Confusion in Public Opinion

It is not strange, therefore, that public opinion is confused and inconstant. Opinion polls, which attempt to report the state of the public mind in regard to a group of related issues, generally report 5 to 8 per cent of the answers as "don't know." In so far as this fraction includes those who don't care, the condition in a democratic society may be regrettable—at least if the question has social implications. But in so far as the "don't know" answer reflects honest hesitation in taking a position on an issue where the information available is contradictory, it is, at least, defensible and, perhaps, desirable. It may be better "not to know" what is not true. Repetitions of the same inquiries show considerable shifts in beliefs and attitudes through time—a condition that may be due to additional information, vigorous persuasion, or returns to earlier positions. Such shifts may be praised as flexibility or they may be firmly censured as fickleness. They may be attributed to events, propaganda, enlightenment, or loss of public interest in social matters and civic affairs.

People's immediate concerns are those of food, clothing, and shelter for themselves and their families, of "social respectability" and mobility, and of escapes into conformity and adventure.[13] It is seldom, indeed, that all, or even a simple majority, are keenly aware of a social problem before it reaches a crisis. Only when a strike of employees threatens the community, an epidemic breaks out, or war is obviously impending does the majority of citizens, even in the United States, feel that the problem requires thought or action on its part. Even then, once the crisis is past, the issues are likely to be quickly dismissed.[14] As Walter Lippman[15] has put it:

> The public will arrive in the middle of the third act and will leave before the last curtain, having stayed just long enough perhaps to decide who is the hero and who the villain. Yet usually that judgment will necessarily be made apart from the intrinsic merits, on the basis of a sample of behavior, an aspect of a situation, by the very rough external evidence.

NONGOVERNMENTAL ESTABLISHMENTS AND THE DIVERSITY OF PUBLIC INTERESTS

In later chapters of this book, an attempt is made to assess what schools and their cooperating institutions are endeavoring to do to stimulate and guide public interest in civic affairs. At this point, however, it is useful to mention typical examples of social establishments that tend to influence people with only indirect relation to state action. These establishments are diverse in purpose and character. They include service organizations (for example, the American Red Cross and other welfare associations, cultural clubs, and various religious societies) and endowed libraries, museums, foundations, and social settlements. Other social establishments, less consistently purposeful, but potent in their influence on some segments of the population, include theaters, the press, sports organizations, and professional agencies. Neighborhood gangs, for example, are sometimes very important influences in the lives of American urban youth.

[13] Cf. Samuel A. Stouffer, *Communism, Conformism, and Civil Liberties,* Doubleday & Company, Inc., New York, 1955.
[14] Witness the immediate wholesale demobilization following World War II and the accompanying chaos in the early stages of military government in Western Germany, Austria, and Italy.
[15] Walter Lippmann, *The Phantom Public,* Harcourt, Brace and Company, Inc., New York, 1925, p. 65. (By permission of The Macmillan Company, New York.)

Nongovernmental meliorative organizations—those which foster active community participation in projects that promote the civic welfare—seek to inform the public regarding the social problems with which each establishment is concerned. By stimulating public interest and inviting general collaboration in their projects, they enliven and guide public opinion. Such informed and aroused publics are likely, of course, to sustain both political and nonpolitical undertakings which are consonant with their objectives. The means used by such organizations to elicit favorable public attitudes and actions on behalf of their projects and the effects of these means on popular thought and behavior are diverse and sometimes ambivalent.

Techniques for Gaining Public Support

Leaders of social establishments of the type under discussion generally realize that whatever support they obtain must come voluntarily from the public. Consequently, they attempt to avoid controversy and rivalry in connection with the measures they wish to promote. Though misjudgments of popular sentiments do occur,[16] voluntarily supported establishments generally emphasize their exclusive adherence to social policies which most men of good will believe should be supported.

Thus, the Red Cross cares for the victims of disasters. The Boy Scouts and Girl Scouts, the YMCA, and other youth-serving organizations furnish leadership for young people. The purposes and activities of anti-tuberculosis, cancer-control, and other health societies are self-evident, as are those of the National Conference of Christians and Jews and the other intercultural organizations. Similarly, associations to combat juvenile delinquency, improve aesthetic conditions, increase healthful recreational facilities, support public education, prevent accidents, restrict child labor, and protect mothers and infants from poverty are assured the good wishes and some degree of financial support of the general population.

The public relations officials of social service organizations generally accept the vagaries of public opinion as a fact. While they strive never to let the people forget what the organizations stand for and what they are engaged in doing, they seek special occasions and times for stressing the critical needs for their peculiar services. If, as Lippmann says, the public does not arrive until the third act, then the

[16] Examples of such errors are the refusal of the American Red Cross to aid the families of coal miners on strike during the 1920s and the publicity given by the Boy Scouts of America to an anti-labor-union harangue by Captain Eddie Rickenbacker in 1943.

drive for support is poised in the third act; press and platform, television and radio, public displays and occasions, costumed and badged volunteer collectors, insignia and window displays for contributors are so mobilized as to heighten the drama and foster desire in each citizen to participate in meeting the emergency.

As a fund-raising procedure, there can be no doubt that the intensification process of such campaigns is effective. Whether or not the effect on the public mind of such "beating of the tom-toms" is beneficial, deleterious, or neutral is a moot question. The overt act in itself may be of value.

In justification of the campaign rhythm, it may be argued that large numbers of the citizenry would never identify themselves with social service projects, even to the extent of a small, money contribution, except as they are brought under the spell of an intensified appeal.[17] Only by occasional emergence from their narrow self-interests into social responsibility would many of these persons come to active participation in community projects. Moreover, once the shell of selfish indifference has been broken by any public service program, the break is unlikely to close completely; the memory of even an occasional generous act begets a readiness to act again in behalf of others.

Ballyhoo and Conformity

It may be that the exploitation of the "crowd process" with its accentuation of conformity, its uncritical assent to programs to be carried out by employees who are assumed to be capable and honest, for purposes more or less comprehended, tends to depersonalize human relationships. Moreover, it may foster a readiness to accept and support any group or movement that effectively uses publicity techniques. Indeed, the emphasis on fund raising may affect the selection of administrators and trustees, so that publicity experts rather than humanitarians come to control, with the acquiescence of the contributors, the practices of the organizations.

The exploitation of similar rhythmic and dramatic devices by commercial establishments heightens the doubts regarding the wisdom of substituting feverish drives for the more leisurely and more voluntary forms of support. The fear is that the services rendered as a result of the methods of fund raising may, in the long run, be much more detrimental than beneficial.

As has already been indicated, the basic devices of clever men for arousing and mobilizing public enthusiasm for their private and public projects are not new. Themistocles, the Gracchi, Peter the

[17] Of course, there is ego compensation in the corresponding recognition obtained in participating.

Hermit, Cromwell, Samuel Adams, Bonaparte, and a thousand others have used them successfully. In the United States, especially, religious sects, political parties, reformist organizations, sports promoters, and their publicity experts have proven, by trial and error, the effectiveness of campaign procedures. Many Americans have undoubtedly been conditioned to uncritical acceptance of ballyhoo, and social service fund raisers have merely exploited this condition for their own ends, worthy or unworthy.

Unfortunately, the acceptance by so many of this pragmatic device for the management of human affairs raises a serious problem. The use of public relations techniques as promotional devices may result in the diminution, if not the elimination, of individual reflection about the causes and solutions of conditions that social service organizations seek to meliorate.

To the degree that such diminution does take place, popular resistance to authoritarian leaders and bureaucracies is weakened. The avoidance of controversy by promoters, whether of social service agencies or of commercialized entertainment, does not encourage men to ask why there should be catastrophic floods, war, poverty, malnutrition, or lack of playgrounds, or why, indeed, human misery, endemic disease, crime, and slums are localized as they are. Noncontroversial publicity campaigns encourage men to give a few dollars to the community chest and to let someone else worry about improving conditions. There may result a kind of generalized emotional glow of good will which serves as an obstacle to fundamental changes in the economic, political, and atavistic jungles of the social system. Money giving now takes the place of the overt act of personal good will which was the mode of yesteryear.

Social establishments are potent conditioners of men's thoughts. Those which are branches of the state and the kinds of nongovernmental organizations discussed above have been, historically, less important than the family and the neighborhood, of course, but in recent decades they have rapidly overcome their historical handicaps. Realistically, each establishment exploits the improved instruments of communication, the relics of childhood pride, loyalties and rivalries, the individual desires for conformity, recognition, and vicarious adventure, funneling them all to support its objectives.

Skepticism as a Safety Valve

In the United States, fortunately, there is a powerful contrary tradition and safety valve—a combination of pride in individualistic nonconformity, a stubborn unwillingness to be stampeded, and a cynical inquiry regarding the private purposes of the promoters of ventures of any kind. "Oh yeah?" "So what?" and "What's your racket?" are expressions that typify the responses of many people to political orations, governmental expositions, all the side-show barkers and their more polished successors of the advertising fraternity, and to emotional appeals for support of institutions and projects.

It is not that this skepticism, social indifference, and airy sophistication are of themselves admirable. They do, however, serve as a counterpoise for the all too smooth lines of many social establishments of varying purposes, ranging from the World Federalists to prize-fight racketeers, from the American Civil Liberties Union to the Daughters of the American Revolution. Conservatism, inertia, stubbornness, and even cynical indifference, in practice, function so as to retard the tendency toward conformity and impersonality wittingly or unwittingly fostered by so many social establishments.

Americans are constantly subjected to the play and counterplay of establishments and the forces of individualism which are so much a part of the American culture. No man can escape the impress of his social contacts and the patterns of his culture upon his mental and emotional responses. And yet it is the peculiarly American dream that each man can create a self of his own, his own values, and even his own practices—all this, somehow, without denying his social group.

THE CHALLENGE FOR PUBLIC EDUCATION

It is precisely at this point that the educator faces the enigma that he seeks to solve. This enigma is the subject matter of the later parts of this volume. At this point it suffices to state the generalization. The educator recognizes the limitations both of the crowd process of communicated, accelerating excitement and conformity and of selfish indifference, cynical abstention, and stubbornness which rejects suggestion. He seeks not so much a compromise or a middle way between mass mobilization and individual abstention from social action as he does a fresh and quite different approach.

In a word, this new way consists of encouraging every individual to find incentives and satisfactions in personal services and friendly relationships whereby he can, through experience, come to appreciate, understand, and judge his fellow men. Let this generalization serve as a firm hypothesis. It can be a major guide in the exploration of those social ideas and their symbols which at once support school education and set all too narrow limits to it.

SUMMARY

In earlier chapters of this book, the developmental controls of community practices and values over individual and group behaviors and attitudes were surveyed. Certain of the important social establishments to which all members of our society respond have been more specifically treated. It is through selective interaction with these varied establishments that individual personalities, social purposes, and accomplishments are shaped.

The challenge to the modern educator is (1) to be informed about the various forms in which social establishments appear, (2) to recognize the necessity for youth to learn as much as possible about their society, (3) to encourage the learner to experience living in his own local community and so to understand its structure and processes, and (4) to give substance and support to the idea that the school can be a very valuable laboratory for learning to live adequately within the society.

If social establishments as here conceived are to have meaning for educators, then checks and balances such as operate between different interests and social segments will need to be recognized and understood, and patterns of acceptable nonconformity will have to be evaluated. It will have to be understood that many parents' standards will require adaptations as their children come in contact with a set of mores different from their own. Such items as these lie within the province of the educator who seeks to understand his community's structure, function, and needs.

SELECTED REFERENCES

Chase, Stuart: *The Proper Study of Mankind,* 2d ed., Harper & Brothers, New York, 1954. An interesting approach to the social sciences and especially to individual interpretation of the social mores.

Dahlke, H. Otto: *Values in Culture and Classroom,* Harper & Brothers, New York, 1958. Contains good chapters on "The Legal Order and Education" and "Special Interests and Education."

Dewey, Richard, and W. J. Humber: *The Development of Human Behavior,* The Macmillan Company, New York, 1951. A treatment of group psychology and its influence on the process of growing up.

Lowie, Robert H.: *Social Organization,* Rinehart & Company, Inc., New York, 1948. Brief summaries on man's institutions and sodalities.

Lundberg, George A.: *Can Science Save Us?* Longmans, Green & Co., New York, 1947. Scientific concepts applied to human relations.

MacIver, Robert M.: *The Web of Government,* The Macmillan Company, New York, 1948. A search for a formula that provides for individual needs for autonomy within a framework of government that both limits and safeguards the rights of all individuals.

Mitchell, Elmer D., and B. S. Mason: *The Theory of Play,* The Ronald Press Company, New York, 1948. A good study of the implications and influences of the concept of recreation on the mechanisms of man's establishments.

Ruesch, J., and G. Bateson: *Communication: The Social Matrix of Psychiatry,* W. W. Norton & Company, Inc., New York, 1951. Communications as related to culture, values, human relations, and mental health. An invaluable work on individual, group, and culture.

Skinner, B. F.: *Science and Human Behavior,* The Macmillan Company, New York, 1953. The techniques developed by man in adjusting to and controlling his environment.

Willing, M. H., and others: *Schools and Our Democratic Society,* Harper & Brothers, New York, 1951. A description of the social role of the school and what democracy demands of it.

DISCUSSION QUESTIONS

1. To how many formal associations and organizations do you belong? Do your memberships in some of them correspond to or determine what policies or espousals you tend to support or to oppose?

2. Does the repetition of exposés of adverse conditions (for example, slums, destruction of natural resources, and accident hazards) dull your feeling of personal concern and responsibility for them? Does the very existence of social establishments which deal with such matters through public relations officers, executive strategies, and pressures on governmental agencies both to correct and to defend existing conditions encourage you to stand aside and let "them fight it out" while you alternately watch and forget the struggle?

3. Throughout the United States, as well as the rest of the modern world, consumers, distributors, and producers, either separately or through collaboration, have joined in cooperatives in order to bring under control economic disadvantages they could not otherwise handle. In some cases, however, the cooperative establishments have been guilty of the same kinds of serious abuses they originally sought to control (for example, the Dairymen's League of New York State in January, 1947, admitted illegal rigging of butter and milk prices to the disadvantage of consumers). Do such unethical, if not always illegal, practices indict cooperatives and cooperators as frauds? If not, how do you account for the anomalous situation?

4. Why does it happen that our governmental establishments become more and more paternalistic while nearly every influential government spokesman declares his firm opposition to government interference with private enterprise? Can American private business engage

in international trade, now that so many commercially active countries have state-controlled economies? Is it possible that the United States might develop a state-controlled economy under slogans of private enterprise?

5. On March 15, 1947, French Foreign Minister George Bidault asked, at the Moscow meeting of representatives of the United States, Great Britain, the Union of Soviet Socialist Republics, and France, that his nation be permitted to adopt many thousands of German children in order to bring them up as Frenchmen. This, he said, would offset the relatively greater decline in population in France than in Germany, her century-old rival. Is the implied belief that cultural controls can make a Frenchman out of a German justifiable? If so, what becomes of the statements that the German people are peculiarly warlike or sadistic (or masochistic) "by nature"?

6. Those who argue for limiting the school to its residual function of imparting traditional knowledge sometimes imply that the school has actively sought to take over responsibilities that "belong to" the home, church, and other social agencies. Apologists for the school's expanding role assert that public sentiment has *compelled* the school to coordinate other institutions and to compensate for their shortcomings. Consider the situation regarding physical and mental health, aesthetic appreciation, human relations and citizenship, and practical knowledge and skills. Are either the critics or the apologists justified? Are both partly right?

6

Social Ideas and
the Communication of Values

SOCIAL IDEAS AND INDIVIDUAL DEVELOPMENT

Every community has its own peculiar norms which govern behavior. Each individual, if he is to find a sense of security and well-being, must conform in some degree with the standards which organize his own local community. Moreover, these standards are typically expressed as symbolic (especially verbalistic) abstractions. It is the purpose of the present chapter to examine more specifically than was done in earlier chapters certain important aspects of these abstractions.

The individual's behavior is typically judged to be "normal" or "abnormal" according to the adjustments he makes to standards which are acceptable to other people in his community. An idea of what is right or wrong, desirable or undesirable, consequential or inconsequential in one social group or establishment may not be applicable to another one. Similarly, the significance or appropriateness of an idea varies from one set of social circumstances to another. What is correct at a formal dance or a religious service may not be applicable to other situations. Ideas that carry simplicity of value judgments in each of the many specific settings are "sound" ideas, that is, they evidence "normality."

98

In the broadest sense, all ideas have social connotations and hence may be construed to be *social ideas*. All are verbally or otherwise symbolically conceived and communicated. However, in this chapter, a somewhat narrower definition of social ideas is utilized. The concern here is primarily with ideas that rather directly affect group behavior and personal relations and with the communication of such ideas in a democratic society.

The kind of docility which their early family experiences foster among "normal" children generally influences strongly their later responses to school personnel, policemen, employers, and many other adults. "Normal" behavior is any kind of adjustment which develops individual security and a sense of well-being and, at the same time, wins adult approval and the satisfaction of desires. Such "good behavior" is rewarded by the kinds of commendation and privilege that "normal" children cherish.

Every ordinary individual is a favor-seeking being and tends to act to some extent in accord with the social standards he knows. Implicit in this conception is, of course, the idea that various individuals in the community live under a certain pressure to conform. This tendency toward social conformity is, however, offset by two potent, interrelated factors. The first is the apparent desire of every individual to experience what is new and untried—that is, the wish for adventure—and his need to assert a unique selfhood. The second is the social idea that every individual, whatever his age, occasionally has a strong impulse to act in defiance of the social norms. The desire to assert oneself, either mischievously or defiantly, is fostered by older youth and by literature, drama, comic strips, and "funny" stories told by adults. It is established as a variant of "normal" behavior.

The general cultural pattern is often blurred by such inconsistencies as those illustrated by the examples above. But even more confusing and contradictory social ideas have force as expressions of approval and disapproval among people.[1] In the contemporary United States, for example, public opinion exalts volunteer service for public welfare as a standard for judging the acts of men. At the same time, it

---

[1] The anthropologist and the social historian who examine cultural patterns of primitive peoples and of social epochs among civilized populations are struck with the conflicts between taboos and tolerances toward their semisecret evasion. See Robert H. Lowie, *An Introduction to Cultural Anthropology*, Rinehart & Company, Inc., New York, 1940, pp. 374–380, John Lewis Gillin and John Phillip Gillin, *Cultural Sociology*, The Macmillan Company, New York, 1948, chap. 27, and Kingsley Davis, *Human Society*, The Macmillan Company, New York, 1949, pp. 137–139.

honors ruthless self-seeking by individuals and organized groups so long as their conduct falls short of obvious violence and defiance of the law. Obviously, the second type of prestige is given without reference to social welfare.

Indeed, some apologists for the ascendancy of self-interest in the motivation of individual and group behavior assert that the public good is served by the "free enterprise" of rugged, insensitive men who would "let the devil take the hindmost" in a competitive world. It is, they say, this strife and competition that has made the United States the great and technologically progressive society it is. Constant war, declared or undeclared, between man and man, man and group, group and group, and group and the state, they assert, compels the efficiency required for national survival.

Need for Awareness of Inconsistencies

There exist simultaneously popular tolerance and even enthusiastic support for such antithetical social ideas. American children, like children everywhere, inherit conflicting social patterns. And the personality of every American of whatever age is largely a resultant of his interaction with other people in the context of generally valued ideas. In some degree, if "normal," he is compelled to incorporate all aspects of the cultural complex known to him into his own sets of values; hence, his own mental world, to the extent that what he knows is inconsistent, is also certain to be confused and conducive to contradictory behaviors.

This disturbing reality is the premise on which the educator must build any program for aiding young people and their elders in the understanding of the social nature of the self. It is true that no man, simply by taking thought, can clear his cosmos of conflicts and compromises. Through effort, however, he may in considerable degree increase his awareness of the nature and power of the social ideas that play constantly on his own personality and on those of other men.

Such awareness promotes tolerance of others' shortcomings and may help the individual to see himself somewhat as others see him. It is likely to be a sedative for arrogance and overt self-justification; no one so enlightened can thank God that he is not as other men are.

He will then appreciate his own uniqueness as merely a slight deviation from a norm. He is the product of a biological inheritance conditioned by the interplay of endlessly complex practices and ideas over which he, as an individual, has little control. Even though the product is such that he can be assigned to a type—introvert or extrovert, megalomaniac, or paranoid, for example—he is, nevertheless, generally more like than unlike his fellow men in his habits and value judgments.

The Temper of the Times and Individual Valuations

The multiform and constantly changing environment of things, customs, and ideas to which adjustments must be made compel the adult to be capable of multiple adjustment. In wartime, for example, he is likely to identify strongly with the nation and to act in accord with that identification. In time of postwar prosperity, he may succumb to the slogan that "only boobs work" and that clever men attach themselves to "rackets." In time of depression, he may be a radical, a progressive, or a conservative according to the groups with which he identifies.

Economic peaks and valleys and the popular moods that accompany them have been intensified in the United States, as elsewhere in the Western world, with the predominance of the mass-production economy. Both those who are overly optimistic in boom times and those who are overly pessimistic in recessions typically go no further in their analysis of social and economic factors than the search for personal devils. "Radical agitators," "reformers," "intellectuals," labor-union leaders, and the "monster state" are favorite devils of many conservatives; Wall Street, brass hats, and "soulless corporations" are the devils of many liberals.

Paradoxically, perhaps, the mood of fear tends to be dominant during prosperity while the mood of hope gains ascendancy during depression. It is during boom times that "radicals" are purged and reformers lose influence. It is during periods of unemployment and financial instability that the most insistent demands for social reforms and the boldest plans for insuring human welfare are heard.

THE INDIVIDUAL AS ARBITER OF SOCIAL VALUES

The common failure of Americans to feel, think, and act consistently in their own long-term interest can be most readily accounted for by the number and diversity of impacts made on their minds. It is conceivable that if the ordinary citizen could and would devote a considerable share of his attention to the workings of a single establishment he might come to reasoned conclusions regarding its actual purposes, the adequacy of its functioning, and the alterations which would more effectively insure his own goals.

The typical individual cannot possibly perform in this way, however, even though, in theory, democracy expects him to do so. He is busy earning a living, bringing up a family, "keeping up with the Joneses," being loyal to church, political party, and club, improving his property, and following his hobbies. Nevertheless, he finds himself in the anomalous position of being a member of the court of last resort to settle an amazingly wide range of issues about which he has no special knowledge or reasoned opinions. These issues range over health measures, sex morals, community aesthetics, religion, economic production, matters of world government, and many more. In addition to these social issues, he must include a multiplicity of personal problems which have to be resolved.

The individual must pass judgment on all these matters. Conscious evasion of an issue does not free him from passing judgment because his behavior toward any establishment in some degree implies an attitude of support or of opposition. Moreover, because most of the issues are interrelated, his opinions and acts in regard to any one of them are indicative of his feelings, if not his considered judgment, concerning other establishments and their problems. For example, his response to appeals for support of the American Civil Liberties Union implies an attitude of acceptance or rejection of practices of racial segregation, coexistence of competing ideologies and national aspirations, technological and material aid for relatively primitive peoples, and religious toleration.

THE SURVIVAL OF SOCIAL IDEAS

There are some long-term trends and problems that cannot be settled by the citizen, no matter what he decides. If he approves of forethought and planning of the nation's economy, the public park system, or his household budget, the planned program may in some degree fail because of unforeseeable factors. As a result, he may lose faith in further planning. If he favors planlessness, some degree of chaos will surely follow. Even though he believes that a combination of planning and improvisation is a solution, he will often see one concept dominant when the other possibly should be.

Trends That Govern Survival

Whatever his notions concerning alternate courses of action in dealing with personal and social problems, eventually he is compelled to tolerate measures that are in line with the long-term trends of his society. In time *veto by the fact* condemns erroneous programs, whatever majorities may support them and however apologists may symbolize them.

Bingham[2] notes five of these long-term trends:

1. The revolt of the common man against inequality and oppression.

[2] Alfred Bingham, *The Practice of Idealism*, Duell, Sloan & Pearce, New York, 1941, chap. 2.

2. The transformation of the economic system by the technical revolution.

3. The search for new political techniques appropriate to contemporary needs.

4. The obsolescence of nationalism.

5. The decay of traditional religious beliefs and the demand for a more positive faith.

If these are, in fact, the true trends, they will act as roughhewers of purposes and practices of all the social establishments that will survive in the years ahead. Every institution that does not shape its course to them will wither away, be it religion, government, school, or family. Institutions are always in process of change; ideas concerning their character and function inevitably change *pari passu*.

Consequently, the institutional loyalties, rituals, and creeds to which man has been indoctrinated require reorientation if they are to survive. To be sure, obsolete shibboleths are mouthed by men even after their conduct has adapted itself to change. Eventually, however, creeds and concepts have to be justified in terms of present realities rather than of past establishments and relationships.

Such reorientations of faiths and concepts, even though partial, are of supreme significance for a democratic society. Democracy requires tolerance and compromise in cases where attachment to absolutes might lead to isolation or violence. In time, the dead past gets interred.

Science and the Survival of Ideas

Both science and the aspirations of the common man are relatively new in the world.[3] They are interrelated and their importance in the affairs of man constantly increases. That they are disturbing and disruptive of old, established orders is beyond doubt. For the past four centuries, they have figured strongly in revolutions and counterrevolutions. Most assuredly the end is not in sight.

In time, archaic practices, authorities, attitudes, and creeds are swept over by the tide of events. Despite apologists, threats, and violence to maintain it, slavery as an institution has ended throughout most of the civilized world. Legal and ecclesiastical condemnation of strikes, even of membership in labor unions, has given place in most instances to toleration and even collaboration and support.[4] The British people,

[3] "What characterizes medieval in contrast to modern society is its lack of individual freedom . . . But although a person was not free . . . neither was he alone and isolated . . . He was identical with his role in society . . ." Erich Fromm, *Escape from Freedom*, Rinehart & Company, Inc., New York, 1941, pp. 41–42.

[4] Cf. Clarence E. Pickett, *For More than Bread*, Little, Brown & Company, Boston, 1953, chap. 1.

while still maintaining the monarchy as a symbol of their common history and aspirations, are governed by representatives of the common man—the Labor party or the (in fact, liberal) Conservatives.

Scientific Emphasis on Tentative Conclusions

The scientific outlook provides both the mood and the ideological framework for the common man's aspirations. Its orientation toward final truths is that they may be goals to be sought but never completely attained. Even the "laws" of science are revised and refined to apply adequately to newly discovered facts. Science predicts that, under a given set of circumstances, certain results can be expected. Science does not attempt to evaluate the outcomes as good or bad.[5]

When this outlook toward absolutes penetrates the religious, political, and economic establishments which exalt established creeds and codes formulated in the past, the results are disturbing to old ways of thinking and behaving. Dogma, tradition, and authority are no longer unquestioned. The scientific attitude demands operational applications of verbal "truths"; if the creed, code, label, or "law" lacks meaning when applied to needed action, intelligent men tend to disregard it. To be sure, they may still defend their group's esoteric creeds when they are challenged; such emotional attachments may indeed have value in forestalling chaos. But irrelevant absolutes have little significance for man's greatest adventure—the creation of a world fit for an evolving truth.

Adaptations to Social Change Versus Absolutes

It is, however, in the multifarious derivations from science and human aspiration that changes in the conditions of man become most conspicuous. Most obvious, of course, is the technological advance of the past two centuries. From home to shop, to local factory, to specialized plant, to international organization, manufacture has carried in its train drastic changes in man's wants and their satisfaction, in family life, in geographic and social mobility, in governmental intervention, in labor and employer relations, and in the means of communication. It is these things, predominantly, which have made the individual willy-nilly a citizen of the world.

This interesting complex of processes may or may not be synonymous with "progress"; philosophers disagree according to their conceptions of the "good life." It must be recognized, however, not

[5] The scientist seeks, in his investigations, to eliminate any influence of his own conceptions of what is good or bad. In his role as citizen, however, he forms opinions of what is good and bad and often rises with his fellows to be counted when the time is appropriate.

only that the technical revolution proceeds irresistibly but also that it stultifies man's thoughts and dreams at the same time it frees and enlightens him, provides him with food, shelter, and clothing, and increases his longevity.

But human habits and institutions are stubborn. Irresistible requirements for change meet almost unchangeable customs and attitudes. What then? Man invents a shorthand of symbols and clichés. Through them he ostentatiously expresses his modernity, while still he subconsciously harbors his tribal, prescientific mysticisms. He accepts the symbols of democracy, universal brotherhood, and magnanimity. But he owes a first loyalty to his family, gang, firm, church, and clubs; on their behalf he may be deceitful, coercive, and hateful toward members of out-groups.

Word Symbols of Social Ideas

In most cases, modern man does not consciously recognize the antithesis between his in-group behavior and the implications of the symbols of science and democracy which he knows. He accepts the precepts of his group and those of science and democracy even though they may be inconsistent. He may rationalize the paradox by verbal legerdemain, by glorifying family unity, by identifying religion with virtue and brotherhood, or by accusing out-groups of being subversive or otherwise dangerous to world peace or democratic institutions. More likely, however, he makes no attempt to face the paradox intellectually. He just feels and acts on many occasions according to tribal codes. At other times, he expresses sentiments attuned to twentieth-century ideology, but his behavior responds laggardly to his realistic sentiments. The multitude of impacts experienced within his society impel him to think and act incongruously.

Thus it comes about that the same man may despise men because of color, ancestry, nationality, or philosophies that differ from those he calls his own, while at the same time he sacrifices money, time, and even life itself on behalf of democratic, scientific, and religious institutions and tenets which his primitive self rejects. People say of him—and by that they mean almost everyone—that he is humanly inconsistent, poorly informed, and, to say the least, stubborn in his convictions.

SOME AMERICAN SOCIAL IDEAS

Prestige Patterns and Status Seeking

What order there is in the American culture is not primarily caused by an intentional or reasoned system of ethical ideas regarding human relationships. It is rather a resultant of a hodgepodge of prestige values, offices held, equipment owned, behavior exemplified, realization of needs, and adjustment to less than expected achievement.

The roots of respect and adulation for our varied and inconsistent elites extend far back into primitive life; the chieftain, the fighter, the gloriously garmented, the rich, and those equipped with special knowledge and skills have been accorded honors from time immemorial. Ordinary people, in large numbers, continue now, as they always have, to seek the favor of such elites and, so far as possible, to emulate them. Indeed, the aspiration to attain elite status for oneself and one's family is one of the major dynamics in a democracy. The cultural values represented by these elites may be well or ill founded; in either case, however, they operate to provide goals to which many ordinary men and women aspire.

Imitation, of course, has widely varying results. It may drag men down to the brute level of the gangster; it may lead them to the heights of intelligence and good will. In the case of most, it does neither for very long. Alternately, perhaps simultaneously, men honor and in some degree emulate the behavior of the kindly, the clever, the defiant, the foresighted, the crude, and the polite. Sometimes people seek status by feeling and acting like "everyone else"; at other times they emphasize individual uniqueness as an attention-getting device.

Glorification of Wealth Getting and Display

In the contemporary United States, moreover, the dominance of economic motivation has led to two very significant alterations of the earlier patterns of prestige, aspiration, and imitation. The first of these alterations is that wealth getting is dynamic not so much for economic security or even for the comforts, luxuries, and chivalric honors that it may help men attain but for the *process* of wealth getting and, hence, the attributes of the successful wealth getter, which attain prestige for themselves. The mere possession of wealth is undoubtedly less important in firing the imaginations and hopes of many Americans than are the day-by-day manipulations and exploits of those who gain the status of being "in the money"—financiers, industrialists, corporation lawyers, movie actors, prize fighters, and publicity experts.[6]

The second innovation is closely related to the first. Through the various mass media—television programs, news articles, and drama, for example—prestige values adhering to things, ideas, and people are built up until they become what is "worth knowing" by anyone who wants to be up-to-date. Brands of frozen food, the scores made by

---

[6] The tastes, behavior, and opinions characteristic of established, wealthy families do still determine in great degree those of aspirants for high social status, of course.

professional golfers, the pronouncements of congressmen, the plays in which an actress has had a leading part, the wisecracks of a television comedian, and the latest in clothing fashions are examples. Not to know such things may be more embarrassing than ignorance of chemistry, Shakespeare, the history of France under Louis XIV, musical classics, or "Ohm's law." It is not surprising, therefore, that among people continually pounded by publicity tricks, the intellectual, the clergyman, the public servant, and the inventor, however able and whatever his services, may have less popular recognition and esteem than a home-run swatter, a gangbuster, a movie queen, or a political grandstander.

Since prestige so largely governs aspiration, it is not surprising that people who seek high status should want to get into money making and conspicuous pursuits. To many of them, civic service, homemaking, research, and art seem dull.

Probably far more important than the quantity of adulation produced by public relations experts is its transitory quality. The synthetically built-up "heroes" usually leave little impress on the cultural patterns; they have their little days and depart; only the specialist keeps a file of yesterday's glamour lads and lasses.

It is the never-ending succession of superficial personalities touted by publicity that stultifies the American prestige and emulation processes. No individual figure blown out of proportion by publicity campaigns counts for much from decade to decade. But the ever-ready public accepts successor after successor to fill the places of yesterday's Miss America and Mr. Movie Hero.

American Class Stereotypes Largely Limited to One Class

A democratic society has faults that almost inevitably accompany its strengths. In the United States, housekeepers, factory hands, clerks, and agricultural workers and their children increasingly participate in the comforts and luxuries, the impulses and conformities that in other countries and other times have characterized alone the employer, professional class, landed aristocracy, and merchant princes. Thus, there have been released driving energies to attain the equipment and modes of living which in more rigidly stratified societies have differentiated upper classes from manual workers. Since neither a landed aristocracy nor a nobility has ever firmly established itself in the United States, the American society has become almost universally bourgeoisie.[7]

[7] The exceptions, noted by Warner and his followers are a tiny element of upper-upper class families and the depressed lower-lower class of urban and rural slum dwellers. The use of varying terms in different researches sometimes creates difficulty in inter-

Historically, the bourgeoisie has been a striving class imitating the leisure occupations of the aristocracy. In the United States, with no authentic aristocracy to imitate, the society uncertainly turns in on itself. Many Americans try to do what they think would typify a nobility, if there were such a thing. Their attempts at such identification include dainty clothes, night clubs, ballroom etiquette, poses of superiority (or what they imagine they might be), the patronizing of athletics, a superficial interest in music and art, a few French phrases, and an ability to demand service in organizations where servants "know their place."

In modern American urban and suburban life, there are vaguely recognizable classes, statuses, and coteries. But no ideas and stereotypes are *rigidly* characteristic of the upper statuses.[8] The upper-upper class member may be a liberal reformer, may dress carelessly, may work pridefully as gardener or cook (but not for wages), and may associate in sincere friendship with members of the middle classes who share his interest in fine arts, golf, or business.[9]

Other Prestige Carriers

In the United States, there are other prestige carriers than wealth and social class. The numbers of people whose behavior and aspirations relate to these other prestige items is relatively small; there is likely to be a permanence, possibly a smug complacency, among them, however. As a rule, they neither defy nor openly protest the American standard stereotype of wealth and social status; they differ chiefly by not being enslaved by it.

---

preting the results. Centers, for example, makes a distinction between "working class" and "middle class." Nevertheless, an overwhelming proportion of Americans evidently does identify itself with something that can be thought of as a "middle class." See Richard Centers, *The Psychology of Social Classes,* Princeton University Press, Princeton, N.J., 1951.

[8] Some differences in economic, political, and ideological attitudes have, of course, been found among classes (as defined by occupational level). Centers, for example, found that upper-class occupational groups showed a stronger leaning toward private ownership of property and toward individualism, and against "more power for the working people," than did lower-class occupational groups. *Ibid.,* p. 63.

[9] Cf. W. Lloyd Warner and Paul S. Lunt, *The Social Life of a Modern Community,* Yale University Press, New Haven, Conn., 1941, and Robert S. Lynd and Helen M. Lynd, *Middletown,* and *Middletown in Transition,* Harcourt, Brace and Company, Inc., New York, 1929 and 1937.

Exemplars of this somewhat aberrant culture pattern are most readily identified among university faculties, the medical and related professions, civic employees, judges in courts at all levels, scientists, and artists in many fields. There are also many inconspicuous common men and women who do not fit the stereotype of the American wealth and status striver. They may be rich or poor, but they do not honor others in terms of social or economic status; nor are they themselves often so evaluated. They are not uninterested in the consumption patterns of their generation, neither are they obsessed by them. Their wants are relatively simple; they work and spend for the satisfaction of these simple wants with little regard for what goes with a station in life. In a word, they have little desire to keep up with the Joneses. But they are concerned about such matters as public welfare, social policies, community planning, beauty and order, neighborly intercourse, and the frontiers of learning.

Frequently, they are so individualistic that their effects on contemporary prestige standards are impossible to generalize. Nevertheless, they do serve significantly to offset the fickle sweeps of popular esteem in our rather rootless society. It is such men and women who provide the best examples of the objectives of American schools.

They differ from their class-conscious contemporaries in their orientation toward life. The adjective "spiritual" is often used to differentiate them from their "materialistic" fellow men. Semantically, however, these are unprecise terms. Too often spiritual connotes mysticism or revealed religion, and materialistic frequently implies a gross disregard for friendship, beauty, and civic righteousness. Obviously, so understood, the terms are not applicable to differentiate the types of people here discussed. Probably the concepts secure and insecure are more applicable if it be understood that the security referred to is internal or psychological rather than economic (though the latter doubtless plays a part in the former).

Selective Response to Popular Morality

Psychological security requires toleration of individualism. Hence, a flamboyant defiance of contemporary practices and slogans is avoided. The individualist, however, chooses the moral influences to which he will conform. He tends to disregard, to a greater extent than many of his contemporaries, the ephemeral fashions of his day.

The uniqueness of each individual is a postulate of democracy. Uniqueness is relative to self-adjustment in a culture that requires much conformity both in kind and degree. The emancipation of the individual from indiscriminate acquiescence to crowd morality is, however, precious to the democratic society. All invention, all truly reflective thinking, and hence all progress toward the attainment of American social goals depend on freedom to challenge contemporary social ideas and, within limits, institutions and actions.

Consciously purposeful agencies of democracy, both governmental and voluntary, have, therefore, a dual function. They endeavor to encourage and guide each "to make the most of himself" as a unique individual within a variable and flexible culture, and they foster by precept and example a respect for individuality among all sections of the public that they reach. Both these functions promote communication and mutually sympathetic understanding without which a democratic society would be impossible.

COMMUNICATION OF SOCIAL IDEAS AND VALUES

Communication a Two-way Process

The instruments by which states of feeling and thinking are communicated among individuals and groups are many, varied, and complex. The same overt symbol—yellow caution traffic light, oral or written phrase, gesture or manner—may transmit somewhat different meanings to individuals and groups in various settings. Every society develops conventions by which desires, permissions, warnings, threats, and the rest are expressed symbolically and are interpreted by those who respond to them.

The two phenomena of communication and response typically interact. The reaction communicates itself to the original communicator who in turn reacts to it according to his momentary array of moods, knowledge, and intentions.

Communication of competing ideas is emotionally conditioned. Attitudes of loyalty, nostalgia, affection, and hostility, already present in the respondent, color the reception of what he observes, reads, hears, and imitates. The individual responds most readily to whatever idea, or fragment or symbol of an idea, is most familiar to him and, hence, is in degree already accepted by him. Seldom is he quite objective in his response.

Communication is thus a two-way process. What one person says, writes, or does is never precisely what another person hears, reads, or observes.[10] The symbols—words, gestures, voice, rhythm, metaphors,

[10] Semantics is a name given to a science devoted to language as a precise instrument of communication. The gist of semantics is, first, a consciousness that words are *symbols,* not *things,* and that as abstractions they have meaning only with reference to specific instances or "referents"; second, that terms have meaning when applied to action or operation not to other verbal abstractions. Cf.

environment, and art forms—do not have quite the same relationship and meaning for the one who imparts the message as for the one who receives it. What the latter most readily accepts and assimilates is most likely to be related to and consistent with his own system of moods, beliefs, and doubts.

Nevertheless, communication, however imperfect, is integral to community. It carries the burden of formulating and transferring ideas. By means of it, personal and social decisions and more subtle adaptations are arrived at. In any society, and most especially in the modern complex one, communication makes possible all social arrangements; through it, the purposes, processes, and values of the group are determined, interpersonal relations defined, and most social behavior expressed.

Denotive, Connotive, and Emotive Characteristics of Words

All words used in speech and writing carry some implication of value; if they did not, they would be meaningless. Descriptive adjectives and their adverbial forms and in many cases nouns and verbs not only denote condition or instance but also connote concomitant and secondary attributes. They may have emotional implications of approval or disapproval. Only in meticulous scientific exposition is objectivity of verbal usage attained; technical, almost esoteric, language is necessary.

Language abounds in words, phrases, and figures of speech borrowed from one setting for use in a different one, thereby expanding original meanings. Metaphorical language abounds in inferences, connotations, and inflections which call forth various emotions. The context in which it appears and the use of pictures and cartoons typically reinforce (though they sometimes limit) the emotional force of the written language. Voice, gesture, and "stage setting" do the same in oral communication.

The ordinary man is, then, enmeshed in a communication system which is shot through with connotation and emotion. It is accordingly too much to expect that he can or will weigh objectively the impacts on his mind of all the stimuli which call him not only to reflection, but to feeling and action as well. Nevertheless, a reasonable degree of skepticism and reluctance to accept an inference or partake of an emotion without examining the evidence and the alternatives is surely desirable and, in degree, achievable.

Stuart Chase, *The Tyranny of Words,* Harcourt, Brace and Company, Inc., New York, 1938, pp. 9–17, and S. I. Hayakawa, *Language in Thought and Action,* Harcourt, Brace and Company, Inc., New York, 1949.

Devices for Communicating Ideas and Values

The means for propaganda and indoctrination are age-old. They have been used to foment and to control revolts, to throw off outmoded conventions, and to fortify them. Whatever the future may hold, it is improbable that any movement for human welfare can now succeed without some exploitation of the propaganda techniques which have been made possible by technological advance in communication.

Whatever the purposes and effects of propaganda devices, and however necessary they may be to obtain popular response, their use implies a contempt for man's intelligence and individual worth. If at present they seem to be essential as tools for cultural cohesion and social direction, the most (and the least) that educators can attempt is to increase the ability of men (starting with themselves) to recognize propaganda when they see or hear it. It may be fun to get fooled, but it is just as pleasurable, and surely safer, to be at least half-aware that one is being made a fool of. Gradually, the more gross and obvious tricks of advertisers and publicity experts, orators, dramatists, and the whole array of opinion manipulators would decline in power if enough people were adequately taught about them.

The "seven common propaganda devices" explained by Miller[11] provide minimum intellectual equipment for anyone who seeks to judge propaganda messages. The *name-calling device* uses "poison words" to discredit an opposing or inconvenient individual, group, or idea; for example, the scholar is called a longhair or an egghead; the liberal, a Communist fellow traveler; the business executive, a tycoon. The *glittering-generality* or *rosy-glow* device uses emotionally accepted symbols, such as mother, home, honor, and loyalty, to win approval for a brand of beer, a social policy, or a political candidate without the examination of evidence. The two devices of *transfer* and *testimonial* are related to each other. By getting the audience to associate a respected figure—church or ethnic-group leader, popular actress, or a handsome and convincingly "sincere" salesman—with whatever he is "selling," whether cigarettes or foreign policy, the propagandist is likely to get acceptance of his assertions. The *plain-folks* device is a pretence of identification of the propagandist with his nostalgic audience; stock symbols of rugged simplicity—the woodpile, tinkering with the old Ford,

[11] Clyde R. Miller, *What Everybody Should Know about Propaganda,* Methodist Federation for Social Action, The Commission for Propaganda Analysis, New York, 1949. See, also, Alfred McClung Lee and Elizabeth Bryant Lee (eds.), *The Fine Art of Propaganda,* Harcourt, Brace and Company, Inc., New York, 1939, pp. 23–24.

a breakfast of flapjacks and sausage, caring for a sick child—serve to establish rapport.

The *card-stacking* device is probably the most vicious one. It generally involves half-truths, suppression of facts, and often actual deception, self-righteousness, and effrontery. Evidence, perhaps the bare assertion, of evil or inadequacy of the condemned men or philosophy are contrasted with the virtue or beneficence of the "cause" the propagandist serves. The *band wagon* device is so obvious and familiar that it is surprising that it retains its efficacy; it exploits the sheeplike quality of human beings, that is, their readiness to follow the crowd and their fear of being different. Man's moral conditioning readies him to fall victim to this cheap pressure.

COMMUNICATION AND EDUCATION IN A DEMOCRACY

The democratic process is an attempt to provide experiences in two-way communication so that ideas, desires, agreements, oppositions, and criticisms may be transmitted and received in a spirit of comity, calm consideration, and toleration of individualities. In a rigidly stratified society, indoctrination, command, and compulsion are exploited as one-way communication; favored responses are docility and obedience; resentment and hostility are ignored or, if openly expressed, are punished. The difference is, however, one of degree; the propagandist responds to his audience's reactions to his attempts at indoctrination; he modifies his future tactics in the light of past success and failure.

Free Communication Basic to Democracy

One tenet of the democratic faith is that if men are exposed to variant opinions, prejudices, "truths," and proposals, they will, as individuals and as groups, reach the kinds of conclusions and consensus that will favor experiment and modification rather than rigidity in their social relations. This tenet is, of course, the basis upon which freedom of expression and belief is justified. Freedom to portray individual belief in a wide variety of ways, and to seek to persuade, indoctrinate, and propagandize others (within some limits of sexual morality and political loyalty) is ensured to all. There is a faith that, in the long run, the outcomes of public opinion will accord more closely to truth than to falsehood and that what will not work out to the satisfaction of the majority will not long be approved by them.

The democratic faith has justified itself to date. Unwise decisions have, of course, been made. False conclusions have been frequent. Violence and coercion have been experienced. Sabotage and defiance have been tried out. But "fact the dictator" intervenes; compromises and conciliations are achieved. And these very experiences communicate themselves throughout the population; they infiltrate the social heritage.

Civic leaders, including of course professional educators, are morally bound to promote the democratic practices of presentation and consideration of arguments for alternatives. Parliamentary procedures are required in a democracy to pervade debates, conferences, and open forums to permit advocates to persuade audiences with a minimum of molestation and infringement. The free press must report events and arguments with at least a considerable degree of objectivity and open its letter columns to those of varied opinions. Broadcasting systems, under federal compulsion, have to give equal facilities to speakers for opposing sides of controversial political questions.

A democratic society, therefore, attempts to meet the challenges to exact communication which are presented by the very nature of language. Semantic purification of language usages is a dream and, indeed, some improvements can be made. But, even so, the non-language instruments of communication—music, the plastic arts, religious ritual, the theater, and design—employ symbols and settings that successfully invite emotional participation and identification so subtly and pervasively as to make language reform of itself a partial cure at best.

If "the truth is mighty and will prevail," it is because the truth works well in the long run and untruth does not. So within the limits of fraud, libel, obscenity, and treason (all legally defined), no check or hindrance can be officially applied in a democracy to the advocacy of any belief, measure, or service so long as it is not accompanied by illegal action.[12]

In the American society, no social question has been finally answered or is finally answerable; no problem is finally solved or solvable. Both good and evil are relative; they are not absolutes; they cannot be personified as devils and angels, as Communists and free men, or as any other dichotomy. Scapegoats do not remove shortcomings from American shoulders. The road is open for social ideas and for all instruments of communicating them throughout the population. Individually and collectively, citizens of democracies meet their problems from day to day as best they can; they do not yield to them, but they know that revision and compromise are the tools with which they must work.

[12] In time of war, or threat of war, official action is less limited. Utterance of beliefs and freedom of action that are believed to lessen national unity or diminish national security are restricted by executive, legislative, and judicial actions.

Encouragement of Two-way Communication

Conscious two-way communication is as yet an aspiration rather than a fact. Pioneering intellectuals, since the days of the Athenian democracy, have attempted to realize a two-way process of communication among different segments of the citizenry. Even in Athens, however, the two-way process was tolerated by frightened conservatives only within narrow limits. Asking for explanations and justifications for assertions and commands retains the taint of immorality within many families, churches, and nations. Intelligent inquiry and reflective thinking corrupt moral conformity today as they did in Socrates's time.

Intercommunication of democratic ideas is implicit in the acculturation of Americans. The self-restraint, toleration of differences, readiness to cooperate, and the devotion to all other democratic ideals are learned by experience. The intercommunication of attitudes, moralities, and ideas goes on from birth to death. Imitation and conformity to the ways of associates is offset by the self-assertiveness of individuality and by a morality of "live and let live."

Cultural fragmentation is thus enabled to exist side by side with cultural unity—a unity that permits and highly values fragmentation within the limits of the right of all subgroups to their own faiths, modes of dress, and other peculiarities. The communication of such toleration and cooperativeness is, to be sure, far from perfect; the assuredness of some in-groups that "we are right" implies that all who differ are "wrong" and, hence, must be set "right" by persuasion, evangelism, or coercion. When hate or fear dominates the country or a region of it, one-way communication temporarily dominates; apologetics of the ideas and acts of the feared or hated figures are likely to be equated with subversion or disloyalty.

Nevertheless, science, the genius of modern civilization, marches on. Objective examination of all institutional taboos and customs proceeds. Questions are asked that demand intelligible answers. And both the spirit of inquiry and the institutional adjustments of creeds and regulations are communicated to common men. Blind adherence to shibboleths of a prescientific, class-structured society becomes more limited year by year. Emancipation is gradual and as yet only partial; an individual's emotional security still requires gross conformities to the "ways of the herd." Vocalized unbeliefs are morally disapproved even among many who themselves have political, economic, and religious doubts.

Political rule of the people for and by themselves implies intelligent popular inquiry and reflection. Only thus can causes and effects of measures and events be identified and evaluated. In so far as

individuals respond reflectively and with open minds to the challenges
so implied, they act scientifically. And, however uncertainly and
inconsistently their judgments take shape, their search for rationality
and objectivity fosters inquiry in other than political and economic
spheres. Hence, persuasion and open argument increasingly supplement
dogma and authority.

Intercommunication Characterizes Modern Education

Schools, libraries, museums, hospitals, and other meliorative
institutions have made strides toward overcoming their comparative
weakness. The centuries-old dependence on oral telling and printed
pages to communicate information, ideas, skills, and attitudes is increasingly being supplemented by demonstration, example, participation, and experimentation. Emphasis on the initiative and individuality
of the learner has subordinated obedience and stimulated cooperation.
Guided self-activity tends to replace the one-way communication form
of instruction.

These changes in the spirit and mode of communication have
greatly modified educational tools and procedures. In schools at all
levels, movable classroom furniture encourages socialization of work,
group collaboration, cooperative planning by teachers and pupils,
alternating leadership, and the other socially dynamic processes that
will be discussed in Chapter 8. Visual and auditory devices for encouraging moods and attention propitious for the educational purposes
of civic, health, and other organizations are many and varied. They
range from architecture and interior decoration to exhibits, moving
pictures, recordings of music, debates, and drama. Always a major
intent is to enliven and improve interaction among members of the
publics the establishment seeks to serve.

In a broad sense, such education is as truly propagandistic as
is advertising or political persuasion. It differs from them, however, in
two very important ways. It has no ulterior or hidden motivation, and
it promotes the desirable processes of democratic communication. The
social ideas so indoctrinated are interwoven with respect for differing
opinions, with tentativeness of judgment, and hence with loyalty to
freedom of thought, with tolerance for individual tastes and outlooks,
and with a devotion to a search for best answers rather than the
acceptance of ready-made formulas.

The Meliorative Function of Education

The meliorative agencies of democracy have a selective ideological and communicative function. Because their frame of reference exalts
the fundamental rights of all individuals to life, liberty, and the pursuit

of happiness, their social mandate is to keep communication open, not only from platform to audience and audience to platform, but also among platform partisans and among the members of audiences; not only from press to readers and from readers to press, but also among editors, writers, and readers; not only from teachers to pupil and from pupil to teachers, but also among teachers and among the pupils. The social ideas of supreme importance to democracy need no further indoctrination than adequate two-way communication. Consensus arrived at through the free competition of ideas and self-interests may not be "the truth," but it serves to keep the ground ready so that the truth is free to emerge.

The meaning of the adjective *meliorative,* which the authors have used in this and preceding chapters, should be clear from the contexts in which it has appeared. Nevertheless, it is so obviously a value word that some clarification may be desirable.

The basic assumption of educators is that the universe is meaningful; that is, that the processes of nature, including human social nature, support and condition group and individual life and that man, individually and collectively, can and does choose from various goals those he believes are more likely, in the long run, to favor his security and happiness. These goals are teleological. They provide the framework within which temporary goals and measures are to be evaluated.

Meliorative, then, connotes teleological orientation. As such, it has emotive implications for educators because professionally they require goals toward which to direct their efforts; the purpose is barren if it has no referents or if the referents it does have are vague and inconsistent.

Public education in the United States is an agency of political democracy. Accordingly it finds its referents in the ideals and justifications of political democracy. Political democracy connotes, indeed, it almost denotes, an abrogation of social-class privileges and arbitrary economic compulsion, an assertion of the dignity of the individual, and a faith that people themselves can and will provide for their own common welfare. The meliorative function of education, therefore, consists of fostering the realization of these tenets.

America itself is a dynamic social idea! It is an expression of self-assertion and of faith by and in the common man. The public school, in collaboration with all other similarly mandated agencies of democracy, is to be primarily engaged in equipping individuals and groups with the confidence and competence that come from repeated success in planning, executing, evaluating, revising, and so learning how to manage their own affairs.

SELECTED REFERENCES

Albig, William: *Modern Public Opinion,* McGraw-Hill Book Company, Inc., New York, 1956. Perhaps the best recent textbook on public opinion and mass communication.

Berelson, Bernard, and Morris Janowitz, eds.: *Reader in Public Opinion and Communication,* enlarged ed., Free Press, Glencoe, Ill., 1953. A collection of papers on communication and public opinion.

Bridgman, P. W.: *The Intelligent Individual and Society,* The Macmillan Company, New York, 1938. Individual appraisal, evaluation, and reaction to social communication.

Chase, Stuart: *The Tyranny of Words,* Harcourt, Brace and Company, Inc., New York, 1938. General work in semantics.

Dewey, John: *Experience and Nature,* W. W. Norton & Company, Inc., New York, 1925. Understanding the environment.

Katz, Daniel (ed.): *Public Opinion and Propaganda,* The Dryden Press, Inc., New York, 1954. A book of classified readings compiled by the Committee for the Society for the Psychological Study of Social Issues.

Korzybski, Alfred: *Science and Sanity,* Science Press, Lancaster, 1933. An excellent treatment of the practical aspects of communication.

Lee, Alfred McClung, and Elizabeth Bryant Lee (eds.): *The Fine Art of Propaganda,* Harcourt, Brace and Company, Inc., New York, 1939. A useful and fascinating analysis of the techniques of the propagandist.

Lumpkin, Katherine Du Pre: *The Making of a Southerner,* Alfred A. Knopf, Inc., New York, 1947. A self-emancipated Georgian, examining her own and her family's experience, explains how the mores and myths of plantation aristocracy were made absolute standards ensconced in rural Southern morality.

Lundberg, George A.: *Foundations of Sociology,* The Macmillan Company, New York, 1939. Contains a good discussion of the role of symbols and symbolic systems in society and in science.

Mead, Margaret: *And Keep Your Powder Dry,* William Morrow & Company, Inc., New York, 1942. An evaluation of some cultural elements which people care enough about to want to preserve.

Merton, Robert K.: *Mass Persuasion: The Social Psychology of a War Bond Drive,* Harper & Brothers, New York, 1946. One of the best studies yet published on mass persuasion. An analysis of a war-bond drive by radio performer, Kate Smith.

Morris, C. W.: *Signs, Language, and Behavior,* Prentice-Hall,

Inc., Englewood Cliffs, N.J., 1946. General semantics in the art of expression and communication.

Murray, Henry A. (ed.): *Myth and Mythmaking,* George Braziller, Inc., New York, 1960. Origin and meanings of current myths and the possible nature of a mythology to come.

Ogden, C. K., and I. A. Richards: *The Meaning of Meaning,* Routlege, New York, 1936. A description of communicable techniques which people use in satisfying their needs.

Sapir, Edward: "Language," *Encyclopedia of the Social Sciences,* The Macmillan Company, New York, 1935. Probably the best brief account of language in existence.

————: *Language,* Harcourt, Brace and Company, Inc., New York, 1921. The classic anthropological discussion of the nature and forms of language.

Seipmann, Charles A.: *Radio, Television, and Society,* Oxford University Press, New York, 1950. A provocative, though sometimes debatable, work on the nature and effects of mass communication.

DISCUSSION QUESTIONS

1. Few "enlightened Americans" would admit a faith in magic. Nevertheless, astrologers, numerologists, spiritualistic mediums, purveyors of charms, and faith healers find many followers among "educated" people. Can you explain this paradox? Is it a kind of cultural lag—a tendency to retain and use social ideas of the past long after they have been shown to be invalid?

2. Do social ideas as evidenced by popular preferences determine the character of reading matter, drama, television programs, fashions, and modes of doing business? Or is the former the result of the latter? Or does the majority of people docilely accept whatever is, paying attention to such parts of it as they enjoy? Do Americans in fact have "thirteen-year-old intelligences," as some have asserted, because the people who provide their mass-communication messages treat them as though that is their level? Or is it true that, because they have moronic or dull-normal mentalities, the mass of Americans will not have their interest engaged by any communication keyed to a higher level?

3. Can political and social democracy evolve in orderly fashion unless the society maintains a system of folkways, many of them crystallized into laws, which restrict any individual's or group's freedom to act "immorally," or, in degree, even to support such action?

4. In the United States and elsewhere, too, men occasionally

win acceptance as leaders by giving adherence to radical or to reactionary shibboleths and programs in order to head them off. Does the definition, "politics is the art of the possible," find a justification in such a process?

5. Modern commercial journalism, drama, and television, depending as they must on large-scale voluntary support, are compelled to use the language, ideas, symbols, and prejudices of their audiences. If those who control these instruments propose to modify popular conceptions, they are likely to act with subtlety; they "slant the story," "color the news report," and use cartoons and slogans that awaken folkway-sanctions for the opinions they desire to shape. Cite examples from the current press, radio, television, and movies which illustrate either pandering to popular prejudices or the exploitation of public stereotypes to foster support for special purposes.

6. Is the communication of values inevitably a two-way process? Or may an individual passively absorb moral, aesthetic, and social status standards and aspirations without conscious choice? Is poise in social relations possible if one fails to conform to fashion, whether of clothes or of ideas?

7. The term "code of ethics" is frequently used within the medical, teaching, and other professions. There are unwritten codes that control most research scientists, many artists, and all gentlemen. The code of giving primary loyalty to the company, for example, affects the management of large industrial and commercial establishments. Are these varying codes really "the rules of the game" by which the group protects whatever is dear to its members? Can you cite examples wherein the welfare of mankind seem uppermost in the practices fostered by the codes? Examples wherein reaction, stupidity, or evasions of truth or of law seem to be sanctioned by the codes?

PART THREE

The American School:
Its Heritage, Roles, and Processes

7

The School
and Its Heritage

LEARNING PATTERNS IN PRIMITIVE AND MODERN SOCIETIES

The pupil-teacher system upon which modern scholastic institutions are built exists in primitive as well as in modern societies. The primitive child learns from his parents and other adults the skills, beliefs, and knowledge that assure him social acceptance. He achieves much of this learning by imitation, of course, but intentional instruction plays an important part, especially by pointing out what elements of the social inheritance are valued in the society.

A child usually learns many skills and values from his siblings and from other children. Indeed, in some primitive societies, every pupil becomes a teacher in some situations. But since all these young people are culture-bound, adult authority determines what shall be taught and learned. Whatever the nature of the educational agency in the primitive society, it develops as a cell of the social structure; there is no artificial separation of a skill, a ceremonial observance, or a subject from the social life.

The institutional form of the teacher-pupil relation among primitives is sometimes limited to special occasions and functions. Prepara-

123

tion for initiation into adult membership generally requires formal instruction and examination. Youths selected for leadership usually undergo a rigid training and selection process whereby fitness for full-fledged
citizenship is proved. The criterion for adequacy is what is conceived by
the people to be important to the welfare of the community. Thus in
one society, resistance to fatigue, bravery, and proficiency in ceremonials
are peculiarly valued; in another, civic and military training; and, in
a third, "good form" in manners and knowledge.

In the contemporary American society, technological competence is added to some of the qualities just mentioned.

In modern societies, the old is mingled with the new and
cultural vestiges with newly invented or borrowed techniques and knowledge. These vestiges and recent additions to culture sometimes conflict
with one another; sometimes they are reinforcing. One result is that
rigidity of learning patterns is largely lost. The child in the modern, as
in the primitive, society is culturally conditioned; the modern child is,
however, more typically subjected to inconsistent and conflicting conditioning. For example, he may be admonished never to quarrel with
his playmates but also strongly urged to be self-assertive.

Culture Patterns and Social Differentiation

It is obvious, of course, that the mingling and conflicting of
cultural patterns have been accelerated and intensified, not only by
social mobility, but even more fundamentally by factors that have
fostered such mobility. Both in antiquity and in the modern world,
whenever differentiation of labor and of castes developed, especially as
cities grew, new functions had to be performed; hence, new virtues and
new vices have been recognized. Many tribal mores have been outmoded.
Civilization requires its own discipline. Laws and law enforcement pro-
hibit many primitive acts that might still be tolerated among families
and other face-to-face groups; for example, acts of revenge, stealing
from out-group persons, and unsanitary practices become "antisocial"
behavior. Popular attitudes somewhat laggardly approach conformity
with the patterns approved by the public opinion they foster.

Civic conformity, to be sure, has great survival value for a
society. The dangers involved in the fragmenting of society and in the
emotionalized defiance of law and order are apparent. If a society is
to survive, it must, to some reasonable extent, forestall and offset nonconformity to accepted attitudes and establish an emergent code of
accepted behavior. To these ends, enlightened political leaders have
encouraged the development of economic, civic, and domestic competence, and have fostered good will toward fellow citizens. As men and
women of variant cultural backgrounds have mingled in civic, economic,

and leisure activities, increased tolerance has tended to break through the barriers of sectarian, racial, and clannish loyalties and mores. The desire of leaders to accelerate and direct such trends, as much as anything else, is what led to the development of public education.

THE DEVELOPMENT OF SCHOOLS
IN WESTERN EUROPE AND AMERICA

Training for Elites

The development of formal schools has been one of the major means of social control in all civilized societies. In Europe, prior to the democratic and scientific revolutions of the seventeenth and eighteenth centuries, institutional training was prescribed only for a select few. They were taught the knowledge and techniques that would assure them eminence. In such status, they were expected to set up a scheme of prestige, belief, and behavior that accorded with the society's safety and the aspirations of its rulers.

The Spread of Formal Schooling to the Middle Class

Following the Renaissance, technical skills, adventure, and entrepreneurship became highly valued. New problems of human association had to be met, new interests asserted, old "rights" defended; new loyalties to craft and guild harmonized with those deep-rooted in neighborhood, family, faith, and habit. Increased production and the availabilty of petty luxuries—both of which are causes and results of new wealth, specialization, and exchange—excited men's hopes and ambitions. Hence, self-respect and boldness, often fostering enlightened self-interest and cooperative shrewdness, characterized a new urban elite, the middle class or bourgeoisie. The economic and class basis of modern political democracy and intellectual liberalism, the union of technology, capitalism, and free inquiry, was in process. Hence, the middle class sought and obtained formal schooling.

Religion and the Broadening of the School Base

The Protestant Reformation, the Catholic Reaction, the mutual dependence of city and national state (to offset the power of the feudal lords), and the somewhat uncertain triumph of empiricism among politically and economically emancipated men were reflected in educational innovations during and following the sixteenth century. The religious motivation of the Protestant Reformation accounts for its emphasis on universal literacy and secular success. Each person must be able to read and interpret the Bible for himself; this required that he learn to read in his own language. Leadership and power must pass into the hands of temporal rulers who could resist the Catholic Church. Hence, there had to be established primary schools for the majority of children and "realistic" secondary schools emphasizing science, leadership, and the differential training of individual abilities. The Catholic Reaction met the threat by seeking to develop instructional systems which would be more efficient for its purposes than those developing under Protestant auspices.

The Progressive Orientation of Eighteenth-century Education

The schools founded and maintained by liberal, skeptical, and humane men who did not "take sides" in the religious controversy were even more significant. They exemplified what was fundamentally revolutionary in the new science and technology—a faith in the inevitability of further discoveries and a better world on earth to be created by man himself. From Sturm and Comenius in the sixteenth and seventeenth centuries to Franklin and Spencer in the eighteenth and nineteenth, they advocated the discipline of science, toleration and intellectual freedom, practical and sophisticated leadership, and conscious recognition by the learner of his own problems and needs. The various realistic educational institutions and programs utilized some of the same educational ideas that Protestant and Catholic leaders espoused. Conversely, some schools of religious sponsorship were decidedly realistic, especially in their associational life and in their acceptance of the cultural values of the new order—national patriotism, wealth, high social status, and the plaudits of contemporaries.

Meantime, technological training, at first passed on from father to son, developed into an apprenticeship system, and much later into professional and trade schools. Such developments were made in response to the evolving patterns of hope, faith in progress, self-imposed discipline, ambition for "success," and institutional effectiveness.

The survival values of these innovations account for their emergence and development from the shifting, complex, and often contradictory activities and mores of feudal and agrarian societies. In an industrial society, effective living requires a high degree of individual adaptability. The basic drives are ages old: the personal will to live, to rear a family, to earn a livelihood, to support social institutions, and to "adorn" oneself with the attributes which carry prestige. But these drives had to find expression and fulfillment in the emerging social order.[1]

[1] Herbert Spencer, *Education: Intellectual, Moral, and Physical,* D. Appleton & Company, New York, 1860, esp. chap. 1.

Diverse Cultural Bases of American Schools

From the foregoing historical résumé, it is obvious that the contemporary school functions in large part as an instrument for carrying out diverse social and cultural purposes. It retains the functions of acculturation: the inculcation by example, imitation, and institutional regimen of habits, attitudes, and skills approved by adults of the community for young people of different age levels.

Adults in the United States exhibit a generally unacknowledged faith in the power of the school as an agency for accomplishing their loftiest ends.[2] This faith is characterized by an almost sacred quality. The inversion of this American faith, incidentally, may account in part for the phenomenon of mutual intolerance between low-brows and high-brows in the contemporary United States. Education—especially pure, abstract, or nonutilitarian learning—is assumed to have a "spiritual" value for leaders in whom no contamination by earthly or materialistic considerations is desired.

Somewhat inconsistently, education is popularly valued because it increases the prestige, economic status, and urbanity of young people, thereby bolstering their inner security, self-esteem, and confidence. This valuation is peculiarly important in the milieu of a capitalistic, competitive culture which encourages people to "succeed," that is, to get ahead of one's fellows.

Intellectual Justifications for Education

Mingled with the values named above are intellectual justifications. Science, reason, skepticism, objectivity, and hence moderation and self-control are goals highly honored in the abstract in Western societies (although there may be little enthusiasm for them when they lead to conclusions that conflict with individual prejudices or purposes). Nevertheless, in modern industrial society, some approbation is accorded the "unworldly" experts whose scholarly attainments create new machines and lead to new discoveries in the fields of medicine, war making, economic control, and aesthetics.

These attitudes—varying from popular toleration and vague acceptance of acculturation, to magic, self-advancement, and reason—are limited in contemporary Western culture by an almost universal fear of the unknown factors already at work in man's midst and likely to control his future. New ideas—such as racial equality, the emancipation of unskilled labor, world government, and "one world" of economic plenty and brotherly cooperation—unsettle complacency.

[2] Cf. Wilbur B. Brookover, *A Sociology of Education,* American Book Company, New York, 1955, pp. 37–46.

The desirability of some of these goals is not often challenged, but people dread casting off their moorings in a past that seems now to have been knowable and not entirely unsatisfactory. So people would keep an anchor to windward by exalting patriotism and maintaining faith in the past—the truths espoused by the founding fathers, the emotionalized loyalties to the flag, old systems of morality, and old slogans, however they conflict among themselves and however inapplicable they are to the world of tomorrow.

THE INITIATION OF YOUNG PEOPLE

Large and influential sections of the American public are characterized by nonreasoned hesitancy and insecurity. It is obvious, then, that the heritage of the school, maintained by the public to foster social stability and orderly progress toward the goals of American democracy, is endlessly complicated by this inconsistency and insecurity. It is anomalous that so many citizens should so distrust the institution that they themselves have created to initiate and control children and youths. It might, however, be observed quite as justly that educators are rather naïve to presume that they will be quite free from criticism if they teach the young to want better homes, better politics, better economics, or better leisure-time practices than the vocal members of the adult community have or practice.

The public school and its personnel are forced to accept a compromised mandate. They have to accept all the children of all the people, except those who are institutional cases and those whose parents prefer private schools or tutors. As representatives of parents, individually and collectively, and of the bodies politic, educators initiate young people gradually into participation in a somewhat innocuous school process—one that the public seems likely to find acceptable.

This rather obvious and certainly uninspiring generalization applies to the formalities of the school. For both good and ill, there are far more kinds, and far more dynamic kinds, of acculturation taking place in the school and its social environment than are readily controlled by formal organization. Children and youths learn from each other and from each other's siblings and parents quite as truly as they learn from class instruction, orchestra rehearsals, guidance conferences, and other aspects of the formal school.

The enrollment of almost all American children and youths in public schools is a most important means of fostering the integration of the people. In much of the country, such complete enrollment is being approached. The acculturation processes in public and private schools and in schools for exceptional children (delinquents, crippled, and mentally or emotionally abnormal) are not dissimilar. Through instruction, guidance, student activities, and school regimen, such knowledge, interests, ideals, habits, and powers are fostered as the teaching profession advocates and as public opinion tolerates.

Public Opinion and Educational Planning

The inculcation of what is valued and the formation of personality traits that do not offend adult stereotypes for all children and youths is itself a program that requires insight, sensitivity, and teaching skill. A hundred gremlins lurk to disrupt the best-laid plans that educators may make. Teachers, pupils, administrators, custodians, coaches, and parents are but human beings. Each individual who participates in the school's acculturation process has moods and immediate concerns that influence, if indeed they do not dictate, what he approves or disapproves, ignores or responds actively to, praises or blames, proposes or forbids.

Moreover, the climate of public opinion within which the school's program must function sometimes changes swiftly in response to a dramatic event, a propaganda drive, or the letdown that follows zealous effort. School officials count on the active support of the adult community, or at least its tolerant approval, to reinforce their efforts. This support or approval, because of some occurrence outside the school, may turn suddenly into active hostility.

Such apparently sudden shifts in public attitudes do not often mean that the general adult population has consciously changed its position significantly with respect to some aspect of acculturation. It is enough that a vocal minority, hitherto uninfluential, has become a force potent enough to veto whatever the school has been attempting. For example, public enthusiasm for international organization may be succeeded by nationalistic intolerance; support for price control may shift to antagonism toward all bureaucracy; tolerance of minorities may be followed by witch-hunts; pride in the achievements of cooperation between labor and management may be superseded by taboos on the expression of favorable judgments regarding organized labor.

The most potent obstacle to the efforts of school officials and teachers, however, is the fact that recruits for the teaching profession usually are not drawn from young people who themselves are much concerned with social problems and social actions. Furthermore, many persons on the staffs of teacher training institutions are specialists who are quite satisfied with such aspects of the *status quo* as guarantee their security so long as they confine themselves to their specialities.[3] Finally, teachers everywhere are certified, licensed, and employed in formal terms of grades and subjects. Teachers so recruited and so trained, whose certificates and contracts are defined as they are at present, do not respond readily even to the most resourceful and determined supervisory agents who are inclined to persevere in the face of public criticism.

Freedom for Educational Planning

When one examines the school's function as the public's accredited agency for selective acculturation in the light of these uncertain, if not actually unfavorable, conditions, it is clear that the task of school people is difficult. Fortunately, however, there is much in the culture which is noncontroversial and which is motivated by nonideological aspirations that schools can and do transmit with a good deal of success.

The prestige value of cleanliness, orderliness, attractive personal appearance, and courtesy assures public support for habit and attitude promotion in these aspects of the popular culture. Similarly, the patterns of work and play among American adults are such that cooperation, alternating leadership and followership, fair play, special consideration for the beginner, the weak, and the less able, and a readiness to share one's special advantages with others all fit in with values overtly subscribed to by almost all adults.

Moreover, the fragmented and inconsistent culture patterns of contemporary American society present favorable conditions within which ideas and tolerance of differences may be, and often are, successfully fostered. In sports, the arts, and scholarship, participants are honored in terms of ability and achievement, with little regard to economic status, race, religion, ideologies, or social class. Within the limitations of codes governing good taste and restraint, similar disregard of origin and status characterize popular attitudes toward dress and personal appearance, social graces, civic services, political alignments (if not too radical), and institutional loyalties. Hence, the school can accentuate similar attitudes among pupils and those adults it may influence.

[3] Cf. David Riesman's account of the University of Chicago professor who demanded a kind of "intellectual tariff" to protect the field of economics against the encroachments, in the search for students, by sociology, psychology, and human-development study. *Constraint and Variety in American Education*, Doubleday & Company, Inc., New York, 1958, p. 79.

The social ideas just mentioned are relatively permanent and widely accepted among American adults. There are, however, many aspects of social aspiration and behavior in the contemporary United States in which these values and standards are less consistently found. Values regarding skills and achievements in the areas of wealth and its acquisition, political manipulation, and showmanship are flexible and variable. Attitudes toward law enforcement and the avoidance of legal restraint are often inconsistent. Many Americans, as a further example, see no inconsistency in traveling by public roads to meetings in tax-supported school auditoriums protected by city police in order to applaud an apologist for "free enterprise" who denounces "socialism."

Mixed Cultural Patterns and the School

Even in a relatively homogeneous and isolated culture there develop socially approved beliefs and behavior that are, or seem to be, incompatible with the general culture pattern. In the Zuñi pueblo of New Mexico, for example, although aggression, anger, and authority are suppressed, a jealous wife may physically attack her rival without risking social disapproval. Among the Zuñi, also, a candidate for the "war cult" (protectors and policemen of the people) must have killed someone to be eligible; this implies a tolerance for violence if it leads to expiation and service to the group.[4] Conversely, among the Plains Indians, whose dominant culture pattern was individualistic and violent, gentleness, voluntary cooperation, submissiveness, and personal affection had a place in the culture, however inconspicuous and subordinate they may have been.[5]

Incompatibilities in relatively simple cultures such as these serve only to warn against absolutes in definitions of the American way of life and the school's objectives and processes in relation to it. If there are paradoxes in primitive and isolated cultures, they may be expected a hundredfold in the culture of a "melting pot" society, characterized by a high rate of social mobility and rapid technological and scientific change.

There are primary values in the United States, but they are contradictory and often competitive. The survival complex, with its emphasis on rivalry, ambition, risk taking, self-reliance, and callousness, is dominant in many American social relations. Generally, these qualities and the activities associated with them are considered admira-

[4] Ruth Benedict, *Patterns of Culture*, Houghton Mifflin Company, Boston, 1934, chap. 4.
[5] Cf. Abram Kardiner and others, *The Psychological Frontiers of Society*, Columbia University Press, New York, 1945.

ble, or at least excusable, and they are ordinarily given credit for the "greatness" stereotyped in popular phraseology regarding Americans as individuals and as a nation. Scholarship contests, much classroom recitation procedure, athletics, forensics, and "tryouts" for drama, musical, and other student exhibitions all accord with this competitive motivation. To succeed or fail, to beat or be beaten, to get or lose, to attain or to be pushed aside, to face cruel life realistically, and to be a hero in the strife—these are all prominent in American life. Or are they?

Certainly, such values are quite out of harmony with the humane sentiments espoused by most Americans in more religious or senti-mental moods. Within limits, most Americans affirm the brotherhood of man—all men. They applaud unselfish service to civic organization, to the unfortunate everywhere, and even to abstractions like beauty, truth, and science. They honor the good neighbor, the gentle, the cooperative, the unassertive member of the community who may himself be unaware of his own contributions to gentle living, tolerance, and affection. They salute the American flag and pledge allegiance to it as the symbol of liberty and justice for all. They proclaim faith and loyalty to the sentiments articulated in the Declaration of Independence, in the Preamble to the Constitution, in Lincoln's Gettysburg Address, and in the other canons of American democracy.

The American school accepts all this, too, as a mandate, side by side with its antithetical "survival motivation."

Cultural Vestiges and Education

Subordinate to this great conflict of primary values are many fragments of other values, to several of which the school makes at least a gesture of agreement and support. These fragments are usually vestiges of cultural patterns once wholeheartedly accepted in the forerunners of contemporary schools.

The American verbal and ceremonial obeisance to the abstrac-tions of learning and scholarship is a case in point. These tags are fetishes whose magical power is seldom questioned by teachers or patrons—even those (perhaps especially those) who have little learn-ing and who make little sustained effort to get more. By implication, the tags usually stress those forms of erudition that are associated with the stereotype of the "scholar"—a somewhat unworldly character, in-troverted, even seclusive, working calmly and unhurriedly in library or laboratory. The vestigial quality of this fragment is at once obvious. In the cultural pattern of the medieval and early Renaissance periods, such a "scholar" was a figure of great significance.

The point is that, while learning and scholarship continue to have undoubted value for the contemporary society, conventional reverence for these attributes is not based so much on their significance as on tradition. It is almost scholastic blasphemy for a teacher openly to challenge the validity of this notion, although few of them feel any urge to seek great erudition for themselves. Elsewhere in this book, some aspects of the more or less unconscious exploitation of this vestigial respect for "learning" are examined.

Other relics of the past similar to this academic stereotype can only be named here. "Discipline" in the sense of obedience to rules and commands is in degree a relic of patriarchal authoritarianism. Marks, promotions, examinations, graduation ceremonies, and school insignia have roots in the past, when selectivity and cultism were far more in harmony with the general cultural patterns than they are in the mid-twentieth-century United States. The study of the English classics, the solution of some mathematical puzzles, the premium put on foreign-language credits for admission to some colleges (which then proceed to ignore what the student knows), and the memorization of historical facts are in great degree vestiges from former periods when such things were highly esteemed among leisure-time castes.[6]

EDUCATIONAL REFORMS AS RESPONSES TO SOCIAL CHANGE

Prophets and interpreters of institutional change may accelerate reforms and affect their forms of expression, but they do not themselves cause the reforms. Only when the time for their ideas is propitious do their recommendations come to have long-term significance. Socrates, Plato, Jesus, Vittorino, Luther, Comenius, Rosseau, Pestalozzi, Thomas Arnold, Parker, and Dewey spoke for ideas that sooner or later found wide support. When times were ripe, when the accepted values, popular aspiration, the nature of leadership, and the economies made the ideas workable, fundamental changes took place.

Major Areas of School Response to Change

The contemporary school is in transition, as indeed all social institutions now are and have been since the Renaissance. It maintains a

[6] That in some instances these learnings have much personal and social value is not questioned here. It is the "protective tariff" of prescription and tradition by which they are artificially fostered that is criticized.

framework inherited from diverse former cultural patterns, but it also develops two sorts of change in response to contemporary social forces.

The curriculum of the schools—from the three R's of the elementary grades to the science seminar in the graduate division of the university—maintains continuity with the culture of the past. Nevertheless, in varying degree in different schools, the actual content and method of teaching and the rewards and standards associated with academic success are often of revolutionary newness. The teacher continues to instruct his pupils as he always has. But instruction, as such, is limited to the techniques and facts which the learners need to achieve the goals which they themselves accept as desired ends. Their objectives are to solve problems, master difficult skills, and gain status before their chosen audiences; instruction is welcomed by them because it makes such success probable. In this revolutionary cultural context, the "master" becomes an instrument; by his instruction, encouragement, and criticism, pupils gain readiness and ability to think reflectively and independently and to judge "right" and "wrong" conclusions and achievements on the basis of their usefulness in meeting needs or desires.

Such a revolutionary process is a response to the spirit of science and invention which regards truth as something to be discovered rather than something revealed in the past. It is a response to democratic equalitarianism, which asserts the right of everyone to create his own world of functional truth. It is in part a response to the economy of abundance now emerging, wherein the good things of life are potentially obtainable by all. And it is, as already said, a recognition of individuality and multiplicity in society. The good things, the truths, and the beauties of life are inward expressions of millions of eyes, ears, brains, and glands. Right and wrong, good and bad, even logical and illogical, have become relative terms.

The other area of school revolution, not unrelated to that of subject change, is the so-called extracurricular. Radical change in this area of school life has been less restricted by institutional traditions and structures than in the area of subjects wherein standards, marks, promotions, and teachers' personal favors have retained importance. However shot through they may be by infantilism and exhibitionism and whatever exploitations are practiced by coaches, administrators, and local boosters, student activities generally provide rich opportunity and encouragement for young people to create their own personalities. These tentative personalities may often seem ridiculous, even stultifying, to many adults; they may shock the puritanic moralists; they may, indeed, be dangerous to health and to social adjustment. But they cannot be entirely avoided, certainly not forbidden, if full maturity is to be attained by the individual student.

The social environment of the school provides the potential nexus between the teaching and learning function of the school and the rather unselective and multifarious developmental influences of community experience. It offers the most favorable opportunity for the school to foster situations typical of social life somewhat idealized and purified—the sole dynamic by which institutional preparation for active community membership can be given. Moreover, it provides richer opportunities than does the conventional class-management process for the promotion of loyalty to school ideas and of identification with leaders who exemplify these ideals. It is in this setting that moral guidance is most effective.

The Spirit of Reform

Care must be taken not to assume that recent and current innovations in the school are something brand new. The extent of the contemporary scientific and economic revolutions in American society are unique and unprecedented, and inevitably they dictate radical changes in the establishments that educate youth. Cultural revolutions have, however, taken place many times in the past, and to each of them schools, churches, governments, and other institutions have been adapted, grudgingly or eagerly, actively or passively, consciously or unconsciously.

The most conspicuous and enlightening forerunners of current reforms may be found in the relatively recent past. The emergence of the famous English public schools is intimately associated with the development of the industrial and financial capitalism of the British Empire in the late eighteenth and nineteenth centuries. These schools, variously founded as royal and religious institutions, charity schools, and as guild provisions for the sons of members, came to enroll sons of landed gentry, manufacturers, entrepreneurs, financiers, and successful artists. They took advantage of the new leisure, the high hopes, the social aspirations, and the aggressiveness of these parvenus to develop in their sons the code of the English gentleman: loyalty to church, throne, and empire, ability to handle men, class consciousness, and identification with the aristocracy.

The revolutionary instruments used were, first, a relatively inapplicable classical training, a potent instrument for protecting an elite from being swamped by intruders and, second, a school regimen of dormitory life and athletic games for social education and for the nourishment of emotionalized habits and attitudes. In dress, posture, voice, pronunciation, reticence, discipline, and assumptions of superiority, the product of the English public school was, as a type, different from any other man on earth. It was he whom Kipling glorified. It was he who was more royalist than royalty itself. It was he whom Shaw and Wells ridiculed. It was he who for two centuries ruled the British Empire and Commonwealth with both amazing success and stupendous failure.

The later efforts to extend the process by admitting to the ancient schools the sons of colonials and scholarship youths selected by examination from the less privileged classes have not been so successful. The cultural revolution has moved too fast for the cautious recruitment of potential protectors into the caste system. The present leaders of the British government and economy are not limited to public school graduates; they include former municipal schoolboys and those of little or no schooling. New revolutions demand changes that former revolutionary schools find it difficult to make.

Public Education a Radical Idea

A most significant example of radical institutional change in the United States is the emergence of the publicly supported "educational ladder." Taxation on the basis of ability to pay in order to provide free schools for all the children of all the people has come about only in the last hundred years. Prior to the nineteenth century, some colonial and state legislatures and the national Congress had provided tax exemption and appropriations for educational institutions. But the major expense of rearing children, including school education, fell on their parents.

The concept that all children belong to the community, and hence that their welfare and preparation for adulthood is a community responsibility, is so generally held today that its revolutionary nature is overlooked. Yet it is not universally or consistently adhered to. "The partial confiscation of one man's property to educate another man's child" is as wrong in the eyes of some contemporary men of property as it was to those in Rhode Island in Henry Barnard's day.

It was the cumulative effects of nationalism, urbanism, democratic ideology, and the organized aggressiveness of common people that eventually overwhelmed the opposition of economic and sectarian conservatives. Universal education is not yet achieved, to be sure, but resistance to it grows halfhearted. Ability and determination, rather than financial or family status, are the attributes that increasingly decide how far and how fast an individual shall proceed in education.

The Paradox of Conservatism through Radicalism

Popular unrest and vivid ideas are likely to flower in periods of marked social change. The day-to-day experiences of men seldom accord with the preachments of moralists and the purveyors of obsolete "truths." Again and again, pioneering individuals and institutions have sought to bridge such gaps by reforms and outright innovations. Statesmen, playwrights, clergymen, philosophers, and teachers have used the instruments and establishments they serve to foster changes in popular thought which, they believe, will make it more consistent with reality.

During periods when hope has dominated the social scene, these pioneers have fostered intellectual inquiry and humane sentiments, individual assertiveness, and toleration of diversity. Thereby they have sometimes frightened apologists for established political and religious faiths who have sought to suppress free inquiry and public expression of unorthodox conclusions.

Such futile attempts to moor a dead past in a world of revolutionary ideas have ancient precedents. Though no intelligent Athenian of the fifth century, B.C., actually believed that the sun was a chariot which was driven across the sky by Apollo, Anaxagoras was imprisoned for denying it. Two millennia later, Bruno was burned at the stake and Galileo imprisoned because they asserted that the earth moved in relation to the sun even though the intellectuals of the church hierarchy no longer believed in an earth-centered universe. And in the twentieth-century United States, some teachers have lost their positions because they have questioned the dogmas of classical economists, political parties, and religious fundamentalists, though such doubts were common among school patrons.

But martyrdom or even the willingness to risk popular disapprobation is not characteristic of human beings. And the teaching profession has always recruited a large proportion of cautious men and women. In their hands, even radical ideas soon lose their aggressive qualities and may, indeed, become associated with reactionary programs.

An example of such perversion of ideas is the present propaganda for "the humanities." This term signified in the fifteenth and sixteenth centuries an interest in persons and things currently observed; it was a revolt against dogmatism and authoritative "truth." It was the *progressive* education of the time, the individualistic inquiry into natural and social phenomena, the elevation of facts and their interrelationships above the repetition of statements made by authorities. Men were dismissed from university staffs because they espoused humanism very much as their counterparts are today suppressed or at least criticized because they espouse "socialism," sex freedom, pacifism, or the affiliation of teachers with labor organizations.

More recently, the sciences entered the university and later the high school curricula as fighting faiths. At first, indeed, science masqueraded as natural philosophy. It was challenged and opposed by "humanists" who had now grown tory, and who revered "erudition" and "discipline." The emotionalized antipathies toward scientists during the first three-quarters of the nineteenth century seem almost incredible today, partly because established religion and classicism have lost much of their dogmatic prestige, but even more because the processes of science and science teaching have themselves become rather esoteric.

Iconoclastic scientists continue to disturb those who wish the world would settle down to an acceptance of the "eternal verities," and true humanists continue to speak out for the rights of man to think for himself—his right to be wrong. But scholastic apologists for the sciences and for the humanities are sometimes major opponents of true science and humanism.

Social Stability and Orderly Progress

The paradox of conservatism through radicalism in educational evolution is readily resolved if it be realized that, consciously or unconsciously, schools are maintained *primarily* to perpetuate the social heritage. Every parent and every society is justifiably concerned with preserving the results of social experience for the children. The time-binding and space-binding attributes of human beings find their advantages in the fact that the young can apperceive much of the wisdom and experience of the race through the exercises of home, school, and the rest of community life, and through vicarious experience.

Whatever innovations find their way into school curricula and school regimen—however they may be supported by enlightened citizens and to whatever degree they may have counterparts among the ideas and practices of adults—must nevertheless face an anomaly. The age-old primary function of training institutions for children and youths is social stability. And many adults, however skeptical they may be in private, believe that young people should not think for themselves until they have mastered through docile learning what was known and believed by their forebears.

In large part, the widespread approval of obedient lesson learning by school children is itself a social heritage; it is considered the business of child-training institutions. It is the "picture in the mind" of classroom processes for many adults, even for many who themselves experienced much independent activity in their own school days.

The high popular valuation put on the inculcation of knowledge and habits by teachers is doubtless reinforced by the consternation felt by many parents and other adults when children do act independently. In every age, young people's behavior and opinions have seemed to threaten the beliefs and customs to which many contemporary adults themselves have given merely formal and verbal acquiescence. The encouragement of independent thinking and nonconforming behavior by younger people has been rather consistently condemned as "heretical" and a "corruption of the morals of youth."

It is not strange that in the twentieth-century United States, in the midst of a bewildering climate of social and technological change, the demand that the school train children in docile obedience, orthodox loyalty, and conventional information and skills should be widely supported by insecure adults. For them, the school's primary function is the provision of a kind of cultural anchor so that the oncoming generations may thus avoid being swamped by untried and untested innovations in morals.

SUMMARY

Fortunately for the school's mission, most active persons in contemporary American society are compelled to a considerable degree to think and act independently. The almost daily emergencies of life challenge everyone to try some adaptations and applications of his repertory of knowledge, skills, and attitudes. In however rudimentary a stage the processes of hypothesizing, choice, trial, and evaluation of result may be, the elements of science as a way of life are present. While it must be granted that habit, custom, and predisposition dominate the adaptation in most instances, each situation presents some variable that calls for self-reliance and independence.

Considered pragmatically, American associative life is itself an effective school for initiative and independence. Paradoxically, conformity to the technological environment and to the resolution of cultural forces compels individuality of response. Consistent following of patterned behavior would be ineffective amid challenges to deal with such varied emergencies.

The choices made on any occasion may be inadequate. But trial and error encourage reflection and modification as similar situations reappear. Success and failure are determined as much by the admiration and disapproval of the peer group as by the objective accomplishment. Generally, achievement and audience response reinforce each other and so are difficult to distinguish. Completing a forward pass, self-decoration to attract the attention of age-mates, overhauling an automobile engine, or entertaining guests may, because they call forth expressions of approval from peers, stimulate quite as much self-discipline, reflective thinking, and initiative as anything the school has to offer in its conventional program.

To a very great extent, therefore, the school fulfills its educational mission by following and exploiting the adaptive practices that young people are engaging in anyway. Children and youths, like adults, are social beings, and they live in a world of associations with their fellows. If the school is to fulfill its mission effectively, its officers, teachers and patrons need to recognize the social character of young people, and organize the school regimen, instruction, and guidance in such a way that account is taken of their learning experiences outside the school.

SELECTED REFERENCES

Allen, Francis R., and others: *Technology and Social Change,* Appleton-Century-Crofts, Inc., New York, 1957. An informative and readable textbook on the relationships of technological and social change.

American Education Faces the World Crisis, American Council on Education, Washington, 1951. Includes discussion of most of the major aspects of education as they relate to world problems.

Brookover, Wilbur B.: *A Sociology of Education,* American Book Company, New York, 1955. Part Two of this text includes a good discussion of the social context of the school.

Counts, George S.: *Education and American Civilization,* Bureau of Publications, Teachers College, Columbia University, New York, 1952. The meaning of the scientific and technological revolution for American schools.

Cox, Philip W. L.: *Curriculum Adjustment in the Secondary School,* J. B. Lippincott Company, Philadelphia, 1925. A pioneer text dealing with the high school curriculum as an instrument of social betterment.

————, and Forrest E. Long: *Principles of Secondary Education,* D. C. Heath and Company, Boston, 1932. Twenty-five principles explaining the scope, processes, and functions of the high school.

Dewey, John: *School and Society,* University of Chicago Press, Chicago, 1902. The explanation and philosophical justification of the laboratory school at the University of Chicago at the turn of the century. Probably the most influential single book affecting the orientation of the modern school.

Hofstadter, Richard, and C. D. Hardy: *The Development and Scope of Higher Education in the United States,* Columbia University Press, New York, 1952. A history of American higher education.

"Long-range Issues in Education," *The Educational Record,* January, vol. 35, no. 1, 1954. Important addresses given at the 1953 annual meeting of the American Council on Education.

Mead, Margaret: *The School in American Culture,* Harvard University Press, Cambridge, Mass., 1951. A brilliant critique of school responses to present and impending cultural changes.

Mercer, Blaine E., and Edwin R. Carr: *Education and the Social Order,* Rinehart & Company, Inc., 1957. A text of readings which contains chapters on the school as a social institution and on the school and the community.

Miel, Alice: *Changing the Curriculum,* Appleton-Century-Crofts, Inc., New York, 1946. The elementary school in process of modernization.

Murray, R. W.: *Sociology for a Democratic Society,* Appleton-Century-Crofts, Inc., New York, 1950. Describes the development of social organizations.

Nordskog, John Eric: *Social Change,* McGraw-Hill Book Company, Inc., New York, 1960. A useful collection of forty-eight professional papers on social change.

Myers, Edward D. (ed.): *Education in the Perspective of History,* Harper & Brothers, New York, 1960. The concluding chapter, "Education: The Long View," by Arnold J. Toynbee, is especially useful in explaining how the formalization of once meaningful education makes it an esoteric monopoly of a learned minority.

Pounds, Ralph L., and James R. Bryner: *The School in American Society,* The Macmillan Company, New York, 1959. Chap. 3, entitled "The Historic Relationship of Schools to Their Societies," is especially relevant to this chapter.

"Promotion and Interpretation of Free Public Education," *Phi Delta Kappan,* Special Issue, vol. 24, no. 9, June, 1953. Interesting issue devoted to the interpretation of public school programs.

Riesman, David: *Constraint and Variety in American Education,* Doubleday & Company, Inc., New York, 1958. The second in this collection of three long essays is a provocative discussion of "Intellectual Veto Groups" in American education.

Rodehaver, Myles W., and others: *The Sociology of the School,* Thomas Y. Crowell Company, New York, 1957. Contains some good chapters on the social context of the school.

Spaulding, Francis T.: *The High School and Life,* McGraw-Hill Book Company, Inc., New York, 1938. Recommendations for high school reform based on the findings of the Regents' Inquiry into the Costs and Character of Education in New York State.

Thurston, L. M.: *The Role of Education in the Development of the American Way of Life,* University of Wisconsin Press, Madison, Wis., 1952. A lecture in the Knapp Lecture Series.

DISCUSSION QUESTIONS

1. Bertrand Russell [7] asserts that the state and the family have generally been hostile to each other, and, hence, the state was clothed by divinity and sanctioned by religion as a means of overcoming family resistance to it. The exception to this antagonism that he cites is the Roman conception—the impersonal state and the religion of public spirit requiring the dedication of the family to the welfare of the state. Since Americans retain no symbol of divine rulership, they espouse the Roman ideal of the impersonal state. But the legal authority of the teacher is *in loco parentis,* not *in loco communitatis* or *in loco statutis,* even though school education is defined as a state function and is controlled by state laws. Can you resolve this paradox?

2. In earlier chapters, it was explained that the anthropologists' and sociologists' concept of culture includes all the man-made knowledge, things, techniques, habits, and attitudes of a definable group. Quotation marks have been used ("culture") when the word refers to the bookish, eruditional, and artistic values and practices of a society. What constitutes "culture" has varied from age to age. For example, it was not until late in the history of Athens, despite the emphasis on beauty, that artists were accepted as equals of literary men. In the very restricted aristocratic "democracy" of Athens, work with one's hands was incompatible with "culture." This Greek concept has retained currency among many Americans. Can you identify elements of it in college and high school programs and policies?

3. Are there some areas of belief and behavior of great importance to individuals in which there are problems for which the school is blocked from seeking solutions? For example, it is widely understood that most people reach sexual maturity long before they are economically able to maintain a home and support children. Can the school and young people discover a solution to the problems which grow out of this fact? Or take myths, religions, and patriotic loyalties dear to parents and to members of powerful associations. Can the school foster critical inquiry regarding them? Would it be desirable for it to do so if it could?

4. It is sometimes asserted that elementary schoolteachers lack status equal to that of many other professionals in the United

[7] *Education and the Modern World,* W. W. Norton & Company, Inc., New York, 1932, chap. 5.

States. If you agree, evaluate such possible explanations as the following: (a) their analogies to the servile pedagogues of Graeco-Roman families, to the English nurse-governess, and to the stereotype of the unmarried teacher of nineteenth-century American schools, (b) the social and economic class origins of many recruits for elementary schoolteacher training, and (c) the contrast between the contemporary admiration for "strong" executives and other dominant men whose characteristics seem antithetical to those of efficient elementary teachers. Does the university faculty member lack prestige as compared with his contemporaries in other professions? As compared with successful businessmen? If not, is it because his work is intrinsically of greater social value than that of the elementary schoolteacher? Or for some other reasons? How do you account for the present high esteem for athletic coaches? Music directors? Conductors of research? University presidents?

5. On April 9, 1941, the teachers of Norway, having been proclaimed by the Quisling government automatically to be members of the *Laerersamnandet* (Nazi Teachers Front), opened their school day by reading to their pupils slowly and with feeling a statement, a part of which follows:

> The teacher's vocation . . . is not only to give the children knowledge. He must also teach the children to believe in and desire that which is true and just. He is therefore unable to teach anything which is in conflict with his conscience without betraying his calling . . . I will never ask you to do anything which I consider to be wrong, nor will I teach you anything which in my opinion is not in accordance with the truth . . . I believe that I shall then be in agreement with the great majority of the people who have entrusted me with my educational duties.

In reprisal for this and other resistance to Nazi regimentation, 500 key teachers were crowded into a derelict vessel by Quisling police and, after severe torture, were carried to Kirkenes, the town farthest northeast in Norway, where all of them suffered and some died. Heroic? Surely! Emotionally thrilling to read about? Yes, indeed. An act characteristic of patriotic loyalty? Reflecting a myth of individual freedom and responsibility to be maintained at all costs? An exception to the course of compromise, evasion, and postponement typical of middle-class people in a democracy? Was this gesture of defiance an aspect of the mental and emotional configuration which war experience develops?

How do you account for such sacrificial action by these Norwegian teachers? Do you know any American teachers who would make such an issue of conscience if it could be avoided? If you do, would you care to estimate what fraction of all teachers they represent?

8

Group Processes
in the School

THE ROLE OF THE GROUP IN PERSONALITY FORMATION

Young people undoubtedly learn as much from each other as they do from adults and, because of this, it is essential for the educator to know the processes and relationships which characterize pupil associations and to understand how to use them.

Each individual in an association is significantly affected by the emotional atmosphere of the social situation. His moment-to-moment moods and values are responses to the combined responses of his fellows. And his expressions of approval, rejection, and indifference, in turn, affect their reactions.

When any aggregate is unified by common purposes and collaborative activities it becomes a cohesive group. For good or for ill, cohesive groups are of major importance as instruments of social control; in large part they shape the personality of members and, in lesser degree, of those nonmembers who are significantly affected by the groups' behavior and attitudes.

It is possible to control the formation and processes of certain groups which are important to personality development. Perhaps the school's most persuasive influences operate through such control. It is thus possible for the school to exert an influence on the development of personality so that it tends to conform to patterns of attitudes and behavior which are highly valued by those directing education.

Self-expression and self-discipline are complex adjustments by the individual. They are significantly affected, to be sure, by his prior conditioning and his biological equipment, but always they are stimulated and largely controlled by the groups with which the individual identifies. Even the forms of attitudes and behavior which deviate from community norms are significantly affected by the group; in other words, deviancy is predominantly cultural.[1] Nonconformity to the standards of the group itself, of course, may be due to faulty interpretation of group values, feelings of inferiority, faulty goal setting, inadequate adjustment technique, or poor judgment.

A considerable degree of self-assertion and resistance to group pressures to conform are surely necessary if the individuality so highly esteemed in a democracy is to be fostered. Mature adjustment calls for the neat compromises learned mostly within groups. School personality guidance consists in helping each student to express himself and to discipline himself as he responds to the means, purposes, attitudes, and behavior of the groups with which he associates.

Adjustment and the Maturation Process

The "normal" or "healthful" personality has purposeful, meaningful, and satisfying interactions with others. The young person creates his role and develops his ego ideal experimentally by "trying out" behavior; his associates' responses prove satisfying or frustrating, in varying degrees, and he adjusts his behavior and self-perception accordingly. Individual children, then, are not isolated, discrete entities but personalities in constant process of adjustment to others.[2]

These associates include out-of-school persons, some of whom may, indeed, exist only in fantasy. Because so many of most children's group relationships are related to the school, however, school experience is often in the very center of their adjustment processes. Hence, the professional staff can significantly influence and control the process through which the individual pupil develops a "self."

[1] Cf. Robert K. Merton, "Social Structure and Anomie: Revisions and Extensions," in Ruth Nanda Anshen (ed.), *The Family: Its Functions and Destiny*, rev. ed., Harper & Brothers, New York, 1959, pp. 275–312.

[2] Cf. Charles Horton Cooley's concept of the "looking-glass self." *Social Organization*, Charles Scribner's Sons, New York, 1909, pp. 23ff.

One aspect—perhaps it may be called "positive"—of the process of self-extension consists of the incorporation of concern for other people's conditions (sentiments, activities, goals, and welfare). "What one loves becomes a part of him" applies almost equally to persons, institutions, ideals, and whatever else one internalizes, that is, adopts into his system of values and motives. Thus, as time passes, the self, which is largely conditioned by biologically inherited characteristics and by experiences in the in-group, is transformed, through an ever-widening complex of interaction, into an autonomous, socialized self. Ethical maturity consists largely of planning for the welfare of others as well as for the self and in executing such plans.[3]

Because such self-extension has to develop, has to begin and grow satisfyingly where others' responses and conditions are sensed and in degree understood, the family, church, club, team, and other face-to-face groups provide favorable opportunities for guidance by adults. The capacity to identify the self in the context of others, grown effective in primary groups, broadens as the individual adapts to new and more inclusive groups and as he comes to feel sympathetic membership in groups with which he has no immediate contact.

The processes of identification with primary and secondary groups and with individuals, real or imaginary, are the same whether the emerging ego ideal, judged as a whole, is "good" or "bad." Justification or encouragement of a youth's identification with a predatory gang, a nationwide hate organization, a sophisticated beauty queen, or an immoral big-shot can generally be found somewhere in the American value system. An immediate challenge to the school and other establishments concerned with socialization is to be found in this harsh fact.

The effective school arranges a purified and somewhat idealized environment wherein the processes of identification of the student with primary and secondary groups and with real and imaginary individuals may be favorably controlled. The school thus reinforces those cultural influences that foster self-realization in terms of civic welfare, aesthetic sensitivity, and the democratic ethic, and so it competes with and offsets those influences that promote self-realization in terms of behavior, tastes, and values which are judged by educators to be undesirable.[4]

As the individual becomes socially mature, his identifications become increasingly and more consciously selective. He chooses among

[3] Gordon W. Allport, *Personality: A Psychological Interpretation,* Henry Holt and Company, Inc., New York, 1937, pp. 217–220.
[4] Cf. Philip W. L. Cox, *Creative School Control,* J. B. Lippincott Company, Philadelphia, 1927, pp. 11–15.

his many possible selfhoods those that seem likely to be most satisfying.[5] Since satisfaction depends in large part on a feeling of adequacy and on expected recognition by those whose opinions he values, the choices he makes during his early years have a prophetic quality. The selfhoods developed during school years do not wholly determine adult personalities, but they do give promise (or threats) of them.

COHESIVE GROUPS IN THE SCHOOL

Transmission of Democratic Values through Groups

School administrators are coming to foster democratic group cooperation. In many schools, teachers and pupils now play considerable parts in educational policy making and in the operation of the institution.

In classes, clubs, councils, and less formal associations, matters of school and community concern are evaluated; plans for studying them are made; tentative solutions are advocated and, when feasible, experimentally tried. Thus, the school increasingly enhances initiative, reflective thinking, toleration of differences of opinion, and compromise, all of which are aspects of group cooperation and of the democratic process.

The school is, of course, only one of the social agencies by which the morality basic to a democratic associational life and civic competence is developed and transmitted. Arrangements for young people and adults to experience and so to learn those habits and customs that undergird the American democracy characterize, however inconsistently, most families and other institutions.

The school intentionally fosters certain group processes both because they are favorable to its efficiency and because they characterize those establishments and informal associations of the community which are democratically oriented. In varying degrees, school objectives may be different from those of church, family, 4-H club, Grange, or gang, but the group processes of all are similar. They thus provide a background of experience and understanding among teachers, patrons, and pupils for the school's ventures in group control of policy and practice that are related to the value concepts of the society.

Young people, as well as adults, have a need to be independent and self-determining, and the modern school encourages them to create their own value concepts, ego ideals, and personal compromises within group relationships where they are sure to be meaningful. It is in terms

[5] William James, *Principles of Psychology,* Henry Holt and Company, Inc., New York, 1899, vol. 1, pp. 291ff.

of peer-group influences that the behavior and value judgments of an individual of any age are best understood. In school, the interaction of pupils, teachers, and other adult associates proceeds in classes, clubs, corridors, lunchrooms, assemblies, councils, and many other situations. Interpersonal relations are component parts of every group. As the individual comes to identify himself more fully with a group, it typically comes to have an increasing influence on the development of his personality. The school, therefore, endeavors to promote cohesion among pupils, teachers, and patrons in support of the school's aims. These aims are embodied in, and given substance and meaning by, various group activities.

Transforming Aggregates into Groups

The intentional transformation of mere aggregates of pupils, teachers, and patrons into groups requires consistent and intelligent efforts of many kinds.

Contiguity, though fundamental to group life, does not of itself assure the development of cohesive relations among individuals. The exigencies of school administration require the assignment of pupils and teachers to face-to-face groups, each with some stipulated purpose, for example, to master the curriculum set forth for a grade, to develop a football team, to present a play, to plan and carry out institutional regimen, or to have a party. Both pupils and teachers bring to these associations not only valuations, customs, and aspirations derived from other, usually earlier experiences, but also, of course, their unique biological inheritances. The development of cohesive, meaningful relations in such groups is fostered by common purposes, the achievement of which requires cooperation, compromise, and tolerance.

Social Isolates

Sociometric investigation of classes and clubs generally reveals that there are "isolates," that is, individuals who are avoided by others. In addition, the repeated and varied use of sociometric questionnaires and diagrams can reveal to the teacher information about the extent to which individual members of the group are accepted and rejected by their fellows. The usefulness of sociometric data, of course, is limited to situations which are defined by the nature of the questions used. Sociometric data also throw light on several other interpersonal relations: the existence of subgroups and cliques, patterns of boy-girl relations, and mutual choices for partnership in several or in all associated activities.[6]

[6] Helen H. Jennings and others, *Sociometry in Group Relations,* American Council on Education, Washington, 1948, and Hilda Taba,

Many other devices are useful for supplementing and perhaps for correcting judgments regarding the patterns of interaction among pupils. They include pupils' diaries, personal records kept by teachers, correspondence, interviews, replies to open-end questions, teacher logs of class or club procedures, and home visitations. Whether the time and energy required for these undertakings are likely to be justified by ensuing improvements in pupil relations must be decided by the teacher.

Social Obstacles to Group Cohesion

The school and its professional personnel do not operate above the battle. Conflicting ideas, aspirations, and political positions, both of local and of more remote communities, impose moral imperatives and prohibitions, the outright rejection of which is impossible. Institutions that serve the public, whether supported by taxation or by fees and contributions, must be acceptable to their clientele. One public may demand an innovation while another opposes it; paradoxically, in some cases, the same persons may, on different occasions, belong to both publics. The school's freedom of action is thus limited by popular consensus of social ideas and by the somewhat spasmodic, and often inconsistent, compromises between ideals and customs that characterize the views and behaviors of "publics."

Students, in some instances, are able to select some of their associations—school orchestras, art clubs, and literary organizations are typically of this sort. In such associations, the common purposes of the pupils and teachers are quite likely to forestall group disorganization which could result from some strongly self-assertive behavior. These self-selected associations, therefore, readily become purposive peer groups which fix certain standards of behavior and attitudes to which each member must conform if he is to find personal security among his fellows. One very important member of these peer groups is the sponsor—teacher, coach, or director.

In other cases, pupils are assigned membership in certain organizations. In arbitrarily assigned associations, the development of purposive relations becomes more difficult. Here contiguity is often the major cohesive factor until or unless common purposes become intrinsically motivated; that is, until the class becomes united by a desire to put on an assembly program, to solve a problem, or to discuss a book. Once group motivation is effected, acceptance and interaction among all members is largely assured; anyone who would break the pattern of

Diagnosing Human Relations, American Council on Education, Washington, 1951. She pp. 150–152, below, for a detailed discussion of sociometric techniques and their use in the school.

"we-feeling" is quickly isolated; the boastful or otherwise aberrant act is obnoxious and hence avoided. The responses to group purposes and undertakings by individual members of the class, however variant they may have been in the beginning, tend to become patterned to accord with the prestige values of the group.

It is obvious, of course, that the successful development of cohesive, purposeful interactions, whether in assigned or voluntary associations, is facilitated or hampered according to the over-all spirit of the school and of the local community it serves. Young people respond hour by hour, not only to immediate classroom and club conditions, but also to the atmosphere of the entire school and of its immediate background of families, neighborhoods, gangs, churches, and the rest. If community "we-feeling" dominates these associations, it tends to penetrate the small group, becoming a norm which orders the relations of the members.

The faculties of forward-looking schools, with whatever help they can get from parent-teacher associations and other civic groups, foster purposeful collaborations involving, if possible, representatives of all identifiable subgroups of the local community. Gradually thereby, the in-group loyalties of members of ethnocentric groups become diffused; they attach themselves little by little to members of other groups and join with them in common projects.

Measuring the Cohesion of Groups

Even in relatively cohesive groups, however, there is considerable variation in acceptability and affection among the members. In order to study the extent and degree of attraction and repulsion of group members toward each other, several devices have been developed to supplement judgments of teachers. The two most commonly used are the social-distance scale and the sociometric tabulation and diagram.

The social-distance scale, developed by Bogardus, measures the degree of social acceptance between the individuals and cliques within a group. Adapted for school use, the questions to which pupils (or parents or teachers) reply cover the probable occasions wherein collaboration is desirable, for example, committee work, team play, and party associations. The scaled answers indicate degrees of conscious readiness to share with associates emotionally, as well as intellectually and behavioristically, in the specified activities. Some skepticism toward replies is needed because verbal assents to partnerships are likely to be more affected by moral sanctions than are corresponding attitudes.

Sociometrics is a technique for determining the degrees of attraction and repulsion that exist among members under specified conditions of association. The reliability of responses to a single question (for example, "whom would you like to have in the same 4-H club with you?") applies only to the specific situation, and, furthermore, they are almost certain to be transitory. If another kind of club or situation were substituted, or if the same question were asked a week later, other choices might be made.

TABLE 1. A SOCIAL-DISTANCE SCALE*

Directions: According to my first feeling reactions, I would willingly admit members of each race or nationality (as a class and not the best I have known, nor the worst members) to one or more of the classifications which I have circled.

Ethnic group	Close kinship by marriage	My club as personal chums	My street as neighbors	Employment in my occupation	Citizenship in my country	As visitors only to my country	Would exclude from my country
English	1	2	3	4	5	6	7
Negro	1	2	3	4	5	6	7
French	1	2	3	4	5	6	7
Chinese	1	2	3	4	5	6	7
Russian, etc.	1	2	3	4	5	6	7

* The social-distance scale is simple to administer and to score and as a consequence, it is a widely used technique in the measurement of ethnic attitudes.

SOURCE: By permission from Marie Jahoda, Morton Deutsch, and Stuart W. Cook, *Research Methods in Social Relations*, Holt, Rinehart, and Winston, Inc., New York, 1951, p. 189.

CULTURAL DISPARITIES AND DEMOCRATIC EDUCATION

Two examples of conflicts between American ideals and American realities that condition the functioning of the public school may be cited. The disparity between the ideal culture patterns of a classless society (affirmed almost universally in American law and ceremonials) and the actual cultural patterns of our class-structured, religion-fragmented, residence-sequestered, ethnically diverse population have been discussed in earlier chapters. The school is compelled to make adaptations both to ideal and to fact. In the long run, however, its dedicated mission

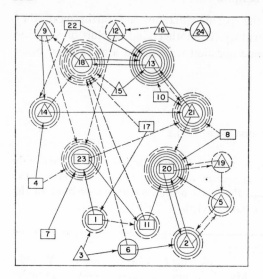

At left, first sociogram shows first and second choices for a discussion group leader during the first week of class.

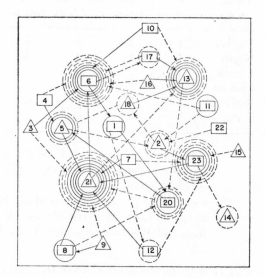

At right, second sociogram shows first and second choices for a discussion group leader at the end of the three-month term.

Figure 1. Changes in Sociometric Choices in a Class in Leadership Training. Solid arrows and circles represent first choices; broken arrows and circles represent second choices. Triangles represent girls, and rectangles stand for boys. Note the changes in the choice patterns from the beginning to the end of the three-month term. (For example, Nos. 8 and 17 were both "isolates" at the beginning of the term but not at the end of the term; for No. 9, the situation was reversed.) Sociograms, courtesy of Mrs. Leone Johnson, Oregon State College.

is to foster among its staff, its pupils, and its patrons both the determination and the competency to make the real patterns conform to the ideal.

This "bootstrap-lifting" operation assumes self-emancipation by those who undertake to stimulate it. But in fact, principals, teachers, and other educators are themselves victims of many of the same stereotypes as are their reluctant masters, the publics who control tax levies and school board elections. Breaking out of the vicious circle demands more than intellectual assent by school personnel, though such assent is fundamental. It requires that educators understand their own prejudices and stereotypes and have the willingness and ability to modify those that interfere with the attainment of democratic aims.

Social-class Status of Teachers

From childhood, teachers themselves have been conditioned by their social environments. Their canons of good taste, respectable opinions, language, manners, dress, knowledge, and a hundred other attributes of "good" membership in the community are affected by class status, religion, and occupation. Indeed, as Warner and his associates have shown,[7] teaching is one of the most accessible and socially visible professions for ambitious women to enter; in the communities they studied, 92 to 98 per cent of the public schoolteachers came from middle-class families. However much teachers differ individually among themselves, most of them bring to their professional work standards of what is "right," fitting, and desirable that spring from their middle-class upbringing. And these standards are reinforced by the school's middle-class symbolism of competition, taboos on physical violence except in sports, emphasis on remote goals, and ambition for personal social and economic success.

Group life within a middle-class–patterned school tends to reproduce the regimen and activities as they are remembered or envisioned by patrons who have themselves attended such schools. They also reflect the stereotyped values and foster the mental and emotional attributes that are agreeable to "respectable" people. In many respects, such orientation is reasonable in that the American so reproduced is

[7] W. Lloyd Warner, *American Life: Dream and Reality,* University of Chicago Press, Chicago, 1953, chap. 3. There is some evidence that a larger proportion of teachers is presently being recruited from professional and business families than was the case early in the twentieth century. See Robert W. Richey and William H. Fox, *An Analysis of Various Factors Associated with the Selection of Teaching as a Vocation,* Bulletin of the School of Education, Indiana University, Bloomington, vol. 24, p. 18, May, 1948.

authentic; that is, the major dynamic of the American democracy continues to be a product and process of restless, middle-class ambition and energy. Hence, the motives, restraints, ingenuities, compromises, and organizations that characterize the society have proved their worth in the growth and survival of whatever stability and freedom Americans now have.

Fortunately for the school's fulfillment of its democratic mission, middle-class teachers, pupils, and patrons have equalitarian values along with their prejudices and narrow institutional loyalties. Almost universal *verbal* support is given, for example, to the right of labor to organize for the exertion of political influence and to the right of Jews and Negroes to equal opportunities in education, business, politics, and the professions, even though many pupils, teachers, and patrons simultaneously favor "keeping Negroes in their place," distrust Jews, and object to organized labor's potent influence in politics.[8] To a considerable extent these inconsistencies work themselves out in favor of the ideals, both out of school and in school, largely because thereby the more dynamic associated undertakings are most adequately served. For example, success in music, dramatics, athletics, creative writing, and forensics becomes in many school situations more highly regarded than class-typed speech, dress, and manners.

Decreasing Importance of Social Class in School Groups

If we use as criterion for judging contemporary educational and other meliorative institutions their exemplification of American social ideals, we are likely to be dissatisfied, perhaps shocked, with their actual achievements. If, however, criteria are less absolute, if they are formulated in terms of trends, there are many evidences of progress.

Snobbish coteries of pupils, teachers, and patrons glorifying esoteric niceties of "cultivated" manners and avocations are, to be sure, conspicuously entrenched in school regimen. Great numbers of children from disadvantaged homes[9] may find little in the curriculum and regimen of their schools that seems to them and their parents to

[8] Gunnar Myrdal, *An American Dilemma,* Harper & Brothers, New York, 1945, pp. 1–25, and Joel B. Montague, "Real and Ideal Culture Patterns as Revealed in Students' Responses to Dichotomous Questions," *The Journal of Educational Sociology,* vol. 24, no. 11, pp. 167–176, November, 1950.
[9] Economically disadvantaged families, frequently equated with the lower classes, may provide more wholesome developmental controls for children than middle-class families do. Cf. Allison Davis and Robert J. Havighurst, *Father of the Man,* Houghton Mifflin Company, Boston, 1947, pp. 11–16.

have much immediate significance for their present or anticipated activities. Teachers of academic erudition, somewhat frustrated by popular disregard for the subject matter they so highly value, do retain great influence in the determination of school requirements and standards. Their academic criteria are attuned to middle-class stereotypes that are verbally honored but practically neglected, not only by patrons and pupils but also by many faculty associates.

Nevertheless, these shortcomings really exemplify a kind of social lag rather than an intentional adaptation toward educational fulfillment. It is to the broadened curriculum of schools, from primary grades through graduate schools, that one must look to identify trends toward universality of opportunity. Here it is that one finds diversity of recognition whereby everyone may discover for himself some contribution that he can make to the group's social objectives, a contribution which may earn him acceptance at least in so far as it facilitates group action. This broader curriculum includes not only what has been conventionally known as the "extra-curriculum" but also many activities and experiences not primarily centered in the school, such as home duties and participation, membership in youth service organizations, and accomplishments gained under private teachers or by self-instruction. These revolutionary changes are dealt with in other chapters.

SOCIALIZATION OF STUDENTS AND TEACHERS

The socialization function of the school is obviously a selective and remedial one. Socialization itself proceeds from birth to old age, independently of intentional social agencies as well as in connection with them. The school seeks to strengthen, weaken, or otherwise modify adaptive tendencies of children as it finds them "in being," to the end that individual personalities and a democratic society reinforce each other.

Socialization takes place in the context of action. Living together implies doing something together—working, enjoying, appreciating, understanding, and even competing cooperatively. Common purposes and common successes motivate and reward such activities. "We-feelings" grow as the successes or failures of an individual member or of some part of the membership come to be considered representative of the group.

The behavior of teachers and other older persons who identify themselves with pupils and the groups they form is most important in the determination of the social and personal attitudes and behavior that evolve in such groups. In varying degrees and at different times, older associates of the group and of its individual members—coaches, subject instructors, siblings, and parents, for example—provide incitement, example, audience, and subtly suggestive influences to which members respond.

Stereotypical Values

These pervasive influences are seldom all beneficent, consistent, or mutually reinforcing. Many times they are not intentional or consciously exerted; they may be unexamined and unevaluated attributes of personalities and institutional mores, for example, evasiveness and rationalization of ethical codes and the exaltation of immediate ends over means or over more fundamental purposes. Stereotyped values imprison most of the group's older associates;[10] they are proud of a winning team; they praise a finished dramatic performance; they admire a go-getter; they esteem cleverness. Their attitudes and behavior speak more loudly than their frequent verbal espousals of altruism and kindliness.

Teachers, no matter how sincerely devoted to their duties and however well prepared professionally, are fallible human beings, driven by the crosscurrents of ambition, competitive striving, and resulting insecurity. Though experience in the schoolroom teaches them to control overt expressions of irritation, they respond in ordinary ways to frustration and opposition.[11] The determination "not to let oneself go," though minimizing the overt expression of agressive feelings toward pupils and other associates and, hence, constituting fundamental self-discipline, is at best negative. Inner tensions remain.[12]

The Emergence of Meliorative Attitudes

The teacher, however, *typically* displaces his authoritarian relationship to his younger associates by identifying himself with the group, and he usually replaces competitive striving with his fellow faculty members with generous mutuality. Thus, meliorative attitudes and behaviors emerge. His new actions tend to remove his personality from a central and dominating position and so foster dispassionate objectivity in essaying the motives and actions of associates. There are some, of course, who "live by their personalities" and never achieve this level of objectivity in their relations with their colleagues.

[10] See James Harvey Robinson, *Mind in the Making,* Harper & Brothers, New York, 1921.

[11] George A. Dorsey, *Why We Behave Like Human Beings,* Harper & Brothers, New York, 1926, pp. 306–311.

[12] E. K. Wickman, *Children's Behavior and Teachers' Attitudes,* The Commonwealth Fund, New York, 1937, pp. 80–116.

Self-identification with group activities and purposes induces kindly consideration and magnanimous understanding of others, freedom from fear related to school experiences, and a minimizing of prejudiced antagonism toward persons and groups whose backgrounds and outlooks differ from one's own. The famous Lange-James dictum applies: feeling follows action at least as truly as action follows feeling; hence if one will act worthily, he is likely to feel worthy. The mind, said James, is what it does.

A resolution to face truth squarely, a philosophy of educational and social service, and the possession of information regarding cultures and cultural processes surely have great value for people who wish to deal effectively with children and adults in a cosmopolitan society. But these attainments are functional only in so far as individuals identify themselves with groups and apply them in social relations. To this extent they are decisive; success is success and failure is failure. And because success alone has survival value in the American school, the effective, wholesome, happy teacher exemplifies in considerable degree the growth of a secure, socialized personality.

SOCIAL ASPECTS OF SECTION ASSIGNMENT

Human relationships within a school must necessarily work themselves out in accompaniment with administrative adaptations devised to facilitate the attainment of some educational goals. One of the most important of these adaptations is the assignment of some pupils and selected teachers to sections—grade classes, home-room sections, and subject classes. If the aggregates of pupils and adults so assigned are quickly and effectively to develop "we-feelings" of group unity with accompanying in-group loyalties and sympathies, decisions regarding which teachers shall associate with what pupils (and their parents and other out-of-school affiliates) are of paramount importance.

Goals in Teacher-Pupil Assignment

Especially in larger schools, where there are several more or less parallel sections of the same grade for subject instruction or for advising, intelligent administrative foresight arranges teacher and pupil assignments so as to foster propitious associations. Some hierarchy of valued goals is obviously implicit in any intentional sectioning procedure. If mastery of subject matter dominates a school's educational philosophy, and if pupil and teacher enthusiasm for such mastery can be assumed, assignments in terms of abilities and aptitudes are indicated. Under such improbable conditions, the American school being what it is, little regard would need to be paid to the more subtle factors of organic and social heritages, prior experiences, out-of-school activities, and peculiar personality traits. If, however, another educational outcome is judged by the faculty to be as important as (or more important than) subject mastery, or if pupil and teacher eagerness for such learning achievement cannot be assumed, the problems of sectioning become far more complex.

The problems that face the school staff in this area of administrative decision are not simple. No solution is effectively applicable as a fixed policy year after year or in different schools. Even within broad philosophical preferences for some form of homogeneity or of heterogeneity within each section, assignments of specific teachers and pupils call for serious consideration, if group consciousness and cooperative behavior are to develop. If group loyalties in a section are dominantly unfavorable, disintegration and hostility among the members are probable. Teachers and administrators then have to devote much energy to acting correctively, negatively, and, too often, futilely.

To be more specific, suppose a minority of the pupils assigned to a section are characterized by language habits, dress, pigmentation, religious observances, and aspirations that do not conform to the teacher's and other pupils' middle-class concepts of what is "of course" right or desirable. Considered statically, misunderstandings and resentment are at least potential in such a situation. Only a teacher and those pupils who are emotionally ready to join with unconventional associates in cooperatively planned projects are likely to develop a we-feeling in such a section.

Chance Assignments of Teachers and Pupils

Alphabetical or other chance distributions of personnel by sections may be successful in a school already characterized by an *esprit de corps* attuned to cultural diversity and to appreciation of the unique contributions of individuals to all-school projects. A football star from a slum quarter, a brilliant Negro debater, and a Jewish student-council president may greatly affect the pattern of acceptance in all sections of the school.

In less happy situations, however, much serious thought needs to be given to the creation of associations of pupils and teachers which are favorable to the development of civic competence, fellowship, and stable, cooperative personalities. It may not be possible, indeed it is not at all necessary, that all associations be planned in these terms. But it is surely desirable that school experiences as a whole should provide many opportunities for boys and girls to pursue collaboratively the objectives that are valued by the group. Such objectives are, of course, minimally affected by social class stereotypes and other divisive factors. A dramatic society, a mechanical drawing class, an orchestra, an athletic team, or a service squad is likely to honor its members with little regard to color, peculiarities of speech, or hair style. In connection with such groups, narrow sectarian, family, and gang loyalties brought from out-of-school associations lose their sharp edges. Individuals become flexible and capable of adapting to the diverse situations and groups which characterize the democratic society.

DEVELOPING EFFECTIVE GROUP RELATIONS

However the multiple sectioning of a school's population may be arranged and fostered, pupil and teacher responses will be group-conditioned. The paramount problem facing the intentional processing of education, therefore, is that of ordering group activities and interactions so that attributes favorable to educational objectives may be frequently and effectively encouraged.

Similarities and Differences among Teachers and Pupils

Such processing requires that the group leader take account of the organic heritages, cultural inheritances, unique group and individual experiences, and the resulting personality patterns of the pupils and teachers who form each association. Fortunately, except for special cases, there is much similarity in the heritages and experiences of young people growing up in the contemporary United States. What is most required, therefore, for the attainment of youthful adaptations in school organizations are leaders who are aware of these similarities and differences and of the nature of the organic characteristics and group experiences from which they rise.[13]

Children and teachers learn a great deal about human behavior through working together on projects, regardless of what the course of study or other overt intention may be. This learning, associated with, and incidental to, the projects, takes effect in behavior and feeling as well as in verbalized form. The subtleties of comfort and discomfort, success and failure, encouragement and inhibition, and high status and low status control the unique experiences of every member. Thus they shape the individual's personality, at least as it expresses itself in the group's processes. And since these experiences and the conditions under which they take place are not very unlike those of the individual's out-of-school group situations, the transfer of the training to out-of-school life is facilitated.

[13] Cf. T. R. Schaffler, "The Process of Socialization," *Phi Delta Kappan*, vol. 36, no. 3, pp. 225–228, March 1953.

Structural Arrangements as Aids to Group Process

In progressive schools, adaptations of rooms and equipment are made to encourage, so far as possible, interactions among pupils and teachers; the settings are arranged so that feelings and behavior valued by educators are likely to accompany the learning of lessons. Movable furniture encourages face-to-face exchanges of ideas. Unit kitchens in a home-economics room, unit shop equipment in industrial arts workrooms, and practice office equipment in business education rooms, encourage collaboration of pupils and teachers in achieving goals and in evaluating outcomes. So, too, do special studios for music and art classes and group-work arrangements in science laboratories and libraries.

These and other structural arrangements are of little effectiveness, of course, unless teachers take full advantage of them to foster and guide the students so that they make something of the potentialities of group work. The implementation of favorable physical factors depends on the readiness, adequacy, and security of both teachers and students in the group.

Any attempt to teach the democratic process in an overtly teacher-dominated classroom is so obviously contradictory as to be almost certainly futile. The pupils' role in that situation is to be quiet and to listen, occasionally to volunteer information or opinion for the teacher's acceptance or rejection—if called upon. The teacher and the text have the "right" answers, regarding both facts and judgments; the pupil disagrees at peril of "failure." He soon learns not to participate as a thinker, an innovator, or a dissenter but to defer to authority and to keep his ideas to himself.[14]

A More Fundamental Basis of Effective Group Functioning

It is the democratic processes of give and take, of appreciation of the diversity of human talents, beliefs, and loyalties, of tolerance for others' idiosyncrasies, of mutual helpfulness, and of assertion tempered by compromise that ought to characterize American schools. A democratic society, as John Dewey always insisted, is a two-way process. In it, all individuals not only contribute but partake of the contributions of others. Furthermore, democratic ends are impossible to attain except through democratic means.

[14] Cf. Morris L. Eisenstein, "Group Work Education—Education for What?" *The Journal of Educational Sociology,* vol. 27, no. 1, pp. 205–214, January, 1954.

In all this there lies a major challenge to educators in a democracy. How can the individual student be encouraged to contribute his best to the group and at the same time obtain the most from interaction with teachers and classmates and from reading, conversation, and observation? Group dynamics or effective group relations are the terms generally applied to the interaction processes favorable to the attainment of these ends; and effective group relations require various adaptations to people's interests, abilities, and statuses.

Some groups are characterized by cooperative activities which call for the expression of individual talent and the alternating of leadership among various members. Such groups ordinarily have little difficulty in developing effective techniques and leadership. In fact, techniques and leadership already exist in some form. For example, if all the members of a group are keenly interested in a mechanical device, or have nearly equal ability for solving geometry problems, or have backgrounds of similar social-class experiences and values, or are in any other respect socially homogeneous, they are likely to develop cooperative behavior. This is to say that such a group responds to the appropriate challenges—to the special interests of the members, their abilities and aptitudes, or their special experiences and values.

The Fostering of Cooperative Action

If a school class has not already achieved this kind of social unity and if it is not homogeneous in any respect, except in contiguity, the fostering of effective group relations requires great ingenuity, patience, and persistence of the teacher or other leader. Indeed, little success in the projected tasks of the group is probable until and unless the skillful leader has somehow established a "we-feeling" among the members and some kind of homogeneity, so that resistance to cooperative interaction decreases.

The obstacles imposed by a lack of group consciousness resulting from varied degrees of interest in a subject and by marked differences in ability and aptitude are obvious. Heterogeneity of social background, although fully as important an impediment, is too often discounted or ignored by advocates of group-dynamics techniques. The perceptions which students and teachers have of themselves and of others vary with out-of-school experiences. This fact helps to explain certain of the detachments, inferiority feelings, and hostilities which characterize some members of minority groups.

More children from lower-status families than from middle- and upper-status ones, for example, apparently feel unable to express themselves well and, hence, dislike to recite or to volunteer in class.

They are often conscious of being unpopular, of being left out of social activities, of having difficulty in making friends, of not having enough time for study, and of an inability to concentrate.[15] It is obvious that these difficulties more commonly arise in some school situations than in others; they are especially frequent in oral classroom activities and in parties and clubs patterned on middle-class stereotypes. Inferiority feelings and status hostilities seldom characterize playground and athletic activities, shop, home-economics, business, and laboratory situations, or those other aspects of school regimen where class-differentiated behavior and attitudes are less in evidence.

There are, in other words, some school activities in which group dynamics is relatively independent of class-related social experiences and traits. Some educators attempt to beat the challenge of assimilating pupils of every social status by bringing together students of heterogeneous backgrounds, interests, and aptitudes in the gymnasium, shop, and laboratory, while maintaining somewhat more homogeneous groupings in academic classrooms. It is the intention of these educators to foster interaction among heterogeneous students where the chances of success are great and to avoid situations where the chances are small.

The Need for Group Interest

Fundamental factors of group organization for dynamic interactions have been discussed at such length because of the great importance of the situation in which universal and mutual participation is to be encouraged. There is needed a group interest in finding the best solution for a common problem or project; otherwise, individualistic aggressiveness motivated by a desire for prestige is likely to discourage some individuals from making contributions of which they are capable. Also, there needs to be recognized that *doing* something is quite as necessary as *saying* something, and that this doing includes not only conciliatory behavior but also experimental manipulation of materials; otherwise, group dynamics is too likely to be narrowly conceived as verbal and abstract discussion. And, finally, there is needed generous recognition of every sincere effort to contribute to the solution, whether or not it conforms to majority opinion.

The democratic group operates in a field of social space.[16]

[15] Joel B. Montague, "Social Status and Adjustment in School," *The Clearing House,* vol. 27, no. 9, pp. 19–24, September, 1952.

[16] Cf. D. M. Hall, *The Dynamics of Group Discussion,* The Interstate Printers and Publishers, Danville, 1950, and U.S. Department of Agriculture, *Group Discussion and Its Techniques: A Bibliographical Review,* no date.

Each member ideally acts and interacts according to some end or ends. No one, not even the leader, is trying to "sell" an already formulated solution. Differences of opinion and values are welcomed so far as they are relevant to the issue under consideration. Individual members may suggest fresh ideas or starts; they may orient, facilitate, harmonize, or encourage the group when it tends to bog down; they may summarize, analyze, and evaluate alternative proposals and positions; they may seek facts or present ideas that bear on the matter at hand; they may recommend compromises or alternatives to break deadlocks; they may propose experiments to test hypotheses. If the desire for the best practical solution dominates the group, all contributions are likely to be tolerated; conversely, most recognition seeking, dominating, blaming, blocking, or other autocratic action is recognized and disapproved.[17]

To the educator, of course, the quality of the decisions reached is important, and he seeks to guide students toward knowledge and understanding. But individuals also learn from the group's experiences. Such learning is also important. The educator sees in it some promise that the techniques of effective group relations can be applied by students with confidence and satisfaction in other school and out-of-school situations.

CONSTRUCTIVE DISCIPLINE AND SELF-DISCIPLINE

The three processes just discussed—socialization of aggregates, wise assignment of pupils and teachers to sections, and the fostering of effective group interaction—are basic factors in developing democratic discipline. All of them promote the successful planning and execution of projects in which every member of the group can gain recognition and acceptance by his peers and teachers. Self-confidence, self-reliance, loyalty, and mutual affection characteristically result. Self-discipline generally is incidental to them.[18]

[17] The roles identified here are those listed by K. D. Benne and Paul Sheats, "Functional Roles of Group Members," *Journal of Social Issues,* vol. 4, pp. 41–49, 1948.

[18] Cf. "Discipline: An Interpretation," Reprint Service Bulletin from *Childhood Education,* The Association for Childhood Education, Washington, 1944, and G. V. Sheviakov and Fritz Redl, *Discipline for Today's Children and Youth,* National Education Association, Department of Supervision and Curriculum Development, Washington, no date.

The Schools' Relations to Other Authority Mechanisms

The enforcement of the prevailing mores upon the younger generation is a task shared by the authority mechanisms of all communities. The mechanisms are usually the same, regardless of the type of community. The authority usually takes the same forms, such as the approval and disapproval of adults, customs, school regulations, concepts of honesty, patterns of demeanor, and the ethics of various occupations.

The local enforcement agencies usually reflect the community pattern with respect to the toleration of certain kinds of deviance. The school which ignores these patterns of tolerance is likely to fare ill. Confusion and frustration result from an individual's misunderstanding of the relation between what he would like to do and what he is allowed to do. Owing to the multiplicity of authority and restrictive mechanisms, the individual sometimes is at a loss to know what to do. One teacher tolerates an act and another forbids it; one officer of the law turns his back upon a minor infraction of the law, while another makes an arrest for the same act; one parent holds firm, the other relents; one judge convicts, and another acquits; one principal admonishes, another punishes. Thus, the individual frequently does not know what to expect as consequence of a given behavior. Authoritative mechanisms are neither unified nor constant.

Because the school is one of the mechanisms within the community which restricts and shapes behavior during a considerable part of young peoples' waking hours, it has a definite responsibility for their development. The school staff is apt to be better informed than most parents regarding the social acceptability of specific behavior patterns. This knowledge supplemented by their training and experience in establishing school regimen and mobilizing peer sentiment to control behavior should be helpful to other social agencies—family, police, church, and civic organizations—which are sometimes confused and contradictory about what they expect of youth.

The Schools' Role in Promoting Self-discipline

Self-responsibility should be the objective of the school in all its attempts to control the behavior of young people. To enable the individual not only to orient himself to the conduct desired of him by the community, but also to develop for himself a way to meet the challenges which face him, it is desirable that the school staff determine what kinds of behavior the school should encourage and what mechanisms exist to interpret and enforce them.

Because the pupil's social milieu is constantly changing, his life becomes alternately the congealing and upheaving of value concepts. It is, therefore, necessary to help him become aware of the gap that often exists between his own value concepts and those set up by the various groups to which he belongs and which are enforced by them. These gaps he must somehow learn to bridge.

Self-discipline and Transitory Values

Every individual has great difficulty in adapting to rapid social change. It is not always possible for the school to interpret accurately the fringe areas of socially acceptable and socially unacceptable behavior. The modern communication of ideas is too rapid and its processes too multifarious and subtle. Radio, television, the movies, and other mass media are no respecters of income, geographical location, or family taboo.

In order to promote rational behavior in young people in a society characterized by flux, the professional personnel of the school not only needs awareness of the social temper of the local community but also must estimate with reasonable accuracy the direction and trend of social change. Only if this is accomplished, is school experience likely to aid the pupil significantly in intelligently modifying his social behavior. The accurate appraising of community temper and trends and appropriate guiding of young people in terms of them are exceedingly difficult goals to attain, to be sure. Nevertheless, failure by the school to make earnest efforts to achieve them is inexcusable in a democracy.

SUMMARY

The American society is a revolutionary one. Appropriate group processes are those which are validated by reference to the ideals, values, and relationships which are at the very heart of a democracy. Schools are willy-nilly involved generally in the direction of group relations and specifically in school associations. In the school, individuals are presented with unusually potent opportunities for developing cooperative adjustments to others and for coming to understand the societal value and importance of such cooperation.

Some community background factors that mold the dispositions and practices of young people are favorable to group relations that are consistent with democratic aspirations. Others are unfavorable to such adaptations. Hence, the role of the school is selective; it seeks to reinforce, guide, and direct the activities of pupils in ways corresponding to behavior patterns which are adjudged beneficent. The school seeks to foster competence, confidence, and satisfaction in democratic group relations. The school, therefore, competes with and offsets those community associations and forces that contradict and undermine democratic processes.

The socialization of pupils, teachers, and patrons calls for social engineering of high caliber. It involves the considered assignment of teachers and pupils to sections or other groups in which the democratic values of tolerance, cooperation, and respect for the dignity of the individual seem likely to be fostered. And it largely supersedes the conventional stereotype of disciplined behavior; it substitutes for authoritarian control a sense of individual and social purpose and the ideal of cooperative group membership. Under such conditions, the learning of subject matter can most effectively take place.

The adjustments learned under conditions of democratic group relations involve much the same compromises between assertiveness and conformity in the school as out of school. The group is a good taskmaster, if at times a hard one. Democratic role playing demands recognition of, and adaptation to, the "rules of the game."

So it is within the school and so it is in the nonschool world of young and old alike. The individual's' own self-realization and his contribution to his society probably depend as much on the kinds of groups he identifies with as on anything his formal school experience can teach him.

SELECTED REFERENCES

Berry, C. A. (ed.): *Activities and Citizenship,* National Council of Social Studies, Yearbook, Washington, 1951. The relationship of extracurricular activities and good citizenship.

Blumer, Herbert: "Collective Behavior," in Alfred McClung Lee (ed.), *New Outline of the Principles of Sociology,* Barnes & Noble, Inc., New York, 1946, pp. 167–222. A famous treatise on collective behavior and group processes.

Borgeson, F. C.: *Elementary School Life Activities,* A. S. Barnes and Company, New York, 1931. The elementary school as an experiential environment.

Bushee, F. A.: "Social Organization in a Small City," *American Journal of Sociology,* vol. 51, no. 3, pp. 217–226, November, 1945.

An empirical study of the nature of social organizations in a small city.

Cartwright, Dorwin, and Alvin Zander (eds.): *Group Dynamics,* Row, Peterson & Company, Evanston, Ill., 1953. A useful collection of papers on the behavior of groups.

Cook, Lloyd Allen: "An Experimental Sociographic Study of a Stratified 10th Grade Class," *American Sociological Review,* vol. 10, no. 2, pp. 250–261, April, 1945. A classic study of a 10th grade Ohio class efficiently diagrammed in sociometric technique.

Cox, Philip W. L.: *Creative School Control,* J. B. Lippincott Company, Philadelphia, 1927. Group processes within the school and school-related community as they may be directed toward democratic experience.

————, John Carr Duff, and Marie McNamara: *Basic Principles of Guidance,* Prentice-Hall, Inc., Englewood Cliffs, N.J., 1948. Positively oriented group guidance toward action outcomes as well as reflective thinking and abstract evaluation.

Frederick, Robert W.: *The Third Curriculum,* Appleton-Century-Crofts, Inc., New York, 1959. The author views the relatively voluntary, predominantly group activities as truly a curriculum as is the program of studies.

Greer, Scott: *Social Organization, Studies in Sociology,* Random House, Inc., New York, 1955. A useful, short theoretical discussion of social organization.

Hare, A. Paul, Edgar F. Borgatta, and Robert F. Bales (eds.): *Small Groups: Studies in Social Interaction,* Alfred A. Knopf, Inc., New York, 1955. A good reader on small group research and theory.

Homans, George C.: *The Human Group,* Harcourt, Brace and Company, Inc., New York, 1950. An informative study of the organization and processes of social groups.

Jahoda, Marie, Morton Deutsch, and Stuart W. Cook: *Research Methods in Social Relations,* The Dryden Press, Inc., New York, 1951. Part 1 of this work contains a description of interpersonal measuring devices which elaborate on the Bogardus Scale.

Jennings, Helen H.: *Leadership and Isolation,* Longmans, Green & Co., Inc., New York, 1950. One of the best treatments of sociometry.

Johnston, Edgar G., and Roland C. Faunce: *Student Activities in the Secondary School,* The Ronald Press Company, New York, 1952. A text on extracurricular activities in the high school.

Kilzer, L. R., H. H. Stephenson, and H. O. Norberg: *Allied Activities in the Secondary School,* Harper & Brothers, New York, 1956. A useful book on extracurricular activities.

McKown, Harry C.: *Activities in the Elementary School,* McGraw-Hill Book Company, Inc., New York, 1938. The value of extracurricular activities in the grades.

Madden, Ward: *Religious Values in Education,* Harper & Brothers, New York, 1953. Commitments to creative social acts as the religious objective.

Mercer, Blaine E.: *An Introduction to the Study of Society,* Harcourt, Brace and Company, Inc., New York, 1958. Chap. 5, "Social Groups and Collectives," contains empirical data on the nature and processes of group relations.

Noar, Gertrude: *Freedom to Live and Learn,* Franklin Press, Philadelphia, 1947. A junior-high school principal explains the day-to-day activities of a core group.

Science Research Association: various pamphlets, esp. *Life Adjustment Series* and *Better Living Series,* Chicago. Pamphlets and monographs on various subjects related to social adjustment.

Strang, Ruth M.: *Group Activities in College and Secondary School,* Harper & Brothers, New York, 1946. The values of group forms of extracurricular activities.

Warner, W. Lloyd, and Paul S. Lunt: *The Social Life of a Modern Community,* Yale University Press, New Haven, Conn., 1949. Widely known field study.

West, James: *Plainville, U.S.A.,* Columbia University Press, New York, 1945. A good description of a small community and its inhabitants. Especial attention is paid to social class.

DISCUSSION QUESTIONS

1. "Society may now be defined as the social heritage of habits and sentiments, folkways, and mores, technics and cultures, all of which are incident or necessary to collective human behavior." (Robert E. Park and Ernest W. Burgess, *Introduction to the Science of Sociology,* University of Chicago Press, Chicago, 1924, p. 163.) Does this definition apply to a classroom group? To a street-corner gang? To a school assembly? To between-period corridor-passing pupils? To a lunch-room aggregate? Justify your answers.

2. Everyone is said to belong to two worlds: a microcosm (the world within himself) and a macrocosm (the world outside himself). The former is assumed to be the epitome of the latter. To the degree that this is a true statement, is it possible for an individual to be nonsocial?

3. Third generation Americans are said to be a rootless lot, characterized by the needs and stresses of persons who move often,

live in strange cities, have few ties to kinfolk, neighborhood, or locality. Their commonality lies in temporary job associations, admiration for the same athletes and movie and television stars, and patronage of the same commercial establishments, all of which are substitutions for relinquished home-town ties. (J. J. Corson, "Need Is an Anachronism," *The Survey,* vol. 86, no. 3, pp. 134–135, March, 1950, and Margaret Mead, *And Keep Your Powder Dry,* William Morrow & Company, Inc., New York, 1942.) How do pupils tend to compensate for and to elevate the commonality of otherwise rootless families?

4. Community actions, which are always particular experiences, lead to consciousness of common possession of values, talents, and needs; they must proceed and accompany verbal communication regarding them. "The community is inalienably concrete." (Baker Brownell, *The Human Community,* Harper & Brothers, New York, 1950, p. 224.) Apply this generalization to the school as a "pilot plant" for community building. What preplanning is desirable? And what provisions are necessary for taking advantage of "particular experiences" as the projects move forward?

5. Allison Davis and Robert J. Havighurst in *Father of the Man* (Houghton Mifflin Company, Boston, 1947), conclude on the basis of case studies that on the whole children growing up in lower-class environments are likely to develop more wholesome, outgoing personalities than are those from middle-class homes. Are there lessons or implications to be drawn from this conclusion for the socializing processes of the schools?

6. Many lower-class parents have themselves had little or no successful school experience. They sometimes believe that the school experience is a waster of their hard-earned money and of their children's time that would better be spent in earning money to help out the hard-pressed families. Would frequent social success for lower-class pupils, stemming from their contributions to athletic, musical, artistic, or service projects of the school be likely to improve the esteem for the school by lower-class adults?

7. Lower-status families often exemplify some patterns and standards of behavior that are quite as understandable, justifiable, and admirable as those of the middle-class families which the schools generally standardize as the "right" ones. The generosity of the poor to those who have met misfortune is proverbial. Even the realistic behavior typical of slum neighborhoods is often characterized by courage, boldness, and hope. Read Betty Smith's novel, *A Tree Grows in Brooklyn* (Harper & Brothers, New York, 1947), to identify some of the attributes of the character that the school might well foster for the general population.

8. "It is always true," says Walter Lippmann, "that individuals cannot be free if their community is not independent." (New York *Herald-Tribune,* November 3, 1938.) Does this statement apply to pupils in a school club, class, home room, or assembly? If so, what are the implications for school administration?

9

The Coordination
of Educational Forces

THE SCHOOL AND THE FUTURE

The educator is a social engineer. Accordingly, he seeks out those community institutions and establishments which support the school's means and purposes.

In the process of seeking such support, the educator discovers many usages and valuations which are inconsistent with, or directly contrary to, those which the school seeks to foster. In varying degrees, through guidance, by providing opportunities for many sorts of accomplishments, and by providing prestige for varied achievements, the school competes with these conflicting forces. The educator tries to offset these adverse influences without arousing the ill will of the individuals and groups who create and support them. No matter how tactfully and persistently the school proceeds in this matter, however, its effectiveness is narrowly limited unless other vigorous community establishments are engaged in parallel efforts.

The educator, therefore, endeavors to integrate the programs of appropriate establishments with that of the school whenever their aims are the same and the means for promoting them are consistent. If, for example, the objective is a high quality of individual and com-

171

munity life, the educator almost certainly can count on the support of municipal officers, medical societies, service clubs, social workers, and, indeed, all other enlightened citizens. Similarly, if the objective is the improvement of intercultural relations among pupils and various subgroups in the community, the educator readily discovers civic groups and individuals eager to participate. In both cases, of course, the school's projects will have to be made clear, the cooperation of interested citizens sought early, and their "place in the sun" assured.

Limitations on the School's Program

Even when the school's program is directed toward the accomplishment of such generally approved ends, however, the educator recognizes the limitations set by the inertia of public indifference, the assertiveness of excessive self-interest, and the dynamics of personal and group rivalries. Any one or any combination of these may upset the best laid plans. The motives of men are not only complex and inconsistent, but are also frequently irrelevant to the issues; their actual motives are often unacknowledged by those involved in debate over school policy. Moreover, the force of these motives is often ephemeral.

Nevertheless, the educator cannot absolve himself from his social responsibility persistently to endeavor to carry out the school's mission. His strategy and tactics involve "calculated risks" as truly as do those of the military officer, the athlete, the governmental official, and the judge. He gauges the opportunities and the obstacles facing each major educational venture; he assesses the favorable and unfavorable factors as they already affect the attitudes of those whom the school seeks to influence. He endeavors to make sure that as many as possible of those whose cooperation is needed—teachers, pupils, patrons, and youth-serving and other civic groups—identify themselves with the planning, execution, and evaluation of the project. He makes sure that every sponsor has a chance, and knows that he has a chance, to perform some concrete act for the success of the project, and he makes sure that there is recognition for the service.

Scholastic Institutionalism

Despite the modern school's orientation to the future and its consciousness that its educational objectives cannot be attained except through the mobilization of the planned efforts of many individuals and organizations, the school typically retains its institutional character. As such, it is embedded in an organizational stereotype of classroom recitation, lesson learning, examination passing, teacher authority, and pupil conformity. In the conventional school, stereotyped virtues—unquestioning acceptance and memorization of "facts," obedience to rules and commands, and institutional loyalty—are all considered ends in themselves. These virtues provide somewhat artificial criteria for judging success and failure and, hence, for justifying reward and punishment.

There are four related phenomena which typically accompany this institutionalization. (1) Often the curriculum is characterized by verbal and manipulative techniques abstracted from the valued skills and knowledge of yesteryear; modifications in the light of changing values and needs are resisted by many teachers and patrons. (2) The related instructional stereotype suited to docile lesson learning still persists. (3) Institutional training is an entree for admittance to the professions and other preferred occupations and, in degree, is a criterion of social status. (4) Consequently, school success is regarded as a social ladder by which ambitious people can transcend the limitations of the common life. The cumulative result of these four interacting developments is that there is danger that schooling itself might become an abstract measuring device isolated from the uncertainty and confusion that characterize the American society.

THE EFFECTS OF CHANGE ON EDUCATIONAL STEREOTYPES

The life of the community has always penetrated the school. Democratic aspirations and pressures, reinforced by changes in the values of a technological society, have compelled the school to broaden its curriculum and to modify its criteria for judging success. In the United States, free play and organized recreation early became approved supplements to the classroom; in time, the spirit of the former enriched that of the latter. Expressive and constructive activities gained admittance to the institutional process, at first as noncredit activities (sometimes called extra-curriculum or even fads and frills) and later as integral parts of the broadened curriculum. Today, the inclusion of art, music, practical and household arts, dramatics, and pupil participation in management and policy making is almost nowhere rejected.

The Public School and Other Educational Agencies

"Education," says George S. Counts,[1] "is always a function of some particular civilization at some particular time in history." A heterogeneous and heterodox nation is the American's particular civilization and the present is his particular time in history. There are three sets of interacting variables which spring from deep in our civilization

[1] *Education and the Promise of America,* The Macmillan Company, New York, 1945, p. 23.

and time and which affect the varieties of American education. These are: (1) the great number of philosophies and prejudices that characterize the public; (2) the personalities of the individual teachers and other adults who influence pupils' activities; and (3) the biological and social capacities of pupils to alter their personal values and ego ideals.

The school's great contribution to the American civilization has relatively little to do with programs of study, scholastic credits, and institutional mechanics. The school's major role has been, and promises to continue to be, that of a great coordinator and stabilizer in American life. It has accepted generation after generation of young people of diverse cultural background, encouraged their association, tolerated both originality and imitation, and inspired and guided young people. The public school is to be appreciated best as a dynamic environment encouraging rapid acculturation of young people.

Some Limiting Factors

Children do not leave their homes and neighborhoods behind them when they set forth for school. Their parents, siblings, and playmates, their religious attitudes, the residues of their vicarious experiences, their fears and hopes, and the other products of living come to school along with the pupils.

And neither are teachers and other adults of the school independent, detached, spiritual embodiments of education. They, too, bring to the school all their personal hopes and triumphs, frustrations, fears, problems, victories, and defeats. Teachers' personal traits are every bit as important as their words and actions in the creation of admiration, distaste, and other reactions in the minds of those who associate with them.

The Public's School

That the school belongs to the public is a truism. But it is valid only within the frame of reference of popular devotion to the common welfare and to the rights of individuals to self-determination. The public school reflects American aspirations—sober second thoughts regarding long-term desires rather than impulsive excitements.

Even so, public judgments are affected by the diverse prejudices, loyalties, and self-interests which circumscribe the criteria by which the school's functions and processes are evaluated. And ignorance or misunderstanding of what these processes and functions actually are often results in temporary "public opinions" that are not based on facts. Moreover, the crowd character of much of public opinion frequently finds expression in criticism and denunciation of the school (and in the readiness to accept them undiscriminatingly) as an outlet for frustrations that are not clearly connected with institutional education.

Nevertheless, these criticisms and irrelevant judgments of the school's efficacy reflect a vague, almost mystic, faith in its potentialities as a determiner of individual and group erudition, behavior, and values. However skeptical it may be regarding the immediate goals, standards, and methods believed to be characteristic of the school, the public assumes that if the school were maximally effective, the shortcomings of youth, and in time of adults, would be largely overcome.

This faith, however vague and preposterous it would be if explicit, presents a social force that educators selectively exploit. It assures stability to the school, if only because there is no alternative universal institution in the United States to guide the growth of all the children of all the people. Hence, if any influential public envisions a desirable form or aspect of social belief or behavior, it is almost always presumed that the school can materially aid in its achievement.

MINIMIZING COMBATIVENESS AND ANTI-INTELLECTUALISM

The dynamic forces that have to such a remarkable extent wrested political and economic power from the "upper classes" in the United States have brought popular tolerance of the tactics of emotional arousal and crude ridicule little restrained by reasoned judgment. Hence the power of the "raucous voices" which H. G. Wells[2] has warned are the final masters of negative, inarticulate men; they are, he says, "the residual heirs of America."

Men and women who have shouldered their way through hardship, defeat, conquest, law evasion, duplicity, and compromise have openly or secretly admired the tough, determined, and resourceful characters who have met their obstacles head on, whether by forthright attack or by clever manipulations. Crude satires directed at established figures—for example, diplomats, intellectuals, industrial magnates, and society matrons—have always delighted most Americans. They express the suspicion and hostility felt toward those who are believed to be critical of popular assertiveness.

The Values of Mutual Aid

Nevertheless, limitations on intemperate combativeness have emerged *pari passu* with tolerance for the "raucous voices." Both the spiritual and pragmatic values of love, brotherhood, and mutual aid

[2] *The New America the New World,* The Macmillan Company, New York, 1935, p. 77.

have mellowed and humanized American life. Ideologically and sentimentally, the combative heritage has been relegated to staged contests that people "enjoy." Momentarily, to be sure, the "raucous voices" may dominate the American scene; but the futility of mere attack and satire in the face of need for constructive action is readily apparent to almost everyone.

Among the establishments characterized by a feeling of civic responsibility, the public school is unique. It minimizes promiscuous combativeness and exalts reasoned conclusions and mutual trust. Its immediate function is to prepare young people to meet the exigencies of the present and the future, endeavoring thereby to make them ready to deal with specific problems that do not yet exist by use of tools and resources that can as yet be only vaguely envisioned.[3] Obviously, neither the school's goals nor its means of promoting them can be defined solely in terms of facts to be learned or specific processes to be mastered.

As an agency for cultural integration, the school truly faces a Herculean task! There is no clear line of demarcation between the ethic and practices of humanistic democracy and the dog-eat-dog private-enterprise anarchy which is sometimes exemplified in business, professional, political, and, it must be reluctantly admitted, even in school relations.

The School and Its Contradictory Masters

Whatever its legal sanctions and however "spiritual" its aspirations, the school cannot altogether escape its heritage of rivalry and antagonism. The half-conscious popular esteem for victory in combat tends to transform the school's humanistic and mutual-aid functions into a milieu of attempts by pupils and teachers to outdo and humiliate rivals. In athletics, journalism, debate, studies, personal adornment, popular leadership, and sophistication, efficiency is judged by victory. Teachers who may themselves transcend this childish adulation of victors are aware that denunciation of such antihumanistic values offends the vested interests of many articulate patrons, upperclassmen, and fellow teachers who attribute their individual success to winning out over rivals.

The public school inevitably responds to what the public values. Hence, the experiences and activities that it tolerates and generally ap-

---

[3] The courts, the press, the church, political parties, and labor unions, for example, in some cases intentionally foster climates of opinion favorable to reason and restraint, thereby supporting the school in one of its major purposes. (See Margaret Mead, *The School in American Culture,* Harvard University Press, Cambridge, Mass., 1951, p. 41.)

proves are mixtures of human aspirations for mutually helpful associations and of competitive struggle. It thus combines the functions of child welfare and civic service with that of preparing young people to "make good" in a world which tolerates sharp practices and rewards competitive success.

THE SCHOOL'S SELECTION AND COORDINATING FUNCTION

Whatever the advantages implicit in the central position of the school, it cannot by itself purify the multifarious social inheritances represented among pupils, teachers, and patrons. Fortunately, the school has many potential allies and reinforcements in its efforts to prepare individuals for a cooperative, interdependent society and to help close the gap between narrow loyalties and prejudices and intergroup collaboration for the common weal.

"Gold Is Where You Find It"

The scope, aims, and processes of some of these potential allies are in many respects almost identical with those of the school, for example, those of several youth-serving organizations, many religious groups, and private and public welfare agencies. Other potential allies offer only occasional and partial reinforcement of the school's efforts to guide individuals toward scientific objectivity, social understanding, fellowship, and high standards of moral conduct. Within families and ethnic groups, patriotic societies, labor unions, employers' organizations, political-party clubs, and other associations, despite their often polemic intensities, there are values, practices, and attitudes which can be exploited by the school.

The school courts and welcomes whatever public approval it can find for its efforts to fulfill its role. Its meliorative mission cannot wait until special evolution develops an ideal common life independently of the school. The good life for all men which it seeks to foster is already approved in principle and is exemplified in at least some practices by the majority of all civilized people. The school's strategy, therefore, is to provide opportunities for appropriate organizations and individuals of its local community to sponsor, help plan, and participate in important educational projects.

Educational Potentials of Community Life

School and community life are as varied as they are referenced to the future. Today's acts and attitudes obviously affect, if they do not altogether determine, tomorrow's weal. With varying adequacy, every individual and every establishment is compelled to assess present decisions and deeds in terms of their probable future effects.

Each of the almost infinite combinations of valuation and action provides the individual with opportunities for self-realization, civic competence, economic efficiency, and interpersonal adjustment. Every success is liberating and satisfying; every failure annoying, perhaps frustrating. The school's contribution is to provide its quota of such opportunities to pupils, teachers, and patrons and, so far as possible, engineer each undertaking so that success may be frequent and satisfying.

In a word, the school enters into the stream of life, increases its momentum, and, in collaboration with other social establishments and enlightened men of good will, it endeavors to direct the stream. Its purpose is to make it as probable as possible that life experiences in the American society will teach, to young and old, the same basic virtues as those that define the school's mission.

The Best Defensive Is a Strong Offensive

The major, often interrelated, obstacles to human progress are ignorance, fear, outmoded stereotypes, ill health, reliance on coercion, and sloth. For thousands of years, mankind has partly defied and partly succumbed to these age-old enemies. Men have revolted, migrated, formed sectarian societies, colonized, and even isolated themselves in order to free themselves and their progeny. The earliest schools in America were established to aid one such effort.

Contemporary schools continue the effort to minimize the obstacles to human progress, both by direct attacks on ill health, ignorance, sloth, outmoded stereotypes, fear, and reliance on coercion and by creating so varied and such engaging opportunities for voluntary participation that all members of the school community will be challenged to make contributions to the social weal. In so far as the latter effort is vigorously and efficiently managed, the need for direct attack diminishes.

COOPERATION BETWEEN THE SCHOOL AND LOCAL GROUPS

Many community organizations have objectives that in great measure parallel those of the school. Some of their programs are general and continuing, such as those concerned with health, character building, recreation, and intercultural relations. Others are relatively specific, for example, observation of Flag Day, beautification of a park, and ratification of a municipal charter. The opportunities for collaboration between the school and the sponsors of such undertakings differ according to the size, type, and cultural complexity of the community.

Rural and village schools frequently engage in projects which are initiated by nonschool organizations. For example, the local garden club may agitate for the elimination of ragweed, for roadside beautification, or for landscaping the grounds of public buildings. Boys and girls belonging to 4-H clubs, Scouts, and similar organizations typically share in carrying through the project. The school may support the undertaking in one or more of several ways: school credits and honors may be awarded to participants, exhibits or assemblies may be devoted to it, and appropriate subject classes or clubs may adopt the project.

Educators are likely to find many patrons in village and rural areas who recognize the importance of work experience as a supplement and corrective for the conventional bookishness of high school and college programs. The possibilities for flexibility in the regimen of small schools are favorable for both formal and informal sharing by pupils and teachers in the work of the community.

Limitations on School-Village Cooperation

There is little danger that the village and rural schools will go overboard in participating in community projects. They are subject to uniform state requirements regarding curriculum, attendance, and teacher certification. Many of their pupils, with parents' enthusiastic approval, regard school education as a means of escaping the drudgery associated with machine operation, poultry raising, serving customers, and house cleaning. Moreover, the school itself recognizes the reality that many students will live as adults in urban and suburban communities, paying for goods and services with money earned as wages and salaries rather than furnishing them by their own labor; indeed, it is generally understood that this way of life increasingly invades rural areas.

Other Collaborative Services

Fortunately, there have developed some transitional services, equally aplicable to rural and urban cultural enrichment, that invite collaboration. The traveling public library, for example, brings to rural homes and schools the books and magazines of contemporary interest. The health nurse, home-demonstration director, youth-serving organizations, and church-related social service agencies have counterparts in urban and in rural communities. Newspapers, radio and television broadcasts, moving pictures, automobiles and service stations, mail-order merchandising, bus, train, and boat transportation, hospitals, doctors' and dentists' offices, beauty parlors, and supermarkets, all are similar except in the most remote areas. In so far as the school selectively accommodates its program to these common and transitional establishments, it prepares for city as well as for rural and village effectiveness.

Urban and Suburban Communities

The opportunities for school and nonschool educational collaboration in urban and suburban areas differ from those of village and rural areas chiefly because of the greater fragmentation and impersonality of human relations in the case of the former. City clean-up and sanitation crusades, for example, are carried through on such a scale that there is little chance for pupils actually to participate in their operation. Labor unions may prevent pupils from working, for educational purposes, on the construction and repair of buildings and equipment. On-the-job training in offices and shops requires somewhat elaborate arrangements. Associative youth activities, for example, boys' clubs, which seek to provide wholesome substitutes for gang activities have their own camps and recreation centers. School educators approve these provisions and often serve them as officials or as advisers; but it is difficult to maintain close coordination between them and the school's program. Civil defense, Red Cross programs, projects for the diminution of racial discrimination, and United Fund drives are likely to be initiated and managed by adults; schools are invited to publicize and otherwise to support them, but they seldom can share in their planning or execution.

The urban school's effectiveness as an active agency for community stability and betterment is likely to be somewhat indirect. Adult educational projects—classes, lectures, forums, and exhibits, for example—influence civic and cultural affairs. Parent-teacher associations frequently publicize conditions which require remedial measures and may take the lead in mobilizing the forces of government to bring the recommended measures into being. School administrators are usually included in the membership of the coordinating councils formed in urban centers to foster cooperation among agencies which endeavor to combat juvenile delinquency, improve intercultural relations, remedy unsanitary conditions, provide recreational facilities, and foster aesthetically satisfying surroundings.

Community and Classroom

Alert teachers of the social sciences, science, English, art, and other subjects do, of course, seize upon such community concerns as opportunities to motivate their classwork. The understanding of the processes by which civic and cultural betterments are attained and the experience of evaluation of alternatives sometimes have two desirable outcomes: pupils and teachers gain the self-confidence which enables them to enter into discussions of community affairs; and some pupils become fired with the vision of a community guided by intelligence, an enthusiasm which they carry with them throughout life.[4]

Urban Life Accentuates Some Adjustment Problems

The character of urban living results, at least temporarily, in confused valuations, clever evasions, restlessness, and sometimes in mental aberration. Sharpers operate both "within the law" and by breaking or evading the law; influence peddling infiltrates political and economic life. "Success," however attained, is highly respected and hence eagerly sought. Competitive economic enterprise is to a great extent channeled toward display, toward winning personally favorable attention, and toward attaching one's prospects and services to an already successfully established corporation as a salaried employee.

The alienation of men's ideals of workmanship and integrity from their means of winning economic success is a correlative of the amorality of those who "live by their wits," whether legally or illegally. That "everybody has a racket" and that "only boobs work" are grotesque exaggerations, but they do reflect a general tolerance of the substitution of clever manipulation for sincere and guileless workmanship. Law evasion, delinquency, and crime become definable not so much in terms of ethics and integrity as in terms of the toleration of certain activities by those social groups who have the power to enforce compliance with the social codes. Hence, the borderline between what one can and what one cannot "get away with" becomes hazy. Bold, adventurous, and resourceful individuals frequently risk crossing the line of demarcation.

THE YEA SAYER IN AMERICAN SOCIETY

It is obviously an oversimplification to classify people as "yea sayers" and "nay sayers." An individual, for example, may be an unorthodox pioneer in his business while holding firmly to orthodoxy in religion or to father-domination in his family life. Still, it is obvious that some persons and groups (the yea sayers) are more ingenious and more willing to undertake bold new attacks on social problems than are others (the nay sayers) who look to the *status quo*.

[4] In later chapters, several instances of urban schools are cited in which pupils and teachers do enter into improvement projects as active participants.

The American environment has encouraged bold actions. Geographic and social mobility, the near absence of an hereditary elite, freedom from inclusive ecclesiastical authority, the vigorous interplay of communication facilities, and the near universality of the franchise have all favored cooperative action programs.

Ambivalent Motives for Social Action

The readiness to respond actively to challenges and opportunities is, of course, not limited to those for whom concern for the general welfare is uppermost. Excessive self-interest has been quite as frequently a mover of men as has concern for the common weal. Thus, civic amorality is transmitted to youth, justified by the American consecration to "success."

The social assets and liabilities of self-interest motivation are not argued here. The immediate interest is its influence on youthful attitudes and behavior. Self-interested ambition may seek satisfaction within the community's codes and institutional framework—scholarship standing, money making, and conspicuous consumption—or by the evasion of rule and law.

Almost inevitably, the spirit of self-interest infiltrates all youth groups. So long as its expression keeps within the bounds of morality and law observance, it undoubtedly stimulates individuals to productive effort. Unfortunately, however, outward evidence of success may be gained by clever evasion and by bold defiance of codes and laws. The school cannot afford to ignore their frequency, and even "normalcy," in the American culture.

The Social Ethic Is Compromised

Organizations for youth cannot cut themselves free from the cultural contradictions of the time. What they can do is to attach the prestige of success to those attainments which, if they do not actually benefit one's associates, at least do not appreciably harm them. To achieve an outstanding performance whether in a history class, a community orchestra, or on a football team obviously contributes to the group's accomplishments while assuring the individual performer the glow of personal success.

Following an analogous procedure, the youth-serving organization may provide many opportunities for gang morality to function within the bounds of the welfare of the association of members and their community. The boldness, loyalty, and ingenuity, honored in in-groups among youth and adults, can find free play. By means of its counseling system, the youth organization may help each member to find his place in the sun—to seek to achieve both prestige and affection among his peers. His self-image thus includes both his self-interest in success and his desire for the security and response to which his contribution to the common good entitles him.

THE SCHOOL REFLECTS A DYNAMIC CULTURE

Progressive schools respond to the values and practices which characterize twentieth-century America. American attitudes and behavior, while complex and variant, are themselves responses to the impacts on human lives made by an industrial civilization. Most middle-class adults undoubtedly believe that tomorrow will be better than today, that opportunities are waiting to be seized, and that prestige can be obtained by anyone who is in the right place, at the right time, with the appropriate competence and credentials.

Americans are optimistic, assertive, and independent. They value and practice freedom to direct their own lives, to move from job to job, place to place, and group to group, and the alternation of leadership and followership. All these express the American people's desire for security, their readiness to adventure, their eagerness for recognition, and their longing for sympathetic understanding by their fellows. They transmit these moods and behavior to their progeny.

The School and Cultural Transmission

Publicly supported schools cannot avoid becoming major transmitting agencies for the values and usages that characterize the adult population. Just as conformity to codes and rules is voluntarily acceded to by the majority of citizens, so the regimen of schools is so planned and managed as to make voluntary conformity to institutional norms highly probable. Just as a democratic society tolerates the individual's right to choose his values and behavior, checked only by moral pressures, legal restraints, and his own foresight regarding probable consequences, so the school accords similar rights to pupils, teachers, and patrons in matters pertaining to its program.

In order to accord freedom, to encourage voluntarism, to recognize varied achievements, and to minimize insecurity due to failure, the school, like the society it serves, carries on its constructive program within a somewhat vague configuration of cultural and emotional norms. Serious misdemeanors are regarded as symptoms of maladjustment; the welfare of the majority may require the restraint or elimination of offenders, but only after extensive and ingenious efforts have failed to lead them to act as normal persons.

Major Modifications in School Regimen

During the twentieth century, progressive schools have made many changes in the attempt to harmonize their educational programs with the changing practices and outlooks of the American industrial society. The change in the general orientation of the school has been noted. In the following paragraphs, somewhat more specific modifications in the program of studies, so-called "extracurricular activities," and guidance processes are considered.

Within the program of studies, at all levels, insistence upon uniformity of achievement has come to be limited to the knowledge and skills which most pupils and their parents recognize to be of fundamental importance either for personal adequacy or for further educational achievement. With respect to these, there is generally voluntary acceptance of school requirements. Even in these prescribed learnings, however, the progressive school depends less than its traditional predecessor on teacher authority and extrinsic rewards and punishments. It relies more heavily on the teacher's preparation of the pupils' readiness and capabilities to undertake the assigned tasks, on pupils' initiative, and on their enhanced sense of accomplishment. For the enrichment aspects of required courses and for all elective subjects, dependence is put chiefly on pupils' motivations and purposes; the teacher aids the pupil to undertake jobs, to plan and execute his own projects, and to evaluate his own products on the basis of appropriate criteria.

Because the stereotypes of "subjects" and "promotion" have limited the school's freedom in diversifying its curriculum, there have developed many noncredit educational opportunities for self-realization and for winning institutional honors and the esteem of fellow students. These extracurricular opportunities include assistanceships to teachers and custodians, membership in traffic squads, clubs, teams, and editorial boards, participation in assembly programs, student government, parent-pupil events, and many forms of collaboration with nonschool establishments. Successful participation in any of these undertakings requires individual responsibility and assiduous endeavor and fosters initiative and originality. Their effectiveness, therefore, depends not only on the nature of the tasks undertaken, but also on their voluntary character and on the transfer of pupil control from teacher authority to group morality.

Teachers increasingly forsake the enforcement of orders for a growing emphasis on guidance. In consonance with the spirit and processes of contemporary civil life, the school seeks to enlighten and persuade rather than command. Pupils, teachers, and patrons are helped to set up goals which seem to them reasonably attainable and worth the effort. The guidance officer, whether he acts as supervisor, counselor, classroom teacher, coach, club sponsor, or parent-teacher association official, helps individuals and groups to attain *their* chosen objectives by purposeful planning and vigorous endeavor. To the degree that he is successful in fulfilling his guidance role, he is usually eagerly sought by those he would aid.

These Modifications Are Interrelated

It should be understood that curriculum reform, student activities, and guidance are interrelated. The spirit and processes of each infiltrate the others. As decision making becomes a responsibility of each individual and group concerned in any aspect of the school's program, critical mindedness and voluntary cooperation replace docile conformity to ukase. Authority becomes a function of competence, not of institutional regulation or hierarchical position. Authority is voluntarily accorded to those who are capable of giving instruction by those who seek and welcome it.

Hence, the school administrator and the classroom teacher in their roles as institutional managers give instruction to persons who accept it as reasonable, justifiable, and necessary if the objectives of class and school are to be achieved. But the requirement for uniformity is limited to that knowledge and to those acts and skills which justify standardization. Many curriculum activities are characterized by the spirit of voluntarism, individual responsibility, and desire characteristic of extracurricular and guidance processes. One evidence of this transfer is the occasional inclusion of the extra-curriculum (in such cases as music, drama, journalism, and athletics) and of orientation and group-guidance classes in the program of studies.

Similarly, the sponsors of clubs, coaches of teams, and faculty representatives on student councils do not hesitate to give their charges instruction on appropriate occasions, though their main reliance is on pupils' spontaneous desires to participate in organizational projects. These desires obviously provide infinite occasions for guidance.

And so, too, in those areas of school activities marked off as guidance, because of the desire for assistance in establishing goals and in making decisions regarding their attainment, instruction plays an important part. It is often welcomed by the person seeking guidance; the special knowledge and the broader experience of the guide provide security for the adventurer on untried paths.

OBSTACLES FACING THE SCHOOL

Both from within the educational profession and from conservative or ill-informed segments of the public, objections to the modifications sketched above are expressed which are as vigorous and persistent as they are, under present conditions, futile. It is, of course, possible that the dynamics of the American industrial democracy may some day weaken. Widespread poverty could induce the kind of docility which characterized some immigrant groups in years past. Or, less likely, in a continuing "garrison state," the popular mentality could come to equate patriotism with scholastic lesson learning, as it is alleged to have done in the Soviet Union. Or it is possible, but scarcely conceivable, that some powerful elite might persuade the people to give up their demands for participation and individual decision making and to submit to social arrangements satisfactory to "their betters."

Unless and until one or more of these most unlikely conditions come to pass, however, it seems almost certain that the moods and the usages which characterize the American industrial society will have counterparts in public schools. Parents and their children who daily experience freedom to decide their courses of action and to accept responsibility for their choices and conduct will not long submit to authority based on nothing more reasonable than institutional regulations or more substantial than prejudice.

The School as a Scapegoat

Momentary aberrations will upsurge to plague the school. Here and there progressive schools will be cast in the role of scapegoats for juvenile delinquency, lack of scientists, failure of citizens to vote, the fact that "Johnny can't read," and many other actual and alleged shortcomings of the nation. Temporarily, some schools will be forced by public opinion, perhaps by official action, to a vain effort to revert to an authoritarian type of prescription, superimposition, and, of course, elimination of the stubborn and the less academically able pupils.

The certainty that such upsets can be only sporadic and temporary is based on the actualities of a changing industrial society. Pupils and patrons effectively demand reasonable explanations of, and justifications for, prescriptions, commands, pupil failures, and expulsions. Nowhere in civil life do they blindly accept authority as binding on themselves; they will not do so in the public school. And they have the political power to support their protests.

THE SCHOOL AND THE EVOLUTION
OF SOCIAL POLICY

The school does not work alone. It is part of a state and society which is referenced to the future. The democracy it serves is wrestling with problems very similar to those of the school. And in that democracy are many forward-looking men and women who are seeking to discover the roads which an industrial society should follow. They are to be found in religious, social welfare, international policy, labor, commercial, industrial, legal, and educational organizations. And they are found, too, among men and women who are not attached to any planning groups but who, within their own families and neighborhoods, exemplify and value the attitudes and behavior that accord with democracy and believe that with enlightenment and opportunity free men will learn to be good men.

These optimistic citizens are, of course, not altogether in agreement regarding specific goals or the methods by which their goals should be pursued. But their orientations are the same as that of the forward-looking school. In most cases, moreover, their espoused goals and methods are tentative and not dissimilar to each other or to those of the school. It is the cultural momentum which they represent to which the school finds itself attached. And it is a momentum that cannot be seriously checked, certainly not reversed, so long as the technological revolution continues.

The School as Coordinator

The school's coordination with nonschool social processes and establishments is selective. It seeks to understand and to be understood by those who believe that the American nation can realize its ideals only as the people who compose it adapt themselves to the opportunities and needs of a rapidly changing world society. Such men know that industrial, financial, legal, religious, political, and all other social institutions are profoundly affected by the enlightenment and assertiveness of common men everywhere. They know that the educational programs of most social establishments foster sympathetic popular understanding of, and consent for, the measures they undertake to harmonize their institutions with world realities. They recognize, therefore, the similar impact that schools experience. In most cases, they are disposed to regard favorably educators' considered efforts to gain the enlightened cooperation of patrons and pupils in meeting the exigencies and opportunities presented by social change.

PERSONALITY TRAITS AS FUNDAMENTAL
OBJECTIVES OF EDUCATION

Though the teaching of skills and information has been and continues to be a major function of the school, the expected outcomes of schooling have seldom if ever been limited to such learning. The hoped-for character traits derived from schooling have perhaps always had a mystical quality, but the human product was expected to exemplify them. In the progressive school, character modifications are of primary importance to attain the school's social objectives. The basic qualities which make for successful living, whether as parent, physician, teacher, homemaker, businessman, farmer, or engineer, or any combination of these, are much the same. In all important fields of human activity, there are needed men and women who can get along with each other and with their superiors and subordinates, who can persevere in the face of jealousy and friction, who can withstand ridicule and unjust criticism, who will not wilt under discouragement or flare up in anger and pitch their jobs. However important specialized knowledge and skills are, they become futile in associative undertakings unless underlain by temperamental adjustability, whether native or acquired.

More than mere adjustability is needed, however. Optimism and social purpose are typically characteristics of those vigorous persons who know that community life can be made better than they find it and who stand ready to help improve it. And the best chance to develop these qualities for most people lies in active participation in the creation of better institutional life during the years of childhood and youth.

Inertia and Change

In a democratic society, the pendulum swings between public inertia and demand for change. These swings are very largely influenced by the relative contentment and discontent of great numbers of youth and young adults. Most American social establishments are so flexible, however, that many of the alternate swings are perceptible only through overt efforts made to forestall overt public protest.

The school inevitably reflects these alternating moods. Together with other stabilizing agencies, however, it endeavors to exemplify in its own regimen relatively conservative standards of "good taste," toleration of diverse opinions, and reasoned judgment. To this degree, at least, it tends to restrain those youths and young adults whom it influences from extremes, whether of conspicuously unconventional behavior or of ill-considered beliefs. Questions and controversies that arise in the school are generally discussed in an atmosphere of controlled tempers. Emotional partisanship is minimized by the insistence upon objective argument and by the treatment of advocated measures as hypotheses, always subject to analysis, experimental application, and probable modification.

To maintain such a reasonable posture requires considerable resistance to those extreme pressure groups which believe that the school should openly espouse their particular set of values, even at the expense of objective facts. In times of tension (for example, during political campaigns, periods of labor-union agitation, international crises, and delinquency scares) vociferous demands on, and harsh criticisms of, educators by one group or another are to be expected. Although they cause great discomfort for those responsible for the school program, extreme groups generally cancel each others' pressures. To surrender the schools' objectivity and reasonableness to the demands of one group is to court disastrous counterblasts from another.

Continuity of the School's Program

In the long run, the continuity of the school's program is safeguarded to the degree that representative civic groups and influential individuals of good will have participated in its formulation and, hence, have become sponsors of its purposes and general character. The public school thus allies itself with the aspirations and behavior of forward-looking men. It seeks to interweave its own processes and objectives with those of individuals and groups which promote humane social relations, the spirit of self-determination, civic competence, and economic efficiency. As such mutuality of purpose and program is progressively achieved, support for one agency becomes support for all; attack on one is resisted by all.

It is because the objectives of the community-coordinated school are strongly reinforced by the objectives and values of citizens and establishments referenced to the future that their attainment is ultimately assured. The attributes of the successful pupil, teacher, and patron of the school are ordinarily much the same as those of other respected citizens; hence, they feel secure, gain companionship in adventure, find warmth of response and generous recognition in the community.

THE SCHOOL AND THE PURSUIT OF HAPPINESS

In response to the changing nature of American life, the school has become less and less a "social isolate." Although it is still restricted by stereotyped ideas, practices, and relationships persisting from previous decades, it is compelled to accommodate its regimen and curriculum to new patterns of family, community, and national life. In other words, the modern educator and his charges face the future together with other citizens of all ages and from all walks of life. And the democratic educator seeks to attune the school to the most persistent and compulsive of human aspirations—the pursuit of happiness.

It is not a wholly self-centered happiness that the individual in a democracy pursues. Repeatedly, hour by hour, he faces the reality that only as one's associates are well disposed in a relationship can an individual ordinarily find pleasure. The pragmatic justification for the Christian ethic is discovered and rediscovered, applied and reapplied, in common life. Hence, cooperative adjustments to other people characterize all normal personalities.

It must be recognized, of course, that such adjustments are not yet complete. Fragments of Old World loyalties and hates, class antagonism, racial, ethnic, and religious prejudices, and even vestiges of regional parochialism remain potent; occasionally they afflict minds that are in most other regards enlightened. These atavisms challenge all democratic agencies, but peculiarly the public school.

Education and Leisure

The professional educator's special equipment and opportunity include not only the regimen of the school, but also his knowledge of children and their parents and other associates. His school ought to exemplify the correlative happiness of young people and their elders. Because the educator recognizes the determinative quality of avocational wants and their satisfaction in an industrial society, his school encourages leisure-time occupations, for young and older people, that are harmless or, so far as feasible, that are constructive of democratic individualism and voluntarism. Because just such avocational pursuits of happiness already are general in community life, the school's effort integrates with those of many similarly oriented extra-school agencies and individuals.

Humane concern for the maladjusted and disadvantaged are thereby fostered, not so much in terms of charity and beneficence as in terms of human rights and of community tranquillity. In all professional relationships, whether primarily concerned with pupils and faculty associates or with school-related publics, the educator seeks to encourage his collaborators to set up for themselves worthwhile objectives which are reasonable, practical of attainment, and not in serious conflict with the legitimate objectives of others. He recognizes the rights of all people to their private scales of values and objectives; but he fosters reexamination of these values and objectives through reflective thinking, group decision, and cooperative action.

Community Reinforcements for the School Program

Community life reinforces the lessons the professional educators thus endeavor to teach. In families, neighborhoods, labor unions, churches, chambers of commerce, boards of directors, and a hundred other situations, group decisions and collaborations based on reflective thought are more satisfying and successful, and hence more pleasurable, than is obedience to ukase. Once common purposes are established and facts are clearly apprehended, choices of ends and means are usually reasonable, and in application self-corrective. Maladjusted and disadvantaged members of associations are drawn into collaboration and eventually into group processes of decision making, if only because their exclusion endangers the success of the common endeavor. Brotherly concern is good, not so much because it is ethically mandated as because it is efficient.

Decade by decade, as populations have changed, domestic arrangements have been modified, child labor has decreased, and mechanical improvements have altered all aspects of American life, the public school has, partly by foresight, but chiefly by trial and success, adapted its curriculum, regimen, and philosophy to provide opportunities for all its pupils. School-sponsored recreation, emphasis on personal qualities, acceptance of student activities into institutional life, the introduction of new subjects and the refinement of established ones, and the partial replacement of instruction by guidance and pupil-teacher planning have contributed to the creation of the American character.[5]

SUMMARY

The establishments of all the professions—for example, law, medicine, architecture, engineering, and religion—change to meet the challenges presented by the social milieu in which they have their being. If they do not, they languish into futility. The school is no exception. It is a purposeful social agency. Its mandate is to foster stability and orderly progress.

But stability and progress themselves are by-products of social evolution. It is change, perhaps more than anything else, which makes the modern school necessary. It is a culture in process of accelerating change that the school endeavors to transmit and, as far as possible, to qualify. Obviously, the school cannot itself solve society's problems. Indeed, in many cases, the problems are insoluble in advance of a

[5] Cf. D. W. Brogan, *The American Character*, Alfred A. Knopf, Inc., New York, 1944.

social evolution which will respond to forces that are, as yet, not even clearly foreseeable.

Nevertheless, the school ought to act in the present in the light of those factors and those trends which can be discerned. Its measures may, indeed, be only "the least erroneous answers to insoluble problems," as Justice Cardozo defined the Supreme Courts' responsibility. Educators, therefore, look to the sciences which deal with individual and group behavior and to any and all other fields for assistance in *understanding the proper mission of the school in a democracy*. In the light of such understanding, educators themselves become critical of their established practices and values.

They cannot, of course, start *de novo* to reconstitute the school. But they can, and in many instances they do, reorient the curriculum and regimen of the institution. They can thus reinforce the desired, and counteract the undesired, behavior and attitudes which pupils learn from experience outside the school. In doing this, the school helps its clientele find some degree of wholeness in community life by striving toward the achievement of democratic and Judaeo-Christian ideals and by making whatever compromises with unavoidable custom and compulsion they must, but knowing why they so act.

The social and economic framework within which the school builds continues to be transitional. Popular demand and common consent for legislatures, courts, and administrative agencies to adapt their acts to already changed conditions come slowly, but they do come. The democratic discipline that typifies American character is complex; it involves persistent agitation and pressure, patience in disappointment and defeat, and flexibility to adapt oneself and the institutions with which one identifies in the light of what is possible as well as what is desirable. Ideological inconsistencies are subordinated to practical considerations; class structure in a theoretically classless society thus persists so long as it does not preclude rich opportunity for upward mobility; "true religions," however vigorously propagandized, are protected, provided their adherents tolerate other sectarians. Science and technology affect men's attitudes and behavior in a thousand immediate contingencies and, in time, undermine their socially inherited, stereotypical beliefs. To all these the school falls heir and with them it must work in its mission of preserving social stability and order in progress.

SELECTED REFERENCES

Bear, R. M.: *The Social Functions of Education,* The Macmillan Company, New York, 1937. Chap. 14, "Education and Social

Change," is a good discussion of the role of the school in a rapidly changing society.

Bridging the Gap between School and College, The Fund for the Advancement of Education, New York, 1953. A description of some of the experimental programs in use.

Brookover, Wilbur B.: *A Sociology of Education,* American Book Company, New York, 1955. Esp. chap. 6, "Education and Intergroup Relations." Contains an evaluation of intergroup education.

Brown, Francis J.: *Educational Sociology,* 2d ed., Prentice-Hall, Inc., Englewood Cliffs, N.J., 1954. Chap 11, on the family, 16, on other agencies, and 22, on planning, provide valuable reading for the student on the place of the school in social change.

Conant, James B.: *The American High School Today,* McGraw-Hill Book Company, Inc., New York, 1959. Report of a leading educator's analysis of the strengths and weaknesses of the American secondary school system.

————: *Education and Liberty,* Harvard University Press, Cambridge, Mass., 1953. Description of a plan for higher education.

Dahlke, H. Otto: *Values in Culture and Classroom,* Harper & Brothers, New York, 1958. Part 6, "The School in the Center of Controversy," contains good chapters on the school's relation to special interest groups and to the law.

Davis, Allison: *Social Class Influences on Learning,* Harvard University Press, Cambridge, Mass., 1948. If the curriculum were drawn more predominantly from the daily life of pupils and if the curricular experiences were more intense, they would more significantly influence the American society.

Douglass, Harl R. (ed.): *Education for Life Adjustment,* The Ronald Press Company, New York, 1950. Out-of-school community processes, as well as the subjects, student activities, and the guidance programs of the school, may be intentionally directed to aid in life adjustment.

————: *The High School Curriculum,* 2d ed., The Ronald Press Company, New York, 1956. Chap. 5, 6, and 9 are especially relevant to this chapter.

Educational Policies Commission: *Education for All American Youth: A Further Look,* National Education Association and American Association of School Administrators, Washington, 1952. An updating of the idealized community schools recommended in the earlier publication, *Education for All American Youth,* Washington, 1944.

Fortune, Editors of, with R. W. Davenport: *U.S.A., The Permanent Revolution,* Prentice-Hall, Inc., Englewood Cliffs, N.J., 1951.

Esp. chap. 8 about the problems of free men, with a note on technological revolution. Description of changes in American capitalism in the last few decades.

Havighurst, Robert J.: *Human Development and Education,* Longmans, Green and Co., Inc., New York, 1953. The developmental process in human motivation.

Johnson, Martha F.: *Parents as Partners,* University of Kentucky Press, Louisville, 1953. Especially valuable in describing family cooperation with the school.

Klein, D. B.: *Mental Hygiene,* Henry Holt and Company, Inc., New York, 1944. Esp. chap. 16 on educating for mental hygiene. A description of how schools can promote mental health.

Koopman, Margaret O.: *Utilizing the Local Environment,* Hinds, Hayden, and Eldredge, Inc., New York, 1946. Techniques for community study by secondary schools.

Mannheim, Karl: *Freedom, Power, and Democratic Planning,* Oxford University Press, New York, 1951. Social planning and social engineering.

Mead, Margaret: *Culture Patterns and Technical Change,* UNESCO, Paris, 1953. Shows the influence of technology on changing social values.

Mercer, Blaine E., and Edwin R. Carr (eds.): *Education and the Social Order,* Rinehart & Company, Inc., New York, 1957. Chap. 7, "The School as a Social Institution," and chap. 11, "The School and the Community," contain selections applicable to the relations of the school and the larger society of which it is a part.

Merriam, C. E.: *Civic Education in the United States,* Charles Scribner's Sons, New York, 1934. Esp. chap. 4, "Concurrent Agencies in Civic Education," chap. 5, and 6, "Integration of Civic Education with Social Training."

Moore, Clyde B., and William E. Cole: *Sociology in Educational Practice,* Houghton Mifflin Company, Boston, 1952. Chaps. 5–9 include a treatment of education with respect to related aspects of the institutions of religion, economics, and government, and with respect to community life. Chap. 17, "The Role of Education in Social Change," describes culture as a product of associated group living and points out the futility of leaving social change to chance.

Mumford, Lewis: "The Social Responsibilities of Teachers," in *Culture and Social Elements in the Education of Teachers,* National Education Association, Commission on Teacher Education, Educational Policies Commission, Washington, 1940. An essay by a famous American humanist.

Olsen, Clara, and N. D. Fletcher: *Learn and Live,* Alfred P. Sloan Foundation, New York, 1946. How rural elementary pupils and their teachers tried to improve the diet, clothing, and housing of their communities.

Peters, Charles C.: *The Curriculum of Democratic Education,* McGraw-Hill Book Company, Inc., New York, 1942. Part 2 is especially good for illustrations of the operation of a socialized curriculum.

Rodehaver, Myles W., William B. Axtell, and Richard E. Gross: *The Sociology of the School,* Thomas Y. Crowell Company, New York, 1957. Chap. 2 of this short volume is a discussion of the relation of the school and the values and practices of the contemporary American society.

Sirjamaki, John: *The American Family in the Twentieth Century,* Harvard University Press, Cambridge, Mass., 1953. A delightfully readable short book which emphasizes the changing structures and processes of family life in the United States.

Stratemeyer, F. B., and others: *Developing a Curriculum for Modern Living,* Bureau of Publications, Teachers College, Columbia University, New York, 1947. Concrete cases of pioneering ventures.

Teggart, Frederick J.: *The Idea of Progress: A Collection of Readings,* University of California Press, Berkeley, Calif., 1949. A leading scholarly work on the nature and meaning of progress.

DISCUSSION QUESTIONS

1. There are a number of master ideas or myths regarding the American culture which may serve as criteria for judging contemporary human relationships and legal arrangements, for example, *e pluribus unum;* life, liberty, and the pursuit of happiness; justice for all; and the "general welfare." These values are held to be binding on the state, the neighborhood, and the individual. Failure to conform to the master ideas are all too frequent. But each such failure leaves in the minds of some citizens a regret, even a feeling of guilt, that such a lapse has occurred. What, if any, are the proper roles of the pulpit, the press, civic organizations, and public education in challenging the public to recognize the lapses and to rectify them? Is it probable that the suppression of guilt feelings because realities fall short of ideals will encourage people to rationalize their behavior or beliefs in an especially aggressive way? Or project the blame for shortcomings on the injured parties?

2. To what neighborhood groups definable as gangs have you belonged at any time since you were about eleven years old? Review your own leisure-time relationships with other children prior to adoles-

cence. Can you distinguish between your feelings and behavior during pre-adolescent play associations and those during later gang memberships? What of group cohesions and of alternating leadership?

3. In your elementary, junior high, or senior high school experience, were you a member of an active home room, club, service squad, or civics class that developed such cohesive in-group loyalties, standards, and codes that it could properly be termed a gang? If so, can you identify the means by which the teacher or sponsor cultivated and exploited the gang spirit? Or did the gang spirit itself get out of hand, create hostile rivalries or priggish exclusiveness, or express itself in destructiveness or defiance? Apply these questions to college or high school secret societies.

4. List ten or fifteen examples of miseducation that sometimes characterizes developmental activities of families and neighborhoods, for example, crude table manners and incorrect language habits. Are local school standards so divorced from common practice that pupils tend to lead dual lives, conforming to the teacher's requirements in school and to family and neighborhood practices and values when outside the school? Is a middle ground between popular culture and "polite" culture feasible or desirable?

5. What aspects of the American heritage of attitudes, ideas, and behavior seem to you of greatest immediate importance for educational institutions to preserve? In preparing to reply to that question, consider such features as correct use of language, national patriotism, human sympathy, physical well-being, appreciation of beauty, neighborly cooperation, stable ego ideals, ambition for upward social mobility, skepticism toward the mores, foresight, optimism, scientific attitudes and reflective thinking, and religious beliefs.

6. It is generally considered desirable for young people to understand and to adapt themselves to the inconsistent, emotionalized attitudes and behaviors of adults and for adults similarly to understand and deal with children. Is occasional recourse by teachers to impatience, blame, and punishment as responses to their own fatigue and frustration therefore justifiable? Should a teacher ever apologize to his pupils for his own occasional lapses into such emotionalized behavior?

PART FOUR

Dominant American Cultural Patterns and Trends

10

Wealth, Prestige, and Power

THE HIGH REGARD FOR WEALTH

Educators, like most other citizens, believe that the American state is purposeful. They are accordingly deeply concerned with the values and hopes that motivate men to individual and collective effort. So far as men act rationally, their values and hopes determine which experiences and ends they seek and which they avoid. In the American society, as in any other, there is wide variation among individuals and among groups about what they find desirable and what undesirable; nevertheless, there are some values which can be said to dominate any given society at a particular time. In the United States, as in other contemporary Western societies, the desire to attain wealth, prestige, and power is an important force in the lives of most people.

The American society is, to a considerable extent, a "this-worldly" one, attuned to the present rather than the past. It has, throughout its short history, always been oriented to its present, a fact which, perhaps, springs primarily from the nature of the origins of the American state: born in revolution, it sought to break with the past it rejected. Place such a new nation on a half-explored continent abounding in natural wealth yet to be exploited, and it is not difficult to understand

199

why economic considerations became so early in the national life major reasons for assigning individuals and groups to places of high prestige and power.

Sources of the Regard for Wealth

The American people turned with ready will and great hope to the transformation of a wide expanse of the North American continent into a land of material comfort and plenty. It is not strange that they came to value most those men who took an active and easily observed part in this task, the doers, the builders, those who wrought wealth from the storehouse of nature and those who designed and commanded business organizations which produced and distributed economic goods and services.

It is largely for reasons of history, therefore, that private economic enterprise has been one of the major cultural dynamics of the American nation. It is because of the dominance of economic enterprise that the language and concepts of business have attained so significant a place in social affairs, while ethical and aesthetic values are typically subordinated to and limited by economic considerations. To the man in the street, even "value" is most likely to mean economic value and "motive" to mean economic motive. Still, he knows that man does not live by bread alone, and he sometimes feels, and more rarely acknowledges, the ambivalence he experiences.

The Role of Economic Values

It is generally true that in Western European and American societies, economic pressures and values have played important, and sometimes dominant, roles in human relations—in political, religious, educational, and social-class organizations. The influence of economic considerations is felt, too, in such aspects of life as those involving health, law, and the relations of ethnic and racial majorities and minorities. One question that the social realist always finds it necessary to ask about any public question or project is: Whose economic interests are behind it, and whose economic advantage will be enhanced by the proposal being made? [1]

In the United States, prestige and power are intimately related to wealth and its pursuit. It is not enough simply to know that this relationship exists; understanding of these major dynamics of American

[1] Charles A. Beard, *The Economic Basis of History: An Economic Interpretation of the Constitution of the United States,* The Macmillan Company, New York, 1935, p. xvii. Beard, in this instance, referred only to theories of national power and states' rights.

life requires analysis of the background and historical development of this relationship.

The "economic man," acting under the stimulating hope of material gain and the fear of material loss, was postulated by some English economists of the eighteenth and nineteenth centuries. Although mitigated somewhat by the belief that in the clash of innumerable self-interests some would offset others and ultimate benefit would redound to society, personal selfishness came to be elevated to a status of inevitability and, in degree, to respectability. Such elevation of individual selfishness appealed especially to those oftentimes energetic and efficient business leaders who thus justified their personal acquisitivism.[2]

FREE ENTERPRISE PROTECTED AND FOSTERED BY GOVERNMENT

The irrepressible advance of the commercial and industrial revolutions in the eighteenth and nineteenth centuries undermined the effectiveness of legal structures that had protected the great land-holders. It also weakened the influence of the ecclesiastical morality which monarchs and landed aristocracies had established. If economic and civic anarchy were to be avoided, some revisions of state and church regulations were obviously called for. How to make such revisions realistically and intelligently became a primary challenge for liberal intellectuals.

What these thinkers sought was freedom from economic restrictions without the loss of private ownership and security of property. This somewhat inconsistent combination implied a dependence on government and on other institutions to assure property rights while, at the same time, there was to be no interference with, nor condemnation of, anarchic business practices. To resolve this paradox, the "classical" economists formulated a rationalization—free enterprise and *laissez faire* restrained by "natural law." [3] Government, according to this verbalism, would still protect property at home and abroad and act as umpire if entrepreneurs disagreed among themselves; otherwise, it would let the economic machine and its machinations alone.[4]

[2] Cf. Marquis W. Childs and Douglass Cater, *Ethics in a Business Society,* Harper & Brothers, New York, 1954, p. 38.

[3] Cf. Thurman W. Arnold, *The Folklore of Capitalism,* Yale University Press, New Haven, Conn., 1937, chap. 1.

[4] As noted later in this chapter, however, Smith, Mill, and other apologists for *laissez faire* assigned important constructive and corrective functions to the state.

This rationalization was not generally a conscious intent to deceive or harmonize what is fundamentally disharmonious or to make the worse appear the better reasoning. Indeed, Adam Smith, David Ricardo, Jeremy Bentham, John Stuart Mill, Robert Owen, Pierre Proudhon, and other philosophic economists were humanitarians, sympathetic with the oppressed and unfortunate. Their hypotheses and recommendations seemed to them most likely to foster a society dedicated to human welfare.[5]

The Ethics of Christianity

The great difficulty lay in the fact that Christian morals and ethics were basically antagonistic to business morals and ethics, however alike the slogans and aspirations of humanitarians and economists. Almost everyone in Europe and America claimed to adhere to Christianity, with its emphasis on self-renunciation, service, and simplicity. However, the economic *Zeitgeist* drove many self-assertive people to act in what they conceived to be their self-interest, to seek comforts and display, and even to acquire a degree of cynicism regarding the motives of those whom they served. Thus, there resulted a fundamental dichotomy within Western culture. The Christian admonition to "take no thought for the morrow" was antagonistic to the bourgeoisie morality of industry, thrift, foresight, and money making, *but the same individuals, often with complete sincerity, subscribed to both!*

This paradox called for solutions, at least partial ones. Many lawyers, clergymen, and scholars sought to supply them. Hence, a fabric of superficial doctrines and shibboleths developed which tended to provide peace of mind for the self-seeking Christian. The early Protestants espoused faith rather than works as the basis of redemption. This was easily transformed into a justification of pious protestations by men who were addicted to devious planning and a variety of compromising activities. Charity and endowents by the rich provided some relief to the poor and unfortunate, who could thereby be persuaded that humbleness and "virtue" during the earthly span would assure them glory in life beyond death. Hence, it seemed to the philanthropists that only the carper and the ingrate could point the finger of scorn at the benefactor. Even the term "enlightened self-interest" became respectable and was used by many as a justification for distrust in the good faith and honesty of their fellow men.

As a matter of fact, the outstanding theorists of "classical" economics recognized that happiness sought by economic means is psychological and hence attributable to many influences not narrowly

[5] Wesley C. Mitchell, *Lecture Notes on Types of Economic Theory*, A. M. Kelley, New York, 1949, vol. I.

definable as economic; for example, affection, health, and energy. Indeed, the concept of the "economic man" was challenged at the time as purely theoretical. Nevertheless, the assumption that man is in general moved only by the practical question of what's in it for him when he makes a significant decision attained, and has retained, widespread acceptance in Western societies.

The classical assumption that each man's striving for his own advantage would in the long run benefit society as a whole has, to be sure, considerable historical justification. It was, for instance, the economic success of individual artisans, merchants, and professionals in the towns of medieval and Renaissance Europe which led to their ultimate self-assertiveness as a class. Thus it was ultimately individual striving which led the bourgeoisie to question feudal and ecclesiastical establishments and encouraged their enunciation of democratic ideas and aspirations.

The Defiance of Free Men

Such an eruption of defiance of a repressive social order is nowhere better exemplified than in the Massachusetts Bay Colony. The men who had landed at Salem and Boston in 1629 and 1630 were impoverished and in debt for their passage to America. When they became free men, owning the land they had cleared and cultivated and the dwellings they had built, they straightway asserted their right to control their own religious and civic affairs in spite of the established theocratic colonial government.[6]

The flexibility of the American society is, in considerable measure, the product of a long process of change in economic arrangements. Values related to occupational specialization, technology, wages, money and credit, private ownership, and competition interrelate with most personal motives and values. Hence, the evolution of economic institutions and generalizations must be analyzed if contemporary American aspirations are to be understood. Emerging social ideas and legalisms are in many instances rationalizations of obsolescent economic "laws." The social revolution out of which was born the present Western world has been in vigorous process for 400 years. The resurgence of the mechanical arts and the development of protection for market places in the towns of Europe during the twelfth to the fifteenth centuries ushered in the modern capitalist economy. Political influence along with economic power passed from the feudal nobles to the guilds of artisans,

[6] Although victory for local autonomy was not fully achieved until 1689, it was as early as 1642, only twelve or thirteen years after the arrival in the New World, that the General Court (legislature) conceded considerable local jurisdiction to town congregations.

merchants, bankers, and professionals and to the monarchs whose purposes these emerging power groups served.[7] The bolder town dwellers freed themselves, bit by bit, from the encumbrances which the old feudal class system had imposed upon them. They thus stimulated other common men to aspire to similar conditions of freedom.

So the stage was set for the expression of individual ambition, the assertion of human rights, and the great struggle for political and social democracy. The revolution is still going on.

Economic acquisitivism has been readily instrumented by ingenuity, purposefulness, and assiduity; it has served many people as a shortcut to self-respect and superior social status. Material wealth is not, however, the final goal for most people; they ultimately seek the social status and power which they know ownership insures.

Power and Emotional Security

Emotional security requires some belief that one has power to satisfy his immediate wants and to assure some degree of control over his future needs. In the contemporary Western society, however, personal ownership of commodities gives less definite assurance than do investments in securities, which are claims against the future production of wealth. This projective, time-binding quality accentuates the *power* aspect of wealth. It provides the mechanism by which masterful men dominate an expanding economy. It promises them control even of the activities of men as yet unborn.[8] Nevertheless, it entails also a fear of present and future losses as well as profits; hence its ambivalence. It fosters a mixture of optimism and caution and of adventurousness and conservatism.

Acquisitivism as Means and Acquisition as an End

Acquisitivism is a dominant motivation in American life. Conspicuous success in business is generally accorded high prestige and great monetary reward. Financially succesful men and their families

---

[7] Though monarchs and nobles sometimes combined to check the growing influence of the bourgeoisie, the Crown found more effective help in the long run among bankers, merchants, and industrialists because economic power was in their hands.

[8] One justification for inheritance taxes—and even for the outright confiscation of decedents' property—has been the questionable social effect of unlimited claims against future production and, hence, power over future human beings and associations. The classical economists foresaw the need for limitation on the inheritance of great wealth; for examples, see the works of Jeremy Bentham, John Stuart Mill, and Herbert Spencer.

typically exert strong influence on American culture patterns; often, indeed, they are objects of undiscriminating adulation. Economic solvency is a minimum condition for "success" in the popular view.

Even the recurrent failures of the free enterprise system may indeed be credited with significant contributions to American practices and cultural values. The protests of those frustrated individuals and groups who have been disadvantaged in the competitive struggle have significantly affected public attitudes and policies. At times, such protests have been instrumental in the development of a public opinion which compelled governmental action to regulate business enterprise.

Acquisitivism is deeply embedded in the American ethos, but its continued dominance is neither secure nor unchallenged. Its increasing dependence upon claims against the future requires an ever-expanding spiral of production and consumption if the claims are to be realized. But every technological development is likely to upset some aspects of the economy; every political and social change in the restless populations of Europe, Asia, Africa, and Latin America threatens the assumptions of unlimited expansion of markets; every drastic and long-continued curtailment of purchasing power in any considerable segment of the American population may involve eventually almost the whole economy.

Hence, an "acquisitive society" [9] is not a secure one either for individuals or for the population as a whole. It is, indeed, peculiarly vulnerable as it becomes a kind of game wherein "victory," symbolized by pecuniary gain, prestige, and power, becomes an end. Satisfactions accruing from commodities are limited for an individual to what he and his dependents can consume during their lives, plus gifts that he may make to others. Excess acquisitions must, therefore, inevitably take on a somewhat fanciful character—black ink on paper symbolizing claims on an unknowable future.

[9] The term "acquisitive society" refers to that aspect of a capitalistically dominated culture that places high valuation on the creation of more and more wants and the enlargement and intensification of industry and commerce to satisfy them. It is a relatively recent phenomenon, a complex substitution of means for ends.

"Like a hypochondriac who is so absorbed in the processes of his own digestion that he goes to the grave before he has begun to live, industrial communities neglect the very objects for which it is worth while to acquire riches in their feverish preoccupation with the means by which riches can be acquired." By permission of the publishers from R. H. Tawney, *The Acquisitive Society,* copyright 1920 by Harcourt, Brace and Company, Inc., New York, copyright 1948 by R. H. Tawney, pp. 183–184.

Characteristics of Power and Prestige Acquisitivism

There is some evidence that acquisitivism as it operates in business is not always directly related to the accumulation of wealth. Among the managers of large corporations, according to one study, acquisitivism and wealth seeking are curiously estranged. What most corporation executives really seek, according to Elmo Roper, who bases his opinion on extensive surveys, is emotional security, the ingredients of which are: (1) recognition of achievement; (2) autonomy of management; (3) dignity of position; and (4) rewards paid in leisure. Money reward seems not to be the prime consideration. If needs for security and status, as defined above, are cared for, the individual's drive for profit would probably disappear once a minimal level of income and assets were achieved.[10]

Whether this conclusion is applicable to people other than corporation managers is, of course, uncertain. It nonetheless seems a reasonable guess that, for most businessmen, the fear of loss and hope of gain are attenuated by the more potent motives of reputation both for "sound" business judgment, energy, and foresight and, quite as important, for "smooth" human relationships.[11]

The American society, to a large degree, is business-dominated. The way the honored businessman relates himself to his environment— how he dresses, greets people, and avoids friction, and the nature of his house, his recreation, and his philanthropic interests; even the attributes of his wife and children—influences American social standards and the concept of the "desirable" personality. Often unconsciously, indeed, an individual puts himself up for sale; the hoped-for price includes not only a financial return but also promotion, prestige, and power.

The "Salable" Personality

The main features of the kinds of personality which are "salable" are repeatedly delineated in articles and speeches prepared by public relations experts who are employed by the status-seeking, successful businessman. The public press and other mass-communication media depend largely upon advertising for revenue; they therefore pound the stereotype of the business leader by playing continually on his great abilities and services along with his recreational interests, estates, and philanthropic contributions. This constant reiteration of the "successful

---

[10] Albert Lauterbach, *Men, Motives, and Money,* Cornell University Press, Ithaca, N.Y., 1954, p. 19.

[11] T. K. Quinn, *Giant Business: Threat to Democracy,* Exposition Press, New York, 1953, esp. chap. 15.

business personality" establishes the major goal for most ambitious youths.[12]

It is not that the figure so popularized is not reasonably close to the truth. Outstanding business executives are characteristically good organizers. Their security typically involves ambition and compulsive work without neurotic tensions; they generally seek and enjoy being busy under pressure. To them, profit is frequently viewed as a standard of achievement rather than an end in itself. They are usually conservative in their single-mindedness on the job and in dress and manner, but quite the opposite regarding technological and administrative matters. They ordinarily have the ability to make other people work effectively and the gift for avoiding antagonism. They are typically convinced that their services help to satisfy human desires.[13] Profit seeking as an end is more generally a preoccupation of stockholders than of business executives.[14]

Acquisitivism and Other Motivations

Two other traits, already mentioned, must be noted, since they somewhat modify the rather universal characteristics of the "successful" executive type. In some cases it is an instinct for contrivance or an instinct for workmanship that must find satisfaction. In other cases, it is the adventure of gambling that beckons. Occasionally, these two kinds of urges combine in a single personality.[15]

Another caveat should be entered against the oversimplification of the successful businessman's motivations and overemphasis on acquisitivism. The basic, if somewhat hidden, conflict between democratic and religious ethics and competitive self-seeking makes for a fundamental dichotomy in valuations. Though money is generally accepted as at least a minimal element in the standard of "success," there is, nonetheless, a more or less hidden charge of guilt against wealth as a standard of success. This sense of guilt about money sometimes reflects jealousy on the part of the less successful. It sometimes expresses the ideological disdain for wealth seeking which is inherent in American religious and democratic tradition. In either case, it foments a malaise of conscience in many financially successful people. This guilt feeling is exemplified in the common aversion to accepting money gifts and

[12] *Ibid.*, chaps. 4, 19.

[13] Lauterbach, *op. cit.*, p. 12.

[14] *Ibid.*, p. 22.

[15] Cf. F. W. Taussig, *Inventors and Money-makers,* The Macmillan Company, New York, 1915, p. 11, and Thorstein Veblen, *The Instinct of Workmanship and the State of the Industrial Arts,* The Viking Press, Inc., New York, 1914, pp. 103–104.

the social stigma of tips (or, recently, when gifts are large, payola) for services and favors. An inversion of this charge of guilt is an illogical stigma attached to financial failure; a businessman who does not succeed is usually regarded with disdain.

Man is universally an insecure being. From the time he emerges from his mother's womb until his death, the typical individual is engaged in a search for security. He takes joy in adventure, but he also longs for recognition, human affection, and sympathy. In a word, wealth grants him little security if it is not associated with public respect; the adventure of seeking the one involves the risk of forfeiting the other.

The "purely self-assertive" animal, the stereotypical rugged individual, the product of unlimited private enterprise and competition, has seldom, if ever, emerged as a personality. The corporation businessman is restrained in his search for monetary success by two factors. He may recognize that ruthlessness within his organization and among his business associates is self-defeating; he must play the game according to the rules or accept ostracism. Furthermore, there has developed, especially since the depression of the 1930s, a public demand that businessmen accept the idea that social responsibility ought to accompany economic power.[16] The businessman is reasonably apt to be aware of this public demand. This demand and its recognition are as yet only partially realized, but the trend is unmistakable; indeed the very survival of capitalism will depend in part on the extent to which economic power becomes socially responsible, not only in the United States, but wherever else it exists in the world.

BACKGROUND OF THE ACQUISITIVE SOCIETY

As industrial and financial capitalism develops and expands, the outright ownership of natural resources is supplemented and in large degree replaced by ownership of leases, concessions, and franchises which give legal sanction for the exploitation of property. The

[16] Such maturity of judgment is more common among businessmen attached to long established industries than it is to the *nouveaux riches*, for example, men who have made a killing by gambling, whether in stocks, oil prospecting, or rackets. By and large, the same variation is likely among the wives and progeny of moneyed men. Cf. A. A. Berle, Jr., *The 20th Century Capitalistic Revolution*, Harcourt, Brace and Company, Inc., New York, 1954. Exceptions to this proposition can be found, of course: for example, the collusive price fixing which resulted in the jailing in early 1961 of several high-ranking officials of large firms in the electrical industry.

present unresolved questions of public versus private development of water power, forests, mineral resources, water-fronts, and other resouces in the United States are counterparts of the contemporary problems of land-hungry peoples of Asia, Africa, and Latin America. The exploitation for private advantage of economic opportunities that exist independently of an individual's efforts is increasingly being challenged.[17]

Changes in the Forms and Meaning of Ownership

As the character of Western civilization changed through the centuries, the forms and meaning of ownership also changed. In Athens, for example, power and prestige passed from the landed aristocrats to the commercial oligarchs and then to popular leaders of the citizens; in each stage, the art forms and religious institutions agreeable to those in power were encouraged. In the Roman Republic and Empire, military conquest played the important role in providing property advantage and, hence, power and prestige for successive elites. In medieval and Renaissance Europe, the landed nobility, both secular and ecclesiastical, were undercut by the monarchical state and the rising bourgeoisie, whose partnership lasted until the democratic revolutions of the eighteenth and nineteenth centuries.

As pecuniary advantage, political power, and social prestige are transferred from one section of the population to another, a strange kind of lag develops. The actual characteristics of those who have lately come to power do not at once become the symbolic indicators of their dominance. Instead, each segment of the population, as it rises to dominance, seeks to fortify its class status by appropriating the customs and accouterments of the upper class. Thus, as the industrial revolution progressed, wealthy bourgeoisie became landlords, maintained country estates, endowed hospitals, schools, and charitable institutions, sought political honors, and adopted the forms of leisure pursuits, dress, speech, and other aspects of the manners and codes of the aristocracy.

An interesting ambivalence in outlook often resulted. Efforts of men-on-the-make to acquire prestige by infiltrating the ranks of the socially select have encouraged civic responsibility, "good taste," and conservatism, whereas measures for acquiring material wealth and economic power have demanded opportunistic adventures with new ideas, techniques, and social controls. This ambivalence influences the institutions successful businessmen dominate. The codes embodied in

[17] Differential rent (land values depending on high fertility, mineral or power resources, or location favorable for business advantage) is in some degree taken into account by government in levying taxes. Absolute rent is abolished in the case of government ownership and utilization for public purposes.

Protestant churches, service clubs, public and private schools, the rituals of government, and the "gentlemanly" codes of leisure-time pursuits all exemplify more or less inconsistent ideals: that of winning immediate victory through innovation and ingenuity and that of the moral, spiritual, and intellectual exaltation associated with religion, learning, justice, and sportsmanship.[18] Such ambivalence has been a fruitful source of rationalization for seemingly contradictory acts and attitudes.

The Concept of the "Culturally Inferior"

The cleavages between social classes in Europe—and, in lesser degree, the United States—remain as a relic of feudalism. Upward mobility requires some counterpart of serfs to whom middle-class people can feel superior and, hence, to whom can be attributed inherent and cultural inferiority. The stigmata of such attributed inferiority may be pigmentation, foreign language and customs, or religious sectarianism. Racial, ethnic, and religious minorities thus serve as substitutes for peasants, the traditionally "inferior" segment of European societies.

Prestige seeking is, however, somewhat self-defeating in a society characterized by a dynamic economy and democratic politics. Individuals and groups to whom inferiority has previously been attributed attain economic competence and political power so frequently and rapidly that they themselves become socially mobile.[19] Their eagerness to share in the patterns of possession and "style of life" which they associate with the upper classes makes them important consumers of economic goods and services and, hence, in considerable degree the arbiters of what goods and services shall be produced. In one sense, therefore, they effectively influence, if they do not quite determine, the

[18] These "aristocratic" codes are, to be sure, quite unrealistic, except as abstractions. In actual fact, historical aristocracies have been quite as predatory and oppressive in their behavior toward inferiors as the *nouveaux riches* of the capitalist revolution. Lip service to the ideals of *noblesse oblige* has been, however, a major symbol of aristocracies; and this symbolism has been very potent in shaping the codes to which socially mobile people have attached importance. The sincere and effective services contributed by businessmen as laymen of religious institutions and as unpaid members of government commissions, service clubs, and youth-serving organizations are in large part expressions of their civic codes.

[19] Regarding social and occupational mobility, see W. Lloyd Warner and J. C. Abegglen, *Occupational Mobility in American Business and Industry*, University of Minnesota Press, Minneapolis, 1955, and C. Wright Mills, *White Collar*, Oxford University Press, New York, 1953, esp. chap. 4.

courses of action of entrepreneurs of upper- and upper-middle class status. So far as social prestige depends on widely distributed economic power to provide a mass market for consumer goods and on political power to affect the quality of civil and economic rights, prestige based on restriction of luxuries to those whose families have already "arrived" becomes relatively meaningless.

Transition from Free to Managed Economy

A relatively loose-knit economy characterized eighteenth- and nineteenth-century Western Europe and America. In such economies, the venturesome expression of acquisitivism by the entrepreneur served a constructive social purpose. The entrepreneur participated in obtaining the money required by his business, buying or renting a factory, shop, and machinery, and hiring superintendents, sales representatives, and laborers. Generally, his productive and distributive activities bore direct relation to the equation of supply and demand.[20] If and when he miscalculated potential demand for his product, or was underpriced by his competitors, he made the necessary correction if possible; else, he soon was eliminated. Thereby the more efficient entrepreneur survived.

It was to the workers' advantage if production and distribution increased; to their disadvantage if they shrank. Under conditions of unrestricted free enterprise, however, employees lacked power as voters and consumers and they had not yet developed bold, calculating, disciplined unions. Discharged laborers found other employment if they could, or they and their families became charity cases. Labor was considered a dispensable commodity, like wool or shoes, purchasable as needed; the welfare of workers as human beings was not the entrepreneur's concern.

So long as the acquisitive culture was limited to relatively small segments of the population, it was an excrescence on an economy pri-

[20] The law of supply and demand assumes that price varies directly, but not necessarily proportionately, with demand for a commodity; that is, increase in demand favors higher price, which brings to the market an increase in goods or services to meet the demand; decrease in demand tends to lower prices and so discourage marginal suppliers. The operation of this law is most clearly recognizable in the case of perishable goods; for example, strawberries "in season" are relatively low in price to create large demand lest they spoil; out-of-season demand would exceed supply except that a higher price eliminates marginal consumers. More durable goods respond less immediately to the law because they may be held in reserve in the hope of a more favorable price situation. Even perishable goods may be held by means of refrigeration and preservatives until a glut is over.

marily concerned with the production of food, shelter, and clothing. It provided supplementary goods and limited luxuries for purchasers who were both able and willing to pay for them rather than to produce them for themselves. And thereby a new, and perhaps transitory, economy took shape.

In twentieth-century United States, and in somewhat lesser degree throughout the Western world, the major challenge to the people of large as well as small communities, has become how to live in a society dominated by acquisition. As technological invention and specialization transformed the patterns of production, employment, and consumption, the populace has come to be increasingly regimented as to when, and how, they shall work, what they shall wear, what find amusing, what eat, and what approve.

The Business of Public Relations

Selling the people on what to buy and trying to sell them on what to believe and what measures and organizations to support and on how to speak, behave, and vote have become a specialized applied science in the hands of public-relations experts—a business, generally quite amoral, conducted for the purpose of making money for the expert. Attempts are made to avoid price competition and hide the identity of the content of products under brand names and then to feature insignificant if not wholly fictitious differences by means of soap operas, slogans, jingles, colorful displays, and any other forms of exploitation of natural or man-made facilities that the expert can control. Mass purchasing must be developed to support mass production; hence, mass appeal through mass entertainment is directed almost inevitably to the lower levels of intellectual and "cultural" appreciation. Only the hardy and somewhat isolated individual escapes conformity either by cynicism or avoidance or by creating alternative patterns of consumption.[21]

[21] "The major count in the social indictment of advertising in the United States is not the amount of our resources which it employs, or the specific deceptions which it practices. No, it is rather that, despite the tremendous social influence which it exerts, it has no social goals and no sense of public responsibility, short of avoiding flagrant violations of truth and decency. It is this lack of social responsibility coordinate with the power which it holds that has made advertising a cause for concern in America." Charles M. Hession, S. M. Miller, and Curwen Stoddart, The Dynamics of the American Economy, Alfred A. Knopf, Inc., New York, 1956, p. 183. Used by permission.

Acquisitivism and Ownership

The structure of ownership of the modern corporation also contributes to the dominance of acquisitivism. Stock and bond ownership is widely dispersed through a large fraction of the American population; a considerable part of corporate investments is now made by ordinary wage and salary earners who invest either directly in corporate securities or indirectly as holders of insurance policies, pension fund contributions, or bank deposits. And the plain fact is that individuals and trustees who purchase stocks and bonds do not typically do so because they are interested in the production or distribution process of their companies, but because they hope or believe that dividends or interest will be forthcoming.

The Common Man: Master or Victim?

Acquisition rather than the processes of production and merchandising is the primary concern of the typical investor. He is ordinarily not himself an entrepreneur. His "private enterprise" consists of having funds at his disposal and of estimating the hazards of different alternatives for "putting the funds to work."

Once he has purchased securities that seem to him to hold financial promise, he finds it difficult, if not quite impossible, to judge objectively the social effects of the policies and practices of the business to which he has entrusted his treasure. Indeed, the transactions of large-scale businesses are so complex that the technical facts, the bookkeeping entries, and the economic motives involved in the decisions of corporation managers are beyond the ken of the typical investor. The effects of these decisions on the industry, on society in general, and on the prospects of the investor can only be evaluated in terms of confidence in the competence and honesty of the management.[22]

Both as consumer and as investor, the common man's decisions become increasingly oriented to the future. He frequently buys goods by promising to pay for them in months, even years, to come. The securities in which he invests are valued in terms of anticipated future earnings of corporations. These corporations, in turn, use their resources in large part to modernize and expand their plants and to purchase securities in other enterprises in the expectation that future earnings will justify their present investments. Judgments have to be made re-

---

[22] State and national laws and supervising agencies endeavor to protect investors and even gamblers against dishonesty, machination, and gross error of judgment by managers in whose hands other people's money is placed.

garding future supply, demand, domestic and world political and economic conditions, the strength and attitudes of organized labor, political parties, consumer organizations, and a host of other factors.

Hence the paradox: collectively, the common man conditions, if he does not altogether determine, the future of the acquisitive economy; individually, however, he is almost helplessly subject to it. His immediate competence and power to affect decisions of management are slight, but as citizen, consumer, and worker he ultimately confirms or denies the adequacy of those decisions.

His acquisitivism requires risk, and risk implies insecurity. His employment and his income vary with the conditions of prosperity or recession. His investments capitalize judgments and hopes regarding future events. And no one can predict with certainty the future of the economy.

The unavoidable risk can be somewhat lessened by certain governmental fiscal policies, social planning, and the formation of cartels in industry. But each of these devices limits free enterprise and regiments acquisitive men. The justification for any one of them is that it helps guard against the potential chaos of uninhibited power and prestige seeking by cunning and energetic men who may not realize that their own security depends on the welfare of common men.

Humane Sentiments Still Powerful

Despite the dominance of self-seeking in American life, there are much older and more fundamental attitudes and valuations which in the long run serve as criteria for judging and limiting economic freedom. There are many attributes that have their being apart from "economic man." Among them are consciousness of community interdependence, the efficacy of mutual aid, high regard for the "Christian virtues" (which are really as ancient as the Stone Age), and loyalties to institutions devoted to human brotherhood. In a sense they are beneficent "cultural lags," [23] inheritances from the precapitalistic world of interpersonal concerns, a world in which family, neighborhood, religious congregation, and even the manor presupposed the mutual acceptance of responsibilities.

These attitudes provide bases for checking the excesses of acquisitive men by reenforcing popular dissent regarding the extension of corporative power and privilege. Thus, by a framework of moral and legal sanctions, they set limits on competition and conflict and help to determine what kinds of power hierarchy are endurable.

[23] That is, the relatively slow change of social ideas and practices compared to that of technology and economic organization.

Popular attachment to the slogans and ideals of humane religion and social democracy restrains ruthless men, not only as individuals, but also as managers of impersonal organizations. "A decent regard for the opinions of mankind" remains pervasive in American culture; it acts as a conservative check on callous self-interest precisely because it generally diminishes the prestige and power of those who disregard it.

The general "cultural lag" of moral imperatives is supplemented by a more specific code of elite values derived from medieval aristocracy. To this aristocracy, business morality was the "great heresy." It defied many of the ideas and standards of the privileged classes, sanctioned by God and church and justified by the teachings of Greek and medieval philosophers. Elite morality was surely inconsistent with universal humanitarianism, but it did impose on its devotees a code of chivalry and an ideal of *noblesse oblige*.

Aristocratic Attitudes

Residues of aristocratic attitudes remain in contemporary upper-upper social classes and in those who aspire to admittance to that charmed circle. The negative aspect of the heritage is a snobbish disdain for those directly engaged in trade. The positive and far more important aspect is the "gentle tradition"; that is, "well-bred" persons are unobtrusive, considerate of others, responsible for community welfare, and restrained in giving vent to passion. In a mobile society, these qualities associated, or believed to be associated, with upper-upper class members are criteria which are significant in the determination of class membership.

People interested in high prestige have typically sought to exemplify the characteristics of the elite. Although the dynamism of acquisitive men has threatened the *status quo* of privileged elites, their revolutionary influence has been greatly diminished by their tendency to exalt many of the ideals of religion and chivalry. The infiltrations have worked both ways; while acquisitive, mobile men have absorbed elite morality, these same elites have come to accept, even to condone, practices which they previously rejected.

Continuing Conflict between Self-interest and Ethics

In the United States, the absence of a cohesive aristocracy and the dominance of Protestant sects have encouraged much rationalization and accommodation between elites and acquisitive men. There are, however, certain historical factors in this accommodation which antedated even the growth of medieval towns. Indeed, the triumph of Christianity during the Roman Empire of the third and fourth centuries resulted from the church's success in working bigger and better miracles than its rival religious orders quite as much as it did from its recognition of the equality of men in the sight of God.[24] That is to say, the hope of temporal security, self-respect, and material gain was as truly a basis for the support of the Christian revolution of fourth-century Rome as was any grasp of the ethic of Jesus or the hope of reward in after life.

The temporal claims and assertions of authority by the higher clergy—bishops, cardinals, and popes—carried a paradoxical union of earthly glory and humble acceptance of God's will by the faithful. St. Benedict, St. Francis, and others might withdraw from the conflicting ideologies, teaching their followers to disregard earthly rewards and to work humbly and humanely with their God. Albigenses and Waldenses might accept the consequences of their challenge to church discipline and doctrines. But the dichotomy was not resolved.

The Inquisition

The sale of beneficences rationalized the purchasing during life of surceases from suffering after death. The church elevated dogma above reason and thus set a pattern of censorship to protect vested interests. Imposed orthodoxies and conformities, favors for institutional benefactors, and exaltation of dogmas still characterize much of Western culture.[25]

In a word, neither the capitalist nor the Protestant revolution made a clear break with the past. Customs and stereotypes remained, no matter how irreconcilable with each other or with whatever might be new in the revolutionary ideas and practices. The "truth" of a Luther or a Calvin might accommodate itself to realities of political and economic power, but it could brook no ideological challenge to its own "self-evident" validity. Capitalistic apologists might vaunt freedom and human rights, individual enterprise, and competition, while, at the same time, the individual capitalist might endeavor to limit the freedom of employees and of rivals, to ignore human rights by considering labor merely as commodity, and to suppress the enterprise and competition of those whose success might injure him.

[24] Cf. S. J. Case, *Origins of Christian Supernaturalism,* University of Chicago Press, Chicago, 1948.

[25] Analogous authoritative impositions long preceded those of the Christian religion. They are exemplified by the supernatural sanctions for power and taboos among primitives. They had been in practical effect in Greek and Roman religious and political structures. They were approved in Plato's *Republic* and *Laws.*

Man Universally a Rationalizer

What has been noted here is in large degree a phenomenon of social and individual psychology. Every individual tends to see things and to interpret causes and effects according to the impact that the event or fact makes on his desires and concepts of well-being. Hence, the historical manifestations of human institutions give only color and form to the expressions of the original nature of man. Man is richly endowed to find justifications that seem reasonable, albeit often superficially so, for believing and acting in accordance with his own interests. Capitalism did not invent this practice; it has, however, made fully as extreme and effective use of it as any antecedent system of power.

Though born of challenge to restraint, capitalism, once supreme, has entrenched itself in law, government, and folklore. It imposes tariffs and other restraints of trade. Corporations limit individual liability and substitute a fictitious personality and a synthetic moral code for individual conscience. Business concerns subsidize political parties and maintain lobbyists and experts to influence governmental officials and legislators. Economically favored men in all good conscience thus foster their private interests.

Profits which have heretofore been justified as bait for enterprise and boldness are now demanded as "rights" for all business undertakings whether or not social contribution, ingenuity, or venture characterizes them. The slogan of free enterprise publicized by promoters, financiers, and organizers is sometimes directed in practice to the suppression of new ventures (by individuals or by the people as a whole through government) if such ventures threaten established economic practices or institutions.

There is, of course, no implication that these attitudes and activities are consciously and intentionally fraudulent. They are, as already asserted, rationalizations by which "good" reasons (or at least plausible ones) are found by human beings in order to harmonize their desires and self-interests with social and ethical canons. They often involve no more than a subtle shift of words and concepts to settings in which they do not in fact fit—as in the examples just cited of *assured profits* as *rights* for investors and business adventurers and the *limitations on new ventures on behalf of free enterprise,* if such ventures threaten established investments.

In a word, when investors find that their risks would be minimized or their chances of success increased by appropriate social action or public opinion, there is, of course, strong economic motivation to bring about such sentiment and action. There frequently results a project or program that employs the high-flown phraseology of democracy, religion, and ethics calculated to bring about the desired sentiment and action. Classic examples of this kind of rationalization and propaganda are the Puritan and bourgeoisie–common-man revolutions of seventeenth-century England and eighteenth-century America and France,[26] the establishment of the Amercian government,[27] the revolt of the manufacturer and financier against the Southern planters' aristocracy—the Civil War[28]—and more recently the establishment of the Liberty League during the depression to minimize the popular support for the New Deal.

Emphasis on the exploitation of sentiment and political action by "big business" and its sycophants must not be allowed to obscure the somewhat parallel assertiveness of more humble property owners and economic venturers. Sometimes, as noted above, they have made common cause with their wealthier contemporaries. At other times, the interests have been in conflict, as in the case of the successful political revolts of farmers and artisans resulting in the bloodless revolutions of 1800 and 1828, "the social-justice" agitations and reforms of 1885 to 1914, the continuing subsidization of agriculture, and the demands for a larger share of government contracts by small businesses.[29] Indeed, the political and public relations campaigns of farm organizations, labor unions, cooperative societies, and regional pressure groups are in most cases economically motivated propaganda to offset that of "big business."

Meaningless Phrases Become Accepted Shibboleths

Under the excitement of such propaganda and action campaigns, it is almost inevitable that outdated slogans and terms should become significant, though in fact meaningless, rallying points for one side or the other. Thus "state capitalism," "government competition with" private business, and "paternalism" are opprobrious charges sometimes flung by corporation propagandists. Yet these same corporations have government charters which are based on the assumption that the businesses exist for social service; their patents, privileges, and property depend on government administrative and legal institutions; in many cases they have been benefited by protective tariffs; and in time of emergency, they are obliged to depend upon state patronage.

[26] Cf. George Soule, *The Coming American Revolution,* The Macmillan Company, New York, 1934.
[27] Cf. Beard, *op. cit.*
[28] *Ibid.*
[29] Cf. Charles A. Beard, *The Rise of American Civilization,* The Macmillan Company, New York, 1927, chap. 18.

Inconsistencies of Puritan Morality

The confusing application of terms and slogans to conditions that they do not fit is not new in history. Nowhere has it been better exemplified than in seventeenth-century England. There religious dissenters and businessmen challenged the established order of which the church and the crown were guardians. Puritans, Presbyterians, and Separatists found support among small landholders, merchants, manufacturers, and shopkeepers—common men of the industrial revolution. Religious protest and economic revolt found common ground in resistance to restraint. The outcome was the Puritan revolution and the establishment of English liberties.[30]

Victory did not resolve the inner contradictions of the capitalist-Protestant partnership, however. The objectives of businessmen, as such, were earthly treasure and the accession to the equipment and luxuries of the nobility and clergy; whereas the motives of Puritans and Separatists, as such, were religious sincerity, austerity, and justification to God through faith and good works. *But in large degree they were the same men!* Hence, within their individual personalities there grew up divisive and contradictory values which could only be reconciled by the most strained rationalization.

So matters stood through the eighteenth and half the nineteenth centuries. Pietism and self-denial went hand in hand with the values of industry, thrift, and profit. Moralism and patriotism flourished along with exploitation, smuggling, sharp practices, and "watching the main chance."

The substantial citizen gained in social respect over the merely virtuous one. "For the Protestant," says Mumford,[31] "business became holy, not least because it tended to become more and more odious in its performance . . . To save money by paring the costs of production, to sacrifice present goods for future rewards, to drive one's self for the good of one's soul, and to drive others quite as unmercifully for the sake of *their* souls; all this was the very essence of the new Puritan morality."

[30] Carleton J. H. Hayes, *A Political and Cultural History of Modern Europe,* The Macmillan Company, New York, 1933, vol. I, pp. 440ff.

[31] By permission of Harcourt, Brace and Company, Inc., New York, from Lewis Mumford, *The Condition of Man,* copyright 1944 by Lewis Mumford, p. 199. The term Puritan morality frequently has application to the low-church Anglicans known as Puritans. It applies, however, to all bourgeoisie groups whose rationalizations of spiritual and material conflicts required them to challenge the doctrines of the medieval church and nobility.

The idea of laying up treasures in Heaven for advantage in life beyond death was subtly transformed into providing for rainy days on earth and for piling up wealth for purposes of prestige and power in later years—or even for tomorrow if one were clever enough to leap into the saddle by means of a quick deal.

SUMMARY

The preceding pages indicate how it has come about that acquisitiveness and corporate industry play a dominant role in the lives of Western peoples. When, as is peculiarly the case in the United States, an entire population depends on technology for its daily occupations and leisure, governments at all levels are obliged to make sure that machines are supplied with materials, that there are workers of sufficient skills to manipulate them, that there are markets where products will be purchased, and, sometimes, that there are guarantees of credit. Legislative, judicial, and administrative agencies accept as their primary mandate the support of technological processes because the very sustenance of the population depends on them.

Whatever the ideas and ideals of a nation, they must be instrumented within the framework of its economy; else, there is no nation. The dual challenge to American government is, therefore, how to fulfill its covenant to foster life, liberty, and the pursuit of happiness, to establish justice, insure tranquillity, and promote the general welfare and at the same time safeguard and expand the technology which undergirds the economy.

Economic feasibility and the dominant motivations of acquisition, power, and prestige effectively control the ideas, principles, and, in large measure, the actions of government and of other social institutions. More is required of governments, family, church, and school, however, than acting as umpire or as policeman. Planning and the effecting of plans are called for.

Vigorously intelligent American citizens need to examine and evaluate both their democratic ideology and their technological organization if their judgments regarding social policies and programs are to be soundly based. This is the subject matter of the next chapter.

SELECTED REFERENCES

Beard, Charles A.: *An Economic Interpretation of the Constitution of the United States,* The Macmillan Company, New York, 1935. The classical interpretation of the United States Constitution as an economic document. This edition has a new introduction.

————, and Mary R. Beard: *The Rise of American Civilization,* The Macmillan Company, New York, 1927. Vol. I covers the cultural, economic, and political conditions almost to the Civil War. Vol. II explains the complicated interplay of economic and political forces from 1850 to 1925.

Childs, Marquis W., and Douglass Cater: *Ethics in a Business Society,* Harper & Brothers, New York, 1954. An intelligent and lucid inquiry into the applicability of the Christian ethic in an economically competitive society.

Clark, J. M.: *Preface to Social Economics: Essays on Economic Theory and Social Problems,* Farrar & Rinehart, Inc., New York, 1936. Treatment of the relative truth and falsity of earlier economic theory by a scholar who acknowledges the ethical responsibilities of the social scientist.

Commager, Henry Steele: *The American Mind: An Interpretation of American Thought since the 1880's,* Yale University Press, New Haven, Conn., 1950. The impacts of social and economic developments in recent decades on cultural and political practices and theories.

Hayes, Carleton J. H.: *A Political and Cultural History of Modern Europe,* The Macmillan Company, New York, 1935. Volume I is particularly germane to this chapter. It explains the political, economic, intellectual, and religious developments and conflicts of sixteenth-, seventeenth-, and eighteenth-century Europe and the emergence of the nation states. The author's judgments are conservative in temper.

Huberman, Leo: *Man's Worldly Goods: The Story of the Wealth of Nations,* Harper & Brothers, New York, 1936.

————: *We, the People: The Drama of America,* rev. ed., Harper & Brothers, New York, 1947. Both of these works by Huberman are persuasive interpretations of the economic and political developments in Europe and America.

Hazlitt, Henry: *Economics in One Lesson,* Harper & Brothers, New York, 1946. An apology for orthodox economic principles.

Lauterbach, Albert: *Man, Motives, and Money: Psychological Frontiers of Economics,* Cornell University Press, Ithaca, N.Y., 1954. A penetrating and lucid explanation of economic institutions and their backgrounds in men's aspirations and fears.

Lerner, Max: *America as a Civilization,* Simon and Schuster, Inc., New York, 1957. A comprehensive and readable explanation and evaluation of life and thought in the United States.

McConnell, John W.: *The Basic Teachings of the Great Economists,* The New Home Library, New York, 1943. An enlightening exposition of theories and of the cultures to which they applied.

Mitchell, Wesley C.: *Lecture Notes on Types of Economic*

Theory, A. M. Kelley, New York, 1949. Two volumes of lectures which deal not only with the evolving theories of economic philosophers but also with the societies which affected their beliefs.

Mumford, Lewis: *The Conditions of Man,* Harcourt, Brace and Company, Inc., New York, 1944.

————: *The Culture of Cities,* Harcourt, Brace and Company, Inc., New York, 1938.

————: *Technics and Civilization,* Harcourt, Brace and Company, New York, 1934. These three volumes by Mumford provide discriminating explanations of the development and contemporary state of Western culture.

Ross, Edward A.: *Sin and Society,* Houghton Mifflin Company, Boston, 1907. A book that strongly influenced the progressive reforms in twentieth-century United States. Organized society, Ross wrote, deals with obvious sins with some adequacy, but it neglects the impersonal, modern sins, such as child labor, stock manipulation of a dishonest character, and misleading advertising.

Tawney, R. H.: *The Acquisitive Society,* Harvest ed., Harcourt, Brace and Company, Inc., New York, 1948. This classic study of property rights was originally published in 1920.

————: *Religion and the Rise of Capitalism,* Harcourt, Brace and Company, Inc., New York, 1926. A famous study of the relationship of Protestantism and capitalism.

Weber, Max: *The Protestant Ethic and the Spirit of Capitalism,* trans. by Talcott Parsons, George Allen & Unwin, Ltd., London, 1930. The classic essay on the relation of the ethic of Protestantism and the development of capitalism.

DISCUSSION QUESTIONS

1. Identify six phenomena in a local community known to you that exemplify vestiges of feudal economy, for example, class structure, religious creeds, subservience to "betters," payments in kind, subsistence economics, and parochial loyalty.

2. Howard Mumford Jones, in the book *The Pursuit of Happiness* (Harvard University Press, Cambridge, Mass., 1953), traces the evolution of contemporary emphasis on mental and emotional adjustments to environment as "happiness" from the aristocratic-elite concepts of eighteenth-century Americans and Europeans. Read this little volume and try to identify and evaluate the "happiness" most eagerly sought by you and by several of your associates whose values you think you know well.

3. Does it seem true to you that the insecurity characteristic of wealth-seeking men who are ambitious for high status leads them to grasp alliances indiscriminately? If so, do their alliances predominantly attach to innovations and reform movements, or to arrangements which are conservative? Cite concrete cases.

4. The federal and state courts are said to interpret laws progressively to accord, bit by bit, with social and economic conditions and trends. To the extent that this assertion is correct, is such adaptation of legality to reality justifiable? If so, does it make of the court a legislative body?

5. In the foregoing chapter, it has been noted that to religious leaders of the Renaissance, capitalism seemed to be the "great heresy." How has it come about that the equation of American spirituality with private enterprise and material prosperity is so generally approved? In our folklore have God and Mammon become identical?

6. In the light of current capitalistic organization in commerce, finance, distribution, and production in the United States and in Europe, does it seem to you that free enterprise and economic competition have a vigorous future? If you think not, what kinds of changes do you think are required in order to ensure a future for the capitalistic system in the United States and elsewhere in the world?

11

Important Economic Factors
in American Life

MOTIVES AND GOALS IN AMERICAN SOCIETY

From Colonial days to the present, most Americans have been characteristically motivated by two great aspirations. They have sought to better their economic lot, and they have striven for personal freedom. Whatever has seemed to them to thwart either of these ambitions has aroused their pugnacity. Americans have raised their voices in protest *against* men and organizations at least as frequently as they have directed their energies *toward* constructive measures to accomplish their ends. And, of course, the men and organizations so challenged have fought back at the "troublemakers."

Successive Stages of Business Motivation

In the United States, four overlapping stages of economic motivation are distinguishable. American business developed from a predominant concern with commodities in which the major objective was the production and exchange of goods and services. The next stage was individual or partnership business motivated by the hope of profit; goods and services were produced and sold mainly to increase the wealth of the entrepreneur. With the emergence of corporations, managers have come to strive not only for wealth but also for prestige and power; the businessman increasingly sees wealth as a means of increasing his influence and reputation. Finally, municipal, state, and national governments have come to participate in critically important businesses and have assumed some of the management functions.[1]

The slogans and stereotypes of earlier stages have continued to polarize men's minds in support of, or opposition to, conditions that no longer exist. For example, the principle that a man owns what he has produced by his own labor and his own tools is basic to American culture, but it is largely irrelevant in modern industrial society. "Ownership" now generally refers to wealth produced through machines, factory organization, transportation, sales techniques, and credit manipulation. The rewards for private enterprise, clever contrivance, and profit seeking, obviously justified in a business-for-profit economy, have little precise application to an economy directed toward power and prestige or to one regulated by government.

In mid-twentieth-century America, all four stages of development can be seen. The commodity-centered economy, as exemplified by the craftsman who uses his own tools to produce for his family's use, is now of relatively slight importance, except perhaps for operators of "family-sized" farms. But even individual farmers seldom really own their tools or their products; both are frequently mortgaged to credit institutions. Another important exception is that of home maintenance and handicraft, the "do-it-yourself" activities of part-time production and repair.

The second stage, that of business conducted almost purely for profit, is still widespread. It is exemplified by individually owned and small corporative merchandising and manufacturing shops, by independent farmers and miners, and by the practices of professionals—physicians, lawyers, artists, architects, and engineers. Quite obviously, however, the investments in these cases are not clear-cut; they consist as truly of experience, skill, and personal qualities as they do of tools, equipment, and accessories; incomes are properly assignable to wages as well as to profits. The laborer may be classified here, too, though perhaps somewhat tenuously; his success in obtaining greater participation in the product of business (in the form of wage increases, shorter hours, pensions, and paid vacations) may justify such inclusion.

> [1] State intervention in business is usually a response to the ambivalence implicit in individual or coterie power over the economy, whose guardian is the state.

Power- and Prestige-oriented Business

The third stage of development, in which business is for profits but organized and directed toward power and prestige,[2] is one that students of the contemporary American and European economies find most complex and significant. The immediate and primary purpose of this newer emphasis in business organization is the prevention of unlimited competition with its waste, confusion, and inconvenience.

The methods used to "bring order out of the economic chaos" have varied widely. The classic device for attaining power in the market —economic strangulation of those competitors who cannot defend themselves—has been used successfully by able and ruthless men for two centuries and more. Only since the Civil War in this country, however, has the emergence of power-seeking men forced much of the society into the mold of power getting.

"Profit making" as a term retains its place in the vocabulary of business, but in increasing degree, the profits referred to result from manipulation of private and public affairs rather than from production and distribution as such. Technical know-how is still of great importance in productive enterprise, but usually it is purchased through salaries and wages by a power organization, a board of directors representing thousands of almost anonymous investors. The technical experts do not share in the profits, other than as bonuses in especially good years, though their salaries may be large. They are really high-grade workers who replace less-trained and less-skilled workers as machines and processes become more involved and complex.[3]

The profits of the corporation are derived quite as truly from trademarked goods, patents, manipulations of credit, and other power instruments as from the productive processes as such. Indeed, many

[2] Power-oriented business infiltrates and to some extent replaces business-for-profit, as such, whenever the predominating motivation of entrepreneurs and investors becomes prestige, influence, and credit symbols. The peculiar significance of power orientation in contemporary large-scale business lies in its interrelationship with modern technology and the world's political economy. International business cartels exert great leverage on national political economies; in some cases for good, in other cases for ill, from the point of view of the student of social life. Cf. R. A. Brady, *Business as a System of Power*, Columbia University Press, New York, 1943.

[3] Technical experts do at present participate in managerial policy determination to a greater degree than do laborers, but organized labor increasingly and effectively asserts its concern with policy problems.

huge business organizations have become essentially credit and merchandizing institutions which purchase interests in smaller productive
corporations that are already going concerns. The agglomerate corporation provides the subordinate units with the power and prestige of the
over-all organization, a sustained profitable market for their products,
and the advantages of great financial resources.[4]

The basic techniques of this business-by-power are, however,
readily copied by other types of economic organization. Hence, there
have grown up analogous power organizations among workers, professionals, and consumers. They, too, pool their resources, bind their
memberships to uniform action, hire militant executives and competent experts, maintain communication services to enlist public support, and form pressure groups to try to control legislation and to gain
favorable action by public administrative and judicial agencies.

Security and Insecurity in a Power-oriented Economy

Profit seeking is just as truly a major purpose and necessary
condition of contemporary "big business" as it has been for the
"business-for-profit" economy. What is new is the manipulation of
financial devices, communication instruments, marketing agreements,
and political institutions as important means for securing and multiplying profits. Business management seeks to maximize profits and reduce
risks through numerous tactics. These include the control of credit
facilities, patents, franchises, and markets, the procurement of government subsidies and contracts, rate fixing that guarantees a "fair return
on investment," and, in degree, influencing the manners and moods
of the public through the avenues of communication (including "education").

So long as there is prosperity, many thousands of others share
in the benefits incidental to such business management. Largely because
profits are (or seem to be) assured, labor successfully organizes for
economic and political power and so asserts its claims to higher standards of living. And, partly as consequence and partly as necessary accompaniment, the consuming public is supplied with goods and services
almost to the point of surfeit.

[4] T. K. Quinn, *Giant Business: Threat to Democracy,* Exposition
Press, New York, 1953, chap. 8, and chap. 24. Peter Drucker argues
that the modern corporation is more truly to be interpreted as a
political than as an *economic* organization. *The Future of Industrial Man,* The John Day Company, Inc., New York, 1942, p. 74ff.

Business-for-power and Education

For the professional educator, the impact of the business-for-power aspect of contemporary American life on the attitudes of young people is of great importance. To most young people, employment by a corporation that has impressive establishments of plant and personnel, great financial resources, and has attained power in the market place seems very attractive. Such employment offers promise of larger opportunity and less risk than independent entrepreneurship or some other individualistic career, as well as greater chance of success than is likely to be won through individual enterprise.[5] To be sure, within the large corporation, there remains considerable competition among junior executives, salesmen, and other employees. Such competition, however, is usually moderated by the fact that success depends on the cooperation of potential rivals; the lone wolf is rejected by his peers. This limitation is accepted because job security, adequate income, self-esteem, and social standing seem likely of attainment. These probabilities speak more convincingly than textbooks, newspaper advertisements, and platform oratory glorifying free enterprise and competitive business.

Business consolidation, then, tends to stabilize the economy, at least superficially, as compared with its business-for-profit predecessor. More inclusive organization enables it to absorb minor failures. A loss at one point may be compensated for by a gain elsewhere. Increased costs may be offset by higher prices or decreased services,[6] especially in cases where state and national governments are able and willing to intervene to protect the industry.[7] So long as comparative prosperity enables most consumers to pay the higher prices and to make substitutions to replace the decreased services, no great maladjustment follows.

The maintenance of faith and confidence in the economy requires that nice adjustments be made between the business structure and its credit practices. If interest rates change only slightly and

[5] Employment in government services promises somewhat similar advantages, though prestige is less often extended to individual teachers, scientists, administrators, and other experts employed in public agencies than to ambitious young businessmen.

[6] For example, cash-and-carry merchandising, cafeteria and "automat" restaurants, fewer trains or busses for passengers, limitations on toll-free telephone calls, and "extra" charges for equipment generally desired by automobile purchasers.

[7] For example, rate fixing for public services, cost-plus contracts, underwriting of loans, tariffs, subsidies, and favorable tax considerations.

gradually, if demand notes are seldom called abruptly, if technological unemployment is not serious, and if subsistence and minor luxuries are within the reach of the great majority of citizens—if, in a word, no significant segment of the population gets seriously hurt or frightened—all goes reasonably well.

Stabilizing Role of Government

The competition among officers of large corporations for power and prestige through the accumulation of wealth carries the economy farther and farther into the realm of abstract credit and debt symbols. Great wealth vested in an individual or a corporation has little counterpart in concrete equipment, goods, and services. It consists largely of claims on hoped-for future production. Such orientation to the future requires optimism not only on the part of the claimants but also on the part of the public.

The people's representative is government. Confidence in legislators, executives, and justices and in their foresight in creating and enforcing regulations that set safe limits on the financial manipulations, is essential in a world wherein disagreements are rife even among "experts." Which corporation operations are judged constructive and which destructive in their over-all effects on the common welfare must be decided year by year by political agencies.

The time-honored term "political economy" indicates a relation between the guardian state and economic institutions. Every political measure, whether preventive or remedial, wise or unwise, is likely to disturb some economically motivated segments in the society. Hence, efforts to forestall, pervert, or accelerate state intervention are common both among wealth and power seekers and among workers and consumers who are skeptical about the political agitations of various industrial, trade, and finance groups. To discover principles by which political and economic institutions should be evaluated and coordinated has been a historic concern of social philosophers and statesmen.

ASSUMPTIONS OF THE SOCIAL SCIENCES AND ECONOMIC CHANGE

All science is based on the assumption that the world is ordered and that its order is observable. The social sciences are concerned with the observation, classification, and interpretation of the facts of human relationships and with prediction based upon these facts.

Because man is chiefly a product of the culture to which he belongs, he and all his institutions vary as the culture changes. Hence, observable facts do not remain constant. And so the definitions, laws, dicta, interpretations, and applications of the social sciences at any one time are not necessarily of universal validity and reliability through all time.

The needed objectivity of fresh observation and reassessment of facts and the necessary revision of premises and conclusions are hampered by several difficulties. In the first place, scientists themselves do not think and observe in a social vacuum; they are culturally conditioned. The values which dominate the contemporary social scene are as likely to be accepted by scientists as by other citizens. In the second place, there are barriers to communication and understanding among different literate segments of the population. These barriers result from a kind of cultural lag; definitions and generalizations which are radically different from those which are familiar to a particular group tend not to be accepted. Hence, promising hypotheses may be ridiculed or censored while the "tried and true" doctrines are intensively publicized. In the third place, the impact of new assessments and interpretations of matters of great import is diffused and thereby weakened by the frequently polemic disagreements regarding trivia.[8]

Nevertheless, obsolete assumptions, "laws," and slogans, no matter how firmly entrenched in popular thought, do eventually lose their potency as the symbols of fighting faiths. They do not accord with the aims and values of the people brought to power by new conditions. Hence, their defenders lack a significant audience.

There are many interpretations, assessments, forecasts, and proposals regarding human institutions which are ignored or condemned by the general public which does not even pretend to understand their rational foundations. On the one side, there are the decentralists, communalists, anarchists, and syndicalists, all of whom reject the coercions of government. On the other side, are Marxian socialists, nationalists, militarists, fascists, and planned-economy enthusiasts, all of whom would utilize powerful governmental agencies to bring about the reforms they separately favor. Today in the United States all radical programs are rejected out of hand; tomorrow any one of them may strike a responsive chord in popular thought.

Classical Economics, a Reflection of the Nineteenth Century

The classical economists contributed much to the understanding of the economies of their time. But the economies have changed. Moreover, new insights have been achieved which outmode the "principles"

---

[8] Cf. Robert S. Lynd, *Knowledge for What?* Princeton University Press, Princeton, N.J., 1939, esp. chap. 1.

of earlier interpreters.[9] Consequently, the justification of twentieth-century practices and proposals by reference to eighteenth- and nineteenth-century economic "truths" is at best questionable. They were temporarily true in great degree; they are not eternal truths.

When Ricardo, Bentham, Mill, Jevons, and Marshall made their contributions to political economy, cities were relatively small; factory units were independent; mass production was hardly conceived; labor, so far as it was organized at all, was structured by crafts; economic power was diffused; mass communication was limited to the newspaper and platform; popular entertainment was typified by the theater and informal playfield. At the time of the earlier writers, indeed, slavery, child labor, colonialism, and an illiterate populace were taken for granted.

Nevertheless, good will, optimism, and reformism characterized these philosopher-scientists. If they miscalculated the future, it was not because they lacked hope for a better world. In part, their failure was due to an assumption that what was good for the English political economy would be good for all nations. Except for Marx, they could not foresee that industrialists and financiers, freed from restrictions by the state, might be quite as authoritarian and restrictive, once they gained power, as ever the landed aristocracy had been. And, most important, none of them, again with the exception of Marx, appreciated the potentialities of organized masses of men for good or for ill.

Emergence of the Masses as a Powerful Economic Factor

Among social philosophers, as well as in common parlance, the term masses generally refers to those men in an industrial society who lack power to influence decisions and acts that seriously affect that society. Within the American legal and moral framework for stability and orderly change, such a definition is justified. But it leads to an undervaluation of the actualities, and still more of the potentialities, of the faceless majorities to upset the applecart.[10]

Mass man is the ultimate consumer, not only of the goods and services provided by factory, farm, and store, but also of the symbols of his culture and society, of government, of the church, of communication agencies, and of social prestige. If he cannot buy the goods or will not accept the symbols, the power structure is threatened with collapse. Fears and discontents may sometimes be assuaged in degree by bread

[9] For example, value as a product of labor gave place to value as utility, that is, the ability to satisfy a human desire.

[10] Jose Ortega y Gasset, *The Revolt of the Masses,* W. W. Norton & Company, Inc., New York, 1932.

and circuses, by political franchise and synthetic loyalties and hatreds toward abstractions, but not always. From the Peasants' Revolts of the sixteenth century to the fascist, communist, and racist eruptions of the twentieth, mass man has always stood ready to mobilize for revolt when the coincidence of frustration and of wily and bold leadership have occurred. Unwittingly and unwillingly, the failure by acquisitive people to assure sufficient income for the masses of men and thus provide a profitable market for production would bring our vaunted mass-production system to an end.[11]

The Decisive Role of the Consumer

In the early days of the industrial revolution, entrepreneurs directed their major producing and marketing efforts toward meeting the tastes, desires, and needs of rather restricted classes of potential buyers—nobles, wealthy bourgeoisie, and fellow capitalists. Journeymen, peasants, and, later, machine operators and small farmers seldom entered the market to purchase much more than the basic necessities of life.

During the eighteenth and nineteenth centuries, however, as machine industry expanded, larger segments of the population came to be served. Providing transportation and commodities for colonists, traders, farmers, miners, sailors, fur gatherers, craftsmen, and shop owners required attention to what common men could and would buy. These services for "little men" became so profitable to bankers, industrialists, merchants, and shareholders in large enterprises that they ushered in the mass-production revolution of this century. Today, the consumer is *potentially* supreme in determining the goods and services to be produced, and in degree, at what prices.[12]

[11] Cf. Robert L. Heilbroner, "Who Are the American Poor?" *Harper's Magazine,* June, 1950, pp. 27–33. In the prosperous year, 1948, "one family in ten and one single person out of every two must eat and dress . . . on $20.00 a week."

"In a country with the unbelievable annual personal income of $393 billion (as of February) [1960], there are still 32.2 million people living on less than $50 a week for a family of four. Included in these 32 million are one-fifth of the nation's children, and 8 million over 65 years of age." James Reston, in the Denver *Post,* March 26, 1960, p. 10.

[12] However, in practice, the price of commodities, so fundamental a factor in determining demand and hence supply, according to classical economic theory, is of decreasing importance. In contemporary merchandising practices, the prices of relatively standardized commodities tend to be uniform. By agreement between producers and distributors, supported in many cases by state and

Accompaniments of Mass Consumption

Two accompaniments of the recognition of the consumer's importance are of primary significance. One is the orientation of mass communication toward enticing the public to more elaborate wants. The other is the belated recognition that, in an industrial society, the employee is the most potent consumer; the amount and continuity of his wages make the difference between general prosperity and catastrophe.

The practical consequences of the ascendancy of workers' families as consumers are diverse and conflicting. The ascendancy undermines the remnants of the old status system. It increases the importance of mass entertainment. It enhances conformity. It destroys docility. It diminishes the fears and hopes of an after life as compensation for sin and virtue in the present world. It compels governments, by laws and their enforcement, and organizations of businessmen, by the adoption of "ethical" standards, to censor and otherwise supervise dangerous and morally reprehensible practices.[13]

The dawning of an economy of potential abundance profoundly modifies the ways in which motives and values are manifested. Necessities and comforts that are available to almost everybody may still be valued highly as utilities even though they no longer contribute to the owner's distinctive prestige. Adequate food, clothing, and shelter, and many extras—fishing rods, cigarettes, and automobiles, for example—have ceased to provide "class" identification in this country.

Pecuniary factors do, however, retain significance in determining prestige. But financial status and material possessions are probably of lesser importance than reputation, tradition, inheritance, and erudition. Indeed, social distance lessens among "classes" as shared experiences in a great variety of activities increase. It is a phenomenon that works ambivalently and multifariously; the entire gamut of sports, the arts,

---

federal laws and regulations, fair-trade and price-fixing practices restrict competition to alleged superiority of one trademarked brand of goods and services over another for flamboyantly popularized special purposes. The prices of gasoline, toothpaste, and transportation, for example, vary relatively little from one brand or conveyance to another. Whether one is really better than another is seldom known except to subscribers of nonprofit testing services. The control of the consumer over price is, in large degree, limited to his refusal to buy commodities if he considers the price too high.

[13] Edward A. Filene, *Successful Living in This Machine Age*, Simon and Schuster, Inc., New York, 1932.

costume, and equipment is shared in with little distinction among social classes and with decreasing limitations due to differences in pecuniary resources.[14]

CONFLICT BETWEEN FACT AND OUTMODED ECONOMIC ASSUMPTIONS

So long as men get along, they tend to go along. Vague feelings of insecurity, even though substantiated by the memory of hard times, are suppressed. Indeed, man usually resents reminders that what goes up is likely to come down, that, like the bubble it is, credit and debt wealth may burst, and that the unthinking acceptance of untrue shibboleths may prevent the taking of corrective measures by a popularly chosen and supported government.

Semantic confusion is reinforced by the historical association of ideological "liberals" with private economic enterprisers. Liberalism, during the century of democratic revolutions, was "the religion of the middle classes." Because central governments, established churches, landed aristocrats, and guild monopolies then served as coercive instruments hostile to all social change, the demand for freedom from restraint brought diverse groups into collaboration. So it came about that the battle cry of *liberty* and the virtuous aura of *liberalism* became associated with many men who favored specific liberties but not liberty in general.[15]

Stereotypes Exploited by Mass Communication

What are the roots and forces which interplay to foster the equating of liberalism and conformity, of liberty and restraint, and of freedom and suppression? In part, they are to be found in the unconscious assumption that, since all men are presumed to be equal politically, they are in other regards alike. (Any unlike person is a disturbing challenge to be met by ridicule, threat, and violence.) In part, too, they are responses to the suppressed fear of conditions that

[14] Obviously, an economy of abundance has world-wide as well as domestic significance. Money values depend in great degree on scarcity and on potency of demand. But scarcity may come to exist only in economically backward countries whose own craft economies have been ruined by industrial imperialism; hence, they have little or no potent demand.

[15] For example, Alexander Hamilton, who exalted freedom for America from the British sovereign and freedom for economic enterprise from state and national restrictions, had little confidence in popular liberty.

seem likely to get out of control; the radical critic and innovator may seem to be "rocking the boat" in very uncertain waters.[16]

The public relations "professionals" function to cultivate mental and emotional readiness to accept the slogans, rationalizations, and arguments put forward on behalf of clients. Experts in manipulating the verbal, visual, and auditory symbols to which most people respond in predictable ways, they play upon the minds and hearts of their publics. They draw upon popular beliefs, faiths, and loyalties and seek to attach them to their clients' products and services. Conformism to the patterns of thought and feeling highly valued by those who hire the services of the public relations experts become to a considerable extent the standardized attributes of "loyal Americans."

To be sure, the utilization of what "everyone" knows to be desirable and moral in order to win support for the *status quo* is as old as history. Thurman Arnold [17] cites numerous cases from ancient and medieval times which parallel those of twentieth-century American dependence on accepted "truth" and "principles" to justify the continuance of measures that had already become obsolete. Many advancements in science, technology, law, and other fields were retarded because they were considered immoral in the sense that they conflicted with folklore and "right" principles.

Common Sense as a Safeguard against Extreme Folly

The obfuscation of these social forces is disturbing. Nevertheless, however it may postpone, it cannot indefinitely prevent needed social changes. The two safeguards against extreme folly in social life are: first, what won't work, won't work; second, the common sense of common men eventually undermines the obsolete beliefs held by "authorities" who are trapped by their own stereotypes, broadcast by publicity experts, and regrettably, often taught by captive schoolteachers.[18] The compromise and opportunism that promote security typically dilute and eventually replace abstract "laws" that provide no solutions for man's dilemmas.

In times of social crisis—for example, wars, depressions, and acute class conflicts—not only does the cake of custom crumble, but also many so-called "laws" and "principles" come increasingly to be

[16] Cf. H. H. Wilson, "The Individual and Civil Liberties," *Fellowship*, October, 1952.

[17] *The Folklore of Capitalism*, Yale University Press, New Haven, Conn., 1937, chap. 3.

[18] See Merle Curti, *The Social Ideas of American Educators*, Charles Scribner's Sons, New York, 1935, esp. chap. 6.

questioned and, in degree, discarded in practice. Whatever people think needs to be done will be attempted, no matter how "unsound" in principle. Action taken under such stress may not prove to have been the wisest possible measure; very likely it will be ambivalent or worse in its long-time effects. Such errors, however, are in time self-corrective; radical social change mellows; bitter antagonisms soften; life moves forward and yesterday's passionate loyalties give way and new ones are formed.

New Meanings for Old Labels

Less dramatic, but perhaps more fundamentally important, are changes in economic practices that occur so gradually that people are hardly aware of them. Economic ideologies may become quite outmoded in practice without any overt challenge to their terminology.

Embodied in the fight for shorter hours, higher wages, and fringe benefits, for example, is the implicit recognition that the skilled worker is a manager of equipment which has replaced employees. His improved income is in little degree compensation for his direct application of muscle and intellect. Chiefly, he collects a share of the production of the mechanism that he manages. He is essentially a submanager in the productive process and is paid accordingly. In some industries he has an "escalator" clause in his contract guaranteeing his participation in the product of foreseen improvements in manufacture and sales. Increasingly, he shares in the profits of business and is awarded preferential options to purchase stock. Through shop stewards or representatives on labor-management committees, he codetermines policies. He is now seeking an annual wage. In the United States, all of this is taking place without challenge to the accepted terminology of business organization.[19] The "prerogatives of management" continue to be watered down to cooperation and collaboration, with dependence on government mediation in case of stalemate.

[19] Joint labor-capital management has become an established practice in the coal and steel industries of the Ruhr district of postwar Germany. It is these industries that are spearheading the extraordinary economic recovery of West Germany and neighboring areas. In the United States, despite the rather ephemeral success of labor-management, conflict continues, with notable exceptions. The "guaranteed annual wage," if generally realized, may gradually compel a resolution of such conflicts. See H. J. Ruttenberg, "Pay by the Year: Can the Unions Afford It?" *Harper's Magazine*, December, 1955, pp. 29–33.

Confusion of Roles in an Industrial Society

The roles of the acquisitively motivated, prestige-seeking man and of more humane citizens are endlessly confused. This is true, in large degree, because acquisitive man and humane citizen are in many cases the same person. They are products both of democratic, Judeo-Christian morality and of the struggle for personal economic advantage and for higher social status. Their purposes and means, for example, improved health, wholesome family life, reduction of violence, harmless uses of leisure time, and economic efficiency (which all humanists and many acquisitive men espouse), commonly merge and overlap and reenforce each other.

It is over extremes of behavior that disagreements develop. Extreme cases of exploitation and chicanery by acquisitive men arouse the fighting spirit of humanists. To the former, however, the latter frequently seem to be starry-eyed do-gooders and theorists.

The difference between acquisitive men and humanists, however, is really one of degree. The emotional drive of the former focuses their attention on production as the outcome of economic enterprise. The social effects of their behavior may be obscured by their wishful thinking. The humane citizen, in turn, may be so predominantly concerned with man's welfare that he undervalues the incidental beneficent effects of the spirit of economic adventure, management, and even ruthlessness in competition. He may even espouse social policies that endanger the economic foundations of such welfare as has been achieved.

Nevertheless, the income of wage workers is determined in significant part by social policy[20] and by the political and economic power of organized labor. The members of the upper-lower class are affected by middle-class standards in such matters as clothes, manners, and amusements, and in the means by which these standards may be attained. Their insistence on the minima of necessities and luxuries determines their conception of what is an acceptable standard of living.[21]

[20] Social policy manifests itself in many ways. Legislation sets minimum wage rates and limits the work of women and young people. Public opinion, stimulated by philanthropic foundations and public administrators, is potent in the support of measures that promote adequate annual incomes for depressed segments of the population. The interrelation of wages, production, and consumption challenges public policy makers.

[21] In a dynamic society, aspiration to achieve the minima of necessities and luxuries determines living standards acceptable to most people.

THE ECONOMIC BASIS OF THE CLASS STRUCTURE

One result of the constant impacts of upper-class symbols on middle-class and lower-class attitudes and activities is the rather confusing equivalence of the terms socioeconomic groups and social classes. The implications of these terms are somewhat different because not all the symbols of class differentiation are socioeconomic in character or derivation. Although wealth, lineage, taste, and formal education do usually qualify social acceptance at higher levels, individualism of interest and the active pursuit of civic and aesthetic goals and, hence, association with others similarly occupied, regardless of socioeconomic status, frequently serve the same end.[22]

Many Americans admire and emulate other characteristics of elites than those of conspicuous consumption and the exhibition of economic power. Among upper-class members, the attributes of self-restraint, avoidance of conspicuous behavior, and high esteem for intellectual, aesthetic, and professional achievements are frequently to be found. These qualities tend to modify, if they do not quite set, a pattern of values for the middle classes; their values in turn influence the standards toward which aspiring members of lower classes move.

Public and private schools supplement magazine and newspaper

[22] Political scientists, economists, and other students of society use other classifications of populations in addition to that of social class. These other rankings, though they interrelate with social-class distributions, are independently potent in affecting popular aspirations for improved standing in the community. One such classification includes landlords, entrepreneurs, and workers, with subdivisions and some overlapping. Whoever has a considerable investment in a natural resource is to that extent a landlord; if he risks his wealth to exploit the resource, he is a capitalist; if he himself engages in managing the enterprise, he is an entrepreneur; if he accepts a salary for his services, he belongs in the worker category (a white-collar worker). An independent farmer may be a landlord, a capitalist-entrepreneur, a laborer; on his farm, the workers might include "hired men," tenants, sharecroppers, and even peons. Prestige and disdain are related to one's rank in the income-distribution hierarchy.

Within professions and craft trades are other explicit and implicit classifications of hierarchic character. For example, in law, from Supreme Court justice to local justice of the peace, and from partner in a firm to law clerk; in military organization, from admiral or general to worker in a labor battalion; in a trade, from licensed master craftsman to apprentice.

articles and advertisements, movie, radio, and television programs, shop displays and sales counsel, and other more subtle communication media for standardizing and "upgrading" popular tastes and codes. The lines of demarcation that are presumed to define class memberships are thus blunted. The desire to conform to patterns of "well-bred"—or at least of sophisticated—people characterizes many members of lower socioeconomic families and neighborhoods.[23] Such a desire may be spasmodic and inconsistent in expression; the results may be clumsy or, sometimes, even ridiculous imitations of "wrong" models, or they may be faulty interpretations of what does characterize "well-bred" behavior. But the impulse to conform to elite modes is a strong force in the American society. Individual ambition to acquire prestige and power fosters the mastery of the techniques, not only of commercial, mechanical, and professional processes, but also of group leadership and collaboration for specific purposes. Hence, technological competence and social adaptability, rather than inheritance of wealth or lineage are increasingly honored.

Flexibility Resulting from Wealth as a Status Criterion

Largely because of the continuing dominance of qualities derived from wealth in defining social classes, financial acquisitivism often bemuses the nonelect. Money symbols present a more concrete goal for achievement than do the "cultivated" tastes, intellectual preoccupations, and ethical codes attributed to elites. And because wealth-getting as such is an amoral pursuit, the energy and enterprise of the aspirant to elite status are often directed toward his goal with little regard for ethical niceties.

The frequent attainment to positions of prestige and power by tough-minded men, although it dilutes the "gentle tradition" of elite responsibility for ethical standards, does perform a positive function in a democracy. Any aristocracy based in such large part on material possessions as it is in the United States can never become rigid or self-perpetuating for very long. In times of prosperity and technological advance, members of middle and lower classes move upward in the hierarchy; in times of adversity, there is downward movement. "Three generations from shirtsleeves to shirtsleeves" may be an exaggeration as applied to American mobility, but it contains more than a kernel of truth. Hence, the democratic aspirations of the American society are

[23] See Bernard Barber, *Social Stratification: A Comparative Analysis of Structure and Process,* Harcourt, Brace and Company, Inc., New York, 1957, pp. 135–167, for a discussion of the "symbolic indicators" of social classes in the United States.

unlikely to be completely frustrated because of obstructions placed by an economically vested elite.[24]

The Extent of Occupational Mobility

During the 1930s and into the 1940s, it was common for students of the class system of the United States to assert that social mobility (usually defined as occupational mobility) was declining. The comment that the "channels of mobility were becoming clogged" was often heard. One wag remarked that Americans were "developing arteriosclerosis of the occupational arteries." These assertions were based on arguments that (1) the frontier had disappeared, (2) the upper classes were beginning to reproduce themselves to a greater extent than formerly, (3) great corporations were falling into the hands of a relatively few families or other closed groups, and (4) the new psychology of security was hardly capable of producing the spirit of competition which encourages upward social striving.[25]

These assertions have more recently been disputed. A number of studies present evidence either that the extent of social mobility earlier in American history was probably overestimated or that the extent of such mobility at mid-century probably matches that of earlier decades.[26] While the question is still argued in some quarters, it is probable that most students of the subject would now agree that social mobility (especially as measured by occupational mobility) remains high in the United States. There are many who believe that it is easier

[24] To be sure, large-scale industry and commerce foster individual competition only within a framework of coordination and co-operation to advance corporative interests. But personnel managers are alert to discover employees, regardless of socioeconomic origin, whose personal qualities make success in specialized jobs probable. A present tendency for large corporations to recruit and train promising college and professional school graduates for managerial positions may somewhat offset the upgrading of workers to executive positions. But the door of opportunity is not yet closed for them.

[25] See, for example, Joyce O. Hertzler, *Society in Action,* The Dryden Press, Inc., New York, 1954, esp. p. 34.

[26] See the following: Ely Chinoy, "Social Mobility Trends in the United States," *American Sociological Review,* vol. 20, no. 4, pp. 180–186, April, 1955, for a good review of these studies to that date; Natalie Rogoff, *Recent Trends in Occupational Mobility,* Free Press, Glencoe, Ill., 1953, esp. pp. 44–45; and W. Lloyd Warner and James C. Abegglen, *Occupational Mobility in American Business and Industry,* University of Minnesota Press, Minneapolis, 1955.

for more people to "climb the social class ladder" in the 1960s than at any other time in the twentieth century.

The American people, as already noted in an earlier chapter, are preponderantly middle-class in attitudes and aspirations. They strive to better their economic lot and social status according to the opportunities that an industrial society provides. They rally in support of "causes" with which they think their interests are identified; but, because they have so many conflicting interests, their patterns of enthusiastic support and of opposition are kaleidoscopic. Hence the paradox that middle-class attitudes toward political and economic measures are, in some cases, extremely conservative and, in other cases, extremely liberal and largely influenced by self-interest rationalized as public policy.[27] Nevertheless, in the long run, their very pragmatism makes them adherents of compromise, toleration, and conciliation, lest bitterness interfere with business.

American political institutions (including the public school, which in one sense is political) are middle-class products. They ride out the repeated dramatic antipathies which often seem irreconcilable. Enlightened self-interest eventually requires acceptance of, and adaptation to, social change.

But change is never accepted wholeheartedly! As the middle classes adapt to change and so, because of their dominance in the society, come to control it, they tend to carry into the new order some of their old values and patterns of action. Hence revolutionary changes are rarely fully realized. Radical movements, instigated and supported by middle classes (for example, the revolutions in England, France, and America and the eruptions of radical Protestantism) have been, at some stage and in some respects, transformed by their former supporters into conservative and even reactionary movements.

While the general statements regarding the middle classes set forth above are justifiable, it would be a serious mistake to leave them

---

[27] Albert Lauterbach, *Man, Motives, and Money: Psychological Frontiers of Economics,* Cornell University Press, Ithaca, N.Y., 1954, pp. 6–7. This statement, of course, refers to variations within the middle class. Studies show that there are some important political and economic differences between the upper classes and the lower classes when they are compared. Compare with Centers' findings that upper-class urban occupational groups exhibited a stronger bias toward private ownership and individualism and a stronger bias against more power for working people than did lower-class occupational groups. Richard Centers, *The Psychology of Social Classes,* Princeton University Press, Princeton, N.J., 1949, p. 63.

without qualification. The middle classes are endlessly heterogeneous. They are composed of kaleidoscopic groupings and regroupings of inconsistently conforming and nonconforming individuals. Rivalries and antipathies among groups and individuals are as characteristic of them as are collaboration and agreement. It is their adaptability, their pragmatism, and their spasmodic alternation of quasi radicalism and quasi conservatism that characterize the evanescent groupings of middle-class people and those who identify with them.

Middle-class Control of and by Business

The combination of buoyant utopianism and inherent economic insecurity that characterizes the middle classes largely determines the course of the American economy. When the incomes of white-collar workers, professionals, and political office holders provide generous margins for the purchase of luxuries, their optimism knows almost no bounds. While many of them are sufficiently cautious to save money for a rainy day, the majority purchase durable goods—houses, equipment, and luxuries—on installments, thereby pledging their expected future earnings. Moreover, the day-by-day expenditures for food, clothing, entertainment, and services tend to be made with abandon, partly because the spenders need "to keep up with the Joneses," and partly because they believe there will be more money available next week to replace what is spent today.[28]

Not only does the average income of middle-class families rise during periods of prosperity, but the number of such families increases both relatively and absolutely. Hence, there develops an amazingly increased market for industry, commerce, and government services. Popular desires, tastes, and choices provide the targets for fashion designers, advertisers, contractors, salesmen, politicians, and for all concerns that seek their patronage. Middle-class families thus indirectly control the capital expenditures and the character of bank loans and investments in stocks and bonds.

The growth of middle-income families since World War II has been so rapid that the American economy is sometimes referred to as a "one-class" market.[29] As of 1953, the families with $4,000 to $7,500 of disposable income comprised 35 per cent of all American families; they received 42 per cent of the total consumer cash income.

[28] A wisecrack currently going the rounds is to the effect that it is, in fact, impossible to catch up with the Joneses, because "just when you think you've done it, they refinance and start the whole thing over again!"

[29] Gilbert Burck and Sanford Parker, "The Changing American Market," *Fortune*, August, 1953, pp. 98–99.

They tended to live in suburban developments and in small towns, so that the social habits and standards characteristic of these localities become of dominant importance in determining the demands for luxury goods and services and the patronage of private and public institutions.

The enthusiasm of such families for specific styles of consumption is rather fickle (a fickleness encouraged by rival producers and merchandisers); hence, they accentuate the changeability of both private and public enterprise. Ranch houses succeed colonial-type dwellings, station wagons replace limousines, costumes and home decorations change according to fashion, civic improvements are alternately demanded and neglected, clubs and other social groups form and dissolve, and specific kinds of recreation boom and languish. The nature of these middle-class desires and tastes not only supports the high volume of production, but increases the instability of the economic flow.[30]

Moreover, the dynamic impetus that the energetic and restless middle-income families exert on the economy encourages the growth of mass-production and mass-distribution corporations whose junior executives move from one residential area to another as they climb the promotional ladder. These executives accentuate suburban and small-town mobility.

SUMMARY

Education as a public meliorative agency attunes its processes to the dynamic motives and goals of the human beings it would influence. In the contemporary United States, people seek the good life, as they conceive it to be, for themselves and their progeny. That the conception is in some degree superficial and inconsistent is true. The eagerness to achieve the respect of their associates and to play admired roles before their actual and vicarious audiences involves risk and insecurity; but somewhat paradoxically, the effort to attain such approval provides the only hopeful road toward emotional security.

In the American society, the admired roles are many and diverse. Because of the dynamic quality of economic factors in the United States, however, prestige in most roles carries with it, whether as cause or as result, a material accompaniment. Few persons conceive the good life to be achievable apart from comforts and some luxuries. Voluntary poverty, even very simple living by choice, is regarded as a mark of eccentricity.

If educators are to foster spiritual and intellectual values and goals among those they seek to influence, they must take practical

[30] William H. Whyte, Jr., "How Suburbia Socializes," *Fortune,* August, 1953, pp. 120–122, 186–190.

account of cultural factors which condition prestige and status in the society. It is futile to expect that academic requirements can make many youths or adults content to wear hair shirts as esoteric and dedicated scholars.

Nevertheless, it would be even more futile for the educator to surrender to the superficial values and goals which characterize mid-twentieth-century America. If the school is to foster status seeking at all, it ought to be for prestige based on contributions made to group life—family, church, occupation, and country. The acquisitive motivation is thus subtly transmuted; individual pecuniary considerations are subordinated to the common welfare.

SELECTED REFERENCES

Adams, James Truslow: *The Epic of America,* Little, Brown & Company, Boston, 1932. A beautifully written, short, social and intellectual history of the United States.

Allen, Frederick Lewis: *The Big Change: America Transforms Itself, 1900–1950,* Harper & Brothers, New York, 1952. The transformation in the American capitalist system during the first half of the twentieth century.

Arnold, Thurman: *The Folklore of Capitalism,* Yale University Press, New Haven, Conn., 1937.

————: *The Symbols of Government,* Yale University Press, New Haven, Conn., 1935. Influential analyses of the leading symbols and faiths in government and business.

Becker, Carl: *New Liberties for Old,* Yale University Press, New Haven, Conn., 1941. One of America's leading historians analyzes the changes in the American conceptions of liberties.

Davis, Jerome: *Capitalism and Its Culture,* Rinehart & Company, Inc., New York, 1936. A critical look at the ethics and practices of a capitalist economy.

Galbraith, John Kenneth: *The Affluent Society,* Houghton Mifflin Company, Boston, 1958.

————: *American Capitalism: The Concept of Countervailing Power,* Houghton Mifflin Company, Boston, 1952. Provocative analyses by a leading American liberal economist.

Kapp, K. William: *The Social Costs of Private Enterprise,* Harvard University Press, Cambridge, Mass., 1950. Some of the important social wastes of capitalism.

Hofstadter, Richard: *The Age of Reform: From Bryan to FDR,* Alfred A. Knopf, Inc., New York, 1955. A leading historian describes the social reforms in the fifty years prior to the New Deal.

Lippmann, Walter: *The Good Society,* Little, Brown & Company, Boston, 1937.

————: *The Phantom Public,* Harcourt, Brace and Company, Inc., New York, 1925.

————: *Public Opinion,* Harcourt, Brace and Company, Inc., New York, 1922.

————: *The Public Philosophy,* Little, Brown & Company, Boston, 1955. Four books on public opinion, its making, and its consequences by the dean of American political commentators.

Mills, C. Wright: *White Collar: The American Middle Classes,* Oxford University Press. New York, 1953. A provocative description by a sociologist of the American middle class at mid-century.

Quinn, T. K.: *Giant Business: Threat to Democracy,* The Exposition Press, New York, 1953. A polemical, but powerful, book on American big business.

Riesman, David, and others: *The Lonely Crowd: A Study of the Changing American Character,* Yale University Press, New Haven, Conn., 1950. An influential, provocative book which spells out a theory of change in the American personality.

Sorenson, Helen: *The Consumer Movement,* Harper & Brothers, New York, 1941. A good history of the American consumer movement.

Soule, George: *Economic Forces in American History,* William Sloane Associates, New York, 1952. An economic historian traces the effects of economic ideas and actions on the course of American history.

Wright, D. M.: *Capitalism,* McGraw-Hill Book Company, Inc., New York, 1951. A description of the workings of the capitalist economic system.

DISCUSSION QUESTIONS

1. List the names of five businessmen concerning whose economic standing you have considerable knowledge. For each one note whether his business income is chiefly in the form of salary, commissions, direct profits, or interest and dividends. Would you classify him as an entrepreneur, a manager, an inventor, a technician, or in some other category?

2. Consider the changes in sources of income of a family in your local community that has been "well to do" for two or more generations. Perhaps the grandparents were successful farmers, manufacturers, or sea captains, whereas the grandchildren's major income is dividends, interest, rents, royalties, or honorific fees (a fee paid for permission for a business firm to use a respected name).

3. Bourgeoisie morality has placed high value on hard sustained

work. C. Wright Mills (*White Collar,* p. 220) asserts that the "new middle class" does not accord with this work ethic and therefore, in that respect, is nonbourgeoisie in mentality. Do you believe his assertion is valid? If so, does it account to great or little degree for contemporary moral attitudes and standards in the United States?

4. Cite as many examples as you can of individual entrepreneurships in a local community you know well. How does the volume of production and sales of these private ventures compare with those of corporations in similar lines of business which are owned by stockholders, few of whom are local residents, and managed by employed executives?

5. What is the justification for the plea to consumers that they "patronize home industry"? Is it more valid in the case of local entrepreneurships or consumers' cooperatives than it is in the case of branch stores or factories of large corporations?

6. Examine the current issues of representative national magazines, for example, *Harper's Magazine, The Atlantic, The Nation, The New Republic, The Reporter, The Progressive, Time, Newsweek, Life,* and *Look.* In terms of number, space, prominence, and repetitiveness, what relative importance do editorials, articles, pictures, and advertisements seem to you to assign to social and economic questions as compared with aesthetics, ethics, recreation, and romance? How many of the social and economic items are controversial in character? Among the writers who strongly approve and those who strongly dissent from a proposed change in social policy (federal income tax rates, for example) are the authors' definitions and assumptions evident?

7. Does any business establishment in your local community engage in profit sharing, granting of bonuses, incentive pay, awards for workers' constructive suggestions, or management-labor committees on policy and grievances? Do the executives of any establishment still assert the prerogatives of management to make decisions without interference by labor's representatives?

12

Commonwealth: A Basis of Social and Economic Organization

COMMONWEALTH AND THE ECONOMY

Many important changes take place in social arrangements just because there is nothing else that can possibly correct obviously unsatisfactory conditions. Sometimes, indeed, the changes are already well under way before statesmen and political leaders grasp their importance. Their belated pronouncements, justifications, and admonitions regarding the change may then appear to be statements of principles to be followed in controlling the inevitable and already half-completed change.[1]

In the United States, the national, state, and local governments all postulate the common welfare as their controlling mandate. In the

[1] For example, the end of British mercantilism, the abolition of slavery in the United States, the gaining of independent legal status by women, job security for organized labor, the ending of horse cavalry in army formations, and the replacement of superimposition and coercion by motivation and cooperation in public school education.

247

sphere of private economic activities, however, the mandate has had only vague reference to the public advantage; private incentive and reward have been esteemed in terms of individual virtues, rights, and benefits. Whatever contribution private enterprise might make to community welfare has been blandly assumed to derive incidentally from a competitive struggle.

As the national economy has become increasingly integrated, and as "free individual contractors" themselves have largely lost their economic identities to corporative establishments, there has developed a general awareness of the basic community of interest in a stable economic, as well as a stable political, society. A severe depression threatens every element of the entire social fabric.

Interdependence in the Industrial Society

People in an industrial society are so interdependent that the welfare of each segment of the population is essential to all the others. A failure at any point threatens the expansion and stability of an economy which depends on a growing rate of consumption of goods and services and on hope, confidence, and general good will. Consciousness of this interdependence, though as yet transitory and incomplete, is an important force in the creation and maintenance of many social and economic organizations.[2]

These organizations, which may be thought of as "partial commonwealths," are products of the interplay of conflicting social pressures. The frequently inconsistent purposes of economic organizations are disciplined by the compulsion to make concessions to the probable effects of its decisions on other economic associations and on public opinion. Unless all the related institutions and groups benefit (or, at worst, escape injury), the organization is less than optimally effective.

It is a major concern of business, taken as a whole, to foster mass consumption. Its continuing prosperity depends not only on expanding demand but also on the stability of political institutions, social mobility, and community morale.

A large corporation is, indeed, itself a limited commonwealth. Its productivity means potential prosperity to investors, workers, consumers, suppliers, and many small businesses that directly and indirectly

[2] Political democracy itself is as yet an aspiration, an ideal, and a symbol; it is a great adventure based on the hope that men may respond favorably to an assumption of equality in responsibility and in human rights. Political democracy attempts merely to "unstack the cards" by assuring all men a "square" or "new" or "fair" deal.

serve its processes and personnel. Hence, the management which makes its corporation a success automatically fulfills a political role. The organization of economic forces, people, and materials may create or may destroy communities; many decisions of management are therefore affected with public interest. Getting people to do what is in their common interest is a political function, as truly as it is an economic one.

Like successful corporations, labor unions are also governmental organizations requiring support and conformity of their members, public understanding and acceptance of their policies, and continuing stability and prosperity in the society. Hence, however obscured by bargaining strategies, their long-term interest is in high productivity which alone makes possible higher wages and salaries, plentiful consumption, shorter hours of work, and full employment.

Resolution of Labor-Management Conflicts

Management of organized labor shares political and social responsibilities with management of corporations. The internal life of an enlightened labor organization, like that of a socially responsible corporation, may be a new American frontier. The tensions implicit in the relation of a man to his work—fear of unemployment and desire for recognition and promotion, for example—are faced by union officers as well as by management. And, as on every frontier, there is continuous experimenting with new ways to resolve these tensions. Labor organizations are webs of conflicting interests, both among actual and potential officials and among those members whose status may be changed by technological developments or changes in shop rules. Similar conflicts are, of course, also characteristic of management.

There is some evidence of enlightenment about the nature of management and employee relations in the large corporation. Many of the day-to-day problems that concern workers are coming to be accepted by employers and workers alike to be primarily the responsibility of union officials. To this degree, then, the union itself becomes part of the "control apparatus" of industry. Shop stewards not only explain the grievances of workers to management but also the points of view of management to workers; increasingly they function to promote understanding and reasonable adjustments, decide questions of seniority rights, regulate shop discipline, and advance the interests of union members in harmony with those of management.

This hopeful realignment of responsibilities is not without its difficulties. Some of the hostility that has become traditional for employees to feel toward management tends to shift to stewards and other union officials.[3] And there is, of course, a tendency among these officers to avoid blame and opportunistically seek self-advantage.[4] Nevertheless, the potentialities for greatly decreasing traditional antagonisms are significant.

Cooperative Organizations

Impatience with laggard and often ineffective governmental action to protect the interests of consumers, independent producers, and credit institutions has encouraged the growth of cooperatives. National and state laws have been enacted to encourage them. By pooling their resources and making systematic arrangements for servicing their dealings, they have in degree overcome their dependency on the decisions made by the management of large corporations.

In some cases, such as credit unions and retail stores, the cooperatives have severely restricted their functions. In many cases, however, either through necessity or opportunity, they have combined related productive, distributive, and consumer functions. Thus farmers' cooperatives have successfully manufactured, distributed, and consumed fertilizers; dairy cooperatives have processed and sold milk and milk products. Plywood cooperatives not only manufacture and sell their product, paying wages and dividends to their members, but also own or lease their own forests and equipment to supply the logs to be peeled; and they expand into the processing and disposal of by-products. Petroleum cooperatives own wells, refineries, and service stations.

Side by side with such organizations have grown up cooperative insurance, cooperative prepayment health, medical, and hospital services, cooperative housing, and cooperative recreational facilities. Moreover, "intentional communities" are growing up in which as much as feasible of the social and economic activities of the group is carried on cooperatively, freed from the profit motive of any individual.

Within all such organizations, the acquisitive motivation is minimal. But it may be of major significance in motivating the association as a whole and, hence, in stimulating individuals to join and

[3] "The Heart of Unionism," *Fortune*, September, 1953, an editorial. For a report on differences as well as similarities in views regarding union activities and policies (in one large union) among officials, stewards, and rank-and-file members, see R. A. H. Rosen and H. Rosen, *The Union Member Speaks*, Prentice-Hall, Inc., Englewood Cliffs, N.J., 1955.

[4] Corrupt union officials and corrupt management officials do sometimes make deals for the pecuniary or other advantage of both, thereby shortcutting the slower and more uncertain processes of representation and conciliation concerning grievances and demands.

support the organization. Producers' and distributors' cooperatives may indeed be almost indistinguishable from private-profit corporations in so far as they affect the consumer public. A fruit growers' or a dairymen's association may be as consciously profit-seeking as any private or corporative enterprise. What differentiates the cooperative (if it is of the Rochdale type[5]) from the conventional corporation is that participation is conscious and voluntary and, especially, that all members have equal voting power, regardless of the amount of stock each owns. Both corporation and cooperative are forms of ownership and enterprise by which it is intended that advantages shall be maximized and shared and risks minimized and shared.

GLORIFICATION OF POWER AS A THREAT TO HUMAN WELFARE

So long as human society was composed of relatively disparate units, the effects of power hierarchies in political, economic, ecclesiastical, and other institutions were ambivalent. Gradations of authority tended to promote institutional stability even though they disparaged the dignity of subordinate individuals.

In the contemporary, interdependent society, however, power systems foster organized rivalries. The rivals may be corporations or industries, big labor unions, political parties, gangster mobs, or ethnic organizations. Power politics is not only international, but also interindustrial, interideological, and inter-economic-class. The glorification of power distracts critical inquiry and social judgment regarding the means by which power is attained and the effect of these means on popular liberties, self-esteem, and interpersonal relations.

The adulation of power is peculiarly confused in the contemporary United States. The American political and economic power units are not individual men, but fictions—corporations, legally termed "individuals," interlocked and subdivided into subsidiary corporations formed for special purposes. Nevertheless, these depersonalized "individuals" claim the attributes of their forerunners, the entrepreneurs of the

[5] In England, the Rochdale Society of Economic Pioneers, inspired by Robert Owen's doctrine, established a retail store in 1844. Its principles have been adhered to by many of the cooperative organizations in Europe and the United States—especially the principle of rebating to each member in proportion to his purchases (or analogous participation) such excesses of income over expenses as the members through their elected representatives authorize. Thus, not ownership, as such, but participation in the form of utilization of services is rewarded.

nineteenth century. Top management and boards of directors of huge modern corporate agglomerations ("owned" by numerous stockholders, most of whom have little actual control of the business, indebted to bondholders, with their policies heavily influenced by financial organizations) are products of a unique economy. Their analogy to the masterful organizers of yesteryear is strained. Entrepreneurship has become a collective, institutionalized process.[6]

The Business Bureaucrat Replaces the Entrepreneur

The outstanding business leader in the contemporary United States is typically an efficient business bureaucrat rather than an individual entrepreneur.[7] His incentives are salary, bonus, job security, reputation, and promotion; profits accrue to his employers. As a bureaucratic employee, he is a holder of important power; his incentives, his services to his employers, and the potentialities for his foresight and managerial ability to affect the emerging social configuration, not only in the United States, but in other nations as well, may deserve admiration and trust. But such respect should be accorded him in terms of his own role, not that of a stereotyped character—a free-enterprising, risk-taking entrepreneur who emerged in response to the opportunities and conditions of previous centuries.[8]

[6] Labor unions and cooperative organizations exemplify some of the same power attributes as corporations. Many decisions are made by executive officers, without prior consultation with the members, that are binding on them. Ratifications of such decisions by referendum are generally *pro forma.*

[7] William Miller (ed.), *Men in Business: Essays in the History of Entrepreneurship,* Harvard University Press, Cambridge, Mass., 1952. See, also, the editorial entitled, "Who Owns Business?" *Fortune,* September, 1952, p. 87. "What is most shocking, perhaps, is the apparent lack of appetite for stocks among the men who run U.S. business . . . only 45 per cent of the 'administrative executives' in the country own corporate stocks . . . it is hardly a reassuring statement of management's confidence in its own ability to turn a profit."

[8] The competitive drive for positions of power within the large corporation is frequently intense. It encourages the striving of restless, ambitious men who find in the struggle, as Lawrence Frank has asserted, "some sort of alleviation for their acute personality problems that otherwise might have driven them insane." Success in attaining a position of power often requires ruthless maneuvering of personal relationships as well as administrative competence. T. K. Quinn, formerly vice-president of General Electric Corporation, in *Giant Business: Threat to Democracy* (Exposition Press, New York,

The "managerial revolution" compels the corporation executive and directors to act in a quasi-public capacity. They are not free agents. In an extreme sense, they are depersonalized instruments of an impersonalized society. No one wills that they should have such great power over this generation and probably the next; but industry, finance, and governments, being what they are, allow management sufficient power to control the economic mechanisms to a very large extent.[9]

Practical Checks on Arbitrary Decisions

There are, to be sure, at least five counterpoises that rather effectively check the power of business management. Four of them tend actively to reenforce each other to make management act cautiously. They are organized labor, governmental law-enforcement agencies, buyer resistance to higher prices and lessened quality, and competition within domestic and world-wide markets.

A fifth counterpoise that induces managerial restraint is enlightenment and intelligence in its various aspects. Intelligence obviously plays important roles in management's dealings with the checks on arbitrary decisions that were mentioned in the preceding paragraph. In the modern, complex society, moreover, and peculiarly in the United States, industrial and financial executives have in many cases accepted the discipline of intellectual inquiry concerning long-term effects of corporate policies and practices.

These effects sometimes have to do with public confidence in the intentions and competence of the management of a specific corporation or industry or with public confidence in the economy as a whole. They sometimes center in the related areas of attracting investment

---

1953), after describing the power struggles among and within large corporations, concludes, "The awful vice of the age is the lust for power over men and nature. Power is being worshiped above truth, beauty, and love, which are all greater, finer ideals. One man of good will, kindness and humility is worth to humanity a thousand aggressive, power-mad emperors, bosses, or leaders. Learning these lessons will stop the spreading of the seeds of war."

[9] Other power elites than that of the business managers have developed, in some cases interlocked with it and sometimes as a countervailing force to it. Most obvious are those of military and other governmental bureaucracies, political machines, labor organizations, and criminal organizations. It is, of course, possible to conceive of circumstances wherein one or more of these elites might come into a position of sustained power comparable to that of business managers. At present, however, they are not so firmly ensconced.

capital and of maintaining and increasing buyer demand for products and services. Attention is sometimes directed to personnel policy in the realization that loyal, cooperative, and hopeful employees are more useful than sullen, antagonistic workers. Intelligence sometimes leads management to recognize the interdependence of adequate incomes for the masses and the continuing prosperity of corporation managers, other employees, and investors.[10]

Organized business can, however, do little to control so amorphous and complicated a mechanism as a prosperity market.[11] Business is subject to two diametrically antithetical pressures—immediate profits requiring expanding plants, equipment, and credit and long-term economic stability being threatened if the expansion proves excessive when demand for goods and services slackens. To guard against this contradiction by governmental fiat, by the development of cartels, or by mass abnegation would be a denial of free enterprise itself. The choice between the aggressive bettering of a firm's competitive position and immediate profits, on the one hand, and enlightened self-interest over the "long pull," on the other hand, is a difficult one; nevertheless, it is one that cannot be avoided. Diversification of products and services, to insure that reasonable demand for some of them may be expected even during recessions, requires that part of the productive resources serve low-profit markets during prosperity to the temporary disadvantage of stockholders.[12]

Once recession threatens, the negative aspect of plant investment becomes of crucial importance. A sudden major cessation of capital outlay is all too likely to plunge the economy into a disastrous depression. In that case, the federal government would have to intervene again as it did during the 1930s, and as, indeed, it has not ceased to do during the 1940s, the 1950s, and into the 1960s. A wholesale intervention in case of the collapse of the contemporary government-

[10] Elliott Haynes, "The Businessman's Revolution," *United Nations World,* November, 1952, pp. 41–44.

[11] An assertion attributed to David Sarnoff, President of the Radio Corporation of America, is to the effect that the American economy lives by obsolescence. The implication is that products must be constantly replaced, not because they are no longer serviceable to meet the needs for which they were provided, but because desires have been created for new and "improved" goods and services.

[12] The editors of *Fortune,* September, 1953, p. 92, take a somewhat pessimistic view of this matter. They report that the consensus among businessmen is that private firms can do nothing to stabilize investment without assuming risks inconsistent with their responsibilities to stockholders.

protected enterprise system might transmute large-scale "private enterprise" into "state capitalism."

BUSINESS CYCLES AND SOCIAL WELFARE

Organizations purposely established to promote the welfare of a part or the whole of society require public support if they are to function effectively. Apart from belief by the community that the organization is desirable and important, the adequacy of such support varies with public ability and willingness to assure welfare agencies sufficient financial means to carry out their purposes. Because public education responds to public moods which vary with alternating periods of economic prosperity and depression, it is important for educators to understand the character of business expansions and recessions.

The phenomenon of successive periods of prosperity and depression, though experienced throughout civilized history, has causes peculiar to the processes of capitalism. "Booms," in modern times, have been responses to new economic opportunities connected with developments of commerce, invention, enterprise, and mining and have often been stimulated by war.[13]

In addition, the stability of the economy is influenced by advances in science and technology, by domestic and international crises, and by competition among rival capitalist organizations. If the economy gets out of hand, a catastrophic depression may follow; a downward spiral of underemployment and consequent underconsumption threatens not only capital investment but also social stability.[14] "Busts" have regularly followed "booms."

The combination of specific causes that "trigger" each recession is unique. Attempts to generalize regarding causes of recession have, therefore, been unsatisfactory.[15]

[13] A chart prepared by L. P. Ayers, of the Cleveland Trust Company, shows twenty-three major depressions in the United States from 1790 to 1932. "Normal" business years scarcely existed. Upswings and downswings about equally divide the time span.

[14] Even assuming an insatiable popular appetite for commodities, which is questionable, purchasing media—money and credit symbols—must balance the flow of goods and services to market. And wages and salaries constitute the firm basis for purchasing power; interest and dividends are of minor significance. See "Why Do People Buy?" *Fortune*, April, 1952, pp. 104–107, 194–198.

[15] Cf. J. W. McConnel, *The Basic Teachings of the Great Economists*, The New Home Library, New York, 1943, chap. 9.

It is generally recognized that high price levels stimulate optimistic and often speculative overdevelopment by industrialists, farmers, and financiers. Modern theory about business cycles, therefore, puts major emphasis on the role of consumer demand in maintaining price levels, and, hence, on the importance of continuing full employment and adequate income of workers to provide a profitable market for goods. Unfortunately, however, high prices stimulate inventions and enterprises that make craft skills and occupational advantages obsolescent and so threaten full employment, high wages, and consumption.

Conflicting Loyalties and Moralities of Management

Despite the relatively enlightened character of much contemporary business practice, there remain significant elements of manipulation and clever intrigue within many business organizations and in their dealings with the public. To be sure, the stereotyped "boss"-manager, defiant of restraint and disdainful toward public opinion, is outmoded. He was a phenomenon of the transition from personal entrepreneurship to modern management. Temperamentally, he has proved unadaptable to the limitations imposed by an occasionally aroused democracy.[16]

The basic outlooks and attitudes of the "boss"-manager have, however, persisted within some modern corporations. These corporations frequently make uneasy peace with organized labor, accept government supervision (and funds), use devious means to meet competition and to evade federal, state, and local taxes, and employ public relations experts to present extravagant claims both for their products and for their contributions to progress and public service. They carry on warfare (sometimes hidden, sometimes open) against liberalism in legislation, education, and all other channels of communication. Their contempt for political democracy is evident in their all-too-successful efforts to corrupt it.[17]

The debasement of a political agency takes many forms. Some of these forms are quite within the framework of legal and popular toleration; others are clever, "within-the-law," but popularly condemned practices. Boldly illegal measures, such as direct bribery, falsification of records, and cheating, although not infrequent, are disapproved by reputable businessmen and the public.

[16] The executive officers of some labor organizations continue their arbitrary sway. But they, too, are transitional figures.
[17] Cf. Edwin H. Sutherland, *White Collar Crime,* The Dryden Press, Inc., New York, 1939, and Marshall B. Clinard, *Black Market: A Study of White Collar Crime,* Rinehart & Company, Inc., New York, 1952.

Legal corruption of democratic processes takes place in areas of institutional activities that have not as yet been adequately publicized. Corrective measures and legal prohibitions await some egregious miscarriage of public business, whether of courts, legislative bodies, or administrations; the shocking effects of such miscarriage mobilize irresistible public protest.

Popular toleration of special economic-group pressures on governmental agencies that are presumed to serve all segments of the population equitably is implicit in an evolving society. That rich clients will have ingenious and skillful lawyers and lobbyists when their affairs are dealt with by the courts or other departments of the government is accepted by the public as a somewhat regrettable fact. Similarly, the fact that campaign contributions to political parties by individuals representing corporations or other economic organizations are likely to be related to hoped-for favors is generally shrugged off as inevitable under current political practices. And so the recruitment of high-level personnel by national and state administrative departments from the very circles or organizations that have direct stakes in the governmental decisions that they are in position to influence is not often openly protested.[18]

In the long run, however, these legal corruptions of political democracy are likely to be self-defeating. Gradually, they undermine public confidence in business management, so that in time of crisis or of flagrantly maladroit tactics, governmental action to remedy the evils and to control powerful economic organizations is likely to be demanded by an aroused citizenry.

Such governmental intervention and such loss of public confidence is exemplified by cases of national and international cartel agreements. Great corporations have frequently agreed to share their information and patent rights, parcel out markets or otherwise control distribution of products, establish priorities for needed materials, and manipulate prices. Secrecy or avoidance of formal organization may temporarily protect such a cartel from prosecution under antitrust laws.[19]

[18] Harlan Cleveland, "Survival in the Bureaucratic Jungle," *The Reporter*, April 5, 1956, pp. 30–31.

[19] Corporation mergers and concentrations continue despite the Sherman Antitrust Act of 1890, the Clayton Antitrust Act of 1914, the Federal Trade Commission, established in the latter year to prevent evasions of these acts, and the Federal Power Commission, established in 1930 to supervise utility-corporation practices.

Political Institutions Favor the Economically Powerful

It is in the realms of morals and law that the cultural lag is most clearly revealed. Despite the shibboleths of political democracy, a distinctive class morality and class justice retain social sanction. Courts of law frequently make distinctions in favor of "standard business practices" with little regard for social ethics.

In the American class-structured society, *the power to enforce* is a realistic determinant of what shall be forbidden and punished and what shall be ignored and permitted. A criminal (or a juvenile delinquent) is one who is guilty of an act believed, by a group that *has the power to enforce* its belief, to be injurious to society and therefore prohibited.[20] Until and unless the social classes which are now disadvantaged by ruthlessness, chicanery, and caprice in higher economic and governmental circles come to believe and *gain power to enforce their belief* that the same code of law and morals shall apply to the "upper" as well as the "lower" economic strata of the population, delinquency and crime will continue to be a characteristic of low economic and cultural status.[21]

The struggle of ordinary people to gain sufficient power to force equality in law and morals has been a mark of Western democratic societies. Every step in the economic revolution, from the organization of medieval town populations to the development of international business cartels, has been accompanied by surges of protest from disadvantaged people who have sought for themselves the power to assert their "natural" rights to share equally in the good things of community life. In the United States, there has been a parallel between industrial and financial invention, on the one hand, and the advancing frontier and popular assertiveness, on the other.[22]

[20] J. L. Gillin, C. G. Dittmer, R. J. Colburt, and N. M. Kastler, *Social Problems,* 4th ed., Appleton-Century-Crofts, Inc., New York, 1952, p. 418.

[21] Harry Elmer Barnes and Negley K. Teeters, *New Horizons in Criminology,* 3d ed., Prentice-Hall, Inc., Englewood Cliffs, New Jersey, 1959, pp. 147–153. Recent investigations suggest the possibility that there may previously have been some overestimation of the relation of low socioeconomic status and high rates of juvenile delinquency and crime—or that this relation has changed somewhat in the last few years. See F. Ivan Nye, James F. Short, Jr., and Virgil J. Olson, "Socioeconomic Status and Delinquent Behavior, *The American Journal of Sociology,* vol. 63, no. 1, pp, 381–389, January, 1958.

[22] Charles A. Beard and Mary R. Beard, "The Industrial Revolution," *Basic History of the United States,* The New Home Library, Washington, 1944, chap. 13.

The thrust for power by the disadvantaged has had numerous effects. Many energetic and ambitious individuals, accepting the world as they have found it, have made their bid for power by industrious and resourceful efforts within the multiform organizations that have grown so extravagantly in the United States. Public education opened the gateways to the professions, politics, and employment in hundreds of different lines of manufacture, selling, publicity, and recreation. Vocational success, for those who have attained it in marked degree, has in many cases required more than assiduity and institutional loyalty; *savoir-faire,* cleverness, venturesomeness, and often considerable ruthlessness, have been needed in the rough-and-tumble competition with rivals.[23] But good faith and trustworthiness toward colleagues and others who have had the power to enforce their demands for honesty have had to be preserved side by side with cleverness in "outguessing" those who have lacked the power and toughness.

Government is not carried on in a vacuum. Every decision and act of an official requires support, or at least toleration, by all sections of the population; else, evasion, defiance, and defeat ensue. In many cases, however, decisions are more than passive responses to the momentary resolution of pressures; political leaders court the active support of powerful groups for policies and for specific acts that they wish the government to undertake. Whether the resulting decisions are wise or foolish, selfish or unselfish, corrupt or honorable, they must be justified before some bar of public opinion—a fact that provides a field day for rationalization, half-truth, and lies. So it has been for three millennia; so it is now.[24]

There is vast interplay of partly conflicting and partly complementary motivations of power-seeking groups in finance, industry, agriculture, and political parties, on the one side, and legislative bodies, courts of law, and public administrators, on the other. The scene is endlessly confused, not only because there are dissenting subgroups in the power organizations, but also because other segments of public concern must be placated, whatever decision is arrived at by government.

The individuals who compose these power groups and other public segments are themselves motivated by inconsistent, often irreconcilable, values. They are consumers as well as producers, investors in corporate ventures as well as employees, members of families, churches,

[23] Oscar Handlin, *The Uprooted,* Atlantic Monthly Press, Boston, 1951, chaps. 8 and 9.

[24] Kings, tyrants, popes, triumvirs, dictators, and even successful reformers have characteristically made policy decisions agreeable to power groups; else, they have not long retained the ability to make their decisions stick.

and civic and recreational groups as well as of veterans' organizations, political parties, and taxpayers' associations. What they favor in one role may be the antithesis of what they find acceptable in another.

The actual role of government, at all levels, is to maintain stability supported by a high degree of common consent to a trial of whatever decisions are made. Only in times of emergency is the government free to act boldly, and, then, only because the power seeking groups have temporarily lost their assertiveness.

Transition from Corporate to Public Economy

An acquisitive society is inevitably pragmatic at least so far as profit is concerned. Private investment quickly dries up if prospects of profit dim. Moreover, the social stake in the solvency of many corporations is so crucial that their failure would threaten the public welfare and safety.[25] Hence, some preventive measures are obviously required to forestall failure; if failure comes in spite of these safeguards, measures of state intervention must follow. So it comes about that municipal, state, and national governments are participants in the affairs of corporations.

At least three forms of such "public-business" intervention may be distinguished. (1) The government contracts to purchase the product or service of a corporation, assuring a reasonable profit on the transaction, lending its credit, allowing rapid "depreciation" and "amortization" of equipment for tax purposes. Requirements regarding labor policies may be specified. This arrangement goes, nevertheless, by the name of "private enterprise." (2) A "public corporation" is established by legislative action to carry on a socially mandatory business that private investors would shy away from. Deficits are met by appropriations from tax funds; profits may be used to improve plant and services or transferred into the public treasury. (3) Municipal, state, or national governmental agencies take over a business, usually by negotiated purchase, from the titular owners and their creditors; public officials then carry on the business, the criterion for policy being adequacy of service rather than profit.

Almost without regard to this classification, federal, state, and

[25] A prolonged shutdown of General Motors automotive plants, for example, not only would seriously endanger their suppliers of parts and the distributors and servicers of their products but also would depress the production of basic materials, such as steel, rubber, oil, coal, copper, and lead. The accompanying unemployment and reduction of dividend and interest payments would so undermine the demand for all commodities that the shutdown might act as a "trigger" to a serious deflationary spiral.

local governments, independently or in combination, have intervened to correct malfunctioning, to encourage business ventures and practices considered desirable by legislators, and to meet emergencies. Some intervention has taken place without specific legislation, either under general enabling laws or "implied" powers or by request or consent of the organizations concerned. In all cases, of course, public toleration for such an act by an administrative agency or by a court has been a basic consideration.[26]

THE AMERICAN ECONOMY AS A MIXED TYPE

Reference to the American economy as "free enterprise," "capitalism," "creeping socialism," "social fascism," "the monster state," or any other neat term or phrase is, in general, inaccurate.

The American economy is a straggling, hit-and-miss, inconsistent, and tentative congeries of structures and processes. The lack of over-all plan and doctrine is caused not by any lack of ideas, but rather by their superabundance and competition with one another. Any specific legislation, administrative action, or judicial decision which affects the economy is almost certain to be held "dangerous" and "un-American" by some citizens. Hence, disagreement, conflict, and divisiveness over economic affairs have been superficial but blatant characteristics of Americans.

Diversity Possible under an Experimental Economy

Regardless of noisy criticism and opposition, legislators, executives, and others who have responsibility for action have made pragmatic decisions one after another. Creeds have been revised, public schools established and modified, labor conditions and relations controlled, immigration policies changed, tax purposes and burdens shifted, national income increased and redistributed, and thousands of other alterations made at all levels and in all kinds of social organizations.

To the cloistered ideologist, it doubtless appears that the United States, like Leacock's famous horseman, is riding off full tilt in all directions at once. The people demand from their representatives both individual and group freedom and also protection from the excesses of others' freedoms. And so compromises are necessary in all larger group decisions reached in whatever boards, councils, committees, legislatures, and executive offices have, or assume, jurisdiction. Inconsistencies are taken as a matter of course.

[26] See Richard Hofstadter, *The Age of Reform,* Alfred A. Knopf, Inc., New York, 1955, esp. chaps. 3 and 4.

From bottom to top, in families, school organizations, religious bodies, and governments, Americans foster not only individualism and decentralization, but also social controls that severely restrict them. The goal is not fixed and precise, though it is generally circumscribed by the values subscribed to in the Declaration of Independence, the Preamble to the Constitution, and other canons of popular welfare. As a people, Americans do not try to "hurry history" too much.

If state and national governments assume far more power than the founding fathers foresaw, they do so because the public consents in the belief that its welfare is thus fostered. If not only roads, hospitals, post offices, and lighthouses, but also nominally private organizations— railroads, steel corporations, banks, labor unions, and large farms— should become parts of the public economy, it would be because such a development becomes, in some degree, inevitable.

Every Governmental Intervention Sought by Some Group

In increasing degree, rather than to fight out their disagreements and so threaten the very existence of a profit-making industry, all interested parties—employees at all levels, directors, stockholders and creditors, and the consumers of the product—look to government for decisions, regulations, subsidies, price fixing, purchases, and loans. Somewhat grudgingly, perhaps, they respond to leadership and guidance by governmental agencies—legislative committees, Presidents', governors', and mayors' *ad hoc* commissions, labor-relations boards and conciliation services, and the Federal reserve banks. And all of the interested groups set up advisory and pressure organizations to promote and protect their own interests and, in some cases, the public welfare. It may be rather easy for them to confuse the two.[27]

At present, anyway, there seems to be general agreement in the United States, both among those primarily interested in corporate business and those most concerned with "general welfare," that the production of many forms of goods and services is likely to be more efficiently carried on, for profit, under the direction of "privately" employed managers and technicians than it would be under a governmental bureaucracy. That issue is not permanently settled. There is, for

[27] A statement attributed to former Secretary for Defense, Charles E. Wilson, that what is good for General Motors (whose president he had been and in which, at the time, he still had a large interest) is good for the country has been widely ridiculed. Nevertheless, there is more than a grain of truth in his assertion. Had he said that what is good for the country is good for General Motors, his statement would have been unchallengeable.

example, little sentiment favorable to turning schools, post offices, parks, and roads over to profit-seeking enterprises.

SUMMARY

For more than five centuries, Western man has been influenced by an accelerating industrial revolution. Increasingly large segments of the population have been drawn into a struggle, first for survival and then for an equitable share in the economic product. The attainment of property, social acceptance, self-assertion, and political influence have been major and immediate objectives of many assertive people.

Workers, weighed down by frustration and hopelessness in an economy rigged to keep them impotent, tended to accept the world as they found it, sometimes seeking compensation in orgiastic excesses. Militant minorities of disadvantaged men, however, challenged the system everywhere in Europe.

The American nation has been a special case. It has differed from its European antecedents in fundamental ways. Here land hunger was in great degree appeased. Here the factory system did not become dominant until after the majority of common men had experienced, and so had come to treasure, relative independence. Here the spirit of protest and nonconformity was irrepressible. Here the flamboyant catchwords of social, political, and economic democracy were honored. And to America came immigrants, many of whom had great ambition, energy, and a spirit of protest.

On the North American continent, an agricultural economy for use and exchange was frequently associated with land speculation, that is, with business for profit. Craft production for use and exchange was succeeded by employment by an entrepreneur. By the end of the eighteenth century, with the beginnings of power-oriented organizations as federal and state governments collaborated with commercial and finance capitalists, use economy merged with profit economy.

During the second half of the nineteenth century, power-oriented business came to dominate the American economy, as it already had done in England. So overwhelming was its impact on the American culture, so shocking to moral sensibilities, so threatening to the security of farmers, laborers, and independent businessmen, and so indifferent to the consumers' welfare that public limitations were imposed. And thus the negative aspect of governmental participation in business became accepted practice.

Positive measures followed immediately, for power-oriented business had already become a major, though unofficial, political instrument. Its continuing success was essential to national prosperity. It could not be displaced; but it could be tamed and made to function with modest regard for the national interest. War and depression, each in its way, made the federal government part owner of giant corporations; guidance, supervision, encouragement, and guarantees of profits became governmental functions. Organized workers, farmers, consumers, and other pressure groups gained analogous roles in government.

In the United States, men are gradually attuning themselves to contradictory slogans and conflicting social and cultural facts. Residues from preindustrial economies still are current, for example, "private property," "the right to the product of one's labor," "the prerogatives of management," and "free competition." But the public is not altogether fooled by the tags. A half-century and more of governmental economic activity has made the terms mean something that the words themselves do not explicitly signify.

The social scientist is an empiricist; he seeks constantly to adapt the categories and generalizations of his discipline to what he observes. He is peculiarly and properly much concerned with the mental and emotional structures of American middle classes. He is especially concerned with their dependence upon an expanding economy, their search for social esteem as a *raison d'être,* the incongruity of their desire for individual freedom and their negation of that freedom, and their vain frenzies to fill up the hollownesses of their own personalities with diversions that seldom satisfy them for long. The scientist seeks the significance of such phenomena to evolving social patterns, their derivations, meanings, and trends. In doing so, he directs his attention to the evolution of political, economic, religious, ethical, scientific, and technological institutions, organizations, and inventions, and to the conflicts and compromises that characterize the society. He assesses neither praise nor blame; as scientist, he has no moralistic function. His judgments regarding the social by-products of the trends he distinguishes are always based on clearly stated criteria.

As a citizen, he probably fulfills a broader and more militant function than he does as scientist. He often contributes valuable information, methodology, and a "spirit of tentativeness" to group efforts to solve social problems. He seeks to help his contemporaries look at human affairs objectively and dispassionately. His opinions are therefore worthy of respect. But he is not the authority; he knows no final truth about the future.

The authors of this volume, though in fact social scientists themselves, consider that they have a function that differentiates them from the social scientist as such. They are concerned with the motives and goals of the American people and with the adequacy of the institutions and organizations through which they seek their goals. Their mandate is that of all American educators: to aid men in achieving their democratic ideals.

The fate of theories and proposals concerning the future of man in society is, to be sure, largely at the mercy of events. The major social changes take place amid circumstances that can only be dimly foreseen. Philosophers, statesmen, and professional educators may persuade their fellow men to act intelligently in the light of what is both possible and desirable in any given set of conditions, that is, to consent to facts and to measures that adequately take account of them. To the extent that they succeed in their persuasions, they promote orderly progress and social stability.

SELECTED REFERENCES

Barnes, Harry Elmer, and Negley K. Teeters: *New Horizons in Criminology,* 3d ed., Prentice-Hall, Inc., Englewood Cliffs, N.J., 1959. An authoritative volume on crime, its prevention, and its treatment. Contains good discussions of the socioeconomic factors in criminal and delinquent behavior.

Bendix, Reinhard: *Work and Authority in Industry: Ideologies of Management in the Course of Industrialization,* John Wiley & Sons, Inc., New York, 1956. A scholarly work on the ideologies of management.

Berle, A. A., and G. C. Means: *The Modern Corporation and Private Property,* The Macmillan Company, New York, 1933. An influential book on the characteristics of the modern corporation.

Harwood, E. C.: *Twentieth Century Common Sense and the American Crisis of the 1960's,* American Institute of Economic Research, Great Barrington, Mass., 1960. An argument for a retreat to national isolationism and free enterprise.

Heilbroner, Richard L.: *The Future as History,* Harper & Brothers, New York, 1960. A projection of the potential assets and liabilities of technology, democracy, and capitalism into the world of tomorrow. Implications for public adult education if the drift toward disaster is to be controlled and redirected.

Knox, John B.: *The Sociology of Industrial Relations,* Random House, Inc., New York, 1955. An informative, easy-to-read textbook.

MacIver, Robert M.: *The Web of Government,* The Macmillan Company, New York, 1947. A famous book on modern governmental structures and processes.

Mayo, Elton: *The Social Problems of an Industrial Civilization,* Doubleday & Company, Inc., New York, 1945. A provocative volume by one of the leading students of the effects of industrialization on society.

Miller, William (ed.): *Men in Business: Essays in the History of Entrepreneurship,* Harvard University Press, Cambridge, Mass., 1952. A good collection of essays on the history of business.

Moore, Wilbert E.: *Industrial Relations and the Social Order,* rev. ed., The Macmillan Company, New York, 1951. A good textbook on industrial sociology. Contains discussions of changing conceptions of property rights in the United States.

Rosen, R. A. H., and H. Rosen: *The Union Member Speaks,* Prentice-Hall, Inc., Englewood Cliffs, N.J., 1955. A research report which emphasizes similarities and differences in the views regarding union activities and policy among officials, stewards, and rank-and-file members of a large mechanics' union.

Schneider, Eugene V.: *Industrial Sociology: The Social Relations of Industry and the Community,* McGraw-Hill Book Company, Inc., New York, 1957. A useful textbook which reports much of the research in the field of industrial sociology.

Tocqueville, Alexis de: *Democracy in America,* trans. by Henry Reeve, Oxford University Press, New York, 1947. This provocative work, first published in 1835 and 1840, still remains the most insightful study of the sources of the American commonwealth.

DISCUSSION QUESTIONS

1. Are cooperative consumer, producer, and distributor organizations classifiable as "collectivistic," "capitalistic," "decentralist," "democratic," or "anarchistic," either in fact or in trend? Perhaps they have all these characteristics in some regard?

2. Some mail-order firms and department stores sell goods under their own "brand names" that are identical with articles that are widely advertised under standard brand names. The prices charged are usually lower than those of the famous trademarks. The practice is legal. Do you believe that it is unethical?

3. Is centralized administration of businesses an inevitable accompaniment of large organization? Is it in fact characteristic of either successful businesses or of state and national governments?

4. In your local community, have two decades of almost full employment markedly reduced the relative number of families whose living conditions are substandard? Do slum areas continue to exist? If both your answers are affirmative, how do you explain the implicit contradiction?

5. One basic disagreement among economic advisers of federal and state legislatures concerns the priority in importance of encouraging the consumption of goods and of services, increasing the potent demand for producers to satisfy profitably, and encouraging capital investments to expand production, thereby increasing job opportunities. How would you expect each school of advisers to react to proposals for an increase of public works, deficit financing, incentive taxation, guaranteed jobs, minimum wages, maximum hours of work at basic wage scales, elimination of child labor, and creating new and enlarged wants?

6. The alleged imbalance between money spent for private purposes and that spent for public purposes is causing much controversy among students of the nation's economy. Since public services are for the most part supported by taxation, and since taxation diminishes the privilege of the taxpayer to spend all of his income for private purposes, he may believe that any more than minimal expenditures for public services amounts to an unwarranted restriction of his freedom. What do you think about it?

7. The astounding increase of purchasing media in this country since the end of World War II has been characterized by dramatic increases in commercial and noncommercial private debt monetized as Federal reserve notes and as checking accounts. Are these credit-debt symbols of wealth legalized and hence supported by public consent? If so, may consent be withdrawn if the system ceases to be equated with the common welfare?

13

Science, Power,
and Freedom

APPLIED SCIENCE AND HUMAN FREEDOM

Freedom from want has always been a basic aspiration of Americans, as of all other people. The scientific and technological revolution now, for the first time in history, makes material abundance a possibility.

Civic leaders everywhere have always hoped that the blessings of material plenty would free men from many of the anxieties, fears, hates, and parochial prejudices that have attended the struggle over wealth. To a considerable extent, the force of these atavisms has been decreased. But they have not disappeared because man, even when his basic wants are satisfied, is not altogether free to choose his beliefs and behavior. He carries with him into the new era the search for status, the loyalty to institutions, and the ghosts of obsolescent antagonisms. Inevitably he is a spectator rather than a participant as dramatic events unfold and as basic political and economic conflicts develop; he often feels impelled by public opinion or by old loyalties to take sides regarding issues about which he is ignorant or indifferent.

It is appropriate to consider at this point a number of the yet unresolved problems with which the American society is now confronted. The measures now in use and the goals now sought by civic leaders and educators who endeavor to resolve these problems are to be evaluated by their probable contribution to the realization of *natural* [1] rights of all men to life, liberty, and the pursuit of happiness. Progress in a social democracy is defined as a "conscious moving on toward purposes which are felt to be worthy of human faith and human endeavor." [2]

Science and Progress

"Science represents the office of projection and control in new experience, pursued systematically, intentionally, and on a scale due to freedom from limitation of habit. It is the sole instrumentality of conscious, as distinct from accidental, progress." [3] This statement holds true whether the scientist's purpose is the modification of an abstract hypothesis, the improvement of a technical process, or the adaptation of a social agency.

The goal sought by the instrumentation of science, however, may be equated with progress in one set of circumstances; it may be destructive of social progress in another circumstance. Projection and control in the fields of electronics and atomic energy are obvious cases in point.

It has seemed to many social critics that the technological revolution had gone farther and faster than it should have.[4] But with so many variables functioning, there have always come "breakthroughs."

The secluded mathematician or laboratory scientist, engaged in the high-level play of satisfying his curiosity, comes to some esoteric conclusion, states it as a hypothesis, and perhaps makes a laboratory apparatus to try out his theory; this may be as far as he is interested in following the matter.[5] But enough applications of scientific hypotheses

---

[1] The question regarding the justification for calling these rights "natural" is not germane for American public educators. Within the American political and ethical framework, the rights are posited. The role of public education is to aid in their achievement.

[2] Attributed to E. H. Carr, the English philosopher.

[3] John Dewey, *Democracy and Education,* The Macmillan Company, New York, 1916, p. 266.

[4] From Bentham, Mill, Owen, Ruskin, Samuel Butler, and Tennyson in England and the Brook Farm group in America to some of the present day "decentralists," humanists, and satirists, the maleficent effects of technological advance, actual and potential, have been matters of concern.

[5] For example, the classic story (perhaps apocryphal) of Faraday's reply to Gladstone's skeptical query regarding the practical im-

and inventive insights do eventually "find a market" so that progress toward automation in manufacture, commerce, agriculture, and transportation continues.

Dislocations Due to Technological Improvements

Each major technological advance makes obsolescent or obsolete the skills of some specialized workers, machines, and processes in which capital has been invested, and entire factories, ships, and even cities which are ill-adapted to the new technology. New capital investments develop other regions, require new kinds of skilled employees, call for better-adapted buildings, machines, and fabricated materials, and often greatly increase the production of goods.

Many dislocations due to technological improvements are in time compensated for. New demands for old skills develop. Workmen are retrained. The people move from one place to another. The increased production of goods and higher wages which are characteristic of technological specialization increase the demand for many kinds of services. Nevertheless, the dislocations can be locally and temporarily severe.

Service occupations, which cannot be economically and efficiently mechanized and for which automatic substitutes cannot be created, may in considerable degree take up the slack in employment. In such fields as health, education, recreation, art, government, and sales, the advantage of personal qualities cannot be replaced by those of robots. But service occupations, like all others, depend on demand, only part of which will probably be supplied by "taking in each other's washing," or by the incomes of six-hour-day and four-day-week workers in offices and factories. Under some guise or other, public subsidization of economically nonproductive activities may be required. Today's compensated military and other civic service, subsidized post–high school education, unemployment compensation, and social security allowances may be forerunners of more general "paid leisure."

The Role of the Educator in Expanding Applied Science

There are, however, even more disturbing questions posed by the "progress" of applied science. What beneficent or maleficent effects do accelerating economic and geographic mobility accompanying the applications of science to industry have on man? Can man avoid being submerged by the products of automatic production? Can society develop a culture that does not depend on compensated productive work

---

portance of electrical induction: "Perhaps some day you can tax it." The political and economic applicability of his discovery did not interest Faraday, the scientist.

to give meaning to life? Will the stultification fostered by the hucksterism of advertising, uniformity of amusements, multiplicity of equipment, crowd attitudes, and stereotyped "normalcy" overwhelm individualism? Will one or several bold, ingenious, and ruthless men come so effectively to control economic institutions, instruments of communication, international policies, the administration of courts and police, and the moral climate of the nation that unquestioning submission to an elite of power will be equated with "good citizenship"? [6]

The social thinker cannot avoid such questions. His concerns with society put him in the midst of efforts to control people's minds. His mandate is to understand the character of the forces that affect the standards and aspirations of men for good or for ill. It is his role to estimate their potency and their potentialities. And in the light of his conclusions he formulates educational measures that seem to him not only meliorative, but within the framework of the American ethos.

For these purposes, the educator considers applied science as much his ally as his foe. The facts of economic abundance, mass communication, and group norms of conduct, clothing, and shelter may ennoble personalities or they may stultify them. In some regards, these facts are personal and social *wealth;* in other regards, personal and social *illth.* In any case, they are present and continuing realities. Education functions well only if it fosters the better effects and offsets or diminishes the worse.

The educator has high regard for that "freedom from limitation of habit required for the projection and control of the new experiences" which characterizes the informed man in a society that exalts science. The problems that must be solved with public consent and support require that information, awareness, and reason characterize men generally and in each specific instance.

Individual Freedom, Reason, and Emotion

The long struggle for freedom from slavery and serfdom, from coercion by arbitrary authority, and from unremitting poverty has in varying degrees been won in the Western world. No man, however, can be fully free from the morality of his group. His interdependence with his fellow men is essential to his being; human beings live and have their being as members of groups.

The truly free man seeks to live a life of reason. He complies

[6] See J. Robert Oppenheimer, "Prospects in the Arts and Sciences," *The Reporter,* January 13, 1955, pp. 32–33. "What is new in the world is the massive dissolution and corruption of authority in belief, in ritual, and in temporal order." Also, C. Wright Mills, *The Power Elite,* Oxford University Press, New York, 1956, chap. 6.

with most of the mores, to be sure, because it does not seem reasonable to flaunt them; indeed, he finds in them some encouragement of independence. The right to differ from the obscurantisms of traditional morality is itself a norm of democratic culture. Respect for rationalism goes hand in hand with high regard for science; together they have pioneered the ideas of, and justified progress toward, individuality.

Limits to the Desire for Freedom

The emergence of such freedom as man has attained is complicated by the fact that only evanescently have individuals wanted to be free. Most men, most of the time, feel more secure in doing and believing what is approved by their fellow men. Even though intellectually they may reject the mandates of tradition and the morality taught them in childhood, they follow the path of least resistance by conforming to the mores of their peer groups and to patterns that are exalted by the mass media.[7]

Only the autonomous man chooses consciously when and with what he will conform and to what degree he will avoid conformity. He alone actively and spontaneously participates in creating his own self-hood and in helping to shape a society that permits and encourages individual self-determination. Once such a character has taken form, any behavior in line with its spontaneous activities will be at the same time psychologically satisfying and practical from the standpoint of successful personality.[8]

There is no blinking the fact, nevertheless, that such independence is usually uncomfortable for the individual. It entails feelings of aloneness and some degree of social ostracism. In a tradition-bound cultural climate, differences seem dangerous to morality and stability; nonconformity frequently leads to economic reprisals, imprisonment, banishment, and bodily injury.[9] Even under such circumstances, however, if the autonomous man can make his adaptations without sacrificing his solidarity with men in general and his spontaneous activity, love,

[7] See David Riesman and others, *The Lonely Crowd,* abridged ed., Doubleday & Company, Inc., New York, 1953, pp. 35–38. The authors distinguished three types of American character structure: "tradition-directed" (conformity), "inner-directed" (parent-induced morality), and "other-directed" (peer-group and mass-media control). The first two are infantilistic; only the third provides much opportunity for the individual's self-choice.

[8] Erich Fromm, *Escape from Freedom,* Rinehart & Company, Inc., New York, 1941, pp. 284–285.

[9] W. L. Miller and David Halberstam, "People in Mississippi," *The Reporter,* December 15, 1955, pp. 27–32. An account of the persecution of two welfare workers in a tradition-bound community.

and work among them, he achieves unity with his world as a free and independent person. He is free to act according to his own will because he knows what he really wants to be.

Awareness of personal selfhood, the basic ingredient of inquiry and spontaneity, is deeply embedded in the structure of human personality. The following questions arise in infancy: Can I? How can I? Why can't I? And despite continuing cultural conditioning and indoctrination, these inquiries are never quite stamped out. These questions are most often and insistently asked when a command, a law, or a custom thwarts the attainment of personal goals.

Such self-interest questions do not necessarily encourage intellectual objectivity in seeking answers; but they may compel the inquirer to face problem situations for which no clear and ready answers are available and regarding which various opinions, tinged by desire and rationalization, are held and propagandized. Even special pleading requires intellectualization both to support one's own plea and to refute opposing pleas. Moreover the debate implies recognition of much freedom to think and to express conclusions.

Of greater immediate social significance, probably, is the awareness that conclusions, whether individually or group-derived, can be effectively instrumented only by collaboration with and organization of those of like mind. And because individual desires and beliefs regarding the problem are unlikely to be identical, feasible compromises are necessary if a common effort is to be forthcoming.

Freedom and Group Action

Voluntary compromise to attain unity of argument and action does not of itself vitiate individual freedom of inquiry. Group action and organized pressure to accomplish agreed-upon purposes do, however, encourage the emergence of leaders and official representatives whose personal interpretations and decisions all too quickly replace thinking by individual members. Unless the individuals give loyal support to their leaders and representatives, group action is almost sure to be futile, and the assurance of loyal support encourages surrender of the right and duty to examine and criticize the opinions and acts of the official spokesmen. Hence, programs, platforms, "principles," and tactical decisions of most political, labor, corporative, and social service organizations become far removed from the general membership which participates in them only vicariously.[10]

Participation in decision making by those directly affected by

[10] See Morris R. Cohen, *The Faith of a Liberal*, Henry Holt and Company, Inc., New York, 1946, pp. 132–133 and Clay P. Malick, "Let's Join a Lobby," *Colorado Quarterly*, pp. 292–301, Winter, 1953.

the judgments is feasible only when relatively small numbers are concerned and when the matters under discussion can be readily grasped by the participants. Such conditions are unlikely to apply to quandaries faced by large organizations whose executives must make decisions to which they hope those affected will submit. The factors which must be considered by the decision makers are frequently so varied and recondite that even intelligent and benevolent officials can do no more than determine what they believe to be in the best interest of the organization, utilize expert advice, and take into consideration whether potent elements among those affected will accede to their judgments.[11]

Individuality, Loyalty, and Freedom

If individuality is ever to be generally attained, all human institutions will have become attuned to freedom. Authoritative superimpositions of dogma, codes, and obedience will have to give way to consent and cooperation based on common goals.[12]

Despite the contradictions, the inconsistencies, and the complexity of human beings and their cultural patterns, the faith that man can think and act rationally remains firmly ensconced in Western culture. The myth that nothing is ever settled until it is settled *right* justifies a rational rather than an emotionally charged approach to the solution of social problems.[13]

Centuries of meeting emergencies realistically have convinced most Americans that the disinterested pursuit of truth is not incompatible with the permanent interests of society.[14] It seems better that

[11] Occasionally, the individual member may exercise his right to challenge such a decision either vocally or by an act of disobedience. But he does so conscious of the fact that the organized government can usually overwhelm him by executive and judicial action and by its control of "loyal" opinion—through its domination of communication instruments.

[12] The quandary of achieving democratic freedom thus becomes similar to Plato's quandary in seeking to formulate and transmit what he conceived to be an ideal social heritage: How can distorted adults be kept from corrupting the personalities of the young so that they may be fit to inherit a purified culture? Plato's solution was most unrealistic, but one that must sometimes occur to professional educators. He proposed that a tyrant gather together a whole generation of children to grow up under the care of an elite of uncorrupted adults while all other grownups were banished!

[13] Henry Steele Commager, *The American Mind,* Yale University Press, New Haven, Conn., 1950, pp. 26ff.

[14] Cf. American Historical Association, Commission on the Social Studies, *Conclusions and Recommendations,* Charles Scribner's Sons, New York, 1937, p. 8.

men should live with the insecurity of doubt characteristic of reason than that they "know" what may not be true. Even the emotional factors, optimism and pessimism, must be subject to disinterested inquiry and judgment.

Loyalties to institutions, values, and established customs are themselves facts. People frequently rationalize their resistance to change in opinion or policy in terms of such loyalties. But the moral mandate to hold to one's prejudices is weakened both by the pragmatic test of their effectiveness and by repeated contacts with other beliefs.[15]

In practical affairs, therefore, men again and again are compelled to examine their specific beliefs. The validity of these beliefs on each occasion has to be tested by what probable or actual effects would follow the application of each belief and preference.[16]

So in the larger field of reference (if the whorls of superstition, ignorance, and retrogression be disregarded) Americans are frequently engaged in liberating themselves from emotionally charged, stereotyped beliefs. Indeed, such liberalizing is the national hope and pride.[17] Political, educational, and economic institutions would be feeble things without widespread loyalty to this mission of American democracy.

In brief, individual liberties are subject to civilized restraints. Though freedom of thought and belief are not affected by the nature of these restraints, their expression as utterances or acts is limited if the public consensus judges them harmful to the general welfare. Not only are violent and coercive acts forbidden, but also incitations to panic and mob action and the publication of personal defamations. Most nonconformities of opinion and behavior are permitted even though not popularly approved; somewhat paradoxically, indeed, consensus upholds social establishments (for example, the American Civil Liberties Union) which have the express purpose of protecting nonconformists' lawful freedoms. Despite recurrent hysteria, it is recognized that liberal democracy itself is in no small degree indebted to men who have spoken and acted in accord with beliefs which were at the time considered dangerous to the public order.

Planning and Propaganda in the American Society

No one can tell for sure what the future of the American society will be or even what it should be. There are far too many important variables and exigencies that shape the ends. Moreover, knowledge of biological inheritance and of social psychology is still incomplete.

[15] Cohen, *op. cit.*, pp. 70, 358.
[16] John Dewey, *Problems of Men,* Philosophical Library, Inc., New York, 1946, p. 360.
[17] Cf. Robert M. MacIver, *The Ramparts We Guard,* The Macmillan Company, New York, 1950, chap. 3.

Nevertheless, the aspiration for a "good society" is the basic qualification for popular government. "We, the people" *in order to accomplish general purposes,* "do ordain and establish" agencies with defined and limited powers to act for us, subject to our continuing tolerance and approval, for the progressive attainment of these purposes. In a word, planning for the continuity of efforts toward accomplishment of purposes is integral to the American society.

American representatives act, with popular consent, in such varied areas as transportation and communication, incentive and redistributive taxation, subsidization and supervision of industrial and financial organizations, development and conservation of natural resources, administration of justice, international relations, sanitation and other health measures, aesthetics, recreation, and formal education. The principle of popular consent stands as a basic criterion for assessing the operations of popular sovereignty in the United States.

Private purposes, inefficiency, and ignorance among legislators, public administrators, and judges do, of course, corrupt democratic processes. Citizens are too often inadequately informed and apathetic. In times of crisis, however, corrections of neglects and abuses are compulsory for the state; an aroused populace demands planning by its representatives.

Planning, of course, requires support, and the sponsors of planning measures seek to mobilize public opinion. In seeking to persuade, they frequently engage in communication in which the borders between enlightenment and indoctrination are shadowy. All persuasion involves a spirit of propaganda. Apathy can be overcome, or even lessened, only by some degree of emotional arousal. Efforts to enlighten men who do not care are likely to be futile.

Propaganda and Democratic Government

If a propagandist is defined as anyone who intentionally stimulates another to feel, think, or act differently than he otherwise would, it must be obvious that democratic processes are inevitably in large part propagandistic. Reason and objectivity serve as limitations and correctives as citizens respond to competing appeals, not only by weighing pro and con arguments, but also by injecting their own desires and stereotypes to tip the balance. In so far as the totality of these responses satisfies the criterion for judging American government—that it be referenced toward the attainment of the purposes for which it was established—they are functionally sound; that is, they exemplify the process of popular sovereignty.

It must be emphasized that the United States is a special case of democracy. Elsewhere the driving energy that sustains a momentum "to go places and do things" may not be quite so dynamic a force. There is nothing in the *logic* of popular sovereignty that assures either liberalism or reference to the future. In other nations, in fact, popular majorities are frequently quite satisfied with the *status quo;* they may acquiesce in policy control by one or another elite; they often support chauvinism and imperialism; they seldom question class privileges. None of these conservatisms has characterized popular sovereignty in the United States. From colonial days to the present, the American society has been dominated by the faith that tomorrow can be made better than today and that the government and, indeed, all institutions exist to help citizens fulfill their faith.

The Right to Protest and to Be Consulted

That American agents are subject to the shortcomings that typify human beings may not be overtly acknowledged by most citizens. The frequent errors the agents commit and their acts of self-interest are accepted as part of the price of representative government.[18] Americans tolerate much in the way of private failing so long as they feel sure that the goal of general welfare is, on the whole, kept clearly in view.

Assured of the right of organized protest and public persuasion, Americans fix operational limitations on the acts of their agents. If the "Providential State" [19] fails in some regard to provide for the common welfare, public clamor typically compels changes in governmental policies and practices.

What Americans hope for and accept from nongovernmental civic, economic, and other organizations parallels what they hope for and accept from government. They insist on being consulted on decisions

[18] No one acquainted with realistic treatments of American government and power-group conflicts from pre-Revolutionary War days to the present can be shocked by the integral part that human frailties play in a democratic state. Cf. Charles A. Beard, *An Economic Interpretation of the Constitution of the United States,* The Macmillan Company, New York, 1935, and Blair Bolles, *How to Get Rich in Washington,* W. W. Norton & Company, Inc., New York, 1952. Though not often overtly acknowledged, it is generally recognized that legislators, executives, and judges are frequently part-time, and generally relatively short-term, public officials; in their other roles, they are businessmen, heads of families, and members of various social groups.

[19] Cf. Walter Lippmann, *The Good Society,* Little, Brown & Company, Boston, 1937. "The Providential State," Lippmann believes, must function within narrow limits in so complex a society as America increasingly becomes. He does not, however, deny its mandate to act for the general welfare.

that affect their goal of abundant living, even though they necessarily accept, in lieu of prior consultation, apologetics and justifications for *faits accomplis*. Such acceptance may be acquiescent or apathetic, cynical or protesting.[20] The principle of consultation, however, retains vitality and, in considerable degree, restrains decision makers from acting arbitrarily.

INSTITUTIONAL RELIGION AND HUMANE RELIGION

Religion functions in emotion, intellect, and behavior quite apart from any association with a religious establishment. An individual may be a deeply religious person regardless of either his belief in a supernatural deity or his membership in a religious congregation. The terms "institutional" and "humane," as applied to religion, merely call attention to these facts and do not imply any necessary opposition between two clearly separated bodies of doctrine and practice.

The term "religion," as here used, refers to the humility which comes from a sense of infinite powers beyond human ken, to the charity and love which springs from a sense of the mystical strength in fellow human beings, and to the spirituality which grows from a sense of the limits of all the material, actual, and attainable. Such are the religious attributes assigned by Morris R. Cohen to the philosophy of Spinoza.[21] They may be taken to apply to all humane religions, whether related to any organization or not. Truly religious men have various faiths; they may believe in immortality, in revelations, in miracles, in a "one true" religious creed, or they may reject one or all of these beliefs. If, however, they are characterized by humility, charity, love, and spirituality, they are humanely religious.

There are, of course, "religions," organized and unorganized, that give little or no emphasis to such attributes. In one or many respects,

[20] Decisions made without adequate preparation for gaining popular consent may arouse a furor among those to whom the decision comes as a surprise. Thus the statement attributed to Secretary of State John Foster Dulles early in 1956 that three times in the recent past his diplomacy had carried the United States to the brink of war, all unknown to the public, set off such a wave of protest that he saw fit to disavow the statement. Similarly, in 1937, it was widely believed that the executives of General Motors Corporation intended to utilize the hunger of strikers and their families as a means of breaking a sit-down strike. Public protest against such possible callousness, in which some stockholders concurred, led to denials of such intent.

[21] Cohen, *op. cit.,* essay on "Spinoza: Prophet of Liberalism."

indeed, they may place high value on pride, intolerance, antipathies, and aggressiveness toward other human groups and faiths. The individual who verbally subscribes to humane values and temporarily acts in accordance with them may, at some times and in some moods, react in terms of in-group hatreds toward anyone who seems to him to threaten his religious organization. To some sectarians, indeed, the inability to conceive of an anthropomorphic God is sufficient ground for condemnation.

Anthropologists generally find in the geographical and historical conditioning of isolated primitive societies at least partial explanations of their faiths. The "good man" exalted by the Buddhists, the Zuñi Indians, and the Quakers is much the same as a type; however, the cultural conditioning, the mixture of tradition, class structure, economics, external dangers and pressures, and the characters of founders in the three cases are very different. Similarly, the peace of mind of the devout Mohammedan and Hindu, and of some Jews and Christians, would be difficult to equate in terms of cultural background.

Religious Attitudes and Behavior

The importance of religiously sanctioned attitudes and behavior is, however, primordial. In so far as they are alike, they frequently provide a platform on which different groups come to common understanding and common effort. In so far as they are radically different among the people of a society, however, they may become barriers to cooperation in the interest of humane, democratic ends.

Few human beings can reconcile themselves easily to the imponderable facts of nature. Infinity of time and space are such facts. Conception, birth, life, and death have emotional concomitants which cannot be quite defined by science. Human associations, whether intimate or relatively impersonal, encourage men to create some transcendent faiths by which their relations may be guided. When crises occur that cannot be resolved by human effort, man is humbled; hence, he seeks an explanation.

The processes by which faiths become sanctioned cultural patterns are the concerns of anthropologists and religious historians.[22] What especially interests the student of contemporary societies is the emergence of highly valued rules for associated living. These rules of conduct are religiously sanctioned, in the sense that religion is a "deep-seated harmonizing of the self with the universe."[23] They provide a collective

---

[22] Bronislaw Malinowski, *Magic, Science, and Religion,* The Macmillan Company, New York, 1925, esp. chap. 4.

[23] John Dewey, *A Common Faith,* Yale University Press, New Haven, Conn., 1934, p. 19.

ethic, subscribed to by all men who are attuned to the transcendent values of their society. They are thought habits acquired through the process of living and doing things in association; they have been validated by experience.[24]

Were it not for the supervening power of the common core of humane ethics, an American *society* would be inconceivable. The multiple allegiances of each to his "one true religion" would entail such vigorous missionary spirit, so emphasize creedal differences, so foment parochial hostilities, and so exalt primitive intolerance of "heretics" that the common faith in freedom would be submerged.

Instead, the very dangers of divisiveness and coercion have in practice required both governmental and popular assurance of the right of every individual to his own religious creed and institutional loyalty. Americans ask, or ought to ask, only that men shall abide by the moral laws of civilized society. "The American way is the most comprehensive religious way because it insures the freedom of commitment for all sorts of different beliefs." [25]

Religion implies, among other things, working in behalf of a better world. Such direction of effort requires that men of good will subordinate irrelevant differences of creed, nationality, race, and social class to humane values and goals.[26]

[24] The outstanding example of commonality of a humane code is "The Golden Rule." In Brahmanism, "This is the sum of duty: Do naught to others in ways that you yourself would find hurtful." In Christianity, "All things whatsoever ye would that men should do to you, do ye even so to them." In Confucianism, "The maxim of loving kindness: do not unto others what you would not have them do unto you." In Islam, "No one of you is a believer until he desires for his brother that which he desires for himself." In Judaism, "What is hateful to you, do not to your fellowman. That is the entire law; all the rest is commentary." In Taoism, "Regard your neighbor's gain as your gain and your neighbor's loss as your own loss." See Lloyd Morain and Mary Morain, *Humanism as the Next Step,* The Beacon Press, Boston, 1954, p. 3.

[25] Horace M. Kallen, "Faith in Action," an address over the National Broadcasting Company, quoted in *ibid.,* p. 15.

[26] Thus, in the depression years of the 1930s, Rev. John A. Ryan, staunch defender of the Roman Catholic faith, Professor Morris R. Cohen, the "medievalist" philosopher, and Dr. John Dewey, naturalistic and pragmatist prophet could and did support each other in the struggle for social reform and the maintenance of civil liberties. See Charles A. Beard and Mary R. Beard, *America in Midpassage,* The Macmillan Company, New York, 1937, p. 910.

CULTURAL CONFLICTS AND CULTURAL INTEGRATION

In a competitive society, conflicting norms tend always to create friction and dilemmas. Emphasis on personal ambition, characteristic of middle-class Americans, accentuates the strivings of individuals. Individualism fosters insecurities which drive most people to seek like-minded associates to compensate for their aloneness. Their unasked questions of those with whom they are thrown are: Are you the same sort of person I am? In what respect can we belong to an in-group? What things and men are we for? And what ones against?

Ethnocentrism and Human Relations

Ethnocentrism is deeply embedded in human relations. No staunch member of any in-group strongly doubts that its beliefs, motives, and actions are *right,* and hence there is suspicion that those of out-groups are *wrong.*

Fortunately, most people belong to several in-groups whose patterns of value and behavior are not uniform. Thus, divided loyalties tend to water down the moral certainties that characterize in-groups when they are mobilized to perform some specific project; for example, a team during a game, a gang preparing for a fight, or a religious sect during a ritual.

Indeed, within most in-groups there are conflicting emotional states both among the members and within each one. In the family there is frequently both fear of, and covert hostility toward, the father and affection for, and security with, the mother; in exceptional cases these attitudes may be reversed. A father figure outside the family—a male teacher, a scoutmaster, a clergyman, or an office holder—may find himself substituting for the feared and hated father, thereby relieving a youth of a guilt feeling.[27] Similarly, fears, frustrations, and smothered hatreds toward members of other groups may be attached to individuals in other settings. Unconsciously, the frustrated persons may find self-justifications in a scapegoat—an individual, a sect, a race, or a social class—which they burden with that part of their own emotions, intentions, and acts that make themselves uncomfortable; they can then hate and attack the scapegoat in good conscience.

Obviously, within humane family circles fear, hostility, and frustration are minimized. The atmosphere of affection fosters the de-

[27] Similar transfers may, of course, make a male or a female teacher or other adult associate the recipient of affection and admiration. These transfers, however, are not relevant to cultural conflicts.

velopment of tolerance and readiness to cooperate with others regardless of color, creed, or social status. Community activities, especially in heterogeneous neighborhoods, provide many opportunities for such expression of tolerance. For children fortunate enough to come from such stable and affectionate families, play, school, and religious associations present goals to be achieved by collaboration; for their elders, civic, and recreational projects serve the same purpose. Because members of such families are little burdened by half-suppressed hostilities toward parents and siblings, they do not feel the need for "scapegoats."

Community spirit and events may override family influence, however. With the nation at war, for example, in-group virtues are often extended to include those who would at other times be members of out-groups; the cleavages between social classes, religious sects, and ethnic groups are temporarily minimized by a compulsory inclusiveness based on a common effort.

Other Sources of Atavisms

Regrettably, other common passions besides those of war, may sometimes sweep many people into atavistic moods and actions. Sweeps of anti-Communist, anti-Negro, anti-Catholic, anti-Semitic, antistriker, or antiemployer emotion may be such that for an individual to hold views different from those of the crowd is to risk criticism or social ostracism. The deviant may become a community isolate; indeed he may be popularly equated with the hated "enemy." The crowd tends to think in patterns and symbols, not in concepts. Balanced judgments are therefore suspect.

In their effect on wholesome human relations, crowd sentiments may be desirable, vicious, or ambivalent. They sometimes favor toleration and collaboration among groups which are often irrationally hostile to each other; for example, the vigorous efforts of some labor unions to minimize racial discrimination. They sometimes foster fear of, and hatred toward, out-groups—for instance, religious dissidents, political radicals, ethnic minorities, or migrant workers. They sometimes promote conformity and escape, thereby providing people the anonymity of crowd obsession with sports, fashions, and vicarious adventure.

Technology and Tensions

An advancing technology doubtless eliminates certain causes of group tension and parochial mindedness. The increasing provision of creature comforts, physical well-being, and, in general, a considerable familiarity with the phenomena and methods of science tend to undermine crowd-minded attribution of evil to ethnic groups, ecclesiastical bodies, economic organizations, and regional populations. Man's attention becomes more frequently directed toward the national and world scenes. The need for collaboration and planning for the general welfare becomes more apparent, thereby creating a wholesome substitute for "the negative and merely compensatory expression of fear, jealousies, and frustrations." [28]

Government and Group Tensions

Private hatred and intolerance toward individuals and out-groups cannot, of course, be proscribed though they may be assuaged. Governmental intervention to protect the civil rights of the victims of discrimination is frequently required, for example, the Fair Employment Practice Code and the unanimous decisions of the United States Supreme Court that racial segregation in public schools and parks is unconstitutional. Mob action, the outgrowth of mass hostility, presents crucial problems for police and judiciary. The state's authority, as such, can compel manifest obedience, but it cannot directly command sentiments to conform to law.

It is the state's educational and forestalling functions that are called into play whenever crowd sentiments threaten to result in mob behavior. Social-psychological insight is needed to recognize the symptoms in advance if effective measures are to be taken to minimize the likelihood that an event, blamed by the crowd on one or more members of a distrusted out-group, will spark mob action.[29]

[28] President's Committee on Civil Rights, *To Secure These Rights,* Government Printing Office, Washington, 1947.

[29] The contrast between responsible and irresponsible behavior of community leaders is indicated by two reported cases involving deep-seated cultural antagonisms. In Canada, the French-speaking Catholic residents of Quebec Province have maintained a culture apart from their Protestant English-speaking countrymen, but their ethnocentrism has smoldered harmlessly. However, sportswriters and club owners, in 1955, whipped up excessive loyalty to the Montreal "Canadiens" hockey team. When the star, Richards, was disqualified by the English-speaking Canadian President of the Hockey League for violently attacking both opponents and officials in a game with the Boston "Bruins" on March 13, 1955, the "sports fans" of Montreal, *abetted by the Mayor,* evidenced crowd hysteria. Four nights later at a game which President Campbell attended, a bomb was thrown at his box, the game broken up, and a mob formed that destroyed property, injured policemen, and brought hockey into disrepute; all French Canada felt ashamed. Sidney Katz, "The Rocket Richards Hockey Riot," *MacLeans' Magazine,* September, 1955, p. 8.

By contrast, in Philadelphia, in August, 1954, a Negro cou-

Nature of Cultural Conflicts

Civic leaders, especially professional educators, need to identify the cultural conflicts that frequently give rise to critical situations, to know the backgrounds of the attitudes, behaviors, and beliefs that characterize the people involved in each situation, and to formulate programs which can operate to assuage the antagonism and distrust founded in ignorance and emotion.

Conflicts are sometimes classified into four categories: social-class, religious, ethnic, and regional. But there is great overlapping among the categories. For example, in times of full employment and business optimism, conflicts between social classes less frequently result in overt action, while in times of economic insecurity, overt conflicts are often rife. So too ethnic or regional distrust is often an important element in religious hostility.

In the codes of sports and political parties, symbols and stereotypes characteristic of gang warfare are blatantly publicized and uncritically accepted; not only are name calling, taunting, and bare falsehoods complacently permitted but even coercion and hatred for opponents are vaunted virtues! Indeed, a school that boasts of its constructive intercultural program of academic studies may complacently encourage gang morality in its interscholastic athletic contests.

Inconsistent Codes of Behavior

Such inconsistency is characteristic of the American society, as of others. In varying degrees, indeed, cultural conflicts occur in most associations and within the personality patterns of most individuals. Marriage, for example, requires tolerance and compromise on the part of each spouse if it is to avoid the strains which so frequently figure in divorce. Typically, the wife and the husband bring to marriage separate and somewhat inconsistent behavior codes. Their experiences (includ-

---

ple purchased and prepared to move into a ramshackle house in a middle-class Irish and Italian neighborhood. A crowd formed and did some damage; but the police and the staff of the city Commission on Human Relations moved swiftly and effectively to keep the situation under control while groups of white and colored citizens met separately with the Commission staff to work out a reasonable solution. Assurance was given that the property would be improved; the legal right of the owner to live in his house was established; property values in the area proved not to be lessened; mob violence was forestalled; and the local community returned to its accustomed tranquillity. Hanna Lees, "How Philadelphia Stopped a Race Riot," *The Reporter,* June 2, 1955, pp. 26–29.

ing family and religious training, ethnic conditioning, and education) have been different. They have, in fact, been reared in different "cultural worlds." Their offspring learn elements of the culture fragments brought by each parent; the resulting hodgepodge is what seems "right" or permissible to youths as they in turn grow up and marry.[30]

These individual and in-group cultural conflicts, though disruptive of personal and organizational security, seldom carry serious threat to the stability of society. On the contrary, they sometimes foster a readiness to compromise when important social conflicts occur.

The cultural conflicts that challenge the canons of universal liberty, equality, and the pursuit of happiness are those that arise from group egoism.[31] The fantasies of cohesive in-groups frequently give moral sanction to ruthlessness, hate, and hooliganism. They provide fertile ground for self-seeking agitators to cultivate support for organized attacks not only on out-groups, but even on an essential of the American faith—the spirit of "live and let live." In-group members, when so aroused, often reject the bonds of the society which make possible the group's own existence. Their embittered ideologies foment contrary ones in the groups they attack; their attempts at coercion breed violence in reply. Anarchy is the logical result; it is forestalled only by the power of the police, who are supported by property- and status-conscious citizens who dread mobs.

Lethargy of "Respectable" Citizens

In many instances, support for "law and order" by "respectable" members of the community is regrettably tardy. Before fear has stabbed them awake, they frequently are unconcerned when teachers, clergymen, and other civic workers are attacked from platform and press by socially irresponsible spokesmen for in-groups which seek to force their particular values on others. Nevertheless, belated as it frequently is, civic support for the enforcement of law is generally made known.

The student of the social foundations of education, conscious of the character of cultural conflicts, is much concerned with the meliorative processes of cultural integration. He sees the disruptivenesses of group fragmentation, but he also appreciates the constructive processes which are at work in American life. He finds that, in spite of the competing values inherent in their different economic, ethnic, regional, and ecclesiastic backgrounds, most persons most of the time make reasonable adjustment to the demands of a heterogeneous culture. Their preoccupation with jobs, consumption, sports, organizations, and social status

[30] Cf. Margaret Mead, *And Keep Your Powder Dry*, William Morrow & Company, Inc., New York, 1942, chap. 3.

[31] Cf. MacIver, *op. cit.*, chap. 8.

leaves little time or energy for ideological crusades. The processes of cultural integration may not be on a very high level, but they are omnipresent and powerful.

Education and the Community of Faith

One function of public education is to foster those integrating activities that harmonize with the American community of faith. The symbols of common aspiration for abundant living and universal freedom should be exalted in the school. They ought to be identified for all men as tokens of the life each one can create for himself in common with his fellows. The symbolic "good man" conforming to American aspirations for magnanimity, self-responsibility, and self-determination ought to become the image that each student holds for himself.[32] The genius of the American people is the remarkable extent to which, historically, they have accomplished this aim through mass education.

NATIONALISM, PATRIOTISM, AND AMERICAN IDEALS

In American ideology, a basic qualification of the "good man" is that he be a national patriot. Nationalism and patriotism are held to command devotion of all "good men" comparable to that paid by all pious persons to their God.[33] Indeed, the symbols of nationalism and acts of service to the nation (especially in wartime) carry a religious aura and a divine sanction which is reflected by ecclesiastical institutions and in public opinion.

This equation of the "good man" with devotion and service to the organized group has its historic exemplifications in city-states, military organizations, and cults. These examples indicate how nearly universal is man's willingness, at least in times of crisis, to surrender his private interests to what he considers those of the group. National patriotism as we know it is, however, of comparatively recent origin.

With the emergence of the domination of monarchies in Western Europe, royal families seized much of the symbolism and ceremony of

[32] See L. I. Chatto and A. L. Halligan, *The Story of the Springfield Plan*, Hinds, Hayden, and Eldredge, Inc., New York, 1945, for the story of a comprehensive community educational enterprise to minimize group antagonism. Also, W. H. Kilpatrick and William Van Til, eds., *Intercultural Attitudes in the Making*, Harper & Brothers, New York, 1947, part 1, chap. 9.

[33] Cf. Carleton J. H. Hayes, *A Political and Cultural History of Modern Europe*, The Macmillan Company, New York, 1933, esp. vol. I, p. 696. Also, Carleton J. H. Hayes, *Essays on Nationalism*, The Macmillan Company, New York, 1926, essay 4.

the church, thereby endowing themselves with the mystery and sanctity of religious establishment. The "good man" became the loyal and obedient subject whose personal and private wealth and whose life itself belonged to his "divinely appointed" monarch. As the secular state came to limit and replace the personal monarch, religious sanction was transferred to the nation, of which the king or emperor became the symbol. The "good man" became a loyal subject to a mystical entity, a "body politic," a sovereign state, a nation. The "father figure" of the king became largely replaced by that of "patria," the native land, the fatherland.

The state, whether organized as city, province, or nation, is an uneasy resolution of competing power groups. The making, interpretation, and enforcement of law becomes the prerogative and the responsibility of dominant interest groups, each seizing such opportunity as it can, and each equating its policy and program with that of the state to which all "good men' owe obedience. Thus state sovereignty defines roles people are expected to play.

Nationalism as a World Force

Nationalism is certainly one of the most dynamic social forces in the world. In advanced societies, there is some merit to the claim that its expression is generally in the public interest, although always potentially dangerous. Elsewhere, however, it forms a witches' brew; desire for popular sovereignty, lack of technological and liquid capital resources, and impatience to attain national aspirations can result at best in confusion and frustration as established governments are undermined. Northern and Central Africa and the Middle East and Southeast Asia present very disturbing nationalistic revolts both against political and economic dominance by imperial states (specifically British, French, Belgian, and Portuguese empires) and against dominating ethnic groups in newly organized states or those aspiring to self-government.

Groups of people in stable states also frequently take on something of a nationalistic spirit as they struggle to retain their established position or to assert demands for more opportunity. Thus conservative groups among the peaceful Hopi Indians, resisting compulsory assimilation into the Anglo-American culture, assert their natural, that is, "national," right to self-rule in cultural affairs. And so, too, many planters and other advocates of white-supremacy in some Southern States assert their (subnational) "right" to segregation and subjection of Negroes in defiance or circumvention of the national state.

Characteristically, the "good man's" belief in the divine sanction and specific divinity of the sovereign monarch has had to be transferred to the collective personality of the representatives of an entire population. Such transfer has obviously involved semantic difficulties and legal fictions. The transition is accomplished, so far as it is successful, by retaining many of the symbols and ceremonials of the "by-grace-of-God" monarch, for example, the national flag, the accouterments of law courts, and "the right to petition for redress of grievances."

Considered realistically, however, the transfer is less revolutionary than might appear. Even the absolutism of a monarch is limited, in fact, by the capacity and willingness of subjects to obey and by geographic and economic factors. Similarly, in states governed by popularly chosen representatives, the facts of human willingness and capacity and of resources place realistic limits on government.[34]

The interrelations between governmental stability, religious and class establishments, and economic processes have continued to be a major concern of every civilized state. Men may not live by bread alone, but they will not tolerate social arrangements that do not make bread winning possible—unless they cannot help it. Hence, as popular unrest, protest, strikes, and revolts have modified political and economic systems, the partnerships between governments and established classes and churches, which have almost necessarily supported the *status quo,* have also been challenged.[35] Popular sovereignty places the ultimate control of industry in national and state governments which, with every emergency, are compelled to intervene in economic matters.

In many national crises—wars, depressions, major strikes, and instances of violent race conflict, for example—action by the state forestalls the possibility of anarchy. Dissension frequently develops between two regions and between corporations and their employees; it also de-

[34] Political scientists distinguish the "nation" from the "state." The nation, like "nationality" and "patriotism," is primarily a psychological phenomenon. These terms imply bonds of affection due to commonality of ancestry, living places, cultural patterns, and, usually, language and religion; often their dynamic expressions are heightened by fear of, or aggression toward, "oppressors." Such a culturally homogeneous social group "at once conscious and tenacious of its psychic life and expression" becomes a state only if it is politically organized within a given territory. A state, however, may consist of several nations or national fragments, for example, Great Britain, which is a state encompassing Welsh, Scottish, and North Irish nations. Cf. Arthur Holcombe, *The Foundations of the Modern Commonwealth,* Harper & Brothers, New York, 1930, chap. 4, and Harry Elmer Barnes, "Nationalism," *Encyclopedia Americana,* 1919.

[35] Nevertheless, residues of the historical partnership remain. In this country, rituals of national anthems, salutes and pledges, invocations, and oaths continue despite the Constitution's clear separation of the state from religious establishment.

velops frequently among owners of wealth, operators of business organizations, among cultural minorities, and religious leaders. In all such cases, the responsible officers of the state need the authority and the emotional aura that nationalism and patriotism foster if they are to mobilize the economic and "spiritual" resources of the community to meet the situation. Governmentally controlled mass-communications instruments overwhelm popular dissent. Obduracy entails public condemnation.

Dangers of the Mobilization of Government

There are, however, grave dangers attending such mobilization of government. The effects of heightened state authority and of patriotic fervor extend into postemergency periods; hence, there is widespread popular intolerance of nonconformity to "proper" political, economic, and religious opinions, and such bigotry is cleverly cultivated and exploited by demagogues for their own purposes. Hence, too, there is the continued dependence of organized labor and of corporation managers on governmental agencies to avoid serious stoppages of industrial processes. And as another consequence, science and technology are to a considerable extent directed to immediate political and economic projects to the relative neglect of long-term social goals.

Perhaps the most damaging postemergency effect, however, is the prostitution of the instruments of communication that in the war emergency had been used so potently by the government to arouse popular support for its measures. Press, radio, television, motion pictures, and billboards come chiefly into the service of those who can and will pay for them in order to create more wants and insure the consumption of standardized goods and services provided for profit. A stultifying conformity of opinion and taste submerges, to a frightening extent, individuality in the American society.

Democratic Nationalism an Anomaly

Democracy not only implies tolerance of individuality and variety but also places high value on the expectation that important cultural contributions are most likely to come from the diverse talents of individuals who collaborate and compete. Nationalism, however, thrives on international conflict, aggressiveness, and emergency; it puts a premium on traditional loyalty and conformity.

"Democracy," MacIver points out, "cannot afford to rest on tradition. If it does not look forward it decays. When it becomes hallowed it becomes untrue to itself." [36] Nationalism, however, would be a

[36] MacIver, op. cit., p. 62.

vacuous thing if the nation were not hallowed and if the tradition of obedience and of all-out support in time of emergency were not assured.

In times of peace and prosperity, the paradox has been rather well resolved in the United States. Most Americans are too busy earning a living, seeking economic and social advancement, and pursuing harmless pleasures to get "steamed up" over international tensions. Their frustrations and aggressions typically originate, and are expended locally, in family, neighborhood, shop, and office. The democracy that they personally experience is an alternation of dog-eat-dog competition and of good-natured accommodation; but it is generally referenced to the future.[37]

Even the first- and second-generation European-Americans generally make the transition from the traditional bellicosities and the relatively fixed standards of their ancestral homelands to the unknown standard of the future by which Americans measure themselves.[38] To be sure, they are likely to retain elements of their native language, religious orthodoxy, hostility and suspicion toward out-groups and a certain spirit of intransigence, each of which provide fertile ground for demagogues to cultivate.

National unity requires a considerable amount of vigorous governmental propaganda, not only to enlighten self-centered and inadequately assimilated people, but also to stimulate them to the active support of national policies. Several difficulties and some dangers, however, attend such efforts to control the minds of the people.

Dangers of Governmental Propaganda

Majority-party policies are not necessarily national, state, or municipal policies; in fact at a given time, popular sentiment may be unsympathetic to them. But the majority party, since it has dominant control of the governmental channels of communication, is likely to confuse its interests with public policy. The situation is even more serious when a vociferous segment of a majority party jockeys itself into a position from which it seems to speak for the state. Its propaganda may then endeavor to rally "patriotic citizens" to support disingenuous purposes by identifying them with national, state, or municipal policy.

National and state bureaucracies, often with the best of intentions, tend to override the autonomy of local governments and individual citizens. The combination of their power to allocate money and their usually persuasive propaganda is likely to make resistance seem

[37] Oscar Handlin, *The Uprooted,* Atlantic Monthly Press, Boston, 1951, chap. 4.

[38] Mead, *op. cit.,* chap. 5.

futile. The contemporary antipathy toward "monster government" is the protest against this tendency. Another, and a more serious, popular response, is the passive acceptance of what seems inevitable, the readiness to leave it to the state and national governments to look after local affairs—health, education, control of delinquency, farm and home practices, and even community organization.

Defense of Government Activities

In extenuation of state and national governmental intervention in local affairs, it may be asserted that executive and legislative agents have broader jurisdictions and responsibilities than their local counterparts. Because of this, they are more likely than local officials to have an over-all view of the general needs and welfare and also to have more nearly adequate resources and expert advice to fulfill their responsibilities. In cases of emergency, these justifications are compelling.

Emergency action is, however, all too likely to become routine for nonemergency situations. Nationalism, patriotism, and "good citizenship" are often equated with docility and passive acceptance of official apologetics. The objector is too often labeled either a "crank" or an undesirable nonconformist, perhaps even "un-American."

Except in wartime (including the predeclaration mobilization of public opinion and the postwar hysteria) the spirit of skepticism and inquiry are, nevertheless, generally tolerated. Men of spirit and intelligence continue to ask: Why? By what authority are they and their fellows told what is good and what is bad, what desirable and what undesirable? They dare to amend, and even to defy, regulations from which they dissent. They assert their right to appeal to their own reason. And as yet, provided that their acts do not prevent the autonomy of other men, no governmental institution successfully denies them the privilege of criticism. To this degree, at any rate, Americans retain "government by consent."

The Right to Dissent

The civil right to dissent and to refuse to conform, so far as an act does not prevent others from acquiescence and conformity, is in large measure protected by the American courts of law. Thus one governmental agency acts to limit the intrusion of other governmental agencies on the privacy of the individual citizen. The courts have a dual function in this respect: that of conserving and protecting the individual rights established by law in the past and that of continually adapting the word of the law and the precedent decisions of courts to meet contemporary social conditions. Somewhat paradoxically, the conservative character of law sometimes becomes the ally of liberty.[39]

Neither democracy nor nationalism provide easy roads to follow. Together they present complex quandaries for the individual and for society. The understanding of either, or of the interaction of both, requires attention to their applications in everyday life rather than to abstract justifications. The public educator is concerned with the secondary as well as the immediate effects of each application of the spirit of democracy and of nationalism. Does, for example, the emotional glow which comes to children who pledge allegiance to the flag or sing "America the Beautiful" foster attachment to the cause of individual liberty and justice for all men? Or does it heighten the disregard and hostility for real or imagined "enemies" of the nation? And is it desirable or even safe to turn fervors on and off like a water spigot?

SUMMARY

If educators would promote intelligent behavior, must they encourage independent judgment, including the privilege of nonconformity? If they would foster both democratic citizenship and national patriotism, what treatment should be accorded to the dissenter from the mood and the policy being encouraged by national propaganda at one time or another? These are among the most important dilemmas faced by public school educators.

No school officer can, of course, act quite independently of the public temper in such matters. He may, however, identify and assess the strength of elements in contemporary society which favor or minimize intelligent behavior. These elements are found both in long-term challenges that the state at all levels must meet and in the contemporary agencies and forces which exemplify intelligent behavior.

The irreversible progression of technology and science compels governments to act constructively to deal both with their many opportunities and with the nation's serious social dislocations. Warnings are provided both by popular discontent and by an awareness on the part of power groups which significantly influence government that disaster is probable unless intelligence and planning characterize public policies.

The outcries of those who seek to exploit national patriotism for private profit or for political advantage are loud and blatant, to be sure. But they are in the long run irrelevant to the problems that the

[39] Cf. Arthur E. Sutherland, "The Supreme Court and the Private Schools," *Harvard Educational Review*, Summer, 1955, pp. 127–131.

state must resolve. Even though the appeals of special interest groups may be momentarily triumphant, as policies, they are generally self-defeating in a society dedicated to science and technological change.

Happily, within the "body politic" there are many influential citizens who strive to understand the complex character of the changing world in which they live. They participate in planning and act intelligently in their civic lives.

The public school can function effectively in fostering social intelligence. It ought to exemplify at appropriate levels the attitudes and methodology of science as a way of life. It is thus attuned to an age that is committed by events and by intention to intelligent foresight and planning.

SELECTED REFERENCES

Ackerman, N. W., and Marie Jahoda: *Anti-Semitism and Emotional Disorder,* Harper & Brothers, New York, 1950. Forty cases of emotional disorder that revealed social pressures which foster anti-Semitism.

Allport, Gordon: *The Nature of Prejudice,* Addison-Wesley Publishing Company, Reading, Mass., 1954. A comprehensive study of the origin and nature of prejudice.

Baker, G. Derwood (ed.): "Economic Education," *The Journal of Educational Sociology,* vol. 23, no. 2, March, 1950. An issue devoted entirely to problems and practices of economic education in the schools.

Beard, Charles A., and Mary R. Beard: *America in Midpassage,* The Macmillan Company, New York, 1936.

————— and William Beard: *The American Leviathan: The Republic in the Machine Age,* The Macmillan Company, New York, 1930. Two volumes on recent American history which emphasize economic determinants.

Boulding, Kenneth E.: *The Organizational Revolution,* Harper & Brothers, New York, 1953. A leading economist analyzes changes in American economic organization.

Brown, Harrison: *The Challenge of Man's Future,* The Viking Press, Inc., New York, 1954. A challenging book on the social, economic, and political future of the human race.

Callahan, R. B.: *An Introduction to Education in American Society,* Alfred A. Knopf, Inc., New York, 1956. Contains an enlightening exposition of science, technology, and the contemporary culture.

Cohen, Morris R.: *The Faith of a Liberal,* Henry Holt and Company, Inc., New York, 1946. Esp. Essay 13, "Minimizing Social

Conflicts," a philosopher's views on techniques for reducing conflicts and tensions.

Dewey, John: *A Common Faith,* Yale University Press, New Haven, Conn., 1934. Analysis of the American faith which transcends religion and other divisions.

————: *Democracy and Education,* The Macmillan Company, New York, 1916. The role of education in promoting the ends of democracy.

Fromm, Erich: *Escape from Freedom,* Rinehart & Company, Inc., New York, 1941. Argues that modern man seeks authoritarianism as an escape from the responsibilities implied in freedom.

Goodman, Paul: *Growing Up Absurd,* Random House, Inc., New York, 1960. Crime and delinquency, like other social problems test and criticize the society in which they occur. In terms of "field theory," contemporary America does not provide adequate opportunities and goals that make constructive growth of youths probable.

Handlin, Oscar: *The Uprooted,* Atlantic Monthly Press, Boston, 1951. A famous book on the "rootless" in America.

Hayes, Carleton J. H.: *A Political and Cultural History of Modern Europe,* The Macmillan Company, New York, 1933. A rather conservative, but still one of the most useful, social and political histories of modern Europe. Excellent for European backgrounds of American social thought.

Hofstadter, Richard: *The Age of Reform: From Bryan to F. D. R.,* Alfred A. Knopf, Inc., New York, 1955. Social and intellectual history of a reform period in the United States

Holcombe, Arthur: *The Foundations of the Modern Commonwealth,* Harper & Brothers, New York, 1930. Still one of the best works on the bases upon which cooperation may be founded.

Kerr, Clark, J. T. Dunlop, F. H. Harbison, and C. A. Meyers: *Industrialism and Industrial Man,* Harvard University Press, Cambridge, Mass., 1960. The contemporary industrial metamorphosis is diverting men's lives into new channels.

Kilpatrick, William Heard, and William Van Til (eds.): *Intercultural Attitudes in the Making,* Harper & Brothers, New York, 1947. The problems and techniques of developing attitudes of intercultural cooperation.

Laski, Harold J.: *Reflections on the Revolution of Our Time,* The Viking Press, Inc., New York, 1943. A great British Socialist and political thinker analyzes the major revolutionary currents of the twentieth century.

Leighton, A. H.: *The Governing of Men: General Principles and Recommendations Based on Experience at a Japanese Relocation*

Camp, Princeton University Press, Princeton, N.J., 1945. Research report on problems of governing a war relocation camp.

Lerner, Max: *America as a Civilization,* Simon and Schuster, Inc., New York, 1957. Large, informative book on American culture.

MacIver, Robert M.: *The Ramparts We Guard,* The Macmillan Company, New York, 1950. A provocative series of essays by a leading liberal political philosopher and sociologist.

Malinowski, Bronislaw: *Magic, Science, and Religion,* The Macmillan Company, New York, 1925. An anthropologist's discussion of the interrelations of magic, science, and religion in primitive societies.

Mead, Margaret: *And Keep Your Powder Dry,* William Morrow & Company, Inc., New York, 1942. A polemical, provocative book on American cultural inconsistencies.

Mills, C. Wright: *The Power Elite,* Oxford University Press, New York, 1956. A provocative discussion of the American power structure.

————: *White Collar: The American Middle Classes,* Oxford University Press, New York, 1953. A sociologist discusses the characteristics of the "new middle classes" in the United States.

Morain, Lloyd, and Mary Morain: *Humanism as the Next Step,* The Beacon Press, Boston, 1954. A prediction of and plea for, humanistic religion.

President's Committee on Civil Rights: *To Secure These Rights,* 1947. An influential report on the extent and limits of the American attainment of civil liberties. Contains many data.

Rugg, Harold O.: *Foundations of American Education,* World Book Company, Yonkers, N.Y., 1947. Informative textbook on the social context of the American school system.

Sandburg, Carl: *The People, Yes,* Harcourt, Brace and Company, Inc., New York, 1936. The democratic philosophy of one of America's leading poets of the twentieth century.

Sweezy, Paul M.: *The Present as History: Essays and Reviews on Capitalism and Socialism,* Monthly Review Press, New York, 1953. A collection of essays on the topics in the sub-title.

Whyte, William H.: *The Organization Man,* Simon and Schuster, Inc., New York, 1956. A best seller on American conformism.

DISCUSSION QUESTIONS

1. It is sometimes charged that the American people's preoccupation with new-model cars, theatrical entertainment, athletic sports, political rivalries, and religious creeds diverts them from thoughtful attention to the problems of foreign policy, conservation of natural resources, the growth of economic agglomerations, and social welfare

measures. If true, is the practical consequence desirable or undesirable as it affects the need for the individual's self-assertion in a complex society? Consider the effects of these preoccupations on intercultural (interethnic, intersectarian, inter-social-class, and inter-economic-status) relationships.

2. There is continuing competition for public attention to varied concerns for which only a few men have sufficient information to permit them to arrive at objective judgments. Superficial opinions and emotionalized attitudes regarding many proposed measures are thereby developed; they are expressed as pressures to influence legislative bodies and administrative officials. Does the ephemeral character of men's excitements about controversies serve as a social safeguard? Is the long-term effect of these transient excitements the promotion of the "vigorous moderation of mind" and "a steadfastness of conduct and consistency of opinion" so highly valued by Walter Bagehot as typical English virtues?

3. "Exhausted and bewildered by dint of false and dehumanized philosophy, reason confesses its impotence to justify any ethical standards," says Jacques Maritain, the Catholic philosopher (*Education at the Crossroads,* Yale University Press, New Haven, Conn., 1943, p. 93). He does, however, advocate a "natural morality," based on reason, that "feels most at home and least deficient in the field of our temporal activities, or of political, civic, and social morality; because the virtues proper to this field are essentially natural ones, directed toward the good of civilization; whereas in the field of personal morality, the whole scope of the moral life cannot be comprehended by reason with regard to our real system of conduct in actual existence, without taking into account the supratemporal destiny of man. So the teaching of natural morality will naturally tend to lay stress on what we may call the ethics of political life and civilization."

Assess the educational practices or the best public school or individual teacher or administrator known to you as they relate to the promotion of natural morality as defined by Maritain. Do you agree that reason is impotent to justify any ethical standards? If not, relate one or more moral standards to ethical principles.

4. In the famous "100-day" legislative period of Congress in 1933, measures became law, with bipartisan support, which drastically affected many economic establishments and practices that had become installed by law and custom during the previous decades. These revolutionary acts included those entitled: The Emergency Banking Relief Act, The Civilian Conservation Reforestation Act, The Act Abandoning the Gold Standard, The Act Establishing the Tennessee Valley Authority, The Agricultural Adjustment Act, The National Employment

System Act, The Home Owners Loan Corporation Act, The National Industrial Recovery Act, and The Act Establishing the Public Works Administration, among others. Many of these measures were denounced both by conservative businessmen and by professional social scientists as contrary to economic laws, sound institutional processes, or Constitutional guarantees. President Roosevelt, whose advisory "brain trust" had formulated the measures, distrusted much of economic theory and vested business practices. Regarding each measure whose enactment he recommended, he said (according to Ernest Lindley, who "covered" him for the press), "Let's try it and then change as necessary."

Were Roosevelt's attitude and acts more scientific or less scientific than the attitudes of those who would have limited legislative enactments to measures that accorded with economic "laws" and to precedents of Constitutional interpretation?

5. Is there an important interdependence between freedom of the individual from coercion, fear, and material want and his freedom to choose what he believes, how he behaves, and what he values? Do the products of science and technology imprison men's minds by so setting the mental and emotional scene that most men are free to choose only among those alternatives that are pecuniarily profitable to those who control the instruments of public communication?

6. Immanuel Kant stated his famous categorical imperative as the basis for moral behavior as follows: "Act as if the maxim of thy will were to become, by thy adopting it, a universal law of nature." Compare this statement with The Golden Rule and its equivalents. (See footnote 24, above.)

PART FIVE

America and the Search for a Humane World Order

14

The American Quest for the Good Life

Compared with the stable structure of the predemocratic and preindustrial society, the contemporary American society is relatively loosely organized. It is, however, this very looseness of organization that stimulates social intelligence. Americans experience alternations of prosperity and recession, of national aggressiveness and international conciliation, of responsibility for government from one political party to the other, and of adulation and adverse criticism of leaders of industrial, labor, educational, religious, ethnic, artistic, and recreational organizations. Such changes compel men to make judgments. Often, to be sure, these judgments are superficial and inconsistent; opinions are crowd-processed, mere repetitions of those heard or read; facts are disregarded and motives unfairly assessed; irrelevant factors tip the balance. But whenever an individual makes judgments and defends his opinions, he is exhibiting some awareness of his importance and hence of his responsibility as a citizen in a democracy. He at least recognizes the fact that he has a stake in the outcome of the plebiscite of public opinion.

301

The Importance of the Plebiscite

The great importance of this plebiscite is indicated by the public relations programs of public organizations. Political party campaigns have, of course, long been characterized by efforts to gain support for candidates and platforms. In recent years, however, mass-communication facilities have come to be used by corporations, labor unions, and educational, religious, military, and ideological organizations in their efforts to convince the populace that their programs and proposals are justifiable and their motives above reproach. Indeed, judges, courts, executives, and legislators often frankly justify their decisions on grounds of public acceptance.

It is a disorderly panorama that the professional educator surveys. The intrinsic merits of many social issues are not understood by the public. Many people have neither the knowledge nor the trained ability required to make judgments based on reflective consideration; nor the inclination to give sustained attention to debates. Nevertheless, they influence the makers of decisions; they confirm or reject the decisions when made; they occasionally overturn policies which formerly they had approved.

Democracy is the great adventure of mankind; and all adventures are dangerous. It is a tolerable disorder, and it is tolerable because of two factors.

Self-restraint and Accommodation

The first is the fact that, however their values and standards vary, people do have in common the search for the good life—a somewhat vague notion, but one that serves as a criterion for judging the probable effect of one outcome of an issue as compared with another. The search for a good life for oneself and one's immediate associates exerts a steadying influence on judgments; it reduces, though it does not prevent, capricious expressions of emotional rancor or adulation. It encourages "second thoughts" about matters that might affect job security, safety of person and property, military service, and the attainment of necessities and comforts.

Tentative Decisions Are Modifiable

The second factor which makes our disorder tolerable is the referendum—the privilege of overthrowing a regime, of reversing a policy, or of sanctioning its continuance. By historical necessity, Americans have learned to apply the pragmatic criterion in assessing instruments and outcomes in all matters that they believe affect their welfare. In the political sphere, frequent elections provide formal opportunities to affirm or reject policies which candidates sponsor. But public opinion does not wait until election time to let decision makers know popular sentiments.

Scoffers at democracy sometimes ridicule the idea that the voice of the people is the voice of God, that the wisdom of a decision should depend on its acceptability by the ignorant and fickle masses, and that business "go-getters" should be permitted to control the economy. They fail to understand that in applying the criterion of their own well-being, people judge empirically with little reference to "truths," "principles," and "theories." Part of the experience on which they draw is the knowledge that there is at best only partial agreement among experts regarding these generalizations or their application to specific social problems. Faced by contradictory advice by those who admittedly are better informed in their special fields than is the man-in-the-street, citizens are emboldened to use their own scales to decide the adequacy and inadequacy of the men and measures they are called upon to judge. They are aware that such decisions involve risks, but they are accustomed to risks. And they have learned to make the best of an unsatisfactory choice, patiently awaiting the day, never far in the future, when new choices can be made.

Controversies and Compromises

Controversies rage. There are differences of opinion on almost every issue, sometimes so tightly drawn that deadlocks temporarily develop. Tempers get out of control; threats are sounded; occasionally violence occurs. Groups with interests vested in the going order are likely to resist changes, even those they admit in time will become inevitable. The ethnocentric group loyalties of religious sects, ethnic segments, and economic organizations clash with those of other groups. Progressives and boosters frequently square off against conservatives and reactionaries. And once he has taken sides in a controversy, the individual typically feels committed, and saving face makes compromise difficult.

Nevertheless, compromises do eventuate. The paralysis of deadlock is intolerable even to the most intensely committed adherents of one or the other side of most controversies. In other roles and group relations they must secure the consent and cooperation of their fellow men. Merchants, politicians, civic officials, educators, social service personnel, and labor leaders, for example, cannot function effectively in a strife-torn community.

In varying degrees, indeed, conflicts often have constructive outcomes. Their resolution brings about a we-feeling among most members of a community because they have become conscious of their stake in comity and accommodation and in the discomforts that accompany social tensions. The right to disagree is not denied, but the flare-ups of hatred are eventually brought under control.

CONTINUING MAJOR DISORGANIZATIONS IN AMERICAN SOCIETY

In a mobile, competitive, and fragmented society, tensions and strains follow one upon the other. Pent-up emotions of doubt and fear too often find release in faultfinding and hatred. Confidence in self and in social arrangements wavers, and intellectual objectivity under emotional stress is difficult.

In periods of prosperity and high hopes, the paths toward achievement and elation are too many and too inviting for most individuals to devote much time to recrimination. Optimism encourages accommodation and comity. Upward mobility creates hope, attainment, and self-confidence; fears, doubts, and suspicions remain, to be sure, but they tend to be sporadic and minor.

Permanent bitterness and hatred are more frequent among the defeated and the downwardly mobile. They form the hard core of extremist groups.[1] In times of depression, protests are rife, charges of blame are excessive, and emergency action becomes mandatory.

Revolutionary Effect of Emergency Action

Emergency action, however, has long-term, quasi-revolutionary effects. It is irreversible, though subject to later modification. It therefore calls for foresight and planning based on understanding and prediction of the conditions and forces that are producing social disorganization. Considered emergency action is thus a propitiously timed aspect of all intelligent social planning to deal with actual and potential socal disorganization.

[1] For example, unemployed white-collar youth in Post World War I Germany were recruited as Brown Shirts, and many frustrated college students and graduates in the United States embraced Communism during the depression. Hannah Arendt points out that the Nazi Party in Germany and various Communist movements in Europe after 1930 received their early support from a "mass of apparently indifferent people whom all others parties had given up as too apathetic or too stupid for their attention." *The Origins of Totalitarianism,* Harcourt, Brace and Company, Inc., New York, 1951, p. 305. In Europe between the two world wars, as in the United States, there were many persons who saw no future for themselves in the programs of moderate political parties and so turned in their frustration and bitterness to extremist parties.

The assumption that the United States and most of the rest of the world will maintain organized societies, however varied and however much in process of change, is a justifiable postulate. Nevertheless, it is only a postulate. There are reasons to doubt that it will hold true. The habits, attitudes, and accommodations that characterize men in social organizations are both brittle and malleable things. Their stability and predictability are far from certain.

Sometimes they break down suddenly in response to crises, at other times, more slowly, but no less seriously, in response to social change which in some degree outmodes moral restraints. The former has been exemplified many times in our own country by local and regional disruptions. Examples are the Boston Tea Party, Shays' Rebellion, The Whiskey Rebellion, wartime disasters to cities and other areas, the looting following the San Francisco earthquake, Iowa farmers threatening judges and preventing foreclosures of mortgaged farms early in the depression of the 1930s, the violent disregard of legal instruments both by the private police of industrial corporations and by strikers in Pennsylvania and elsewhere, and the acquittal of known murderers of Negroes by white juries in Mississippi.

Cases of disorganization due to progressive social change, while less often as dramatic, are more likely to be of continuing importance. Rapid urbanization compounded with the employment of women and youths in factories, stores, and offices, and hence their relative economic independence, has made drastic changes. The impersonality and privacy of apartment dwelling, the horizontal age groupings for leisure-time activities, and the accessibility of contraceptives, liquor, and automobiles have accelerated, if not caused, a general decay in the mores that characterized the small town, village, and rural life from which many urban adults have sprung. The relaxation of restraints on personal behavior is observable in the increasing tolerance of sexual freedom, new forms of delinquency, decreasing religious ritual in the family, and the general lack of esteem for thrift.

SORE SPOTS THAT THREATEN THE QUEST FOR THE GOOD LIFE

Educators do not fail to recognize the dangers of disintegration either among segments and regions or in the American society as a whole. They are disturbed by the general apathy in a people whose public opinion is so important in sanctioning or vetoing whatever actions governments, corporations, organized labor, reform societies, political parties, and other special-interest groups undertake. They recognize that the competition for popular attention to the multiform aspects of a complex and confusing life is such that public affairs can at best command the concern of individuals only spasmodically.[2]

They are well aware that democracy must exist dangerously in a world undergoing great change. They know too that democracy usually proceeds by trial and error, making correction for mistakes and neglects when they become acutely evident. Nevertheless, they fear that some phases of our social revolution may move so fast as to get out of hand.

Hence, students of education seek to identify those lags and sore spots which seem likely to develop into threats to social organization. There are a number of quandaries that especially concern them. These quandaries are discussed in the next few paragraphs.

Suspicion and Hostility toward Other Peoples

Granted that the situation might be expected to be worse than it is, cultural tensions, frequently exacerbated by real or imagined economic conflicts of interest, too often become seriously acute. Such attitudes are not limited to ethnic, religious, and regional out-groups. There is currently a widespread rejection of individuals and groups who espouse foresight, who seek to forestall and otherwise meet emergencies not momentarily evident. "Intellectuals" are frequently referred to by the derogatory term "egghead." Acceptable thought and action are all too likely to be at a low level of intellectuality. Hence, racism is enforced in the Southeastern states; "anticommunism," only vaguely and uncertainly defined in much of the country, as is anti-Semitism and anti-Catholicism among various segments of the population.

Regional Lags in the American Economy

The continued exploitation of "stoop-labor" migrants and tenants, sometimes held in peonage by debt, fosters a vested interest among their employers to continue the ignorance and poverty of agricultural workers. That the latter occasionally fight back lawlessly, and lawlessly are subdued, follows almost inevitably. So, too, do their occasional orgiastic outbursts, abetted by liquor or religious excitement, and their propertyless proclivity to squalor and petty thievery.

>   [2] It is argued by some observers that, seen in large enough perspective, the safety and stability of social organization in the United States is benefited more than it is endangered by popular indifference to proposals, movements, and laws. To the extent that this hypothesis is justified, the evanescence of public moods, opinions, and competing in-group loyalties may be the bulwark that prevents a fascist or class-status revolution in America. If so, perhaps school and community preoccupation with sports, romance, chatter, and prestige seeking is a prerequisite to stability in a democracy.

The Uneven Distribution of Postwar Prosperity

Despite general improvements in living standards, it is obvious to anyone that ugly slums remain, that the diets of large numbers of people are insufficient, that not all old people are adequately covered either by public assistance or social insurance, that provision for health, sanitation, and medical care are insufficient, and that family-sized farms and other small-scale entrepreneurships are in serious difficulty.

The Tenuous Character of Postwar Prosperity

This prosperity depends in large degree on a garrison state's defense and public works expenditures, on the production and distribution of "new-model" luxuries, comforts, and hobbies (largely purchased on the installment plan), and on the concomitant expansion of public and private debt. A serious jolt to popular confidence in our blown-up credit structure might be disastrous to social organization.

Economic Domination by the Federal Government

At one time or another in past years (usually in regard to *specific* spheres of legislative and administrative action), farm organizations, organized labor, the exploiters of natural resources, and great production corporations have successfully dominated government policies and actions. And with less success, consumers' organizations, ethnic groups, and liberal reform associations have sought to bring the pressure of public opinion to bear on executive and legislative bodies. All of this is quite in accord with the principles of representative government. But there exists the possibility that one segment of the economy might become so powerfully ensconced that defiance or submission would be the only alternatives for other men and organizations. Either alternative would exemplify social disorganization in America.

The Geographic Mobility of Men and Industries

Mobility upsetting social stability is, to be sure, not a new occurrence in Western societies. Since 1940 in the United States, however, several events and situations have combined to make conditions more acute. Wartime industries drew workers from far-distant places and from many occupations, changing radically the modes of life and standards of living of both the newcomers and the old residents. The rapid growth of already huge industries, the widespread locations of their plants and offices, and their tendency to abandon obsolescent facilities and replace them at other sites compelled frequent shifting of workers' residences, caused the decay of areas from which industrial plants had moved, and promoted centralization of control in huge labor organizations. Within each of these transformations are the potentialities of disorganization —unemployment, broken homes, strikes, ethnic strife, the demotion of workmen whose skills are made obsolete by technical advances, conflicts of moral standards, and increased juvenile delinquency.

Lack of Understanding of American Dependence on the Rest of the World

Can the American people, accustomed to viewing their country's political, economic, and military power as invulnerable, be educated to face the fact that their country is now, and will increasingly in the future be, dependent on the material wealth and good will of the 2¾ billion people who live elsewhere? Can the American people be prepared to play a realistic role in a world economy in which the United States may increasingly be a "have-not" nation with regard to many raw materials, and a less dominant country with regard to military manpower? Unless the people are prepared for the changing role of their country, scapegoats will undoubtedly be sought, blame will be assessed in an irrational manner, and independent thinking will be endangered.

None of the disruptions of the national or local community life may ever reach a critical stage. And if one or more should do so, it is reassuring to recall that the American society has survived drastic disorganizations in the past without long-time serious ill effects. But no man of good will would desire the recurrence of such crises if they can be foreseen and forestalled.

American Ideals as Functional Criteria

Nothing less than the great ideals of the American nation can provide the criteria required for judging the factors in contemporary American life which promise or threaten its quest for the good life. These ideals have been summarized by the Educational Policies Commission of the National Education Association under ten headings: (1) respect for the human personality; (2) each person's responsibility for the consequences of his own acts; (3) institutional arrangements as the servants of man; (4) mutual consent, rather than coercion and violence; (5) the human mind liberated by access to information and opinions; (6) the fostering of excellence of mind, character, and creative ability; (7) all persons judged by the same moral standards; (8) the concept of brotherhood given precedence over selfish interests; (9) maximum opportunity for each person to pursue his own happiness; (10) emotional and spiritual experiences which transcend material aspects of life made readily available.

This list of values provides one frame of reference for educators and other civic leaders to use in defining the elements of social promises and problems of American life and to help chart the course by which present success may be exploited. It is true that the mandates implicit in charting such a course cannot actually be fulfilled in detail, largely because emotional states cannot be accurately estimated. Nevertheless, foresight is inherent in quest. Its only alternative is to drift.

AREAS OF SPECIAL CONCERN TO EDUCATORS

Educators seek to identify and assess the importance of many phenomena besides those discussed thus far. All social phenomena inter-relate, however; hence, an investigator must consider many institutions and trends.

It would require endless duplication to deal in this text with each promising approach to prophesy and diagnosis. But the following list of topics and subtopics with brief comments regarding their prob-able importance in a rapidly and fundamentally changing society may prove useful.

Population Trends and Problems

The rapid increase in population in much of the world during the last two centuries has been looked upon with fear, with enthusiasm, and with indifference by different diagnosticians and at various times. Basic assumptions regarding food supply, industrial capacity, and fate have colored men's attitudes toward population growth.

The educator is primarily concerned with the *qualities* of the human beings who comprise the population of his community. He knows very well that the qualities of the present generation will largely determine the "goodness of life" thirty years hence, and he knows that no easy solutions for increasing the effects of desirable present qualities or for offsetting undesirable ones (such solutions, for example, as longer school attendance or sterner police surveillance) can be very effective. At the same time he knows that the common people, those who most recently and perhaps incompletely have come to share in the "good" material and spiritual aspects of the community, will produce the majority of the next generation. Herein the educator finds quandaries with which he must deal in cooperation with all individuals and associa-tions which seek optimistically to safeguard and to improve the social inheritance.[3]

[3] See E. L. Thorndike, *Your City,* Harcourt, Brace and Company, Inc., New York, 1939. Also, *144 Smaller Cities,* Harcourt, Brace and Company, Inc., New York, 1942, and *Education as Cause and as Symptom,* The Macmillan Company, New York, 1939.

Older People

Concern with this fundamental quandary leads the educator to consider many other problems and opportunities connected with population trends. The increasing numbers of older people make his concern with geriatrics and gerontology compulsory. Hence, he advocates and cooperates with measures for the security of older people, including preretirement counsel, programs for health insurance, visiting nurses and rest homes, and plans to insure the continued participation of retired persons in the civic, economic, and cultural activities of family, neighborhood, and community.[4]

Infant Care

The educator is interested in the care of infants and preschool children. He realizes that much of the development of traits, good and bad, takes place before institutional education starts and continues side by side with it thereafter.

The Status of Women

The changing role of women demands his attention. The conspicuous participation of women in civic and political affairs, in professional, industrial, commercial, and leisure-time occupations, their influence in shaping the market for services and products, and the many half-sublimated expressions of their sex urges do not blind the educator to the facts of squalor, drudgery, and inferiority of status from which great numbers have not yet been emancipated.[5] What inheritance of submissiveness, defiance, and carelessness do they now and will they in the future transmit?

Safeguarding the Approved "Culture"

The educator's awareness of the plurality of cultures in American life is obviously involved in his study of population characteristics. So, too, is the agitation for measures to minimize the danger of a stamping out of "higher" cultural ideas, activities, and mores by those of "lower" cultures. These proposals include those of slum clearance, state custody of seriously disadvantaged children, birth-control clinics, and, in cases of extreme biological inadequacy, sterilization.[6]

[4] Committee on Ageing, *Selected References on Ageing: An Annotated Bibliography, 1955*, Government Printing Office, 1955.

[5] Cf. U.S. Department of Labor, *Employment and Economic Status of Older Men and Women*, Bulletin No. 1092, 1952.

[6] "The New Eugenics and Education," *The Social Frontier*, vol. IV, pp. 113–117, 1938.

One aspect of the pluricultural complex is of peculiarly immediate concern for the educator: the differences in standards of morality, manners, language, diet, and other customs among people of different social-class levels. Whatever their explanations (and they are complex),[7] they are likely to differ from those fostered by the public school. Historically, the middle classes have sponsored the educational values and program of public education; teachers have been trained and selected to personify and to perpetuate these values. The standards of middle-class oriented schools, therefore, reflect both the business virtues—for example, obedience, accuracy, and promptness—and the language usages, etiquette, aesthetic taste, and code of honor assumed to characterize the upper-class culture emulated by the middle classes.

The School and Class-approved Standards

Children from lower-class homes attending middle-class schools must, therefore, lead double lives if they are to behave in accordance with their differential cultures. It is not surprising that they frequently exemplify in school situations the crudeness, callousness, aggressiveness, carelessness, and language solecisms (or worse) that are characteristic of their homes and neighborhoods. Rigid enforcement of conventional school standards in their cases, including condemnation, classroom failure, disgrace, and punishment, is likely to be met by defiance and truancy. School discipline, thus, may be a contributory cause of juvenile delinquency and a general rejection of authority.

Class and Crime

The existence of criminals and delinquents, of course, derives from far more basic conditions than those that the school alone can control. Indeed, the distinction between law-abiding, law-evading, and lawbreaking sections of the population is difficult to defend. If the definition of "crime" is an "offense punishable by law," then at one time or another almost everyone has been a criminal. Indeed, a competitive, acquisitive society condones law avoidance and law evasion by its emphasis on ingenuity, risk taking, and boldness.

That the men and women who have been convicted of a crime by a court come disproportionately from lower-class neighborhoods may give some justification for speaking of "crimogenic" neighborhoods and "a criminal class," but the terms should not blind one to the truth that much of the difference implied in them is due to the fact that conviction is often a function of financial inability and of ignorance of pro-

[7] They may reflect the culture of one or more ethnic groups mediated through, and mixed with, attitudes and practices tolerated in the slums.

cedure to assert one's legal rights.[8] It is true that the middle-class regard for property and for conventional behavior does discourage acts of violence, thievery, and destruction of property, a moral pattern less observed among lower classes. Middle-class morality is, however, tolerant of "fixers," "inside dopesters," [9] and other clever men who know what can be done without fear of arrest and conviction and whose connections are such that they can get disputed cases settled by agreement, thereby avoiding the stigma and expense of court trials.

Lower-class neighborhoods are disproportionately characterized by squalor, deprivation, broken homes, street gangs, and hopeless, shiftless adults. These facts have stimulated public support for slum clearance and housing projects, social services, recreational provisions, free health clinics, and legal aid for disadvantaged people.

Foreseeing School Enrollment and Related Problems

Educational administrators and the civic groups whose cooperation they cultivate are primarily interested in the provisions that must be made for oncoming generations of students and, less insistently, for adult education and community recreation. In economically stable localities, the birthrate, rates of migration, and grade school enrollments permit the reasonably accurate forecasting of needs.[10]

Other phases of population trends that concern the student of education have already been discussed under other topics. The effects of migration in its several aspects call both for surveys of present conditions and trends and for provisions for minimizing the undesirable and exploiting the favorable behavior and traits. To the familiar (though seldom adequately solved) problems of European and Asiatic culture fragments persisting into the third generation of immigrant populations, there have been added those of rural Negroes from the Southern states who move into industrial areas of the Northern and Western states, Puerto Rican and Mexican workers, the removal of native and foreign-born families to places of new employment, and, most recently, the almost constant state of movement of mechanized farm gangs in the

[8] Edwin H. Sutherland, *Principles of Criminology,* J. B. Lippincott Company, Philadelphia, 1947, pp. 138–146.

[9] These terms are used by Max Lerner, *America as a Civilization,* Simon and Schuster, Inc., New York, 1957, pp. 650–652. After David Riesman and Nathan Glaser, *Faces in the Crowd,* Yale University Press, New Haven, Conn., 1952.

[10] Cf. "Forty Million in School," *School Life,* vol. 38, no. 10, pp. 5–6, 1955, and C. V. Newson, "Some Population Statistics and the Problems of Higher Education," *The Journal of Educational Sociology,* vol. 29, no. 2, pp. 233–239, 1956.

grain-raising states. Add to these confusing phenomena the restless movements of many young adults who find jobs of brief duration in one community after another and whose children attend school a few weeks here and a few weeks there. The restraints exerted by local mores on transients are both slight and ambivalent; if they are to be supplemented and given a semblance of continuity and system, the public school and its allies have a real challenge to meet.

The educator cannot be unconcerned about popular opinions considered as *qualities* that affect the readiness of the young people to become informed and active citizens. A survey of information and opinion of the American people indicates a general lack of knowledge and absence of positive opinion regarding any of the critical issues and persistent problems that the society faces.[11]

The Future of Rural Life in America

Cities and their suburbs have grown so rapidly and their economic and cultural activities have come to dominate the social scene to such a degree that the continuing importance of village and rural life is seldom given the attention it deserves. Most urban dwellers have brought to their city many of the outlooks, values, and codes that they, their parents, and their grandparents learned in a rural or village environment. In considerable degree, despite the crowded facilities for work and transportation in the great centers of employment and recreation, there is little sense of community as a whole. Fragmental loyalties to church, ethnic segment, club, and family retain in-group characteristics. But the roots of these relations are derived from the emotional warmth approved and practiced in smaller communities.[12]

City living does offer many real advantages over rural living. Services, public and private, are available and relatively cheap; "cultural" resources are plentiful and at hand, and personal growth and sophistication are more readily available to those who value them. But there is often an insecurity where so much is inchoate and where services and contacts are mediated through mechanisms and dead-pan officials —subway workers, clerks, policemen, and the rest. Hence, perhaps, the nostalgic glorification of country living by many urbanites.

Village and rural facilities and comforts, of course, no longer lag far behind those of cities. Not only do the great networks of communication and transportation create a "rurban" country life, but also

[11] Samuel F. Stouffer, *Communism, Conformity, and Civil Liberties,* Doubleday & Company, Inc., New York, 1955.
[12] Cf. Robert S. Lynd, *Knowledge for What? The Place of Social Science in American Culture,* Princeton University Press, Princeton, N.J., 1939.

the state and federal agencies and national civic and social societies have active branches in many village centers.

Moreover, there is in many cases a relationship between the local community and these agencies and societies for which urban cultures have no counterpart. The church, the Grange, the Farm Bureau, the public school, and the elected and appointive officers of local government are known to residents who also know each other personally and who share many social and economic experiences. Alternating leadership is generally awarded on a friendly and personal basis; the physician, the auto mechanic, the farmer, the schoolmaster, the minister, and the town officer—each is accorded recognition when his peculiar competency is needed; he is *primus inter pares*—his authority is granted, not asserted.

Agriculture, the basic economic occupation of rural dwellers, is, however, undergoing revolutionary change. The traditional freedom and independence of the family-sized farm is in some degree being surrendered to organization as the price of survival. Economic realities being what they have come to be, the production of tangible commodities by man power supplemented by horsepower and inexpensive machine power is profitable only for the specialist in luxury goods production. Costly machines are practical for the farmer only if they can be frequently used—which fact advantages the owner of great tracts of land, and such an owner is frequently a corporation.[13]

There remain several alternatives for the operator of a small farm. A group of operators may form a cooperative, with or without government encouragement and assistance, thereby decreasing individual costs for machinery and perhaps for processing and marketing products. A farm family may content itself with a subsistence farm, exchanging the surpluses for other supplies, and perhaps supplementing income by part-time employment in industry. They may as best they can seek to convince legislatures that family-sized farms, and the rural and village life that they foster, have such a cultural value for the state that they should be subsidized.[14]

[13] Two million of the 4.7 million farmers in the United States produce 91 per cent of all the farm products marketed. The other 2.7 million farmers sell only 9 per cent of the nation's farm product; they are primarily subsistence farmers. *Report of Committee for Economic Development,* December 9, 1957.

[14] See Harold S. Sloan, *Farming in America,* Harper & Brothers, New York, 1947, Paul H. Landis, *Rural Life in Process,* McGraw-Hill Book Company, Inc., New York, 1940, and J. H. Kolb and E. de S. Brunner, *A Study of Rural Society,* 4th ed., Houghton Mifflin Company, Boston, 1952,

The social scientist has no firm answer regarding the survival of rural institutions. The frequently expressed opinion that cities are "naturals" for modern man, that small farms are economically wasteful and, therefore, individual farming as a way of life should be discouraged [15] may seem as ridiculous again as it was two decades ago when the "flight from the city" took place.

The Future in Urban and Industrial Centers

Because the impact of applied science and technology is so forcefully felt where men's livelihoods are so dependent on wages and salaries as they are in industrial and related occupations, the upswings and downswings of the economy have more sudden and extreme effects on urban than on rural people. Urban transactions are relatively anonymous. If layoffs from jobs occur, unemployment insurance benefits make neighborly help unnecessary. If serious sickness comes, the patient is taken to the hospital where family and friends may visit but not otherwise be helpful. If gadgets get out of order, the owner sends for a repairman or takes it to his shop; he does not ask his mechanically gifted fellow apartment dweller to lend a hand. If a worker in factory or store feels he has a grievance regarding his job, he goes to a shop steward of his union to present his case, not to his foreman or employer.

The Worker and His Job

More serious than the impersonality and anonymity of so much of urban life is the alienation of the worker from his work. Professionals and managers do, of course, generally live with their work, thinking about it if not actively engaging in it evenings and weekends as well as during office hours. But the wageworker finds little stimulus or satisfaction in out-of-hours concern with his job as such. The fault is not his; he is typically a wage earner rather than a craftsman; he sells his muscle and skill at so much per hour or per piece and with it his independence for the hours he works. Therefore, he is unlikely to express his personality in his work activity.[16] He typically has only his tiny part in the productive process to perform; what else goes on before need not concern him.

[15] "The farm population has been declining at an average rate of 800,000 a year since 1949. At this rate it will be down to 5 per cent of the national total before 1975." John D. Black, "Nineteen Fifty-Eight on the Farm," *The New Republic,* December 30, 1957, p. 9.

[16] C. Wright Mills, *White Collar,* Oxford University Press, New York, 1953, pp. 224–228.

The alienation of the worker from his job is now being accentuated and accelerated by automation. It not only replaces much of what skills and judgments have remained, but also it tends to do away with the jobs themselves. And yet the expensive, electronically-run machines must operate constantly, turning out goods and performing other services, else they do not justify the investment in them. And these goods and services must be bought in considerable part by those whom the machines have replaced—men and women ever further removed and alienated from their highly paid short-hour jobs which would disappear like chaff before the wind if the economy faltered.

Economic Instability and Occasional Crises Probable

Urban centers will doubtless be cleaner, more sanitary and aesthetically satisfying, as electric power and automatic machinery increasingly replace steam power and workmen in factories. Leisure hours will increase and frenzied efforts be made to commercialize them. Money will come easily, if at all, and will be freely spent. "Distress areas" will occasionally develop where prosperity had been in full bloom.

As technology continues to advance in production, distribution, and finance industries, the decreasing number of operators and supervisors of the automatic machines will have to be highly selected on the basis of natural ability and technical training. It seems probable that two critical problems will require careful consideration. (1) Unless these fewer employees receive sufficient income so that they can command the services of the equivalent of the displaced workers, the consuming power of the community will be seriously and adversely affected. (2) If, as seems likely, great numbers of skilled and technically trained former employees experience downgrading in their work, dissatisfaction may become rife and dangerous; the unwilling victims will not "take it lying down."

Every considerable crisis will invite panic and protest. Competition for trade outlets will be intense, both in this country and abroad. War spirit, the historic antidote for internal dissension, may be kept at fever heat. Urban man will frequently be anxious. And continuing anxiety may be almost as disastrous as radioactivity from guided missiles.

Status Seeking and the Resolution of Values

Anxieties will spring from status competition within the American society as well as from fear of general disasters, such as war, irradiation, disease, depression, destruction of natural resources, and racial and other ethnic conflicts. The uncertain future of individuals and of society makes considerable insecurity and instability almost inescapable. Men's minds are alternately dominated by self-interested desire for immediate comfort and by many longer-term interrelated concerns, including health, old-age security, the welfare of progeny, and the continuance of a stable economy.

Beliefs regarding both immediate and future conditions determine the state of public opinion. In a polity that requires majority consent for social arrangements and for measures to modify them, public opinion comes to be of crucial importance. Whether the American civilization shall triumph or even survive, or shall degenerate or perish, will depend fully as much on the nature of public opinion as it will on natural resources and industrial technology.

THE STRUGGLE TO INFLUENCE PUBLIC OPINION

Representative government can function only within the limits of public confidence in its good intentions and its competence to improve whatever physical and social conditions are inimical to the general welfare. But public opinion about what governmental programs and activities are favorable to the general welfare varies with time and place.

The General Welfare and Public Opinion

A lack of clarity as to what constitutes the general welfare is typically behind the struggle for public opinion. On the one hand are the often antithetical values of individual freedom and of "standardized progress"; on the other hand are the conflicting aspirations of economic, regional, ethnic, sectarian, and other segments of the population. Different faiths, myths, fears, and hopes, moreover, provide fertile soil for communications experts,[17] who apologize for and exploit various public policies and action.

The American Credo and the Resolution of Varied Interests

Faith in the collective wisdom and alertness of the voters "who have the final word and the final responsibility" and who alone "can and will preserve our liberties, if preserved they are to be," [18] is justified by the general wholesomeness of American society to date and by the

[17] The communications expert may be a gifted political leader sincerely devoted to a constructive course of action. In the acquisitively motivated society, however, he often is a hired agent, "public relations counsel," advertising specialist, or lobbyist, employed to devote his skill to gain support for the purposes or activities of his employer.

[18] Learned Hand, "The Choice Is Ours," *The Progressive,* December, 1952.

historic inadequacy of distrust in democracy. It is a faith that, in the long run something like a moving equilibrium among a virtually infinite number of mutually dependent variables, is achievable. It is a faith that citizens, individually and in the aggregate, will come to decisions that take account of the general good, and perhaps even recognize that their individual self-interests are secure only to the extent that the general welfare is fostered. The faith does not require, however, a brief that citizens will abjure self-interest, that they will be limited to making decisions by logic, or that they will not be swayed by anger, fear, and love.

Happily, there is a substratum of routine in civilized societies; there is a routine that justifies predictions and permits a considerable degree of assurance of popular common sense backed by the indoctrination inherent in community living. If, as Margaret Mead says, "Fourth of July orations are what little Americans are made of," it is largely because big Americans are similarly conditioned. The credo which exalts equality of opportunity has been imposed on the American community "by infinite repetitions surrounded by a hard shell of emotional aura." The credo is an unquestioned, almost unquestionable, faith. A deep sense of guilt is engendered whenever people become conscious that a public policy or act flagrantly violates this American credo.[19]

Somehow, all further propaganda both for private and public ends ought to be grafted on this body of belief if it is to be successful for very long. Glorification of "high living standards" and of "progress" in America raises feelings of guilt among those Americans who are aware that poverty and squalor persist, sweated labor of children and migrants continues, and social stigma is attached to some subcultures. "Snob-appeal" advertisements make many Americans feel uncomfortable, perhaps ridiculous, even as they are entranced by them. Campaigns of hate and suspicion shock them. The disclosure of corrupt practices and private-interest maneuvering among our governmental representatives arouses indignation and condemnation because they violate myths and symbols of commonwealth even though they may conform to work-a-day business morality.

The Competence of the Common Man

Belief in the competence of the common man is a fundamental tenet of democracy. "Give the common man the facts," it has been asserted, "and he will see the reasonable way to act." Hence, "we, the people" have established a government which operates with the consent of those who are *self-evidently* free and equal. "When opinions are

[19] See Lloyd V. Berkner, "Public Interest and the Technological Revolution," *Dartmouth Alumni Bulletin,* February, 1955.

free," concluded Thomas Paine in his epochal apology for democracy,[20] "truth will finally and powerfully prevail." Utilitarian economists and philosophers[21] guardedly assumed that each man could and would act intelligently and (by implication) independently to increase his pleasure and decrease his pain as much as possible, a belief which, when transferred to social action, favored a faith that common men would support measures that were to the advantage of the commonwealth. Faith in the dignity and worth of individual judgments, at least as potentials, has been central to democratic belief. Such faith is found in all the great American defenders of democracy, from Paine, Jefferson, Thoreau, and Lincoln to John Dewey, Carl Sandburg, Franklin Delano Roosevelt, and Adlai Stevenson.

Distortion of the American Credo

Private interests seeking wealth and power may, nevertheless, distort the American credo for their own purposes. National loyalty is sometimes equated with intolerance and hate toward misrepresented ideas and organizations labeled "un-American." Profitable trade in luxuries and superficialities is frequently fostered by the subtle identification of desire for the goods and services with the American myth of opportunity.

It is the *excesses* of imposition of like-mindedness through mass communication that disturb educators. The organization of purposeful men to influence public opinion is itself integral to most social action. In all group efforts, some degree of individual assertiveness is surrendered by many members, either by compromise, acceptance of majority decision, or submission to a dominant minority or a leader.

Common Purposes Favor Consensus

Consensus and cooperation are products of persuasive argument, which is a form of imposition, however mild and well-intentioned it may be. Constructive group purposes are unlikely to be achieved if the membership is seriously disunited. If individual integrity is to be fostered, such desirable consensus and cooperation must be a product of voluntary and intentional acceptance of group policy and program.

In community organizations where men meet in face-to-face groups for consideration of common problems, consensus is often reached with a minimum of superimposition by leaders. Courtesy, good

[20] *The Age of Reason,* 1794–1795.

[21] For example, Jeremy Bentham (1748–1832), David Hume (1711–1776), and John Stuart Mill (1806–1873), who believed man to be rational rather than reasonable.

will, respect for well-informed participants, common-sense judgments of the feasibility of proposed courses of action, and of the competence of candidates for carrying them out, frequently characterize parent-teacher associations, neighborhood-improvement organizations, church societies, and local branches of national civic associations. In such settings, a free competition of ideas and a maximum of individual voluntarism in assuming personal responsibility for carrying out group decisions are probable. To a considerable degree, reasoned decisions, rather than emotionalized loyalties, govern individual behavior, and intelligent cooperation displaces regimentation by slogan.

Some remnants of such individualism of decision do, to be sure, characterize some aspects of mass communication. Press, radio, and television provide platforms for advocates of differing programs and ideas, leaving the reader, listener, and viewer free to accept, reject, or otherwise react to the arguments. The publicity releases and advertisements of political parties and candidates, of commercial and manufacturing firms and associations, and of professional, religious, and educational associations so conflict that they cannot *all* be taken at face value. Hence, the recipients *may*, if their previous loyalties are not too strong, discriminate as to what and how much to believe and what line of action to follow.[22]

Independent voters, skeptical consumers, and intellectual liberals doubtless take advantage of these diverse arguments in forming their opinions. Perhaps a majority of American adults become somewhat aware that there are two or more sides to every story and that not all conflicting claims can be true and complete. Unhappily, however, too many men do not react intellectually to both sides of an argument; they

[22] Profit-seeking communication agencies face a dilemma in undertaking to present both sides of policy arguments to their publics. They depend for financial support on merchandising enterprises. But selling does not thrive on controversy, whereas intellect functions best when faced by a problem for which no clear answer is known and is, therefore, generally subject to some degree of controversy. Hence, commercial sponsors are loath to pay their money in direct support of programs or press reports that invite controversial audience response. Press and radio may, however, present controversial matter either as a public service or to increase their clientele (and hence make their other services more valuable for advertisers). But TV programs are so expensive to produce and broadcast that the lack of a wealthy sponsor is likely to doom a program that might focus the viewer's attention on the topic rather than on the article being advertised by the sponsor. Cf. Marya Mannes, "Channels: The Hot Documentary," *The Reporter,* November 17, 1955, pp. 37–39.

expose themselves only to the headlines and columns of favorite papers and magazines, radio commentators, and the apologetics of one political, religious, or economic organization. Many, indeed, are so bemused by "sport," dress, "wisecrack," personal gossip, and spectacular events that they have little mind to put on social and civic affairs at all.

"Talking sense to the American voters," as advocated by Adlai Stevenson, is fruitless unless the voters "tune in" to receive the sensible message. Similarly the minds of the audience must be made ready to communicate if arguments are to be rationally considered. And "readying" an audience itself often requires an appeal to emotions, through spectacles, music, oratory, and the rest of "good theater."

"Talking Sense" Versus "Rabble Rousing"

As a practical matter, therefore, "talking sense," though it implies a faith in rationalism—a faith that reason is, or can become, a dominating force in popular decision making—must compromise with man as he actually is. Effective communication is a two-way process; responses are conditioned by illogical feelings and faiths, many of which are not readily amenable to reason. Neither communicator nor communicant can quite free himself from the residues of age-old symbols and legends which are basic to human valuations.[23] In-group loyalties, male and female roles, religious mysteries, aesthetic preferences, and moral standards are in large degree either residues that survive from race experience or derivations arrived at by illogical explanations. Although the criteria for judging what is right or what wrong in these matters differ in detail among those whose responses to communication are sought, the nuclei are illogical and almost universal.

The distinction between "talking sense" to audiences and "rabble rousing" harangues is, therefore, one of the degree to which illogical legends and symbols are exploited and for what purpose they are exploited. The theatricals characteristic of a Nazi assemblage addressed by Hitler, of an Army-Navy Day parade in New York, and of a Billy Graham revival play excessively on the symbols and legends residual in human societies, thereby limiting critical thinking by the audiences.

[23] The sociologist Pareto and psychologists Freud and Jung have provided insight into the nature and potency of this "collective unconscious" (Jung) or "residues" and their "derivations" (Pareto). Recent scientific research also supports the contention that the effect of mass-communication messages depends as much upon the predisposition of the audience as upon the dramatic content of the presentation. Cf. Carl I. Hovland, Irving L. Janis, and Harold K. Kelley, *Communication and Persuasion,* Yale University Press, New Haven, Conn., 1953, pp. 260–277.

But a New England town meeting also requires stage setting, moral sanctions, and established procedures which are backed by other residues of associated life.

The Social Quality of Communications

The criterion by which an American educator evaluates the social quality of communications is its probable effect on the communicant's identification of himself with the symbolic "good man" of American ideology. However diverse in some respects "good man" may be, he is rational, economically adequate, and responsive to the call of civic duty.

A symbolic "good man," the concrete embodiment of ideal qualities, is a strong influence in shaping individual character. The "good man" figure varies in primitive societies—from the brave, wily, adventurous Sioux to the peaceful, unaggressive, generous Pueblo, for example.[24] In the United States, with its many subcultures, the "good man" figure cannot be clearly delineated; he is partly "Faustian," partly "Apollonian," and somewhat "Dionysian," [25] that is to say, he resolutely combats obstacles, with minimum recourse to aggressiveness toward his fellow man, but he is nevertheless individualistic, adventurous, and somewhat orgiastic.

The heterogeneous elements of the American society have, as a common denominator, humane culture and a morality of loyalty, sympathy, and collaboration. These are deep-rooted in our "collective unconscious." The compulsions of associative living have, in great degree, disassociated individualistic excesses from the "good man" figure. Hence, despite aberrations and momentary enthusiasm for a moral aggression, Americans commonly revere the figure who, in important matters at least, speaks the truth, is fair to all concerned, strives to build good will, and is friendly.[26]

[24] See Ruth Benedict, *Patterns of Culture,* Houghton Mifflin Company, Boston, 1934, chap. 4.

[25] "Faustian" is Oswald Spengler's term for Western man's self-conception. "Apollonian" refers to the classic ideal of avoiding conflict and excess and valuing order and normality. "Dionysian" man is assertive, craves excitement, is defiant of restraint; Nietzsche defined his character.

[26] Rotary Clubs throughout the country have popularized the "Four Way Test," mobilizing business and labor organizations, churches, and public schools in its support. The "test" asks the following regarding assertions or beliefs: (1) Is it the truth? (2) Is it fair to all concerned? (3) Will it build good will and better friendships? (4) Will it be beneficial to all concerned? R. A. Placek, "Savannah Takes the Test; Rotary's Four-way Test," *The Rotarian,* October, 1955, pp. 32–34.

Almost until the present day, freedom has been limited for most individuals by economic and social-class restrictions. In earlier chapters the effects of the industrial-economic, radical religious, and political revolutions in broadening the membership in a quasi-free society have been explored. In the United States, the process approaches its culmination as ever larger sections of the population attain relatively adequate economic status, political potency, and participation in the educational and leisure-time institutions that have previously been dominantly upper-class privileges. Self-confidence and assertiveness are counterparts of this new status.

The broadening of membership, though potentially encouraging for the quest for greater human dignity, is not without its ambivalences. Man cannot attain freedom from without himself; he must free himself from the mental and emotional habits associated with his own past servitude, including not only his fears of, and hostility toward, out-groups, but also his adulation of shallow practices associated with the "leisure classes." How widespread the popular preoccupation with conspicuous consumption actually is at present is a moot question; it may not justify the lamentations so often expressed by critics. It characterizes a striving for one aspect of a good life, however partial the conception.

The carry-over of hostile attitudes toward whatever institutions and establishments provide targets for his aggressiveness is more regrettable. Antagonisms stimulate counterantagonisms; both disrupt the American quest. They divert popular mentalities and energy from attending to constructive efforts to better the lives of all human beings. The life good to live is found in the process of trying to achieve it, not in defending standards already attained or establishments that skeptics may scrutinize.

The good life in the United States requires means and ends which are consistent with humane religion and humane science. That unwelcome truth is better than cherished error is a value judgment that gives moral significance to enlightened Americanism.

SUMMARY

Americans who approve and support the symbol of the "good man" are thereby committed to science and humane purposes as ways of life. The implicit belief is that mankind's destiny is largely of man's own making. Accepting the fact of the tolerable disorder characteristic of a complex, modern society, they have faith that, by dint of intelligent effort, meliorative measures can be developed which will lessen the dangerous strains which distort individual and collective thinking.

Despite the uncertainties of a changing world, they believe that reason guided by optimism and good will eventually lead most men to seek self-realization in cooperation with the efforts of all other men to "better their lots," not only economically, but also physically and spiritually.

Many of the advocates of reasoned good will and humane progress realize that man is not as predictable as a machine—his reason is often quite unconsciously subordinated to his desires or to the fixations of ideas and loyalties that censor and distort his thinking. This limitation, however, is factual, just as are the facts of population, rural and urban life, and the many danger areas in social organization which have been discussed in this chapter. The complexity and difficulty that these phenomena present do not stop the forward-looking citizen from attachment to reasoned good will, the only way of promise for a good society wherein man can shape his destiny.

The public educator belongs among this elite of hope, reason, and social engineering. He seeks always to understand what makes himself, his coworkers, and his students what they are and how they may effectively be drawn into purposeful participation in a creative institutional life—into the quest for the good life.

SELECTED REFERENCES

Bazeman, A. B.: *Politics and Culture in International History,* Princeton University Press, Princeton, N.J., 1960. Cultural systems of ancient civilizations persist and condition the efforts of new republics to establish national identities.

Buckley, William F., Jr.: *Up from Liberalism,* McDowell, Oblinsky, and Company, New York, 1959. An adverse criticism of contemporary ideological and political liberalism.

Burke, Edmund: *Reflections on the Revolution in France,* Henry Regnery, Chicago, and Liberal Arts Press, New York. Two paperbacked editions of the source book for many of the ideas of latter-day philosophical conservatives.

Chase, Stuart: *Live and Let Live,* Harper & Brothers, New York, 1960. A great danger in our divided world is "pendulum thinking" (either-or, black-white). Constructive thought applied to problems of national sovereignty, the population explosion, and other major challenges requires tentativeness, experimentalism, and compromise.

DeGré, Gerard: "Freedom and Social Structure," *American Sociological Review,* vol. 11, no. 10, pp. 529–536, 1946. An influential sociological treatment of the dependence of freedom on social structure.

Educational Policies Commission: *Education for International*

Understanding, National Education Association, Washington, 1948. A book for people who want to do something about peace and human progress.

Handlin, Oscar: *The Newcomers,* Harvard University Press, Cambridge, Mass., 1959. Report on a factual study of Negro and Puerto Rican people in New York City.

Hartz, Louis: *The Liberal Tradition in America,* Harcourt, Brace and Company, Inc., New York, 1955. A discussion of the liberal search for a humane society.

Lerner, Max: *America as a Civilization,* Simon and Schuster, Inc., New York, 1957. An authoritative and provocative book on the quality of American civilization.

Lipset, Seymour M.: *Practical Man: The Social Basis of Politics,* Doubleday & Company, Inc., New York, 1959. The apathy of American citizens considered as an advantage and as a disadvantage for effective government.

Meadows, Paul: *The Culture of Industrial Man,* University of Nebraska Press, Lincoln, 1950. A collection of essays on human problems and aspirations in the industrial society.

Mills, C. Wright: *The New Men of Power,* Harcourt, Brace and Company, Inc., New York, 1948.

————: *The Power Elite,* Oxford University Press, New York, 1956.

————: *White Collar: The American Middle Class,* Oxford University Press, New York, 1953. Three provocative books by a sociologist on the American power structure.

Packard, Vance: *The Status Seekers,* David McKay Company, Inc., New York, 1959.

————: *The Waste Makers,* David McKay Company, Inc., New York, 1960. The confused equation of the good life with profligacy is discussed in these two books.

Ross, Ralph, and Ernest van den Haag: *The Fabric of Society,* Harcourt, Brace and Company, Inc., New York, 1957. Especially Chapter 47. An extraordinary textbook discussion of public opinion and mass communications.

Smith, Huston, and Richard Heffron (eds.): *The Search for America,* Prentice-Hall, Inc., Englewood Cliffs, N.J., 1959. Outstanding liberal spokesmen identify and analyze the obstacles facing the American democracy and recommend measures to overcome them.

Stouffer, Samuel F.: *Communism, Conformity, and Civil Liberties,* Doubleday & Company, Inc., New York, 1955. Report of an empirical study of the everyday concerns of American citizens.

Sutherland, Edwin H.: *White Collar Crime,* The Dryden Press,

Inc., New York, 1949. Especially important for its discussion of the class differences in "justice."

U.S. Department of Labor: Manpower: Challenge of the 1960's, 1959. Composition of the work force in the United States predicted for the decade ahead.

————: These Are America: A Report to the American People, 1957. Illustrations and explanations of the activities of workers in typical work situations in the changing industrial society.

Vorse, Mary Heaton: Labor's New Millions: The Growth of a People's Power, Modern Age, Inc., New York, 1938. The story of the organization of industrial workers in the United States during the 1930s.

DISCUSSION QUESTIONS

1. Ethnic diversity in the United States is sometimes cited as a major hazard to national unity; it is also occasionally asserted that the processes of cultural assimilation have contributed in large measure to the greatness of this nation. Are both assertions partly true? Or is one of them untrue? Can the United States be properly called an Anglo-Saxon country? A Christian nation? A peace-loving people?

2. Is it true that geographic and social mobility within the American population has been so free and continuous that class and status barriers to commonality of national membership have never attained rigidity and that regional, religious sectarian, and other segmental ideologies have ceased to be "fighting faiths"? If true, do the moods and behaviors induced by expansionism (almost constant growth) account for this? To what extent have democratic ideals been a causative factor?

3. Have similarities of speech, costume, etiquette, luxuries, and recreation, which characterize different groups in the United States, increased sympathetic understanding and expedited upward mobility? Or has it "corrupted" or degraded the aesthetic tastes, manners, sense of civic responsibility, and humane sympathies of upper-class and upper-status members? Or both?

4. Though the money incomes of most working people increase in times of inflation and full employment, those of wage earners, of industrial managers, of financiers, and of merchants (including advertisers and salesmen) increase faster than those of salaried ("white-collar") workers, thereby changing the relative economic power of these groups. Is the temporary disadvantage of the last-named group compensated for by greater job security and maintenance of salary rates during recession and depression? Does salary status carry a prestige value superior to that of wage status that compensates for disadvantage in income? As industrial labor wins guarantees of annual wages will

they tend to approximate the salaried workers' status with its advantages and disadvantages?

5. Apologists for some advertising firms assert that their techniques add value to the products that they promote by increasing the self-esteem of the purchaser and his appreciation of the articles and services he buys. Is this alleged value an economic value? Is the acceleration of obsolescence by means of advertising socially desirable? Do the prestige values attached to ownership of latest-model cars, clothes, and house furnishings contribute to or detract from social and philosophic good, that is, something worthy of being believed and trusted?

6. How do you account for the tenacity of a person's attachment to cherished beliefs which are contrary to facts readily observable to the believer? Social scientists have found in one extreme case that disproving a belief actually strengthened the solidarity of the members of a group and strengthened their belief (see Leon Festinger, H. W. Riecken, and Stanley Schacter, *When Prophecy Fails,* University of Minnesota Press, Minneapolis, 1957). Do you see any similarity between this phenomenon and that of national "balance-the-budget" advocates who, along with most other big-business executives, have thrived for twenty-five years on unbalanced budgets? Or to that of pervasive isolationist sentiment in this country after two world wars?

7. Most labor union memberships are found in manufacturing, especially in large-scale mass production, while, in "white-collar" and agricultural occupations, labor unions are at present weak. In all of these occupations, however, technology and approaching automation are displacing many human skills and so are making revolutionary changes in job requirements and in numbers of employees needed. Do you believe that the welfare of workers in manufacturing will be safeguarded by union negotiated contracts more effectively than that of office workers and farm laborers by individual contracts?

8. "The threat of misused leisure" has frightened some sincere spokesmen for moral and aesthetic standards ever since workers have sought shorter workdays and workweeks. Others, equally concerned for standards, have believed that with greater leisure widespread appreciation of order and beauty are achievable. From your acquaintance with and observation of men and women employed forty or fewer hours a week at their regular jobs, can you make a generalization regarding the effect? In many cases, do workers use the released time to take on second occupations, engage in home improvement, develop hobbies, become spectators of sports and shows, squander their time and money with crude or evil companions, or enroll in self-improvement classes? Read the rather surprising results of the study of Akron's six-hour-day workers. (Henry Swados, "Less Work, Less Leisure," *The Nation,* February 22, 1958, pp. 153–158.)

15

The United States
and the Search for a Humane
World Order

Each man lives in a world society. His membership in the human race is inescapable. Not only his physical security and material welfare but also his humane qualities are affected by the circumstances that condition the lives of all other men.

It is a polyglot, pluricultured, ever-changing world society. It is fragmented by regional, national, religious, and other cultural ethnocentrisms, and by confusing social, political, and economic structures, values, and practices. Conditions of poverty, disease, suspicion, fear, and hate, if widespread and malignant in any part of the world, are disruptive and potentially destructive to the associative life of all men. Physical and emotional insecurities provide fertile ground for rival agitators to cultivate their own immediate interests or those of specific economic classes, nationalities, religious orders, or other establishments.

So long as energy resources, food supplies, technological processes, and scientific knowledge remained inadequate for the possibility of at least the minimal welfare of all men, there may have been realistic justification for the many to suffer in order that the few might survive.

328

But in an age in which the suffering of poverty, plague, and war is no longer necessary, self-interest is not served by exploiting the adverse conditions of any people's life. Only as hope for a better future fires the aspirations and provides the dynamics for community of effort among men everywhere can a world order adequate for a humane society be established anywhere.

The American Experience in Community of Effort

Viewed in this way, it is obvious that America's experience during the past 3½ centuries provides an interesting, if not altogether inspiring, example of an experiment in community building. Here land, food, and freedom were within the grasp of an energetic people. Here hope, aspiration, and opportunity favored collaboration, ingenuity, and order. Here, therefore, compromise and toleration proved more likely to lend support to personal achievement by the majority of men than egregious violence and coercion. And here leadership has been awarded and followership voluntarily extended to those men who have envisioned and formulated the political, economic, and technological instruments which have seemed to the majority of men propitious for the common welfare.

Failure, disappointment, dissatisfaction, and unresolved conflicts have marked the way of the nation's uneven progress. Poverty, disease, suspicion, fear, and hate have not yet been overcome, but they are generally recognized to be unnecessary and avoidable. And the major trends of the society are set determinedly toward melioration of these outmoded conditions. It is, therefore, not only the very real success already achieved, but at least as important, the widespread consciousness among Americans that much more is required to achieve a truly humane community that makes the United States a precursor of a humane world order.

The American nation is itself a polyglot, pluricultured, and multiclass agglomeration of peoples who have wrought out a nationality of their own, who have somehow subordinated their ethnocentrisms to a pride in their national community and to a determination to preserve and extend it. Granted that this pride and determination sometimes lead to excesses of zeal which threaten the very objectives Americans value most, their underlying motivation is for a society that shall prove to the world that common men can live and work together in a nation for the attainment of universal human welfare.

Accomplishments and Potentialities

It is the potentiality as well as the accomplishment of popular control of social destiny that is inspiring. "The shot heard round the world" fired by the farmers and artisans at Concord symbolizes the rejection by the common man of arbitrarily imposed restraint. Only by his own consent would he submit to governmental regulation. It was an assertion that "natural man" would adventure in a "natural society" to secure his "natural rights."

The adventure has not run smoothly; no adventure does. Men's minds and their social institutions do not change suddenly, radically, and consistently. But the "truths" and purposes proclaimed by the founding fathers in the Declaration of Independence and the Preamble to the Constitution have been congenial to the common man. He has found justification in them (and in their confirmation by his experiences of daily community living) for challenging unacceptable prescriptions, whether they be political, ecclesiastical, social-class, or economic.

The progression of science, technology, manufacture, finance, commodity consumption, and urbanization have presented ever new opportunities for the assertion of what the ordinary man has believed to be his "equal rights." Thus the doctrinaire "truths" and purposes enunciated in the Declaration and Preamble have served as an ideological background for practical year-by-year measures undertaken by all social establishments; without consent by those they directly affect, they are futile. Teachers, preachers, and even military officers, as well as governmental officials have somewhat erratically learned to respect the limits of the possible.[1]

Nationalism and Community

The broadening of a sense of community has historically accompanied the development of political societies. Peculiarly in the case of nationalism, a consciousness of membership in a complex geographic and economic structure has fostered a we-feeling among all classes and sections of a nation which is at least an approach to brotherhood. Though this catholicity of sentiment promoted by nationalism induces a sense of loyalty and pride often too narrow and too charged with emotion to make supranational comity and mutual trust readily achievable, it does, nevertheless, indicate the path that a world society must follow.

It is at best a slow and always an uncompleted process. Even after centuries of union, many Scots, Welshmen, and North Irish, though loyal British citizens, are zealous subnationalists. In the United States, regional and states "rights" and fragmental religious, economic, and

---

[1] The debt that Americans have owed to analogous popular participation in resolving social problems in European countries, both before and contemporary with their exemplification in this country, must be recognized, of course. Those developments have been treated in Chapters 10, 11, and 12.

ethnic interests sometimes arouse militant in-group loyalties accompanied by fear of authority of the Federal government. It is obviously predictable, therefore, that the growing acceptance of the concept of a world community will continue to be accompanied by national, economic, and ideological rivalries, constant threats to international comity and collaboration.

The establishment of the American commonwealth may be viewed as a pilot project for a world commonwealth, though the obstacles to the realization of the latter are far more complex than those of the former. Among the thirteen original independent states, language barriers to communication were almost nonexistent, the social heritage of English law and customs pervaded all sections and classes, national police power to enforce national law was in being, and national ownership of most of the Northwest Territory carried with it national responsibility for its development. Nevertheless, there were critical years in which class and regional antagonism had to be assuaged, and many economic problems required constructive solution if a commonwealth was to be firmly established. Its successful achievement, however, has fired the imaginations and hopes of statesmen who seek to draw on the American experience in meeting world problems, always with discriminating attention to the successes and failures that marked the American progress toward commonwealth.[2]

The Achievement of a World Commonwealth

The progressive achievement of a world commonwealth, however, requires more than political establishments. There are, of course, powerful controls other than those of politics that govern human welfare. There are economic "empires," dependencies, and various forms of collaboration that exist and function independently of national states; governments may encourage some and limit or outlaw others, but the flow of raw materials and manufactured goods goes on often with scant concern for their effects on human welfare. There are complex cultural values, varying from religious, dietary, and moral customs to ideas regarding class relationships which determine the acceptability of political agencies' recommendations and mandates.

[2] The British Commonwealth also serves as a pilot project which complements that of the United States. It has met successfully the problems involved in noncontiguous and widely separated population areas, of great differences in ethnic and religious cultures, and of local economies varying from primitive to technologically advanced. In these regards, its experience may be more pertinent for the achievement of a world commonwealth even than that of the United States.

The broadening of a sense of world community depends on the self-discovery and self-emancipation regarding the long-term advantages of intelligently conceived mutual welfare as compared with callous indifference toward, and self-seeking exploitation of, others' needs. Such discovery and emancipation can be expedited by exposition and persuasion and by the clarification and exaltation of humane ideals to which all men of good will give assent. Coercion, however, is not effective in the process of freeing minds from obsolescent stereotypes.

The Enlightenment of Decision Makers

The enlightenment of all men who participate in decision making, whether in political, economic, religious, or other significant areas of group life, becomes a major function of responsible statesmen. In the higher echelons of problem solvers and social planners, frequent service by congressmen, bankers, industrialists, and churchmen on commissions to study various world problems encourages them to reexamine positions and measures that they may previously have advocated.[3] For the general populace, forums, public interviews, newspaper and magazine articles, and broadcast addresses help men become informed regarding controversial questions—at least help them recognize the fact that there may be a reasonable basis for disagreements about them.

The role of public educational establishments in fostering the achievement of a world commonwealth is directly related to this second function of responsible statesmanship. Except at the higher levels of specialization, professional educators and those youths and adults they teach are unlikely to engage immediately in the process of policy making in this field. Their more modest but fully as important function is to foster an enlightened and constructively oriented electorate capable of evaluating the recommendations of statesmen and determined to support those steps which they believe favorable to world commonwealth.

[3] Business and trade union leaders have traditionally favored high tariffs to protect American industry and wage earners from foreign competition. Currently, however, many spokesmen for large corporations and labor unions are among the vigorous proponents of reciprocal trade treaties and for technical and welfare aid by the United States for underdeveloped and financially disadvantaged countries. They believe that it is clearly to the advantage of our domestic economy to help increase the flow of world trade. See, for example, Ken Miller, "New Opportunities for Yankee Traders," *The Reporter,* March 20, 1958, pp. 15–19, and Sidney Hyman, "Mr. Dillon and the Fight for Foreign Aid," *The Reporter,* March 20, 1958, pp. 10–15.

ESTABLISHMENTS AND MEASURES IN BEING

If anarchy on a world scale, potential in international and inter-power-group rivalries, is to be avoided, some supranational codes and laws must exist which cannot be successfully flouted by any nation or power group. Codes governing trade practices and war making have developed over many centuries; compliance with them has been enforced by those establishments and groups whose self-interest has been at stake. Thereby they have come to have legal sanction both within, and among, civilized nations and power groups; though, as in the case of many other laws, their interpretation and their extension to cover changing situations have been often in dispute.

By no means have all these codes and standards achieved the status of international law. Many agreements among nations and power groups apply only to specific occasions or practices, for example, the arbitration of disagreements, cartel arrangements for manufacture and markets, and currency conversion and other financial practices. Other agreements are formalized as pacts, conventions, and treaties among nations and as consortiums among economic groups; their force depends on the opprobrium the violator undergoes.

International Law

International law similarly induces compliance lest world disapproval and retaliation be visited on the nation or economic group which defies it. There is no supranational governmental agency competent to enforce compliance, though some tentative steps have been essayed in recent years.[4] The International Court of Justice is endowed with only such jurisdiction as member states choose to grant it; there is no compulsion other than the pressure of world public opinion for the submission of a question of international law to the Court, and, of course, no administrative agency that might compel compliance with its decisions. The United Nations itself is a structure for world confederation and cooperation, analogous rather to the Articles of Confederation of the American colonies than to the Constitution, which involved

[4] Two examples: In 1951, the UN Security Council (the Soviet representative having voluntarily withdrawn from it) authorized the UN military intervention in Korea; in 1956, with the acquiescence of the nations concerned, the Secretariat was directed by the Assembly to maintain a token international military force to patrol the borders of Israel and some of its contiguous states to make sure that truce conditions were observed.

the surrender of many state autonomies. What the future may hold for the international political structure will depend on world experience. Emergencies which threaten future world conflagrations may require drastic steps to legalize whatever acts are required to enforce compliance with decisions voted by the General Assembly of the UN. If the danger is acute and dramatic enough to make such action obviously necessary, it is improbable that structural difficulties, such as the veto right of every member of the Security Council, will prevent doing whatever has to be done.[5]

United Nations Planning and Welfare Agencies

Information regarding the structure, the history, and the quandaries of the political provisions of the United Nations Charter, of course, interests the educator. His major concern, however, is with those social and cultural agencies associated with the world organization which are immediately directed to the melioration of human conditions. Their efforts are analogous to those of welfare agencies in the United States, one of which is, of course, the public school. Some of the world welfare agencies, such as the International Red Cross and the Save the Children Foundation, are structurally independent of the United Nations, though official provision is made for consultation with their representatives by United Nations agencies. Some associated organizations, including the International Labor Organization, the International Court of Justice, and the Universal Postal Union, antedate the United Nations. Special agencies have performed their function and been discontinued; the United Nations Rehabilitation and Relief Administration (UNRRA) is an example. New occasions and developments have called for new agencies, for example, the Atomic Energy Commission.

The basic and continuing meliorative agencies are less hampered by the political and structural character of the United Nations than are the special ones. They study the needs and opportunities for social betterment, assess the effectiveness of the steps being taken to im-

---

[5] Supranational power to compel compliance with laws and codes have characterized all empires. Of especial interest is the *Pax Romana,* imposed on the then known world, a comparatively enlightened rulership that assured security of property, justice in private economic affairs, and much freedom in religious, intellectual, and other cultural expressions. Following the decay of the Roman Empire, the Holy Roman Empire, headed by the hierarchy of the church, sought to continue control over political and economic institutions as well as personal morality in the Western world, using religious dogma and statecraft to enforce its codes.

prove conditions, and collaborate in carrying out the agreed-upon policies.

INTERNATIONAL COOPERATION
FOR A HUMANE WORLD ORDER

The organizations under the auspices of the United Nations which are engaged in planning and carrying forward projects for human welfare, as distinguished from those which seek to maintain an orderly international political and economic comity, have many forerunners. Religious establishments have rarely limited their memberships or their human concerns to the people of one country. Socialists, pacifists, and the votaries of other ideologies have recruited followers wherever they could. "Learning" has proudly belonged to mankind; its applications, except those kept secret for trade and military reasons, have been gladly shared.

The Economic and Social Council

Happily, much of the determination of meliorative policy is in the capable hands of the Economic and Social Council, composed of representatives of several nations who are professional social scientists. However much their national loyalties and their ideologies differ, they do "talk the same language," and they are conscious of the social and economic consequences likely to follow specific courses of action. This Council early took the lead in establishing nine permanent, and two temporary, commissions to study acute problems and to recommend policies to appropriate agencies. It also brought into official relationship with the United Nations various specialized agencies that had survived the League of Nations—the International Labor Office, the World Health Organization, and the International Trade Organization.

As already emphasized, education is a major function of all these specialized commissions. As they endeavor to feed the hungry, to prevent disease or heal its ravages, to establish standards of human rights, to improve the lot of labor, and to enlighten the ignorant, they also serve to recruit world-wide cooperation among men.

Not only are their aims teleological, but also they provide the means by which disadvantaged peoples are encouraged to participate in their own emancipation from disease, ignorance, poverty, and superstitious fatalism. The discussion here is limited to the programs of four United Nations specialized agencies: the World Health Organization, the Food and Agricultural Organization, the International Labor Office, and the United Nations Educational, Scientific, and Cultural Organization.[6]

The World Health Organization as an Educational Agency

Sound health for all mankind is not only a humanitarian ideal, it is also a very important economic resource. Healthy populations produce more and are therefore more potent consumers of goods and services than people debilitated by malnutrition and disease.

Their domestic and foreign policies compel nations to be concerned with health conditions both in their own populations and in those of allies, of trading areas, and wherever else their military forces and civilian representatives go. Their efforts are assured popular approval, aside from materialistic and policy considerations, because of the dramatic and personal quality attached to the idea of sickness. The morality of caring for the ill and helpless is almost universal; it is at least as ancient as stone-age cultures. Morality and materialism thus reinforce each other.

The World Health Organization successfully directs the attention of the people of member nations to their specific immediate needs; it cooperates with national endeavors to meet these needs; and it independently carries on projects mobilizing the human and material resources available. In cooperation with the United Nations Relief and Rehabilitation Administration, for example, the malaria cases in Greece were reduced from 2 million to 50,000 by the use of DDT and other preventive measures, saving thereby the equivalent of the working time of more than 100,000 workers a year. In Egypt the threat of a cholera epidemic was met by the World Health Organization at the request of the Egyptian Minister of Public Health.

In eastern Bengal, one season's effort in malaria control increased the rice crop yield by 15 per cent. On the Italian island of

[6] Several other establishments related to the United Nations have significant educational functions or implications. The International Court of Justice, if in time it is to function effectively, requires the development, on the part of national governments and of the power groups they represent, of readiness to submit to agreed-upon rules of law of world-wide application. The International Bank for Reconstruction and the International Monetary Fund arrange credit facilities and currency exchange among various countries whose governments and power groups have developed responsible attitudes and organizations to manage their nations' financial affairs. The International Postal Union and the International Telecommunication Organization aid, in obvious ways, the growth of popular consciousness of a world-wide society.

Sardinia, as a result of a campaign against malaria, fertile soil capable of providing homes for a million people has been opened for settlement, thereby furnishing some relief for the crowded mainland. Equally impressive projects are under way in other areas. Sanitation is transforming disease-infected localities into healthful environments for human habitation, increasing productivity, and fostering enlightenment, thus providing conditions favorable for individuals to achieve responsibility, liberty, and to pursue their own happiness.

The Food and Agricultural Organization: Emancipation through Enlightenment

Mutual reinforcement of the World Health Organization and the Food and Agricultural Organization is implicit in the interrelatedness of their objectives and their common emphasis on self-help. The latter cooperates with whatever governmental and other agencies are engaged in improving agricultural processes and the social and material conditions connected with them.

The Food and Agricultural Organization starts with a well-based conviction that an increase in agricultural productivity adequate to keep pace with population growth and to bring a reasonable standard of nutrition to the whole world is technically possible. It is neither lack of resources nor techniques, they say, but economic, social, and political differences which impede the achievement of an adequate diet for all people.[7]

Means of Increasing Production

Six techniques for increasing production in areas where there is a chronic imbalance between population and human welfare are: (1) the development of natural resources; (2) the improvement of domesticated plants and animals; (3) the provision of better equipment for farming; (4) the use of better nutrition for plants and animals; (5) the prevention of losses (through spoilage, for example) in food supply; and (6) the development of better skills on the part of farmers.

In cooperation with the program of Technical Assistance of the United Nations (to which in 1953 seventy nations pledged financial contributions of some 25 million dollars) the World Health Organization and the Food and Agricultural Organization have put 1,600 technical experts to work in areas where specific assistance is much needed and welcomed, and they have maintained 2,100 "fellows" from such areas in training in foreign countries with a view to the trainees utilizing,

[7] Food and Agricultural Organization, *Report to the United Nations Economic and Security Council,* May 18, 1953.

in their home countries, the knowledge, skills, and human attitudes so gained.

These two processes, it must be emphasized, are not necessarily one-way passages. Some countries that need specific technical assistance are well equipped in regard to other techniques to extend help to other needful areas. India, for example, provided eighty-four experts to work in other countries where their contributions are much needed, during the same time she received ninety-one experts from other countries to help the Indian people deal effectively with specific problems. Even the so-called backward societies may have important contributions to make both to other relatively primitive people and to the solution of problems in all countries. Thus Indonesian experts are introducing their highly successful processes of fish farming to other peoples who can profit by their techniques.

The Point Four Program

The efforts of the Food and Agricultural Organization and its allied agencies of the United Nations is supplemented by the United States' Point Four Program, so called because it was the fourth recommendation for constructive world policies in the Inaugural Address of President Truman in January, 1949. This recommendation was implemented by the Act of International Development in June, 1950, and by congressional appropriations since that time.

The Point Four Program has had its counterpart in other lands. The most important of these, the well-known Colombo Plan, is an ambitious undertaking to supply technical assistance to a vast area in Asia. In this region of the earth approximately one-fourth of the world's population subsists. The plan is supported by Australia, Borneo, Burma, Canada, Ceylon, India, Indo-China, Indonesia, Malaya, New Zealand, Pakistan, Thailand, and the United Kingdom. In addition to other forms of development, it is the expectation of the sponsoring countries that 13 million additional acres of land will be placed under cultivation and as a result 6 million tons of food will be produced annually. The estimated cost of the project is between 5 and 6 billion dollars. Seventy per cent of this expenditure is to be devoted to increasing agricultural production.

Examples of successful accomplishments in applying technology to the improvement of food supply are many and varied. They include national, regional, and private projects, some of long standing, as well as international ventures like those mentioned in the following paragraphs.

Examples of Accomplishment

The reclamation of land for agricultural purposes is now being achieved by three modes of attack: the drainage of swamp lands, the irrigation of arid lands, and improved sanitation to combat plant and human diseases. In Africa, wells and cisterns, constructed by the Romans 2,000 years ago, are again in use for irrigation. East Bengal, as early as 1951, had brought 2 million additional acres under irrigation. Russia has reclaimed 34 million acres near Stalingrad. Holland is building dikes in the gulf of Zuider Zee which will increase by 7 per cent her productive land area.

Improvement in the productivity of domestic plants and animals has been phenomenal. The production of rice, the staple diet of 70 per cent of Asian peoples, may be increased in keeping with the spectacular results achieved with corn in America. Nine countries, encouraged by the Food and Agricultural Organization—India, Pakistan, Burma, Ceylon, Indo-China, Indonesia, Thailand, Malaya, and the Philippines—are cooperating in an effort to produce hybrid rice.

Remarkable progress has been made in improving the quality of livestock. Inferior breeds consume as much food as do superior breeds though their yield of milk and meat is small. If the milk yield of cows of Asia and Africa, for example, could approach that in Great Britain, human diets could be rapidly improved. In Northern Africa, native cattle are being crossed with zebus; the offspring are more rugged, better meat and milk producers, and more satisfactory draft animals than are the Sudan breeds.

Food and Agricultural Organization experts have estimated that an increase of 30 per cent in general crop production for the world would result from maximum use of organic and inorganic fertilizers. Known resources which can be utilized for the production of inorganic fertilizer are adequate for many centuries.

In many countries of the world, conditions are not favorable to mechanized farming. In such places, an increase in the quality and number of simple tools that can be made available and simple instruction in their use are the practical steps to be taken.

In Afghanistan, for example, time-consuming and wasteful methods of work are embedded deeply in the poverty-stricken lives of the peasant farmers. The ancient sickle is being replaced with the scythe, hand forks, and hand rakes. A Swiss farm-implement expert and men familiar with hay farming under similar topographical conditions demonstrate their use. These tools will enable each farmer to accomplish five times the work that could be performed with more primitive implements. The local blacksmith is useful in keeping the equipment in repair. Gasoline and oil which could be procured only at prohibitive cost are unnecessary. The capital investment is not large, and the simple economy of the people is not disrupted. Thus feasible action directed toward a limited improvement in the situation is being undertaken.[8]

Better technological methods aid agriculture, and agriculture in turn makes technology possible by releasing manpower for scientific and industrial activity. Living standards cannot advance to a high level in any economy where the vast majority of the working population is engaged in production of food mainly for their own consumption.

The International Labor Office

This organization, established under the League of Nations and adopted by the United Nations, has made, and continues to make, significant contributions to the world community. It serves as research agency, publishing house, and committee of experts for matters pertinent to labor welfare. The delegates who control policy consist of representatives of national governments, employers' associations, and labor organizations. The International Labor Office keeps interested parties throughout the world informed regarding labor conditions and agreements, and on request makes recommendations for action. Not only matters of employment, but also health, housing, adult education, consumer credit, geriatrics, and whatever else concerns the workers of the world, are scrutinized, and approved practices are publicized.

Especially pertinent to the subject matter of this chapter are the "international labor conventions" or treaties drawn up by the experts of the Office, and submitted to the appropriate national legislatures for action. When approved, reports of progress and problems involved in the instrumentation of the convention are cleared through the International Labor Office, whose agents proffer advice on request. These conventions remove many potentially acute issues from bilateral or unilateral governmental action. Adequate communication among nations regarding the achievements and problems of employers, employees, and governments fosters a climate of opinion favorable for general consent to meliorative action. The International Labor Office has no power to enforce the conventions; its functions are education and conciliation.

That this process is effective and far-reaching is shown by the

[8] See, for example, the work of the "Ugly American" in William J. Lederer and Eugene Burdick, *The Ugly American*, W. W. Norton & Company, Inc., New York, 1958.

following quotation from a pamphlet prepared by the International Labor Office for social studies teachers in the United States:[9]

> By September, 1947, 86 international treaties and 82 recommendations had been adopted by the International Labor Conference, over a 28-year period.
>
> But what do these figures mean in terms of the lives of ordinary working men and women? That is the real question. Well, they mean that the family of Jose Garcia in Central America is protected against deprivations as a result of sickness or accidents on the job by a system of social insurance drawn up to meet International Labor Office specifications. They mean that when Pat Nash gets hurt on his job in New Zealand, he is insured to cover his injury. They mean that when Senora Rosita Flores, a factory worker in Chile, has to leave her job to have a baby, she gets six weeks' paid vacation or leave before, and six weeks' after, the birth of her child. They mean that a family in a European country cannot legally take an eleven-year-old son out of school and put him to work in a coal mine. They mean that a textile factory in England cannot ask women to work long hours on the night shift. And they mean that Bill Smith, an American seaman who is shipwrecked, is guaranteed full wages while he is stranded abroad, transportation home, payment for the gear he has lost, and another job with his company. These are only a few random examples of how working people have benefited by the International Labor Office's work.

The United Nations Educational, Scientific, and Cultural Organization

UNESCO attempts to foster the concept of universality in educational, scientific, and cultural activities and organizations. It does this by formulating meliorative projects calling for collaboration of intelligent men everywhere. Because chauvinism has been the major obstacle to such collaboration, immediate emphasis has been put on international understanding and tolerance. The first pronouncement was therefore somewhat naive: "Since wars begin in the minds of men, it is in the minds of men that the defenses of peace must be constructed." [10] However desirable the corollary surely is, the assumption itself is little more than a half-truth; wars, unfortunately, seem to begin in national, economic, and other assertive group rivalries; the minds of men are then propagandized to support the war effort.

Counterindoctrination "to encourage mutual knowledge and un-

[9] *The U.S. and the I.L.O.*, International Labor Office, Washington, no date, p. 2.
[10] Preamble to the Constitution of UNESCO.

derstanding between peoples" should decrease the hatreds that are inculcated by press, radio, and platform orators during "hot" and "cold" wars alike. To chauvinists, however, such encouragement of understanding seems unpatriotic, if not downright subversive.

As in the cases of the World Health Organization and the Food and Agricultural Organization, UNESCO carries forward its admirable program in collaboration with many other agencies. Its faith and its aims are as comprehensive as the potentialities of the human mind. It recruits educators, scientists, and humanists in support of its bold ventures. It engages the talents of experts in radio, films, and the press for effective communication of its purposes and means to all men.

Apart from "top-policy" formulation, these collaborations are specific; the ends sought and the means used to attain them determine the combinations of talents recruited. The projects vary from reconstruction of schools and school systems in devastated and otherwise disadvantaged areas to the translation and distribution of books and the exchange of music, art objects, and science exhibits. And there is always special emphasis placed on finding means to overcome the prejudice, tension, and ignorance that keep people apart.

The supplanting of emotionally charged myths and symbols is more effectively achieved indirectly than overtly. To direct the attention of adults and young people to likenesses characteristic of mankind in their efforts to understand and to deal with factors and problems that are similar the world over can contribute mightily to international fellowship. Vicarious experiences surely contribute to this end; hence, the justification for distributing literature, pictures, transcriptions of music and other recordings, and movies.

UNESCO-approved Measures

Four measures which provide opportunity for collaborative experience are approved and encouraged by UNESCO. International conferences of educators, scientists, humanists, and social welfare representatives usually intensify their world outlooks and have favorable effects on public opinion in the countries represented. The exchange of teachers and lecturers brings students and audiences into personal contact with cultured representatives of foreign countries. Potentially even more intimate associations result from the exchange of students and other young people who may actually live in the homes and participate in work and play activities of youths of the country they visit. Direct contribution to the welfare of other peoples makes probable some degree of self-identification by the giver with the beneficiary of the gift. Such projects include letter writing and preparing classbooks and gifts to be sent to young people in other lands, raising money for CARE packages for relief of needy persons abroad, the "adoption" of individual children or institutions by a school, a town, or a club, and international work-camps where volunteers devote their vacations, and sometimes much longer periods, to collaborations which usually involve physical labor and technical know-how and which foster sincere brotherhood.

UNESCO did not originate any of the modes for improving human relations mentioned above. Instead, it has acted as a clearing-house both within the United Nations organization and among the institutions and national governments that have already engaged in such projects or which may now be encouraged to do so. The Red Cross, Rotary International, the Quakers, the Scouts, 4-H clubs, the National Educational Association and its member organizations, the International Hostel Association, the American Association of University Women, and Save the Children Fund, and the Conference on International Educational Construction are some of the organizations that have pioneered in this field. Within the United Nations itself, several other agencies parallel in one way or another the program of UNESCO: The World Health Organization and the Food and Agricultural Organization, of course, the Commission on Human Rights (whose ringing declaration of the dignity of all men everywhere was adopted by the General Assembly in 1948), and especially the United Nations International Children's Emergency Fund. This latter organization (closely associated with WHO), not only fights malaria, yaws, and tuberculosis wherever they threaten young people, but also strives to stimulate concern for child welfare among adults and their governments in the countries it services.

Fundamental Education

A unique contribution that UNESCO sponsors is called Fundamental Education. Although the Preparatory Commission of UNESCO has not yet been able to declare precisely what the term shall comprehend, its constant objective is clear; it seeks to direct the thought and efforts of men of good will toward helping human beings to thrive in a global ecology—thrive mentally and emotionally as well as materially. Its emphasis presents a clear alternative to suppression, coercion, and regimentation.

There is clear recognition that technology, either in the productive processes or in medicine and dietetics, is but one, albeit an important one, of the forces that govern thinking. Emancipation must be won within each culture; piecemeal contributions cannot effectively be made by a "superior" culture to an "inferior" one; indeed, the "plodding peasant" or the freedom-loving nomad has much to offer to the harried Westerner. Neither health, nor education, nor literacy constitutes "Fundamental Education." Rather, it is whatever combination of factors develops the character of a child or adult and his environment at the same time—the transformation of the community and the development of the individual are reciprocals.[11]

The "advanced" society may be quite as much in need of this sociological orientation as any "backward" society. The roots of war are the same as those of most other violent and defiant behaviors. It is the frustrations of life, the inadequacy to deal with the human and material environments, and the resulting fear and insecurity that make men eager to hate.

Other National and Regional Collaborations

In many areas of the world are found collaborative organizations and projects which in one way or another have been greatly influenced by the experience of the United States government and of the social and economic institutions of this country. Each such organization or project has drawn on American examples according to its own purposes and needs, and it has developed uniquely as it has reflected the peculiar economic, moral, and other characteristics of its own culture.

In Latin American countries, the most obvious borrowing has been the republican structure of government as each nation established itself. Less obvious, because they have not been achieved even in form, have been the aborted movements looking toward union of the countries into one or more federations comparable to the United States, the replacement of feudalism, slavery, and peonage by free labor and a wage economy, the toleration of opposition political parties by the established government, and the clear separation between church and state. Nevertheless, these and other changes are vigorously advocated and in some of the countries considerable progress toward their realization has in fact taken place. In nonpolitical institutions, change has been accelerated not so much by agitation for reforms as by the intrusion of United States and European establishments and practices into the economy of the Latin American countries, for example, banks, industry, transportation, and consumer-goods distribution. Whether resented as aspects of imperialism or welcomed as examples of modern efficiency, the cultural evolution in almost every sphere reflects North American examples.

Collaboration between the United States government and those of all others in the New World antedates the Monroe Doctrine, promulgated in 1823, which, however, may be taken as the formalization of recognition of their common interests. Despite many instances of unneighborly interference in the affairs of other American countries,

[11] *Fundamental Education*, Report of a Special Commission to the Preparatory Commission of UNESCO, The Macmillan Company, New York, 1947.

both political and economic, the government of the United States (often abetted by philanthropic, financial, military, and industrial interests) has sought to foster their stability and orderly progress toward democratic goals.

Much of the progress which has been achieved has been mediated through international establishments such as the International Labor Office, and through the borrowing of one country's successful practices by another. And some significant achievements, such as the *ejido* communal agriculture in Mexico, have no exact antecedents in Western culture. Nevertheless, the spirit of experiment and adaptation and the belief in the feasibility of such projects are characteristic of a people not bound by tradition.

The Pan American Union (which later became known as the Organization of American States), a quasi-intergovernmental establishment, has since 1889 endeavored to keep communication channels open among the public and private organizations concerned with problems and prospects in the Western Hemisphere. The Good Neighbor Policy initiated by Secretary of State Hull during Franklin Delano Roosevelt's first administration fostered a feeling of commonality among both governments and people of the various countries; the control of its internal affairs by each country's own officers was unchallenged, however, and financial, scientific, and technical aid for roads, dams, and other self-liquidating projects was given.

European Unity

After the decay of the Holy Roman Empire, principalities, electorates, and bishoprics were brought into monarchies by means of dynastic and other political and military consolidations. The unification of Germany was brought about as recently as 1871. The indoctrination of popular fervor in support of these nations was successful only after the French Revolution and threats to its security. Among enlightened continental Europeans, national patriotism has been diluted by a consciousness of membership in a European, or even a world-wide, community culture. Though they themselves have not been free from national loyalty, it has seemed to many a rather childish emotion not meaningfully attached to their major cultural concerns. Large business interests have never limited their enterprises or their economic "loyalties" to a single country. Their fervors have been well-compartmented.

Many European businessmen have recognized the advantage that the United States has in a domestic free-trade area larger than Western Europe providing markets, products, and protection by relatively uniform laws and enforcement agencies. Though they have generally approved the exploitation of patriotic fervors and nationalistic

adventures when they have seemed to advantage their countries' economies, they have viewed all Europe and the rest of the world as markets
and as bases for needed resources. The ownership of French, German,
British, Belgian, and Dutch industry is not limited to nationals; hence,
the owners are readily persuaded to support Euratom, the coal and steel
community, the "common market." Indeed, since the close of World
War II and the success of the Marshall Plan in stimulating economic
recovery, Western Europe has "agglutinized," rather than consciously
integrated, into an effective economic community with one industrial
area and its suburbs almost merging with the next, a phenomenon very
like that of the American northeast.

Unsolved Problems of the World Community

If the major obstacles to world community were those of material lacks and complexity, the science, technology, and political institutions developed during the past three centuries might be sufficient to aid
disadvantaged peoples in solving their own problems. Regrettably, both
advanced and retarded nations are seriously hindered by atavistic stereotypes.

Though it is not accurate to say that wars arise in the minds
of men, it is surely true that the fears, hatreds, and stereotyped self-
interests of men provide fertile ground for the threat of war. National
and ethnic loyalties are readily transmuted into suspicion and hostility
toward whomever is thought to be associated with an out-group. This
transmutation is effective even when the rallying cry of loyalty is attached to obvious unreality (e.g., loyal American Legionnaires branding
UNESCO "communistic"). Corollaries of suspicion are fear of reprisals,
tolerance of a garrison state, acceptance of policy making by a military
elite, and the gangster morality of negotiating only from a position of
military strength. Within this configuration of fear, suspicion, and hatred,
aggressive individuals and groups find high status which would be endangered if general assuagement of popular malaise should take place;
hence, their hostility toward conciliatory and intellectual approaches to
the resolution of world tensions.

A second problem that has so far almost defied solution is an
outgrowth of private investment in the economies of "backward" countries in which social unrest and threats of popular uprisings occur.
Compensation for expropriated property owned by foreign investors
may be in dispute, or punishment of citizens of an advanced country
may be summary. Arbitration of claims by an agreed upon "third party"
or an appeal to the International Court of Justice would seem a reasonable solution; but reasonableness seldom characterizes the moods of the
disputants in such cases. On the one side, the aroused people of the

"colonial" country may satisfy their need for a scapegoat by blaming the foreign capitalists for their ills; on the other side, the national government or governments which represent the injured parties respond to the indignation expressed by influential groups among their own citizens by threatening reprisals against, or intervention into, the economy and political affairs of the offending country. In time, the need for new hate objects and the gradual recognition of the futility of threats and bluster may remove the specific quarrel from the center of popular attention, but residues of suspicion remain long after whatever was factual in the situation is forgotten.

A third area of unresolved disagreement is the so-called population explosion, its causes and character, and its prognosis and control. Fortunately, this disagreement does not immediately threaten to disrupt international relations; the quarrel is as yet ideological. The neo-Malthusians assert that at present birth rates and with increasing longevity population will not only outrun possible food supply but will bring about irrepressible attempts at geographical expansion by conquest; their recommended solution is the provision of contraception information and devices among those populations where birth control is not now practiced, supplemented if possible by eugenical selection. Other equally well-informed social economists, while admitting the theoretical validity of the Malthusian thesis, believe that with better nutrition and greater enlightenment, birth rates will adjust without need for paternalistic supervision by advanced societies. Mainland China, despite its dense population, now reportedly suffers a labor shortage! In this connection should be noted the active opposition of the Roman Catholic Church to mechanical contraception.

A fourth complication for which no immediate solution is seen is the unsettling effects of the encouragement of undeveloped countries to engage in economic pursuits which tend to disrupt the economies of other barely viable nations. A long-term solution, of course, is such an expansion of demand for products that all countries can produce efficiently. But the immediate problem requires more than a distant promise.

A fifth challenge which United Nations agencies face in their efforts to encourage the governments and other social establishments of less economically advanced societies is how to foster the welfare of all of the population if control is vested in an elite. The absence of a vigorous middle class of merchants and manufacturers in such societies and the sufferance of poverty and degradation by the lower class makes even timid steps toward self-reliance and intelligent adaptation by the depressed people seem dangerous to the ensconced elite. Financial and material aid granted the government of such a country is unlikely to be used for the direct benefit of the mass of the people unless agents of the United Nations organization (or in case of nation-to-nation subvention, an agent of the benefactor nation) supervises its application. But that intervention is open to the objection that it undermines whatever stability already has been achieved.

The complexities involved in such problems as those listed above helps people to a sympathetic understanding of the dilemmas that must be resolved on a world scale. Counterparts, however, may be identified in the American society. Past and present efforts to resolve our own domestic problems, including our failures to date, emphasize the role of the United States as a precursor of a humane world order. Our experimental adventures looking toward the establishment of social justice, the insurance of domestic tranquillity, the promotion of the general welfare, and the security of liberty for ourselves and our posterity are real and continuing. The American society does exemplify science as a mode for social direction. And it is the successful scientific approach to the solution of human problems that holds most hope for a better world society.

SUMMARY

Hope springs eternal! Else, institutions for popular education would collapse. Like all other enlightened citizens, teachers behave as though they believe that national policies and economic forces will be sufficiently controlled so that, at worst, contemporary stalemates will be maintained even if little progress is made toward solutions.

Nevertheless, there is no blinking the fact that the humane world lives at the brink of disaster. Philip Noel-Baker, Nobel Prize winner and disarmament expert, is quoted by Congressman Charles O. Porter of Oregon[12] as saying in 1959 that as an optimist he believed that universal disarmament was feasible if the nations all decided that they want that equality. But, he added, "I'm also a pessimist in that I believe that in ten years we will all be dead, and the earth will be an incinerated relic." The man standing next to Noel-Baker, a top scientific adviser in the United States government, declared, "I believe so, too."

Neither statesmen, scientists, business executives, nor even most military officers, however, *behave* as though they share this belief, though all of them must acknowledge its reasonableness. Unrestrained national sovereignty under present conditions of science and technology applied to war making amounts to world-wide anarchy. And time is running out!

[12] "Accident or Aggression," *The Nation*, March 5, 1960, pp. 190–192.

Bold gamblers with fate and authoritative personalities retain their potent influence over national political, economic, and ideological policies and programs. The omnipotence of the United States to enforce its will is tacitly assumed. Threats of massive retaliation, or at least of crippling countermeasures if the nation's demands are ignored, are irresponsibly promulgated and receive much support by thoughtless people who find in anger and hatred some relief for their individual fear and helplessness. It is within this configuration of mental and emotional obfuscation that the American teacher performs his educational function.

In some degree, the preoccupation of the American professional educator with immediate problems of instruction is mandatory and justifiable. Arithmetical skills, spelling, laboratory science, and the rest require assiduous effort. Human relations present day-by-day challenges that call for resourcefulness and sustained effort. Unless the educational establishment itself functions competently, its contribution to the solution of social problems will be slight.

The educator has, however, a supervening responsibility to society. He must be a Twentieth-century American—a personality attuned to a kaleidoscopic world in relation to which popular understanding and ideals are insistently required. As such, he represents an America seeking for itself an ordered humane society within a world that depends in great degree on American success and example. He must, therefore, know and assess the major facts regarding the conditions, aspirations, and proposed roads that humanity faces.

Civilized society is faced by a world in which vast regions are overpopulated in terms of present capacity to provide even a minimum of food, clothing, shelter, protection against disease, insects, drought, and flood. Hopeless, sick, and hungry men are generally responsive to mass suggestion; their submissiveness to "fate" is often compensated for by hysteria.

It is, of course, a matter of degree. Western mass man is similarly prone to irrationality. Self-righteous rationalization of attitudes and behavior characterize him as an individual and as a member of in-groups. Such restraints as do characterize him, furthermore, are chiefly due to his superior nurture, both materialistic and educational. Having more to lose by recourse to violence and more to hope for by conciliatory, discriminative attitudes and behavior, he is inclined to assert himself in relatively orderly fashion. As a member of a neighborhood, a labor union, a mutual insurance society, a political party, a church, a state, and a dozen other organizations, he communicates with his fellows and joins them in common ventures and in restraining impetuous and ill-considered impulses.

In fostering such rational, orderly, and cooperative expressions of personality among those he can influence, the educator helps prepare them to welcome constructive ideas regarding the economic lacks and resources, reasonable aspirations, and nationalistic and religious fervors of colonial peoples. Because the typical American highly values literacy, health, magnanimity, adequate material conditions, personal liberty, and security for all Americans, he is disposed to accept similar valuations in other peoples. The educator's further responsibilities in fostering an orderly world, therefore, consist largely in helping those he can influence, on the one hand, to understand sympathetically the programs of organizations looking to world order, their partial success and partial failure, and the problems they face in a world subject to revolutionary changes and, on the other hand, to recognize that continued stability in the United States itself requires a stable and hopeful world.

The process of progressive enlightenment of the American people is therefore essential to the future of the country. And such progressive enlightenment is the function of education broadly conceived to include all instruments of communication and guided experience.

Of supreme concern to the educator is the failure of so large a section of the American public to become informed regarding the fatally disastrous character of atomic, bacterial, and chemical warfare. To the man in the street it simply seems not at all obvious that human civilization cannot be saved by the wholesale murder of millions of people, the mass suicide of our own people, and by the sterilization of millions of square miles of land for centuries to come.

This apathy is somehow confused with "loyalty"; it is esteemed not quite "patriotic" for the citizen to inquire to what actual ends war making would lead. But the America to which the citizen owes allegiance is dedicated to humane values. America as a humane civilization is destroyed to the degree that the nation's intentional instruments of offense and defense are grossly inhumane.

It is granted that the school is not primarily an emergency institution. It is granted that its major power has lain in its long-term encouragement of restraint, tolerance, and empathy whenever social tensions have threatened human fellowship. This the school has done generation after generation and among millions of families. It is granted that it is late in the day to foster public foresightedness when the world is already face-to-face with overwhelming disaster. And it is granted finally that public apathy and "well-padded escapism" provide little support for the school's efforts to present accurate information regarding the United Nations and its agencies, the complementary regional and other mutual assistance pacts, and the nongovernmental and quasi-governmental establishments which foster peace, reconciliation, and human welfare. All of these are granted, and yet the school must act! What it is doing and what it can do is the burden of the exposition of the chapters which follow.

SELECTED REFERENCES

Bowles, Chester: *The Coming Political Breakthrough,* Harper & Brothers, New York, 1959. Three sources of American international problems: rising expectations of the poor—and colored—peoples of the world; the emergence of the Soviet Union as the second greatest world power; and the threat of worldwide suicide through nuclear, bacteriological, and chemical warfare.

Counts, George S.: *Education and American Civilization,* Bureau of Publications, Teachers College, Columbia University, New York, 1952. A readable and stimulating exposition of American society and its potentialities.

Dahl, Robert A.: *A Preface to Democratic Theory,* University of Chicago Press, Chicago, 1956. An excellent discussion of the nature of democracy.

Davis, Jerome, and Hugh B. Hester: *On the Brink,* Lyle Stuart, New York, 1958. Myths derived from prejudices, traditions, and misunderstandings govern popular thinking about the Cold War and national security.

Johnson, Gerald W.: *The American People,* Harper & Brothers, New York, 1951. An examination of the beginnings and progress of the democratic adventure.

Kennan, George F.: *Russia, The Atom and The West,* Harper & Brothers, New York, 1958. An important book on world politics in the 1950s.

Miller, Helen Hill: "What America Can Afford," *The New Republic,* March 7, 1960, pp. 15–23. A review of national needs in the 1960s, pertinent to the question whether the Soviet system or the American system can deal more effectively with the problems that beset mankind.

Muhlen, Norbert: *The Incredible Krupps,* Henry Holt and Company, Inc., New York, 1959. An international industrial complex with vast and unsuspected holdings abroad—"a sort of economic Mafia." Ownership and ultimate control vested in a single representative of the Krupp family, which acknowledges no national loyalty, not even to Germany.

Muller, Herbert J.: *Issues of Freedom: Paradoxes and Promises,* Harper & Brothers, New York, 1959. Human nature as the primary source for social progress.

Myrdal, Gunnar: *Beyond the Welfare State,* Yale University Press, New Haven, Conn., 1960. In the Western world, the pattern of the welfare state is now established. It is nationalistic and introverted and largely indifferent to the world economy; its very success tends to increase the economic disparity between the rich nations and the poor ones. Myrdal holds that a "created harmony" can be achieved in the world economy by application of the same rational coordination on a world scale which has been so successful on a national scale.

Palmer, R. R.: "The Challenge," *The Age of the Democratic Revolution: A Political History of Europe and America,* vol. I, Princeton University Press, Princeton, N.J., 1959. The contribution of the American Revolution to democracy throughout the world was two-fold: a new idea, that the people actually create and contrive the government, and a new institution, the constitutional convention which implements the idea.

Parkes, Henry B.: *The American Experience,* Vintage Books, New York, 1959. How the interplay of historical, religious, and other cultural factors account for the American character.

Scott, John: *Democracy Is Not Enough: A Personal Survey of the Hungry World,* Harcourt, Brace and Company, Inc., New York, 1959. Political democracy is not feasible so long as hunger is general and persistent and so long as the majority of a population remains illiterate. Newly independent people need strong leaders who believe in political democracy and who guide their people step-by-step toward its achievement.

DISCUSSION QUESTIONS

1. Some nineteenth-century liberals believed (at least, they hoped) that if the whole population were taught to read they might master all sorts of opinions and arrive at sound decisions and, in a democracy, elect representatives to give effect to the decisions. (This is a paraphrase of James Mill's opinion as reported by his son, John Stuart Mill.) Can a person master all sorts of opinion? Can he become fully informed? Would many be willing to make the effort to become so? Does the ability to read books, magazines, and newspapers equip a person to judge wisely what he reads? Does it make probable sound judgments? Would the problems of government be wisely solved by representatives who carried out the mandates of their constituents? Has the naïveté of these early liberals carried over to influential enthusiasts for universal literacy? What about advocates for teaching universal (synthetic) language, such as Esperanto?

2. Tourists abroad, student exchanges, international work-camps, Fulbright scholarships and fellowships, international Scout jam-

borees, 4-H club exchanges, and visiting delegations of labor leaders, farm organization officials, and attendants at world conventions, festivals, etc., have been praised frequently as propitious for better understanding among peoples of different countries.

Do you know several persons who have had one or another of the experiences indicated in the list above or similar ones? Can you report to the class regarding their opinions as to the effects of "people-to-people" associations on mutuality of understanding? On differing standards of dress, food, "patriotism," virtue, or aesthetic discrimination? Among your respondents, do you discover any consensus regarding the probable influence of face-to-face intercommunication among persons of varying national, religious, and other ethnic cultures on future popular resistance to "hate" propaganda?

3. Can a "science-for-peace" campaign or its analogous promotion of the sharing of medical, educational, industrial, and ideological knowledge be effective in an age of deep insecurity and fear of "unprovoked," disastrous attack by the "enemy"? Can the people of any nation protect their interests without borrowing on the world fund of knowledge and technology?

4. Much is said among advocates of world government about the rule of law as one of the supreme achievements of Western man, an achievement so obviously beneficent for society that all peoples could be persuaded to accept a world code and be bound by it in their domestic and international affairs. Does the Preamble to the United Nations Charter (which begins, "We, the peoples of the United Nations determined" to bring about stated desired conditions, have agreed, through empowered representatives, "to the present Charter of the United Nations and do establish an international organization to be known as the United Nations" and which was later approved by the member national governments), establish law binding on the peoples or on their governments? Or does it merely provide institutional arrangements propitious for the evolution of such laws?

5. The ten aims of UNESCO, stated in 1951 at its Fifth Session of the General Conference, are:

1. To eliminate illiteracy and encourage fundamental education.

2. To obtain for each person an education conforming to his aptitudes and to the needs of society, including technological training and higher education.

3. To promote through education increased respect for human rights throughout all nations.

4. To overcome the obstacles to the free flow of persons, ideas, and knowledge between the countries of the world.

5. To promote the progress and utilization of science for mankind.

6. To study the causes of tensions that may lead to war and to fight them through education.

7. To demonstrate world cultural interdependence.

8. To advance through the press, radio, and motion pictures the cause of truth, freedom, and peace.

9. To bring about better understanding among the peoples of the world and to convince them of the necessity of cooperating loyally with one another in the framework of the United Nations.

10. To render clearinghouse and exchange services in all its fields of services in reconstruction and relief assistance.

Do all of these aims seem proper, desirable, and achievable for UNESCO? If not, what changes would you suggest?

Would the acceptance of any one of them reflect adversely on an American citizen's loyalty to the government of the United States? If not, how do you explain the hostility of the American Legion to UNESCO, the votes of condemnation by some local parent-teacher associations, and the occasional denunciation of UNESCO as "communistic"?

6. As war spirit flows and ebbs, as former national enemies become allies and vice versa, popular stereotypes of the character of the people who compose the nations change dramatically. Friendly, industrious Germans became "beastly Huns," then a wholesome, cleanly people patiently endeavoring to repair their ravaged country, later a rather stupid melange of sadists and masochists, next a regimented, hate-mongering people, and now thrifty, ingenious producers. Similarly polite, almost obsequious, beauty-loving Japanese became faceless, treacherous robots, and now brave, stoical, and conciliatory people. The Russians were transformed from "sluggish Slavs," to revolutionary extremists, to victims of Bolshevik tyranny, to brilliantly led "brave Ruskis," to brutal suppressors of Hungarian freedom fighters.

The shift of stereotypes is made obvious by the depicting of typical characters in theater, magazine stories, and cartoons. Are they more often to be accounted for as results of changes in popular regard for national characteristics or as causes of the change? How else might the shifts be explained?

7. How do you account for the apparent apathy with which many Americans face the possibility of their own mass incineration in case of another world war?

PART SIX

The Quest for Community: Challenges to American Education

16

Education and the Processes of Change

Largely as a result of the remarkable social and cultural changes of the past century, American schools (like all other institutions) have undergone revolutionary alterations in orientation and method. In part, these changes can be directly traced to the creative leadership of pioneering educators and, in part, to the trial-and-error response to pupils and patrons as they have increasingly come to be understood.

American educators have always sought to fulfill their mission of cultural transmission; in addition, they and the schools they operate have, during the past few decades, increasingly been charged with two other responsibilities: to foster and guide the personality development of their students and to search out and teach techniques of democratic social relations. Along with these heavy responsibilities, educators have continued to face the formidable task of adjusting the school program to the search for the goals which are appropriate for a humane, democratic society.

Unrealistic Criticism of Public Schools

It is because many of the critics of the public schools have not grasped the operational meaning of the school's function to transmit an

357

idealized social inheritance that their demands for abrupt changes in educational institutions have not been realized. Decade after decade, conservative reformers have recommended that the public schools raise their academic standards, that they abandon, or at least minimize, their elective subject offerings, abjure their tolerance of social activities, personality-adjustment objectives, and job-preparation programs. With each such well-publicized demand, influential citizens have responded vigorously, albeit ignorantly. They have called on faculties to cut themselves free from the limitations imposed by the unwillingness of young people and their parents to abide by a regimen which would sharply decrease their participation in "the good life" as they now conceive it to be.

With each upsurge of agitation for "a return to fundamentals," for "more iron in education," for directing (perhaps forcing) bright pupils to study mathematics, science, foreign language, and conventional history, timid administrators, with the encouragement of some of their downwardly mobile and, hence, frustrated teachers, publicly declare their intentions to conform to the recommendations of the unrealistic critics. But after a brief flurry, the schools go on much as before.

The Schools and Real Life

There are several compelling reasons why educational institutions must deal with life as it is rather than as esoteric scholars believe it should be. The primary one is that the academic conception of "excellence" as limited to bookish learning is not shared in practice by the majority of youths and adults who value quite as highly "excellence" in athletics, social organizing, forensics, and etiquette. Hence, any faculty that, by superimposition, attempts to limit its recognition to academic attainments, thus overtly or implicitly scorning other "excellences," cuts itself off from the enthusiasms of many of the youths they seek to educate.

A concomitant result is discontent among those pupils who (often with their parents' toleration if not encouragement) seek their "place in the sun" outside the patterns of approval set up by the faculty. The teachers may then be relatively insignificant; institutional life goes on without its official directors.

All successful American schools are inevitably adventures in a democratically molded social space. They take into account what their clientele values highly. Satisfaction of desires for security, adventure, recognition, and response cannot be denied them if frustrations and distortions are not to endanger the success of the enterprise. These desires, in their multifarious ramifications, will fulfill themselves in any case; whether constructively or destructively depends, in part at least, on how intelligently and competently the school provides opportunities and keeps them under control. The primary grade teacher adapts the reading instruction so that each child realizes growth, supervises games, and appoints monitors. The graduate seminar is a forum where each member "struts his stuff" and meets the challenges of his peers on his own grounds of special knowledge. At no level is subject matter set forth to be learned without concern for the individual's compulsive need to assert his dignity.

The major difference between the process at lower and at more advanced levels of education is a lesser need at the latter for compensating for deficiencies and obstacles derived from out-of-school life. At the elementary school level, the deficiencies and obstacles may be unsatisfactory health practices, uncouth speech or manners, lack of affection, or lack of discipline in the home; these and other shortcomings require something more than obedient lesson learning, no matter how "scientifically" justified. But at the college level as well as the elementary, generous provisions are made for recreation, civic participation, faculty-student association on a peer level, guidance, and job preparation. The frequent spectacle of university professors berating the high school for athletic excesses and for granting credit toward graduation for such "fads and frills" as music, art, and shopwork becomes grimly ironical in view of the programs of their own institutions.

The "Hard" Subjects

What has been said in the preceding paragraphs is not meant to belittle the importance of the sciences, mathematics, history, and foreign languages. The criticism is directed to the attempt to superimpose any of them on the school *without due regard for the values actually attached to other subjects and activities by pupils and their adult associates.* This disregard for the preferred values of great numbers of youths and their elders is reflected in some of the reformers' confusion of the adjectives "hard" with "dissatisfying" or "uninteresting"; pupils work at least as hard, and find accomplishment at least as difficult, in athletic games and in orchestra as any of them do in geometry, physics, or Latin. The recommendation that bright students be urged or compelled to study only "hard" (meaning distasteful) subjects, *without any motivation other than docile acceptance of the will of the administrator,* would almost surely prove disastrous to the school which followed it.

As a matter of fact, it is doubtful that such compulsory or honorific artificialities are required to persuade capable youths to choose voluntarily to study such subjects as mathematics, science, social science, and foreign language. To be sure, some bright pupils will prefer art, music, mechanics, business skills, or even athletics or school government. But in the United States, theirs is the responsibility for choice of their road toward the good life. Even if their start is false, it need not be fatal. Better a belated voluntary change than docile submission to someone else's institutionalized judgment.

Varieties of Prestige

Prestige attached to vocational and avocational competence is varied and not readily classifiable in terms of abstract intelligence, social class, wealth, or occupation. The industrialist may win fame as an art collector, the former actress as a congresswoman, the college professor as a baseball expert, and the brilliant lawyer as a *bon vivant*. People everywhere in the nation admire physical beauty and sexual charm; the erudite scholar, the labor leader, and the department store executive, whether male or female, long for recognition as figures of distinction.

The permutations of familial, ethnic, economic, religious, and class-structured values as they are reflected in the motivations of any individual are endlessly complex and often evanescent. Some are accentuated, others diminished as the public mood changes—as concern over missiles competes with a prize fight, or the excitement of a political campaign is followed by Dior's decision regarding the length of women's dresses. Few persons would attempt to defend their scale of values at a given time as being quite rational; but all Americans would protest against one man's, or one group's, attempt to prescribe what should be the private valuations of another man or another group.

The only limit to each person's liberty to choose his own path toward happiness—his array of sought-for outcomes—is that he not unduly restrict other men in that same liberty. In a situation of such personal freedom, the school functions most effectively as it offers to each unique individual the opportunity to reshape his own valuations of means for winning immediate and future security, recognition, adventure, and response. The school is, however, an intentionally controlled environment; it stacks the cards in favor of those kinds of prestige that seem peculiarly valuable for individual wholesomeness and the general welfare.

The School and Compulsion

The school minimizes, but it does not abjure, compulsion. As in the society it serves, there are fixities and limitations seen by the great majority of teachers, pupils, and patrons to be necessary for the orderly and economical conduct of the school. There is a locus—a school plant with rooms, corridors, and other facilities—and, for activities within this locus, "rules of the road" are required and generally complied with. There are prescribed subjects and assignments. And there are areas of decision making reserved for the administrative and teaching staff as representatives of the society which maintains the school. So long as educators recognize their own proper limitations of use of legal authority, there remains much independence and freedom for the shaping of valued means and ends and for voluntary cooperation and compromise.

In these respects as in others, the school approaches the ideal of the democracy for which it prepares young people by helping them experience democracy.

Personal and Social Adaptability

The problems that a school faces in the areas of personality and human relations are quite different from those inherent in instructing young people in a standardized subject.[1] No teacher or counselor knows with certainty what adaptation is the *right* one for any individual to make in a complex situation; even if he did, he would not know for sure how the individual should proceed to make it. There are far too many variables in every life and every human relationship involved—variables of biological inheritance, infant conditioning, and contemporary out-of-school associations and concerns. All these factors are constantly interacting with, perhaps offsetting, whatever school officials and teachers might prescribe.

What the resourceful teacher can do is to encourage every pupil to set some worthwhile goals for himself that by consistent effort he can reasonably well satisfy. The goal may be complex, or it may be relatively simple and immediate; its locus may be the classroom project or an all-school or school-community undertaking. What is important is that the *desire* to achieve the goal shall be forceful, for effort toward succeeding is necessary if the teacher is to be of much help.

Goal-selection and Achievement

The discovery by the pupil of meaningful objectives is facilitated to the degree that the school and the community engage in and honor accomplishment in constructive civic, aesthetic, and recreational activities that are open to the active participation of young people. Under such conditions, the boy or girl who seriously strives to achieve an objective is assured not only the approval of a peer group, but also recognition and encouragement by his elders who are sincerely interested in the projects in which the youth is engaged. It is the value of the contribution and the spirit in which it is offered that receive recognition;

[1] There is, of course, a background of somewhat standardized behavior conditioning personal and social adaptations, for example, etiquette and "good taste."

the age, pigmentation, religious affiliation, sex, national background, or other irrelevant peculiarity is given little or no consideration. Prejudices and status exclusiveness become relatively restricted to the practices of coteries.[2]

Institutional Responses and Adaptations

Despite the compelling character of the dual mandates, that is, that the school take full account of the nature and immediate needs of the student and that it plan and execute its educational program in the light of valued social goals, the school's very institutional nature prevents it from a thoroughgoing reorientation. The stereotype of "school" is deeply impressed in the minds of teachers, patrons, alumni, and pupils; any radical change in its organization or practices is likely to offend their sense of fitness. Many members of the typical community, indeed, have vested interest in the maintenance of the stereotype; their personal, and in varying degrees their professional, status is fortified by the continuity of traditional school standards and practices.

Nevertheless, the phenomenon of institutional evolution and transformation in the history of American education is fully as impressive as that of institutional inertia. Schools have expanded, both "horizontally" and "vertically" in their enrollments. There has accrued a remarkable diversification and specialization of educational institutions, important modifications of regimen and curriculum have been made, and standards of accomplishment have been made increasingly flexible. However reluctantly these innovations have been undertaken, they have been accomplished, and taken altogether, they add up to nothing short of an educational revolution.

The processes of change in schools at all levels should be considered in perspective. Few, if any of them, are very new. In most cases, indeed, their antecedents or analogs have characterized age-old familial and tribal forms of education. Their near universality is not strange; the pragmatic compulsions implicit in the nature and needs of human beings as contributing members of their cultures have constantly imposed social goals for education. One especially important social and cultural change affecting schools is the recent decrease in the authoritarianism once so characteristic of family, business, and church, especially in the American middle and upper classes.

Extended School Services

Because the American public school grew up to fulfill a residual function, that of teaching the school arts and the traditional academic

---

[2] Some of the problems and opportunities in the areas of personality and human relations are treated in following chapters.

subjects which could not be assigned to domestic, religious, or other civil establishments, its popular acceptance became bound up with stereotypes of accommodation to the institutional practices of a pretechnological society. The most obvious instance of such accommodation is the thirty-eight- (or forty-) week school year and ten-week summer vacation.[3]

As work and living patterns of communities changed, as health protection and recreation became institutionalized as public responsibilities, and as the school's offerings broadened to include subjects and other activities which reinforced and offset learnings in other-than-school situations, the insulation of school services became difficult to maintain and impossible to justify. Early in the twentieth century, pioneering school administrators moved boldly to extend the school day and the school year for whatever educational and other welfare services were appropriate for the school plant and staff and which the public could be persuaded to support.

Among these extensions, adaptations, and collaborations, may be cited the following:

1. The development of elementary school gardens and of high school agricultural projects which necessarily involved supervision during the summer months.

2. The employment of school nurses and attendance officers on an all-year basis who maintained contact and services to children and families.

3. The opening of public library branches in local schools, which accustomed the public to the idea that the school building is a year-round educational resource.

4. The summer use of school playgrounds, gymnasiums, auditoriums, shops, home-economics facilities, and band and orchestra equipment, even though under the auspices of other-than-school establishments, which fostered public acceptance of an all-year school.

5. The growth of concern regarding pupil failure and retardation, whether due to irregular attendance or illness, transfer from other school districts, boredom, or dullness, which led to the provision of remedial and make-up classes during the summer period. For ambitious pupils, summer school has offered opportunities to anticipate term-time instruction, thereby making acceleration possible.

6. The development of much taxpayer resistance to school support, which came with the elaboration of school plants and the increasing

[3] Many fewer weeks of school attendance characterized rural schools in some states until recent years. In some areas, the distribution of the weeks of the school year now take account of seasonal crop-gathering and of difficulties of transportation of pupils.

costs of construction and equipment and of salaries of professional and custodial personnel. One response to public criticism was the frequently-made proposal (and the occasional adoption) of the four-quarter or all-year school somewhat analogous to the practice of a considerable number of universities. In such schools, students have normally attended, and instructors taught, classes during three of the four quarters.

7. The growth of school-related summertime (and, in lesser degree, term-time) activities not limited to school plants. School camps fostering nature study and conservation practices, music and art instruction, and associational living, have provided urban young people opportunities that many of them would otherwise have missed. These camps, like other auxiliary services, in some cases have been supported and directed by voluntary agencies or by municipal governmental departments. Because they have been broadly educational in character, however, the school has embraced their programs as part of its own.

Reactions of School Officials to the Broadened Concept of Education

There remains in the thinking of many educators a resistance to some of these innovations on the ground that they interfere with the "legitimate" program of the school. Moreover, a similar stereotype limiting school education to the already accepted functions is deeply engraved in the minds of the public and its political officers.

Consequently, municipalities and other political units have in many cases assigned welfare and educational functions to other-than-school agencies—park and recreational commissions, and police and health departments. This divorce of responsibility from the schools has been quite illogically resented by professional educational spokesmen who seem somewhat jealous of their assumed prerogatives to determine the scope and character of public education. Perhaps this resentment explains, in part at least, their bias in favor of state supremacy in the direction of education—a reasonable bias if education be narrowly conceived. In general, Congress has compromised with this bias in making educational appropriations; it has made "grant-in-aid" for public education to the states, but it has designated rather specifically for what purposes the aid should be used. The states, required to match the grants from their own tax resources, retained the primary control of the administration of these measures.

Nevertheless, side by side with this policy, Congress has authorized and financed independent public educational establishments, both of emergency and permanent character. Thus in 1862, the Morrill Act provided resources to the states to establish land-grant colleges to provide instruction in agriculture and mechanics arts and appropriate liberal and scientific studies. The Hatch Act of 1887 carried Federal educational influence farther by initiating annual grants for scientific research in agriculture experiment stations at the land-grant colleges; in effect, this made them service stations for the Department of Agriculture, facilitating its later direction of agricultural, home economics, and 4-H extension work through these colleges. A further direct intervention came with the emergency of the First World War, when military training in these colleges became compulsory, equipment and officer personnel being provided by the War Department.

A more radical and more nearly complete divorce between the state and local direction of public education and the national measures came during the economic and social crisis of the 1930s. The immediate need for relief, employment, and vocational training for unemployed youth was met by the establishment of the Civilian Conservation Corps in 1933 and the National Youth Administration in 1935. It seemed obvious to the sponsors of this legislation that public school systems were ill-equipped both as to staff and facilities and as to an educational conception to handle the job. Consequently, both the Office of Education and the state departments of education were by-passed in favor of direct administration by a national bureau. Nevertheless, the Educational Policies Commission and the American Council on Education deplored the centralizing trend these acts indicated.

Realistic Adaptations without Disturbance of Stereotypes

Fortunately, there are devices for carrying through rather drastic changes without undue disturbance of the widely held stereotypes of the school. By maintaining the terminology, ceremonials, regimen, and other symbols of the established order, the school can progressively and subtly modify its internal processes and structure without causing undue public alarm. Thus opportunities for vigorous voluntary participation in potentially educative but nontraditional activities have been designated as the extra-curriculum in the upper grades and as play or social education in the lower grades. The names of subjects and of their subdivisions (for example, grammar, percentages, and the Constitution) have been either retained or only gradually replaced, though the actual contents and conventional recitation-and-test procedures in these curriculum fragments have been drastically modified. Many important changes in meanings and educational effects have been made in graduation ceremonies, promotions, report cards, the nature of classrooms, corridor passing, assemblies, and teacher-pupil relations. Even so, the school has managed to maintain most of the ceremonials, social distances, and other symbols conventionally characteristic of it as an institution.

The School and the Community

Behind these facades of institutional continuity, however, the school responds realistically to the community of which it is a microcosm.

As the practices and standards of the society change, especially those of the locality served, the school adapts itself both to what it must do and to what it can do. Teachers and school serve *in loco parentis;* they function within a "climate of opinion," a consensus of beliefs, standards, and practices of adults and young people. As time passes, modifications occur in the internal organizations, the accepted attitudes and behaviors, the valued skills and knowledge, and the extensions and limitations on individuality that characterize families, churches, factories, stores, theaters, and the rest.

The interrelationships and admixtures of these modifications present both requirements and opportunities for changes in the school. The people of the school, and of the community in general, have to talk the same language; dress, discipline, "respect" for elders and for "authority," "scholarship," and all other standards and virtues must be much the same in school-related affairs as those valued in, or tolerated by, the climate of opinion characteristic of the contemporary local community. Dissimilarity in such matters, of course, breeds distrust and conflict.

Nevertheless, the school is not simply a reflection of evanescent public opinion. It has its own traditions and stereotypes; it has its own valued functions and purposes. It may resist even those behaviors of the young which the community tolerates. It may mobilize potent segments of public opinion by communicating its purposes and program through parent-teacher associations, the press, and other available instruments, and thereby fortify its traditions and its purposes. Occasionally, by taking advantage of a combination of events and public concern about them, the school may establish a position of leadership in fostering constructive measures for such things as wholesome recreation, cultural opportunities, hygienic standards, human relations, and vocational preparation.

It is obvious, however, that any school's responses and adaptations to community opportunities and needs are almost limited to those that aggressive segments of the public will support. The most reactionary faculty or school board must compromise with young people's unwillingness to "learn" assigned lessons if parents have ceased to believe that docility is of prime importance. The most liberal and "progressive" staff must assay sensitively the limits of tolerance of powerful community groups if they are to avoid finding the ground cut out from under their most important projects.

POSITIVE ADAPTATIONS AS SAFEGUARDS TO SCHOOLS

However important sensitivity to moods and opinions may be, the avoidance of social responsibility for meliorating community conditions would be fatal to the school, even were it entirely possible. Young people bring to school attitudes, behavior, and knowledge developed at home. In so far as this pattern of attitudes, behavior, and knowledge is erroneous, harmful, or otherwise undesirable, the school could not ignore it if it would. Its own regimen and authority would be wrecked unless it acted vigorously to correct or offset viciousness and error.

Merely negative or defensive measures would, however, not suffice for long. Even if successful, they would still leave only a moral vacuum. Day by day, the school would have to wrestle with more behavior problems, would have to deal restrictively with misconceptions, antagonisms, and crudities current in the local community. Restrictions, repressions, and punishment, however, often act as challenges to the ingenuity of young people to outwit or otherwise frustrate the guardians of school regimen.

What Consensus Characterizes Peacetime Community?

Social organization is impossible without considerable popular accommodation of beliefs and behavior to a consensus of what is permissible and what forbidden, what honorable and what dishonored. In great degree, this consensus is tacit; it is the almost unanimous acceptance of customs and standards, especially as they have become formalized as public law and legally authorized regulations.

These approved accommodations of behavior to community consensus provide stability and assurance of continuity for social establishments. Their evolutionary changes link together the loyalties and values attached to past and present patterns of belief and behavior with the acceptance of the generic and deliberate adaptations to social changes that seem to be desirable.

The public, tax-supported school, as one such establishment, properly assumes a present consensus regarding its relative permanence, its legal status, its actual and potential role as a beneficent institution, and its responsibility for serving, within the limits of its human and material resources, all persons committed to its care by law or who voluntarily seek its institutional aid. These immediate assumptions are undergirded by three others, somewhat more shadowy but generally secure: (1) the consensus favoring the right of adult individuals to seek a good life, each according to his conception, with the proviso that he accord other men the same right; (2) the consensus favoring loyalty to the state and obedience to its laws; and, (3) the ethical imperative favoring the honest fulfillment of a solemnly given promise of fair dealing and of sympathetic help for disadvantaged persons or groups. These background consensuses are, however, always characterized by relativity and tentativeness; exceptions to their general application are characteristic of many in-groups even when emergencies and conflicts are not rife.

In a world of international and ideological rivalries, of racial and other ethnic conflicts, and of rapidly changing technology, uncertainties and tensions are endemic. The causes of these insecurities are seldom easily defined; or if they are, the individual and his in-group may not find the definition pleasant or acceptable.

Insecure men seek simple, often single, explanations for what they find disturbing; clichés and scapegoats serve to justify exceptions to moral imperatives. Demagogues, opportunists, and, indeed, sincere men who have never approved some aspects of the consensus find in the disturbed climate of opinion conditions favorable for their various purposes. It may be a political party or official which bears the brunt of criticism and demand for change of policy or practice. Or it may be organized labor, or a big corporation, or Negroes, or "pornographic" books and movies, or cheating on television, or (most pervasive in recent years) "communist subversion."

Nevertheless, it is within the configuration of these kaleidoscopic value patterns and their distortions and exceptions that the public school must discover or create consensuses for its programs if they are to function effectively. Like all other political, economic, and religious establishments in the United States, it finds its stability in variety and flexibility. As far as possible, therefore, administrators and faculties try to assuage those critics and sponsors of proposed innovations by making whatever modifications in response to the criticism and importunities they can with good conscience undertake. But quite obviously, their prior commitment to the education of "all the children" sharply limits what the school can do if it is to retain its integrity.

Fortunately, educators know that there are countervailing forces in the community; any drastic cutting back of school services and opportunities would arouse the belligerencies of those who sponsor them and of those who now benefit from them. Consequently, even though the assumed consensus has been disrupted, the disruption is less real than apparent.

The Need for Constructive Participation

Hence, only the institution that encourages constructive participation among its personnel—pupils, teachers, and patrons—is likely to maintain itself with even a minimum degree of security. The American culture is what it is, and the individuals and groups who compose it are what they are; they are the facts that must be recognized and manipulated for ends conformable to the school's function and purposes.

Home and neighborhood invade the classroom, lunchroom, corridors, and auditorium, while the larger community of industry, television, cartoons, and fashions invade home and neighborhood. The school, therefore, faces the problem of meeting the challenges implicit therein by endeavoring to invade the home and neighborhood and, less directly, the larger community. It does this by fostering the skills, knowledge, and attitudes that seem likely to prove both socially valuable and personally satisfying. Such experience, it is hoped, will "carry over" into the organizations and activities of the community.

The School's Emphasis Not Solely Intellectual

Because it serves a popular culture so diverse in backgrounds and spirit, the school in the typical American community cannot emphasize solely the intellectual. Only in rather esoteric circles and among relatively few individuals do intellectualism and aestheticism rouse great faith and passion. For most people, faith and passion are typically inspired by human associations and political, religious, and other sectarian loyalties, and by the gaining of livelihoods and attaining "success." They may be stimulated by communication devices, public assemblies, and flamboyant exhibitionism. Their effects may be unifying or divisive, socially propitious or corruptive, and aesthetically desirable or undesirable.

Schools in a democratic social order have to deal with the basic viewpoints and practices that determine community life as it is. Only as the faiths and enthusiasms of teachers, individually and as organized faculties, are reciprocal in large part with those of pupils and patrons is effective communication of ideas, ideals, and standards probable.

The Barrier of Aristocratic Tradition

The aristocratic tradition in scholastic education has been a stumbling block for professional readjustment. It has retarded the democratic acceptance of the common man, faith in his potential intelligence and virtue, and assumption of his consciousness of community of interest. Like all other political and social instruments, the school must cultivate "the art of the possible"; else it becomes a detached artificiality— it becomes impotent and frustrated.

The interlocking of school and extra-school enthusiasms, faiths, and activities does not at all mean that cultural ideals and practices which characterize the school are not of a different order from those that typify the norms of the community. There is recognition, however, that the reality of compromise is the discipline required for stability and gradualism. Pupils, patrons, and teachers themselves are community-conditioned; they are more than mechanical entities to be manipulated in a social vacuum.

Indeed it is school life as a whole that constitutes the pupil's curriculum. Usually the most potent aspect of this total curriculum is the personality of the teachers and other school personnel, including older pupils. Subjects, regimen, and special events serve best as occasions for human associations, for broadening interests, for guiding responses, and for self-education.

RECENT EDUCATIONAL CRITICISMS AND RESPONSES

The inescapable responsibility to stimulate young people to find satisfaction in democratic, wholesome community life belongs to local boards of education and their agents. But the school's authority and program are also inescapably conditioned by the public's attitude toward the school, by the legal definitions of its role, and by the ethical imperative that its goals and processes be in conformance with the democratic ethic.

It is when these abstract controls are reduced to specifics that the nature of the school's adaptations becomes particularly evident. The public whose consent and support is required is not an entity; public opinion is frequently unstable and public support for specific educational measures evanescent. Indeed, the very criteria by which educational programs or accomplishments are measured are often contradictory. In this flux of frequently ill-informed judgments, there remains the traditional, almost universally accepted, belief that the public school is somehow the most promising instrument Americans have for fostering social cohesion. Hence, however varied, inconsistent, blatant, and insistent are the demands on and complaints about specific school practices, the establishment itself is fully as secure in popular esteem as it is in the constitution of each state. Public, tax-supported education is ensconced as a central element in the American conception of the good life in the community.

Moreover, the shifting public demands on, and condemnations of, school programs, disturbing and unsettling as they often are, are generally more fruitful than harmful. Educators' responses to criticism often call forth from the public energetic champions of the school. The ultimate outcome may then be increased public understanding of, and support for, the public school.

Critiques of Language, Science, and Mathematics Programs

In recent years, public clamor for increases and changes in the teaching of science, mathematics, and foreign languages, and for more attention to the "superior" students has had far-reaching influence not only on the schools themselves, but on other agencies of communication and even on governments. The background of this sweeping and successful pressure was the somewhat hysterical effect of the shock that, in some regards at least, American science and technology have been less quick to develop power fuels capable of sending heavy missiles into space and intercontinental bombs across the oceans than Soviet scientists and technologists have been. With the stage so set, the "softness" of a gadget-happy, affluent American public and, especially, the public schools which such a bored and careless people tolerated have been readily identified as scapegoats.

Just how either an allegedly bemused public or a school system allegedly devoting its major efforts to pupils' mental and physical health and associational living was related to the alleged shortcomings among American men of science has never been made clear. Nevertheless, public pressures for emphasis on academic lesson learning developed and have been made to appear well-nigh irresistible. For what are undoubtedly a mixture of reasons, many high school administrators and teachers have welcomed the public support enlisted for this sentiment; whether opportunistically or as a matter of sincere conviction, their spokesmen disclaim major concern for associational living, family life, mental health, and worthy uses of leisure time and proclaim instead their intention to restore the "college-preparatory" curriculum to a place of honor.

Educational Response to Recent Criticisms

It would not be fair to call this abnegation a retreat to the high school of the 1890s, although it has much in common with it. Negatively, it implies inferior status for nonacademic subjects and student activities, and, hence, for those pupils and teachers whose major concerns are with aesthetics, practical arts, job preparation, athletics, and civic participation. On the other hand, it supplements the traditional social-class basis (including the motivation of upward mobility) for pupils' choice of "college-preparatory" subjects by efforts to identify early those pupils who have the kinds of aptitudes and ability that are alleged to presage later success in the study of mathematics, foreign language, science, and history. Using the results of such measuring devices as a basis for selection, trained guidance counselors are expected to persuade promising pupils to major in these subjects during their later high school years and, presumably, to continue to study them in college.

Government Programs

In furtherance of this "reform," Congress has provided generous funds to meet what it has been persuaded to believe is vital to the national emergency—the alleged lack of capable scientists. In 1954,

Public Law 531, The Cooperative Research Program, authorized the Commissioner of Education to provide financial aid to colleges, universities, and state educational agencies for research, surveys, and demonstrations relative to such things as intelligence, aptitude testing, the identification of gifted children, and kindred matters in the field of education. In 1958, the National Defense Education Act, among its other provisions, emphasized research and experimentation with newer educational media, especially the development of audio-visual and teaching-machine devices and procedures, their interrelationship with the teaching-learning process in general, and their usefulness for individual cognitive learning rather than for information and skills as such.

These national subsidies build on programs and pressures that have characterized American schools and colleges for a half-century and more. Indeed, many of the recommendations of the widely read Conant Report[4] and the Council for Basic Education's *The Case for Basic Education*[5] reflect the same academic–subject-matter prejudices as the Report of the Committee of Seven made in 1893. They evidence little awareness of the findings of psychological and sociological research or of the outcomes of educational experimentation during the nearly seventy years which have intervened. They may not altogether ignore the resources and limitations inherent in the social scene and its valuations and processes, but they certainly subordinate them to those of an insulated institutional regimen.

Educational Uses of Public Pressures

There is much that is inevitably tentative in the responses which educators choose to make to such public pressures. For example, more precise instruments for determining the abilities and aptitudes of pupils may come to provide needed knowledge not only for homogeneous subject grouping and for guidance regarding choice of courses, but also for many other aspects of school regimen, such as curricular provisions for pupils with little interest in present academic offerings. Knowledge of the advantages and limitations of audio-visual aids, and other "automatic-teaching" devices proves valuable in the improvement of classroom instruction. And surely the recruitment of highly capable graduate students into the teaching profession may improve the preparation of college-bound students. The provision of more broadly trained counselors may well benefit pupils of lesser native ability or aptitude who, because of energy and determination, promise quite as much as scholars

[4] James B. Conant, *The American High School Today,* McGraw-Hill Book Company, Inc., New York, 1959.
[5] James D. Koestner (ed.), *The Case for Basic Education,* Little, Brown & Company, Boston, 1959, p. 256.

and as citizens as do those who have higher intelligence quotients. Such counselors may awaken and so rescue late starters, those who do not come to realize until their junior or senior year in high school that a college education may be attainable and desirable.

There is yet another very important reason why pressures on the high school to emphasize academic scholarship should be welcomed by educators. Response to the forces of competing beliefs has been the normal road toward stable heterogeneity in American society. Now one, and again another, school of thought or aggressive group becomes the dynamic of evolution, and most social institutions are at least temporarily compelled to adapt themselves to the *Zeitgeist*. But as no doctrinaire innovation is likely to meet the variety of needs to which the institution has already adjusted, the adaptations to the most recent criticisms will of necessity be limited by a whole host of other public mandates.

School administrators and teachers cannot ignore either patrons or pupils. Scolding them about their customs and values achieves less than nothing. That American youths and their elders do not now consistently pursue excellence in general and that some esoteric intellectuals believe that they ought to do so (their standards of such excellence being limited to the "impractical") are facts. The grotesqueness of the unspoken assumption that populations as a whole in any society have pursued an abstract excellence should be obvious. Perhaps no individual since Leonardo da Vinci has even approached such an impossible ideal.

Anyway, in the United States, the public school will continue to serve a somewhat stubborn and heterogeneous public. Some of its members may be concerned with excellence in golf or cabinet making, and some with accounting, but it is doubtful that any patron, pupil, teacher, or administrator strives for excellence in everything he undertakes. Pursuit implies motivating purpose. And the purposes that fire men's imaginations and zeal derive from the values that their actual, and, in less degree, their vicarious, associates esteem.

The School and the Elevation of Values

No one denies that the school has a responsibility to enrich and elevate the values of the society. But there must be some nexus between the political, economic, religious, and aesthetic values the common man now exemplifies and those that educators seek to foster among their pupils. Even to carry out this modest mandate requires a humble consciousness that few educators themselves are free from superficial and vulgar values.

Whatever may have been the cultural superiority of the school of yesteryear compared with that of today (and except for a very few high schools with restricted admissions, it really was little better!), the near-universal American high school was a great break in academic traditions. Whereas a majority of high school students at the turn of the century came either from upper–middle-class homes or from those in which parents and older children accepted upper–middle-class standards, the contemporary high school has no such pervasive cultural standard.

Although middle-class desires for wealth, prestige, and power, remain with Americans still, there has been much change in the symbols of success and in the means to their attainment. And this change has been signaled by a decrease in the proportion of pupils and parents who have high regard for academic erudition[6] as a symbol of upper-class equipment.

The change from the appeal of high attainment in mathematics, history, language, and science to that of consumption has been evolutionary, rather than revolutionary. The recognition that conspicuous consumption is an upper-class symbol that can readily be duplicated by those who attain wealth has a long history.[7] The important changes in American cultural values, in so far as they are related to the schools, have been associated with the increasing proportion of pupils to whom the pursuit of an abstract and culturally ignored "excellence" in erudition has little appeal.

As secondary education became compulsory for most American youth, it was broadened to include both technological and aesthetic specialties. The eruditional ladder toward the good life in an urbanized society is envisioned to include social graces, mechanical efficiency, aesthetic judgments, and athletic competence of diverse kinds.

There is confusion, too, among those who have ascended the traditional eruditional ladder to "success." One aspect of this confusion is the frequently disinterested amorality and esoteric frivolity of some cloistered scientists. To the outsider, at least, many scientists *seem* indifferent whether their speculations and theorems find application in automatic devices for mass murder or in greater industrial production, in popular soporifics or antibiotic drugs.

The apparent estrangement between science and morality finds some counterpart in other scholarly insularities. With noteworthy excep-

[6] Research Services, Inc., reported an opinion poll of parents and the general public described by the Denver Public Schools in 1959; top priority was given neither to science nor foreign language study. "Science, Languages Low in Public Esteem," *Phi Delta Kappan,* vol. 41, no. 3, p. 286, 1960.
[7] Cf. Thorstein Veblen, *The Theory of the Leisure Class,* The Macmillan Company, Inc., New York, 1899.

tions, the ends sought by advanced specialists in linguistics, aesthetics, and even in philosophy seem to the nonspecialist to be the meticulous codification of erudition, of which the relationship to the experiences of the common man is so remote as to be meaningless.

When the public high school is urged to pressure most of its mentally superior students to the study of advanced mathematics, science, language, literature, and history, to compete for high marks, and to strive for "excellence," it is not strange that many faculty members become bewildered, if not downright cynical. They themselves have not always been selected on account of their purely scholarly attainments but rather because of their competence in human relations. Few of them know what the university professors conceive to be standards of excellence in their special areas of learning; and if they should find out, it would probably seem irrelevant for the youth they teach.

The Social Mandate for Teachers

The social mandate for teachers is primarily moral. They strive to show their young charges how to learn from their school (and extra-school) experiences those things which will enrich their personalities and enhance their civic and economic competence. Teachers, as well as their students and patrons, are products of a childhood in which persuasion and consent dominated family, neighborhood, religious, and many other aspects of economic life.[8] Authoritarianism and coercion have lingered, but they tend either to be denigrated or impersonalized. In a word, the community they have come to accept as "normal" leaves nuclear physics and "games theory" to the mysterious specialists, all-out competition to the social atavists (or to athletes), and metaphysics to the clergy and philosophers.

Most secondary school teachers would probably argue that they did not will the universal high school into being. They accept it as they do public roads, hospitals, and fire departments. It is! Though they frequently have religious, political, and ethnic loyalties of great intensity, most teachers concur, most of the time, with the American consensus that good will and accommodation promise more for the good life than does the investment of ideological problems with moral color and high emotional charge. Disagreements and controversies run their course in the school as they do in the community; they may disrupt, but they almost never destroy, the school's basic mission to enrich the lives of students.

[8] Cf. Margaret Mead, "A New Kind of Discipline," *Parents' Magazine,* September, 1959, pp. 50–51, 86–87.

The School's Future Contribution

As for the future, the best contribution to its democratic evolution that the school can offer lies in making the most of present opportunities. Teachers seek to make the school community one that will serve as a forerunner of the one which students will be creating a few years later.

Sometimes eagerly, sometimes reluctantly, they accommodate to changes which they would be helpless to prevent anyway. If few students elect to study Greek, Latin, or art, the subject eventually is dropped. If there is public agitation for an orchestra, solid geometry, or athletics, the faculty seldom demurs. If governments provide funds to aid and encourage training in vocational arts, science, or mathematics, the faculty generally seeks to qualify the school. If the school is called on to deal with increasing numbers of fifteen- and sixteen-year-olds who continue to attend only because of state compulsory education laws, the faculty generally seeks to handle the problem by modifying the curriculum.[9]

SELECTED REFERENCES

Bobbitt, Franklin: *The Curriculum of Modern Education,* McGraw-Hill Book Company, Inc., New York, 1941. The author was a pioneer in deriving curriculum activities from community practices and standards.

Brameld, Theodore, and others: *Design for America: An Educational Exploration of the Future of Democracy,* Hinds, Hayden, and Eldredge, Inc., New York, 1945. Fleetwood, Minn., juniors and seniors face the future.

Briggs, T. H.: *The Great Investment,* Harvard University Press, Cambridge, Mass., 1930. A challenging arraignment of conventional educational institutions.

Bruner, Jerome S.: *The Process of Education,* Harvard University Press, Cambridge, Mass., 1960. A conservative challenge to some of the assumptions of modern educators.

Dewey, John: *School and Society,* University of Chicago Press, Chicago, 1902. The classic explanation of school reproduction of home and community activities and valuations.

Douglas, William O.: *The Right of the People,* Doubleday &

[9] Curriculum differentiation has been the usual means for adaptation. The "adjustment" curriculum for pupils with little academic interest and with low aptitude for scholarship is one form of such differentiation.

Company, Inc., New York, 1958. Legal justification for liberal interpretations of laws as they affect personal securities and freedoms.

Havighurst, Robert J.: *Human Development and Education,* Longmans, Green & Co., Inc., New York, 1953. Especially helpful in explaining the nature of developmental tasks of children as influenced by peer groups.

Kilpatrick, W. H.: *Education for a Changing Civilization,* The Macmillan Company, New York, 1926. One of the early and most exciting challenges to formal schooling.

——— (ed.): *The Educational Frontier,* Appleton-Century-Crofts, Inc., New York, 1933. A stimulating and influential product of a group of progressive educational philosophers.

———: *Philosophy of Education,* The Macmillan Company, New York, 1951. "The life good to live," says the author, "is one of active adaptation to the challenges and opportunities of community life."

Madden, Ward: *Religious Values in Education,* Harper & Brothers, New York, 1953. Commitments to creative social acts seen as the religious objective.

Mercer, Blaine E., and Edwin R. Carr (eds.): *Education and the Social Order,* Rinehart & Company, Inc., New York, 1957. Contains several selections on the community school and on education and democracy.

Mumford, Lewis: "The Social Responsibilities of Teachers," in *Culture and Social Elements in the Education of Teachers,* National Education Association, Educational Policies Commission, Commission on Teacher Education, Washington, 1940.

Patterson, S. H., and others: *The School in American Society,* International Textbook Company, Scranton, Pa., 1936. Especially Unit 4, "Current Educational Problems of a Dynamic Society."

Raup, Bruce: *Education and the Organized Interests in America,* G. P. Putnam's Sons, New York, 1936. A provocative and stimulating discussion.

Regents' Inquiry into the Character and Cost of Public Education in the State of New York: *Studies,* McGraw-Hill Book Company, Inc., New York, 1938. Contains the following volumes: Gulick, Luther, *Education for American Life,* Spaulding, F. T., *High School and Life,* and Wilson, H. E., *Education for Citizenship.*

Trump, J. Lloyd: *Images of the Future,* National Education Association, National Association of Secondary School Principals, Commission on Experimental Study of Staff Utilization, Washington, 1958. Recommends more flexible assignments and salary scales for teachers, with teacher specialists ("master teachers") highly paid, general teachers adequately rewarded, and "instruction assistants," clerks, and general aides paid on an hourly basis. Much instruction would be aided by visual, auditory, manipulative, and other mechanical devices.

Wey, Herbert, and John Corey: *Action Patterns in School Segregation,* Phi Delta Kappa, Inc., New York, 1959. A project of a commission on the study of educational policies and programs in relation to desegregation. An examination of the community moral resources favorable to orderly progress in desegregation of schools.

DISCUSSION QUESTIONS

1. If the American school reflects, and selectively reproduces, the world of young people, including the morality and values they derive from experiences in their other-than-school lives, is its meliorative function weakened or strengthened thereby?

2. What do you understand "transfer of training" to be? Is it involved in every case of reflective thinking? In every adaptation of behavior? What relevancy have these questions to the conception of the school as a social microcosm?

3. Athletic sports participated in by high school and college youths engage the enthusiastic attention of considerable segments of the public. What are some of the advantages and disadvantages for the young people and for educational institutions resulting from the popularity of interscholastic athletics? How effectively has a school or college known to you exploited the advantages or minimized the disadvantages?

4. Are there aspects of curriculum and regimen wherein the school's function is so mandated by law, by custom, or by other compulsion that the approval or disapproval of patrons can be disregarded? Consider in this connection measures prescribed for health and safety, for care of school property, for school attendance, and for submission to authority.

5. Is there undue duplication of youth services among schools, parks, recreation departments, progressive churches, and such organizations as settlement houses and sponsored clubs for young people? Are rivalries for the time and loyalties of youths frequent or rare? What of effective collaboration?

6. Do contemporary advocates for academic reform of elementary and secondary education conceive of the school as an establishment devoted somewhat narrowly to the "academic discipline" of learning the social inheritance of elite-approved attainments? Is there any evidence that a "demanding education" centered about history, literature, science, mathematics, and English composition does in fact assure the selection and preparation of pupils for creative achievements

in higher educational institutions and in occupational and avocational life?

7. Do the great philanthropic foundations such as the Carnegie Corporation, the General Education Board of the Rockefeller Foundation, and the Fund for the Advancement of Education of the Ford Foundation have a mandate to decide what is good for the American people? If so, is the mandate sanctioned by the money they control? Or by a messianic zeal? Or by the high status intellectual, civic, and professional men who serve as appointees of the foundations? Are the personal judgments of these self-selected elites likely to be free from prejudiced preconceptions? Are they likely to view the learning process from the point of view of the educand?

8. If it be granted that the pursuit of excellence by young people is a desideratum, is such excellence a meaningless abstraction unless it has concrete referents? How many specific excellencies are involved in the functioning of an excellent artist? Baseball pitcher? Geometrician? Poet? Linguist? Mother? Merchant? Is it possible that the publicists who scold the American people and specifically American teachers for their "broken mainsprings" confuse orderly docility with "excellence"?

9. Can morality, self-discipline, initiative, good judgment, empathy, or other desirable character traits be successfully taught by means of lessons to be learned by study exercises to be done at home or in study periods and recited to instructors? Are character excellencies any of the school's business?

10. To the protagonists for "literary" education, vocational preparation at any level below the university graduate school is to be disdained. Is this a kind of snobbery which is a relic of the European class system? If so, is there an inconsistency in the derogation of "the practical" inasmuch as polite learning has been, and continues to be, an instrument of upward mobility? You may be interested in reviewing the "occupational" character of most Greek, Roman, medieval, Renaissance, and eighteenth- and nineteenth-century English and American schools at all levels. Who constitutes the American elite? Are they practically capable men and women? What kind of education leads toward contemporary American elitehood?

11. The responses of the public schools to the growing assertiveness of ethnic out-groups have been modified since the end of World War II and, dramatically so, since the Supreme Court's decision of 1954 outlawing school segregation based on race or color. What degree of success have those school districts which sought to provide truly equal facilities for whites and Negroes in fact had? Has the integration of schools in Washington, Louisville, St. Louis, San Antonio,

and elsewhere resulted in the lowering of scholastic standards or otherwise affected school processes adversely? Do you believe that the nonviolent, noncooperative resistance to continued segregation of public and quasi-public facilities has promoted desegregation more effectively than more militant protests have done? What can you say about the degree and kinds of courage required by each approach? And what of the resolute courage shown by Negro boys and girls, outnumbered several hundred to one by nonsympathetic white pupils, in such "hot spots" as Central High School in Little Rock, Arkansas, in the late 1950s, when the attempt at desegregation was made?

12. Among the responses that most secondary schools and colleges make to the mores and stereotypes of contemporary "affluent" American society is the encouragement of glamorous public behaviors, for example, that of "majorettes" and girl cheerleaders, uniformed marching bands, staged athletics, class proms, dramatics, and choral singing. To some critics of modern schools and colleges, one or another of these and other responses to current popular enthusiasms seems to reflect a surrender of the educational mission of the schools, that of transmitting a purified and idealized social inheritance. How would you reply to such critics? Would you admit the impeachment in the cases of some of the examples cited above but refute them in others? If so, can you defend your position?

17

Some Educational Responses
to Social Change

American educators have responded in a variety of ways to the
great social and cultural changes which have characterized their country
in the twentieth century. Some have sought to lead change, some only to
follow and reflect it in the schools, and some to resist it. But few or
none has successfully ignored the changing character of the American
society.

The importance of reproducing in the school environment situations that are typical of homes and neighborhoods has been recognized
since the days of Pestalozzi and Froebel. In such an environment children practice with pleasure those human relations, and learn those skills
and attitudes, that are considered desirable for wholesome group life.
At primary grade levels, the teacher becomes a kind of second mother;
classmates become like brothers and sisters and neighborhood playmates; mutual helpfulness in work and play tends to outmode authoritative discipline and docile lesson learning. Effective efforts are made to
enlist parents, especially mothers, as partners of their children and their
teachers to the end that home and school learning and practice may

381

reinforce each other. In cases where parents cannot or do not respond, there may be recourse to social service agencies.

Social Projects in the School

Probably the most common adaptation of this sort is the inclusion of a wide variety of social projects similar to those in which many children are engaged in their homes and neighborhoods. They include participation in games, serving of luncheons, care of rooms, making of decorations for school and home, entertaining schoolmates, parents, and others, observing and taking care of plants and animals, collecting and arranging specimens and curios, contributing and distributing food and clothing for the less fortunate, exchanging gifts, and other cooperative undertakings which are thought likely to foster socially desirable behavior and interests.

It is obvious that all such activities introduce and motivate inquiries regarding the physical features and the living conditions of plants and animals, including humans. Buildings and streets, hills and marshes, birds, beasts, and grownups, trains, planes, and automobiles, traffic lights, policemen, and firemen, gas and sewer pipes, electric lines and water mains, parks, sunsets, and night skies—the list of phenomena that impress young children is endless. Opportunistically, the alert and resourceful teacher lives and learns with his pupils.

Homes and neighborhoods vary, of course, from school to school, and often from decade to decade for the same school. And within any classroom group there are likely to be considerable differences in parental language, religious affiliation, authorities, and standards, all products both of chance and of nationalistic and racial backgrounds. Cooperative ventures and antagonisms (sometimes evanescent, at other times relatively permanent) challenge the teacher from year to year— even from month to month. The school's microcosmic role is inescapable; its responses and adaptations are compulsory. Home and neighborhood problems and resources intrude into classroom and playground; they are realities with which teachers must deal; they cannot be ignored.

Primary Grade Emphases

In the primary grades, the emphasis in progressive schools is on behavior and interests of children in relation to the natural and human environment, rather than on precise or exhaustive knowledge about them, or any meticulous evaluation regarding their social significance. Hide-and-seek and big-league baseball, candy stores and factories, spaceships and family cars, personal spending money and the local bank, parental occupations and municipal utilities, household chores and the care of public property—these and a hundred other enthusiasms and concerns are forming the children's minds. They are grist for the school mill.

The progressive school, in its preoccupation with its micro-cosmic role, does not neglect the fundamental school arts. It probably could not do so if it would, partly because most parents and children believe that reading, writing, and number relations belong in the primary school curriculum and partly because the very environment with which the progressive school is so much concerned encourages some skill in these fundamental arts. To the degree that they are culturally funda-mental, they are inescapable.

Street signs and billboards, television programs, newspaper headlines, box scores and surveyors' transits, birthday messages and invitations, prices and change making, and many other objects and ex-periences involving reading, writing, and computation are characteristic of children's environments. Typically children want to read, to write, to spell, and to compute *because* emotional security is in large degree gained by appropriate knowledge and skills that find application and social esteem in their homes and neighborhoods.

ADAPTATIONS IN THE MIDDLE ELEMENTARY GRADES

As children grow older and progress through the upper grades of the elementary school, their own responses and requirements in rela-tion to their physical and human environments change. Innate indi-vidual differences and cultural variations make impossible any clear-cut distinctions between the readiness and adequacies of younger and older pupils. By and large, ten- and twelve-year-olds respond intellectually to geographic, historical, civic, scientific, and aesthetic aspects of their natural and cultural environments somewhat more readily than do their younger brothers and sisters. Like their older siblings, they are proud to show off their acquired erudition, scholastic and worldly, but usually they are more spontaneous and less self-conscious in attaining and in exhibiting their knowledge and skills than adolescents are.

Problems of the Middle Grades

It has been rather more difficult for schools to reorient their programs at "middle-grade" level than in the primary grades. The school's historic inheritance and the stereotyped memories of patrons place much emphasis on superimposed knowledge and skills. Hence, though teachers themselves usually recognize that children learn best when they are free from compulsion, they often find themselves faced by parental or administrative requirements that all their pupils achieve "minimally essential" competence. It would require, therefore, more boldness than is characteristic of teachers to depend altogether on opportunistic learning of these essentials in connection with social and individual projects. Hence, in the upper elementary grades there is usually generous provision for formal instruction, drill, review, and testing.

Nevertheless, much liberalization and innovation characterize the practices of fourth-, fifth-, and sixth-grade classrooms. In progressive schools, it is accepted practice for pupils to participate in the planning, execution, and evaluation of activities, both those of subject areas and those of institutional regimen and community relations. *Pari passu* the assertion of teacher authority tends to become sublimated in the social sanctions that foster cooperation and fellowship. The teacher typically becomes sponsor, helpmate, coach, and friendly critic, rather than "boss."

Importance of Pupils' Interests

The broadened curriculum is built about carefully nurtured interests of pupils—interests that find counterparts in those of respected adults, thereby assuring the children a degree of support and admiration for their accomplishments. While verbalistic erudition retains a prominent place in processes and goals, physical, aesthetic, and manipulative activities are also emphasized. Applications and motivations are found in domestic, church, commercial, and governmental institutions and in the natural environment—in weather, topography, and ecology.

In large part, the responses and adaptations of the elementary school to its role as a microcosm of our culture consist of ingenious and persistent efforts to direct pupils' awareness and resulting interests to the meanings of phenomena with which they are already somewhat familiar. Their daily behavior and observations acquaint them with streets and stores, dress and customs, plants, pets, and wildlife, transportation and safety precautions, homemaking and neighborhood activities, and many other aspects of their environment. The school selects pertinent areas of these experiences for examination and evaluation by the pupils; it stimulates and guides them in their readiness and adequacy to cooperate in the maintenance and improvement of the conditions that are favorable to their interests.

First-hand Intellectual Experience

Increasingly, the school fosters first-hand intellectual experience with many elements of the American culture that might otherwise be taken for granted. For example, the phenomena of topography raise questions regarding drainage, soils, crops, community planning, health, and, perhaps, mineral resources, scenery, and wildlife. How adults earn and spend money may lead to a study of economic processes, budget keeping, housing, and even the role of government in the production, distribution, and consumption of goods and services. Awareness of differences among the people of the locality may stimulate inquiries about pupils' family histories, variations in social practices, employment and labor organizations, racial, religious, and nationalistic prejudices, and neighborhood improvement associations—inquiries that, wisely directed, may foster associational attitudes and collaborations superior to those that otherwise might characterize the local community.

There are several kinds of intermediate techniques useful in raising the observational powers of children to the level of exact fact finding, analysis, and evaluation. Probably the simplest and most common technique is the use of pictures, diagrams, and text material both in books and magazines, posted on bulletin boards or pasted in scrapbooks. School visits by representatives of governmental agencies and of civic and service organizations provide opportunities for explanations and questions, thereby fostering understanding and collaboration between pupils and adult civic and service associations and between the school and influential individuals of its community. Other visitors may include local artists, merchants, clergymen, and representatives of labor unions.

Visits to farms, factories, banks, parks, legislative and executive offices, housing facilities, and museums, either vicariously by means of audio-visual aids or personally in guided tours, are common practices in modern elementary schools. And with these more direct and intimate contacts with the activities of the adult world has come about a revolution in school furniture and regimen; movable desks, art studios, shops, and housekeeping facilities have encouraged the acceptance of purposeful, cooperative activities as a superior substitute for traditional docility, silence, and "order."

ADAPTATIONS IN THE JUNIOR HIGH SCHOOL

There are two major factors which especially affect the nature and program of the junior high school. In the first place, the major function of the junior high school is to serve children at the dawn of adolescence according to *their* capacities and needs rather than solely according to some preconceived program and standard of curriculum; as these children's culturally conditioned interests and needs are modified, so are the activities of the junior high school changed. In the second place, as progressive elementary schools have more and more made the kinds of adaptations described in the preceding pages, the junior high school finds much of its formerly revolutionary methodology and emphases already anticipated; hence, it can build more securely on the readiness ot pupils and patrons to participate in its activities and purposes.

In the early days of the junior high school, its immediate challenge was to provide forms of educational experiences that would engage the enthusiasms and meet the obvious needs of many young people who were bored with academic school processes and whose parents saw no compelling reason for maintaining them in school beyond the compulsory school age, in those days universally fourteen. Hence the emphasis was on overcoming retardation, the acceleration of "bright" pupils, prevocational guidance and training, social, civic, and aesthetic activities, and achievements in social groups.

Special Role of the Junior High School

As state legislatures raised the age of compulsory school attendance, and as meaningful curriculum activities and standards and almost universal promotions became the practice in many elementary schools, it became feasible to postpone the emphasis on occupational preparation and somewhat to stabilize the classroom and school regimen. Fewer pupils on entering junior high school "hated" school and fewer expected to drop out soon; hence, the junior high school tended to become supplementary to progressive elementary education and anticipatory to senior high education.

While the swing away from its earlier revolutionary mission carried the junior high school back to subject-matter emphases in some cases, its inheritance of freedom and spontaneity was seldom lost. Consequently, its role as a microcosm of the community as it affects thirteen- to fifteen-year-olds finds large place for pupil-initiated projects, for constructive partnerships between boys and girls and their sympathetic, interested, and competent elders, and hence for guided loyalties to the ideals which characterize the school.

Mandate of the Junior High School

The uniqueness of the junior high school is the direct result of the interplay of young people in the process of becoming adults and the traits and standards which they accept, or can be led to accept, as typical of adulthood in the society about them. The realization of worthy selfhoods, as they evaluate worthiness, is their major concern. The junior high school is mandated to foster satisfactions among its pupils and their out-of-school associates in human relationships and civic competence that are comfortable to democratic culture ideals.

Such a mandate is not an easy one to carry out in a confused and complex society. To compete with shallow and false valuations that carry prestige among many older youths and young adults requires not only ingenuity and persistence on the part of faculty and parents, but also constant collaboration among all constructive social agencies, public and private, whose concerns include the behavior and attitudes of youths. Consequently, the effective junior high school is compelled to articulate its services with those of governmental and nongovernmental organizations at a considerably more formal and advanced level than that of the elementary school.

In a word, internal readjustments of curriculum and regimen are not enough. The goals of junior high school education can be attained only in social settings that involve adults and older youths in homes, neighborhood organizations, and community associations. These are the loci of the developmental activities by which the characters of boys and girls are roughhewn; and in these settings must successfully be practiced the positive traits—attitudes, competence, and ideals—which are the special concern of educators.

Major Curriculum Changes

From its inception, the junior high school curricula, regimen, and public relations have tended to reflect this orientation. Within the traditional subject areas, there has been a redirection of contents and methods; English, later called "language arts," replaced grammar, spelling, penmanship, and reading; social studies replaced history, geography, and civics; general mathematics replaced arithmetic, intuitional geometry, and the elements of algebra and bookkeeping; and general science replaced nature study, physiology, elementary biology, and physics. In nonacademic areas, the orientation was even more revolutionary; physical education replaced calisthenics and unsupervised play; music and art replaced "singing" and "drawing"; household and practical arts either were innovations or took over the timid beginnings represented by domestic science and manual training.

These changes in terminology have been accompanied by emphasis on activities that typify effective home and community institutions. Games with which boys and girls are familiar and in which skills assure recognition find a place in the physical education program. Home repairs, various hobbies, leisure-time activities, church affairs, and the like provide projects not only for art, music, practical and household arts, and typing classes, but also for classes in science, civics, and literature.

To an even greater degree, the nonsubject activities and regimen of the junior high school have been modified by such community orientation. The list of opportunities and challenges for the constructive exploitation of the interests of young people at the onset of adolescence is almost endless. Clubs, assemblies, home-room advisory periods, social service programs, participation in school government, "drives," parades, and excursions are but a few examples of occasions useful for educating young adolescents in social responsibility. Most of them foster the cooperation of parents and other adults, so that learnings tend to become closely related to the daily experiences of pupils. Such integration of school and community life makes subject instruction meaningful and interesting to the student, on the one hand, and increases the effectiveness of home visitations by teachers, attendance officers, and social workers, on the other.

Trends in the Junior High School

Harl R. Douglass summarized the significant trends in, and characteristics of, 140 junior high schools that he had visited during the seven years prior to June 1953, as follows:[1]

> 1. A tendency to organize subject matter around problems and applications to life situations—in which blocks of subject matter, organized functionally, could be mastered; if there were gaps left no one would worry about that.
> 2. A core-curriculum in a variety of forms is found throughout the country. Perhaps three-fourths of the programs are with upper grades or junior high schools.
> 3. A tendency to develop arts and crafts studios in which youngsters may work upon any one of a number of arts and crafts, or upon several during a year.
> 4. In evaluation, teachers are putting less emphasis on paper-and-pencil tests and more emphasis on observing youngsters and evaluating, among other things, their emotional and social adjustment, status, and growth.
> 5. In reports to parents, greater scope is given to child growth, and the more complete reports are supplemented by personal conferences.
> 6. A tendency to recognize that preparation for college does not consist only of an accumulation of credits in certain subjects, but in definite training along certain lines; for example, improving the size and accuracy of vocabulary, specific study habits and skills, arithmetical skills, and extending intellectual interests.
> 7. Grouping pupils on the basis of individual needs with teachers of special competence in the areas of deficiency, for example, for improvement in reading or arithmetic.
> 8. Replacement of recitation on school-book facts by oral discussion and critical thinking.

[1] Address presented at Junior High School Principals' Conference, University of Colorado, June 1953. Not all of the trends noted were found in any one school. By permission of Harl R. Douglass.

9. An increasing interest in group dynamics, getting pupils organized to work together cooperatively, stimulating and assisting each other.

10. An interest in character and in spiritual education, particularly in the light of the incidence of juvenile delinquency at junior high school ages.

11. A more constructive approach to school discipline, employing modern knowledge of mental hygiene.

12. A pronounced trend to develop better public relations through such methods as home visitation, better reporting, and personal acquaintance of teachers with the people of the community.

13. Laboratory and supervised-study procedure whereby learning activities go on in the classroom; longer class periods to foster such procedures are found.

14. Resource units to replace or supplement conventional courses of study.

15. Longer school days, accompanied by decreases in assignments of homework.

16. In-service teacher improvement centering about the improvement of local schools.

ADAPTATIONS IN THE SENIOR HIGH SCHOOL

Public schools at higher levels have been more gravely handicapped in making the transition from selectivity to universality of their student groups than have elementary and junior high schools. Compulsory school attendance laws came to affect the senior high school much later than they did the lower grades. And because high school academic subjects were the product of many centuries of traditional selection of abstractions, verbalisms, and symbolisms, their liberal arts–trained faculties were often ill-equipped to cope with the radical changes that the industrial revolution made essential.

Nevertheless, the realities have had to be faced. Many modern youths of compulsory school age either would not or could not master the conventional mathematics, science, English, foreign language, and social science materials. Despite reading clinics, homogeneous grouping, special-help classes, and the repetition of required subjects, the efforts to entice, compel, or otherwise get these pupils to meet traditional scholastic standards have been largely in vain. In many schools, the necessary reforms have only reluctantly been made; and in some, they have hardly been made at all.

Extracurricular Activities

The most conspicuous modifications have been in response to new recognition of youths' gregarious nature. Athletics, bands, dramatics, student governing organizations, "pep" meetings, and dances and other parties were at first tolerated, then welcomed, and finally, in some cases, almost totally surrendered to. They have at least provided common ground for the sympathetic meeting of heart and mind of institutionally "loyal" teachers, pupils, and patrons; they thus somewhat assuage the strained relations that might otherwise develop between scholastically entrenched academicians and unwilling lesson learners. Compromises and other adjustments have involved, on the one hand, the nominal maintenance of "scholastic standards" and, on the other hand, noninterference with the group and "private" personal behavior of pupils. In connection with school-related contests and other public events, to be sure, some civic groups do uphold the school's cautious limitations on "unsportsmanlike" behavior of spectators, whether these be pupils, alumni, or other local supporters of the school.[2]

It is indeed rather paradoxical that, for all the resistance to radical change exerted by the school's academic traditions and entrenched subject-centered faculties, the impact of the complex culture of twentieth-century industrialism on youths of high school age and on their elders has been such as to relegate the purely academic subject instruction to a place of minor importance. In so far as verbalistic and symbolistic subjects have retained vitality in the public high school curriculum, their content conforms to the values and skills that spring from middle-class culture. Only as electives and as special technical preparatory subjects are the "classics" of literature, music, and art and advanced mathematics and science maintained at all.

It is in the general curriculum and in the vocational specialities that sweeping changes conforming to those of the American industrial society have taken place. Newspapers, magazines, novels, the theatre, radio, and television enter the English and social studies classrooms, and, in perhaps less degree, science, art, music, and practical- and household-arts laboratories. Job sheets for technical and vocational courses change from year to year as business and industrial machines and commercial practices outmode the class exercises that seemed adequate last year. Successful job experiences, either as employee or as voluntary worker in home or civic service organization, are frequently encouraged, supervised, and awarded school credit. Similarly, private instruction in plastic, musical, dramatic, and other arts receive school recognition both

[2] The high school's role in relation to community planning for physical and social environments favorable to minimizing delinquency, to postschool personnel work, and to continuing participation in civic betterment are important, if not yet frequently successful, adaptations. These and related matters are treated in later chapters.

toward scholastic standing and as special honors. Applicability and employability are criteria by which curricula must be judged if public support for the school is to be forthcoming.

The Selection of Subject Matter

There is in process a surprising revolution in the processes of selection of subject matter. It is passing from a privileged function of the school faculty to one of self-selectivity by the pupils and their parents. Whereas the academic curricula have in the past been adapted to the conceptually superior pupils and motivated semiconsciously by the snobbish title "college-preparatory," there has in recent years been a very marked tendency of pupils with high intelligence quotients to choose technical and vocational curricula. In part, this change is to be accounted for by the fact that college admission and education are no longer altogether dependent on so-called college-preparatory subjects. Basically, however, the cause for the change is to be found in the decreasing esteem for liberal arts education as such. Unless those with "liberal education" are good mechanics or merchants, good parents, good soldiers, good artists, or good participants in social and civic affairs, their erudition and refinement seem merely esoteric or even a little "undemocratic" to the man-in-the-street.

Approaches to Change in the High School

In the light of these observations, the contemporary terminology of, and justification for, change in high school education become readily understandable. Edgar M. Draper distinguishes five major approaches to reform: subject-matter, extracurricular-activities, child-centered, social-adjustment, and synthetic.[3]

Some faculties try to meet the complex challenges they face by modifying the content and methodology of courses of study, either for all pupils or for differentiated groups of pupils, so as to make the instruction meaningful and give them the opportunity to feel successful in pursuing it. Simultaneously, noncredit or "extracurricular" activities are frequently encouraged to foster voluntary participation by pupils in learning and in making personal adaptations.

Other faculties explore the interests and problems that face contemporary high school youth, largely implicit in the patterns of class culture with which they identify themselves or to which they aspire; school and school-related provisions are then made to help pupils satisfy those interests and deal with those problems.

[3] In Harl R. Douglass and others, *The High School Curriculum,* 2d ed., The Ronald Press Company, New York, 1956, pp. 197–211.

The social-adjustment approach differs from the child-centered one chiefly in emphases; it is concerned less with individual aptitudes (except as they affect social relationships) and more with potential political, economic, and cultural conflicts.

The most common approach is the synthetic, usually partial, approach whereby, within any given school, the inescapable need for reform stimulates some teachers and administrators to use two or more of the approaches in combination.

The Terminology of Secondary School Reform

There are many terms applied to all such reforms and they are not clearly distinguishable in meaning. Several refer primarily to classroom instruction in subject matter, for example, *correlation, fusion, integration, broad-field, large-unit, general,* and *core.* Others have broader connotations, for instance, *guidance, student activities, life adjustment,* and *experience curriculum.* In terms of philosophy and goals, however, they all are much alike. Their virtue lies in the fresh approach they offer for teachers and administrators to discover opportunities within the school and its related environments for enlivening the interests of young people in the meanings and processes of the society to which they belong. Hence, even classroom-centered projects necessarily involve extraclass school and community activities; and guidance, student activities, life adjustment, and the experience curriculum, though in conception school-community centered, necessarily invade the classroom. In all cases, if the reforms are more than mere verbalisms, situations involved in the life of the family, neighborhood, and larger community become the background of, if not the actual basis for, classroom projects. And, conversely, pupils, individually and in groups, are encouraged not only to explore, but also to participate constructively in, the domestic, civic, economic, and recreational affairs of the community.

REFORMS IN HIGHER EDUCATIONAL INSTITUTIONS

In several respects, the educational ventures mentioned above are as typical of lower and higher schools as they are of senior high schools. Elementary and junior high schools, in many cases, anticipated the senior school in all these aspects of reform. In somewhat less degree and in different forms, the innovations in modern high school provisions have been shared, if not preceded, by those of the junior and four-year colleges and by universities and graduate schools.

With the rapid growth of secondary education during the second decade of this century, the need for post–high school educational opportunities increased. As early as 1915, seventy-four junior colleges, many of them under private auspices, enrolled 2,300 students. They varied from strictly academic schools, teaching subjects generally prescribed by four-year colleges, to vocational, semiprofessional ones—secretarial, mechanical, and agricultural schools. The local character of many of these junior colleges led to their being renamed "community colleges"; they serve to extend the provision of free public education near to students' homes.

Junior college (and, in lesser degree, senior high school) student achievement is judged primarily in terms of content mastery of academic subjects.[4] Other valued ends, such as character traits, aesthetic and mechanical competence, and ability to get along with others, are frequently recognized as desiderata, to be sure. But they are subordinated to academic proficiency. The social justification for so central a position in the policy decisions of public educational institutions seems doubtful. There are many ladders to successful participation in contemporary political, economic, civic, and other areas of the cultural milieu, not all of which are directly dependent on academic adequacies. No one can now say that one is more fundamental or important than another.

The General Education Movement

The "general education" emphasis, which gained many adherents among administrators and faculties, especially after World War II, has been advocated for college students rather more vociferously than for secondary school pupils. To be sure, the term has not meant the same thing to all its advocates. To some, particularly at the college level, its advantage seems to be the hope that it may rescue from oblivion the traditional "humanities"; to achieve this desired goal, general education courses are organized to bring into the context of contemporary cultural problems significant aspects of comparative civilizations, ancient and modern, including their faiths, philosophies, economies, arts, and political structures. In such cases, passing reference has generally been made to the personal attributes of students, usually in terms of their prospective status as "educated men and women." To other advocates of general education, the personality of the student has been the primary orientation—the well-rounded development of each individual.

It is obvious that, if unity of educational experience is the chief value sought, differences in individual needs are likely to be subordinated to uniformity of erudition and to common appreciation of the historic cultural inheritance. Conversely, if the "well-rounded individual"

[4] Cf. Burton R. Clark, "The 'Cooling-out' Function in Higher Education," *The American Journal of Sociology,* vol. 65, no. 5, pp. 569–570, 1960.

is the valued end product, his choices and talents may in degree undercut the concept of uniformity of curriculum and erudition.

"Student Life" as General Education

It can be argued that their social experiences outside the classroom provide an important "general education" for many, perhaps
most, college students. Debating societies, bull sessions, social service
and religious organizations, union membership of part-time employed
students, and discussions of divergent interpretations among lecturers
and authors in the social sciences—in these and in all other situations
where controversial questions come to be aired, colleges serve as microcosms of a rather distraught world.[5] Loyalties and prejudices developed
in previous associations meet opposing loyalties and prejudices; assumptions that have seemed convincing are torn to shreds by opponents;
even supporting "facts" are met by other "facts" with which they do
not agree.

To the degree that students come to reconcile themselves to
diverse faiths, purposes, and reasoning processes, they prepare themselves to meet differences of opinion and intention with controlled
temper—a condition fundamental to intellectual efficiency. Under the
guidance of mature companions—teachers, fellow students, and counselors—they may seek to reach agreement on facts and the significance of
facts as a basis for conclusions. If so, rancor over differences of opinion
is reduced; table-pounding assertiveness and personal recrimination become "bad manners." The full and fair presentation of "platforms" and
supporting arguments is assured a hearing, however unorthodox the
ideas and acts may be. In a word, the truly liberal college encourages
members of its institutional community to act like civilized men and
women.

In vocational preparatory programs, the emphasis on reproduction of skills and procedures is so obvious that mention is enough. Law
schools deal with enlightened legal processes and purposes; the curricula
of engineering, medical, architectural, business, and other professional
schools are direct responses and adaptations to the opportunities and
needs of special aspects of community life as faculties and students
interpret them.

SOME RECENT GENERAL INNOVATIONS

Elsewhere in this text,[6] the use of television for the enrichment
of curriculum has received comment, and its pervasive influence on the

[5] These situations arise, also, in high school groups.
[6] See, esp., chap. 6.

communication of social ideas has been noted. At this point, some note should be taken of television as a manifestation of public support of pioneering schools.

Commercial television, although licensed by the Federal Communications Commission in accordance with an act of Congress that requires service in the public interest, is a business conducted for profit. Public interest, unless "interest" be defined as enthusiasm for sports, light comedy, "Westerns," and "whodunits," is served by the great networks which dominate the industry chiefly during the hours that advertisers avoid, which, of course, are likely to be the ones which relatively few viewers find convenient. Nevertheless, interpretations of contemporary events and issues, concerts, dramas, and much geographical, political, historical, and scientific information (if not much profundity of knowledge) do have varying impacts on the minds of viewers. Despite the relatively passive attitude induced by television, some reflection may take place after, if not during, a program. Hence, even commercial radio and television provide potential support for pioneering educators. Indeed, some FM radio stations, and an occasional AM one, which seek to reach "quality" audiences for commercial reasons can be valuable allies of modern schools.

It may well be that, with passage of time, the pervasive influence of these "big-audience" media on Americans will decline or at least become more differentiated and selective. The day-after-day repetition of very similar programs, the melange of stock characters, plots, voices, dialogues, tunes, and events, however effortlessly responded to, may pall. After all, man's desire to do something for himself, create something uniquely his own, requires more than standardized acquiescence. This probable reaction, if anticipated, provides opportunity and challenge for alert educators to foster alternative situations, including radio and television programs which are truly educative.

At present, however, radio and television programs furnish a common apperceptive background against which a commonality of educative experiences may function. Although the level of intelligence and taste summoned by routine programs may be deplorable, they are, as Max Lerner says,[7] "the great tying mechanisms of American culture, bringing every part of the nation together instantaneously." May the school not find in this synthetic America evidences of fair play, of respect for individual integrity, of mutual aid, and of other humane sentiments that are grist for its mill?

But forward-looking educators are taking more aggressive action

[7] Max Lerner, *America as a Civilization: Life and Thought in the United States Today*, Simon and Schuster, Inc., New York, 1957, p. 852.

than that. By 1955, fifteen educational television stations, geographically well distributed and reaching areas with 46 million inhabitants, were in operation and eleven more were in various stages of construction. These stations are discovering audiences for a variety of educational programs. They have carried on "market analysis" to discover groups and areas to serve; for example, WQED in Pittsburgh found that an estimated 70 per cent of eligible people of western Pennsylvania do not possess a high school diploma and that 10 per cent of the high school students are failing in some subject each year. Television classes were organized to serve both these groups, and school credit was offered for successful completion. Seventy-one per cent of the first, and 78 per cent of the second, type of enrollees passed the examinations required for credit. During school hours, "master teachers" gave instruction to elementary and high school classes on which parents were invited to tune in. Adult education offerings included utilitarian aid to homemakers, a classical music "discjockey," creative-writing instruction, and dramas. Programs for young children were offered at appropriate hours.

The Educational Television and Radio Center in Ann Arbor, Michigan, a creation of the Fund for Adult Education, films the good productions of these noncommercial stations and makes them available to others. It also produces and distributes, at low cost, tapes of its own excellent and varied programs.

Recently, even more elaborate plans for teaching by television have been put into effect. On the college level, programs of teaching by television (generally well-received by faculty and students alike) have been put into effect at Pennsylvania State University, Miami University, Case Institute of Technology, State University of Iowa, State College of Washington, and San Francisco State College, among others. In the secondary and lower schools, programs have been successfully carried on in Pittsburgh, St. Louis, New York City, and in Washington County, Maryland.[8] But perhaps the most impressive experiment in television teaching is the Midwest Program of Airborne Television Instruction, headed by John E. Ivey, Jr., formerly Executive Vice President of New York University. The Midwest Program began in the fall of 1960 to televise classroom courses from a DC-7 aircraft flying about 20,000 feet over north-central Indiana. It is expected that this program will "help lift quality and efficiency of education in a six-state region with 5,000,000 students and 13,000 schools and colleges." [9]

[8] *Teaching by Television,* The Fund for the Advancement of Education and the Ford Foundation, New York, 1959, pp. 16–25, 34–45.
[9] "New Council Announces Airborne Instructional TV Experiment," *Phi Delta Kappan,* vol. 15, no. 11, p. 85, 1959. See, also, *Midwest Program on Airborne Television Instruction: A Regional Exploration in Education,* Purdue University, Lafayette, Indiana, no date.

The audience problem which all educational television stations face is to determine how catholic their offerings should be. Recognizing that not all men and women (or boys and girls) will come forth voluntarily to be "cultured," the policy determiners do not wish to neglect those who might "move from ham to Hamlet." Nevertheless, they must not devote their resources to catering to the momentary taste of the majority.[10]

This dilemma is similar to that which faces schools and other intentional cultural agencies regarding other instruments of mass communication. Resourceful teachers, with explicit or implicit support of discriminating patrons, have met these challenges with considerable success by encouraging pupils to use these media purposefully and critically. They thus help them to do better those things that they are probably going to do anyway.[11]

Most of the reports currently available on teaching by television indicate successful experiences—but not all do. In the spring of 1960, for example, two school systems, Washington, D.C., and Keene, New Hampshire, reported that their much-publicized experimental programs were being dropped. But most educators remain, if not genuinely enthusiastic about the prospects of educational television, at least somewhat hopeful. Alexander J. Stoddard [12] undoubtedly sums up the guardedly optimistic view of a majority of thoughtful public school teachers and administrators in the final summary statement of his now widely known report:

> The use of television in the educational program, not only to supplement and enrich, but also to perform certain functions heretofore performed by teachers, and to cover areas of the regular curriculum as an integral part, offers great hope for meeting teacher and building shortages, but more important, for raising the level of teaching. There is already no doubt about the great effectiveness of television as a teaching medium. It is being used widely at the college level. Its use in the schools is not very extensive as yet because of problems of adapting teaching techniques, rearrangement of instructional groupings, practical difficulties involving schedule making, and the challenge of presenting dynamic television programs. But these road blocks can and will be surmounted as more experimentation takes place in these areas—they are not insurmountable.

[10] Leland Hazard, "Educational Television," *The Atlantic,* November, 1955, pp. 61–64.

[11] Cf. Thomas H. Briggs, *The Junior High School,* Houghton Mifflin Company, Inc., Boston, 1920, p. 157.

[12] Alexander J. Stoddard, *Schools for Tomorrow: An Educator's Blueprint,* The Fund for the Advancement of Education, New York, 1957, p. 60.

EVALUATIVE CRITERIA AND THE MEASUREMENT
OF EDUCATIONAL QUALITIES

Quality control has a very important place in the processes of efficient production and distribution. The criteria for developing devices to measure the degree to which the standard of efficiency is met can be identified, used experimentally, modified, and so brought close to perfection. The goal of marketability is organically related to the profit motive.

Educators are fully as desirous to evaluate the quality of the processes and products of the school. In the effort to find analogies between the evaluating of problems and procedures of science, technology, and marketing, much of educational evaluation has been based on a mixture of superficial borrowing and adaptation of devices and of uncriticized retention of traditional criteria and symbols.

Educational Goals and Evaluation

In a word, there is almost no connection between the stated goals of education in America and the criteria and devices by which the success of pupils or of teachers is customarily evaluated. A typical statement of educational goals, for example, is that of the Educational Policies Commission: self-realization, civic responsibility, economic efficiency, and human relationships.[13] It is granted that some connection can be identified among competence in theme writing, mathematical computation, familiarity with historical events, and facility with foreign language; but there is little assurance that such masteries have prognostic value for any of the stated educational goals.

Lacking any discriminating justification for the marks and credits they assign, the absurdity is heightened by the mathematical refinements by which their "objectivity" is assured and by the frequency-distribution process by which "standards" of achievement maintained by teachers are presumed to be kept approximately equal.

A similar quandary faces the administrator and board of education when faced with the problem of rewarding the competent teacher more than the incompetent one. A solution is obviously desirable. But the research which has been carried on in the endeavor to establish criteria that distinguish the better teacher from the less good one, gives little prospect for statistically defensible results with traditional devices. A study reported in 1959, sought to find out whether there are easily measured characteristics of teachers which correlate highly with the criterion of "good all-round growth" of pupils. The only close rela-

[13] *The Purposes of Education in American Democracy,* National Education Association, Washington, 1938.

tionship found was between teacher personality and pupils' comprehensive growth. Superior officers were shown to be quite unable to judge their teachers validly in terms of the criterion. Nor were training, experience, or knowledge of the subject taught of any help.[14]

In spite of such a revelation, which confirms conclusions reached by other researchers during the past half-century,[15] some state departments and boards of education, convinced that some form of rating is desirable, will require it no matter how futile and invalid. Educators and the rest of the public may hope that they will be spared such refinements of meaningless measurement as have been associated with pupils' marks and credits in many schools.

SUMMARY

In the United States, the democratic postulate of the potential dignity of all men ultimately defines the orientation of public institutions. The postulate itself is backed by many thousands of years of associational human experience, is energized by the aspirations of disadvantaged men for acceptance and respect by their contemporaries, and is proved reasonable both by the success of bold adventures in social, economic, and political freedom and by scientifically controlled experiments in social space.[16]

The underlying goal of educational institutions in a democracy is to help human beings attain dignity for themselves and to learn to respect the rights of others. Fortunately, the experiences of Americans of all ages provide to considerable degree opportunities, indeed compulsions, for each person to choose and to accept responsibility for his own decisions. At appropriate age and experience levels, therefore, the school endeavors to supplement and guide such choice and acceptance of responsibility.

Elementary school children's experiences include social adjustments to age-mates (techniques of cooperation, sharing, and group decisions, and preadolescent sex roles), physical and mental skills useful in games and in emulating adults, self-control and due modesty as they fit

[14] William A. McCall and Gertrude R. Krause, "Measurement of Teacher Merit for Salary Purposes," *Journal of Educational Research*, vol. 53, no. 10, pp. 73–75, 1959.

[15] Earlier studies are summarized in Philip W. L. Cox and R. Emerson Langfitt, *High School Administration and Supervision*, American Book Company, New York, 1934.

[16] See Kurt Lewin, "Experiment in Autocratic, Democratic and Laissez-faire Atmospheres," *The Social Frontier*, vol. 4, no. 7, 316–319, 1938.

heterogeneous situations involving defeats and triumphs. These experiences determine in great degree children's attitudes and behavior related to their own and their associates' health and happiness and to the different, the unaccustomed, and the unknown as they occur in social contacts with diverse ethnic, religious, political, and economic groups. Through these experiences they learn obedience (or at least accommodation) to rules, law, authority, and the muscular superiority of elders and of some age mates.

As children grow into adolescence and early adulthood, reorientations take place in these developmental experiences. The sex role changes; the establishment of emotional independence from parents and other adult authorities is required for self-assertion; and, in the American society, ambition for economic and social prestige is expressed in many forms.[17]

Because Americans, from infancy to old age, are engaged in developmental tasks, special controlled environments can function effectively to influence the valuations and choices that they make, and also the adequacy of their adaptations with respect to their resulting desires. The school as one such controlled environment provides guided experiences in associational living for all its members. These experiences, varying of course with the ages of those served, correspond to the nearly universal developmental activities of young people. At high school, college, and adult levels, specialization of opportunity is provided, either to overcome deficiences or to gain specific competencies which may be needed by individual students to fulfil their aspirations.[18]

In varying degrees and at all levels, schools respond and adapt to their roles as microcosms of the communities they serve. If the community is restricted, as in the case of a private sectarian school or a public school in a very conservative locality, the school's freedom to prepare its members for the broader community may be restricted to what its patrons will tolerate. If the culture to which any school responds is dominated by fear and hysteria, its role as an instrument of enlightenment may have to be very cautiously played.

By and large, however, American schools function rather successfully to promote good will, health, economic efficiency, associational

[17] Cf. "Children and Youth Today and Tomorrow," *Schools for a New World,* Twenty-fifth Yearbook of the American Association of School Administrators, Washington, 1947, chap. 5, also, Stephen M. Corey, "The Development Tasks of Youth," in *The American High School,* Eighth Yearbook of the John Dewey Society, Harper & Brothers, New York, 1946, chap. 5.

[18] See Philip W. L. Cox, *The Junior High School and Its Curriculum,* Charles Scribner's Sons, New York, 1929.

competence, and the integration of personality. To the degree that the school succeeds, the credit belongs quite as much to the favorable conditions that typify most aspects of American society as it does to the intentional planning and execution of school experiences. Conversely, to the degree that the membership of the school community fails to reach educational goals, the fault lies quite as much in the distraught and contradictory character of a competitive, mobile, and diverse people and their institutions as it does in the lethargy, cowardice, or confusion of educators.

No discerning critic, however optimistic regarding the American society, could be satisfied that the schools at any level are fully successful in reproducing a purified and idealized culture wherein people can practice living in the freedom, creativity, and peace the heart may desire. Such a critic can, however, find in many American schools at some times provisions and practices that come reasonably close to fulfilling such a role.

In the remaining chapters of this book, two trends toward such accomplishments are described, explained, and assessed. The first of these trends is the replacement of the conventional emphasis on instruction, with its implications that right answers and ways are known and that pupils should docilely learn them, by guidance, with its emphasis on self-discovery and self-development. The second of these trends is the emergence of a creative community-centered school, one that approaches the teleological ideal.

SELECTED REFERENCES

Administration: Procedures and School Practices for the Academically Superior Student in the Secondary School, National Education Association, Washington, 1960. A practical program for educating the superior secondary school student.

Alberty, Harold: *Reorganizing the High School Curriculum,* The Macmillan Company, New York, 1947. An excellent guide for curriculum integrators.

Bathhurst, Effie G.: *Where Children Live Affects the Curriculum,* U.S. Office of Education, Bulletin 7, Washington, 1950. Examples of the use of local resources and problems by elementary school pupils and teachers.

Briggs, T. H. (dir.): *Consumers' Education Study,* National Education Association, National Association of Secondary School Principals, Washington, 1945–1946. A series of units for high school students, each dealing with a problem of wise use of consumers' resources.

Bowen, Genevieve: *Living and Learning in a Rural School,* The

Macmillan Company, New York, 1944. How a one-teacher school in Riverside (Bucks County), Pa., responds to community opportunities.

Caswell, H. L. (ed.): *The American High School,* Harper & Brothers, New York, 1946. Especially Chapter 5, "The Developmental Tasks of Youth," by S. M. Corey.

Cox, Philip W. L.: *Creative School Control,* J. B. Lippincott Company, Philadelphia, 1927. An exposition and exemplification of the school's functioning as a creative environment fostering the self-realization of its members within the democratic cultural pattern.

————: *Curriculum-adjustment in the Secondary School,* J. B. Lippincott Company, Philadelphia, 1925. Principles of curriculum modification by which the practices and achievements of conformist, progressive, and pioneering schools can be evaluated.

————: *The Junior High School and Its Curriculum,* Charles Scribner's Sons, New York, 1929. The broadly conceived junior high school curriculum presented in terms of functional objectives. A pioneering book whose orientations have almost become characteristic of dynamic secondary schools.

Dean, Stuart E.: *Elementary School Administration and Organization,* U.S. Office of Education, Washington, 1960. A report of a survey of policies, practices, and trends in elementary education.

Democracy in Action, Michigan State Department of Public Instruction, Lansing, 1941. Describes secondary school students' participations in school-community life.

Douglass, Harl R. (ed.): *Education for Life Adjustment,* The Ronald Press Company, New York, 1950. Chapters 3 to 21 treat adaptations in subject and other areas of secondary education.

————: *The High School Curriculum,* 2d ed., The Ronald Press Company, New York, 1956. Especially Chapters 5, "The Curriculum in an Industrial Democracy," 6, "The Curriculum and Changing American Life," and 9, "Extra-school Agencies Influencing the Curriculum."

Dressel, Paul L., and Lewis B. Mayhew: *General Education: Explorations in Evaluation,* American Council on Education, Washington, 1954. The final report of the Cooperative Study of Evaluation in General Education of the American Council on Education. Enlightening explanation of the major types of general courses and of the attempts to develop satisfactory instruments for evaluation both of the courses and of the achievements of students who take them.

Encouraging the Excellent, The Fund for the Advancement of Education, New York, 1960. Proposals for making the most of the abilities of students.

Ford Foundation and Fund for the Advancement of Education: *Teaching by Television,* Ford Foundation, New York, 1959. An informative report on the experimental use of educational television by various schools and colleges.

Gaumitz, W. H., and G. S. Wright: *Broadening the Services of Small High Schools,* U.S. Office of Education, Bulletin 9, Washington, 1948. Examples of successful ventures in community schools.

Greenhoe, Florence: *Community Contacts and Participations of Teachers,* American Council on Public Affairs, New York, 1941. A research report on teacher involvement in community life.

The High School in a Changing World, Thirty-sixth Yearbook of the American Association of School Administrators, National Education Association, Washington, 1958. Advocates community colleges embracing the increasing heterogeneity of abilities among students.

Hock, Louise, and T. J. Hill: *The General Education Class in the Secondary School,* Holt, Rinehart, and Winston, Inc., New York, 1960. Discussion of high school general education programs.

Johnston, E. G. (ed.): *Vitalizing Student Activities in the Secondary School,* The Bulletin of the National Association of Secondary School Principals, vol. 25, December, 1941. A series of papers on student activities.

Jones, Galen (dir.): *How Children Learn to Think,* U.S. Office of Education, Bulletin 10, Washington, 1951. Elementary school class situations that foster reflective thinking.

Koopman, Margaret O.: *Utilizing the Local Environment,* Hinds, Hayden, and Eldredge, Inc., New York, 1946. Techniques of community study in secondary schools.

Leonard, J. P.: *Developing the Secondary School Curriculum,* Rinehart & Company, Inc., New York, 1946. Clearly stated assumptions regarding community relations and their practical application.

Miel, Alice: *Changing the Curriculum,* Appleton-Century-Crofts, Inc., New York, 1946. A textbook on curriculum adaptation.

Noar, Gertrude: *Freedom to Live and Learn,* Franklin Press, Philadelphia, 1947. A junior high school principal explains day-by-day activities of a core group.

Ohio State University High School Seniors: *Were We Guinea Pigs?,* Henry Holt and Company, Inc., New York, 1938. Account and evaluation of their own six years' growth in secondary school.

Olsen, Clara, and N. D. Fletcher: *Learn and Live,* Alfred P. Sloan Foundation, New York, 1946. How teachers and pupils attempted to improve diet, housing, and clothing in their communities.

Perdew, Philip W.: *The American Secondary School in Action,* Allyn and Bacon, Inc., New York, 1959. Practices characteristic of modern junior and senior high schools.

Peters, Charles C.: *The Curriculum of Democratic Education,*

McGraw-Hill Book Company, Inc., New York, 1942. Especially Part 2, "Illustrations of the Operation of a Socialized Curriculum."

———: *Teaching High School History and Social Studies for Citizenship Training,* The University of Miami, Coral Gables, 1948. A report of an extensive experiment with democratic action-centered education.

Pierce, Bessie L.: *Citizens' Organizations and the Civic Training of Youth,* Charles Scribner's Sons, New York, 1933. An early discussion of the role of community organizations in education for citizenship.

Pierce, Paul A.: *Developing a High School Curriculum,* American Book Company, New York, 1942. An urban school reflects its community.

Progressive Education Association, Commission on the Relation of School and College. Includes the following, all published by Harper & Brothers, New York, 1942–1943: Aikin, W. M., *The Story of the Eight-year Study,* Giles, H. H., and S. M. McCutcheon, *Exploring the Curriculum,* Smith, E. R., and R. W. Tyler, *Appraising and Recording Student Progress.* A final, general volume is: *Thirty Schools Tell Their Story of Participation in the Eight-year Study.*

Richmond, L. M., and E. G. Bathhurst: *Culloden Improves Its Curriculum,* U.S. Office of Education, Bulletin 2, Washington, 1951. An example of community participation in helping children deal with life needs.

Science Research Associates, various pamphlets, especially *Life Adjustments Series* and *Better Living Series,* Chicago.

Sprague, Lucy C., and others: *The People of the U.S.A.: Their Place in the Curriculum,* Progressive Education Association, Service Center Committee, New York, 1942. Units for elementary school children to promote intercultural collaborations.

Stoddard, Alexander J.: *Schools for Tomorrow: An Educator's Blueprint,* The Fund for the Advancement of Education, New York, 1957. A leading educator's report on and evaluation of the educational uses of television. Contains model plans for television teaching in various types of schools.

Stratemeyer, F. B., and others: *Developing a Curriculum for Modern Living,* Bureau of Publications, Teachers College, Columbia University, New York, 1947. Some concrete cases of pioneering ventures in curriculum construction.

They Went to College Early, Evaluation Report 2, The Fund for the Advancement of Education, New York, 1957. Successes and difficulties of the advanced placement program in colleges which received Fund support for the experiment during the years 1951–1954.

Weber, Julia: *My Country School Diary,* Harper & Brothers, New York, 1946. Steps a teacher took to improve the school program.

DISCUSSION QUESTIONS

1. Where voluntary participation has tended to replace compulsion in the regimen and curriculum of the school at any level, has it been accompanied by a decrease or an increase in scholarly attainment by pupils and teachers? Can you cite relevant facts about a specific school to support your opinion?

2. Do you know of a successful effort made by a school to gain support for some part of its program from organizations that in other respects were hostile to "progressive education"? Explain to the class the opportunities that the school seized, the means used to gain the organization's collaboration, and the further developments of significance, if any.

3. Do you know of important failures of a school to communicate its intentions and procedures to community groups whose hostility might have been attenuated or avoided if public relations had been more ingeniously and effectively cared for?

4. Do you think it likely that the selection of "superior" individuals (based on tests of scholarship ability and aptitude, school marks, diplomas, and degrees) unduly exalts achievement, standardization, and conformity above inquiry, originality, and independence? Do "ability" and achievement as criteria of selection for special education accord with equality of opportunity? Are these criteria sufficient for the selection of promising individuals for advancement?

5. Read the results of the comparison of successes attained in college by graduates of progressive and of traditional secondary schools summarized in Wilfred Aikin, *The Story of the Eight-year Study* (Harper & Brothers, New York, 1942). It has been asserted that in so far as these results are favorable to the schools which encouraged pupil participation, the difference was chiefly due to the superiority of the teachers in such schools rather than to the regimen, curriculum, and procedures of progressive schools as contrasted with subject-centered schools. Would such a criticism imply that better teachers use inferior curriculum organization and procedure than traditional teachers do? Can a useful distinction be made between the quality of the results of teaching and the quality of the teacher?

6. In recent years, no pedagogical term has aroused more protest and ridicule by publicists than "life-adjustment curriculum" which critics have juxtaposed with "intellectual discipline." Is the conflict be-

tween the two concepts entirely a figment of the critics' imagination or ignorance? Unless you already know the needs and purposes which the reform that came to be called "life-adjustment" sought to fulfill, acquaint yourself with them before venturing a reply to this question.

7. Does the insistence on lesson learning and academic scholarship ignore the incidental, contingent, and associated learnings that take place in classroom and in class-related experiences? If these related learnings (having to do with self-confidence and self-doubt, mutual aid and rivalry, enthusiasms and distastes, for example) are ignored, does not emphasis on formal information and skills defeat itself? How does the modern school meet this challenge?

8. Have the proponents of restriction of elementary and secondary curricula to strictly academic disciplines rejected the fundamental mandate of all political agencies in the United States—that they promote civic objectives: justice, tranquillity, general welfare, the blessings of liberty, the common defense, and a more perfect union? Or do they assume that these objectives are already assured or that their attainment should be left to other-than-school agencies?

9. Among the reforms of curriculum organization both at high school and college levels have been the institution of "general education" courses in the "humanities" and the natural and social sciences. By the term "humanities" is generally meant the nonscientific studies, including literature, philosophy, art, and humane religion. The basic distinction between science and humanities is the idea that science rests on the assumption that there is an objective world which exists in its own right. The "humanities," however, have to do with human reactions to the objective world, not the qualities that it actually has. But are not these subjective values, "good-bad," "right-wrong," "beautiful-ugly," nonetheless real? Is the reality of science merely different from the reality of the "humanities"? Do humanistic valuations intrude into the interpretations of objective facts? Should they? Do objectivity and accuracy play important roles in the "humanities"?

10. In determining whether gifts to educational institutions shall be tax-exempt, the United States Internal Revenue Service has drawn up a definition of education which it uses as a criterion: "Education is the cultivation, development, or improvement of the capabilities of the individual through instruction or training." Basing its decision on this criterion the Internal Revenue Service denied tax exemption to a mental health organization on the ground that it promoted social action rather than education. Would the application of this criterion deny exemption for contributions to schools and colleges which seek to foster civic concern in students?

11. A learning exercise usually assumes a "right" or "wrong," or at least a "better" or "worse," response or answer. No such certainty, however, is possible in the case of a true *problem;* only tentative conclusions, opinions, and hypotheses are possible. What limitations do these facts impose on the use of teaching machines, audio-visual instructional aids, and evaluative instruments?

12. Such terms as "free enterprise," "socialism," and "capitalism" are so loaded with traditional meanings that they sometimes interfere with communication about current political and economic affairs. In educational parlance, would a similar observation apply to "college preparation," "graduation," "curriculum," "instruction," and "discipline?"

13. The economist J. K. Galbraith has popularized the term "countervailing power" to apply to social responses to forces or trends that emerge in the political and economic life of the nation. Thus, if factory workers are underpaid, their union grows strong enough to compel management to raise wages. Would the concept help to explain the alternation of progressivism and conservatism in educational practices?

18

The Concept of Guidance in American Education

EFFECTIVE INSTRUCTION AND PUPILS' WILLINGNESS TO LEARN

School instruction is unlikely to be effective unless it is intrinsically motivated. In so far as information and skill gained from imposed lesson learning are obviously necessary, instruction under ideal conditions is welcomed by the pupil because it is part and parcel of his own aspiration. The achievement of the pupil's purpose frequently requires far more vigorous drill and concentrated attention than institutional authority alone could possibly command.

The Prime Value of Education

Education's paramount value to the individual lies in its provision and maintenance of worthy purposes. Therein is defined the major goal of guidance in its many forms. There is little less instruction in a guidance-oriented school than in one dominated by the "learn-for-test-passing" stereotype. But to the degree that guidance becomes primary, the instructional process becomes a partnership undertaking—the instructor helps pupils to achieve *their* objectives. The trick, of course, is to ensure that individual purposes are also worthy social ones.

408

If guidance is recognized as a necessary reorientation of school-pupil relationship, so that the volition of the learner is brought into full play, the conflict between the academic goals espoused by traditionalists and the functional objectives set forth by contemporary progressive educators becomes more apparent than real.

The Restatement of Educational Objectives

It is, indeed, to help teachers, pupils, and patrons to perceive and to appreciate the immediate direct relationship between the information, skills, and attitudes fostered by the school and the goals sought for and by the pupils themselves, that the restatement of objectives is best justified. To the degree that pupils, teachers, and patrons *themselves* wholeheartedly accept self-realization, civic competence, economic efficiency, and intelligent human relations as desirable and achievable ends for all normal people, the school's common-sense orientation of subject matter and method should be readily understood. Mystic and ill-defined terms for educational goals—"culture," "disciplined minds," and "how to think," for example—may be recognized for what, in the best sense, they are: vaguely termed desiderata implicit in the statement of functional objectives and applicable only as attributes of them.[1]

It should be emphasized that a sincere acceptance of such functional objectives provides an orientation favorable to collaboration among pupils, teachers, and patrons. All may be assumed to want to foster self-realization, civic competence, economic efficiency, and intelligent human relationships for themselves and for each other. All efforts of the teachers to help young people (and indirectly their associates in the school community) to gain the knowledge and powers favorable to the attainment of these objectives is likely to be welcomed by pupils, parents, and professional colleagues. An environment propitious for learning and guidance is thereby created.

GUIDANCE DEFINED

Guidance includes all measures by which younger and older people are helped to set up objectives that are for them dynamic, rea-

[1] "Much of what passes for appreciation of the arts and letters in some circles is a combination of antiquarianism, a collector's instinct, and the old snob appeal of a gentleman's education. The academic people who pander to these tastes to my mind do a positive disservice to the humanistic tradition, which is in fact the tradition of the continuing triumphs of the creative human spirit." James B. Conant, *The President's Report* for 1951–1952, Harvard University, 1953.

sonable, satisfying, and worthwhile and by which they are aided to attain these objectives so far as possible. The basic postulate of education as guidance is that the reconstruction of experience takes place within the personality of the learner and, therefore, that his motives and purposes determine not only what and how well learning takes place, but also how it is likely to be applied. Inescapably, guidance is inherent in all effective efforts to educate.

The Role of Guidance in Education

It is the recognition of the central role of guidance in education that is relatively new. The role itself has been fulfilled by the great teachers of all ages. It is recognizable as the primary methodology of Socrates, Jesus, Vittorino da Feltre, Pestalozzi, and Thomas Arnold. It was doubtless central in the procedures and personal relations of the "best" teacher that the reader can recall.[2] Most educational psychologists, sociologists, philosophers, and administrators favor the intentional replacement of imposed learning and standards by efforts to engage every pupil in active measures which promote the attainment of effective membership in a democratic society.

Real problems, whether personal or social, differ from school case exercises in that each real problem is unique. It is emotionally structured; it is seldom clearly formulated in intellectual terms. Alternative and tentative solutions are not mutually exclusive; their probable outcomes not only overlap and interrelate, but also imply more problems. The solving of most personal and social problems is far more complex than the use of logical patterns as in geometry originals or the choice between two alternatives and the defense of that chosen—the *sic et non* of Abélard—or even the scientific procedure based on Dewey's analysis of "how we think."

The Transfer of Training

Good as it may be to practice intellectual modes of problem solving, transfer of the training is slight unless the transfer itself is practiced. And specific transfer requires the discovery of the myriad actual personal and social challenges that each person faces as he lives from day to day. As Margaret Mead has phrased the enigma:[3] "We need to

[2] Cf. Frank W. Hart, *Teachers and Teaching,* The Macmillan Company, New York, 1934, John L. Tildesley, *Better Teaching in the High Schools,* Board of Education, New York City, 1926, and Paul Witty, "What Teacher Helped Me Most," *Journal of the National Education Association,* vol. 36, no. 5, p. 386, 1947.

[3] Margaret Mead, *The School in American Culture,* Harvard University Press, Cambridge, Mass., 1951, p. 41.

teach our students how to think, when we don't know what method to use, about a problem that is not yet formulated."

Obviously, so tenuous a process calls for more than simply instruction in precise adaptation patterns and in "correct" responses. The best educators can do is to encourage tentative self-adaptations or choices, followed or accompanied by experimental applications that probably prove to be partially successful and partially unsuccessful. And such encouragement and experimentation call for teacher-guidance rather than for teacher instruction.

MODERN SCHOOLS AND GUIDANCE ADAPTATIONS

Educational institutions themselves are faced with challenging problems analogous to those that their pupils and patrons have to try to solve. Efforts to deal with these problems meet with similar partial successes and partial failures. No final "right" pattern of school management, public relations, classroom procedure, or supervisory technique is possible; each occasion for decision is in degree unique. "A readiness to use unknown ways to solve unknown problems" [4] is required for administrators, teachers, and parents as it is for pupils.

Trends in Classroom Procedures

The trend in classroom procedures is a case in point. The setting of tasks to be performed by pupils—lesson assignments, "recitations" as tests of learning, exercises and drills, all with the goal of uniform mastery of identical knowledge and skill—retains a justifiable educational function, chiefly, however, in connection with the minimally essential techniques and information of specific subject fields. The compulsory character of traditional instruction is softened to the degree that the pupils' docile acceptance of superimposition is motivated by their recognition of the contribution that the achievement of the skill and knowledge makes to their own educational progress. The guidance aspect of the compulsory learning mode is limited largely to such motivation.

The "Development-lesson" Procedures

The "development-lesson" procedures, sponsored by the Herbartians in the late nineteenth and early twentieth centuries,[5] encouraged far more teacher and pupil initiative than the learning of assignments. Hence, far more opportunity and necessity for guidance developed.

[4] *Ibid.*, p. 40.
[5] See Charles A. McMurray and Frank McMurray, *The Method in the Recitation*, The Macmillan Company, New York, 1903.

Preparation and motivation of pupils to assimilate what was to be taught required teachers to encourage voluntary participation and multiplicity of response, and to use questions to stimulate inquiry and evaluation. The "five formal steps" [6] of the development lesson were artificial, of course, but much of the spirit and many of its techniques for fostering activity on the part of pupils and their teachers carry over to the guidance orientation of the modern school.[7]

The characteristic that distinguishes effective teaching in contemporary guidance-oriented schools from that in more conventional institutions is the combination of emphasis on pupils' motives and pupils' purposes, the flexibility of curriculum opportunities, diagnoses of, and adaptations to, pupils' individual capacities, abilities, needs, and differential standards of accomplishment. Self-adjustment, self-adaptation, and self-mastery are processes that encourage partnership activities among pupils, teachers, and parents. They are processes which are shot through and through with guidance opportunities. They call for courage to recognize in advance that all decisions will prove in some respect to be inadequate and hence to require continual examination and revision. Every step in carrying out the individual or group project calls for evaluation, for encouragement, for stimulation, and perhaps for consultation among all immediately interested parties. And these are the very stuff of which guidance processes are made.

GUIDANCE AND THE AMERICAN FAITH

The basic thesis of the school in the United States is that it defines its function and develops its processes in harmony with the rationale and ideals of a democratic society. It is granted that there are disagreements among American citizens regarding both that rationale and those ideals, and that specific schools and individual members of all communities properly reflect and express varying conceptions regarding what the society and its institutions actually are and what they should be; the thesis nevertheless retains its validity.

The Improvability of Individual Lives

One major aspect of the American faith is the belief in the improvability of individual lives. In part, this faith denotes a benevolent

[6] The sequential steps in the recitation were: preparation, presentation, association, systematization, and application.

[7] See Henry C. Morrison, *The Practice of Teaching in the Secondary School,* University of Chicago Press, Chicago, 1927. Morrison recommended as a modification of the "development-lesson" procedure, larger units of work with emphasis both on the mastery of minimal knowledge and on the stimulation and guidance of individual projects.

desire to help the individual to find and create a rich personality for his own pleasure. More significant, however, is a well-founded belief that most men have a spark of potential genius in some regard and that the welfare of all people is advanced to the degree that all human abilities find opportunity for constructive expression.

The primary challenge to educators in the American society is, therefore, how to organize as much of the physical and social environment as they can control or influence so that all the individuals within the school community find a niche in its activities for the constructive expression of their talents.[8] This challenge may seem overwhelming and perhaps disconcerting. But it cannot be annulled on those grounds except by the abdication of the avowed social mission of the school.

PERSONALITY AS A CENTRAL CONCEPT OF EDUCATION

A person is obviously more than a body. He is a product of his desires and hopes, his fears and antipathies, his adequacies and inadequacies, securities and insecurities. His physique and bodily health have important bearing on these states both temporarily and permanently; indeed, they interact with them. At least as important in determining personal characteristics is culture conditioning. Within the configurations of culture, the individual person's stereotypes of success and failure take form.[9]

The Role of the Educator

It behooves the educator to understand the psychobiologic character of individuals and its interplay with the social institutions that shape, and those that might be made to shape, personality structures. The professional educator is in this respect the counterpart of the physician; like the physician, he is little concerned with assessing praise and blame for conditions in the individuals he seeks to benefit. His job is to try to diagnose the conditions, to determine the causes for whatever his diagnosis reveals, and to discover and recommend whatever treatment best meets the needs of the individual, to check on the results of the recommended treatment, and to make the requisite modifications in it from time to time.

[8] *Cardinal Principles of Secondary Education,* U.S. Bureau of Education, Bulletin 1918, no. 35.

[9] See Clyde Kluckhohn and Henry A. Murray (eds.), *Personality in Nature, Society, and Culture,* McGraw-Hill Book Company, Inc., New York, 2d ed., 1953, Abram Kardiner and others, *Psychological Frontiers of Society,* Columbia University Press, New York, 1945, and Douglas G. Haring (ed.), *Personal Character and Cultural Milieu,* Syracuse University Press, Syracuse, rev. ed., 1948.

The teacher's function is, obviously, far more comprehensive than the above analogy suggests. For all but a few, it is also less specialized. The classroom teacher is a continuing associate of his pupils, a substitute parent, a community agent, a contriver and executor of means for evoking responses whereby the pupils may create roles to play successfully. And the teacher's relation to his colleagues and to patrons of the school is such that he often similarly influences them.

The person that the educator thus deals with is a very complex organism. He is continually in process of becoming something different from what he has been. The life process and the changes implicit in it go on inevitably and irreversibly.

The Uniqueness of the Personality

The personalities of no two individuals are alike, however similar they may be in observable traits. Personality is more than the sum total of an individual's feeling, intelligence, and acts, though it is a function of the interaction of these phases of mentality. "It may be centered in one case in a successful drive around some point of superiority, such as special beauty, strength, or intellectual capacity, just as it may be wrecked around some point of inferiority." [10] Although biological inheritance may rough hew the potentialities of each individual's personal qualities, their refinement and manifestations are the products of experience. And it is in the provision and control of experience that the school and all other constructive social agencies function.

Personality the Paramount Operative Concept

Research fully supports what observation and experience has long made obvious to professional educators. Inability or unwillingness to get along with others has been overwhelmingly the major cause for domestic difficulties, vocational failure, and civic infelicity. Each individual personality is the role that he has selected to play (mostly subconsciously and by trial and error); by it he interprets himself to others whose responses affect him in various ways. He may modify his role so as to gain approval, or he may seek self-justification by blaming his audience. Fortunately, modifiability in most cases never ceases throughout life;[11] so there is hope that, except for the extremely abnormal, everyone can achieve a tolerable working relationship with his associates in whatever circumstances he is likely to find himself.

[10] Abraham Myerson, "The Pattern of Personality," *Survey Graphic,* April 1, 1931, pp. 22–23.
[11] Ian Stevenson, "Why People Change," *Harper's Magazine,* December, 1953, pp. 55–60.

More than a barely tolerable personality is of course desirable, though in too many cases even this minimal goal is not achieved. It is on this point of merely acceptable personal adjustment, indeed, that teachers and professional counselors—psychologists, sociologists, social workers—tend, perhaps too much, to concentrate. If many human beings of the present age have lost their sense of belonging to a sustained social order in a coherent world, and hence their personal integrity,[12] it is obvious that meliorative measures call for more than analyses of, and remedies for, maladjustments.

Dangers of Over-integration

For the majority of human beings, the configurations of habits, attitudes, and ideas to which they respond—those of family, job, government, and church—change so gradually that maladjustments are not severe. The "eternal verities" of social ethics, domestic responsibilities, neighborhood standards, and national patriotism retain their potencies as moral mandates. Every individual is under social pressure to become a stereotyped "American"—so much so, in fact, that one function of popular education may be the unsettling of the uncritical adjustments of self to society. In a relativistic, complex society, there is always the possibility that personalities may become too completely integrated in terms of obsolescent social habits and outlooks, that there may be too little consideration by the individual of the kind of person he should be and that there may come to be too great complacency in a role of unquestioning conformity.

The impatient reformer may justifiably ascribe such adjustment to a desire for escape from freedom. The educator, however, seeks to decrease the likelihood of over-adjustment to the static elements in a fluid society by fostering the adjustment by each individual through creative participation in school and community projects.

In so far as such propitious environments can be produced in school and extra-school communities, the personalities of most participants will become actively adaptive. As athlete, artist, 4-H member, actor, politician, cooperative neighbor, and in hundreds of other possible roles, the individual finds opportunities for creative participation.

For all reasonably normal pupils and their adult associates, personality guidance consists mainly in helping them find niches in the democratic life about them, observing their successes and failures in their chosen jobs, encouraging and counseling them to think and act creatively

[12] See Erich Fromm, *Escape from Freedom,* Rinehart & Company, Inc., New York, 1941, and *The Sane Society,* Rinehart & Company, Inc., New York, 1956.

and cooperatively in the light of social goals, and ensuring them satisfaction for achievements that contribute to the group efforts. Within such a framework, most persons will successfully create their own selves!

CULTURAL DISCONTINUITIES AND MINOR CRISES

In relatively stable societies, such as those of some primitive peoples, the divisions between child, youth, and adult activities are less distinct than are those that typify Western industrial societies. Children work and play with their parents and older siblings; all participate in religious ceremonials together; what is moral and what tabooed for one applies to all. Age and sex differences do exist, of course, and special learnings are intensified at the time of initiation to adult membership. In general, however, maturation is gradual; there is far less discontinuity than characterizes Western societies. Nevertheless, even in cohesive societies, minor crises due to incompatibility of precept and example do exist. Tolerances for breaches of proclaimed standards of sex morality and religious performance are in some cases vague and variable.

Discontinuities in Modern Society

In industrialized societies, the sharper differences between belief and behavior patterns approved for children, for youth, and for adults are due largely to the "social lag" of stereotypes. By and large, the adult society sanctions considerable independence of behavior and ideas among grownups while maintaining a myth that young people are to conform to codes that adults are free to flaunt. Among upper-status people, pride in family status and aspiration is a major influence in controlling behavior and standards; among the lower-status population, loyalty to church, gang, or national origin motivates conformity to stereotyped patterns of behavior and belief. The spirit of inquiry and adventure, however, leads youths and, in degree, younger children to challenge, even to reject, unquestioning obedience as part of their role.

Crises in the United States

The frequency and sharpness of crises in the United States are greater than in many other societies because specialization of occupation, more elaborate consumption of goods and services, geographic mobility, and especially an economic-conditioned stereotype of "success," confront young people with conflicting adult standards of behavior and belief. Their difficulty in adapting their personalities to the cultural framework is due to the lack of any over-all frame of reference —unless it be that of acquiring money and goods, "class-structured" prestige, and power.

The difficulty is peculiarly heightened by an unrealistic extension of dependence beyond physical maturation. Biologically mature youths remain economically dependent on their parents and hence subject to the adults' often inconsistent standards of behavior and attitudes for children and youth.

Recognizing the importance of the resulting crises, many parents and teachers seek to soften the frustrations of young people by insulating them in some degree from the hard realities of rivalry, competition, conflict, and failure that characterize the adult world. They would have adolescents accept a long, and a somewhat irrelevant, preparation for adulthood—an artificiality that is frequently rejected by youth.

GUIDANCE IN SELF-ADAPTATION AS THE MAJOR FUNCTION OF EDUCATION

Adults whose services are dedicated to aiding young people in creating integrity of personality in the midst of shifting social values, have both a positive and a corrective role to play. For the great majority of young people, constructive measures adequately foster such self-realization. For only a relative few is there great need for corrective and remedial treatment. In some cases, failure in self-adaptation is due chiefly to biological factors; in other cases, to the shortcoming of environment; in a few cases, to both.

The Constructive Guidance Program

The constructive program requires, above all, the arrangement of propitious conditions whereby the child can progressively do what will be expected of him as an adult, meeting the same kinds of frustration, failure, and disapproval that face the adult, receiving the same kinds of reward for achievement as the adult. Only thus can he make decisions during childhood of the same sort that he will have to make as an adult. Such constructive social milieux are often exemplified in progressive schools, cooperative families, and organizations for youth, such as Scouts, 4-H clubs, and Girl Reserves. Guidance in propitious environments consists of aiding individuals to adapt ego ideals, and to develop personal qualities, that are consistent with the American democratic aspirations. Such creative participation encourages integrity of personality in spite of occasional frustration.

The Achievement of Maturity

Persons achieve maturity by behaving maturely, whether they are aged six or sixty. They remain immature, or regress to immaturity, by behaving in infantile fashion. The corrective and remedial aspects of guidance for self-adaptation grow out of, and supplement, the constructive program, but they do not take its place. Indeed, unless a propitious environment is provided wherein the maladjusted person can find a place for his creative contribution, the remedial undertaking is almost certain to be futile.

AMELIORATIVE GUIDANCE IN THE SCHOOL

In schools, the institutional regimen and curriculum are inevitably somewhat artificial. Hence, adjustment failures of pupils and associated adults—teachers, custodians, parents, and others whose interests and activities are related to school practices—are immediate challenges to the wisdom and ingenuity of professional educators.

Ignoring for the moment the many questionable school regulations, even though they are themselves frequent causes of undesirable behavior, guidance becomes dramatically imperative in three aspects of professional activity. The first concerns mutual relationships among pupils and teachers; the second requires the utilization of objective evaluating instruments by teachers and guidance experts; and the third calls for the interplay of the social services of the community.

Mutual Relationships

Matters of school management, problems of maladjustment, and disruption of morale involve teachers, administrators, and custodians, as well as pupils. The selection and assignment of personnel, avoidance or mellowing of conflicting interests, provision for expert and specialist services, and the opening of opportunities for each person to experiment and to express his individuality as a participant in managerial affairs provide the occasions for interviews, for preliminary cooperative planning, and for group recognition of contributions to school regimen.

Evaluative Instruments

Another obvious starting point for guidance is the discovery and assessment of causes of personality shortcomings and decisions regarding measures to remove or replace them. Five instruments or devices are frequently used in progressive institutions for each case of difficult adjustment. One is a study of test data and other information often provided by cumulative record cards together with a sociometric diagram[13] or other measure of social acceptance. A second is the autobiography and interview technique, whereby social tensions are exposed

[13] See chap. 8 for explanations of sociometry and social distance.

and may be reduced. A third consists of observations of young people in their individual and associative activities and of carefully planned and evaluated play and work therapy. A fourth is the development of differential standards for pupils' success within the school's institutional life. And a fifth, one of underlying importance, is the provision of reasonably wholesome teachers.

Instruments for objective evaluation of pupils' capacities and adaptations are analogous to those in other lay and professional activities. In all cases, a high degree of precision is called for and considerable assurance that different competent people using the device (or the same person at different times and in different moods) will arrive at similar judgments of quantity and quality. In dealing with personal traits, interpretations of evidence and "scores" become very important; often they require the assistance of specialists.

The interview based on such evidence as is revealed by the student's autobiography or diary may provide opportunity for catharsis. Permitting him to verbalize his troubles may ready the advisee for self-examination and self-decision regarding subsequent behavior and attitudes.

The other devices for discovering and assessing causes of personality shortcomings are treated later in this book. Here they are limited to a single sentence each. By observing and questioning young people in their associative settings, their needs for self-expression in work and play projects are discoverable, and opportunities for such therapy are indicated. Tests of various kinds and degrees of achievement are applied and interpreted by teachers, guidance counselors, and pupils themselves, to the end that frequent success in reaching socially approved goals are experienced by each individual. Wholesome personalities of teachers are of primary importance if the inevitably variant characters of pupils are to be constructively treated.

Interplay of School and Community Service Groups

The school can seldom help a young person create an adequately adjusted personality without taking into account the other-than-school factors that influence him. His adjustments depend fully as much on his home and neighborhood traditions and standards and on the economy in which he is immersed as they do on intra-school conditions. Hence it is that coordination and reinforcement of the programs of all official and unofficial agencies concerned with the betterment of family and neighborhood life and, somewhat more remotely, with improvements in the economy are essential if the school's guidance program is to be effective. Therapy confined solely to school configurations is unlikely to be successful if potent extra-school environments are maleficent.

THE REDUCTION OF SOCIAL DISTANCE
AND SOCIAL TENSION

It may at first seem that this consideration of meliorative guidance has unduly stressed its negative and remedial aspects. Such a conclusion would be quite invalid. Correction of personal lacks or unsatisfactory adjustments is largely a process of making the individual's environment such that his feelings and actions are most likely to foster the development of socially functional personality traits. Such institutional controls seek to make certain that satisfaction and self-confidence are the outcomes of school experience.

These traits "are not little deities of mind which act according to caprice . . . They are not intelligent slaves which hasten to act when bidden . . . Nor will indiscriminate practice make them perfect . . . [They] are specialized in their development." [14] If, therefore, accommodation of individuals to individuals and of groups to groups within the school community is to be fostered, collaborative projects will be promoted in connection with the traits—abilities, physiques, tastes—which will prove their value regardless of factors that are irrelevant to success, for example, ancestry and social status.

The Reduction of Social Distance

Social distance (the degree of readiness or unreadiness to associate with others) among young people is generally of minor importance in play and athletic activities, in art, music, and dramatic groups, and in the relatively impersonal associations of transportation, commercial transaction, and occupation. Institutional provisions, parallel or similar to such associations, assure teachers and guidance officers probable success in their efforts to promote accommodation and assimilation among pupils and thereby to reduce the prestige of social-status "pecking orders." [15]

Success gained in such rather specific situations tends to generalize. The athlete, the actor, the cornettist, the associate editor, the artist, the corridor officer, each admired and socially accepted for his effectiveness in his special role, is not likely to be totally ignored or avoided even in school configurations tinged with class consciousness.

[14] Edward L. Thorndike, *Education for Initiative and Originality,* Teachers College Bulletin, Eleventh Pamphlet Series, no. 4, October 25, 1919.
[15] A term borrowed by social scientists from studies of the social life of the hen yard. See W. C. Allee, *Social Life of Animals,* W. W. Norton & Company, New York, 1938.

Social adjustment is a dynamic, ever-changing process. Prestige varies from month to month; ego ideals and selfhoods respond to them.[16] Guidance consists in large part of seizing the opportunities implicit in these changes to aid pupils in envisioning themselves as creative participants in the life of their society, specifically, of course, in that of their school community.

Role Playing as a Remedial Instrument

It is evident that all guidance is in a broad sense corrective, in that it aims at better social and personal adaptations than those that would result from unselected social controls. Some individuals, perhaps some cohesive social groups, require special diagnosis and treatment if they are to attain social acceptability and personal integrity. For individuals suffering from major and long-standing maladjustment, guidance officers require the assistance of specialists—psychiatrists, social workers, and probation officers—and, in some cases, the actual transfer of pupils to a special institution for treatment.

For less serious cases of maladjustment, however, there are effective procedures that can be undertaken in the school to help the individual reshape his attitudes and behavior. One of the most dynamic of these instruments is that of role playing.[17] Such role playing is not limited to formal dramatics, though this form has been chiefly publicized. The role of school receptionist, class secretary, or football referee may be fully as favorable to self-identification with a model of efficiency, tactfulness, and fairness as play acting a dramatic part.

Dramatic Roles as Guidance

As an introductory and preparatory step toward the assumption of civic roles, however, dramatic performances in which the maladjusted pupil finds himself acting the part of ("wearing the mask of") a character who may express feelings and beliefs strange to the actor's conscious self, but which may, nevertheless, resemble those that control his personal fears, hatreds, and prejudices, may provide the victim a

[16] Philip W. L. Cox, "The Home Room," *Creative School Control,* J. B. Lippincott Company, Philadelphia, 1927, chap. 5, and Ellis Weitzman, *Guiding Children's Social Growth,* Science Research Associates, Inc., Chicago, 1951.

[17] Gardner Murphy, "The Mind Is a Stage," *The Forum,* vol. 97, no. 5, pp. 277–280, 1937. A. F. Klein, *Role Playing in Leadership Training and Group Problem Solving,* Association Press, New York, 1956, and J. L. Moreno, "Psychodramatic Production Techniques," in Pitirim A. Sorokin (ed.), *Forms and Techniques of Altruistic and Spiritual Growth,* The Beacon Press, Boston, 1954, chap. 27.

psychological catharsis, a purging of bottled-up emotional states that ordinarily express themselves in maladjusted behavior. Or the actor may adopt the mask of a socially approved character, identifying himself with the role so thoroughly that the mask tends to become reality.

Dramatics, as such, is an instrument; its manipulation for the purposes of diagnosis and treatment is very significant for guidance. Emphasis on memorizing parts and cues may result in a "smooth" performance for the benefit of spectators, but that is incidental and may be deleterious. What is needed for guidance is the immersion of the actor in the individuality of the person he portrays, through whom he expresses his hidden desires, hostilities, or aspirations and in whom he may discover characteristics to avoid and some to adopt as his own.

Other Forms of Role Playing

Role playing is not by any means limited to dramatic acting. Fantasy and allegory, wherein the self is imaginatively expressed, are common in theme writing, art, and, in lesser degree, all other expressive activities of the school. Spontaneity and creativity are essential if the potentialities of the self are to be revealed to guides and to pupils, who may either purge and purify them or attach promising aspects to constructive aspirations and ideals. Once the latter is even partially attained, the task for the counselor is to steer the pupil toward participation in school, family, neighborhood, and community life, helping him plan how to accomplish his self-assumed task, and to encourage him to perform his part in it freely according to his plan.[18]

Other Modes of Alleviating Mental and Emotional Tensions

Classifying human beings as normal and abnormal serves a useful purpose only if the relativity of the terms is kept clearly in mind. Normality (in the sense of wholesomeness, rather than in that of the average) is something that varies widely in degree and kind, not only among different individuals, but also within the fluctuating personality patterns of the same individual. Physical conditions and personal interrelationships cause everyone to feel and act abnormally in some degree or manner day after day. The maintenance of mental health demands hourly self-discipline, partly habitual, partly conscious. People restrain the impulse to judge and to act long enough to examine alternatives to such judgment and behavior. Often individuals are well aware of their own imperfections. A first step in alleviating the mental and emotional tensions in others is a proper humility regarding one's own personality.

Knowing oneself, as well as knowing the almost unpredictable

[18] William H. Burnham, *The Normal Mind,* Appleton-Century-Crofts, Inc., New York, 1924, chap. 9.

vagaries of all other human beings, should restrain individuals from facile condemnation of undesirable behavior resulting from mental and emotional tensions. Guidance-oriented schools have therefore developed (both by trial and error and by borrowing techniques from clinical psychologists) a number of preventive techniques for assuaging tensions and improving human relations.

Choosing the members of one's own work and play groups, long an effective device for improving class and faculty morale (and one that has, of course, characterized good practice in families, neighborhoods, and other social groups) has been refined and elaborated under the name "sociometrics." The discovery by the teacher of the rejected pupils, of the leaders, and of the companionable ones, is thereby made more exact than general observation makes probable.

Diaries and Other Records

At elementary grade levels, pupils are sometimes asked to keep diaries in which often appear unself-conscious revelations of likes and dislikes, parental and sibling relations, enthusiasms and special aptitudes, and real and fancied social roles, all of which expose to the teacher evidence of wholesome or unwholesome adjustment. Interviews with parents may encourage them to give full support to the former and to cooperate with the school's effort to modify the latter. With older pupils, the keeping of diaries has rather specific and restricted values. They sometimes make records of their work activities and employment relationships, out-of-school lessons and practices, hobbies and games, entertainments, diets and apparel, and community participations. Care is necessary, however, not to seem to be prying into private matters of the pupil or of his family or other in-group. Once full confidence in the teacher or counselor has grown, the pupil may confide voluntarily. Until then, information desired about such matters should be gained through official agents such as attendance officers, social workers, and probation officers.

Where evidence of serious social tension is uncovered, the teacher or the guidance specialist may, at least as a preliminary step, attempt to help the student toward self-emancipation. The simplest means—one that for best results requires skill but which is often reasonably effective if used by a patient and sympathetic teacher—is the interview in which the maladjusted pupil talks himself out without meeting obstacles of others' judgments or criticisms.[19] It is another example

[19] See Carl R. Rogers, *Dealing with Social Tensions*, Hinds, Hayden & Eldredge, Inc., New York, 1948, Bernice L. Neugarten, *How to Get Along with Others*, Science Research Associates, Inc., Chicago, 1953, and George J. Mohr, *When Children Face Crises*, Science Research Associates, Inc., Chicago, 1952.

of catharsis; pent-up feelings need to be discharged to relieve tension. Once freed from overanxiety, the student can be drawn into some positive school and community action in connection with which success, recognition, and self-confidence will be forthcoming. The self thereby tends to relegate tensions to evanescent moods, quickly resolved if the momentum of cooperative action is maintained.

Such momentum is explicit in the living, growing school; all school-related frustrations—and, in less degree, many tensions derived from out-of-school experiences—dissolve as the students participate in, and contribute to, projects that are reasonably successful. Therein are frequently attained the adventure, recognition, friendly response, and sense of security which meet the fundamental needs of mental and emotional health.

SELECTED REFERENCES

Adorno, T. M., and others: *The Authoritarian Personality,* Harper & Brothers, New York, 1950. The interrelations of fear and dictatorial attitudes.

Ausubel, David: *Ego Development and the Personality Disorders,* Grune & Stratton, Inc., New York, 1952. How the adolescent's search for independence through self-demonstrations of freedom to make choices often carries with it a painful deterioration of relations with adults.

Cassidy, R., and H. C. Kozman: *Counseling Girls in a Changing Society,* McGraw-Hill Book Company, Inc., New York, 1947. Problems of high school and college girls.

Cox, Philip W. L., J. C. Duff, and Marie McNamara: *Basic Principles of Guidance,* Prentice-Hall, Inc., Englewood Cliffs, N.J., 1948. The guidance role of the classroom teacher.

Dorsey, George A.: *Why We Behave Like Human Beings,* Harper & Brothers, New York, 1926. A fascinating exposition of man's irrationalities.

Guidance for Today's Children, Thirty-third Yearbook of the Department of Elementary School Principals, National Education Association, Washington, 1950.

Guidance in the Curriculum, National Education Association, Association for Supervision and Curriculum Development, Washington, 1955.

Guidance Series, Science Research Associates, Inc., Chicago. About fifty, good, inexpensive booklets addressed to young people to help them solve their everyday problems.

Hatch, R. H.: *Guidance Services in the Elementary School,* W. C. Brown Company, Des Moines, 1951. Techniques and programs for child guidance in the school.

Henry, N. B. (ed.): *Education for the Gifted,* Fifty-seventh Yearbook of the National Society for the Study of Education, Chicago, 1958.

————: *The Education of Exceptional Children,* Forty-ninth Yearbook of the National Society for the Study of Education, Part 2, Chicago, 1950.

Lane, Howard, and B. Beauchamp: *Human Relations in Teaching: The Dynamics of Helping Children Grow,* Prentice-Hall, Inc., Englewood Cliffs, N.J., 1955. A useful text on guidance techniques.

Life Adjustment Series, Science Research Associates, Inc., Chicago. Fifty or so, attractive, inexpensive booklets that help young people to understand themselves.

McDaniel, H. B.: *Guidance in the Modern School,* Harper & Brothers, New York, 1955. Addressed especially to beginners in guidance work.

Myers, George E.: *Principles and Techniques of Vocational Guidance,* McGraw-Hill Book Company, Inc., New York, 1941. A useful textbook.

Newsom, H. W., Harl R. Douglass, and M. L. Dotson: *Living and Planning Your Life,* Harper & Brothers, New York, 1952. Good textbook presentation of modern guidance principles.

Prescott, Daniel A.: *Helping Teachers Understand Children,* American Council on Education, Washington, 1942. A monograph.

Rothney, J. W. N., and B. A. Roens: *Counseling the Individual Student,* The Dryden Press, Inc., New York, 1949. A textbook presentation.

Saul, Leon J.: *The Hostile Mind,* Random House, Inc., New York, 1956. Hostility conceived as a disease to be prevented and cured analogously to smallpox or diphtheria.

Super, D. E.: *The Dynamics of Vocational Adjustment,* Harper & Brothers, New York, 1942. Impacts of social change upon career choices and education of youth.

Willey, R. D.: *Guidance in Elementary Education,* Harper & Brothers, New York, 1952. A textbook.

Williamson, E. G.: *Counseling Adolescents,* McGraw-Hill Book Company, Inc., New York, 1950. Influential textbook on guidance with especial emphasis on the secondary school.

DISCUSSION QUESTIONS

1. Do you think the current emphasis in the published discussions of guidance of high school pupils is too heavily focused on the discovery and encouragement of "gifted" young people? If so, does this indicate a decrease of concern for the pupils judged to have normal or

less-than-normal "capacity to learn"? Is the term "to learn" merely a vague abstraction unless it is limited by concrete referents?

2. Does the emergency-oriented national and state subsidized program to train and employ many more counselors in high schools tend to subordinate the guidance role of classroom teachers to that of testers and individual advisers? If so, does this imply a divorce of guidance from teaching?

3. Must guidance, by its very nature, always be sought by the advisee? If so, how best can a young person be encouraged to seek competent advice? What place do you assign to the prestige values of boys and girls and their out-of-school associates in such encouragement?

4. For at least 150 years in the United States, the enhancement of the individual within the configuration of the general welfare has been the dominant aim of education, though national patriotism has found an important place, too. "Education for defense," however, may become the prime determinant of both guidance and the curriculum. What special problems does this possibility pose for a democratic society? Is not this the orientation of Communist societies? What safeguards to protect democratic civil life might be taken?

5. If "social need" be accepted as a controlling criterion for determining the selective routing of young people's education, is the emphasis on academic educability and achievement too narrow? Is there evidence to indicate that competent businessmen, political leaders, civil functionaries, artists, homemakers, labor organizers, or military officers, for example, have greater academic capacity or achievement than unsuccessful ones? Are robust health, readiness to get along with colleagues, originality, persistence, and initiative at least as important for social contributions as academic educability?

6. The Fels study of the IQs of 300 middle-class children from birth to maturity (reported in *Redbook,* February, 1960) indicates that self-reliance plays a key role in determining whether the IQ will increase, decrease, or remain the same as the child grows older. There were twice as many boys as girls whose IQs increased, presumably because girls are encouraged to retain dependency in our culture to a greater extent than are boys. In school academic achievement, however, the girls' greater docility is to their advantage as the rank list in almost all co-educational schools shows. Have these facts any significant bearing on the problem of selective guidance?

7. Although intelligence tests from which IQs are derived do measure much else beside innate capacity for academic learning, their results are relatively free from variation because of special coaching in preparation for taking them. The Scholastic Aptitude Tests "V"

(verbal) and "M" (mathematical), given year after year to many secondary school seniors, are remarkably reliable in this respect. If scholastic success in college is the criterion, they are also reasonably valid. Do these statements mean that they are *educationally* reliable and valid?

8. Does labeling and pigeonholing pupils according to curriculum interest, ability group, or social characteristics cause teachers and fellow pupils to treat them as stereotypes? Are girls "better students" than boys? Is there a "halo effect" that affects the marks of well-bred pupils?

19

Education for Responsible Community Life

PERSONALITIES AND CULTURAL INCONSISTENCIES

In the United States, as everywhere, people live with inconsistent values, beliefs, and loyalties. Children and adults alike are under compulsion to affirm the peculiar superiorities of sects, races, and even of geographic sections of the community in comparison with the population as a whole. As an American, however, the individual must simultaneously assert and in degree exemplify good will toward all human beings.

The Clash of Values

Another clash of values is found in the identification of success with getting ahead of one's contemporaries in the race for emolument and honors. The mandate to be ambitious in a competitive society presses almost irresistibly on the aspirant to emulate the disingenuous, industrious, clever self-seeker. But the individual is simultaneously under compulsion to be a good neighbor to his fellow man and to sacrifice on behalf of the community something of his private interests in personal success. Hence comes about an insidious bivalency of "personality." It

428

is a commodity to be hawked in the market place of popularity; it is also an inner pattern of good will and aesthetic pleasure.

Somehow each individual must work out his own salvation. Somehow he must satisfy the demands of familial, sectarian, ethnic, local, and national loyalties, while simultaneously espousing universal values which deny these demands. Somehow he must strive for economic "success" and popular esteem while simultaneously developing an individual pattern of values and adequacies that make him unique as a person.

In response to these compulsions, the public school program finds peculiar challenges in six areas of personal adjustment and human relations. The overlapping areas are those of (1) family life, (2) accommodation to intermingling culture fragments, (3) leisure occupations, (4) juvenile delinquencies, (5) political and economic rules and practices, and (6) critical understanding of the melange of prejudices, pressures, aspirations, and ideas that characterize the evolving American culture.

GUIDANCE AND FAMILY LIFE

Two aspects of family life are of peculiar importance to the school. The first and more general one is the duality of developmental and educational loci, the school and the home, implicit in the legal definition of the teacher's authority—*in loco parentis*. The child's personality has already been conditioned before he comes under the school's influence; it continues to respond to the practices, relationships, and values of parents and siblings throughout his school career. The home environment presents, therefore, a primary configuration, sometimes favorable, sometimes unfavorable, to which the school's measures must be adapted. Affections, fears, loyalties, customs, and standards that characterize the child's home are transferred to the school—and *vice versa*. Helping him accommodate himself to both environments by reinforcing the favorable and offsetting or ignoring the unfavorable factors of the home requires great tact as well as deep understanding of the child's and the parents' dilemmas. Hence, there is much emphasis in contemporary guidance programs on parental conferences both in the school and in the home situations and on school activities that are analogous to those of home life.

The second aspect of family-life guidance peculiarly significant for schools is related to heterosexual behavior. The institution of marriage is not only rooted in custom, but is also fundamental to the stability of the society. The difficulties of adapting this honored institution to the exigencies of the economic revolution and of individual

freedom of behavior in America are complicated by the prolonged period
between sexual maturation and the time fixed by law, custom, and economic self-sufficiency for marrying.

Esteem for Sexual Allurement

The impact of this complex on school guidance is usually first
recognized in the cultural mandate on the individual adolescent to gain
the admiration of age-mates. Americans value highly the role of sexual
love as a factor in marriage; consequently esteem for sexual allurement
is projected downward from the age of anticipated courtship to that of
preadolescence. Self-esteem of the young person becomes centered about
his or her attractiveness to members of the other sex and the consequent admiration of those of his own sex. Hence the character of much
of the daydreaming and overt behavior of young people takes on a
sexual emphasis.

At the same time, the taboo on premarital sexual intercourse,
while not effective in preventing "indiscretions," stops the guidance officer from frank discussion of the matter with boys and girls of early
and middle adolescence except in cases of overt breach. Hence the
school's effective measures are likely to be indirect, stressing other
aspects of youthful popularity, such as athletic skill, good taste, artistic
accomplishment, and scholarship. Quite as important is the encouragement of pupils' contributions to those home and community activities
that are likely to provide recognition for "wholesome" accomplishments,
and thereby complement the school's efforts to foster ego ideals that are
not exclusively preoccupied by sex interests.

In senior high schools and colleges, skillful treatment of marital
matters is socially tolerated in increasing degree. The relative immediacy
of the challenge to make a success of married life is the decisive factor.

The success of family-life guidance is likely to be greatest in
those cases where it is least needed, that is, when the persons influenced
by it are reasonably free from serious individual and social tensions.
It is indeed a specialized aspect of the total process of home and school
that is favorable to the development of wholesome personalities. For
individual pupils who have not made adequate adjustments, family-life
guidance may present peculiar opportunities for catharsis of pent-up
personality conflicts and for the encouragement of constructive relations
with other people.

ACCOMMODATIONS TO THE INTERMINGLING
OF CULTURES

"I know of no other situation in history similar to yours [that
of America] in having assembled the vivid and adventurous spirits of

numerous races in an environment favorable to the creation of a great culture, except in the Mediterranean basin of the fifth and fourth centuries B.C. . . . It will be strange if you don't profit by your situation." [1]

The American ethos assumes that, in the long run, equality of opportunity and freedom in so favorable an environment assure a humane "great culture." The national motto, *e pluribus unum,* applies to the cultural entities as truly as to the states that make up the country.

Such integration is an aspiration yet to be achieved—and the public school is advantageously situated to foster its realization. Indeed it has been credited by foreign observers with much of the unity which characterizes the American society. But the goal itself is far from attainment. And, as yet, the school has fulfilled its function only partially. Segregation, not only of races, but also of social and economic classes and religious sects, is common. Middle-class teachers and influential patrons find it difficult to accept sympathetically the uncouth speech and manners of disadvantaged children whose resentment against, and compensation for, disdain and exclusion may be excessive.

Decline of Minority Taboos

Fortunately, in many communities, the taboos and stereotypes attached to ethnic, racial, and social class minorities are losing their absolute qualities. The stage, politics, athletics, music and art, science and technology, and the professions increasingly prize ability above pigmentation and religious affiliation. The school's guidance of individuals toward better accommodation to intermingling culture fragments is facilitated by such examples. And it is a two-way process. The attributes of the successful, socially accepted athlete, artist, scientist, political leader, or educator who came from a disdained minority tend to be transferred, in the view of the public, to other members of the group from which he sprang. Moreover, the peculiar pride that these members feel in the triumphs of their representatives affect their own ego ideals.

The readiness of people to evaluate and to accept their fellows in terms of their abilities, contributions, and character, regardless of other considerations, depends in great measure on their own success in collaborative projects and in their freedom from serious abnormalities, whether biologically or socially derived. Even for relatively adaptable persons, accommodation to differences of race, religion, and class is often gradual; it is likely to be limited to specific situations wherein social taboos are weak. Obviously, an individual liberated from prejudice

---

[1] Alfred North Whitehead, quoted by Lucien Price in "The Permanence of Change," *The Atlantic,* April, 1954, p. 69.

in art, athletic activities, or work might feel compelled by social pressure to avoid "conspicuous fellowship" in situations where taboos retain force, for example, at dances.

Effective guidance for cultural maturity in this area is based on efforts to foster wholesome personalities in general: to make each individual successful in some purposeful project and to reduce so far as possible internal conflicts and tensions. Beyond that, guidance accentuates the tolerance and acceptance of those different from one's self in the school community, thereby accelerating the development of such attitudes outside the school.

GUIDANCE FOR LEISURE OCCUPATIONS

Obviously, much of what has been said regarding domestic activities and the intermingling of culture fragments applies as well to leisure occupations. So too does the recognition that in many school communities there are numerous developmental factors which favor reasonably harmless, if not altogether desirable, behaviors and attitudes. The school's guidance function often needs to be only mildly meliorative and corrective as applied to leisure associations and activities.

Counseling for Leisure-time Activities

Only with pupils who are making seriously wrong leisure-time adjustments—those deleterious to health or morals, for example—need the counselor deal individually. Facts derived from records, diaries, and interviews with these pupils and their teachers and other adult associates provide no more than starting points. For some cases, tension-reducing catharsis and prearranged recognition for efforts to participate in school activities may lead them to redirect their personal choices of leisure occupation. Beyond those steps, the cooperation of whatever agents the local community affords—clergymen, municipal officials, playground supervisors, and social workers, for example—must be sought; even proprietors of poolrooms, soft-drink and candy stores, and dance halls have proved responsive to appeals for help.

Need for Realistic Guidance

Leisure-time guidance is futile if it is not realistic. School recognition for information gained from viewing better television and movie programs may somewhat improve young people's choices; but it is not likely to reduce the time spent in viewing. If "going with the gang" in out-of-school time seems deleterious, substitutions of playground and youth-organization activities may be made, especially if the gang leaders themselves accept the substitution. But the individual who finds his fulfillment in gang membership will seldom choose a leisure-time occupation that is very dissimilar from that embodied in such association.

Drastic changes in ego ideals do take place, of course; occasionally they come with the suddenness of religious conversion. Usually, however, the transition is a process which takes considerable time while the individual develops confidence in his new "looking-glass self." Home-room and other group guidance provide favorable opportunities for the pupil to practice his new role with sympathetic audiences, with the "coach" close at hand to provide needed cues. As the changing ego ideal takes form, indeed, the pupil may voluntarily seek counsel from a teacher or other trusted adult regarding his out-of-school interests and difficulties.

GUIDANCE AND DELINQUENCY

Problems of juvenile delinquency are closely related to those of leisure-time guidance. Young people who get into trouble with the law are not much different from those who do not get caught. The American society, with its high premium on initiative, adventuresomeness, cleverness, boldness, and evasiveness, encourages people to take chances and to depend on luck and vigilance to see them through. Add to that amorality the effects of mobility and the fragmentation of group restraints and group stimulations, and it is not surprising that most people break some laws—generally with impunity.

Delinquency a Relative Term

"Delinquency" then must be a relative term. It denotes a peculiar legal status. The illegal act which is detected and punished is most likely more flagrant than most of the similar acts of those who not only avoided arrest but may have reaped rewards and won adulation from their associates. "Waves of delinquency" in localities may mean that police surveillance has intensified, that group antagonisms have sharpened, or that new challenges to youthful adventurers to steal, to destroy, and to fight have emerged.

The school itself is one of the community's agencies for anticipating and minimizing delinquent behavior. As a social microcosm, it presents to children and youth, in somewhat controllable form, rules which they may obey or break, persons whom they can help or harm, and property which they may safeguard or destroy. Disciplinary infractions are analogous to delinquent acts. Responsibility for the well-being of the school community is analogous to desirable civic attitude and behavior. Guided membership in school-related group life is then the major anticipatory and minimizing function of the school.

Two special aspects of anticipation call for mention. Because detected flagrant defiance of law is far more frequent and serious in slum areas than in middle- and upper-class neighborhoods,[2] schools in such localities are presented with peculiar challenges to coordinate their constructive efforts with those of other agencies concerned with youth welfare and law enforcement. Because repeated serious delinquencies are often associated with maladjusted young people,[3] the guidance-oriented school can in some measure identify in advance those who are most likely to seek self-expression by defiance and evasion. Such identification signals intensified effort to reduce the victim's inner conflicts and to help him find success in whatever constructive school community projects may be made available. Thereby it blends with good guidance practice in general.

GUIDANCE AND ECONOMIC REALITY

Great changes proceed in political and economic institutions. Job securities in obsolescent productive and service occupations vanish; bemoaning their loss will not bring them back. Reference to the future in the guidance program is therefore mandatory. Preparation for yesterday's occupations, yesterday's social structure, and yesterday's antagonisms, prides, and prejudices unfits young people for the world they will live in. Modern technology, finance, and industry transform skilled workers into managers of machine processes. They make government the custodian of social welfare; it alone can intercede to make transitions tolerable.

Organizational Planning

The ongoing social and economic revolution requires that much individualistic activity be replaced by organizational planning and execution. Impersonal corporative enterprise increasingly pushes the individual entrepreneur, inventor, writer, artist, and technician into the role of organizational employee. Accompanying this change, employees and consumers organize to assure themselves full shares in the benefits of the technological and managerial revolution. In such a society social serv-

[2] C. R. Shaw and H. D. McKay, *Social Factors in Crime in Chicago,* National Committee on Law Observance, Chicago, 1931, also *Juvenile Delinquency in Urban Areas,* University of Chicago Press, Chicago, 1942.

[3] Sheldon and Eleanor Glueck report on 500 matched pairs of children in *Unraveling Juvenile Delinquency,* The Commonwealth Fund, New York, 1950, also, in *Delinquents in the Making: Paths to Prevention,* Harper & Brothers, New York, 1952.

ices follow suit; nationwide and, increasingly, world-wide organizations become militantly organized for health, religious, educational, and other welfare purposes.

Role of Guidance

What of guidance in relation to these social trends? Obviously there is required something far more broadly conceived than the traditional arousal of ambition to be a "lone wolf" seeking to rise in the social and economic scale and to gain prestige by "beating out" some competitor. Such atavism is increasingly narrowed to such roles as those of the speculator hoping for a lucky strike, of the self-seeking politician and the fixer, and of the gambler and the gangster; even in these roles individuals would likely be helpless without organizations of some sort.

Cooperative endeavor, supported and supervised by the state on behalf of all the people affected, imposes the pattern in our time. Preference for an individualistic, competitive world is increasingly academic.

GUIDANCE AND CRITICAL MINDEDNESS

The fact that man's political, economic, and social-service activities inevitably become organizational does not mean that the importance of individual decisions is thereby minimized. Quite the contrary. Organizational policies and practices, whether emanating from majority opinion or from managerial decision, are open to question by individuals and by organized minorities. Indeed, fragmentation proceeds *pari passu* with organization; majorities and managers are almost constantly challenged by power groups who seek to get control for their own purposes.

Control and Persuasion

Getting control and keeping it require constant and ingenious persuasion of members of organizations and of the general public, without whose consent no social institution can long survive. Efforts to control the minds of adults and youths involve all the agencies of communication; and the public school is a very important agency of communication. Hence economic and civic organizations make their special pleadings available to schools. Sometimes textbooks and other instructional aids (including the beliefs of teachers themselves) are scrutinized by adults who align themselves with one or another interest group.

Basic to democratic ideology, however, is a faith in human intelligence. Yet, there can be no intelligence apart from its functional operation. Intellect, moreover, is personal, even though it is stimulated and rewarded by the opinions of others. Reflective thinking takes place only when questions for which alternate answers are possible must be decided in order to choose a course of action.

As organization of economic, service, and "spiritual and aesthetic" enterprises grows, however, alternative courses of action are seldom subjects for individual reflection or decision. Under the dual impact of propaganda and of the futility of reflection concerning organizational policies, passivity is fostered; to be a "loyal" Republican or Democrat, Baptist or Roman Catholic, corporation stockholder, union member, subject teacher, club member, Legionnaire, or local "booster" fosters avoidance of discriminative thinking.

Critical Thinking Largely Concerned with Personal Problems

Critical thinking for decision making tends to be reduced to personal problems or relegated to hobbies. Matters of dress, etiquette, buying, job promotion, self-improvement, and human intercourse are surely worthy of reflective thinking. But so also are matters of municipal, state, and national economics, policies of corporations and other large organizations, intersectional and international relations, and the social effects of group cooperation and rivalry.

The implications of this trend for school education, especially for guidance, are obvious. Unfortunately, classroom discussion of public policies is too readily labeled "controversial"; even in times of widespread social insecurity, public opinion gives only halfhearted support for it.

Guidance and Critical Thinking

The guidance interview and informal group discussion do, however, favor consideration of loyalties to institutions and leaders. So long as the counselor limits himself to guidance, he properly encourages independent thinking about social institutions. He aids his advisees to seek relevant facts; he strives to make them examine their own logic; he encourages tentative choices and decisions concerning their applicability. But he does not expound his own opinions as though they were the truth. His role is not that of instructor.

Guidance finds its major challenge in encouraging people to face the organizational world with critical intelligence. As citizen, employee, union member, parent, and church member, the individual can act intelligently only as he faces courageously the fallibility of human beings and their institutions. Such critical consciousness need not imply disloyalty toward organizational policies and programs. But it does comply with the fundamental postulate of democracy that men can and will practice intelligence individually.

GUIDANCE AND THE LIFE-ADJUSTMENT CURRICULUM

Human adjustment would be a relatively simple process if the world to which adjustment must be made were itself fairly rigid. Obviously, however, the basic characteristic of the postfeudalistic world has been cultural and social change. Not only do institutions wax and wane, but also the relations among them are altered. The desire for security and certainty may be universal, but only a recluse or escapist can even approach such oblivion.

Adjustment and Change

Adjustment in a world of impending change requires acknowledgment of grave alternatives. The release of atomic energy is only the most recent of the factors that can add greatly to human happiness and well-being or cause the total destruction of civilization. All important scientific developments, technical inventions, and political opportunisms present men with alternatives regarding what applications should be fostered, which discountenanced, and which accepted fatalistically. Adjustment is not limited to the last of these alternatives.

The acceptance by the school of responsibility to promote self-adjustment of pupils and teachers would be fantastically presumptuous were it not recognized that adjustment is never achieved, that it is a process never complete. What goes on behind the faces of youths and adults? What makes their lives dull or thrilling? What are their great hopes and great fears? What restricts their free use of intelligence? It is with such questions in mind that the counselor approaches his duty and his opportunity to foster the adjustment of young people.

IMPORTANCE OF WHOLESOME TEACHER PERSONALITIES

In order not to confuse the points previously emphasized by discussing two variables at once, the authors have postponed explicit treatment of the accentuation of tension and frustration due to lapses in mental health among the professional staff. Teachers, administrators, custodians, and consultants are subject to the same kinds of strain as pupils. They are attached to standards and stereotypes of what is "right" and "fitting," derived both from their own early home, church, and other neighborhood environments and from their adult associates and institutional attachments. It is therefore difficult for them to evaluate objectively and impersonally the behaviors and beliefs of pupils, associates, and parents that differ greatly from their own standards.[4]

[4] See E. K. Wickman, *Teachers and Behavior Problems,* The Commonwealth Fund, New York, 1938.

Middle-class Teachers and Lower-class Values

The middle-class teacher often resents the diminution of emphasis on the academic "culture" that he is prepared to dispense. He is sometimes shocked by the profanity, belligerency, and callous disregard of pain on the part of lower-class pupils, or amazed at the extreme shame attached to public nudity, in any unconventional degree, among lower-class girls.[5] The "obstinacy," "stupidity," and general "unworthiness" of those pupils and colleagues who do not conform to his own valuations frequently so exceed the toleration of the inflexible middle-class teacher as to outrage and frustrate him. He sometimes counts as professional failure his lack of success in making his pupils and colleagues over in his own image; if so, he may pity himself, isolate himself, or perhaps develop a paranoia. Such a teacher has obviously become a liability to the guidance-oriented school.[6]

The Disturbed Teacher

Some teachers and other school officers suffer from maladjustments derived from their home and other associative conflicts. Like the pupils, they bring to the school personalities marred occasionally or chronically by hostilities and feelings of inadequacy which demand compensation at the expense of pupils, colleagues, or the world in general. It is all too easy for the disturbed teacher to project his faults to others. And as such projection becomes basic to his self-esteem—his own purity of motive and blamelessness—it becomes very difficult to reorient his personality from outside himself.

If guidance orientation is to be central to school education, maladjustments among the guides themselves must obviously be kept at a minimum. Changes in assignment of classes and subjects often prove helpful. As "cats in strange garrets," some disturbed teachers adopt a learner's attitude, a readiness to seek solutions to new problems; they find adventure, recognition, and security in collaborating with pupils, colleagues, and parents in situations where final answers are lacking. In more extreme cases of maladjustment, transfers to other schools or leaves of absence to travel or study may supply the needed new setting for the restoration of health. Psychiatric treatment, or even compulsory retirement, may be required.

If the school has already achieved an over-all guidance orientation, however, fellow teachers and administrators quickly recognize

[5] Allison Davis, "Ability and Survival," *The Survey,* February, 1951, pp. 60–63.

[6] John G. Watkins, "Unreality Reactions in Teacher-Pupil Relations," *Phi Delta Kappan,* vol. 34, no. 4, pp. 279–283, 1953.

symptoms of maladjustment. They give the victim opportunity to talk himself out of his incipient tensions, help him in whatever constructive measure he undertakes to meet his problem, and engage him in collaborative projects unrelated to the human and physical situation wherein his difficulty arose. They know that, for adults as truly as for children, the momentum of achievement itself can often carry the individual safely beyond the disastrous whirlpools of worry, frustration, and self-analysis.

EGO IDEALS AND SATISFYING HUMAN RELATIONSHIPS

In a democracy, there is near identity between the guidance processes and concepts and those of education itself. It is assumed that every individual needs to find happiness, gain and retain liberty to choose and act, and to associate with his fellow men cooperatively and tolerantly. To what extent these are birthrights and to what extent they are the products of culture are of only academic significance for Americans. The great adventure is the trying out of a social theory; the school is one major instrument by which Americans hope to prove its truth. Whatever their private doubts, as public servants educators would be faithless to their mission if they should fail for lack of effort and ingenuity to make democracy realizable.

Intelligent Self-direction

The compelling character of this mandate is a major topic of the following chapters of this book. Here, however, the concern is with the directive that educators foster intelligent self-direction of every individual in the light of the goals he sets for himself. This directive automatically rules out goals where their attainment would deprive others of the privilege of establishing their own ends.

Consequently, the public school—in conjunction, of course, with other similarly oriented agencies—assumes the possibility and the desirability of self-direction. It endeavors to stimulate all whom it influences to choose continually, reflectively, and experimentally the preferred conditions of life. Many, probably most, of these choices are of immediate objectives—position on a team, part in a play, report to prepare for class—but the successes and failures every child experiences in making choices have long-term effects. Little by little, each person discovers which of the desired things it is possible to attain by effort and which of the eagerly anticipated things proves deeply satisfying when achieved.

Freedom to choose becomes effective discipline; it teaches the individual to adjust to realities. Both triumphs and disappointments foster maturation of the self, if they are met one by one, week after week, and year after year.

Role of Guidance in Self-direction

Guidance enters the process at several points: to encourage the timid individual to seize opportunity and to coach him a bit to increase his self-confidence; to help him to assess success or failure in case it has been more apparent than real, and to learn from the experience what to do and what not to do the next time a similar challenge is met; and to acquaint him, if necessary, with relevant examples, exhibitions, and literature that might make future choices and trials more effective.[7]

At the high school and college levels and among out-of-school youths and adults, the career motive becomes of paramount importance for many persons. Here it is that vocational guidance becomes a serious matter. To the extent that those who seek counsel have accustomed themselves to making choices bravely and wisely during preceding years, the role of the guidance officer is to make available whatever objective data are pertinent—test results, rating sheets, job analyses, indications of job opportunities, and interviews with potential employers and with competent practitioners of trades and professions.

Much of the time, energy, and resources of the guidance specialist has to be expended on persons who lack experience in making reasonably firm and enlightened choices of any kind. His professional skills and knowledge are peculiarly needed, however, to aid these immature individuals, because they are unprepared to face the problems that associational life inevitably poses. Success in occupational careers depends on personal maturity fully as much as it does on specific aptitudes and learned knowledge and skills.

SCIENTIFIC INSTRUMENTS AND THE SETTING OF ACHIEVABLE GOALS

In a broad sense, of course, all rational efforts to help individuals and groups to create or modify their goals and ego ideals may be called "scientific." At this point, however, attention is directed to certain objective instruments that provide bases on which adviser and advisee may reason in relatively detached manner regarding goals and personal equipment for attaining them.

[7] See H. H. Remmers and R. H. Bauernfeind, *Your Problems: How to Handle Them*, Science Research Associates, Inc., Chicago, 1953, Bernice L. Neugarten, *How to Get Along with Others*, Science Research Associates, Inc., Chicago, 1953, and N. W. Newsom, H. R. Douglass, and H. L. Dotson, *Living and Planning Your Life*, Harper & Brothers, New York, 1952.

Measuring Devices

By means of objective measuring devices, it is in degree possible to discover biological and social capacities, attainments, specific shortcomings, aptitudes, and potentialities. With varying degrees of validity and reliability of the instrument used, starting points, progress, and prognosis may be estimated both by the guidance specialist and by the persons who are seeking assistance in setting up reasonable and desirable goals. These instruments are analogous to those used by a physician as partial bases for his diagnoses, prescriptions, and advisements; in a few cases they are the same.

For guidance purposes, the need for reliable measuring devices is peculiarly acute because of the subjective quality and general inadequacy of traditional school marks, examinations, promotions, and certificates. All these institutionalized symbols serve as rewards and punishments for school behavior and attitudes as well as crude measurements of abilities and achievements. Moreover, they are found to vary with the moods and personal idiosyncrasies of those whose judgments are the bases for marks and other symbols of adequacy.

Standardized tests and rating scales have, to be sure, greatly refined the processes of evaluation by making more precise the quality and quantity on which judgments are based. More socially significant, however, is the lessening of emphasis on competition among pupils to "beat" someone else; each comes to be judged in terms of relatively impersonal "norms" or definitions. The tendency is to evaluate each according to his starting point, capacity, growth, and promise.

Valuable as these objective ratings of achievement have been, there have nevertheless remained sharp differences between what the school values highly and what contemporary society otherwise requires and rewards. Hence, more exact and valid instruments to measure native aptitudes and emotional factors have been developed.[8] Temperament and aptitude tests and interest inventories are, to be sure, more useful in selecting workers for particular jobs than in aiding individuals to choose suitable occupations.[9] Nevertheless, their virtue for the guidance specialist is great, in so far as they present to the pupil and his parents objective and relatively reliable and valid evidence on which to base their choices.

[8] G. Frederick Kuder and Blanche B. Paulson, *Discovering Your Interests,* Science Research Associates, Inc., Chicago, 1953.
[9] George E. Myers, *Principles and Techniques of Vocational Guidance,* McGraw-Hill Book Company, Inc., New York, 1941, pp. 140–141.

Beyond that the school cannot go. Just as effectiveness of instruction requires of the learner a willingness to abide by instruction, so guidance would be meaningless unless the one to be guided wants the service. And in cases of immature or frustrated individuals—those who peculiarly need guidance—such willingness cannot be assumed.

THE GUIDANCE ORGANIZATION AND ORIENTATION OF THE SCHOOL COMMUNITY

The authors do not discount the importance and the potential value of the utilization of scientific instruments in guidance. Their emphasis, however, is on something far more fundamental. They are concerned that the spirit and procedures of guidance in choice making and in achieving the goals implicit in the choices shall come to characterize education at all levels and in all segments of the population.

Herein is found the sweeping challenge to the administrative and teaching staffs of public schools and to voluntary and official social service agencies. The guidance organization of the school system and of each unit should be so planned, administered, and activated as to encourage choice making at appropriate ages in the light of realities and possibilities; thereby it will foster the maturation of pupils and their adult associates. To accomplish such a goal, guidance staffs need pay much more attention than they generally do to the resources inherent in other community institutions—familial, religious, and civic.

Fortunately, such guidance organization finds counterparts in the voluntary cooperation between adults and young people outside the school. Authoritarianism and compulsion in families, neighborhoods, and municipalities, decrease in frequency, potency, and social approval. Conversely, persuasion, reasonableness, patience, compromise, and experimentalism increasingly characterize public safety, social service, and other reform agencies. Community councils, parent-teacher associations, organizations for children and youth, and even political parties advocate and instrument reasonable choice making. Indeed it is a fundamental tenet of the democratic philosophy that, if given freedom to make their own decisions, human beings will become mature to the degree that they will face the consequences frankly.

SUMMARY

The revolutionary changes that have characterized American social establishments during the nineteenth and twentieth centuries are still in process. The society is future-oriented and dynamic; it places a high value on individualism. The interrelated developments of science, technology, and government have provided both encouragement for human aspirations and instrumentations for their fulfillment. Coercion, whether sanctioned by "authority" or by custom, is called in question; in many cases it is rejected.

Freedom to make up one's own mind, share in the determination of one's own destiny, and challenge all arbitrary compulsions is the American heritage from the humanist past and especially from the evolution of the middle classes in the Western world.

In the United States, great prosperity has relieved the majority of the people from the degradation of poverty and dependence, temporarily at least. Even during economic depression, however, most youths and adults maintain faith that better times and opportunities lie ahead.[10] The right to share in the product of the economy is assumed; with it goes an expectation of participation in decision making. American children grow up in an atmosphere of questioning.

Explanation and persuasion supersede command in all aspects of life where voluntary participation comes to be highly valued. Even in military and industrial organizations, although chains of command and unquestioning obedience to orders properly retain status, great emphasis is put on morale building, "orientation" processes, guidance, and opportunities for each to utilize his peculiar abilities constructively and, in degree, individualistically.[11] In familial and neighborhood institutions—church, club, improvement association, and gang, for example —voluntary cooperation requires persuasion and example.

In such a cultural configuration, the public school undertakes the complex task of educating generations of young people. Academic stereotypes and symbols have little power over the minds of large numbers of these youth. Many of them accept compulsory school attendance reluctantly, both because the equipment of an intellectual elite seems irrelevant to their aspirations and because their American heritage encourages them to demand justification for all rules and requirements to which they are asked to conform.

This condition of affairs is reality. Questioning whether it ought to be so is rather futile, except as an academic exercise. The important problem has been and continues to be how to deal constructively with reality. And it is to this problem that the present chapter has been addressed.

Guidance tends to replace instruction and indoctrination in school because the desire to learn is of fundamental importance to

[10] See Howard Bell, *Youth Tell Their Story,* American Council on Education, Washington, 1938.

[11] "Leadership," *Field Manual,* U.S. Department of the Army, 1951.

effective education. Voluntary action requires the forming of purposes and the adoption of ego ideals which the school can help achieve.

Modern education, therefore, is directed to the stimulation and examination of choices by each pupil (and his responsible elders) of the self he wants to be. These chosen purposes may be for immediate realization or for later life. In either case, the school provides opportunities and encouragement looking toward their attainment. Guidance is defined as encouraging persons to set up worthwhile, reasonably achievable goals and helping them reach these goals.

In the rapidly changing American society, the school and its cooperating agencies for social melioration are especially important in aiding people to create goals for themselves. Human relationships in school, at home, and in the community are analyzed and, where necessary and possible, given special treatment. Objective evaluation of capacities and adjustment is utilized in helping individuals arrive at wise decisions regarding goals and means. And the modern, guidance-oriented school seeks to bring to bear all community resources which are useful in eliminating individual maladjustment.

SELECTED REFERENCES

Bell, Howard: *Youth Tell Their Story,* American Council on Education, Washington, 1938. Maryland youth's depression-years faiths, hopes, and doubts.

Bettelheim, B.: *Love Is Not Enough,* American Book Company, New York, 1950. How emotionally disturbed and delinquent children learn to live normal lives.

Davis, Allison: *Social-class Influence on Learning,* Harvard University Press, Cambridge, Mass., 1948. The relation of class membership and learning.

———, and R. J. Havighurst: *Father of the Man,* Houghton Mifflin Company, Boston, 1947. An influential work on child development.

Fine, Benjamin: *1,000,000 Delinquents,* The World Publishing Company, Cleveland, 1955. The challenge of delinquency in the United States.

Glueck, Sheldon, and Eleanor Glueck: *Delinquents in the Making,* Harper & Brothers, New York, 1952. An enlightening presentation of characteristics of potential delinquents.

Henry, N. B. (ed.): *Juvenile Delinquency and the Schools,* Forty-seventh Yearbook of the National Society for the Study of Education, Part 1, Chicago, 1948.

Horney, Karen: *Our Inner Conflicts,* W. W. Norton & Company, Inc., New York, 1945. A leading psychiatrist aids the layman to understand himself and his fellow men.

Hullfish, H. G. (ed.): *Educational Freedom in an Age of Anxiety,* Twelfth Yearbook of The John Dewey Society, Harper & Brothers, New York, 1953.

Kvaraceus, W. C., and others: *Delinquent Behavior: Culture and the Individual,* National Education Association, Washington, 1959.

————: *Delinquent Behavior: Principles and Practices,* National Education Association, Washington, 1959. The interdependence of contemporary morality accentuating adventure, aggressiveness, and "success," and of youthful patterns of values and behavior is clearly shown in both these works.

"Leadership," *Field Manual,* U.S. Department of the Army, 1951. A military manual.

Murphy, Gardner: *Personality: A Biosocial Approach to Origins and Structure,* Harper & Brothers, New York, 1947. The nature of personality.

Plant, J. S.: *The Envelope: A Study of the Impact of the World upon the Child,* The Commonwealth Fund, New York, 1950. A research study of personality formation.

Prescott, Daniel A.: *Emotions and the Educational Process,* American Council on Education, Washington, 1952. A monograph.

Redl, Fritz, and David Wineman: *The Aggressive Child,* Free Press, Glencoe, Ill., 1957.

————: *Children Who Hate,* Free Press, Glencoe, Ill., 1952.

————: *Controls from Within,* Free Press, Glencoe, Ill., 1952. Three excellent research volumes on disturbed personalities in children.

Shaw, C. R., and H. D. McKay: *Juvenile Delinquency in Urban Areas,* University of Chicago Press, Chicago, 1942. Research volume by two famous authorities on delinquency.

Strang, Ruth: *The Adolescent Views Himself: A Psychology of Adolescence,* McGraw-Hill Book Company, Inc., New York, 1957. The permissive range of the teacher-sponsor's "unobtrusive concern" mitigates young people's desire to assume authority.

Torgeson, T. L.: *Studying Children: Diagnostic and Remedial Treatment,* The Dryden Press, Inc., New York, 1947. Techniques and treatment through guidance.

Wickman, E. K.: *Children's Behavior and Teachers' Attitudes,* The Commonwealth Fund, New York, 1937. Influence of teachers' attitudes on the personalities and behavior of children.

DISCUSSION QUESTIONS

1. Explain an example of role playing by a young person that seems to you to have had marked effects on his personal adjustment, good, bad, or ambivalent. Do not limit yourself to play-acting roles. Does the explanation and evaluation of the example you have selected suggest to you how beneficent role playing might be practiced in other school settings than the one you described?

2. Give three or more examples of successful coordination of guidance efforts of school personnel with those of out-of-school agents, for example, parents, club sponsors, church officers, social workers, and employers.

3. Define the following terms and give examples of their application: project teaching, socialized recitation, group guidance, core-curriculum unit, pupil-teacher planning, and home-room advisement. Considered as instruments of guidance, what similarities and what differences in purposes and processes do you identify.

4. Among the criteria by which the study of mathematics, foreign languages, natural sciences, social sciences, logic, philosophy, and "great books" are justified by their respective advocates is the stimulation and improvement of students' reflective thinking. In the light of your own judgment after reflection on the presentation in this chapter, evaluate the claims for each of these disciplines.

5. The grouping of pupils for instruction either in terms of capacity for academic learning, special talents, or educational or vocational aims has been a bone of contention among educators for a half-century. What are the arguments pro and con? Would homogeneous grouping in any subject assure that the pupils would be much alike in specific skills? Would it make probable a reasonable homogeneity of interest?

6. Failures and drop-outs in high schools are variously attributed to lack of ability to do high school work, to boredom with school regimen, and to antagonistic attitudes toward authority, or to combinations of these with an often rationalized economic necessity. From your acquaintance with pupils who have failed to maintain satisfactory scholastic standings in high school or college, would you be inclined to rank these explanations in order of frequency and of importance?

7. In the case of scholastically talented and ambitious youths, is the prevailing assumption that they should be encouraged to carry heavier academic loads and thereby try for advanced placement on entering college acceptable to you? What of the alternative of enriching their pres-

ent lives with some aesthetic, practical arts, social service, or other more or less nonacademic activities?

8. One strong consensus of participants in a recent Children's Bureau Conference was that "early in the child's life the school system should begin to channel many lower-class youngsters into programs that would help them to develop a successful school career." (See D. J. Bordua, *Sociological Theories and Their Implication for Juvenile Delinquency,* U.S. Department of Health, Education, and Welfare, 1960.) Is such channeling possible in a school that maintains high academic standards? What are some of the opportunities and limitations of the guidance processes in endeavoring to make universal school success possible?

9. American college students are increasingly selected on the basis of results of group-testing programs. Is there danger that, with the burgeoning of such testing practices at high school and college levels, the guidance process will tend to become "norm-oriented" and somewhat mechanical? If guidance in a democracy is to exalt the individual, his values, attitudes, and outlooks, does the selection of students on the basis of group tests endanger the personal counseling function? If so, is money for test programs under the National Defense Education Act truly spent for "the direct guidance of the pupils"? In this connection, read and report to the class on H. J. Peters, "Testing or Testomania," *The Clearing House,* vol. 35, no. 11, pp. 141–144, 1960.

20

The Creative Community
School

THE CHANGING ROLE OF COMMUNITY EDUCATION

Self-determination, individualism, and personal liberty are relative privileges; the degree to which they are acceptable to one's associates is limited in any case and varies with changes in the climate of public opinion. Hence, if public education is to promote efforts by pupils and others reflectively to evaluate, choose, and seek to attain goals, the social environment in which the reasoned life is to be lived must be taken into consideration.

To the extent that the democratic school's spirit, processes, and other institutional characteristics penetrate and become integrated into the culture of patrons—and vice versa—the term "community school" may properly be applied.[1] Such integration, wherever vigorous and effective, is accompanied by volitionally active school personnel—pupils, faculty, custodians, school-board members, and other citizens. School-community collaboration to achieve social purposes within a framework of democratic values encourages the creativity of all participants. Such

---

[1] "Community-centered school" and "community-integrated school" are, perhaps, more precise terms for such an institution.

448

collaboration progressively exemplifies, in purified and idealized form, the processes and aspirations of American democracy.

The Community School and Democracy

The creative community school is a great democratic adventure. It is like a ship launched in uncertain waters. The personalities that are at once its goals and its instruments are fluid, responding variantly to complex and ever-changing stimuli. Every social action (and most actions have social concomitants) is at once the expression of personality, culture, and the social system.[2] Social customs, morals, and other stereotypes set limits to the overt expressions of unique personalities, to be sure, but the inward effects of such limitations on the individual are themselves multifarious.

Somehow, pragmatic resolutions of the varying factors that control human behavior work themselves out. Motivations necessary for societal survival, or for the survival of any segment of humanity, are provided by a matrix of transcendental values, sacred, secular, or both. It is not strange that in such a heterogeneous society as the United States the transcendental values held to be "truths" by one group may be disregarded or even denied by other groups. Hence, there are always potential clashes of opinion and standard.

The tasks, concerns, problems, and ideals of each child, youth, or adult must ultimately be resolved for himself. His solution requires an integration of a selfhood that accommodates itself to the persons and institutions whose approval he values highly.

The school curriculum interjects into the processes of cultural transmission deliberately selected educational challenges and practices that, it is hoped, will enable the individual to achieve adequate self-adjustments within the social configurations of his everyday life. But the modern school faculty is well aware that, for the most part, those self-adjustments must be registered in many interrelated and conflicting social situations, of which the school is only one.

The Role of the State

The intrusion of the state into a social process, which under former cultural patterns was the responsibility of parents, priests, and other purveyors of the mores, has inevitably aroused considerable contention among supporters of religious, class, and family authorities. They do not deny the political importance of formal education. They do, however, assert that state domination is at least potentially dangerous, in

[2] Cf. Talcott Parsons and E. A. Shils, *Toward a General Theory of Action,* Harvard University Press, Cambridge, Mass., 1952, and Talcott Parsons, *The Social System,* Free Press, Glencoe, Ill., 1952.

that it could lead to indoctrination on behalf of interest groups that might control the nation's political life.[3] They maintain that religious values, or family rights, or class mores, or combinations of these, are primary and that the state's interest in the matter is limited to the legal protection of individual safety, health, and morals.

It is the genius of Anglo-Saxon democracy that such conflicts are resolved gradually by compromise. Hence, American law and custom do not deny the rights of parents, of churches, and of status and other special-interest segments to maintain their own educational institutions. Indeed, in some respects, they are encouraged and subsidized: the public school teacher serves *in loco parentis;* private nonprofit schools are tax-exempt; in some states, transportation and health services are provided at public expense for pupils who attend private nonprofit schools. Reciprocally, private schools and family training respond favorably to the same community moods and beliefs that control political policies and acts. Their adaptations are often made laggardly, to be sure, but such conservatism may be beneficent in so far as it preserves traditional values.

The point to be emphasized here is that in the highly industrialized American society, the political role of the school is increasingly important. Such is true not because a "monster government" seeks to impose its will on individuals and sects (although such authoritarianism may be a remote possibility even in America), but because the opportunities and problems that face individuals and groups everywhere require governmental intervention for safeguarding and promoting those transcendent values that give meaning to the society. The day of the self-sufficient individual or locality, if indeed it ever existed, has passed beyond hope of recall. The community school serves community-conditioned individuals and organizations.

"To Govern Is to Educate"

In a society in which "everyman" not only may vote for political candidates and measures, but also may share in deciding what kinds of goods and services will find a market and what "spiritual" and "religious" beliefs and practices will be tolerated, popular government is in large degree popular education. Informal as well as formal referendum is part of the democratic pattern; temporarily at least, it is the court of last resort. "The battle for men's minds," the struggle between "good" and "evil," and confusing misunderstandings and polemics among those

---

[3] The reader is reminded that "political" as here used refers to governmental policies and institutions, not to political parties.

who favor popular indoctrination of "right" beliefs and behaviors and those who put their faith in freedom of enlightened men to choose, all reflect the inescapable force of public opinion.

From the point of view of social stability, democracy is dangerous to its own fulfillment. Competitive, economically insecure, and emotionally disturbed men, bemused with prize fights, glamorous television shows, "keeping up with the Joneses," and equating "the American way" with luxurious living standards, are fair game for the charlatan and demagogue. Professional educators have a double fight on their hands: first, to keep themselves reasonably free from prevailing popular moods that sanction pompous display, hatred, and coercion, and, second, to gain and retain the confidence and support of those organizations and individuals which are in some way concerned with popular enlightenment and freedom of choice. The latter is frequently complicated by the partial character of adherence to freedom; a person may advocate freedom to evaluate in the field of art while denying it in religion, economics, or nationalism.

If the schoolman expects all-out support for all the projects in which the faculty and pupils engage, he will be disappointed. Few men have progressed to a point where they would accord to all their fellow men complete freedom to act or even to believe according to their own reason. The realistic, progressive educator, therefore, solicits support for specific freedoms and enlightenments, in the hope and expectation that successful applications of the logic of enlightened freedom in any human endeavor will soften opposition to freedom in other areas.

Faith that free men will, under propitious conditions, prove willing to grant equivalent freedoms to other men is a basic premise of democratic ideology. Hence it pervades all educational institutions in so far as their processes accord with the American ethos. It characterizes democratic schools, democratic families, democratic churches, and democratic youth-serving organizations. The school and the community are shot through and through with examples of these mutually reinforcing processes, each one perhaps partial and specific, but all potentially contributory to a democratic society.[4]

[4] Even in military organization, that great stronghold of hierarchical authority, education becomes a dominant instrument of control. Though termed "indoctrination" and "morale" measures, enlightenment and persuasion tend to replace the absolutes of command and the negative motivation of punishment. The growth of specialization in the service has especially encouraged these syntheses of education and authoritarianism, for an unwilling pilot, mechanic, or scout is a liability.

THE ROLE OF ELITES IN AMERICAN DEMOCRACY

The democratic evolutionary process has been fruitful for human comity. Consciously and unconsciously, it is based on a faith that variant "truths," if allowed to compete peaceably for general acceptance, will in time evolve into valuations broad enough that elements of all the "truths" may become integrated within an American ethos.

Controversies frequently threaten the very process, to be sure; advocates of a specific "truth" are all too likely to desire to compel its universal acceptance. Such zealots are unlikely to be finicky regarding the means they use to force their faiths on their fellow citizens. Americans are a geographically, genetically, and economically heterogeneous people. Social stability and orderly progress toward American goals are presumed to accompany multiple reconstructions of rather capricious experiences.

It has always seemed necessary to responsible citizens that such chance experiences be supplemented by education in democratic values, lest controversy and exploitation get out of hand. Various elite groups have proposed their own programs for fostering what they have understood to be the general welfare.[5]

The Educator as One of the Elite

In the contemporary United States, the schoolmaster is charged with fulfilling such an elite role. His professional functions are theoretically nonacquisitional; he is presumed to act on behalf of the social will to make democracy work. Similar roles are assigned to, or assumed by, others, for example, statesmen, the judiciary, the clergy, and foundation officials.

That these presumed elites often falter is part of the risk implicit in the democratic adventure. That too frequently their members confuse their idealistic selves with their acquisitive selves is inevitable in a society that grants major prestige to the accumulation and display of wealth.

Sometimes excessive emphasis characterizes these elites. The clergyman may overstress creed; the bureaucrat, administrative efficiency; the schoolmaster, authority. It is not easy for a dedicated person to maintain humility.

[5] John S. Brubacher, "The Public School, an Example of the New Social Order," *School and Society,* vol. 44, no. 12, pp. 761–768, 1936. The author reviews progressive programs to promote responsibility for public welfare through education advocated by elites and eventually accepted by the electorate.

Elite devotion to social welfare may be largely a myth; but if so, it is a good myth. It establishes one standard by which professions and individual citizens are judged. Civic responsibility does assure social recognition.

Democratic improvisation, with its "hits" and its "misses," is held to its ideals largely because these elites, however serious their shortcomings, do fulfill their roles with at least partial success. The opportunistic politician, once he achieves public office, can seldom altogether avoid social responsibility. The lawyer who becomes a judge finds himself accountable to plaintiff, defendant, and public. The relatively self-centered teacher becomes institutionally controlled to foster pupil welfare, parental cooperation, and faculty morale.

AMERICAN LIKENESSES MORE SIGNIFICANT THAN DIFFERENCES

People at all ages are engaged in doing things which are stimulated by their biological drives and social incentives, and which in degree are influenced by "intelligence." The things that need to be done are not fundamentally unlike, though the manner of their doing varies widely in different societies and subsocieties. Getting and spending, homemaking and child rearing, practicing authority and responsibility, mutual aid, competition and conflict, maintaining health, loyalty to institutions, and acceptance of myths and conventions—such behaviors characterize all human communities.

In modern heterogeneous societies, many subgroups are likely to be in process of modification partly by the social effects of the economic revolution. The "resolution of forces" in a particular locality and at a given time seriously influences, if it does not altogether determine, the acts, aspirations, and valuations of most people.

Frame of Reference of the Community School

However great and however desirable are the differences of opinion among Americans, the nation is irrevocably launched on the great adventure of creating democratic ways such that government of, by, and for the people shall establish justice, insure domestic tranquillity, provide for the common defense, promote the general welfare, and secure the blessings of liberty to people now living and to posterity. Herein is found the inescapable framework within which Americanism functions. Anything that lies outside this frame of reference has no place in the program of American education.

However inert and neglectful in action American citizens may be in supporting the achievement of their democratic goals, acknowledgment of their desirability is almost universal. It is on this fundamental likeness that the school and its allies build. Moreover, from this American postulate are derived criteria by which the functioning of schools may be evaluated.

Effective educational institutions, therefore, are intentionally meliorative. The school endeavors to reinforce selectively "moral" behaviors and standards in so far as they are judged to promote the ends for which society supports educational institutions. In ways appropriate to their ages, it seeks to guide children, youths, and adults toward acceptance of these selected moral behaviors and attitudes. It establishes its own regimen so as to make such attributes habitual and satisfying. Thus the school in a democracy fulfills a unique function: that of conservator and critic of personal and social values.[6]

PUBLIC EDUCATION AS A POLITICAL INSTRUMENT

It is by the selective reproduction (within the school and in the extra-school environment) of conditions propitious for "purified" and "idealized" motivations, practices, and satisfactions that the community school functions creatively. Justification of such mission on the part of schools is implicit in the idealized function assigned to government in the Declaration of Independence: governments are instituted among men to secure certain "unalienable" rights, among which are life, liberty, and the pursuit of happiness. Similarly, the Preamble to the Constitution of the United States declares its purposes. Obviously, American governmental institutions, including the public school, have a mandate for positive meliorative action. Mere reflection of the *status quo,* mere transmission of an unselective social inheritance from generation to generation, if it were possible, would be worse than abandonment of mandated function; it would be social treason.[7]

To be devoted to the fulfillment of a uniform social mission does not require agreement among educators regarding specific measures by which the goals are to be reached. The "ways of democracy" are many and diverse; there is no single "truth" regarding means whereby life, liberty, and the pursuit of happiness are best to be fostered. Indeed, there is room for considerable disagreement among men of intelligence and good will regarding precisely what the ideals themselves imply. Cer-

[6] See Charles A. Beard, *The Unique Function of Education in American Democracy,* National Education Association, Educational Policies Commission, Washington, 1937.
[7] Private, nonprofit, tax-exempt educational institutions are assumed to fulfill a similar public function and hence to accept the same social mandate.

tainly, individual differences in capacity and temperament are such that one man's meat may be another man's poison.

HALLMARKS OF DEMOCRATIC EDUCATION

The Educational Policies Commission of the National Education Association and the American Association of School Administrators published in 1940 the results of a comprehensive study of practices in American schools as they related to the promotion of democratic ways of living. From the practices found were formulated twelve "hallmarks" by which effective democratic educational programs can be identified.[8]

1. Democratic education has as its central purpose the welfare of all the people.

2. Democratic education serves each individual with justice, seeking to provide equal educational opportunity for all, regardless of intelligence, race, religion, social status, economic condition, or vocational plans.

3. Democratic education respects the basic civil liberties in practice and clarifies their meaning through study.

4. Democratic education is concerned for the maintenance of those economic, political, and social conditions which are necessary for the enjoyment of liberty.

5. Democratic education guarantees to all the members of its community the right to share in determining the purposes and policies of education.

6. Democratic education uses democratic methods in classroom, administration, and student activities.

7. Democratic education makes efficient use of personnel, teaching respect for competence in positions of responsibility.

8. Democratic education teaches through experience that every privilege entails a corresponding duty, every authority a responsibility, every responsibility an accounting to the group which granted the privilege or authority.

9. Democratic education demonstrates that far-reaching changes, of both policies and procedures, can be carried out in orderly and peaceful fashion, when the decisions to make the changes have been reached by democratic means.

10. Democratic education liberates and uses the intelligence of all.

11. Democratic education equips citizens with the materials of knowledge needed for democratic efficiency.

[8] *Learning the Ways of Democracy,* National Education Association, Educational Policies Commission, Washington, 1940. By permission of Educational Policies Commission.

12. Democratic education promotes loyalty to democracy by stressing positive understanding and appreciation and by summoning youth to service in a great cause.

THE SCHOOL'S CREATIVE ACTIVITIES SELDOM CHALLENGED WHEN COOPERATIVELY UNDERTAKEN

Voluntary collaborations for achieving mutually desired objectives are so characteristic of American life that they are socially sanctioned within all organizations. The community-related school moves on firm ground, therefore, if in each of its areas of educative practices it reproduces selectively and piecemeal, as it were, the motivations, experiences, and satisfactions already discernible and respected in homes, stores, industries, "cultural" circles, and governments.

In large degree, the community-related school thus rejects in practice the "residual" concept of education; that is, that the school should avoid doing for pupils and patrons anything that other social institutions can do for them. Rather, the creative school approaches the ideal as expressed by John Dewey:[9] "what the best and wisest parent wants for his own child, that must the community want for all its children." If the personal and social values which the school fosters accord with the transcendent purposes of America, there need be little fear of duplication of effort. It is indeed by the effective reconstruction of experience and the frequent applications of skills to meet new emergencies successfully, that problem solving progresses and that character is itself formed.

THE CREATIVE SCHOOL EXEMPLIFIES BETTER SOCIAL ARRANGEMENTS

The school, as the community's purposive telic instrument, is likely to function most effectively if outwardly it conforms in gross respects to the public stereotype. There is a school plant—a building of dignified appearance, landscaped lawns, suitable play areas, classrooms, offices, and specialized equipment. There are teachers, custodians, and administrators who are presumed to "know their jobs." At the school are happy and busy young and older people. "Lessons," "student activities," school honors, school hours, report cards, home assignments, and a dozen more fragments are parts of the stereotype. A board of education, representing the public's aspirations and prejudices and its willing-

[9] *The School and Society*, University of Chicago Press, Chicago, 1900, p. 19.

ness to provide financial support, is advised by professional administrators and other educators and authorized by state law to control the operation of the school system.

Professional employees of the board of education seek and find opportunities to promote educational measures for the community that so far as possible do not violate the generally accepted patterns of "the school." They are sensitive to popular moods, gauging when, how fast, and how far to press forward with reforms and innovations that have already been approved by consensus of the staff, the board of education, parent-teacher associations, and other civic bodies. Often, indeed, the professional staff, having arrived at an approximate agreement regarding desirable modifications in school arrangements, becomes the prime mover in stimulating a popular mood to approve and support the change.

The creativity of school personnel—the staff, the pupils and patrons, and the board of education and its lay consultants—is always central in importance. Constructive participation of all school-related persons is fostered, both in anticipation of desired changes and during their execution. Administrative authority is tactfully restrained; in any case, it is merely a delegated authority.

Consultative Character of Leadership

Responsible leadership in a voluntaristic society is chiefly consultative in character. Enlightenment, persuasion, and self-determination require participation of the members in examining relevant factors, estimating needs for change and the probable concomitants and outcomes of changes undertaken, formulating policies and programs, and executing them. Tentativeness and flexibility in the carrying out of the advocated measures permit unconvinced individuals and minorities to give cautious consent to the innovation.

The school system or individual school that thus proceeds exemplifies in great degree the processes by which the progressive American community works out its problems. In the American democracy, consent to change is mandatory, not because "that is the law," but because a militant minority of dissenters can make the reform unworkable. In reproducing within its institutional framework the best characteristics of the community's changes-by-consent, the school engages the creative capacities of very significant sections of the entire population—children, youths, and adult students, the professional staff and their associates, parents and other well-wishers for young people, and civic groups proud of their communities.

Democracy as "Tolerable Disorder"

Even so, cross-purposes, disagreements, and "false" valuations will doubtless develop. After all, democracy is "tolerable disorder." Its very endurability facilitates "second thoughts," amendments, and reconsiderations, the safety valves for hasty action.

It would be naïve to believe that in any society or in any organization of human beings, however favorable conditions might be made, men singly or in association would always and universally act, think, and feel in accord with some preconceived pattern. An acquisitively motivated society, wherein initiative, self-reliance, reflective thinking, and foresight are stimulated and honored, can maintain only such uniformity of behavior and outlook among its members and subgroups as the self-interests of majorities of the population will support and enforce. And in a social and political democracy, the areas of such agreement are rather nebulous and changeable, consisting of verbal symbols for ill-defined moods and aspirations. Abstract as the consensus is, however, it has so far met the pragmatic test; the inevitable disorder has been, and promises to be, tolerable. Certainly no return to absolutism of church or state or to feudalism would be tolerable for an industrialized society.

THE SCHOOL FOSTERS INDIVIDUAL AND GROUP AUTONOMY

The school as an intentionally meliorative agency postulates the tolerable disorderliness of ideas and behavior among pupils, teachers, and patrons. Individually and collectively, to be sure, they adjust in the main to conventional patterns of dress, behavior, verbal symbols for ideas; so a considerable degree of overt order and regimen are attainable. But deviations and "over-adjustments" [10] present constant hazards to uniformity of institutional processes. No two persons or events call for the same treatment, not even the same person or event on different occasions.

The autonomous individual is, of course, influenced by cultural traditions and the valuations implicit in his childhood conditioning.[11] His uniqueness is characterized by his self-awareness, his freedom to choose whether, and in what degree, to conform to social norms, his willingness to reexamine the justification for his in-group valuations, and his

[10] "Over-adjustment" means extreme docility and avoidance of overt self-expression. Cf. David Riesman and others, *The Lonely Crowd,* abridged ed., Doubleday & Company, Inc., New York, 1953, p. 92.

[11] *Ibid.,* p. 29.

readiness to base his beliefs and actions on the outcomes of reflective thinking and experimental adaptations.

Conservatism of Social Systems

Cultures and social systems are by nature conservative. Presumptions favor their mores and structures. Heresies are seldom examined before the heretic is adversely judged. However restrained the autonomous individual may be in expressing his uniqueness overtly, nevertheless he cannot join the conforming members of his set in condemning that which his own reflective thinking evaluates as good.

Autonomy and uniqueness, even when they reflect cogent thinking rather than mere countersuggestion, do present potential danger for public order. One may *choose* to be a thief, a charlatan, a destroyer, a bully, or an exploiter of "individual rights." Selective restraint of autonomy is obviously justified. The fostering of socially advantageous, or at least harmless, personalities by schools is intended to minimize the necessity for manifest restraints on nonconformity.

The Mission of the Community School

The creative community school finds its major mission therein defined. Selectively reproducing the institutional and individual practices and valuations of the community, the school seeks to provide opportunities, guidance, and satisfactions for all persons within its influence. Valuations of the character traits which the school fosters and rewards with social esteem are resultants of both transcendental ideals and pragmatic sanctions. Practicality is compatible with the continuing practice of the "spiritually" valued virtues.

CHARACTERISTICS OF THE CREATIVE COMMUNITY SCHOOL

Varied in activities as the communities they serve, creative community schools have certain common characteristics, which are listed below and then discussed at greater length.

1. The intentionally planned and cooperatively administered school is an environment of multiform purposeful activities engaged in collaboratively by children, youths, and adults, and fostered and subtly guided by professional educators. It is in such an environment that the potentialities for the development and cultivation of socially constructive autonomous individuals are present.

2. The curriculum for such a school environment consists of all the activities and experiences fostered by these educators to help the

participants engage satisfyingly and constructively in school and community undertakings.

3. The faculty of such a school seeks to guide individuals and groups of individuals toward the attainment of worthy characters.

4. Experiences and guidance are planned and executed so as to reinforce those activities and traits judged desirable; and, conversely, to offset those activities and experiences judged undesirable.

5. Within the limits of civic morality, the community school is as inclusive as the society it serves. It accepts all people it can attract, and makes as adequate provision for them as means and ingenuity permit. It encourages success of some sort for each individual, taking due account of his social and natural inheritances.

6. The success of the school is judged by its stimulation of pupils, teachers, and adults in the community to desire to learn, to seek answers for their own questions, to feel secure in their competence to think and act independently, and to desire for all other human beings the liberties and securities they seek for themselves.

7. The provision of opportunities for individual and group initiative and success requires the recruitment of autonomous persons into the teaching profession. Over-adjusted persons who uncritically accept the conformity reflected in most conventional, subject-centered schools are almost certain to feel frustrated if they become teachers in a creative institution. Similarly, persons whose values are closely limited by their childhood inheritances have difficulty in appreciating the desires and standards that are adapted to modern science and technology.

This emphasis on the recruitment of relatively autonomous persons for membership in the creative community school staff does not imply lack of faith in the power of skillful supervisory leadership to help teachers grow toward mature personalities while in service. Rather, it is a plea that progressive schools should not "stack the cards" against the fulfillment of their purposes. It is a difficult enough job to acquire teaching personnel whose characteristics are reasonably well suited to the development of autonomy in their pupils.

Multiform Purposeful Activities

Man shapes himself by his acts; he is the resultant of his behaviors. Education is fundamentally environmental; in controlled situations it fosters adaptations of whatever readinesses, skills, and knowledge each pupil has that seem to him most likely to meet the environmental opportunities and requirements. There is thus a continuity of his experiences in social institutions. Schools attempt to expedite the growth of responses deemed favorable to the socially efficient personality by increasing the probability of frequent and realistic experiences.

461

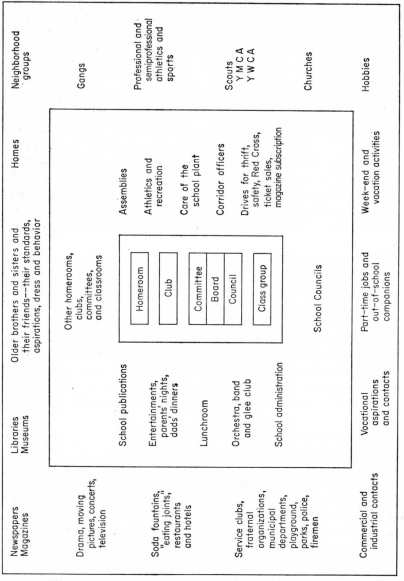

Figure 2. Developmental Organizations and Practices.

Figure 2 should help make this meliorative control of the environment clear. In the outer rectangle of the diagram are named typical developmental institutions and practices with which individuals interact according to their stages of growth. Some of these institutions and practices are intentionally selective and directive, in accordance with multivalent standards. Others have only such educational influence as the peculiar personality of an individual finds stimulating and satisfying. An automobile, for example, may challenge the mechanical aptitudes of one, the aesthetic valuations of another, and a need for release of a third.

Since many, if not all of these developmental factors determine the acts by which each individual creates and modifies his selfhood, analogous institutions and practices must characterize the controlled environments of schools and, in varying degrees and kinds, those of all other educational institutions. Hence the intermediate rectangle names some of the more usual instruments of forward-referenced schools in connection with which pupils are encouraged to contribute good will, talents, judgments, and examples, so that the project may prove satisfying to all concerned. In proposing, planning, executing, and evaluating each undertaking, adults and young people share, with as much initiative and responsibility allocated to the youth as possible without too greatly endangering its minimal success.

For purposes of rather intimate guidance and motivated instruction the school utilizes face-to-face groupings of pupils and teachers. Each group has some primary center of interest related to one or more of the undertakings of school and community life. Both pupils and teachers are selected (preferably self-selected) with this center of interest in mind. Typical primary groupings are named in the inside rectangle.

Curriculum Consists of All Purposively Controlled Activities and Experiences

There are obvious institutional limitations to the degree of interest selection that is possible in subject-class groups, especially in the case of curriculum prescriptions. Hence the need for such radical modifications as the "core" or "integrated" curriculum innovations whereby, for example, language arts, literature, social studies, and personality guidance are correlated under the direction of specially equipped teachers. In elective curriculum subjects, at high school and college levels, there may more safely be assumed a greater degree of voluntary participation on the part of students and, hence, a more willing acceptance of assigned learnings. But in all subject classes, from primary grades to university graduate schools, emphasis on learners' creativity and on appropriate school-related community activities and concerns characterize effective education.

Fortunately, the school at all levels is able to foster groupings that are less restrained by stereotypes than is classroom subject teaching. Interest groups of many kinds are spontaneously formed wherever young people are brought together; their centers of interest may range from playing of games to scientific research, from social-status cliques to civic services, and from mutual admiration groups of art enthusiasts to ventures for economic gain. The creatively controlled school encourages and makes adequate provision for as great a variety of constructive primary groups as feasible.

Guidance Characterizes In-school and Extra-school Processes and Relationships

The continuing association of one professional adult with a relatively small number of young people, as in the elementary classroom, is extended upward in modern educational institutions through the secondary years to graduate work in universities. As a corrective for the fragmentation of pupil-teacher contacts implicit in departmental organization of faculties, secondary schools frequently maintain home rooms; home-room teachers seek to stimulate cooperative (often school-community oriented) projects among their advisees. They seek to help pupils to solve their individual and group problems, sometimes involving school situations, sometimes home and neighborhood conditions, but almost always ensuring their own sense of security and adequacy for successful participation in activities that are highly valued by their peers. In higher education, much the same functions are assigned to tutors, housemasters, and advisers.

School boards and their executive officers, in their relations with the professional personnel, subordinate compulsion and regulation to guidance of cooperative planning and execution of projects. Creative community schools are likely to develop only where state and local educational authorities conceive the teacher's role to be that of a professional practitioner who acts according to his own best judgment on behalf of the community. In a program of multiform purposeful activities involving patrons and pupils as well as teachers, hundreds of discriminating decisions must be made daily, decisions too numerous, too varied, too immediate in many cases for specific reference to "higher authority" or to imposed regulations, except in the most general terms. The school community learns to take minor inconsistencies and errors in stride as inevitable accompaniments of spontaneity and pragmatic adaptation. Analogous mistakes and inadequacies characterize families, churches, governments, and all other institutions.

The Creative School Reinforces Desirable and Offsets
Undesirable Traits and Circumstances

The school cannot successfully instruct anyone as to how he should resolve his own quandaries, but it can (and in the case of the dynamic community-centered school does) act successfully as a coordinating agency whereby selected experiences find encouragement and are assured satisfaction. In the school, there is so great a mingling of prejudices and promises, such eagerness to achieve group success, and such frequent self-discipline as to make effective adaptations of personalities to the alternating and variable roles of leadership and followership probable. The likelihood is great that the emerging characters of pupils, teachers, and associated individuals will tend to correspond to the realities of democratic social life.

Experiments with controlled environments—autocratic, democratic, and laissez-faire—as they affect the personalities and group qualities of children provide clinical evidence to support America's faith in democracy. The "mask" of adaptation, voluntary contribution and conciliatory acceptance of group judgment, and alternating assertiveness and submission, become in degree the "persona." [12]

The composite American, as an ideal and in great degree as actuality, is at once assertive and submissive, self-reliant and resourceful, but ready to shrug off defeat and rejection, curious and manipulative, but complacently conventional in accepting the products of science and technology that he uses without trying to understand them. For good or for ill, he is the product of the totality of the particular America he has experienced.

The farm and village youth and adult, the slum dweller, and the suburbanite differ radically, to be sure. But so nearly universal are mobility, spontaneity, and desire for recognition that in essentials Americans tend to be greatly similar. Technological changes interspersed by social emergencies call for and reward aptitudes, familiarities, and other traits that have been "learned" empirically just by sharing in segments of American life. Thus the widespread practices of tinkering with machines, of "making-do" and creating substitutions, and of alternating leaderships in gangs, sports, and other organizational activities underlie

[12] Kurt Lewin, "Experiment in Autocratic, Democratic, and Laissez-faire Atmospheres," *The Social Frontier,* July, 1938 and *Principles of Topological Psychology,* trans. by Donald K. Adams and Karl E. Zener, McGraw-Hill Book Company, Inc., New York, 1936. See, also, Goodwin Watson, "What Are the Effects of a Democratic Atmosphere on Children?" *Progressive Education,* vol. 17, no. 5, pp. 336–342, 1940.

the ingenuity and adaptability characteristic of American soldiers, work-men, politicians, and executives.

In the multifarious environment in which the "ideal" American creates himself, the community school finds rich opportunities for selec-tive reinforcement. It finds, too, many excesses and imbalances that call for meliorative measures.

The Community School Is as Inclusive as the Society It Serves

The school through its activity program functions first of all as a coordinating and stabilizing institution, by reproducing in the areas of its influence occasions and facilities which enrich and give order to community life as well as foster self-realization, civic competence, and economic efficiency for each individual. School environment and self-selected aspects of community experience thus become reciprocals; what one learns as a family member, an employee, a consumer, or an enthusiast in the realms of sports, health, religion, mechanics, court-ship, the arts, and aesthetics finds counterparts in the school.

As a coordinating institution, the school makes no pretense of being *the* educational establishment. It takes full account of the actual and potential agencies and other factors—ideas, moods, and economic conditions, for example—that affect for good or ill individual adjust-ments and group valuations. Thereby, it influences the development of members of the community.

There remain, to be sure, vestigial popular stereotypes of the school as a social isolate, an esoteric, "ivory-tower" abstraction special-izing in verbalisms, techniques, and symbolisms (including marks, cred-its, and diplomas) peculiar to scholastic education. Such "schooling" continues to be a somewhat artificial prerequisite for conventional social and economic advancement and for the practice of certain technical professions.

These institutionalisms retain prestige, to be sure, but they do not suffice as motivation and reward for students' efforts. Pupils bring their community-fostered traits and values with them into the school environment; the institution may modify and perhaps redirect them but it cannot ignore nor altogether supplant them. Rather reluctantly, extra-school has become accepted as extra-curriculum; in turn the extra-cur-riculum now merges with, and to a degree replaces, the curriculum.

Self-realization and the Life-adjustment Curriculum

From the point of view of the educand, school-related life is the curriculum. If the faculty does not provide opportunities for the practice of adjustments characteristic of the community-culture patterns, pupils introduce them into the school-related environment anyway. If sex appeal, athletic prowess, conversational "lines," gang membership, and sophistication are felt needs for youth in their efforts to gain recognition, the learning of the knowledge and skills required to meet these needs are of first importance to them.

If state laws responding to economic conditions and social and civic aspirations make school attendance compulsory until the ages of sixteen, seventeen, or even eighteen, and if a great majority of adolescents are going to determine their own curricula anyway, not only does the traditional academic curriculum become futile, but also any faculty-determined superimposition is only halfheartedly submitted to by many high school "students." Less dramatic, but scarcely less real, are similar impasses at both lower and higher school levels.

It must be emphasized that any attempt to derive a school curriculum by studying the nature and needs of children, youths, or adults, or by examining the political, economic, cultural, or other social conditions which they do now and probably will continue to face is likely to be somewhat futile unless the educand brings his self-concern into the curriculum. In selected areas of high school and collegiate elective subjects, such self-concern may perhaps be assumed, but certainly not elsewhere. If a problem be not *his* problem or a project not *his* project, his learning is bound to be conformist rather than self-involved.

Personal and Social Concerns of Children and Youths

If we keep this caveat clearly in mind, however, it is obvious that an inventory of actual or probable concerns that characterize human beings as they grope toward maturity may be very helpful to educational policy makers. On the one hand, it should warn of probable failures if some concerns are ignored; on the other hand, it does indicate areas and aspects of the culture wherein adjustment problems imply needs for enlightenment and other character modifications. Such inventories, whether based on replies to a researcher's questions or on systematic analyses of observed behavior, are of course limited in reliability to the time and place and to the social status of the persons studied. Nevertheless, comparisons of results of approximately parallel researches indicate many continuing concerns that are reasonably general for age groups, and, indeed, for the population as a whole.[13]

[13] Committee on Problems Study, *An Inventory Study of the Personal and General Social Problems of 256 Students in Grades Seven to Twelve, Inclusive,* The Ohio State University School, Columbus, 1940, Howard M. Bell, *Youth Tell Their Story,* American Council on Education, Washington, 1938, Donald C. Doane, *The Needs of Youth: An Evaluation for Curriculum Purposes,* Bureau of Publications, Teachers College, Columbia University,

Corey distinguishes five developmental tasks of youth: coming to terms with their own bodies, building new relationships to their age-mates, achieving independence, achieving adult social and economic status, and gaining self-confidence and establishing their own system of values.[14] These tasks are set by our democratic society. Accomplishing them is mandated if mature membership in the community is to be gained. They fulfill the initiatory requirements, as it were, of contemporary society; hence their dynamic quality.

However necessary these achievements may be for personal security and recognition in the community, they are significant to the educator only as minimal essentials for inclusion in school opportunities. He is properly concerned with the kinds and levels of attainment in each task. His valuations take account of desiderata for the "good life" and for the aspirations of social democracy. Therefore he endeavors to establish a school-community environment and to provide adequate guidance and instructional personnel and facilities to the end that people, according to their respective needs and potentialities, may adjust to their own physiques, their fellow men, their strivings for independence, adult status, and self-confidence, all within a configuration of social and personal values consonant with the purposes of America.

Herein are the social-ethical, often termed the "spiritual," justifications for public education. Basic to democratic aspirations are the assumptions that individual freedom can reconcile itself to conformities to law, custom, and good taste, and that the "orderly disorder" implicit in the continuing compromises of such reconciliations may be both stable enough and flexible enough for nonviolent accommodation to an accelerating, relatively impersonal technological and economic revolution.

In the tentative, often evanescent, valuations implicit in such pragmatic adjustments, education's socio-ethical function is somewhat baffling. For there are no precise *right* ways of behaving, *truths* to accept, *knowledge* to learn, *correct* attitudes, *laws* to obey, *rules* to follow, *gods* to fear and cajole, or unquestionable *facts* to accept, except as tentative conveniences, hypotheses, or frameworks of custom to keep social arrangements peaceful.

New York, 1942, Ruth Eckert and T. O. Marshall, *When Youth Leave School*, McGraw-Hill Book Company, Inc., New York 1938, and The Welfare Council, *The Youth of New York City,* The Macmillan Company, New York, 1945.

[14] Stephen M. Corey, "The Developmental Tasks of Youth," in Hollis L. Caswell (ed.), *The American High School*, Eighth Yearbook of The John Dewey Society, Harper & Brothers, New York, 1946, chap. 5.

Professional Personnel for Community-oriented Creative Education

Readjustments of the school institution to coordinate its educational program with those of other meliorative agencies of the community are retarded by various obstacles. The most manifest of these obstacles has been the continued recruitment, certification, and retention of professional personnel whose qualifications are judged in terms of obsolescent educational values and practices. The stereotypes of lesson mastery, formal discipline, and esoteric "culture" are deeply engraved both in scholastic institutionalism and in the minds of many patrons. Indeed, some otherwise progressive school administrators have not clearly distinguished the relation between what they wish the school to accomplish and the qualities of the mediating personnel.

If the community-oriented school is to function most effectively, a dynamic segment (desirably all) of the teachers, counselors, custodians, and other school-related persons who ex officio influence pupils and public should be actively and constructively engaged in community projects and associations. That desideratum is unlikely to be realized unless individuals who compose the personnel are acceptable to potentially constructive institutions and segments of the population. Hence there is need for school staffs to represent catholicity of social-status origins and familiarities and of civic, cultural, aesthetic, and sectarian interests and associations. Flexible, outgiving personalities are essential for an effective school staff.

If community-concerned teachers, attendance officers, guidance specialists, and playground directors are to be predominant in school staffs, teacher-preparatory institutions will be required to recruit and train, cities and states to certify, and local boards of education and administrative officers to select and assign to schools candidates with outgiving personalities and of varied origins and enthusiasms.[15] Once appointed, the staff member must be encouraged to act autonomously among pupils and public. Community schools need some representatives who can display erudition and social graces; but they need quite as truly some staff members acceptable to labor-union groups, cultural minorities, and gangs and coteries of young people in all neighborhoods.

[15] Cf. Philip W. L. Cox, "Should Teachers Be Certified on Credits Earned or as a Result of Examinations?" *New York State Education,* vol. 26, no. 10, pp. 31–33, 1938. And Allen D. Patterson, "Teacher Certification—Credits or Competencies," *Educational Research Bulletin,* vol. 23, no. 12, pp. 233–239, 1944.

DOES THE COMMUNITY SCHOOL SLIGHT THE FUNDAMENTALS?

Conservative educators, though they may approve in principle the community orientation of the school, hesitate to endorse what seems to them to be a revolutionary break from the school's historical functions, those of transmitting the academic social inheritance and of providing the knowledge and skills required for advanced study and for civil and vocational pursuits. They believe that the school should stick to fulfilling its traditional mandate; if other social welfare services are desirable in the community, specific provisions for them should be made by governmental and voluntary agencies.

Conservative Criticisms of the Community School

Except for such groups as the Council for Basic Education which would limit community orientation to imparting such information and attitudes as might be derived from history and literature courses, conservative critics of modern schools are not hostile to efforts to reinforce the programs of such other-than-school agencies. They insist, however, that such collaborations be supplementary to carrying out the historical purpose of the school, that of teaching and learning the facts and processes provided by authority of text and teacher. Such are the espoused "fundamentals" from primary grades through college—and in degree even in graduate schools!

Two kinds of comments seem called for, one negative, the other positive. In the midst of social change, there is no certainty of authority, whether it be sought in religious dogma, good English usage, scientific hypotheses, mathematical theorems, historical interpretation, etiquette, or canons of art appreciation. What was right or correct yesterday may be questioned today and discarded tomorrow; a dynamic society fosters inquiry, reflective thinking, and experiment by its members.

Changing social conditions require changing conceptions regarding what is truly fundamental for meliorative agencies to foster in the community. However complex social interactions may be—indeed, because they are so complex—each person grows into membership in the community by experiencing participation in its ongoing life. This is the *fundamental* process to which all agencies, for weal or woe, contribute.

The Learner Is One

The learner, whether six or sixty, is one person. His adjustments and adaptations cannot be broken into segments and assigned, some to school, others to occupation, church, or recreation. To be sure, one agency may be in more favorable position than another to affect a specific aspect of desirable behavior and knowledge. But to the degree that it attempts to isolate its unique function by disassociating itself from agencies devoted mainly to other functions, it fails even in its restricted field. The transfer of its training to community life requires application to that life. And, conversely, it requires that its training itself must be derived from situations and standards typical of contemporary culture.

The school purifies and idealizes the situations and standards which it reproduces, but it cannot ignore them if it is to function meaningfully. It is they, and not tradition, that determine what is *fundamental* for each person's integration into community life. In all constructive fields of human endeavor, there are needed men and women who can get along with one another and with their superiors and subordinates, who can stand ridicule, persevere in the face of jealousy, resist discouragement, and control their anger. School knowledge and skill unless life-related and applied in the learning are soon neglected and forgotten. Only as they are equipment for the individual's ego image as family member, neighbor, citizen, player of games, and job holder can they be retained and grow.

Humanities, Science, and Practical Arts

At high school and college levels, the term "fundamentals" is less often belligerently used by critics of modern education than it is at the elementary school level. The bias in favor of bookishness and lesson learning for examination purposes and "mental training" is, however, similar to that of advocates of concentration on the school arts in the lower grades.

The conservative stereotype of secondary and higher education goes back to the Greek idea that intellectual wonderment, inquiry, and dialectics constitute a "higher" kind of life than application and experimental experience. In practice, such a divorce has never been realized; it has been certain forms of application that have been denigrated, for example, trade, manufacture, and physical toil. The arts of the military, fine arts, oratory, courtiership, philosophic discourse, and amateur sports have at one time or another belonged to the "of course" category of legitimate goals for the education of adolescents and young adults. They have been encased in the code of the educated gentleman.

Vocational education as a proper function of secondary and higher education has experienced a similar selectivity in popular acceptance. Medicine, law, and theology in the medieval universities carried in their train craft training and "natural philosophy" (the forerunner of science). They fostered observation and classification, pointing the way toward empiricism. And the independent group life of the students, though regretted and resisted, was accepted as inevitable.

Nevertheless, the tradition of the "liberal arts" (linguistics and mathematics) has remained; even in the contemporary United States, with a culture so strongly shaped by technology and experimentalism, the term "liberal arts college" is commonly used for nonspecialized higher educational establishments. In practice, to be sure, these colleges have admitted the natural and social sciences to their curricula, in earlier days, reluctantly because they belonged to the category of "materialism" whereas the "liberal arts" were alleged to contribute to man's "spiritual" nature.[16] Moreover, either by subject election or by designated sub-curricula, college students began specialization looking toward vocations. Nevertheless, the title "liberal arts college" has provided a degree of justification for defenders of the medieval faith in deductive reasoning based on "first principles" or "natural laws" as an "intellectual" and hence a "spiritual" discipline achievable only through the seven liberal arts: grammar, rhetoric, logic (the trivium), and geometry, arithmetic, astronomy, and music (the quadrivium). These were supplemented during the Renaissance by Aristotelian philosophy and Latin and Greek literature (called the "humanities" because they dealt with *man's earthly* life).

"Polite" Learning

Modern liberal arts colleges, despite their inclusion of natural and social sciences in the curriculum and despite the compromises with the applied arts and vocational preparation, retain the prejudice in favor of "polite" learning: what the "educated gentleman" should know and be as one who "looks first of all to his life as a responsible human being and citizen." [17] This humanistic bias infuses the "general education" [18] prescriptions of contemporary liberal arts colleges to preserve so far as possible the traditional conception of liberal education.

This presentation of the "liberal arts" and "humanistic" approach to the education of free, community-concerned citizens is pertinent for consideration of the creative community school both because

[16] This dualism, deriving from the philosopher René Descartes (1596–1650) asserts that human nature, like the universe, is made up of material (body) and spirit (or mind or soul). Only material substances obey scientific and mechanical laws.

[17] Harvard University Committee on the Objectives of a General Education in a Free Society, *General Education in a Free Society*, Harvard University Press, Cambridge, Mass., 1945.

[18] Also called "broad-fields," "fused," and "integrated" courses.

the objective is the same and because of an implicit contradiction between the assumptions regarding the sequence of educational experience. Skepticism of many academic educators concerning intentional community involvement by the school reflects their bias toward deduction as opposed to induction, toward knowledge as erudition as distinct from knowledge as firsthand experience, and toward college preparatory study as a self-denying, docile learning of assigned lessons in textbook or syllabus-organized subjects, chiefly extrinsically motivated. Their adversely critical attitude toward intrinsically motivated social-civic and individualistic school-related experiences, in some cases, includes even general courses in high school analogous to those the colleges themselves organize.

Humanism and liberalism are not something taught by colleges superimposed on a preparation that minimizes immediate human problems and freedom of experience. One learns liberalism and humanism by practice in being free and in association with human beings and their institutions. Within the limits of whatever institutional guidance and protection are needed at stages of maturity, modern humanism is a prime goal of education in homes, churches, governmental agencies, and all other meliorative community institutions, including schools. The humane values fostered by contemporary law, medical, engineering, theological, and educational schools on the graduate level are consistent with those characteristic of democratic families and primary schools. Geology and physics, business management and forestry, history and sociology, all have quite as great a potential as literature and philosophy for liberating man from ignorance, superstition, dogmatism and from narrowness in ideas, doctrines, and sympathies, to a belief in freedom in educational, political, social, religious, and other institutions.[19]

SUMMARY

The school is affected by all the ramifying and kaleidoscopic interplay of feelings and activities in the families and neighborhoods

[19] Cf. J. Crosby Chapman and George S. Counts, *Principles of Education,* Houghton Mifflin Company, Boston, 1924, pp. 486–487: "Knowledge is but one element in the making of a 'free man.' An individual is liberated not by information and by great learning, but rather by an attitude toward life. To be able to see two sides of a question, to realize ignorance, to appreciate expert service, to feel an abiding obligation to study and direct the course of social life, to be public spirited, to recognize the claims of national and international obligations, these are the hallmarks of the man whose education has made him free." By permission of the publisher.

that compose the school community and in intermediate and secondary groups with which families and neighborhood institutions are associated. As individuals and as groups, the people respond to many inconsistent motivations, whose dynamism varies almost from hour to hour among segments of the population.

Because these various motivations (socioeconomic ambitions, fears and fervors, escapes from boredom, and consequent welcoming of excitement) characterize community life and affect the personal adjustments of children as well as of adults, most vital learnings take place quite apart from the traditional school curriculum. Orientation to this situation requires that the public's official educational agency derive its curriculum and practices from contemporary and readily foreseeable motivations and responses. Only so can the school, at any level or in any specialized function, reach potential learners at points where they are actually ready to learn.

In a word, the life-adjustment community-oriented school is concerned chiefly with the personal and social concerns of children, youths, and adults who now compose the population that the school is established and maintained to serve. Because character modifications take place within the highly complex individual organism, all education is self-involved; it is creative for good or for ill.

Because significant learning situations are community-derived and community-applicable and because the learnings are creative self-adjustments in any case, the function of the school is to emphasize selectively those community experiences and values that are already vigorously operative in the individual. The complexes of purposes and activities and the varied satisfactions characteristic of modern life may thus be refined and enriched. The following two chapters of this text are devoted to descriptive explanations of pioneering public educational ventures which, in part or entirely, successfully fulfill the roles of creatively controlled community schools.

SELECTED REFERENCES

American Council on Education: *Cooperative Study of Secondary School Standards, Evaluation of Secondary Schools,* Washington, 1939.

————: *Evaluative Criteria,* Washington, 1950. Continuing the search for and application of standards for schools which seek approval by one of the regional associations of colleges and secondary schools. A basic assumption of the cooperative study group is that each school must determine its own educational philosophy and practices.

Apprenticeship, National Committee on Employment of Youth, New York, 1960. Explains in brief form one aspect of the changing pattern of industrial education.

Barzun, Jacques: *Teacher in America,* Doubleday & Company, Inc., New York, 1954. A persuasive apologia for a rather sequestered literary conception of public eduction. Very comforting to many adverse critics of universal secondary education.

Brophy, Julia R.: "Citizenship Training and Character Development," *Bulletin of the National Association of Secondary School Principals,* April, 1945. A stimulating treatment of these problems.

Brown, Spencer: *They See for Themselves,* Harper & Brothers, New York, 1945. A documentary approach to intercultural education in the high school.

Collier, Paul D.: *The Redirection, Reorganization, and Retooling of Secondary Education,* Connecticut State Department of Education, Hartford, 1944. A program for the reorganization of secondary schools.

Collings, Ellsworth: *An Experiment with a Project Curriculum,* The Macmillan Company, New York, 1923. The earliest scientifically evaluated adventure in community derived curriculum reform.

Conservation in Camping, U.S. Department of Agriculture, 1952. A product of a workshop on conservation of the American Camping Association.

Cox, Philip W. L.: *Creative School Control,* J. B. Lippincott Company, Philadelphia, 1927. The school as an environment favorable for vigorous participation in processes characteristic of constructive community living.

Dunbar, R. M.: *How Libraries May Serve,* Education and National Defense Series, Pamphlet 17, U.S. Office of Education, Washington, 1941. Though prepared in connection with the war emergency, the recommendations hold for contemporary communities.

Education for All American Youth, Educational Policies Commission, Washington, 1943. A prophesy of school-community integration.

Education for All American Youth: A Further Look, Educational Policies Commission, Washington, 1953. A reinterpretation of a study published ten years earlier.

Education in Rural Communities, Fifty-first Yearbook of the National Society for the Study of Education, University of Chicago Press, Chicago, 1952. Useful contributions on community education in rural areas.

Gaumitz, W. H., and G. S. Wright: *Broadening the Services of the Small High School,* U.S. Office of Education, Washington, 1948. A survey of successful practices.

Guernsey, S. K. (chairman): *Education and Florida's Future,* Florida Citizens' Committee on Education, Tallahassee, 1948. A summary report on provisions for education in Florida and potentialities for further steps.

Holland, Kenneth, and E. L. Bickel: *Work Camps for High School Youth,* American Council on Education, Washington, 1941. Program for productive work camps.

Industry Programs for Youth, National Committee on Employment of Youth, New York, 1959. Discussion of industrial education programs and training for young people.

Lorwin, L. L.: *Youth Work Programs: Problems and Policies,* American Council on Education, Washington, 1941. An important statement of problems involved in organizing work programs for youth.

Mearns, Hughes: *Creative Power,* Doubleday & Company, New York, 1929.

————: *Creative Youth,* Doubleday & Company, New York, 1925. Two books that aroused a considerable section of the teaching profession to a recognition of the artistic resources of ordinary youths and adults.

Munro, Thomas, and Herbert Read: *The Creative Arts in American Education,* Harvard University Press, Cambridge, Mass., 1960. Proposals for overcoming the current alienation of art from life.

Olsen, E. G. (ed.): *School and Community,* Prentice-Hall, Inc., Englewood Cliffs, N.J., 1945. A useful textbook.

Programs of the Federal Government Affecting Children and Youth, Government Printing Office, Washington, 1951. The coordination of many federal agencies in several major departments to foster cooperative endeavors to serve young people.

Reller, T. L. (ed.): *The Public School and Other Community Agencies,* in *Annals of the American Academy of Political and Social Science,* November, 1955. City planning to foster coordination of social agencies for better community living.

Sanders, Irwin T.: *Making Good Communities Better,* University of Kentucky, Lexington, 1950. Analyses of community betterment programs.

Stendler, Celia B.: *Field Projects and Problems in Educational Sociology and Social Foundations of Education,* The Dryden Press, Inc., New York, 1956. Helpful units dealing with delinquency, religion, and pressure groups as they interrelate with the school.

Swift, F. H., and J. W. Studebaker: *What Is This Opportunity School?* American Association for Adult Education, New York, 1932. A study of Denver's pioneer tax-supported Opportunity School.

Thornton, J. W.: *The Community Junior College,* John Wiley

& Sons, Inc., New York, 1960. The scope and functions of the local public junior college.

Willis, B. C. (chairman): *Vitalizing Secondary Education,* U.S. Office of Education, Washington, 1951. Report of the First Commission on Life Adjustment Education for Youth.

Youth Work Camps, National Committee on Employment of Youth, New York, 1959. If schools and industry find collaboration in employment and education of youth of high school age, some attention must be paid to the problem of continuing welfare and education of "drop outs." The pros and cons of youth work camps are presented by Hubert Humphrey.

DISCUSSION QUESTIONS

1. In what respects does the best school at any level known to you provide a creative environment for pupils, teachers, patrons, or public, or any combination of them? Set down in paragraph form five of its more dynamic aspects and two or more further measures the school might take to carry its creative program further.

2. Describe and evaluate the collaborations between the high school you attended and one or several youth-serving organizations. Was any constructive measure taken to integrate gang or coterie associations into school activities? If not, might there have been?

3. What anticipatory education should a high school offer for youths who will be called into military service after leaving school? Does military service supplement, reinforce, or conflict with the school's mission to foster civilian virtues? What is your evaluation of President Kennedy's Peace Corps program?

4. As a prospective subject teacher, can you relate your subject to the everyday other-than-classroom concerns of pupils and their out-of-school associates? Explain the opportunities that you as a subject teacher might exploit. How would you deal with the public and professional stereotype that teaching your subject thoroughly is the sole mission of a subject teacher?

5. Whence the term "life-adjustment curriculum"? Has the popularizing of the phrase and the promotional work to actualize life adjustment hastened the modification of school-subject prescriptions, promotion and graduation standards, guidance provisions, and eligibility restrictions of a school known to you? Do such changes as you identify evidence a debilitation of school scholarship?

6. Apply the hallmarks of democratic education to the elementary, secondary, or collegiate institution of most interest to you. Can you justify aspects of its practices that seem to you to conflict seriously

with the hallmarks? What suggestions have you for modifying the institution, the hallmarks, or both?

7. Cite a municipal, state, or national governmental measure which seems to you to depend for success primarily on public education or propaganda. Does such education or propaganda characterize most governmental action? How does the example you cite compare with the adoption, promulgation, and enforcement of school rules that you have been required to follow?

21

The Community and the Pioneering School

BUILDING PUBLIC SUPPORT
FOR THE COMMUNITY SCHOOL

In great degree, every public school is community-oriented, if only by its status as a tax-supported institution. In every local community there is a high correlation between popular sensitivity to social and civic needs on the one hand and the extent of support for public schools on the other. The professional personnel of progressive schools exploit the essentially educational character of all community groups whose endeavors are consistent with popular well-being.

At any given time, a school and the community are likely to present a kaleidoscopic pattern of cooperative and competitive social, civic, economic, and aesthetic projects. Educators take account of abilities of social agencies and groups to collaborate; but also they assess the probable conflicts of interest that may ensue. Educators know that human beings, whether as individuals or as groups, learn best when conflict of interest is minimized. Hence the school's major efforts, at least in the early stages of school-community cooperation, are directed toward goals that are already generally approved.

Such goals exist everywhere and always. Extension and enrichment of recreational opportunities, health and safety measures, eco-

478

nomic self-help, beautification of homes and public buildings, encouragement of educational activities of child and youth-serving agencies,[1] and the fostering of good taste in public dress and behavior are almost certain to enlist approval and support from patrons.

To implement many of the programs designed to offset or minimize adverse conditions and to foster improvements deemed immediately desirable, a number of nonschool organizations are already functioning. Among them may be mentioned the American Red Cross, Associated Charities, Travelers Aid, community chests, various child-service and youth-service organizations, peace and reconciliation societies, and many other associations.

Timing and Choice of Projects

In specific localities and under special circumstances everywhere, public temper sometimes favors school participation in meliorative projects that elsewhere, or at other times, might be forbiddingly controversial. An appropriate committee of the parent-teacher association or a citizens' advisory council, with the consent of the board of education, sometimes serves effectively both in helping to determine what collaboration should immediately be undertaken and also in stimulating vigorous welcome for it among individuals and agencies of the community.

As successful community collaboration is developed, moreover, local and state boards of education and their executive officers come to be chosen in considerable part on the basis of their community consciousness. The assurance of sympathetic understanding by these officials engenders confidence among pioneering teachers. It also encourages local agencies and groups to expect school collaboration and to evaluate the services of school personnel in terms of their participation in community life.

In such school-community collaboration, advantage is taken of acute public concerns, at every opportunity, in order to foster discussion, reflective thinking, planning, and collaboration. Leaders in educational ventures may be parents, municipal officials, civic reformers, members of service clubs, chambers of commerce, college clubs, employers and employees in commerce and industry, or public school teachers. Whoever they may be, they are on occasion members of the school-community "faculty" by virtue of their functioning.

[1] In the cases of agencies offering creedal indoctrination and those devoted to other sectarian beliefs (for example, ethnic groups and political partisans) cooperation is usually limited to noninterference and accommodation.

MECHANISMS FOR BUILDING PUBLIC SUPPORT

In community-oriented schools, four often overlapping, generally successful procedures are distinguishable: (1) the self-survey of local community conditions, (2) patron-teacher-pupil collaboration to determine school and other-than-school responsibilities for children's education, (3) the mobilization of human resources of the community to deal with educational needs and opportunities, and (4) school recognition for other-than-school educational experiences and attainments.

The Self-survey

The community self-survey is a peculiarly useful device for helping teachers and patrons understand the changing orientations of school education. It serves the dual purposes of identifying aspects of community life that call for immediate attention, and of promoting cooperative planning to which citizens of all ages can contribute effectively.

Such a survey may have as its immediate subject a specific set of conditions, for example, the adequacy of playground areas, nutrition or sanitation among slum dwellers, or part-time job opportunities for pupils. Or the subject may be more general, for example, traffic conditions, distribution and mobility of population, government costs, or economic resources. The survey may be initiated and conducted by teachers alone, by teachers and pupils, or by pupils on their own. In many cases, the condition studied requires little more than careful observation, collation of data, and presentation of findings and recommendations to class, staff, or parent-teachers associations. In other cases, more elaborate and meticulous procedures are required.

Such a self-survey is almost certain to arouse the interest of many citizens whose assistance is required in order to gather the desired information, to interpret and evaluate it, and perhaps to collate and present the findings to influential groups. Often some or all these citizens will be concerned with needed public action to correct or otherwise improve situations made evident by the survey. Very likely they will welcome further assistance by school personnel.

Areas of Importance for the Self-survey

Brown[2] suggests eight areas where surveys of community conditions are likely to have important implications for the public schools: (1) population trends and mobility, (2) the composition of population in terms of racial and nationality characteristics, (3) the economic

[2] Francis J. Brown, *Educational Sociology*, 2d ed., Prentice-Hall, Inc., Englewood Cliffs, N.J., 1954, chap. 22.

status of the local community, (4) types and adequacy of housing, (5) provisions for earning a living, (6) service agencies of all types, (7) the organization and functions of local government, and (8) community health, accident rate, or juvenile delinquency.

The school staff generally limits its official efforts to assuring the accuracy of the survey findings and, with official approval, to furthering collaboration with citizen groups which school personnel are invited to undertake. However, individual teachers, like other citizens, may properly act to publicize remediable conditions indicated by the survey and to participate in measures for their improvement.

Collaborative Assessment of Educational Goals and Responsibilities

The determination of the educational goals of a school and the community is the concern of all who are responsible for the promotion of the good life of the community. It certainly is not a private affair of school-centered instructors of subjects.

It is an enlightening experience for intelligent parents to consider the kinds of persons they want their own and their neighbors' boys and girls to be now and in the future. Quickly they become aware, if they are not so already, that the primary responsibility for many of the factors involved in the development of individuals is centered in the home, and that the school, the church, municipal and other governmental and youth-serving organizations can do no more than supplement the home in its efforts to foster desired qualities.[3]

It is equally beneficial for pupils to face frankly what their desired roles in life are and in what ways their present environmental interactions affect the likelihood that they and their fellows will attain their own ego ideals. Their participation in a parent-teacher-pupil collaboration to determine objectives and to allocate responsibilities for attaining these objectives directs their attention to the *other-than-self* aspects of educational outcomes, and it fosters a clear recognition of their personal responsibility for self-education.

Mobilization of Citizens as Resources

It should be evident that effective public and private social service organizations are engaged in much more than the correction of adverse conditions. Their long-term concern is for the betterment of the quality of human life. Only through the improvement of the moral and material environments to which individuals and groups respond is it

[3] If a child's welfare is seriously endangered by parental incompetence or neglect, a court may order more drastic action, for example, commitment, parental punishment, or parole.

possible to eliminate in large degree the sources of social and individual ill-health.

In every locality, even in an economically lower-status area, there are to be found people who desire to improve living conditions within the district.[4] Their immediate concern may be specifically related to sanitation, morals, obedience to law, literacy, or opportunities for aesthetic expression. Or it may be more general, centering on economic aspects, recreational facilities, evening schools, or intercultural relations.

When community-oriented educators collaborate with these alert citizens, they frequently find that the majority of the members of the community exhibit at least spasmodic concern with one or another of these matters. Constructive efforts may indeed already be in process; church societies, youth organizations, art guilds, businessmen's clubs, neighborhood improvement associations, and municipal departments may be eager to collaborate. Overt recognition of their civic spirit frequently intensifies their own efforts and broadens their interest in social welfare.

School Recognition of Out-of-school Education

The fourth mechanism for building community support consists of various official expansions of the school's educational locus to include, for example, experiences in the home, camps, science laboratories, and private businesses. These ventures in coordinating the school's program with experiences away from the school building or outside of school hours frequently result in a high level of community support.

In elementary and junior high schools, recognition is frequently given for services and attainments connected with household duties and with membership in 4-H clubs, Scouts, Camp Fire Girls, Junior Achievement, church-related, and other socio-cultural organizations. At all levels, advantage is commonly taken of popular interest in drama, political campaigns, scientific exhibitions, fashions, and sports, whereby the school may foster selective experiences with communication instruments. Press and platform, exhibits and ceremonials, libraries and museums, and theater—whether experienced directly or through the agency of television, movies, radio, billboards, or conversations—become curricular. In partial fulfillment of scholastic requirements or as substitutes

[4] The Polish-American subcommittee on evening school enrollment at Solvay, New York, in 1914–1916, consisted of a grocer and two saloonkeepers. Not only did they recruit non-English-speaking adults for school attendance, but they also dedicated themselves to support the social-center program of the Board of Education. Moreover, they encouraged their fellow Polish-American citizens to vote in favor of adequate school taxes.

therefor, credit is frequently awarded for approved extramural experiences.[5]

Since school recognition of out-of-school educational attainments implies approval by local and state boards of education, the public may be assumed generally to sponsor the practice. Far more dynamic sponsorship, however, characterizes collaboration in the areas of applied arts—agriculture, industry, commerce, and, less frequently, music, art, librarianship, and youth leadership.

In connection with vocational curricula in high school and college, there are usually advisory committees of citizens representing segments of the population which have special interests in job preparation. In large trade schools, there may be a number of such committees, one for each type of occupation. The practical experience and special knowledge of these men and women serve to assure employers, patrons, and pupils that the requirements and specified experiences of the in-school and on-the-job curriculum are justifiable.

Beyond that, however, the committees themselves are likely to face up to the importance of other-than-technical qualifications that make for job success. If so, they become sponsors for the promotion of higher character traits, specifically for the trainees and generally for all young people. Economic efficiency, they become vibrantly aware, is inseparable from human relations, self-realization, and civic competence. Such is their prestige within intermingling population groups that they may aid influential members of the public to fix major attention on the quality of community life and hence of individual experiences as the goal of all education.

SCHOOL PROJECTS AND PROGRAMS AFFECTING THE COMMUNITY

In elementary schools, school-related community educational activities vary from selling Christmas seals and publicizing other welfare campaigns to gathering and destroying bagworm egg masses and cleaning up littered play areas. They include collaboration with parents and child-service organizations. Health and safety programs of the school require the informed cooperation of police, fire, health, and park departments of local governments, and, of course, of the family and neighborhood adults. Parents and their friends are invited to holiday and other celebrations and parties, for which many of them help formally and informally to prepare. Awards of school recognition to children are in

[5] See Philip W. L. Cox, *Curriculum-adjustment in the Secondary School,* J. B. Lippincott Company, Philadelphia, 1925, pp. 178–179.

part based on approved home and neighborhood services. There are vacation playgrounds, day camps, and other school-related environmental programs for children. Accommodations are generally between school and other child-nurture institutions—religious, health, "cultural" —to eliminate real or feared competition for children's time and loyalties.

The Community as "Center of Interest"

In occasional elementary schools, teachers, pupils, and parents accept a major aspect of the community as a "center of interest," the study of which provides opportunities for activities whereby associational and intellectual virtues are fostered. At the Ballard Memorial School in rural Kentucky, 1931–1934, for example, these interest centers were farms and farming in the first grade, study of the village in the second, pioneer living in Kentucky in the third, coming to Kentucky by trail and river in fifth and sixth, and Kentucky life in 1840 in the eighth grade.[6]

With appropriate modifications and adaptations, similar projects and programs are found in junior and senior high schools and at college and adult levels. Both individually and in associations, people eagerly undertake projects that they equate with high cultural value.

Many youths and adults are seriously concerned with the domestic and foreign policies of their country, concerns peculiarly intensified by the military service required of boys after school graduation. Orientation to contemporary economic problems and opportunities (budgets, consumer protection, supplementary earning skills, development of natural resources, and informed judgments regarding economic trends and potentialities) appeal to many pupils and patrons. Problems that face racial, ethnic, religious, and other groups are very real to many community members. All these varied interests vitalize the curriculum and the related activity programs.[7]

Such interests control procedures as truly as they do content; indeed, the two are in large degree inseparable. It may be fully as important to learn how to conduct a public meeting so as to foster consensus and increase collaboration as to acquire whatever information and to reach whatever decisions may result. How to encourage individual originality and inventiveness while maintaining group stability may be

[6] Elise R. Clapp, *Community Schools in Action*, The Viking Press, Inc., New York, 1939 *passim*.

[7] Paul Hanna and others, *Youth Serves the Community*, Appleton-Century-Crofts, Inc., New York, 1936, and Morris R. Mitchell and others, *Youth Has a Part to Play*, Hinds, Hayden and Eldredge, Inc., New York (reprinted from *Progressive Education*, vol. 19, no. 2, pp. 87–109, 1942).

quite as worth learning by the members of a group as any other knowl-edge and skill. How to mobilize the often latent concerns of local resi-dents on behalf of a constructive undertaking may promise more for community welfare in the long run than the successful completion of the specific project.

TYPICAL SCHOOL-COMMUNITY PROJECTS

Extended description of examples of community-oriented edu-cation is not feasible in this textbook. Each type, indeed each example of each type, would justify a book of its own; in fact, as the citations given on the following pages indicate, most of them have been described in considerable detail in available articles, reports, and books.

The authors here limit their treatment to somewhat unique aspects of examples of ten types of school-related community educa-tional ventures. These types are: (1) curriculum changes as responses to sociological factors, (2) the passing of the stereotype of "homework," (3) lay participation in modifying the school curriculum, (4) school-industry collaboration in vocational education, (5) cooperation between schools and other youth-serving organizations, (6) cooperation between schools and governmental agencies, (7) environmental controls pro-pitious for the constructive development of teachers, pupils, and patrons, (8) city school-community evening social centers, (9) public forums under public and private auspices, and (10) college-community col-laboration. Developments in rural community elementary schools and community-oriented public high schools will be described more fully in following sections.

Curriculum Change in Response to Social Change

For well over a century, the traditional curriculum at all scho-lastic levels has been the object of critical scrutiny, not only by educators, scientists, and skeptical practitioners, but also by many patrons and pupils. On the one hand, they have questioned the contemporary rele-vance of some prescribed learnings, at least for the age levels taught; on the other hand, they have urged the inclusion, either as constants or as electives, of subjects or topics that have obvious applicability to the daily lives of children and adults. Sociological criteria are implicit in these challenges.

In some cases, general observation of human activities and needs has provided adequate justification for the changes demanded. Since the turn of the century, however, relatively exact analyses of social practices and requirements have provided factual bases for many cur-riculum changes that have become almost compulsive. Many experts in educational measurements, minimal curriculum essentials, and curriculum making have relied on such analyses.[8] The criteria are well summed up in Briggs' "First Thesis":[9] The school should first of all teach children to do better those desirable things that they will do anyway. And one implication of this thesis is that information, skills, and other attributes that are not commonly practiced by young people and adults are of secondary concern for curriculum makers.

Scientific studies have been made of acceptable practices of craftsmen, businessmen, homemakers, students, and citizens in general; these studies have not ignored the shortcomings and the ideals characteristic of these various groups.[10] It is assumed that thereby norms and standards may be determined both for the inclusion of knowledge to be taught and for the levels of adequacy to be required of the pupils. Although such analyses are more obviously applicable to the standardized or generally accepted practices than they are to matters of personal taste and aptitude, they are not without relevance even in these individualistic spheres. Taste and aptitude are not exercised in a social vacuum.

It is obvious that in most areas of American life, the subdivision of labor, both in industry and in domestic and civic practices, has increasingly modified what young people will probably do anyway. Activity analyses, whether of plumbers, housewives, or automobile drivers, would not give the same data, or justify the same conclusions, in the 1960s as in the 1910s. A curriculum unit to be pragmatically justifiable must therefore be modified in the light of its probable applicability.

School-assigned Homework

Several concurrent changes in home situations, modified curriculum, the population base, limits of tolerance, and political affairs

[8] For example, J. Franklin Bobbitt, *How to Make a Curriculum,* Houghton Mifflin Company, Boston, 1924, W. W. Charters, *Curriculum Construction,* The Macmillan Company, New York, 1923, C. C. Peters, *The Curriculum of Democratic Education,* McGraw-Hill Book Company, Inc., New York, 1942, Committees on the Economy of Time in Education, four reports in National Society for the Study of Education yearbooks: *Eleventh Yearbook,* Part 1, 1915, *Sixteenth Yearbook,* Part 1, 1917, *Seventeenth Yearbook,* Part 1, 1918, and *Eighteenth Yearbook,* Part 2, 1919, The University of Chicago Press, Chicago.

[9] T. H. Briggs, *The Junior High School,* Houghton Mifflin Company, Boston, 1920.

[10] See Cox, *op. cit.,* chap. 5. Explains typical analyses of occupations, specific jobs, and processes that involve peculiar difficulties to be mastered.

have interacted to outmode much of the formerly conventional assumptions that lesson learning was to a considerable degree an out-of-class process, and that the class period was to be used in large part to discover how well pupils had done their assigned lessons. Most of such changes are so generally recognized, and their effect on the home study of school assignments so obvious, that merely noting them should suffice. Quiet and privacy characterize the evening hours in relatively few lower- and middle-class homes. Prestige for family or for student is not always sought by attaining high marks in school subjects; the mores of lower-status, and most new middle-class, young people and their parents do not generally place high value on studiousness. The newer and more dynamic aspects of the school curriculum—music, dramatics, athletics, business training, and citizenship, for example—do not lend themselves to the kind of home assignments to which begrudging attention was paid by some (not by any means all) young people and their parents half a century ago.[11]

Nevertheless, in community-oriented schools, there are frequent and fruitful reinforcing educational activities carried on by pupils both at school and at home. The effectiveness of class instruction and guidance in such subjects as health, art, home economics, literature, civics, general science, journalism, etiquette, and all vocational areas is judged largely in terms of the carry-over to out-of-school practices. Moreover, the mutual recognition given by youth-serving organizations and the schools for attainments in character, in practical efficiency, in leadership responsibility, and in many kinds of individualistic competence is effective in fostering types of "homework" not commonly called by that name.[12]

[11] It is doubtless true that some senior high school students have already well established goals, the achievement of which requires assiduous private study of preparatory subject material. In their cases, willingness to withdraw from the whirl of adolescent pasttimes and preoccupations in order to master scholastic assignments is certainly one evidence of their fitness to accomplish their self-imposed missions. Such are the vagaries and imponderables of human destiny, however, that this single datum is not conclusive for prognosis. The youth who at sixteen is preoccupied with heterosexual acceptability or athletic prowess may at twenty-two become a very earnest student of engineering, science, or "the humanities." It should also be noted that there has been considerable agitation for increased homework on the part of some school critics since the shock of the first Russian "sputnik" in 1957. Whether these demands are merely flurries which will pass in a few years or represent a relatively permanent desire remains to be seen.

[12] A bulletin issued by the New Hampshire State Education Depart-

At secondary and higher education levels, credit toward the fulfillment of requirements for graduation is awarded for satisfactory completion of many tasks and projects other than "lesson preparation." Such credit may be awarded for "work experience," home projects in agriculture, homemaking, and art, progress made in music, foreign languages, and other subjects pursued under private instructors, in correspondence schools, and for study abroad, in Europe or elsewhere. The justification for the practice is that many school-related accomplishments are feasible only in social settings other than those of the classroom.

Lay Participation in Curriculum Making

As patrons have come to recognize that the attainment of desirable traits by young people is the outcome of many social settings and individual natures, both they and school officials have appreciated that the role of education involves the intelligent cooperation of all adults who are ready to assume the role of educator. An early step in promoting such desirable collaboration is a clearly agreed upon definition of what traits are to be highly valued and at what age levels emphasis should be put on each; also the approximate relative responsibility for their attainment to be assigned to home, school, and to agencies that affect young people's traits. A single instance of such joint endeavor will suffice.

At Shaker Heights, Ohio, a comprehensive study of curriculum problems by pupils, parents, and teachers was carried on over a period of three years.[13] During the first year of the study, two small committees, each composed of pupils, parents, and teachers, studied needs *as pupils feel them* and the educational goals of American democracy respectively. Each committee was assisted by 950 tenth-, eleventh-, and twelfth-grade pupils.

---

ment in 1919 recommended that homework assignments for high school students conform to the types of activities that normally take place in superior homes. Three such types were set forth: (1) reading of books and magazines both in English and in foreign languages, for example, fiction, history, science, travel, biography, politics, and economics, (2) applied arts, for example, repairing, creating, playing musical instruments, singing, and decorating, and (3) social activities, for example, teaching Sunday School classes and participating in youth organizations.

[13] A. K. Loomis, "The Cooperative Study of Curriculum Problems by Pupils, Parents, and Teachers," *The High School Journal*, vol. 22, no. 12, pp. 328–330, 1939. Also summarized in H. H. Giles, S. P. McCutcheon, and A. N. Zechiel, *Exploring the Curriculum*, Harper & Brothers, New York, 1942, pp. 191–193.

Having arrived tentatively at the most important and pressing needs as the pupils themselves saw them, and having grouped them under twenty categories, the first committee asked the pupils, parents, and teachers to estimate whether the school was "solely responsible," "partly responsible," or "not at all responsible" for meeting each of the twenty categories of needs felt by the pupils. After the replies had been tabulated, the categories were again submitted to pupils, parents, and teachers who were asked, for each item: "Does the school now make adequate, inadequate, or excessive provision for meeting this need?" The second committee of pupils, parents, and teachers spent an entire year in a careful analysis of "social needs"; they arrived at ten propositions on which all pupils and parents were invited to express agreement or disagreement.

During the second year, twenty cross-section conference groups of pupils, parents, and teachers were organized. These conference groups considered committee reports dealing with (1) pupil needs, (2) educational needs of a democratic society, (3) types of experience suitable for meeting these individual and social needs, (4) methods of evaluating the outcomes of the program for meeting these needs, and (5) administrative arrangements for the attainment of the proposed goals. On the basis of an analysis of the results of these conferences and the replies to a questionnaire, the third year of the study was devoted to the preparation of a long-term program and the selection of next immediate steps.

The conclusions arrived at through this cooperative effort at Shaker Heights were not unlike those that any group of enlightened school people might have reached. The significant point, however, is not the quality of the conclusions; it is the assumption of responsibility for reflective thinking about purposes and functions of education by pupils, parents, and teachers.

> "Our experience leads us to believe," concludes Loomis, "that the cooperation of parents and pupils is essential in any fundamental revision of the curriculum. We have found the pupils even more helpful than the parents. No plan for community cooperation in studying the curriculum of the schools should fail to use the resources of unbiased, clear-thinking youth."

Often the participation of laymen in educational matters has been warmly welcomed by school personnel only when the need for public support has been rather poignantly felt. That citizens do generally, if somewhat laggardly, respond constructively to such invitations is an evidence of the general good will they hold toward the public school.[14]

[14] The National Citizens Commission for the Public Schools, with state branches, was formed in 1949 to rally support for measures

Lay instrusion into professional matters is inevitable when emergencies arise. It can scarcely be well informed if welcome is delayed until such intervention is unavoidable.

Resourceful administrators and teachers do not wait for emergencies. Public participation in critical appraisal of all aspects of the school's program and in collaborative planning and execution of improvements minimizes the likelihood of hostile attacks, because many vigorous citizens identify their own interests with those of teachers and pupils. In a word, the *modus operandi* of the internal regimen of a creative school and of its community relationships are analogous. In both aspects a "do-democracy" undergirds ideology; civic responsibility, human relations, and self-realization are successfully practiced as they are intellectually justified.[15]

School and Industry Collaboration
in Vocational and Civic Education

In Europe and the United States, much of the training for both trades and professions has emphasized "on-the-job" experience in mastering the techniques and meeting the standards acceptable to master craftsmen. Apprenticeships, internships, and probationary periods, even though in contemporary practice generally postponed until after scholastic qualifications have been attained, continue their essential functions of selection of those aspirants who are fitted by temperament and aptitude for the occupations and of providing needed practical experience.[16]

Part-time employment in commerce, manufacture, and agriculture, under the joint supervision of employer and school representatives (with earned credits granted toward completion of requirements by the school and, wherever labor is organized, by the union) now is general

---

for school improvements to meet the challenges implicit in the contemporary world. The Commission, during the ten years of its existence, rendered effective service in enlightening both laymen and professional educators regarding school needs, practices and potentialities.

[15] See *Do Citizens and Education Mix?* Governor's Fact-finding Commission on Education, Hartford, 1951.

[16] The function of the school in providing the preliminary training and some of the needed information basic to the occupation aspired to is not a new one. The arts of logic, dialectics, and oratory, the knowledge of law, medicine, ritual, mathematics, and languages have had vocational preparatory significance through the ages. Schools have, to be sure, often lagged; they have taught what might have been important for occupations yesteryear rather than in the present and foreseeable future. But their patrons have always assumed that somehow what they taught would have occupational value.

procedure for occupational school programs. Such academic recognition is based not only on technical competence and length of time served, but also on temperament, cooperativeness, and other moral and mental qualities.

Cooperation between Schools and Other Youth-serving Organizations

The developmental tasks of children and youths are carried on in community life regardless of whether adults consciously seek to influence them. In any case, the resulting traits reflect in great degree the values that adults of the family and neighborhood tolerate or exalt. Often these highly valued traits include narrow ethnocentrisms, disregard for inconvenient honesties, callous indifference toward cruelty, and competitive striving with little consideration for ethical niceties. Such often unacknowledged tolerances and exaltations are not by any means limited to the lower socioeconomic strata of the population. In varying degrees, they are almost universal.

Nevertheless, there are large numbers of citizens who have, in various ways, sought to aid youth in adapting to an inheritance of confusing and contradictory adult values.

As a result, many organizations have come into being to provide programs immediately applicable to young people's developmental tasks. Some of them work closely with the institutions they supplement; others develop independently, though eager to collaborate with already established groups. Christian Endeavor and the Holy Name Society exemplify the former; the YMCA and Girl Scouts, the latter.

The catholicity of the independent organizations is favorable for cooperative effort with schools and governmental agencies, since all are engaged in various ways with the same problems. The great advantage of the independent agency is its freshness and consequent freedom from the traditional restrictions typical of institutions. Even though it is supported in large part by public contributions and is therefore somewhat limited in its policies by the evanescent ebbs and flows of public opinion, the immediate appeal of its program, slogans, and symbols is selectively directed to forward-looking, liberal-minded publics. Any general retreat from democratic policies and practices, within its frame of reference, would not only vitiate its organizational activities but also would endanger its financial support.

The Young Women's Christian Association will serve as an example of such an independent youth-service organization. Founded in London by a group of devout women as an expression of "faith in God and love for their fellow-man," it seeks "to build a fellowship of women and girls devoted to the task of realizing in our common life

those ideals of personal and social living to which we are committed
by our faith as Christians." Its program of activities and services, at
first directed toward young employed women separated from their
parental homes, is now also concerned with high school and college
students, young wives, and co-ed groups, without discrimination regarding race, creed, or color. In this country over 300,000 "Y-Teens,"
junior and senior high school students, participate in clubs, classes, and
co-ed groups in programs of their own choosing under voluntary and
professional YWCA leaders. In these young people's organizations, the
spirit and practice of inclusive fellowship leads to the frequent support
of camps for teenagers and conferences abroad, the interchange of
gifts and letters among youths throughout the world, and the emergence
of volunteers who become leaders for younger or less experienced members.

This general pattern of purposeful guided activities, one that
characterizes many other youth-serving organizations, parallels in large
measure that of the creative community school with whose constructive
programs these organizations eagerly cooperate.

Cooperation of Schools and Other Governmental Agencies

The concern of the school for the health, home membership,
citizenship, economic efficiency, and creative enjoyment of leisure time
of young people is also a concern of many political and civic agencies.
Provisions for the physical welfare of citizens of all ages is a major
responsibility of municipal, county, state, and federal departments of
health, sanitation, public safety and order, parks and playgrounds, fire
prevention, and planning. Some of these departments have responsibilities for the prevention of neglect of or cruelty to children and adults,
for the control of potential and actual delinquents, for maintaining and
improving aesthetic standards and practices, for enforcing laws regarding
employment, trade practices, and other economic matters, and for the
provision of adequate recreational facilities for community members.

The faculty of a community-oriented school acknowledges its
responsibility in social organizations for human welfare. They welcome
every project by other public agencies to provide facilities, and other
conditions, propitious for the welfare of the community.

Not only does the classroom work of such a school frequently
draw upon, and contribute to, the projects initiated by other public
agencies, but also the extra-class activities find much of their motivation
and application in them.

In Solvay, New York, in 1915–1916, the occurrence of several
cases of typhoid fever in one section of the village stimulated public
concern about fly-breeding conditions. With the approval of the munici-

pal health and police officials and the board of education, the Junior Republic and the Junior Chamber of Commerce (in this case, organizations of junior high school boys and girls) made a rather meticulous survey, not only of the locality where the disease had appeared, but also of the entire school district and contiguous areas, prepared notification letters for the owners of uncovered garbage containers and other unsanitary places, to be countersigned by the chairman of the village board of health. Sketches of the premises indicated precisely the situations favorable for fly breeding in each case. These notifications were mailed, along with copies of the municipal ordinance applicable to the situation and of a state bulletin explaining both the suspected relation between the fly nuisance and the incidence of typhoid fever and the recommended measures for the control of fly-breeding conditions. In some cases where the nuisances were situated on public property or where private owners welcomed it, the children themselves removed or covered up rotting waste material, most often in their own neighborhoods. Junior high school business pupils typed the letters, obtained the required signatures, and mailed them. An art class made sectional maps of the area surveyed, one for the health department, one for the police, and one for school display, indicating the spots condemned and identifying the character of each. On invitation, representatives from the municipal police and health departments attended joint meetings of the Junior Chamber of Commerce and Junior Republic to express thanks for the assistance and to explain what progress had been made in overcoming the adverse conditions. Wherever resurveys justified it, art-class pupils modified all three copies of their maps, showing by symbols how each "plague spot" had been controlled.[17] The sponsors of the collaborating organizations as well as pupils appeared before school assemblies, parent-teacher association meetings, and civic clubs to explain the project and to receive appropriate recognition.

Environmental Controls Fostered by Concerned Citizens

The fact that the community as a whole controls the development of young people and that its effects are multivalent has long been recognized. Most contemporary boarding schools, vacation camps, "boys' towns," detention homes, and, in degree, country-day schools seek to provide controlled environments.

Analogous to the controlled-environment schools mentioned above, but directed to serve partial culture complexes that are somewhat

[17] Lester Carson, "A Project in the Junior Republic," and Irving Bath, "The Curriculum and the Community," *The Solvay Schools: Annual Report of the Board of Education*, Solvay, 1915–1916.

unique, are full-time and part-time "intentional communities." [18] Workers' schools and recreation centers, for example, recruit teachers, leaders, and clientele from those whose experiences and interests are rather homogeneous. These agencies conduct classes, discussion groups, leisure-time activities, and frankly propagandistic planning and practices that selectively promote attitudes and behaviors which the sponsors believe to be beneficial for workers, and which belong in the configurations of their daily experiences. Thereby it is intended to accentuate a generous, but not all-inclusive, compound of wholesome personalities, associational cooperation and tolerance, social and economic awareness and discriminating group action, aesthetic appreciation, and leisure-time occupation, which the school's sponsors believe desirable for working men and women and their families. [19]

Such controlled educational environments foster attitudes, beliefs, and behavior that reflect the ideals of their sponsors and that characterize, in purified form, the mores to which they wish young people to conform. In so far as these codes characterize the honored peers and adults of the families, coteries, and schools with which the boys and girls identify themselves, they are likely to have effective reinforcement in the several different environments. The codes themselves may be artificial and inconsistent, but, in great degree, they provide a frame of reference for "what is done" and "what is not done." Hence, the frequently identifiable personality patterns of English Public School "old boys," of college students who have "prepared" at a culturally selective boarding school, of convent-trained young women, and of boys and girls who have repeatedly attended long-term summer camps.

Where community reinforcement is lacking, the creation of a controlled full-time environment is less likely to be successful. The codes honored among neighborhood peers are often in conflict with those which even the most adaptable preventive or corrective institution can approve.

One institution combining elements of the workers' school and the intentional community venture, is the Highlander Folk School at Monteagle, Tennessee. Here a humanitarian group, inspired by what its members conceive to be the "social gospel," seek to promote political, economic, and cultural democracy, with particular reference to the conditions existing in the southeastern section of the country. High-

[18] Ralph Borsodi, *Education and Living,* The School of Living, Suffern, N.Y., 1948, pp. 688–702.

[19] Theodore Brameld (ed.), *Workers' Education in the United States,* Harper & Brothers, New York, 1941, and Mark Starr, *Labor Looks at Education,* Harvard University Press, Cambridge, Mass., 1946, pp. 35–36.

lander Folk School is in the tradition of the many effective educational ventures of the Southern Appalachian region, of which Berea College, the West Georgia "College-in-the-Country," the Berry School, and Brasstown Folk School are examples. All are modeled after the Danish Folk Labor Schools.

The Highlander Folk School is supported by contributions from liberal organizations and individuals. The staff of dedicated men and women is supplemented by volunteer leaders of labor and intercultural organizations on appropriate occasions. In addition to six-week sessions for labor leaders, there are conferences of welfare workers and of representatives of Negro and white civic and religious groups.

The curricula are adapted to the needs definitely recognized by the specific student bodies of each session. During a six-week labor school, for example, instruction and activities may be as diverse as public speaking, parliamentary procedure, economics, labor history, mimeographing, journalism, community problems, dramatics, group singing, dancing, and athletic games. The deep-seated prejudices of southern mountaineers and laborers are allowed to mellow by informal association, a process accelerated, of course, by the example of the school's staff.

Compared with such full-time total-environmental institutions as those just described, the American public school obviously labors under disadvantages both of time and of its less selected teaching staff and clientele. And, as has been repeatedly pointed out in this text, the developmental agencies of both local, and more remote, communities represent very heterogeneous cultures. The public school's efforts to inculcate in all its pupils the upper-class "virtues" of polite speech, courtesy, urbanity, and aesthetic appreciation are almost bound to be outweighed in many, if not in most, cases by the influences of extra-school experiences. The sum total of other-than-school learning is more enduring and often more compulsive than whatever codes the school fosters.

Fortunately, however, the task of upgrading the cultures of Americans does not rest on the school alone. Many other institutions and individual citizens recognize a responsibility in meeting the challenge. The upshot in many local communities has been the formation of "coordinating councils" composed of representatives of all concerned groups, including the public schools. A coordinating council, as its name implies, is a conferring and counseling body; it does not itself engage in action. It does, however, minimize rivalries and misunderstandings; it promotes planned cooperation to deal with concrete situations.[20]

[20] See Paul J. Misner, "The Work of a Community Coordinating Council," *Teachers College Journal,* vol. 13, no. 11, pp. 30–32, 1941.

Coordinating councils[21] are often called into being by a general awareness of deleterious conditions, such as delinquency, unemployment, disease, poor housing, lack of recreational facilities, unaesthetic situations, lagging civil defense, and adult apathy or ignorance. Fortunately, however, effective councils soon turn their attention to the over-all conditions of their communities.

Many other organized efforts to promote public consciousness of the fact that *the total* community develops, and therefore by intentional action may educate its members, may be mentioned. Federal and state departments and allied agencies which are concerned with public enlightenment recognize the interrelatedness of the measures each takes to advance its specific program with those of all the others. Agencies as diverse as those concerned with libraries, agriculture, health, parks, resource development, conservation, international policies, and military defense collaborate with educational departments to stimulate and direct community-wide attitudes and actions in which they have mutual interests. In these collaborations, the agencies are supplemented by governmental and nongovernmental special advisory commissions and conferences and by organizations which have formulated broad educational policies having to do with intentional environmental controls.[22]

Besides the organizations directly affecting national and state educational policies and programs, there are other relatively independent groups which foster community education. In this respect, the Tennessee Valley Authority is as truly a cultural and educational agency as it is a political and economic one.[23] State universities, especially those of Virginia, Kentucky, and Montana, have been successful in encouraging community programs in their regions.[24] Important, too, have been the

[21] Other titles for such bodies include "Neighborhood Council," "Youth Council," "Council of Social Work," and "Social Welfare Council."

[22] Over the years, a large number of national governmental commissions or committees and major nongovernmental commissions or committees have made recommendations to Congress or to the President favoring community educational measures. Moreover, educational policies recommended by state and local school officials and educational associations, political parties, industrial and trade organizations, labor unions, farmers' organizations, social welfare groups, church agencies, and women's organizations, many of them vibrantly aware of the importance of environmental influence on people's characters, have been welcomed by public agencies.

[23] David E. Lilienthal, *T.V.A.: Democracy on the March,* Harper & Brothers, 1944, esp. chaps. 9, 10, 11.

[24] Jean Ogden and Jesse Ogden, *Small Communities in Action,* Harper & Brothers, New York, 1940.

"People Act" radio programs, dramatizing successful ventures by civic groups throughout the country in bringing about community reforms and improvements.[25]

Some of the most striking examples of collaboration have been initiated by foundations and philanthropic individuals. The Sloan Fund,[26] for example, has enabled the state education departments and various civic groups of Vermont, Kentucky, and Florida to carry out reorganizations of their rural school curricula and services more promptly and effectively than they otherwise could have done. The Kellogg Foundation[27] has provided personnel and training opportunities and material facilities for great advances in popular awareness and collaborative action to foster child and adult welfare in Michigan and elsewhere; the first joint effort stimulated was in the field of health improvement, but it quickly spread to related areas—recreation, civic responsibility, and social and economic problems. The work of the Ford Foundation and various other foundations is well known.

It must be noted that the efforts of these coordinating agencies are directed along the same lines as those of schools which seek to foster an environment propitious for everyone. Each personality is exalted by the over-all atmosphere of permissiveness and example, the many and diverse opportunities for everyone to engage constructively in the adventures of associative life, and by the assurance of security, recognition, and affection corresponding to the sincerity of his efforts.

School-Community Social and Educational Centers

The utilization of public school buildings and grounds for community purposes other than instruction in school-related subjects is not new. In villages and rural areas, town meetings, "singing schools," and many other gatherings of neighbors have taken place on holidays, evenings, and special occasions. In cities, however, out-of-school-hours utilization of school plants by adults has generally been limited to evening-school classes and to occasional gatherings of patrons for exhibits of school work, school entertainments, and parent-teacher association meetings.

[25] Elmore M. McKee, *The People Act,* Harper & Brothers, New York, 1955.

[26] Clara M. Olson and N. D. Fletcher, *Live and Learn,* Alfred P. Sloan Foundation, Inc., New York, 1946 and M. F. Seay and L. Meece, *The Sloan Experiment in Kentucky,* College of Education, University of Kentucky, Lexington, 1944.

[27] L. M. Thurston, *The More We Get Together: A Report to the W. K. Kellogg Foundation from the Michigan Department of Public Instruction on the Community School Service Program,* Michigan State Department of Education, Lansing, 1949.

Owing chiefly to the agitation carried on by the Russell Sage Foundation, the American Playground Association, and analogous organizations in large cities throughout the country, there developed during the first decade of this century the "social-center movement." As new secondary and elementary schools were built with assembly halls, libraries, gymnasiums, playgrounds, and special facilities, they came frequently to serve as meeting places for youths and adults in the evenings, on weekends, and during vacations.

What started out largely as a provision by boards of education of plant facilities for voluntary community group recreation and other civic activities, developed in progressive school districts into community educational centers supported entirely or in part by public funds and administered by public employees. Autonomous adult and youth groups are increasingly encouraged to initiate and carry on their own projects, so far as these projects are consistent with school-board policies. The services of volunteer adult leaders for activities is usually welcomed, but their participation is supplemented and coordinated with more formal classes and other organized meetings for instruction.

Other governmental agencies participate with the school board in providing personnel and facilities for the "all-day" or "year-round" or "community-center" programs. The park or recreation department of a municipality may actually take over primary responsibility for vacation-time projects, using school plants along with other facilities. In New York City, the Public Education Association and the Board of Education together sponsor and operate "All-day Neighborhood Schools" where "special-group" teachers work with classroom teachers from 11 A.M. until 3 P.M. and from 3 P.M. to 5 P.M.; they serve with adult volunteers to direct the activities of children and youths of the district.

Coordination of the established literacy, citizenship, job-improvement, and homemaking evening school classes and the recreational and cultural activities carried on at school plants when the day schools are not in session has not yet taken the form of an official year-round school. But significant beginnings in the integration of school-hour and extra-school-hour programs with a single administration and teaching force are exemplified in some communities. At Rochester, Minnesota, for example, a complete educational program for youth on a year-round basis was initiated by the faculty with the approval of the board of education and the support of patrons. The school budget had to be considerably increased, of course, because teachers who took part in the expanded program received extra compensation, more employees were required, and plant operation expense was greater.

Trial and error will doubtless guide boards of education and municipal departments in their search for feasible ways to make the school plant serve the community throughout the day and evenings, weekends, and vacations. Too much administrative predetermination will have to be avoided, lest autonomy of civic, cultural, and recreational groups be frustrated, but enough counsel and supervision should be provided to make success for them all probable.

Public Discussion of Contemporary Problems

Myriad challenges daily face the people of a democratic society. For the most part, these challenges are either ignored or dismissed with a stereotyped "answer." Competition for attention to personal and public issues is too overwhelming; reflection and action would be palsied if an individual attempted to reach intellectual conclusions regarding them all. So it is almost inevitable that in a society where everybody is entitled to an opinion about everything, most men grasp for the tags made available by the many and omnipresent communication agencies, television, movies, newspaper cartoons, conversation wisecracks, advertising displays, and the rest. Political propaganda, sectarian religious dogma, labor-union slogans, and ethnocentric attitudes concerning the traits of disdained peoples, are all reflected in the "public opinions" of the American people.

The self-correction of erroneous public opinions is time-consuming at best and is not at all certain to eventuate. To decrease the time lag and to avert the fixing of false judgments in American cultural patterns, public educators seek to stimulate popular interest in, and reflection upon, social problems that seem to them too important to be left to offhand answers. In some cases, these educators have the zeal of reformers; in other cases, they are relatively detached, believing that reasoned answers, regardless of their agreement or disagreement with those affirmed by others, are of primary importance. In many instances, indeed, educators are content merely to inform the public, by means of exposition, exhibits, or both, regarding the conditions, needs, and proposed methods of dealing with a situation. Or they publicize the beneficent product of social endeavor. Such presentations of data, plans, or product, while they lack the "fireworks" of "give-and-take discussion" are effective devices for stimulating people who are already somewhat interested.

It is with regard to controversial questions on which men of intelligence, good will, and devotion to American ideals differ sharply, that rather bitter emotional states are apt to develop on both sides. Many such questions are obviously too hot for the public schools to handle, once such emotionalism has become widespread in a locality. Where pupils, teachers, and parents have engaged, over a period of time, in forum and discussion groups wherein meaningful problems have been faced with civilized restraint, schools are likely to be supported by the public whenever controversial questions arise in social-studies and other classes. Such a school thus finds its chance to exemplify the middle way—that of intelligent inquiry.

A rather different approach to fostering popular understanding of contemporary cultural processes and problems is the "Great Books Discussion Programs." [28] This venture in adult education is based on the premises that people are capable of thinking for themselves, that certain basic problems have confronted mankind in every era, that books written by great thinkers and writers of the past can contribute much to the resolution of present dilemmas, and that reading and discussing these books with friends and neighbors will help people both to deal with their unique personal problems and to act intelligently in matters of public policy and practice. In common with all progressive educators, the program's sponsors believe that education is a continuing activity not dependent on previous school attendance; there are no requirements for participating in the program other than the ability to read and the willingness to learn. In many communities, the public library, schools, colleges, and other local cultural, civic, and business organizations co-operate in promoting and conducting the Great Books program.

More stimulating to many persons vitally concerned with contemporary issues are the "Freedom Agenda" pamphlets distributed by the Carrie Chapman Catt Memorial Fund, Inc., of the League of Women Voters of the United States. They aim to foster informed community discussion about problems of individual liberty. Although their point of contact in local communities is the League of Women Voters, their appeal is quite as great to progressive churches, civic societies, and many liberal teachers.

Doubtless the most effective adventure in fostering public discussion of significant social questions was the Town Hall of the Air. It broadcast discussions of a great many issues of moment to the public. It provided a pattern of rational argumentation of controversial questions.[29] More recently, "Meet the Press" and other television discussion programs have been introduced to carry on the tradition of public service.

College and Community Collaboration

If under the term "collaboration" were to be included either the selection and training of an intellectual elite or the preparation of professionals to serve the community, substantial cases could be made

[28] The Great Books Foundation, 59 East Monroe Street, Chicago, Ill.
[29] H. A. Overstreet and B. W. Overstreet, *Town Meeting Comes to Town,* Harper & Brothers, New York, 1938.

for considering most institutions of higher learning as truly community-centered. Such, indeed, have been their historic missions.

In the United States, however, pioneering academies and later the land-grant colleges conceived their functions in terms of direct service to popular education. Occupational training in agriculture, mechanical arts, homemaking, business, navigation, public speaking, and teaching found an important place in many of these institutions. They sought to serve the common people at whatever point they needed, and were capable of receiving, help.

Privately endowed and state universities, although more restricted by their inner compulsion to "maintain standards," have not lacked consciousness of responsibility for public welfare. Their faculties have participated in many forms of adult education and other community services; they have served in public health projects, as engineering consultants, on park-planning boards, on educational commissions, and on many other community projects.

Indeed, it was the University of Wisconsin which first implemented the vision of a state-wide campus. By the Morrill Act of 1862 and the Hatch Act of 1887, the federal government had granted funds to state universities and land-grant colleges with an implied mandate to foster popular practical education. It was recognized that full-time residence on campus was not practicable for farmers, housewives, mechanics, and merchants, or for many of their sons and daughters. There grew up, therefore, many substitutes for conventional college education. Institutes of two or three days' duration, devoted generally to specific practical problems, were held; short winter courses in agriculture and mechanical arts were offered for young people; lecturers and demonstrators from the college visited towns and villages throughout the state, cooperating with Granges and other agricultural societies, businessmen's and workingmen's organizations, municipal and school officers, and civic groups concerned with matters of health, beauty, and orderly development of their local communities.

In recent years, with federal subsidies, the state-wide campus has become more and more a reality. Agents for home demonstration, conservation, and 4-H club supervision, under the leadership of state colleges, are stationed in many county centers. They carry on educational projects in their appropriate fields with the cooperation of local groups and individuals.[30] College-related state agencies have now attained a primary place in village and rural community development. In cooperation with active civic, economic, aesthetic, and recreational organizations, extension service staffs help communities to attack their vital

[30] See Harold S. Sloan, *Farming in America,* Harper & Brothers, New York, 1947, esp. chap. 1.

problems, for example pasture, crop, or building-structure questions, home efficiency and beautification, hospital and visiting-nurse services, pest control, and wildlife, fishing, and forestry measures. In so far as public schools welcome their aid, they eagerly collaborate with teachers and administrators.[31]

In recent years, many smaller and more locally oriented colleges have undertaken direct service projects looking to popular interest in, and understanding of, community processes and natural and human resources. In these undertakings, representative members of faculties and student bodies have cooperated with local governments, business and cultural leaders, and social service associations. Historical, sociological, economic, geographic, and political surveys have been conducted,[32] and planning and executive commissions and independent economic ventures have been collaboratively established.[33]

Colorado State College, both as an immediate contribution to the welfare of its local community and as a fundamental aspect of its teacher-education program, collaborates with the municipal government, the local school system, and various civic organizations to form the Greeley Community Activities Commission. Organized in 1947, following a survey by a fact-finding committee headed by a college staff member, the Commission employs a full-time director who, as part of his responsibilities, supervises students in the "Community Activities" course prescribed by the College for all undergraduates who are candidates for degrees leading to teaching certificates.

The Commission's activities program is conducted chiefly at a year-round youth center, a former elementary school plant, and on public playgrounds provided by the Park Commission. It includes indoor and outdoor games, athletics, dancing, band and orchestra, swimming, crafts, and story hours. It carefully coordinates its activities with those of the public schools, public library, Scouts, Camp Fire Girls, city parks, church and youth groups, the Philharmonic Society, and the Young America leagues.

Not all of the approximately 125 college students in the "Community Activities" course serve in Commission-directed activities. Some of them choose to engage in church-related youth services, others as Scout or Camp Fire leaders; some are employed by the Park Commis-

---

[31] *Community Developments in the Deep South: Workshop Proceedings,* Mississippi State College, February 5, 1951.

[32] Marietta College Rural Sociology Classes, *New Matamoras in the Mirror* and *Looking at Lowell,* Marietta College, Ohio, no date.

[33] Arthur E. Morgan, *Industries for Small Communities: With Cases from Yellow Springs,* Community Service News, Yellow Springs, Ohio, 1953.

sion. Their community services are all supervised and evaluated by representatives of the college faculty, however, not only during the progress of the course, but also during their practice-teaching assignments in public schools throughout Colorado. Students are encouraged to recognize that the main contribution of institutional education to the community is the improvement of its people.[34]

SUMMARY

In this chapter, specific instances of endeavors on the part of school officers to gain the interest and support of members of their communities in educational projects which the school initiated have been examined and evaluated. The importance of choosing and timing undertakings so as to win favorable community support has been noted. Typical instances of community educational collaboration in which the school is central have been explained—at least from the point of view of professional educators.

In the following chapter, the community problems, challenges, and needs will be treated as central, showing how the school may fulfill a dynamic role as society's agent for fostering public enlightenment and encouraging democratic collaboration.

SELECTED REFERENCES

Aderhold, O. C.: *School Leaders Manual,* Agricultural and Industrial Development Board of Georgia, Athens, 1944. A program of educational development for a southern state.

Anderson, Vivienne, and D. R. Davies: *Patterns of Educational Leadership,* Prentice-Hall, Inc., Englewood Cliffs, N.J., 1956. Chapter 3, "Planning and Developing a Community School," 4, "School Community Relationships," and 5, "Working with Parents," are especially pertinent.

Hanna, Paul, and others: *Youth Serves the Community,* Appleton-Century-Crofts, Inc., New York, 1937. Projects involving youth contributions to civic improvements.

Lund, S. E. J.: *The School-centered Community,* Anti-Defamation League of B'nai B'rith, New York, no date. A program for a "practical school for citizens of today and tomorrow."

McCloskey, M. A., and Hyman Sarakoff: *Schools and Neighbors in Action,* Oceana Publications, New York, 1951. Descriptions of school-community collaboration.

[34] Earle U. Rugg (chairman), *Eighth and Ninth Annual Reports,* Greeley Community Activities Commission, Greeley, Col., 1953 and 1954.

McKee, Elmore M.: *The People Act: Stories of How Americans Are Coming Together to Deal with Their Community Problems,* Harper & Brothers, New York, 1955. Interesting accounts of community approaches to problem-solving.

Moore, Clyde B.: *Problems Confronting Boards of Education,* New York State Department of Education, Albany, 1944. A manual for community participation in educational planning.

Page, W. H.: *The School that Built a Town,* Harper & Brothers, New York, 1952. An example of school leadership in a community.

School Community Cooperation for Better Living, University of Florida, College of Education, Gainesville, 1947. Prepared by staff members in the project in applied economics under a grant from the Sloan Foundation. A handbook of problems and projects for elementary and secondary school classes.

"Schools and Community Improvements," *The School Executive,* Special Issue, vol. 72, January, 1953. Illustrated articles on school communities' action in dealing with immediate problems and opportunities.

DISCUSSION QUESTIONS

1. Consider the scope of welfare concerns of one of the following organizations in a community with which you are familiar: municipal government, recreation commission, public library, a settlement house, Grange, YMCA, Home Demonstration Service, Old Age Assistance, county, state, and national parks, etc. In what respects is the organization you selected already functioning as a "community school"? What is the implication of your judgment for the public schools of the district?

2. H. O. Rugg and others have recommended that the title of the chief executive officer of the Board of Education should be Superintendent of Education instead of Superintendent of Schools. Would the proposed title accord with the responsibilities now accepted by vigorous school administrators? Would such a change of title imply a broadening of the scope of authorities and concerns of a district board of education?

3. Should educators be less occupied with what the school should be and more concerned about what needs to be done by the constructive social agencies of which it is only one? If the latter, are youths themselves competent to participate both in seeking the answers and in discovering the forms of collaboration of these social agencies?

4. That the public school is a composite of publicly favored values is a widely accepted belief among educators. Is the school stopped thereby from having values that are uniquely its own? Is the school something that other community agencies are not? If you find an answer

to that question, consider its significance in terms of articulation of the school with the other agencies.

5. If one considers the horizontal and vertical mobility of urban and suburban populations, and the occupational, recreational, housing, clothing, and other cultural changes that have characterized our relatively affluent society, does it seem reasonable that intelligent persons should be surprised to discover that so restless a people do not characteristically seek excellence as an end in living?

6. A curious contradiction is apparent in the criticisms of contemporary Americans. On the one hand, we are scolded for our preoccupation with getting and spending for gadgets, for conformism, for interest in sports, and it is charged that we ignore international tensions, national problems, and "the future" of the nation. On the other hand, equally respected publicists warn us to calm down, to allay our anxiety, and to go about our business in an uncertain world as though we assume that everything will come out right. What do you make of these two viewpoints?

7. In some urban school systems, many teachers belong to the American Federation of Teachers. In out-of-school time and away from school premises, many teachers engage in political activities, for example, in campaigning for candidates, referenda, and tax proposals. Is such activity "conduct unbecoming a teacher"? What of school support by members of organized labor?

PART SEVEN

Education and Planned Change

22

Experiments in Community Education

COMMUNITY ORIENTATION IN THE ELEMENTARY SCHOOL

Each public school reflects the tolerances and aspirations of a constellation of subcultures—those of families, sects, ethnic groups, economic segments, political coteries, and cultural and recreational sets. These subcultures are not mutually exclusive. Indeed, in the United States, they all belong within the general stream of tolerance and aspiration which characterizes the American ethos. The interpretations and expressions of the basic values may be so conflicting, confused, and evanescent as to seem chaotic; prestige, for example, may be accorded to an individual as statesman, as athlete, as racketeer, as artist, as religious leader, or as best-dressed man.

One may view sympathetically the distressed cry of the scholastic that the modern school reflects the chaos of contemporary culture, that there is too little popular respect for "learning," and that the public ought to limit its demands on and its expectations from the school to scholarly achievements, and to judge the school only in terms of this mandate. But such a public as this exhortation is addressed to is an unrealistic abstraction; it is "the little man who isn't there."

Public aspirations, public demands, public needs, and public

509

dissatisfactions are fragmental and evanescent. But they are current realities to which the school must respond if it would restrain excesses and mobilize sentiment in favor of civic competence, humane relations, economic efficiency, and characters attuned to American ideals.

In making such responses to the complex realities, the educational establishment has the great advantage of broad popular acceptance as the major instrument of upward social mobility. Like other tax-supported social service institutions, it is generally accepted as a benevolent and beneficent fixture on the American scene. It is this public acceptance that assures to schools at all levels their continuing popular mandate to do what needs to be done to secure and improve community living.

It is this mandate which the creative school accepts as its primary control. The goals of American life, and hence of American education, provide its broad framework of purpose and hope. Indeed, the stereotype of what a "school" should be and what it should do retains a firm place in controlling its regimen. But the community school's first concern is with what now needs to be done in the area that it serves to make living conditions more nearly conform to the good life. It is on behavior as well as information and scholastic skills, that emphasis is put.

By mobilizing and coordinating community enthusiasm for the school's purposes, the modern educator can ensure the continued prestige of the educational establishment. With the momentum of such involvement in broad public support, the school is in a favorable position to foster scholarly and aesthetic standards that may not currently find exemplification among its clientele.

The elementary school faculty seeking to achieve a community orientation to education has both advantages and disadvantages as compared with that of a secondary school. On the one hand, it shares the lives of little children with parents during the years when children are dependent on adults for personal care. Teachers acting *in loco parentis* are expected to be concerned with the personal traits of their charges; that expectation encourages a feeling of mutuality between teachers and parents. On the other hand, the traditional special role of the elementary school has been to instruct pupils in fundamental scholastic information and skills; the popular stereotype of "class-time procedure" consists of instruction, drill, recitation, and tests. There is often suspicion that teachers are neglecting their primary function if they direct children's class-time activities toward anything other than the mastery of subject matter.

The community-oriented elementary school minimizes the implicit conflict between this stereotype and the concern for child welfare by engaging the efforts of nonschool adults. Adults who collaborate with the school for the fostering of the objective of child welfare seldom distrust the school's concern for pupils' mastery of the three R's.

RURAL COMMUNITY ELEMENTARY SCHOOLS

The "little red schoolhouse," whatever its other shortcomings, was a community possession, a social center where parents and children found common interests and activities. Frequently it served as a meeting place for entertainment and public deliberation. The very isolation of the patrons, together with their common poverty and thrift, almost compelled the teacher to share in local domestic and occupational activities.

Early in this century, national interest in the potentialities of rural life for the conservation of human values was abetted by a spate of literature glorifying the village and the farm; there was much praise for rural cultural settings, personal relations, and relative freedom from the depersonalized regimentation of urban living. The reports of the Country Life Commission, appointed by President Theodore Roosevelt in 1907, responded to and accelerated this interest. Largely as a result of this enthusiasm, state colleges and normal schools and many educational officers were encouraged to foster rural elementary school reform, looking toward integrating the activities characteristic of farm, home, market, church, and recreation into the school's curriculum. In this school and community interaction, the influence of John Dewey's *The School and Society*,[1] published in 1899, was particularly important.

Housewives and teachers began to collaborate, for example, to teach meal preparation, preserving, and housekeeping in farm and village homes as well as in schools. Similarly, the elements of carpentry, machine maintenance, animal husbandry, bookkeeping, merchandising, music, dramatics, organization of play, and many other social and personal proficiencies were practiced wherever the situations were favorable. In school districts that responded to this reform movement, credit for home and community service was given in the form of recognition if not of grade advance.

Evaluation of a Reoriented Rural School

School-community projects usually started with problems and opportunities already obvious to children and adults. The prevalence of typhoid fever in a school district, for example, was one of the challenges used by Ellsworth Collings in the early 1920s to stimulate children and adults to survey health and work conditions in the neighborhood and its surrounding area and to agitate for improvement. He was the first to keep adequate records and make comparative evaluations of outcomes of such

[1] University of Chicago Press, Chicago.

community-centered curricula. He reported that on academic tests the children succeeded better than in more conventional schools; greater numbers continued their school education; pupils and their parents evidenced appreciation and support for the school and took active part in community life; health conditions improved; and farm income increased.

Many other reorientations of rural elementary schools have been reported. Only one of them can be described here.

Nambé Rural Community School

At Nambé, New Mexico, a ditch brings water from the Nambé River to the fields. It is called *La Comunidad*. Maintained by the shared labor of fathers and sons for almost $3\frac{1}{2}$ centuries, it is symbolic of the community heritage of oneness—an ambivalent heritage of language, religion, superstitions, obsolete health and sanitary practices, primitive domestic and agricultural customs, and generous concern of one for all.

The impact of the modern industrial world, with its money economy, its commercial farming, its strange English language, its state-imposed regulations, its social mobility, and its compulsory school attendance, has been disruptive in its effects. In degree, the traditional rural school had epitomized compulsion to docile acceptance of out-group standards; its curriculum had little counterpart in the mores of home, work, or worship.

Aided and inspired by the benevolence of Mr. and Mrs. Cyrus McCormick, who established a residence in the area, and with government assistance, 150 families contributed labor to build a new school plant. The University of New Mexico and the Santa Fe County Board of Education cooperated to propose a community educational program to be submitted to the people of Nambé. On its acceptance, an adequate staff, including a community nurse, was selected.

The approach in this school, as in all other community-oriented ones, was less on what an elementary curriculum should be and more on what needed to be done to help community members to appreciate one another's attitudes and values as well as their difficulties and needs. Only in this way could language and health and leisure-time practices be acceptably modified.

A single example must suffice. Open privies bred flies which spread diarrhea. Almost all residents belonged to the local Catholic Church whose toilet facilities left much to be desired. So an early start was made to engage adults and children, now familiar with the new school's toilet facilities, to make their church equipment equally adequate. Adults engaged on this project responded to their children's desire for equivalent facilities and approved practices at their own homes. And the readiness to learn why and what to do in this regard transferred itself, somewhat haltingly to be sure, to confidence in the advice offered at the public clinic by nurse and doctor.

One characteristic of this and many other examples of school-community leadership should be emphasized. Encouragement of older and younger people, through the successful achievement of concrete projects, to welcome expert aid in any regard helped them accommodate to modern American culture, its economic, technological, and social welfare planning. All starts were made in the light of the Nambé community's resources and needs, both of which were of great importance. But the goal was membership in an idealized American culture [2]

THE ROLE OF ELEMENTARY SCHOOLS IN "THE SPRINGFIELD PLAN"

Despite the wide and well-deserved public approval of the civic, especially the interpersonal, achievements of the community-oriented schools of Springfield, Massachusetts, those responsible for the processes and their outcomes have avoided the use of the term "The Springfield Plan." What the Springfield school community attempted, and so significantly accomplished, involved a series of plans, projects, policies, and techniques directed toward community welfare in general and toward intercultural understanding, altruism, and cooperation in particular. In connection with these undertakings, individuals varying in age from tiny tots to senior citizens, and belonging to diverse establishments and informal and *ad hoc* groups, collaborated in dealing with interrelated problems and challenges.

Fundamental to all the projects coordinated in "the plan" was the basic belief that children and adults learn the lives they lead. Hence, the challenge for the policy makers and technical advisers was to discover the available, or potentially available, human resources for success and to find ways of drawing resourceful people into the stream of civic betterment.

In Springfield, this challenge presented less difficulty than it might meet in many cities, for Springfield's long history has been one of relatively slow but sustained growth, civic honesty, and varied cultural interests and achievements. As the city grew, newcomers from rural areas north and south and from Canada, Europe, and Asia brought with them diverse religious and other cultural practices, to be sure, but the tradition of community tolerance and rectitude was strong enough to minimize bitter rivalries and tensions among the various social segments.

Springfield, however, did not escape the ebbs and flows of pros-

[2] L. S. Tireman and Mary Watson, *La Comunidad,* The University of New Mexico Press, Albuquerque, 1943.

perity and crisis, tensions and conflicts among special interest groups, and nationalistic and other prejudices. Following the long and deep depression of the thirties, accelerated perhaps by war preparations, racial, religious, economic, and political tensions became evident here as elsewhere. In Springfield, however, the schools, under the leadership of Superintendent John Granrud, took the initiative in rallying liberals to deal with the mutual problems of school and community.

Cooperation among teachers was the first goal sought. Their committees and discussion groups concluded that (1) pupils must be led to understand the historical backgrounds and the contributions to American life of all the constituent groups of the population, (2) that the weaknesses in the democratic processes should be pointed out and ways of eliminating them discussed, (3) that pupils should know and assess the forces that are playing on their minds, and (4) that since most prejudices develop outside the school, education for democracy should reach the adult world which profoundly affects the child's thinking.

Instrumenting these purposes was first entrusted to teachers already enthusiastic and eager to participate. As their success aroused the interest of fellow teachers, their example and guidance were made available to all. Parent-teacher associations and the Adult Educational Council readily cooperated; newspapers and radio stations provided constructive publicity; church groups, service clubs, and other civic and cultural groups invited representatives of the school system to explain the program. Teachers who adventured into the areas of intercultural education were thus assured of considerable sympathetic support for, and appreciation of, their efforts.

Living and Learning Together

Although the exposition of the accomplishments of "The Springfield Plan" are limited to those centered about the elementary grades of the public schools, it should be borne in mind that parochial and other private schools carried out similar projects and that the junior and senior high schools and the three collegiate institutions of the community engaged effectively in the program.

As already implied, the relations among administrators, supervisors, and teachers in the elementary schools of Springfield had long been characterized by friendly collaboration; superior-inferior status distinctions had been minimized and teachers dealt with as individuals, their unique personalities respected, their talents welcomed, and their contributions highly valued.

Because faculties were already accustomed to learning from each other as they worked together, each teacher's integrity was respected whether or not he acted boldly or timidly in one or another aspect of the school program.

Objectives of the Springfield Plan

The five groups of objectives of the elementary schools of Springfield were formulated by the faculties and then accepted as applicable to all levels of the school system. These five kinds of educational emphases, it should be noted, are not revolutionary; in considerable degree they characterize all schools that are attuned to American aspirations. They are:

1. The development of each pupil's individual personality, his physical, mental, and emotional health standards, and his growth in ability to think, make decisions, and to distinguish between facts and opinions.

2. To teach the art of living, working, learning, and thinking together, to develop wholesome and natural experiences in relationships with children, teachers, and others of different races, religions, and nationalities, both within their own school and in association with those of parochial and private schools, and to encourage the acceptance of a share of responsibility for group welfare.

3. To develop an understanding of the contributions of men and women of different occupations, interests, and talents in the community.

4. To teach a conception of the roots of the American way of life and an appreciation of what it means to be an American.

5. To foster the beginnings of an understanding of other countries and their people through a study of different nationality groups in the local community and of the life of children in other lands.

Procedures and Devices

If these objectives were to be attained, more than mere changes in curriculum was needed. Pupil participation in school and community affairs was fostered by active membership on committees and councils, in leaders' clubs and such special purpose organizations as Junior Red Cross, thrift clubs, traffic squads, and teacher-pupil committees. These devices were not unique; they characterize most progressive elementary schools in America. What was noteworthy was their conscious and intentional utilization.

So far as feasible, children were treated as though they were mature persons. By living and acting in mature fashion, they learned the ways of maturity. They took great pride in the fact that they had a real part in school and community affairs; kindergartners as well as sixth-graders took their individual duties and committee projects very seriously. A single example of their mature attitude toward responsibility illustrates the kind of outcome the elementary schools of Springfield sought.[3]

The Library Committee, made up of seven children representing the six grades was holding an emergency session which was overheard by one of the school secretaries who was so impressed that she took down in shorthand what they said. Following is an unedited report:

> *The Chairman* (a fifth-grade girl about twelve years old): You will notice that we have a few magazines here. A girl brought in a magazine from her church. There are a few verses from the Bible and then it has some stories. We wondered what you thought about putting it in here because it comes from a particular church and we want to be sure that it is perfectly all right, because if we find that it really is right then we want it.
>
> *George:* I don't think we should put the magazines here unless we ask if she wants to keep them.
>
> *Chairman:* She is perfectly willing. We just wondered if you thought it was all right to put a magazine in here that comes from a certain kind of religion.
>
> *Mary:* I think we should ask the principal.
>
> *Chairman:* If she is willing does this committee want it here?
>
> *Edna:* I think we ought to know what the paper is.
>
> *Chairman* (showing the paper): Right here is a story. There is nothing about religion. And here is another story that isn't religious. This seems like a little poem. There is another different kind of story. Here is a verse about the stories of Paul. Each week they have a crossword puzzle.
>
> *Mary:* I think it is a good idea to get the children to read what comes out of the Bible.
>
> *Anthony:* It is my opinion that there are interesting stories and we don't have to pay any attention to the things we don't believe in.
>
> *Ruth:* I think it is nice though that you can learn about the other person's religion. It might not seem interesting to you, but you might get more out of it than you think and you learn those things from the Bible. I think it would be interesting to learn about other people's religion as well as your own.

[3] By permission from C. I. Chatto and A. L. Halligan, *The Story of the Springfield Plan*, Barnes & Noble, Inc., New York, 1945, pp. 26–27. See, also, Alexander Alland and J. W. Wise, *The Springfield Plan: A Photographic Record*, The Viking Press, Inc., New York, 1945, and Marie Syrkin, *Your School, Your Children: A Teacher Looks at "What's Wrong with Our Schools,"* L. B. Fischer Publishing Corporation, New York, 1944, pp. 208–221.

Chairman: The main thing is we didn't want them reading that if their religion doesn't believe in it. There are all kinds of religion in this school and we don't want other people to be insulted about it. I think we should take a vote on it. We might as well have a hand vote. All those who want to have the magazine in here raise your hands. Have you got your hand up, Dorothy? That's everybody. I'll see the principal about it.

COMMUNITY-CENTERED HIGH SCHOOLS

The mushrooming of urban and suburban populations, the frequent movement of families into cities and suburbs, the shifting ethnic composition of the residents of many areas, and changes in the economic character of many districts present serious problems to educators. Frequently they have had to redefine their service areas and populations; their pupils may come from districts far removed from the site of the school building; many of them may be transients; cultural backgrounds, out-of-school occupations, and recreations may be quite different from those familiar to most of the teachers.

In village and rural areas throughout the country, the enlargement of high school districts to replace local ones has presented different but fully as difficult dilemmas for administrators and teachers. Pupils may come by bus at school opening time and depart at closing time, their homes and neighborhood lives and their out-of-school associations little related to conventional school experiences. Indeed, whatever success the school may have in rallying the loyalty and enthusiasm of these youths for the school's activities and codes is likely, in degree, to conflict with what is expected of them at home.

Resourceful educators, however, have had considerable success in dealing with these rather staggering challenges. Each solution is unique, of course, but it also has elements in common with all others. It consists first of all in discovering the potentials of the diverse cultural settings of pupils and patrons, and of engaging their efforts in cooperation with the school and with each other to discover and exploit the resources and opportunities of the community for the common good. Four concrete examples of such "educational statesmanship" will make the processes clear.

The Story of Holtville

Of all the creative community schools in the United States, the one that has been most justly celebrated is doubtless that of Holtville, Alabama. It does not detract one whit from the school's stature to note that its able and resourceful faculty built on the successful programs of forerunners, the pioneering white and colored schools of the region, and that the opportunities and freedom from hampering traditions and certification regulations were favorable. Most village and rural high schools have somewhat similar advantages and in many regards scarcely less freedom. Only a few, however, have approached closely the integration of education, community forces, and human resources achieved at Holtville.[4]

The school in Holtville led in the transformation of the economic and social life of a district of 180 square miles containing seven small centers. "Agriculture has become more diversified; traditional cash crops are still grown but in a more efficient and economical manner; more and better livestock is produced. Small community-owned and operated manufacturing projects are supplementing farm incomes. More young people are better fed, better clad, better housed, healthier, wealthier, and happier; all due to the influence of a functioning school-community program." [5]

James Chrietzberg, the principal, gives major credit for the development of the community program to the vocational agriculture teacher and the supervisor of community services, but he recognizes also the contributions of many others—all the teachers, trustees and school-board officers, federal and state educational agencies, representatives of the Southern Curriculum Study of the Southern Association of Colleges and Secondary Schools, and a succession of students and their parents.

Holtville High School was already community-oriented in 1938. But then a "new look" started with a two-hour daily period providing opportunity for students to work in groups on "ways to improve life in the home, school, and community." Teachers, pupils, civic leaders, and many parents had ideas about what needed doing, and in some cases were too impatient to wait for factual surveys to be completed. Interest groups began to form and were permitted to plan and carry out projects pretty much on their own once their plans had received approval. Course prescriptions were discontinued. Students sought instruction and advice from faculty members and from citizens of the community, thereby enlisting much volunteer help from competent adults. The twin objectives of community improvement and personal achievement attracted the support of many people. A dozen kinds of shops, laboratories, and work-

[4] Whilden Wallace, James Chrietzberg, and V. M. Sims: *The Story of Holtville,* privately published, Deatsville, Ala., 1944.

[5] S. E. T. Lund, *The School-Centered Community,* Anti-Defamation League of B'nai B'rith, New York, 1949. Quoted from *Hearings on Agricultural and Economic Problems of the Cotton Belt,* 80th Cong., 1947.

rooms and many books became insistently needed; pupils, patrons, and teachers collaborated to get them. And they succeeded.

Many of the interest groups became economically productive, for example, those involved in a barber shop, in agriculture, arts and crafts, refrigeration, a hatchery, a printing plant, and a cannery. In varying degrees, these groups have been able to supplement their own instructional equipment and supplies. Other interest groups have presented entertainment or contributed from individual earnings for a similar purpose.

Patrons and teachers had at first some difficulty in accepting so revolutionary a school. Presession conferences and emphasis on voluntary services soon won over the faculty; nationwide recognition of their school has, of course, helped greatly. Parents' meetings at school and reports on pupil progress and school accomplishments have supplemented the students' enthusiastic participation in community projects. The result has been pride and support from the public.

Maplewood's Indirect Approach to School-Community Identification

A more indirect approach to community and faculty enlightenment as a means for integrating community agencies may lead to remarkable accomplishment. In all such programs, adult education and youth education are coordinated and their natural parallelism is accentuated.

To those educators who have intentionally used an indirect approach, it seems that education is all of a piece. Youths cannot grow optimally unless they live in communities that are characterized by civic pride, aspiration, and growth. Schools cannot serve youths adequately unless the community is engaged in serving them adequately. Youths cannot be expected to accept seriously civic and cultural responsibilities toward the school unless similar opportunities for such responsibilities exist in their homes and their other out-of-school associations.

To the degree that community institutions and forces can be enlisted in a coordinated movement to enrich and protect the life activities of all citizens, young and old, the school's functions become clear and mandatory. Hence, curriculum reform ceases to be insulated from other aspects of school and community reform. They all move together with a minimum of conflict, confusion, and waste motion, and with a maximum of security and, probably, of permanence.

In the spring of 1932, when the unsettling effects of the depression were being very seriously felt in the suburban community of Maplewood, New Jersey, Ross O. Runnels, principal of the junior high school and director of child welfare, persuaded the executive committee of the parent-teacher association of his school that its major responsibility was the education of the community, the improvement of mental, emotional, recreational, health, cultural, aesthetic, political, and housing conditions of all the people. He did not encourage the parents to study meticulously the school's functioning as such; it was his belief that such study was best conducted by specially trained, experienced professionals.

Under the skillful encouragement and guidance of Runnels, there developed in the ensuing years the Maplewood Adult School (later expanded into the South Orange-Maplewood Adult School) in which many thousands of adults have studied government, international affairs, economics, art, music, literature, homemaking, commercial subjects, and recreation, in hundreds of courses. Members of the successive executive committees of the parent-teacher association have become influential leaders in many phases of community life, serving on official boards, on advisory committees, and in voluntary capacities. Cooperation among the schools, governmental agencies, and civic organizations has become notable. Problems of youth protection and education are met constructively rather than remedially.

Indeed, all Maplewood became a school; all citizens were potential members of it. Children grew up in an environment characterized by educational interest and growth. The school fitted in unobtrusively as one factor in the conditioning of children for self-fulfillment in their human relationships, their civic responsibilities, and their economic activities. Adults who themselves were engaged in the voluntary and pleasurable study of human relationships, civic responsibilities, and economic problems grew equally in ability to understand, tolerate, and encourage efforts of the school to furnish parallel opportunities for the children of the community.

The school's printed program of studies would scarcely interest the very progressive educator; it contains the titles to which patrons have long been accustomed. Indeed, the content and methodology in many classes are little better than conventionally good. But no sensitive person could step inside the door of the school without knowing that he was in a most unusual environment. The true curriculum in such a school is the human relations among pupils, teachers, custodians, administrators, governmental officers, parents, and visitors. It is the civic responsibilities accepted and executed in classes, corridors, lunch room, playground, and the extra-school community by youths and adults in whatever capacities they find themselves. It is the solution of economic problems and the wise expenditure of time, energy, equipment, and resources. It is, indeed, the growing self-realization of youths and adults through hundreds of individualistic and cooperative adventures which only in part and for convenience are located within the walls of a school building.

McKinley High School Community-related, Student-Teacher Management

An adventure in cooperative management of the school community at McKinley High School, Honolulu, begun during the principalship of Miles D. Carey and continued during that of W. D. Geiger, made a fundamental contribution both to community-curriculum orientation and to decentralized and democratized administration.

McKinley High School is a spaciously situated and housed senior high school in a remarkably polyglot community. In 1947, 75 per cent of its 3,850 pupils were of Oriental descent (Japanese, Korean, Chinese, or Filipino), yet more than 95 per cent of them were American citizens by virtue of their birth on American soil. Other pupils included Hawaiians and part-Hawaiians, and descendants of other Polynesians and of European immigrants. Their linguistic and other cultural inheritances were in many important respects so at variance with the practices that characterize mainland American school communities (which in idealized form serve as standards for those of Hawaii) that great stress at McKinley has been put on associational living and on good oral and written expression.

This school makes rich and varied provision (in both day and evening schools and on Sundays) for aesthetic and vocational education for young and old. A single facet of its vast and effective program, that of self-education by day pupils in the skills and attitudes of democratic living, exemplifies the spirit of the whole.

The evolution of the administrative arrangement at McKinley has been in the direction of devising an organization that would make possible the most effective participation in school affairs by students and teachers. Each student is in a "core-studies" class, meeting two hours daily. The work of these core-studies classes is organized around current, critical school and community problems that these young people face, for example, eradicating tuberculosis, setting and budgeting school-government dues, revising the school-government constitution, slum clearance, and military service.

Each core-studies class sends a member to the school representative assembly to participate in dealing with school problems and in making school policy. Important matters are referred back to the core-studies rooms for discussion and decision. What is done in the way of policy making is always undertaken experimentally. If a particular move is ill-advised, it is not long before the shoe begins to pinch somewhere and a proposal for reconstruction is heard from some quarter.

Remarkably successful efforts are made to engage every pupil and every teacher in some important functional group project, many of them enlisting patrons and municipal officials, museum and library staffs, and leaders in civic and cultural organizations. Typical collaborative undertakings include a health program, campus upkeep and beautification, the conduct of forums in which students, teachers, and civic leaders participate, the cooperative planning and execution of the courses of study for every core-curriculum class and for such subjects as home economics, shop, art, and agriculture, the collaborative planning and direction of the parent-teacher association program, community relations, job placement, the school's athletics program, and student publications. As new problems and needs arise, special committees are appointed by the School Assembly representing appropriate grades, core classes, and student, teacher, and parent organizations.

Each group within this complex organization is a going concern. No committee, club, or office is carried on after its usefulness is over and the enthusiasm it aroused has ended. Consequently, the organization of the school undergoes constant scrutiny and change.

Housing Challenges Benjamin Franklin High School

The Benjamin Franklin High School of New York City is located in East Harlem where a population of about 200,000 people lives on some 150 city blocks. Established as a community school under the principalship of Leonard Covello, it quickly came to grips with some of the major problems that faced the people it served. The staff sought and found vigorous allies—social workers, political leaders, city police, fire, and health departments, court officials, and some property owners, merchants, labor-union officials, and spokesmen for ethnic, religious, and economic groups. The new school sought to make common cause with all for every measure that promised a better environment.

One of the problems that commanded the attention of all civic-minded people of the school's service area was that of housing. The congestion in East Harlem was extreme. It was characterized by squalid, dilapidated buildings with sanitary conditions of the worst types. Lack of recreational facilities, poverty, high rates of tuberculosis, high delinquency rates, and acts of violence were interrelated phenomena.

The population was extremely heterogeneous. The diverse subgroups suffered from many maladjustments to American life. The contiguity of 70,000 first- and second-generation Italians (not at all homogeneous among themselves), 20,000 Negroes, 25,000 Puerto Ricans, and various other Spanish-speaking, Slavic, and Middle East peoples fomented suspiciousness and rivalries. The customs and appearances of these relative newcomers were resented by many persons of Irish and German descent who still lived in the area.

The low prestige of residents of East Harlem raised social barriers that separated them from the city as a whole. Moreover, there were discrimination and antagonism within the neighborhoods of the area, some brought from the "old countries," others fanned by political and economic propaganda and religious loyalties. Except for political electioneering, there was little leadership and organization that crossed the lines of these subgroups, although social service workers and some labor officials were attempting it.

In general, there was a lack of democratic tradition and little sense of community. Insecurity and fear of strange customs and of economic rivalry were magnified by language barriers. The need for social education was acute. And constructive agitation for better housing was peculiarly fitted to serve as the vehicle for such education.

The attempt to rehabilitate the physical community aroused popular enthusiasm for a common cause among the diverse groups within the local district. Political leaders, labor organizers, merchants, and members of municipal departments welcomed the support of all citizens of the community. Schools, settlement houses, and other social service organizations found in the spirit of collaboration many chances to provide encouragement and service.

The project was, indeed, an excellent opportunity to introduce ill-assimilated people to the processes of democratic action. Pupils, teachers, and patrons served on active committees for health, for racial and ethnic cooperation, for better leisure-time activities, for prevention of delinquency, and, most pertinent, for the improvement of housing conditions. On these committees, by intention, various religious and ethnic groups and social service agencies were represented. Their "good neighbor" approach to their projects was a decisive factor in stimulating community-wide interest in their enterprises.

Exhibits showing old and new concepts of housing were prepared by students and teachers; models were large enough to show significant details. Social studies, English, art, and modern language departments were especially active in support of the common concern. School assemblies and parents' association meetings dealt with questions relating to land use and values, taxation and rentals, poor housing as a factor in crime and ill health, aesthetic standards, and public versus private housing. As civic organizations and their leaders took up the housing project, the school worked with them and was influential in coordination. The resulting East Harlem Housing Committee and the Harlem Legislative Council, collaborating with the Mayor's Committee on City Planning, brought about the construction of the East River

Housing, accommodating 1,300 families. The clearance of old slums has had revolutionary effects on community pride, on lessening of friction and antagonism, and on the improvement of privately owned tenements.

Much remains to be done. New population influxes have come, other antagonisms have flamed, and predatory gangs, corrupt politics, and organized crime have continued to infest the area.

But East Harlem experienced success in a collaborative effort to deal with one set of interrelated problems. And the Benjamin Franklin High School helped its community to deal with one complex problem after another in the years that followed.

SUMMARY AND EVALUATION

The examples of community education, directly or indirectly related to schools, which have been presented in this chapter, vary considerably in scope, purpose, setting, and procedure. In each case, however, it may be noted that the seven characteristics of a creative community school are present, that is, multiform purposeful activities on the part of those the school seeks to influence, the expansion of the curriculum concept to include all the personal and group experiences fostered by the school, guidance of individuals toward social maturity, the reinforcement of desirable and the offsetting of undesirable traits and community influences, the stimulation of the desire to solve problems and of self-confidence in dealing with them, and the selection and development of leaders whose personalities are consonant with the purposes of each venture.

It is obvious that no uniform pattern of collaboration among those whom the school seeks to recruit for its projects is feasible. A sympathetic awareness of the problems and aspirations of members of the community and of the opportunities and obstacles they face is fundamental. Quite as important for American educators is the conviction that the ways in which people go about seizing opportunities and overcoming obstacles can strengthen or can weaken the fabric of democracy. The community school is challenged to foster those popular aspirations that harmonize with the American ethos and to aid individuals in reaching their goals with reasonable regard for the rights of all other men.

In the American society, fortunately, the democratic discipline of cooperation and compromise is of necessity practiced in all stable families, neighborhoods, and voluntary associations. It is necessary because it alone works out well. It survives because in the long run it is more efficient, at least in the American configuration, than is authoritarianism or force. The harmonizing of reasoned objectives and nonimposed methods is the key to democracy. Business, politics, administration, and recreation all exemplify competition within a framework of cooperation and good will—or they fail to achieve even their immediate objectives. Indeed, if American groups were not generally characterized by a willingness not only to "get along with others," but also to wish them well and to assist actively in many of their projects, the structure of government, economy, and all other associations could not exist.

In the United States, most social innovations start at the periphery. Individuals and small local groups sense a problem, define it, and agitate for solution. Bold school administrators and teachers make evident their readiness to cooperate with such individuals and groups. Frequently this cooperation involves adaptation of school curriculum or regimen. These innovations are then adapted for use in other communities where patrons and teachers recognize similarities of needs and possibilities. After a bit, the pioneering educators find wide recognition, their community supporters gain prestige, perhaps political office, in local and state affairs, state and district educational officials recommend that all schools achieve community orientation, and by various devices provide assistance and recognition for those whose sustained efforts make the community school a reality.

This sequence was interestingly exemplified in New York State during the first part of this century. The collaboration of the Russell Sage Foundation and the Playground Association of America with progressive educators and other alert citizens of New York City, Rochester, Solvay, and other school systems attracted to their schools many professional and lay visitors and otherwise assured much favorable publicity. In the years that followed, many of these educators and citizens won national recognition. As school superintendents, professors of education, school-board members, members of municipal and state legislative bodies and administrative agencies, they effectively advanced social welfare provisions, including, of course, creative community schools.

A consideration of the examples set forth in this chapter, and of the many others which might have been cited, provides convincing evidence that community-oriented educators need not, indeed cannot, work alone.

Educational "statesmanship" consists chiefly in enlisting the cooperation of men of good will wherever they can be found in sustained efforts to maintain and energize the processes of humane living. These processes are mostly humble ones; they are the trust, faith, and kindliness of democratic families and neighborhoods extended to wider circles of town, state, nation, and world. They are the discriminating adaptation of means to consciously valued ends. They are the vigilance to identify and assess both opportunities to achieve and the dangers to avoid or eliminate. They are the discipline of self-identification with others in a common effort to make an environment fit for civilized men to grow and live in.

These men of good will are not limited to an intellectual, economic, or aesthetic elite. "Goodness" in some regard or another is an attribute of most of mankind; it has had survival value throughout human history. Social education functions in helping all persons to direct and express this goodness effectively and to obtain satisfaction and recognition, and hence security, in cooperative efforts to create "things." And these may as truly be things of the spirit as material things; they may be institutions and environments as truly as machines.

The creative community school is potential in the personalities and associational behaviors of the great majority of Americans. Its function is that of selective encouragement and reinforcement of those individual traits and social configurations that correspond to American ideals.

SELECTED REFERENCES

Alland, Alexander, and J. W. Wise: *The Springfield Plan: A Photographic Record,* The Viking Press, Inc., New York, 1945. A photographic presentation of educational situations in a community-oriented school system.

Bowen, Genevieve: *Living and Learning in a Rural School,* The Macmillan Company, New York, 1944. The successful adventure in school, home, and community cooperation in rural school education.

Chatto, C. I., and A. L. Halligan: *The Story of the Springfield Plan,* Barnes & Noble, Inc., New York, 1945. One community's total war on prejudice.

College in the Country and *The Family Comes to School,* New Dominion Series, nos. 118, 119, 1950. Achievements of two adult education projects, West Georgia College and Brick Rural Life School.

Essert, P. E., and R. S. Howard: *Educational Planning by Neighborhoods in Centralized Districts,* Bureau of Publications, Teachers College, Columbia University, New York, 1952. Scholarly discussion of community planning for education.

Everett, Samuel (ed.): *The Community School,* Appleton-Century-Crofts, Inc., New York, 1938. Examples of successful community schools of the 1930s.

Gray, W. S., and others: *The Opportunity Schools of South Carolina,* The American Association for Adult Education, New York, 1932. An experimental evaluation of elementary education for adults among mountain folk of South Carolina.

Ogden, Jesse, and Jean Ogden: *These Things We Tried,* University of Virginia Extension Division, Charlottesville, 1947. A summary of the experiments in community development initiated and carried out by the Extension Division of the University of Virginia in the early 1940s.

Ogg, Elizabeth: *The Rise of Community Welfare Councils,* Public Affairs Pamphlet 277, Washington, no date. Explanation of the purposes and procedures of an educational agency which parallels and reenforces the program of a community-oriented school.

Tireman, L. S., and Mary Wilson: *La Comunidad,* University of New Mexico Press, Albuquerque, 1943. Description of a justly famous school-community program.

Wallace, Whilden, and others: *The Story of Holtville,* privately published, Deatsville, Ala., 1944. The story of the accomplishments of a successful community high school by those who most actively participated in it.

Wright, G. S., and others: *Education Unlimited: A Community High School in Action,* U.S. Office of Education Bulletin 5, Washington, 1951. An explanation of the work of East Hampton, Conn., High School.

DISCUSSION QUESTIONS

1. Cite a municipal, state, or national governmental measure whose success seems to you to depend primarily on public education and/or propaganda as a precursor or accompaniment of legislative or administrative action. Does such preparation and communication characterize most governmental action? How does the example you cite compare with the adoption, promulgation, and enforcement of school rules that you, as teacher or as student, have been required to follow? Does your conclusion suggest desirable changes in the administration of schools?

2. Describe some school-community program you know about. What does it have in common with those described in this chapter?

3. Do you know of a city or other district for which the results of a recreational survey has been published in recent years? If so, first list the recreational opportunities in such an area that come to your mind; then compare them with those dealt with by the survey. What important ones had you overlooked? Had the surveyors omitted or slighted any that you included? If the survey report included recommendations for better facilities or services, was the school's contribution to them emphasized?

4. *Life* magazine published on October 16, 1950 a list of sixty-three criteria to give parents a practical way to measure the education

that children are getting in schools. Three of the criteria pertinent to community orientation are: "All students study community, including municipal government, through visits and participation." "The high school has an adult education program." "There is a person specifically employed to work at least half-time as a director of adult education program." Perhaps you know of a parent-teacher association that used these criteria. Would the consideration of these items stimulate a board of education and school administrators to accelerate community-centered projects?

5. In a Uniontown, Pennsylvania, junior high school some years ago, one noontime a week was devoted to hobby clubs attended and sponsored by nonschool adults. In an elementary school in Atlanta, each core-curriculum unit was sponsored by an interested patron, for example, "transportation" by a passenger agent and "airplanes" by a ground mechanic. The sponsor furnished exhibit material, helped in its organization, and attended occasional class meetings. What advantages might accrue for public tolerance for "fads and frills" which are, in fact, truly educative, from such programs?

6. If *The Peckham Experiment: A Study in the Living Structure of Society,* by I. H. Pearse and L. C. Crocker (Yale University Press, New Haven, Conn., 1945) is available, prepare a report on this comprehensive health center, emphasizing its implications for public education. What school reorganizations would be necessary if public education were to recast its programs in terms of family integration?

7. In cities in which public housing projects have been accompanied by social engineering insights, a wide range of recreational and mutual-aid programs are in process. Can you report to the class on one such instance of community education, noting any evidence of school cooperation with it?

23

Education and Planned Community Change

THE SCHOOL AND THE COMMUNITY

Without the reinforcement of other social institutions, the school's function can be only residual, that is, to teach those behaviors, skills, and information conventionally valued as school arts.

Each of the community schools described in the preceding chapter reacted creatively to challenges and opportunities that were discoverable in the milieu in which it functioned. In each case, the leaders discerned in the traditions and aspirations of the people they served not only desires and aspirations, but also some institutional attitudes and behaviors consonant with the ideals of American democracy. These they sought successfully to mobilize as inspiration and as reinforcement for school-related programs.

In each case, however, the leaders recognized adverse factors such as unsanitary conditions, ethnic conflict, selfish indifference, and lack of confidence that undesirable conditions might be remedied. These defects and threats served as rallying points for educators and other citizens who "caught" their enthusiasm.

In a word, school and community moved together. If they had not done so, the school by itself could have accomplished little. The self-centered establishment, whether church, lodge, ethnic association, social-class club, or school, must find allies, thereby sacrificing its self-centeredness in some degree, if it is to have much influence on community affairs.

Gold Is Where You Find It

In the case of Nambé, the social inheritance of communal ownership and responsibility for the water supply, the intelligent beneficence of the McCormicks, and the competence of University of New Mexico educators, all contributed to the success of the community school. But so also did the obviousness of needs: the health and sanitary deficiencies, the poverty, the illiteracy among adults, and the lack of confidence that characterized the people. These provided the challenges and hence the goals to be achieved.

In Springfield, there were widespread civic concern, a high quality of present and past educational leadership, a substantial economy, and a general confidence that well-conceived plans could be carried out successfully. The immediate challenge to be met was that of social fragmentation and its accompanying conflicts.

The school district of Holtville, characterized by a farm and village economy, had already accepted the leadership of agricultural extension agencies, in which the agriculture teacher had a very important place. There were also examples of pioneering educational establishments in the rural South which favored public acceptance of the school's role as a focus for cooperative efforts for domestic, economic, civic, and other social improvement. The challenges were closely related to the hopes and values of many parents: how help adolescent boys and girls to attain maturity by accepting adult purposes and responsibilities?

Maplewood serves to exemplify the school's opportunity to rally generally unrecognized capacities among the citizens of an upper-middle-class suburb to participate wholeheartedly in a social welfare program. Somewhat unique in this venture were two significant developments, the arousal of enthusiasm and self-confidence of many unemployed or part-time professional workers and their families during the depressed thirties and the culmination of the project initiated for the patrons of a specific junior high school in an area-wide adult education program. In the process of its development, the junior high school where the community education project started became a minor, almost an incidental, factor—but always an effective one.

The case of McKinley High School is also unique. In Honolulu, the need for integration of a polyglot population and its Americanization became so evident in the years immediately before World War II that all socially responsible persons were concerned with the problem. The community resources on which the McKinley faculty drew included a tradition of missionary service by Christian congregations devoted in early years to the welfare of Polynesian, and later to Oriental, peoples, the energy, industry, and ambition of first- and second-generation immigrants, and something that may perhaps be attributed to climate and topography—gentleness, conviviality, freedom from inhibitions, spontaneity, and aesthetic sensitivity, all sufficiently general to be the normal and expected pattern of behavior and attitude. The spirit and the activities promoted within the school community reflected those of this gracious social complex while at the same time pupils worked earnestly to master the English-American idiom, to meet college entrance requirements, and to achieve the competencies needed for success in business and industry. They found in the school American challenges, the American belief in the essential dignity of all human beings, and the American desire that every person have his chance and know that he has this dignity. Because the school had taught them to seek and to expect similar personal and institutional attitudes and behavior in their out-of-school relationships and because these expectations were in considerable degree fulfilled in the Hawaiian community, students and alumni of McKinley (and of other Honolulu high schools which are similarly organized) have been characterized by dignity, self-respect, and loyalty to American ideals.

In great degree, Benjamin Franklin High School expressed the social concern of the majority of New York citizens who rallied to the support of the reform administration of Mayor Fiorello LaGuardia. Indeed, the municipal government itself was at that time an undertaking in community education; the departments of police, fire, sanitation, and welfare directed much effort to information services and to winning public cooperation. In this configuration, the new high school in East Harlem was planned as an *ad hoc* institution; its mandate was to stimulate community pride and responsibility, to foster the setting up of civic goals and to provide guidance in their refinement and attainment, and to cooperate with, and to help coordinate, the programs of municipal departments, social settlements, and the many other establishments devoted to the promotion of human dignity. The school building provided a material base for the program. And the school's faculty discovered, and built upon, the readiness, aspiration, friendliness, and cooperativeness that were waiting to be called upon. In many purposeful community ventures, alumni, pupils, and many other citizens, all eager for the success of the projects, associated cooperatively; through such association, the demarcations between school education and community melioration tended to dissolve.

Heaven Is Not Reached in a Single Bound

In explaining the successful adaptations and reconstructions of creative schools as "engines for social betterment," we are well aware that attention should be called to the fact that success has been partial and relative. Ignorance, excessive self-interest, cultural antipathy, and distorted personalities are too many and too specific to yield quickly and permanently to any treatment that the school can provide. The word "success," as used or implied in these expositions, refers to encouraging bits, incidents, orientations, trends, and collaborations that seem to conform closely to an idealized conception of the democratic life. Such "success" indeed may indicate nothing more exhilarating than a lessening or retardation of forces that threaten communal welfare. Even so, every success improves the chance for regenerative forces to function in the on-going sequence of promises of and threats to life, liberty, and the pursuit of happiness.

You Worse than Senseless Things!

Shakespeare has the tribune, Marcellus, thus assail the "commoners" of Rome whose undiscriminating, joyful enthusiasm in any occasion which would provide a rallying point for likemindedness he despised. So today in the United States, the "orgies" and conformities of the populace are decried by those who are, or who fancy themselves to be, members of minorities whose tastes, erudition, or cultural practices and standards are pitched toward valuations of higher order.

It is not because mass culture, whether exemplified in "the arts," recreation, or civic affairs, is on the whole of a lower or coarser quality than in earlier periods that sincere critics are disturbed. Rather, it reflects a disappointment that the potentialities for good taste, discriminating choice, and understanding of issues, which it might be hoped would accompany the common man's release from exhausting labor, seem so inadequately realized.

In many cases, the grounds for criticism are quite unrealistic. The vaunted standards of elites both of the past and of the present have been spotty—great appreciation of beauty and refinement of manners often combined with callousness toward human suffering among social "inferiors." Increased leisure and consuming power have presented people with other opportunities than that of the pursuit of traditional "culture."

Idleness, stagnation, and infantile dependency may seem satisfying especially to those whose aspirations have reflected a desire to escape the compulsions that hunger or fear exerted. The pastimes and equipment of the idle rich have been enticing to many as they achieved comparative affluence; display, luxurious food, sexual excitement, and gambling have seemed to provide a sudden leap into the ranks of the envied upper-middle class. Nevertheless, many families have used their greater leisure and purchasing power for more wholesome food and houses, for "do-it-yourself" projects, for participation in serious art groups, adult education classes, political and campaign activities, and neighborhood improvement. Such freely chosen uses of their resources and opportunities may be truly considered a gain in a democracy.

The odds against such worthwhile choices, however, are great. In the United States, we are all commoners; our many and diverse social inheritances transmit many conflicting ideas regarding what is "right" and what "fitting" in one or another situation. And these ideas only gradually become blurred as they find little occasion for expression and as they rub up against differing ones.

Relatively fixed ideas and irrational justifications for them characterize segments of the population that are both insecure and relatively homogeneous. In Boston, for example, the defensive intransigence and in-group loyalty of Irish Catholics have been successfully exploited by demagogues. In some small towns of the Deep South, advocates of white supremacy play on the myths regarding Negro characteristics and on the irrational anxieties of insecure whites and Negroes alike.

Democracy is characterized not by a single mass mind, but by a kaleidoscopic complex of overlapping and interacting segmental "mass minds." Moreover, in each segment, "commonplace minds" [1] bulk so large that they usually impose commonplace beliefs and standards on all members who would avoid ostracism. Those who wish to be effective in decreasing or modifying such cultural taboos cannot disregard the limitations they impose; rather, the only hopeful strategy is to discover common elements of social experiences, beliefs, and aspirations which are supportive of the goals of a democratic society.

Unfortunately, many resourceful individuals and groups who are little concerned with fostering democracy use similar strategies to accomplish their ends. There is a kind of communications elite seeking the power to sway men's minds and selling their successful skills to the highest bidder. There are economic, political party, and military elites whose interests intertwine and who employ the services of the communications elite to achieve power positions in society.

Less threatening to the achievement of democratic goals, but nevertheless pervasive in the American society, are the plaints of art elites—often nostalgic and in some cases esoteric—who decry the in-

[1] The term used by Ortega y Gasset as applied to "mass man." *The Revolt of the Masses*, W. W. Norton & Company, Inc., New York, 1932, p. 19.

ferior tastes of "commoners" in the fields of appreciation, recreation, and erudition. For the most part, they stand somewhat outside the main stream of American life; they are apologists for a gentle tradition—the ways of life of the intelligentsia and leisure classes of the past. The practical effects of their very real influence on social processes are ambivalent. On the one hand, their high regard for individual intelligence favors tolerance of differences of conclusions and a freedom from prejudice; on the other hand, their disdain for commonplace minds seems to provide justification for the selfish exploitation of common men by power elites.

It is not easy for public educators to steer their courses in such a way as to keep in focus both their ultimate goals and the only methods they can use. Somehow, they must seek universally wholesome human relationships and individual self-realization through utilization of the same popular experiences, beliefs, and aspirations which are exploited by power elites and art elites for purposes quite contrary to those of democratic education. It must often seem to educators that they are engaged in a quixotic enterprise, ever tilting at enemies which prove to be windmills, fostering hopes and skills which the society makes futile.

PUBLIC EDUCATION AND PUBLIC EDUCATORS

Throughout much of this book, we have dealt with the school establishment as though it were central in the processes of popular education. Such an orientation is justifiable to the extent that the school is defined as the *formal and intentional* organization through which the society endeavors to preserve its stability and to progress toward its goals. In a democratic nation, a composite of many diverse subcultures, the school serves as a primary coordinating and integrating institution, systematically fostering the attitudes, enlightenment, and powers that community consensus approves.

In carrying out this mandate, the school collaborates with, and thereby reinforces, whatever institutions and associations effectively parallel its own practices and purposes. Its stabilizing and meliorative functions require the school also to seek to correct, to offset, and to foster satisfying substitutes for those attitudes, behaviors, and beliefs which are judged by responsible educators to be threatening to the success of community living.

The School as an Agency of Social Polity

It is very important, however, that we keep in mind that from other points of view the school is not central. Rather, it is the agency of social polity and of the many establishments and institutions which carry on the processes of social life. Thus, the family may be considered central; to it is assigned responsibility for the basic socialization of children.

Again, the state, manifested through government, may be considered central. In the United States, the state embodies the sustaining purposes of the people who delegate to it the authority to assure not only that their objectives are not ignored or distorted, but also that experimental steps are taken toward their progressive realization. The school is only one of the educational agencies established by the state to carry out its over-all purpose. The total educational effect of nonschool governmental efforts may be fully as important as those of schools.

From still another point of view, the selective conservation of the cultural heritage seems central both for stability and for ordered progress. All social establishments—churches, government, and family among others—express and transmit the values preferred by dominant segments of the American population. The standards and aspirations so expressed and transmitted are widely variant, to be sure, but they must be attuned to the goals and ways of American life if they are to be popularly accepted. They thus have a pragmatic common denominator, an awareness (however occasional or partial) that the continued autonomy of any group is interdependent with the right to self-determination of other associations.

The Social Function of the School

In this complex of establishments and usages, the school's function is to reproduce, purify, and idealize situations and processes typical of social life. The school is one of many controlled environments in which children and adults mingle and learn from each other. If it is not to insulate itself from the values and practices of other dynamic environments in which personalities take shape, it keeps the lines of communication open. The values common to the democratic way of life are exalted and practiced within its institutional environment so that people of all ages may recognize and support the same virtues whenever opportunities are offered in all their other environments.

In the many and varied child and family welfare organizations, including most families themselves, the school finds and welcomes the same intelligent interest in and affection for persons that it seeks itself to exemplify. Similarly, schools find many "American ways of life" practiced in the hundreds of youth-serving organizations, both those attached to governmental agencies and those administered by voluntary societies.

America Is People

The most significant of the other-than-school-centered conceptions of education is that which focuses on the individual characters of the American people. These are the human entities—living, volatile, critical, desirous, unsatisfied, competitive, and cooperative by turns. Somewhat absentmindedly and often falteringly, they are engaged in the great adventure of community, the common concerns and measures for safety and order, for subsistence and comforts, and for the pleasures and aesthetic satisfactions of associated life.

Though natural resources and political and economic establishments are necessary if community is to be had at all, the means for achieving community are *people,* and the chief obstacles to such achievement are also *people.* People qualified by knowledge, skill, and determination manipulate geographic resources and social establishments and instruments for purposes that may be favorable, unfavorable, or ambivalent as they affect community.

Paradoxically, however, even "bad" purposes cannot succeed if the structure and processes of community are destroyed or seriously disrupted. The excessive self-interest of the exploiter is limited by the willingness of the community to be exploited. Extreme partisanship, whether political or sectarian, is self-defeating if it fragments community. Evasion and withdrawal are emotionally dissatisfying if they lead to community rejection.

Community Living Is Educational

In the long run, therefore, the day-by-day experiences of life among fellow men provide a pragmatic mandate that rejects excessive indolence, selfishness, and partisanship.[2] The major function of democratic institutions is to refine and vitalize valuations and processes that are already in being to the end that men as individuals and as associates shall think, feel, and act as community members.

To carry on this function, policy makers and program planners of these institutions deal with men as they find them already adapting themselves to community limitations on the expression of their abilities and desires. Coercion and restraint of seriously maladjusted persons, when necessary, are the responsibility of law-enforcement authorities, but their correction and rehabilitation, rather than their ostracism or incarceration, are the approved objectives. Except for such necessary minimal restraints and compulsions, democratic associations treat all men as though they were good citizens of the community on the assumption that, by so dealing with them, the chance is improved that they will find such forms of self-expression as will, in fact, make them good citizens.

The response elicited by such fostering of socially constructive personalities varies widely. Some adults and some young people, because

[2] See James Bryce, *The Hindrances to Good Citizenship,* Yale University Press, New Haven, Conn., 1909.

of native or social inheritance and of successful experience in community life, are already eager to contribute their abilities and efforts to community welfare; their self-realization is enhanced by being used. Others may be half-frustrated and undecided how best to act to achieve recognition and status—for them the variant and evanescent prestige attached to money making, display, and personal power is likely to seem more concretely attainable than the more general and less tangible public approval for community service. For this latter group—and they are by far the great majority of people, young and old—community establishments must seek to provide opportunities for achieving satisfactions within the framework of community welfare.

Organizations for the advancement of popular enlightenment and civic collaboration are themselves institutions of public education. But their programs are far from being limited to those with which the school can deal directly. Each organization may, and usually does, approach its program making in the light of one or a cluster of specific needs and of specific opportunities to help deal with these needs. Progressive labor unions' educational projects, for example, provide health maintenance, wholesome recreation, and aesthetic, political and economic education for their members, as well as preparation for union responsibilities. Enlightened industries encourage individual self-adjustments and self-expression for their employees, as well as job training. Youth-serving organizations focus their efforts on influencing the nonschool and postschool lives of young people toward constructive community membership, emphasizing perhaps the values and institutional virtues of particular sponsoring sects or groups but not restricting their educational measures to them. The national and state nonschool educational programs function in similar spirit; the local representatives of soil conservation, home demonstration, university extension, 4-H clubs and Future Farmers clubs, and county agents encourage and depend on the cooperation of adults and young people in the locality for the initiation and execution of appropriate projects.

Americans as Joiners

Group and intergroup organization comes about rather readily in the United States. The readiness may be accounted for on several bases: the ease of communication due to common experiences, the universality of adult franchise, experience with community-owned facilities, familiarity with similar material possessions, economic and civic group interests which cut across narrow in-group loyalties, and, of course, a common language. Doubtless, our heritage of pioneering has established a tradition that common purposes require community of planning, accordance of leadership and fixing of responsibility, and the fulfillment of jobs and duties assigned to members of the organization. Even the parochial loyalties of immigrant groups and sectarian associations may teach their members much of value for more general voluntary organizations.

The key to American organizational proclivities and skill, however, is ultimately to be sought in the many and diverse problems and challenges that people are free to solve. Any individual or group of individuals who believes that a social problem or opportunity is not being adequately dealt with (or even that the treatment proposed or in being is not satisfactory) is free to advocate a different course of action, agitate and propagandize for it, and to organize, with those he convinces, a protest, pressure, or achievement group to bring it about.

The objectives of such organizations and the overt and hidden (perhaps unconscious) motivations of the advocates and agitators vary from personal self-interest to social ideals. The campaigns they conduct may be characterized by exposition and logical argument or by ingenious distortions of fact, the fostering of self-assertion, anger, and fear, or by the selective uses of both straightforwardness and ingenuity. One very important effect of the frequent success or near success of these organizations, however, is the prevalence of confidence among the American people that if they do not like what is happening, they can do something to change it.

Meliorative Nonschool Educational Organizations

It may be useful at this point to note the most important nonschool educational organizations. The following list of examples is restricted to those which most professional educators undoubtedly believe to be in harmony with the philosophy of human improvability through reconstruction of experience.

1. Organizations for, and of, young people which encourage and guide their members toward constructive participation in community meliorations: (a) Protestant, Catholic, Jewish, and nonsectarian religious youth-serving organizations in so far as their policies and activities are directed toward humane ends, for example, intercultural understanding and collaboration, the development of altruistic self-images, and such personal competencies—physical, communicative, organizational, mechanical, and aesthetic—as make these self-images achievable. (b) General character-building organizations not affiliated with (though often encouraged and sponsored by) churches. In some cases, the basis for membership is relatively specific, as the Junior Red Cross and Junior (American) Humane Societies, the programs varying from ceremonials and dues collection to preparation of materials for specific projects. In other cases, such as the 4-H clubs, Boy Scouts,

Girl Scouts, Camp Fire Girls, YMCA, and YWCA, the basis is as broad as the potentially constructive interests of young people; their programs so multifarious as to provide opportunities for learning experiences as diverse as leadership training, social amenities, job improvement, family-life improvement, recreation, health and safety, and world comity. (c) There are also character-building youth organizations which combine rather specific areas of operation with many-phased programs of activities, for example, Future Farmers of America, Junior Achievement, Incorporated, Fellowship of Reconciliation, American Youth Hostels, Incorporated, and the Association of the Junior Leagues of America.

    2. Nongovernmental organizations of young people and adults which are concerned to make their local and wider communities wholesome places in which to live and raise their children: (a) The most obvious examples of such organizations are those of service clubs, for example, Rotary International, Kiwanis, Lions, the American Legion, VFW, Grange, Farm Bureau, the League of Women Voters, various local art and musical societies, community coordinating councils, and chambers of commerce. (b) *Ad hoc* organizations which frequently develop when a need or opportunity becomes evident, for example, fund raising for specific occasions or establishments, citizens' budget committees, publicity committees for local celebrations, and human relations councils to assuage ethnic tension. (c) Aggregates of locally influential individuals whose associated civic activities form and dissolve. These informally organized groups confer with each other and with representatives of community organizations, and their counsel and support is often eagerly sought, but they seldom affiliate themselves with any organized groups. Nevertheless, whether they approve, disapprove, or are neutral regarding a specific community project, their judgments potently affect its success or failure. In some cases, their positions as clergymen, bankers, judges, or merchants may make overt affiliations seem to them unwise. In other cases, it may be political canniness that warns them to avoid close association with avid supporters or vigorous opponents of controversial measures.

    Individuals, *ad hoc* groups, and service organizations do not consistently separate their civic participations as the above classification might seem to imply. Service organizations frequently initiate specific projects; their special committees become potent *ad hoc* groups. The somewhat remote "city father" may be an elected or appointed official, in which role he seeks the support of service clubs and other groups whose enthusiasms are closely related to his official responsibilities. And an *ad hoc* volunteer, if not already group conscious, is likely soon to find satisfaction in groups with sustained programs.

The People, Yes

The public educator inevitably thinks and plans in terms of people. It is the traits—the knowledge, interests, ideals, habits, and powers—of persons that are the object of his concern. This concern requires him to identify and diagnose the processes by which those traits take form and which are consistent with wholesome human relations, self-realization, civic competence, and economic efficiency.

In the United States, the frame of reference for the educator's valuations of traits, and hence of processes, is the democratic ideology as expressed in our historic faith in people. His immediate responsibility is, therefore, to know and to try to understand how and why human characters are modified by social experiences. But understanding purely as an intellectual exercise would be futile, even if it were possible.

The public educator is an active agent of his society. Understanding, for him, requires more than fact finding, fact classifying, and generalization drawing. He uses such scientific method, but he refuses to be limited by it. His inquiry is frankly biased by his commitments to his faith in the improvability of man, both as an individual and as a species.

His understanding of man, therefore, is directed to the potentialities of his nature and of associative behavior, not only in the present rather disconcertingly inconsistent milieu, but also in relation to what he believes to be an attainable future.

The public educator neither avoids nor glosses over the indolences, narrow self-interests, and segmental antagonisms so obviously present in the American society. And he is well aware of man's original capacity for anger and fear. These are liabilities for him to take into account as he proceeds to fulfill his educational function.

His necessary optimism focuses his attention on phenomena that exemplify man's affection for his fellows, the tolerance of differences in values, beliefs, and behaviors and in pigmentation, and the willingness and ability to collaborate in the achievement of worthwhile purposes, a process that calls for bargaining, compromise, acceptance of alternating leadership, and for some degree of empathy and brotherhood with associates.

It is a basic tenet of the democratic faith that the more men can successfully practice such affection, tolerance, and vigorous collaboration in ever more inclusive configurations—interfamilial, interregional, interracial, international—the less will be the strength of irrational hatreds and fears. Optimistically, the public educator identifies, examines, and evaluates the partial successes and partial failures of associations of men as they deal with the opportunities and obstacles in community life. He endeavors to provide many and varied opportunities for collaboration and for favorable situations so controlled that men may learn by experience how to act more consistently, more intelligently, and hence more successfully in solving human problems.

His own awareness regarding the impending possibility of human self-destruction in a world of almost inexhaustible energy and power presents a crucial test for his optimism. He cannot blink the stupendous challenge. He is conscious of the fact that local adventures, disasters, and stalemates have limited effects on men's attitudes and behavior in broader and longer-term configurations and that intergroup collaboration and friendliness inspired by, and realized in, the meeting of recognized needs, opportunities, and emergencies is likely to be specific. He knows how many and how complicated are the differing self-interests, subdued and quieted by the immediate requirement of unanimity for the success of a project, but ready to spring into activity whenever the requirement is relaxed. And he knows the potency of myths and stereotypes that constantly corrupt the conclusions and attitudes that should logically follow from successful experiences in fellowship.

The Elite Role of Public Educators

If world-wide reconciliation and human brotherhood were mere abstract desiderata, waiting for their fulfillment on the discouragingly slow growth and extension of in-group morality to more and more inclusive communities of purpose and achievement, the role of the public educator would be modest indeed. But the desiderata are no longer sentimental objectives only. They are the alternatives to incineration!

Public education becomes, therefore, the role of every social establishment which hopes for survival. Governmental, industrial, and religious leadership are all subsumed under the role of elite leadership—leadership by men of intelligence, boldness, and good will toward their fellow men. Recognition of the impending danger, dispassionate reflection regarding constructive steps to prevent, or even to postpone, disaster, and persistence of loyalty to the human race by citizenship in mankind—these are the hallmarks of the only elite which can fulfill the role the world cries to have filled.

There is fear of failure, of course. But it must drive us neither into paralyzing fright nor into blind and ill-considered action. Fear may, indeed, be beneficent if it accentuates the urgency for intelligence in planning and action. Anger, too, is a concomitant of anxiety—but pitting our hatreds against devils is antithetical to the way of intelligence.

If there is to be a future for civilized man, it calls for the creative energies of wholesomely imaginative people—men who can construct instruments that will serve universal human purposes in some such way as the formulators of the constitutional government of the United States did for our national peoples. And just as the Constitution found acceptance because it reproduced the spiritual and mechanical counterparts of popular aspirations and arrangements for satisfying them, so whatever institutions and establishments may be envisioned for human brotherhood will require counterparts in family life, in school communities, among religious congregations, on the street and playground, in commerce and industry, and in government service. The fragmentation of society, to whatever degree justified as an expression of variety of values and experiences, must not make unity of man's over-all purposes too difficult to attain.

Fortunately, there is ample room within such institutions and establishments for many social myths, many institutional loyalties, and many individual idiosyncrasies to find some opportunity for expression. Whether the overt objective be a neighborhood playground or a world federation of states, there is involved a more fundamental end to be sought along with the means to harmonize with that end. This end is the establishment and maintenance of social momentum toward meeting tomorrow's problems confidently and calmly; resolutely taking the next step is essential whether the problem is getting the family washing done or the substitution of reasoned compromises for threatened obliteration. And the means to that end is the successful practice of reasoned compromise and of alternating leadership voluntarily accepted.

There is undoubtedly urgency. The momentum of science and technology applied to production, communication, and destruction threaten to outrun man's readiness and competence to conceive and achieve human brotherhood. *But there can be no short cut.* The alternative to consensus which is consonant with the democratic faith is, ultimately, destruction. And the fostering of such consensus is education. It is both means and end.

The school may fail. Family, church, the state, and the superstate may fail. But fear of failure is no excuse for not trying. In terms of geography, population, and cultural complexity, the present challenge is greater in scope than those man has met with tolerable adequacy before. But it is not essentially different from those that have preceded it. And the processes of popular enlightenment and of successful trial-and-error experience by which man has thus far escaped disaster "by the skin of his teeth" can be improved and accelerated.

SELECTED REFERENCES

Benne, K. D., and others: *Group Dynamics and Social Action,* Freedom Pamphlets, Anti-Defamation League of B'nai B'rith, New York, 1950. Program and techniques for social action.

Bishop, Claire H.: *All Things Common,* Harper & Brothers, New York, 1950. In some communities of Western Europe, independent groups of workers' families of different faiths and ideologies are building together a way of living wherein valued social contributions of individuals are not limited to economic production.

Borsodi, Ralph: *Education and Living,* The School of Living, Suffern, New York, 1948. A decentralist philosophy and program.

Brameld, Theodore: *Philosophies of Education in Cultural Perspective,* The Dryden Press, Inc., New York, 1955. Following expositions and evaluations of three currently advocated and criticized educational philosophies—progressivism, essentialism, and perennialism—the author advocates a purposeful reconstructionist role for American schools.

Broudy, Harry S.: *Building a Philosophy of Education,* Prentice-Hall, Inc., Englewood Cliffs, N.J., 1954. A problems approach and suggested solutions for problems in the areas of aims and values of educational enterprises. His criterion is the common good.

Brownell, Baker: *The Human Community: Its Philosophy and Practice for a Time of Crisis,* Harper & Brothers, New York, 1950. An appraisal of the conflicts between and the interdependencies of the culture of specialism and the human community as exemplified in Montana.

Cook, Lloyd Allen, and Elaine Forsyth Cook: *A Sociological Approach to Education,* McGraw-Hill Book Company, Inc., New York, 1960. The second revision of *Community Backgrounds of Education,* a standard textbook.

Counts, George S.: *Education and American Civilization,* Bureau of Publications, Teachers College, Columbia University, New York, 1952. Social foundations of American schools.

Dahlke, H. Otto: *Values in Culture and Classroom: A Study in the Sociology of the School,* Harper & Brothers, New York, 1958. A competent analysis of the school, with especial attention to social values and their expression.

Dewey, John: *School and Society,* University of Chicago Press, Chicago, 1899. The justification for the community-related curriculum of the University of Chicago Laboratory School at the turn of the century.

Douglass, Harl R. (ed.): *Education for Life Adjustment,* The Ronald Press Company, New York, 1950. Especially Chapter 2, "Breaking with the Past," and Chapter 20, "The Community in Education for Life Adjustment."

Gassner, John: *Human Relations in the Theater,* Anti-Defamation League of B'nai B'rith, New York, 1949. Racist, religious, and other cultural stereotypes presented to audiences.

Gregg, Richard B.: *The Power of Non-violence,* J. B. Lippincott Company, Philadelphia, 1934. An explanation of a candid dialectical process, characteristic of the Quaker approach to controversial questions, which has proved its practical effectiveness. It is especially suggestive for educators seeking to modify stereotyped school processes and orientations.

Hall, D. M.: *The Dynamics of Group Discussion: A Handbook for Discussion Leaders,* The Interstate Printers and Publishers, Danville, Ill., 1950. Theory and examples of group discussion of problems of community life.

Handbook in Community Development, Furman University Press, Greenville, S.C., 1941. Common problems in southern communities and the means of dealing with them.

Henry, N. B. (ed.): *The Community School,* Fifty-second Yearbook of the National Society for the Study of Education, University of Chicago Press, Chicago, 1953. The prevailing thought, practice, and problems of community-oriented education. "The Impact of the Power Age on the Community School Concept," by Robert Naslund, and "Overcoming Barriers to the Development of Community Schools," by Maurice Seay and John Wilkinson, are especially valuable.

Homans, G. C.: *The Human Group,* Harcourt, Brace and Company, Inc., New York, 1950. Possibilities for voluntary community cooperation in modern societies.

Ivey, John E., Jr.: *Channeling Research into Education,* American Council on Education, Washington, 1944. Resources of southern states, community needs, and educational programs.

Katz, Daniel, and others: *Public Opinion and Propaganda,* The Dryden Press, Inc., New York, 1954. A book of readings, concerning the psychological basis of opinions and the group processes by which they take form and are modified.

Kilpatrick, W. H.: *Philosophy of Education,* The Macmillan Company, New York, 1951. "The life good to live" is one of active adaptation to the challenges and opportunities of community life.

Mead, Margaret: *The School in American Culture,* Harvard University Press, Cambridge, Mass., 1951. The demands of an unknowable future must somehow be met through the educational experience of pupils.

Melby, Ernest O.: *Administering Community Education,* Prentice-Hall, Inc., Englewood Cliffs, N.J., 1955. "The prime 'know how' of the administrator consists in knowing how to release the creative capacities of individuals and how to mobilize the educational resources of communities."

Mercer, Blaine E.: *The American Community,* Random House, Inc., New York, 1956. A short presentation of the structural and functional characteristics of American local communities.

Moving Ahead for Children and Youth, The National Commission on Children and Youth, Washington, 1949. Family life, housing, health services, educational opportunities, recreation facilities, guidance and job placement, social services, and legal protection are considered.

Murphy, Campbell G.: *Community Organization Practice,* Houghton Mifflin Company, Boston, 1954. A good introduction to the organization and planning of community welfare services.

Nisbet, R. A.: *The Quest for Community: A Study of Order and Freedom,* Oxford University Press, New York, 1953. The transition from face-to-face moral relations and interactions to those of mass-oriented, interest-associative loyalties.

Professional Administrators for American Schools, Thirty-eighth Yearbook of the American Association of School Administrators, National Education Association, Washington, 1960. The prestige of membership in A.A.S.A. is such that the eligibility requirement after 1964, adopted by the Association in 1959, promises great advance in the professionalization of school administrators.

Public Education and the Future of America, National Education Association, Educational Policies Commission, Washington, 1955. An appeal for renewed attention to the values and practices of democratic education.

Rosenberg, Bernard, and David M. White (eds.): *Mass Culture: The Popular Arts in America,* Free Press, Glencoe, Ill., 1957. A source book of exposition and appraisal of literature, motion pictures, television and radio, "divertissement," and advertising. A good source for study of the modes of communication and expression through which public education must in part realize its aims.

Sanders, Irwin T.: *The Community: An Introduction to a Social System,* The Ronald Press Company, New York, 1958. A systematic and scholarly presentation of the generic characteristics of all communities. Includes good chapters on community planning and development.

Selznick, Philip: *T.V.A. and the Grass Roots: A Study in the Sociology of Formal Organization,* University of California Press, Berkeley, Calif., 1949. The tendency of organizational power and prestige to subordinate democratic processes to quick attainment of objectives.

Voss, J. E.: *Summer Resort: An Ecological Analysis of a Satellite Community,* University of Pennsylvania Press, Philadelphia, 1941. An interesting account of the interrelations of community associations.

Youth: The Nation's Richest Resource, Their Education and Employment Needs, The Interdepartmental Committee on Children and Youth of the Federal Government, Washington, 1951. A useful committee report.

DISCUSSION QUESTIONS

1. The Daughters of the American Revolution, the Citizenship Committee of the American Legion, and various spokesmen for other extremely nationalistic organizations have denounced UNESCO, the World Federalists, and other organizations which espouse participation by the United States in world-wide collaboration for the advancement of human welfare. In some cities and states, they have pressured parent-teacher associations and school boards to condemn textbooks and library books which present in favorable light the measures for social better-ment and educational reform advocated by these organizations. How have school boards, school administrators, and classroom teachers of social studies, literature, foreign languages, and science responded to these pressures? Have internationalist and liberal organizations and groups effectively built up counterpressures in support of school person-nel who have resisted the demands of narrow nationalists?

2. The League of Women Voters, the Federation of Women's Clubs, and the American Association of University Women have wide memberships which, though their immediate concern may be with the advancement of the status of women and with child welfare, are for these reasons deeply interested in community betterment and hence in public education. Interview the officers or other active members of one or more of these or similar organizations and plot in a diagram the inter-related civic activities represented by their standing and *ad hoc* com-mittees and projects. Do you find evidence of effective collaboration between these organizations and local and state systems of public educa-tion? Do some of their espousals aim independently for social goals which are also the concerns of public education?

3. Sometimes conflict rather than mutual reinforcement char-acterizes the efforts of energetic and ambitious citizen leaders and those of school officers even though both assert that they are concerned only that schools function effectively. Do you know, or can you learn of, cases where such conflicts have been minimized or liquidated by encouraging the antagonistic critics to sponsor school-related innovations consonant with their recommendations on an experimental basis?

4. According to Benjamin Fine, it is more often the citizens of a school district than it is the professional educational officers who en-vision the kind of schools they want for their children. If true, the major problem facing educational officers is one of communication and mobili-zation of potentially constructive publics. Reviewing the examples of progressive attainments of community-related schools presented in previous chapters, can you classify or otherwise set forth systematically

the means utilized by school leaders successfully to create effective public opinion in support of the innovations they espoused?

5. "For many elements of social living, the community or small region is a normal scale for pilot plant operation. . . . Most of the fundamental processes of social life exist in the small community, and most new social methods originate there and can be tried there without the waste and risk of disaster of experiment on a national scale." (Arthur E. Morgan, "The Community as a Pilot Plant for Society," *Community Service News,* January–February, 1951.) The author cites as examples of such successful pilot-plant operations those of primitive Christianity, the Rochdale Cooperative, and the use of electric distribution systems. If Morgan's thesis is valid, what, if any, suggestions does it stimulate you to formulate regarding the frame of reference for the community-related school?

Appendix. Selected Periodicals

Discussions of the functions of educational institutions in fostering popular knowledge and attitudes attuned to the American concern for universal social welfare have found place in magazines, books, and platform addresses for almost 200 years. The thrusts and counterthrusts of the protagonists of intentional efforts to move directly toward the goal of human welfare and of those who favor laissez-faire evolution continue into the 1960s. Readers of this book are, therefore, referred to the daily, weekly, and monthly output of periodicals wherein articles, editorial comment, and even paid advertisements seek to enlighten or stimulate the interest of readers. Also, many useful and stimulating books will have been published after this volume has gone to press; hence, the reader is urged to follow the book review columns for information and comment.

Many of the most enlightening accounts of school responses to the challenges presented year after year by events and changes in the climate of opinion will be found in periodical literature. Of the 1,981 educational periodicals currently published in the United States and listed in the Twenty-seventh Yearbook of the Educational Press Association of America, it is possible to mention only a few of those of general distribution which will be found in many college and larger public libraries.

Adult Education, Adult Education Association of the U.S.A., Chicago.
The American Teacher, The American Federation of Teachers, Chicago.
The American Teacher Magazine, The American Federation of Teachers, Chicago.

Audio-Visual Instruction, Department of Audio-Visual Instruction, National Education Association, Washington.

California Journal of Secondary Education, California Association of Secondary School Administrators, Burlingame.

The Clearing House, Fairleigh Dickenson University, Teaneck, N.J.

Education, The Bobbs-Merrill Company, Inc., Indianapolis.

The Education Digest, Ann Arbor, Mich.

The Educational Forum, Kappa Delta Pi, Tiflin, Ohio.

Educational Leadership, Association for Supervision and Curriculum Development, National Education Association, Washington.

Educational Record, American Council on Education, Washington.

Elementary School Journal, Department of Education, University of Chicago, Chicago.

Harvard Educational Review, Graduate School of Education, Harvard University, Cambridge, Mass.

Journal of Educational Sociology, School of Education, New York University, New York.

Journal of General Education, University of Chicago, Chicago.

Junior College Journal, University of Texas, Austin.

NAEB Journal, National Association of Educational Broadcasters, Urbana, Ill.

NEA Journal, National Education Association, Washington.

National Elementary Principal, Department of Elementary School Principals, National Education Association, Washington.

The Nation's Schools, Chicago.

Overview, Buttenheim Publishing Corporation, New York.

Phi Delta Kappan, Phi Delta Kappa, Bloomington, Ind.

Scholastic Teacher, Scholastic Magazines, Inc., New York.

School and Society, Society for the Advancement of Education, New York.

School Life, United States Department of Health, Education, and Welfare, Washington.

School Review, Department of Education, University of Chicago, Chicago.

Social Education, National Council for the Social Studies, in collaboration with the American Historical Association, Tufts University, Medford, Mass.

The Social Studies, McKinley Publishing Company, Philadelphia.

Teachers College Record, Teachers College, Columbia University, New York.

Name Index

551

Subject Index